P9-DGR-148

Chester
Library
DISCARD
250 West Main Street
Chester, NJ 07930

Berlin on the Brink

BERLIN ON THE BRINK

The Blockade, the Airlift, and the Early Cold War

Daniel F. Harrington

Scholarly publisher for the Commonwealth,
serving Bellarmine University, Berea College, Centre College of Kentucky, Eastern Kentucky University, The Filson Historical Society, Georgetown College, Kentucky Historical Society, Kentucky State University, Morehead State University, Murray State University, Northern Kentucky University, Transylvania University, University of Kentucky, University of Louisville, and Western Kentucky University.

Editorial and Sales Offices: The University Press of Kentucky
663 South Limestone Street, Lexington, Kentucky 40508-4008
www.kentuckypress.com

16 15 14 13 12 5 4 3 2 1

Maps by Richard A. Gilbreath, University of Kentucky Cartography Lab

Library of Congress Cataloging-in-Publication Data

Harrington, Daniel F.
Berlin on the brink : the blockade, the airlift, and the early Cold War / Daniel F. Harrington.
p. cm.
Includes bibliographical references and index.
ISBN 978-0-8131-3613-4 (hardcover : alk. paper) —
ISBN 978-0-8131-3614-1 (ebook)
1. Berlin (Germany)—History—Blockade, 1948-1949. 2. Cold War. I. Title.
DD881.H318 2012
943'.1550874—dc23 2012004169

This book is printed on acid-free paper meeting the requirements of the American National Standard for Permanence in Paper for Printed Library Materials.

∞

Manufactured in the United States of America.

Member of the Association of
American University Presses

To Sylvia, Elizabeth, and Laura,

who bring light and love

to the corridors of my life

Contents

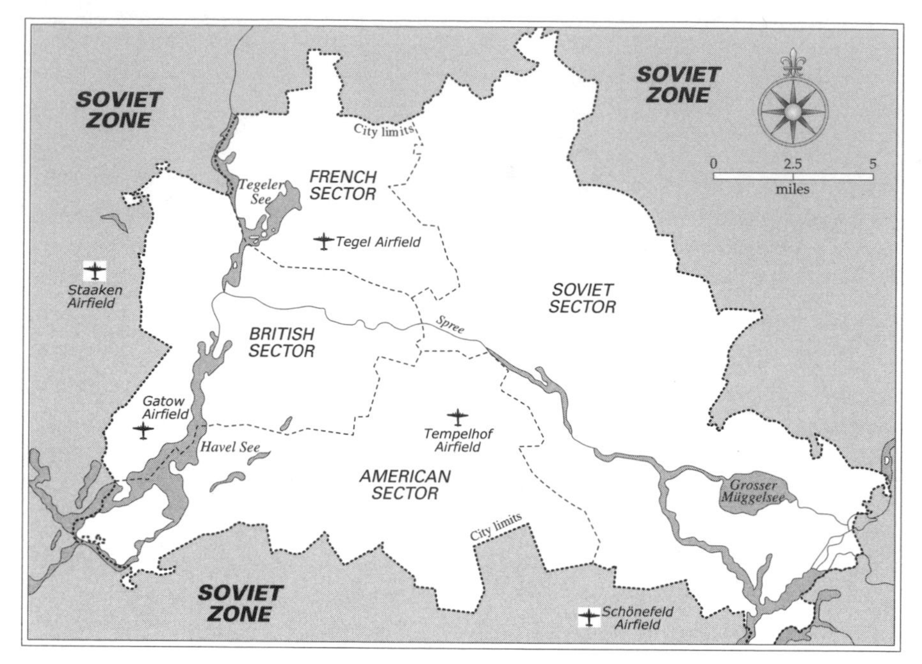

Occupied Berlin

Germany during the Berlin blockade

Introduction

NO PLACE SYMBOLIZES THE COLD WAR more than Berlin. In July 1945, the wartime Allies met on the outskirts of Adolf Hitler's ruined capital and barely managed to paper over their differences. Three summers later, Berlin brought them to the brink of war. Crises in the late 1950s and early 1960s created a new symbol of their conflict—the Berlin Wall—as Soviet and American tanks faced each other at Checkpoint Charlie. The city later acted as a barometer, measuring the change in atmosphere as tensions eased. The 1971 quadripartite agreement ushered in the era of détente, and the opening of the Wall in November 1989 signified the Cold War's end.

The tanks at Checkpoint Charlie have only one competitor as an iconic image of Cold War Berlin: a cargo plane flying over the war-ravaged city during the Berlin blockade. From June 1948 to May 1949, the Soviet Union isolated the western half of the city from its normal sources of supply. The other occupying powers, the United States, Great Britain, and France, sustained their sectors by flying in coal, food, and other necessities. For generations of Americans and western Europeans, the contrast between Joseph Stalin's ruthless blockade and the West's humanitarian airlift offered eloquent proof of Arthur Schlesinger's contention that Western Cold War policies were "the brave and essential response of free men to communist aggression."[1] Westerners still find inspiration in the airlift as the most dramatic mobilization of military technology to save lives in the twentieth century. Claiming parallels between their actions and Harry Truman's, recent presidents have invoked the airlift to bolster support for their policies.

Although an enormous literature exists about Cold War Berlin in general and the blockade in particular, aspects of the crisis remain obscure. One noted historian of the blockade has declared it "one of the most ambiguous and least understood events of the Cold War."[2] No consensus exists about its causes, context, or consequences. No one has offered a convincing explanation of why planners created Western enclaves in Berlin, surrounded by the Soviet zone, without well-defined access rights to them. Nor have scholars looked at how these access arrangements, such as they were, functioned between 1945 and 1948, or at Western efforts to expand access after 1945. Historians do not explain why Western officials did little to reduce the city's vulnerability as tensions increased in late 1947 and early 1948.

Another question is the airlift's place in Western policy. According to most accounts, officials quickly settled on an airlift as their counter to the blockade. Yet historians also claim that Western leaders at the time believed Berlin could not be supplied by air. In other words, Western governments chose the airlift as their response, expecting it to fail. That does not make sense. What, then, was Western policy, and how did the Western powers expect to prevail against the blockade?

THIS BOOK TRIES TO CLARIFY such issues by examining the "Berlin question" from its origin in wartime plans for the occupation of Germany through the 1949 meeting of the Council of Foreign Ministers in Paris. Although the blockade and the airlift form the centerpiece of this story, the narrative puts them in a broader context. It examines the origins of the Berlin problem during the Second World War, looks at how East-West cooperation in Berlin and Germany broke down between 1945 and 1948, and then turns to the crisis itself. It covers the diplomatic maneuvering, the evolution of the airlift, and events in the blockaded city. It concludes by describing the foreign ministers' meeting in Paris, which ratified the division of Berlin and Germany and established the framework for decades of cold war in Europe.

Diplomatic histories tend to concentrate on the high and the mighty. This account is no exception. At one level, it is a case study of how governments behave during crises. Yet the outcome did not turn solely on what national leaders planned and decided. It depended just as much on the actions of airlift pilots and the residents of Berlin. Only by examining the intertwined topics of national policies, the airlift, and life in Berlin can we understand how this confrontation erupted, evolved, and was resolved.

While drawing on secondary literature, the study rests on research in British, American, and Canadian archives, ranging from Berlin sector records to presidential and prime ministerial files. Postwar Berlin has become too familiar in some ways, encrusted with unexamined assumptions and myths. Stories have come to be accepted as true through constant repetition, when their factual basis is questionable. Memoirs are selective, sometimes misleading, occasionally distorted. I went back to the primary record whenever I could. Here I must add an embarrassing caveat. My lack of fluency in French, German, and Russian means that this is not the definitive account I wish it was. I tried to compensate by drawing on studies of Soviet policy that have appeared in English in the last two decades, and I used a handful of works in French and German. The lack of primary material in these three languages weakens my analysis. I can only hope that my work will encourage others to provide a better-rounded account than I have offered here.

Despite its limitations, my research calls into question existing views of the blockade and its origins. The failure to secure written guarantees of Western access to Berlin seemed the height of folly after 1948, and critics were quick to blame the problem on naive trust in Soviet goodwill on the part of Franklin Roosevelt and his advisers. Yet the plan that left Berlin surrounded by the Soviet zone was a British product, not an American one. And although the belief that the Russians would cooperate did influence wartime plans, other considerations were just as important, such as the expectation that the zones would exist for only a short time, the notion that forces of the Allies would move freely in all zones, and the idea that Western access routes would sustain only the garrisons, not Berlin's entire population.

The blockade is best understood as a confrontation among the occupying powers, not as a conflict with local origins. Great-power decisions determined the city's unique postwar history. Had the Allies not chosen to establish a special occupation regime for Berlin, events there would have paralleled those in Dresden or any other city in the eastern zone. Absent the Western powers, the Soviets would have coerced Berlin's socialists into a merger with the communists in the spring of 1946. That merger would have made it impossible for the socialists to claim victory in the city elections that autumn, which turned out the communist-dominated city government installed by the Soviets in the summer of 1945. Furthermore, matters came to a head in 1948 not because of a local contest for power but because of Western plans to create a separate government in west Germany and Stalin's determination to thwart them. As leaky as the blockade proved to be, and as ingenious as Berliners were in circumventing it, had the airlift not placed the material and moral support of the Western powers squarely behind west Berliners, the city would have succumbed to the Soviets. Berliners' ability to resist communist coercion depended on a Western presence.

Standard histories of great-power conflict in Berlin err in a variety of ways, the greatest being a misunderstanding of the airlift's place in Western policy. Most scholars depict Western leaders as weighing options in classic rational-actor fashion and choosing the airlift as their preferred solution to the crisis. Others portray the decision as resting more on intuition than logic, but the conclusion is the same: the powers resolved to stay in Berlin and to rely on the airlift to do so. Dangerous alternatives were on the table. The American military governor, General Lucius D. Clay, wanted to challenge the blockade with an armed convoy, but scholars depict Truman as choosing the airlift instead. The sense is that the administration assessed its alternatives wisely, then selected and pursued a winning strategy.

Such interpretations assume that the airlift would succeed and that Western officials knew it would. Success always looks preordained in hindsight. Doubts about the airlift went much deeper and lasted far longer than scholars have realized. What we now see as inevitable, people at the time thought impossible. No one in June and July 1948 regarded the airlift as a course of action, preferable to other alternatives, that would resolve the crisis. Well into the autumn, Western officials believed the airlift would fail, and no one knew what their governments would do when that happened. This hardly exemplifies sound processes, rational choice, or coherent strategy.

The airlift was a masterpiece of improvisation, not a calculated policy. Scholars have assumed that one decision was made at the start. But the decision to begin *an* airlift was not a decision to begin *the* airlift as we understand that term, and scholars have confused the two. The British and Americans started sending supplies not to break the blockade but to stretch stocks for as long as possible, in the hope that diplomacy would resolve the crisis in the meantime. Yet the odds were against the diplomats. The West remained committed to creating a separate west German government, while Stalin made it clear that abandoning that project was his price for lifting the blockade. The best Western officials could hope for appeared to be open-ended deadlock—perpetual blockade and perpetual airlift—something Berliners could not endure forever. Nor could contemporaries rule out the possibility that Stalin might forcibly disrupt the airlift. Today, we regard the airlift as a virtually risk-free path to success; they could not. Strategy reconciles ends and means. In that sense, the West had no strategy—no policy that offered a reasonable prospect of producing a favorable outcome.

Diplomatic historians and political scientists have treated the airlift as a conscious strategy for several reasons. One is hindsight—the airlift succeeded. Another is the influence of decision-making models. In offering simple outlines of choices and courses of action, these models have predisposed scholars to detect a pattern of behavior during the blockade that did not exist. Third, scholars have not examined the details of implementation, concentrating instead on policy deliberations and decision making. Logistics seem mundane. To understand the airlift's place in Western policy, we must examine how it grew, over weeks and months, into the full-scale, organized effort some believe existed from the start.

Dismissing doubts about the airlift obscures important aspects of Western diplomacy, particularly coalition unity. The powers found it hard to stay in step in at least three key moments during the crisis. Doubts about the airlift were one cause. Europeans feared the Americans wanted to bring the crisis to a head, a step likely to trigger war. We tend to see Europeans' worries as exaggerated, believing that Truman had overruled the most dangerous proposal put forward during the crisis—Clay's convoy plan. But American officials regarded the airlift as the prelude to Clay's armored column, not an alternative to it. *When* the airlift failed, which some expected as early as October, the West would face a choice between withdrawing from Berlin and challenging the blockade with Clay's tanks. Western Europeans were relying on American power to prevent a war with the Soviet Union, not prevail in one. With no ocean between them and the Red Army, Europeans understandably dwelled more on the likelihood and consequences of war than Americans did. They were more willing to let diplomacy spin out and less willing to gamble on the airlift than Americans were.

Diplomatic efforts to deal with Berlin continued after the Soviets lifted the blockade on May 12, 1949. Foreign ministers met in Paris on May 23 and agreed to disagree, bringing this Berlin crisis to a close. Stalin had suffered a serious defeat. He had failed to derail the west German government. He had not captured Berlin. The blockade had alienated Western public opinion, strengthened anticommunist sentiment in Germany, and hastened the North Atlantic alliance.

In the West, the only "lessons learned" seemed to be hard-line ones. The blockade fixed in the public's mind an image of the Soviet Union as an aggressive, expansionist, and ruthless totalitarian state. The most dangerous times during the crisis had come during negotiations; the only safe course was to build positions of strength. Other lessons could have been derived from the blockade. Although firmness and resolve defeated Stalin, Western diplomacy succeeded because of other virtues, too—above all, prudence and a refusal to rush to judgment. Western leaders chose to cross bridges when they came to them, not before. In postponing choice, they unwittingly gave the airlift time to prove itself. None of this was conscious or deliberate or even intuitive. As he drifted, Truman could not acknowledge what he was doing. Instead, he reassured himself with tough declarations about "staying period" and not passing the buck, declarations historians have accepted at face value ever since. The Western policy of avoiding long-term choices seemed illogical well into the autumn of 1948, and it was never the model of rationality some scholars describe. In the end, results proved its wisdom, if not its logical consistency. The policy worked.

CHAPTER 1

Opportunity

The agreements that divided postwar Germany into zones and Berlin into sectors seem to defy common sense. Although the Soviet zone surrounded the city, the accords did not define Western transit rights across it. This omission seemed criminal during the Cold War, and many sought explanations. The most common was that, during the war, few Westerners had given much thought to access, and those who did were overruled by others who naively trusted Soviet dictator Joseph Stalin. Dwight Eisenhower summed up these views when he told GOP leaders in 1952 that the problem resulted from Franklin Roosevelt's concessions to the Russians, which he derided as "bribing a burglar."[1]

As all good detectives know, opportunity alone does not result in crime; motive must accompany it. Eisenhower saw no need to explain Soviet motivations. Convinced that Stalin's mind buzzed with larcenous thoughts, he assumed that opportunity alone was a sufficient explanation. Yet decisions made during the war did not cause the blockade; they only made it possible. A full explanation must combine opportunity and motive, the goal of this chapter and the next.[2]

The broad outlines of how Germany came to be divided into zones are well known. In what remains the best short introduction to the subject, State Department historian William Franklin chronicled a series of missed opportunities and assumptions disproved by time. The United States and Great Britain began discussing the postwar occupation in 1943. Planning quickly became entangled in bureaucratic quarrels between the Department of State and the Pentagon, and it was distracted by a disagreement between Roosevelt and Prime Minister Winston S. Churchill over which country should occupy northwestern Germany. Meanwhile, a European Advisory Commission (EAC)—created at a meeting of the British, American, and Soviet foreign ministers in Moscow in October 1943—worked out a zonal plan that omitted provisions for Western access to Berlin. The Yalta conference approved this EAC plan. The French joined the EAC in November 1944, and at Yalta they were granted a zone of Germany, a sector in Berlin, and a seat on the Allied Control Council (ACC), the committee of military governors charged with overall responsibility for the occupation. Franklin described how approaches to the Soviets in 1945, culminating in a meeting among Soviet Marshal Georgi K. Zhukov, U.S. Lieutenant General Lucius D. Clay, and British Lieutenant General Ronald Weeks on June 29, 1945, left Western transit arrangements ill-defined.[3]

Yet Franklin did not explain why the Western powers paid so little attention to ensuring their ability to reach Berlin. Exploring Western plans and assumptions, this chapter argues that the failure to work out access arrangements had sources other than naiveté or gullibility. In sketching out what would become the boundary of the Soviet zone, British planners in 1943 simply overlooked the issue. They expected a brief occupation, assumed that zonal boundaries would merely mark where each country stationed its troops, and believed that each power's forces would move freely in all zones. The EAC did not correct the British omission. The French joined the commission too late to affect the zonal protocol, the Soviets had no interest in expanding outsiders' presence in their sphere, and no American alternative to the British proposal reached the commission. Roosevelt toyed with a scheme whereby the U.S. zone would abut Berlin, but he abandoned it after learning that the Russian representative in the EAC had endorsed the British plan. Shortly thereafter, American officials debated making free access to Berlin a condition of American acceptance of the boundaries in the British plan, but they later set aside the idea. Once the commission agreed on a zonal protocol, those worried about access did not push hard to resolve the issue, and those who approached the Russians about access met polite evasion.

ALTHOUGH EISENHOWER AND other Cold War critics blamed the Roosevelt administration for the opportunities provided to the Soviets by wartime plans, those plans originated in London. From the start, British planners believed the Allies would have to occupy all of Germany. Partial occupation after 1918 had not worked; only complete occupation had any chance of success this time. Total occupation could take one of two forms: stationing small contingents from all the occupying powers throughout Germany, in what was known as a "mixed" occupation, or dividing the country into zones, one for each occupying power. The British chose the latter.[4]

By mid-October 1943, the Post-Hostilities Planning Sub-Committee under Gladwyn Jebb of the British Foreign Office had drafted a plan that included a "Combined Zone" around Berlin, as well as a map detailing zonal boundaries. The most important line on Jebb's map—the western boundary of the Soviet zone—would divide Germany throughout the Cold War. Jebb's proposal made no mention of Western transit across the eastern zone to Berlin.[5] Following review by a committee chaired by Deputy Prime Minister Clement R. Attlee, Sir William Strang submitted the plan to the EAC on January 15, 1944.[6]

Time would treat harshly the assumptions underlying the so-called Attlee plan. Its authors expected that a peace conference would convene quickly, as had occurred after the First World War, and replace the zones with more lasting arrangements. British officials thought the military phase of the occupation, and hence the zones, might last between six and twenty-four months (U.S. Army officers thought it might last no more than two months).[7]

Nor did planners expect the zones to become exclusive preserves. In Jebb's view, the zones would exist for garrisoning purposes only and would have no effect on day-to-day life. The prospect of "rigid international frontiers wandering up German hills and down German valleys," as one of his colleagues put it, was the furthest thing from anyone's mind.[8] Strang's proposal envisaged that each zone would have an international staff under the host commander, as well as token forces from the other zones. The idea of token forces suggests why the British took access to Berlin for granted. With Western troops moving freely throughout the Soviet zone, special provisions for Western transit to Berlin must have seemed superfluous.[9]

Planners did not see the access routes as west Berlin's sole lifeline, which now seems instinctive to us. Rather, they assumed the city would draw its supplies from the area surrounding it, as it always had done. As a senior staff officer of Eisenhower's Supreme Headquarters Allied Expeditionary Force (SHAEF) put it in mid-April 1945, "Berlin must, from the supply point of view, be treated as part of the Russian Zone." The access routes would support the Western garrisons, not the German population. Soviet insistence in July 1945 that each occupying power furnish food and coal for its own sector came as an unwelcome shock and made access much more important than any planner had imagined.[10]

Yet the main reason why access seemed unimportant was that Westerners did not expect the Soviets to make trouble. Wartime planners approached the occupation from a perspective different from ours. The major purpose of the occupation was to prevent renewed German aggression, which officials regarded as an overriding common interest that would bind the wartime Allies together far into the postwar period. They began their work in the summer of 1943, when optimism about postwar cooperation with the Soviet Union was at its height. They did not—could not—know that the Grand Alliance would collapse. Optimism was no mere planners' conceit; it was government policy, set at the highest level, and it was not called into question until the spring of 1945.[11] By then, the zones were a fixture of Allied diplomacy, and not even Churchill could compel a reconsideration of them.

NO AMERICAN ALTERNATIVE to the British proposal emerged before the EAC convened or for weeks thereafter. Planning for the occupation, by its nature, united categories that Americans put in separate mental compartments—wartime and postwar, military and diplomatic—and the U.S. government lacked the mechanisms to consider it coherently. They found themselves working in isolation on two zonal plans—the British one in the EAC, and a military one called Rankin (or, more precisely, its third variant, Rankin C), being considered by the Joint Chiefs of Staff (JCS). Roosevelt was the only one who could have pulled things together, but he thrived on the lack of system, had an instinctive distaste for postwar planning, and gave no lead.[12]

Scholars have erroneously conflated Rankin and the Attlee plan. Drawn up by British Lieutenant General Sir Frederick E. Morgan's Anglo-American planning staff in London, Rankin outlined Western military responses should Germany collapse, as it had in 1918. Under Rankin C, the plan's most ambitious variant, troops would fan out across Europe to disarm the Wehrmacht and the SS. What they did later was of no concern to the Rankin planners. Rankin C was, in short, a plan for the war's last phase, not the occupation's first, and it covered all of Nazi-occupied western Europe, not just Germany. It divided the Continent into three great "zones" that radiated out from the heart of Germany: the southwestern zone, consisting of southwestern Germany, France, Italy, and Austria; the northwestern zone, consisting of northwestern Germany, the Low Countries, Denmark, and Norway; and the eastern zone, including all the countries to the east, which would be left to the Soviet Union. Morgan allotted the southwestern zone to the United States and the northwestern one to Britain, paralleling how they would deploy in his other major plan, Overlord.[13]

In a famous meeting with the JCS on the battleship *Iowa* in mid-November 1943, Roosevelt insisted that the United States occupy the northwestern zone. His stance had nothing to do with Germany and everything to do with France. "France is a British baby," he declared, and he would accept no commitments there. He went on to outline the zones he wanted in Germany. His quick strokes on a National Geographic map carved out a huge American zone that reached as far east as Berlin and as far south as Frankfurt. The Russians would occupy the area to the east, the British the area to the south.[14]

The joint chiefs, naturally enough, took this as a directive from their commander in chief and asked Morgan to rewrite Rankin. Churchill and the British chiefs of staff resisted, triggering a deadlock that would continue until September 1944, when Roosevelt relented.[15] No one could object when Roosevelt and the JCS argued with Churchill and the British chiefs of staff over what shape Rankin should take. However, the argument took on ramifications outside military channels when, months into the debate, the EAC began considering postwar occupation "zones" in Germany. The American chiefs of staff (and FDR himself) could not distinguish between the two types of zones, insisting that all zonal planning was a "military matter" and hence none of the diplomats' business. Furthermore, they interpreted all questions regarding zones against a background of suspicion and hostility toward the British.

After more than a half century of extolling the Anglo-American "special relationship," it is difficult to recall how distant the two countries were in the early days of the Second World War. Ironically, tensions increased after Pearl Harbor, due to quarrels over the Mediterranean. The British wanted to expand operations there, while the Americans regarded it as a strategic dead end.[16] The War Department connected the EAC with these disagreements. Even before the foreign ministers decided to create the commission, Assistant Secretary of War John J. McCloy had warned his boss, Henry L. Stimson, that the British were reviving a scheme to "run Eisenhower" in the Mediterranean; Stimson passed the story on to Roosevelt.[17] McCloy had mistakenly interpreted a request to have Harold Macmillan, Britain's resident minister at Eisenhower's headquarters, serve as "the channel" between the general and London for reports about political developments in Sicily as a plot to put Macmillan in Eisenhower's chain of command; furthermore, McCloy was sure that only his tough response had thwarted the scheme.[18] Another transatlantic argument soon followed over the relative authority of civil affairs planning groups in London and Washington. This bureaucratic donnybrook and the quarrel over Rankin were in full swing when British Foreign Secretary Anthony Eden won approval for the EAC at the Moscow foreign ministers' meeting. McCloy and his colleagues in the Pentagon jumped to the conclusion that the EAC was yet another maneuver to make London the center of wartime and postwar planning.[19]

The vagueness of the commission's charter did not help. It was to make recommendations on "European questions connected with the termination of hostilities" that were referred to it by the governments involved—specifically, terms of surrender and the control machinery to enforce them.[20] McCloy saw this elastic wording as a deliberate move to create openings for the commission to meddle in operational matters. Armistices and surrender terms were traditionally military topics, and issues "connected with the termination of hostilities" could have military implications. The occupation would begin when Allied troops entered Germany, which could be months before a final defeat. In other words, control measures devised by the EAC for the occupation might begin during the war, not after it, and might tie commanders' hands. McCloy had no doubt that the commission was simply the latest scheme to subordinate wartime coalition strategy to the postwar goals of the British Empire, and British assurances to the contrary fell on deaf ears.[21]

Roosevelt's senior military adviser, Admiral William D. Leahy, warned that the EAC "will mean nothing but trouble for us," a prophecy that proved self-fulfilling.[22] Obstruction by the Pentagon made Anglo-American consultations impossible in the weeks before Strang introduced the British proposal. The timing was critical. Once the British plan was on the table, any American alternative that put postwar access on a sounder basis would have required the Soviets to give up population and territory. As Franklin noted years ago, "This would have required some hard bargaining and/or considerable compensation."[23] Neither was likely. Thus, any American alternative had to reach London in time to influence British planning *before* Strang's submission. Morgan's American deputy, Major General Ray W. Barker, made just such a plea, urging wide-ranging bilateral consultations before the commission convened.[24] The Pentagon's suspicions of the British ensured that this did not happen, even though there was time to consult. The U.S. Army chief of staff, General George C. Marshall, had a copy of Jebb's plans by November 3, and (contrary to Franklin's claims) the State Department had copies two weeks before that.[25] Leahy and the joint chiefs talked over British plans with the president in mid-November. When the Department of State tried to establish an interagency Working Security Committee to coordinate instructions to the U.S. EAC delegation, army and navy planners did their best to paralyze the group. Echoing McCloy's suspicions, they complained that the commission would meddle in questions that "would normally go to the Combined Chiefs of Staff for consideration" and demanded to know what "safeguards" would be created to "avoid shifting the center of policy decisions on civil affairs matters from Washington to London." They insisted on complicated clearance procedures and would commit their departments to nothing.[26] Instead of a venue for expediting U.S. actions in the EAC, the Working Security Committee became a forum where initiatives were talked to death.

State Department planner Philip Mosely recalled a vivid and telling example. He had drafted a plan to divide Germany into zones that included an overland corridor connecting Berlin with Western-controlled areas, and he shared it with a colonel in the army's Civil Affairs Division. Days passed. Finally, Mosely visited the Pentagon to inquire about his suggestion. The officer pulled open the bottom drawer of his desk and pointed. "It's right there," he said. Leaning back in his chair, he put both feet into the drawer and continued, "It's damn well going to stay there, too."[27] Mosely's plan never reached the Working Security Committee, much less the EAC. Preoccupied with wartime plans such as Rankin, and obsessed by fears of British machinations, the American military blocked efforts to deal with postwar issues, including access to Berlin.

WHEN STRANG PRESENTED the British proposal to the EAC in mid-January 1944, his American colleague, Ambassador John G. Winant, was awaiting instructions because the Pentagon had blocked all action in the Working Security Committee. The situation was unchanged a month later when the Russian delegate, Ambassador Fedor T. Gusev, offered his government's plan, which accepted the western boundary of the Soviet zone outlined by Strang. Assuming that Winant had also submitted a plan, FDR asked Acting Secretary of State Edward Stettinius for details of the three proposals. He needed to know, he wrote, to ensure that the American submission "conform[ed] with what I decided on months ago." What he had decided was a mystery to Stettinius, and it remained a puzzle when the president offered an explanation three days later. His memo delineated no zonal boundaries in Germany and bore no relation to anything under consideration at the EAC. It would have made perfect sense to Morgan and the Combined Chiefs of Staff, however, because it was Roosevelt's rationale for swapping the European-wide zones envisaged in Rankin C. But thanks to Pentagon secrecy, no one at Foggy Bottom knew that.[28]

Word that Roosevelt had given the Department of State even this small glimpse of his thinking regarding Rankin broke the logjam in the Working Security Committee. A Pentagon staffer suggested that the committee be given a copy of the December JCS paper calling on Morgan to reverse his zonal allocations and incorporating the Pentagon's version of FDR's *Iowa* map. The army representative, Lieutenant Colonel Edgar P. Allen, was careful not to give away too much. His "impression" was that FDR had approved these papers, but he would not (perhaps could not) explain their background or context. All he knew was that the JCS wanted them sent to Winant.[29]

Stettinius's dispatch to Winant included Allen's papers and a map comparing the zones the JCS wanted and those already approved by the British and the Russians. With tongue in cheek, Stettinius described the JCS papers as "self-explanatory" and waited for Winant to explode. The ambassador did, saying he could not advocate these proposals in light of the British-Soviet agreement on boundaries. He was sending his assistant, George F. Kennan, to Washington for fuller explanation.[30]

When Kennan reached the White House, he found the president focused on the dispute over the northwestern zone. The conversation ran on for some time before Roosevelt understood that Kennan had crossed the Atlantic to talk about an entirely different topic: the boundary of the Soviet zone. As Kennan outlined the problem and described the JCS map, Roosevelt suddenly laughed and said, "Why that's just something I once drew on the back of an envelope." Adding that the British zonal proposal was "probably a fair decision," he authorized Winant to accept it, as long as he continued to insist on American occupation of the northwestern zone.[31]

The Working Security Committee set to work drafting new instructions to Winant. In the process, it produced the only documented attempt to write access into the EAC protocol. The committee's initial draft reflected Roosevelt's instructions, authorizing the ambassador to join his colleagues in accepting the zonal boundaries but insisting on the northwestern zone for the United States. Roosevelt's *Iowa* plan would have assured Western access to Berlin; his abandonment of it left access uncertain. That troubled someone on the committee, and its second draft added a paragraph that tied American acceptance of the zones to agreement that "freedom of movement between the respective zones and such central zone as may be established in Berlin or elsewhere will be accorded, without restriction of any kind, to all forces and other such personnel of the Governments participating in the occupation and control of Germany." The committee dropped this sentence two days later.[32]

Unfortunately, the committee's files do not indicate who urged the addition and who insisted on its removal. The odds are that someone from the Department of State—Mosely or James W. Riddleberger—suggested the insertion, and the military deleted it. Comments by Colonel George A. "Abe" Lincoln, one of Marshall's top planners, reveal the military's indifference at the time to zonal boundaries and their implications. The location of the western boundary of the Soviet zone was, in Lincoln's opinion, "a matter for very little moment from a military standpoint." As it was, the Civil Affairs Division put the cable in final form, and Riddleberger, who, as secretary of the committee, had drafted all three versions, concurred for the State Department. Then it went to the White House for FDR's approval.[33]

The British plan's merits were another reason why no alternative emerged in the EAC. As Roosevelt said, it was "a fair decision," a straightforward approach to the problem at hand: preventing renewed German aggression. The Soviets accepted it at once because it offered them more territory than their own plans did, and its equity and logic forestalled challenge.[34] In terms of equity, it divided Germany, within its 1937 borders, into three roughly equal zones—one each for Britain, the Soviet Union, and the United States. To avoid confusion, the boundaries followed existing administrative borders wherever possible. The British drew the zones in such a way as to encourage separatism, leaving the way open for permanent partition or dismemberment if the Allies decided on either. At Yalta, the Big Three would approve the plan without debate, although Churchill would persuade Roosevelt and Stalin to amend it by giving France a zone and a seat on the ACC.[35]

The EAC accepted the Attlee plan in part because Strang and Winant shared many of its authors' views: the zones would be temporary, a peace conference would soon convene, and in the meantime, the zones would not become exclusive preserves. Strang recalled, "It was not our expectation that the zones would be sealed off from one another." Some officials expected that a central German administration would survive and keep the country united. Others expected that the ACC would wield more power than the individual zonal commands. As Winant commented in January 1945, planners assumed that governments or the ACC would set broad overall policies, with zonal commanders retaining merely "the residue of powers."[36]

Like the planners, Winant and Strang (and their political superiors) assumed good relations among the victors. This was not a naive faith in Soviet goodwill or confidence that Western leaders could "handle Uncle Joe." Everyone realized the war would leave the Soviet Union weakened but without rivals on the Continent, and many were apprehensive about Russian intentions. France was powerless, Britain exhausted, Roosevelt determined to limit postwar American responsibilities. Western leaders realized the Soviets would do as they pleased in eastern Europe and saw the unity of the Grand Alliance as the best means of restraining them. Nowhere was cooperation more important than in Germany, where the victors shared a vital interest in preventing renewed German aggression. Discord would allow the Germans to evade controls and once again threaten world peace. Given the presence of Soviet armies in Germany, cooperation was not only desirable; it was unavoidable. Whether one trusted the Russians or not, presidential adviser Harry Hopkins argued, "it is certainly a risk that we have to take."[37]

The commission's work seemed to strengthen prospects for future cooperation. Strang recalled no serious misunderstandings or broken promises, while Winant felt a sense of trust and "common purpose."[38] The commission formally discussed access to Berlin only once, and Gusev's stance was encouraging. The topic came up in a roundabout way. When Roosevelt relinquished his claim to the northwestern zone, Churchill responded by ceding control of the ports of Bremen and Bremerhaven to the United States and promising unimpeded transit to them across the British zone. U.S. Army officials demanded a detailed agreement on transit, triggering a tedious and drawn-out negotiation with the British.[39] This squabble threatened the completion of the zonal protocol at an awkward time. France would be joining the commission soon, and the three delegations wanted to finish as much as they could beforehand. To speed things along, Gusev urged the insertion of a general proviso on transit to the ports, leaving the details for military officials to settle later. In support of this idea, he remarked that similar arrangements would be made regarding Berlin. According to the British record, Gusev merely discussed procedures (who would decide what), while according to the American record, he pledged that arrangements "will be made, providing United States and United Kingdom forces and control personnel full access to the Berlin zone across Soviet occupied territory."[40]

Winant's post-blockade critics—among them Major General John H. Hilldring, wartime chief of the Civil Affairs Division—would condemn him for taking Gusev's assurance at face value. Yet they all took the same position in 1944. When it came time for the U.S. Army to approve the zonal protocol Winant had negotiated, Hilldring pointed out that it made no provision for Western transit across the Soviet zone to Berlin. "The agreement is weak in this respect," he commented, "but I suppose that we may take it for granted that such facilities will be afforded. No change in the agreement in this particular is believed to be desirable." McCloy agreed.[41]

Another of Winant's critics, Robert D. Murphy, claimed that when Riddleberger urged that the zones converge on Berlin like slices of a pie, Winant rejected the idea. Murphy and people close to him would later suggest that the ambassador had assumed that the right to be in Berlin included the right to go there and that he had taken Soviet good faith for granted. Timing ranked higher in Winant's calculations, however. The EAC had completed the zonal protocol a few weeks before, and, as noted earlier, the three delegations wanted to nail down as much as they could before France joined. Winant believed it was too late to reopen the text.[42]

Thus the zonal protocol, completed by the EAC on September 12, 1944, and approved by the three governments the following February, contained no provisions for Western transit across the Soviet zone to Berlin.[43] Western access would depend on whatever arrangements could be made in a separate agreement; several apparent missed opportunities developed in 1945.

IN JANUARY 1945, the joint chiefs proposed raising the subject of postwar access to Berlin at Yalta. The Foreign Office preferred to wait until the three governments decided whether France would receive a zone and an ACC seat. The French would not be at Yalta, and any tripartite access accord reached there would have to be renegotiated if they joined the occupation regime.[44]

Western representatives did not raise the issue with the Russians at Yalta, although the Americans discussed it among themselves. Military planners urged that the United States seek Allied acceptance of "the general principle of freedom of transit across zones of occupation" and in Berlin. Leahy grumbled that he would submit the idea to FDR, although he "questioned the president's interest." When the document was ready, he changed his mind, claiming the paper "unnecessarily burdens the President and took [*sic*] up his time." Thanks to Leahy's obstruction, the proposal went to London and Moscow without the weight of the Oval Office behind it. The British accepted, the Soviets never responded, and the joint chiefs did not press the issue.[45]

The JCS put forward their proposal as an "interim military measure" pending broader agreements on transit, which, they commented, "may be expected from the European Advisory Commission." This remark prompted the planning committee of the U.S. EAC delegation to draft such an agreement, only to have Mosely stifle the initiative at a delegation meeting on March 23.[46] His reasons are not clear. The committee's draft was little more than a paraphrase of the JCS proposal and would have been superfluous if the Soviets accepted that document. Mosely may have thought that an agreement based on this vague paper would preclude a more specific accord. In the spring of 1945, he was drafting such an agreement, which would have allowed the American commander to choose any two railroads and highways. Under his proposal, the Americans could also repair railway lines, roads, bridges, and signals as they saw fit, plus operate gasoline stations, rest areas, and repair patrols along the routes. If any route became unavailable, the Soviets would provide an equivalent. Mosely thought his proposal was more likely to win acceptance in Moscow than one allowing Western forces to wander at will in the Soviet zone. That expectation, pride of authorship, and the notion that an agreement along these lines would better protect Western interests probably led him to oppose the committee's draft.[47]

When no opportunity arose to submit his draft accord in the EAC, Mosely shared it and a memo summarizing the background of the access issue with the chief of the U.S. Post-Hostilities Planning Section on Eisenhower's staff, Colonel Charles R. Kutz, in mid-May. Although historian Daniel Nelson thought matters ended there, Mosely's handiwork did influence the military's thinking, and it would reach the Russians twice in modified form.[48]

Meanwhile, what many have regarded as the West's best chance of guaranteeing postwar access had come to naught. In the spring of 1945, Churchill sought to persuade the Americans to race the Russians to Berlin, but they would not listen. One may question the widespread assumption that, had the Western powers reached Berlin first, postwar access would have been assured. No one has suggested that the Western governments would have set aside the zonal protocol. The armies would have withdrawn to the agreed zonal boundaries, leaving the city surrounded by the Soviet zone. The Western powers might have secured a "better" access agreement when they left, but we cannot be sure. In any case, postwar transit depended on Soviet cooperation. If relations soured, arrangements secured after a withdrawal from Berlin would have been no more secure than those actually obtained in 1945, when Eisenhower's armies evacuated portions of the Soviet zone they had overrun in the last weeks of the war. The postwar situation would have been the same.[49]

There was one other possibility: establish the seat of Allied government elsewhere. The British toyed with this idea in the spring of 1945, but by then, all four governments had endorsed the EAC's zonal protocol and its special Berlin enclave. The city's symbolic value made it almost inevitable that the Allies would govern Germany from there. The destruction in the city at the war's end, horrific as it was, did not cause them to reconsider.[50]

By the time Berlin fell to the Russians on May 2, access to Berlin and the withdrawal of Western armies from the Soviet zone had become linked. From mid-April onward, Eisenhower had wanted to withdraw Western armies and turn the zone over to the Russians as soon as the tactical situation permitted, but Churchill persuaded the new American president, Harry S. Truman, to leave the troops where they were. The zonal protocol took effect the moment Germany surrendered, but V-E Day came and went with no sign of a Western departure. The Soviets concluded that their partners intended to ignore the protocol and keep the territory they had captured. At a meeting of the four Allied commanders in chief in Berlin on June 5, Zhukov refused to discuss setting up the control council until Western forces evacuated his zone. Eisenhower, Clay, and political adviser Robert Murphy persuaded Hopkins, in Frankfurt on his way home from talks with Stalin, that it was time to withdraw. Clay drafted a cable for Hopkins to send to the president calling for withdrawal to begin June 21. Simultaneously, Western forces would move into Berlin "under an agreement between the respective commanders which would provide us with unrestricted access to our Berlin area from Bremen and Frankfurt by air, rail, and highway on agreed routes."[51] With Churchill's grudging approval, Truman sent Stalin the Hopkins-Clay proposal on June 14; the prime minister dispatched a similar telegram the following day. Stalin's replies delayed the troop movements until July 1 and said nothing about access.[52]

Clay directed Major General Floyd L. Parks, who had been appointed to command the U.S. Berlin garrison, to fly to Berlin and confer with the Russians about withdrawal from the zone, Western entry into Berlin, and preparations for the Berlin summit conference. Parks was to secure "continuing running rights" on the Helmstedt and Frankfurt autobahns, "effective at once," including the right to detour "as required" and freedom from "all customs duties, inspection and the like, and from any and all stoppage or interference . . . without exception." In addition, Clay wanted a "continuing right of movement, effective at once," over two rail lines, also free from inspection. American aircraft could use two airways, one from Frankfurt and the other from Bremen, without restriction. SHAEF forwarded this agenda to the U.S. military mission in Moscow on June 21 for presentation to the Soviets, the first time a version of Mosely's transit proposals reached them.[53]

After several days of haggling, the Americans obtained permission to bring troops forward to survey the summit site (which Westerners expected would be in Berlin). The Russians agreed only after Ambassador W. Averell Harriman twice assured them that the group would not exceed 50 officers, 175 soldiers, 50 vehicles, and 5 aircraft—numbers provided by SHAEF. Parks flew into Berlin with a small group of aides. He also commanded a larger ground force that was to set up a compound in the city for the American summit delegation. This unit's leader, Colonel Frank L. Howley, also commanded the U.S. military government unit destined for Berlin, and the dual assignment caused trouble. Parks's instructions to Howley were unclear, and the colonel brought his military government detachment as well as the summit survey team. Russian soldiers at the autobahn bridge near Dessau, halfway to Berlin, denied passage to his swollen column, citing the numerical limits agreed on in Moscow. Howley had never heard of the numbers and thought the Russians were being obstructive. He argued with them for several hours before receiving instructions from Parks to comply with their demands.[54]

The incident had long-lasting effects. Howley commanded the American sector during the blockade, and in his memoirs he treated the episode at the bridge as proof that the Soviets had been hostile from the start. He never knew the numbers had come from SHAEF, and Western historians continue to repeat his version of events. The Russians interpreted the episode as an American attempt to move troops into Berlin early, violating the Truman-Stalin agreement that withdrawal from the Russian zone and entry into Berlin would occur simultaneously. Howley's actions reinforced the Soviets' mistrust of the West, and Parks's meeting failed to advance the American agenda. When he tried to raise the Clay-Mosely points dealing with access and transit, the Russians would discuss summit preparations only.[55]

Preparations for evacuating the Russian zone and entering Berlin gathered momentum. The Americans had been pressing for a meeting with Zhukov, and it was finally arranged for June 29. Major General John R. Deane, chief of the U.S. military mission in Moscow, and Parks reported that Zhukov "urgently" wanted a list of subjects the Western representatives would discuss. Eisenhower's deputy, Air Marshal Sir Arthur W. Tedder, responded with a detailed list including the now-standard proposals for access. The Western powers wanted immediate and unrestricted use of two autobahns and two railroads, with the right to repair and maintain them. Western officials would train railway crews and supervise them, even in the Russian zone. Western traffic would not be subject to search or control by customs officials or military guards. The Western powers would enjoy unrestricted air traffic between their zones and Staaken, Tempelhof, and Gatow airfields in Berlin and exclusive use and occupancy of the first two bases. Parks gave this second version of Mosely's ideas to General Sergei Kruglov of the People's Commissariat of Internal Affairs, who promised to pass it on to Zhukov.[56]

Clay, his British counterpart General Weeks, and their staffs landed at Gatow on June 29 and drove to Zhukov's headquarters. For over four hours, Clay, Zhukov, and Weeks discussed the issues Parks had been unable to raise: withdrawing Western troops from the Russian zone, moving Western garrisons into Berlin, and Western transit across the Soviet zone. The meeting was businesslike and productive, the atmosphere cordial and relaxed.

After arranging Western withdrawal, the generals turned to access. Zhukov complained that Western control of roads and rail lines to Berlin would divide his zone and create "an extremely difficult administrative problem." He thought one railroad, one highway, and one air corridor would be enough for the small Western contingents. Clay countered that he and Weeks were not seeking exclusive use of the routes, only "freedom of access" under "whatever regulations are set down." After Clay and Weeks accepted the Magdeburg-Berlin railway and autobahn, Zhukov asked them to drop their request for other roads. Clay agreed but reserved the right to reopen the subject. Zhukov countered that "possibly all points discussed at this conference may be changed." Both sides thus regarded the day's results as temporary and subject to revision.

Talk turned to traffic control. Clay asked for "unlimited access to roads," a concept Zhukov professed not to understand, although according to one record of the meeting, he agreed that British and American troops could use the Helmstedt autobahn "unrestrictedly." The generals agreed that Russian road signs and military police would control traffic "in the normal way," according to Murphy (who was not there and received the news secondhand). The Russians would check identity documents but had no interest in inspecting cargo, Zhukov said; his people did not care "what was being hauled, how much, or how many trucks were moving."

Airfields and air routes were next. Everyone agreed that Tempelhof would be under American control; it was in the U.S. sector. There was confusion about Staaken and Gatow. Weeks thought Gatow would be Russian and Staaken British. Zhukov said his maps showed the reverse. The two set the issue aside to be settled later (which it was, along Zhukov's lines). With Berlin's airfields allocated, the next question was how to reach them. The Americans wanted to fly anywhere in a triangle bounded by Berlin, Hamburg, and Frankfurt. Zhukov insisted on an air lane twenty miles wide from Berlin to Magdeburg. There it would divide, one part going to Hannover for the British, the other southwest to Frankfurt for the Americans.[57]

Clay later claimed that Zhukov offered to sign a transit agreement but he decided not to accept. A document that confirmed access on any and all routes was one thing, but what Zhukov offered was far less. An agreement granting access along some routes by implication denied it on all others.[58] Clay's story seems unlikely. Parks's copious notes of the meeting contain no such offer. SHAEF's position for the past six weeks had been that it wanted transit rights along specific routes, not a general right of transit in the western reaches of the Soviet zone. Clay had been part of that process. The cable he had written for Hopkins had not asked for free transit, only passage along "agreed routes."

The Cold War and the Berlin blockade made this meeting appear to be a missed opportunity. Clay would blame himself for not insisting on free access as a condition of withdrawal from the Soviet zone (an admission that undercuts later Western claims that access had been a prerequisite), while others complained he should have obtained a written agreement safeguarding access.[59] Neither alternative would have made much difference. If Clay had obtained either, the West might have had a stronger legal case against a blockade. Yet it is hard to see how that would have been an advantage. When the State Department claimed in July 1948 that free access had been a condition of withdrawal, Moscow ignored the argument. What mattered was not whether the agreements were written or oral, conditional or unconditional. The fundamental facts were ones of geography and political will. The Soviets controlled the ground. Once East and West saw each other as enemies, Moscow could impose or lift restrictions whenever doing so seemed politically advantageous, and there was little the West could do in response, short of armed force.

American military leaders, like the British planners and the EAC negotiators, did not push for more because they shared the general optimism about the future of East-West relations. Eisenhower remarked in May 1945 that Western relations with the Russians were at the same stage as British-American contacts had been in 1942. Just as Anglo-American cooperation had grown, he predicted, "the more contact we have with the Russians, the more they will understand us and the greater will be the cooperation." In his memoirs, he would describe Berlin as "an experimental laboratory for the development of international accord."[60] Worries about bribing a burglar never crossed his mind in these months; nor did they trouble Clay, who was determined to do all he could to make four-power rule in Germany succeed. "It's got to work," he told a gathering of reporters. "If the four of us cannot get together now in running Germany, how are we going to get together in an international organization to secure the peace of the world?"[61]

THE ACCESS ARRANGEMENTS that would be so roundly condemned in later decades worked well for more than two years. As Clay recalled, road, rail, barge, and air traffic moved to and from Berlin without Soviet interference until the end of 1947.[62] If the Soviets resisted attempts to expand Western access, they made no effort to disrupt it.

As Clay, Weeks, and Zhukov expected, the access arrangements they worked out on June 29 proved temporary. On September 10 the ACC approved a paper authorizing sixteen Western freight trains to transit the zone daily, supporting the Western garrisons and delivering the West's share of coal and food for the city.[63] Daily service would grow to twenty-four freight and seven passenger trains by October 1947. Road and rail traffic rested on the June 29 verbal agreements and on an October 1946 ACC directive. Soviet officials allowed the Americans and the British to open repair stations on the Helmstedt autobahn in January 1946, and at their invitation, the British operated a small railway service detachment at Magdeburg from late 1945 through the following summer.[64] A May 1946 ACC agreement set up procedures for routine Allied interzonal travel by road. The Soviets rejected a similar four-power directive regulating barge traffic on canals and waterways. Canals linked their zone with the British zone but not with the American or French, and they insisted on a bilateral agreement.[65]

These rail, road, and barge accords are less well known than the November 1945 air corridor agreement. Clay, Zhukov, and Weeks had approved air corridors connecting Berlin with the western zones, but the arrangement had not worked well, for two reasons. First, the British and the Americans thought the generals had approved a Y-shaped airway originating from Berlin and dividing at Magdeburg, with one arm continuing toward Frankfurt and the other to Hannover. The Russian understanding was that there would be two ruler-straight corridors—one linking Berlin and Bremen, the other linking Berlin and Frankfurt. The Soviets complained of wholesale Western violations before the source of the misunderstanding was identified, and even then, the Russians insisted on their interpretation. Second, aircraft in the corridors flew under national control; that is, British controllers at Gatow directed their planes, while Americans at Tempelhof controlled U.S. flights—hardly the safest procedure.[66] The British wanted unrestricted flight west of Berlin, subject to reasonable notice and safety considerations. Their eventual goal was freedom of flight over all Germany. Washington liked the idea, and the American air commander, General John Cannon, promised to instruct his representative in the Allied air directorate, Major General Robert Harper, to work out a common position with the British. Instead, Harper undermined British efforts by circulating a plan for an expanded corridor system.[67]

Over the next few weeks, the air directorate drafted a plan that followed Harper's ideas. This proposal would establish a Berlin Control Zone, a cylinder 10,000 feet high and 40 miles across centered on the ACC building. A four-power air safety center would control traffic in this zone. Corridors 20 miles wide would radiate from the zone to Hamburg, Hannover, Frankfurt, Prague, Warsaw, and Copenhagen. The Soviets objected to the latter three as being international arrangements beyond the ACC's purview, but Zhukov assured his colleagues that these corridors would be established "in due course." Whereas the Western powers spoke of corridors to satisfy the "requirements of the Four *Powers* for flights over the occupied Zones," the Russians always described the Hamburg, Hannover, and Frankfurt corridors as supporting "the needs of the occupation *troops* in the zone of Greater Berlin" (emphasis added). The plan approved by the ACC on November 30, 1945, contained the three German corridors as well as the two conflicting rationales. The different emphases doubtless seemed unimportant at the time, but they would become the subject of much learned disputation later.[68] The corridors took effect December 19, 1945; the Berlin Air Safety Center started operation April 15, 1946. Under flight rules worked out later, aircraft of the occupying powers could use the corridors without prior notice.[69]

Historians have treated this agreement as if it were unique. This written accord, so the argument goes, protected the airlift against Soviet interference in 1948, while the lack of written guarantees regarding surface access invited obstruction.[70] Yet the ACC did reach written agreements on road and rail traffic. The air agreement carried no more—and no less—legal weight than the other accords. The September 1945 rail accord had precisely the same standing as the air corridor agreement; both were numbered papers approved by the control council. In addition, the air corridor agreement said nothing about a Western *right* of access; like the other transport accords, it established practical procedures for travel. The Russians interfered with surface travel in 1948 and abstained in the air not because the air agreement was more binding than the other accords. They could impede surface travel relatively easily, through new "implementing regulations." In contrast, interfering with Western aircraft ran serious risks. That is what protected air traffic to and from Berlin and made the airlift possible, not the written nature of the November 30 accord.

Western air traffic was not, as is commonly supposed, restricted to the corridors. As one American observed in January 1946, "we can fly over the Russian zone in other directions by giving notification 48 hours in advance." A Russian report indicated that this practice was continuing more than a year later.[71] The Russians cooperated in other ways, helping the British and French acquire their own airfields in Berlin. In August 1945, Zhukov gave the British all of Gatow airfield, which the EAC protocol had divided between the British sector and the Russian zone. Zhukov's deputy, General Vasily D. Sokolovsky, ceded land to the French some weeks later to give them room for an airfield.[72]

Despite such examples of cooperation, the Soviets' general approach was to restrict the Western presence in their zone. At Potsdam, the British sought approval for the principle of freedom of movement by Allied citizens throughout Germany. The Soviet foreign minister, Vyacheslav Molotov, blocked the suggestion, insisting that the ACC study it first. The foreign ministers agreed to refer the matter to Berlin without, unfortunately, recording the decision in the protocol or communiqué.[73] When Field Marshal Sir Bernard L. Montgomery raised the subject, Zhukov would not even discuss passing it on to the staff for study, saying he was too busy. Sokolovsky echoed his chief.[74] British Foreign Secretary Ernest Bevin tried again at the London foreign ministers' meeting, asking Molotov to remind Zhukov of their decision at Potsdam. Molotov promised to look into the subject but claimed that "no concrete decisions" had been made at Potsdam and contended that the military governors were in the best position to decide when to consider the matter.[75] Despite the high-level interest in London, members of Montgomery's staff regarded the issue as of "no intrinsic urgency" and linked it to interzonal travel by Germans, which they opposed due to security worries, lack of accommodations, and fear of a mass exodus from the Russian zone.[76]

In December 1945, the Americans revived the British proposal—derailed by Harper two months earlier—to give military aircraft of the occupying powers "complete freedom of transit over Germany." The Russians opposed both that idea and a March 1946 effort to expand the corridors.[77] When the Americans revived the free-transit proposal in November 1946, Sokolovsky countered that the existing corridors were more than sufficient for the needs of the Berlin garrisons. After all, he continued, "tanks, infantry, and all other types of armed services of the Allies were in the zones allocated to them and did not roam in other zones. He did not see why this right should be granted to aviation." The issue was one for governments, he continued, shrugging off suggestions that he ask Moscow for authority to deal with it. His colleagues had no choice but to withdraw the paper. Another attempt in February 1947 met a similar fate.[78]

Sokolovsky proved equally unyielding regarding surface routes. He denied a December 1945 request for direct routes to Berlin from the American zone, writing to Clay that the highways and railways in his zone were "extremely overburdened." Clay revived the subject twice more; Sokolovsky would not budge. Even so, there was an informal arrangement at the working level, starting perhaps in 1946 and confirmed in October 1947, that allowed four freight trains a day to enter the Soviet zone from Bavaria, carrying meat for the Kommandatura, the four-power committee in charge of Berlin.[79]

Despite the Russians' uncooperative attitude, Clay recalled few problems over access. Banditry was the biggest problem in the early months. Delays were frequent, with trains taking two or three days to reach Berlin from Helmstedt. Armed gangs, often in Soviet uniforms, boarded stationary trains and stole whatever they could. Others stopped trucks on the autobahn at gunpoint, leading the Americans to escort convoys with armored cars. A request that the Russians provide train guards to work alongside Americans went unanswered. In January 1946, two drunken Soviet officers tried to force their way aboard an American train. A military policeman opened fire, killing one intruder and wounding the other. Clay complained to Sokolovsky three months later that "outlaws masquerading . . . as Soviet soldiers" had been stealing supplies from American trains in the Soviet zone; he asked the Russians to suppress the marauding bands.[80] He lodged another protest after the Russians began removing Germans traveling on American military trains. Sokolovsky insisted on the right to check German passengers crossing his zone. Clay denied that the Russians had a right to enter U.S. military trains and assured Sokolovsky that the trains would carry only American citizens and Germans employed by the U.S. military. If all else failed, Clay added, he would station "fifty soldiers with machine guns" on each train, with orders to shoot anyone attempting to board. The two eventually reached a gentleman's agreement. Sokolovsky would not waive his right to inspect Western military trains but would not enforce it, while Clay reiterated his promise to bar Germans who were not affiliated with the military government.[81]

The gentleman's agreement may have prompted the British to allow their German employees to travel on British military trains to and from Berlin. Passengers could not leave the trains in Soviet-controlled territory, and passenger lists would be available for Soviet inspection, but Russian guards were not to check passengers or remove them. Advised of this procedure when it began in July 1946, the Soviets raised no objections. Twice, in October 1946 and February 1947, Soviet soldiers inspected passengers and sent those without interzonal passes back to Berlin. The British reacted strongly, warning that their guards had instructions to prevent, by force if necessary, Soviet officials from boarding their trains, and they would carry out those orders "regardless of the consequences." The Soviets blamed overzealous junior officers and let the matter drop until January 1948.[82] By then, the diplomatic climate had changed dramatically, and Stalin was willing to exploit the opportunity provided by the wartime accords.

CHAPTER 2

Willingness

Wartime mistakes are only half an explanation of the causes of the Berlin blockade. The other half can be attributed to Stalin's motivations. If opportunity alone mattered, he would have imposed the blockade in 1945. Instead, he acted as a result of worsening East-West relations in general and deepening disagreements over the future of Germany in particular.

The European Advisory Commission's plans for postwar Germany rested on Western hopes; Stalin's fears shaped postwar realities. Spurred by mistrust of his Western allies, Stalin resolved to establish a security zone beyond the southern and western borders of the Soviet Union. He believed the Western powers would acquiesce, and they did, to a degree. But the exclusive influence he demanded and the methods he used to achieve it revived old stereotypes, leading Western officials to see Soviet policy as hostile and aggressive. They, in turn, embarked on policies that deepened Stalin's mistrust: resumption of an active U.S. role on the Continent, economic revival of western Europe, a separate regime in the western zones of Germany, and a transatlantic military alliance. By mid-1947, officials on both sides of the "Iron Curtain" were seeing the world in bipolar terms.

Germany contributed little at first to this spiral of disagreement, yet the victors' failure to work out common policies for the country during the war eventually poisoned their postwar relations. Several authors have suggested that the Cold War might have been avoided (or moderated) had the victors agreed to divide Europe into spheres of influence. Fraser Harbutt, for example, believes the British and Russians were close to such an understanding by 1944, and Marc Trachtenberg has argued that Secretary of State James F. Byrnes had a similar arrangement in mind at the Potsdam conference. Germany made such an amicable parting of the ways impossible. The Allies never agreed during the war how the country might fit into a divided Europe. The EAC was one logical place to work out a common position, but neither the Soviet nor the American government took the commission seriously. Anglo-Soviet discussions of what Harbutt terms the "Moscow Order" skirted Germany's future. Byrnes's efforts ran afoul of what Trachtenberg has shown to be a fundamental fact in the postwar world: the Soviet Union, fearing a resurgence of German power, could not give the Western powers a totally free hand in western Germany, while the West, troubled by Soviet actions in eastern Europe, was increasingly inclined to abandon four-power control and revive Germany. Germany, in short, could not be fitted into a clean division of Europe that satisfied all the victors.[1]

Adding Germany to the Cold War dynamics of mutual fear pushed the spiral into overdrive. A Germany allied with the wrong side posed unacceptable risks. By the summer of 1947, both sides saw German recovery in Cold War terms. British and American officials, fearing that the slow pace of European economic revival would open the way to communist revolutions, saw salvation in spurring German recovery. An economically revived Germany would hasten European reconstruction, bolstering political and economic stability and containing communism. If the motivation was defensive, the consequences, as the Soviets saw them, constituted an attack on Moscow's position in central Europe. Soviet leaders regarded German revival under Western auspices as the first step toward another invasion, and they looked for a way to stop it. Stalin thought he had found it in Berlin.

THE COLD WAR BEGAN when the Allies could not agree on the future of Poland and eastern Europe. Stalin was determined to restore the borders Molotov had negotiated with the Nazis in August 1939. Those borders, as Stalin told Eden in December 1941, were "what the whole war is about."[2] He also intended to extend Soviet influence westward to provide a security zone in eastern Europe. Stalin was in some ways an old-fashioned man, equating security with territory: the more land Moscow controlled, the safer it would be. Realizing there was little they could do to prevent it, the United States and Great Britain accepted Soviet control but sought to persuade Stalin to allow an "open sphere," one in which eastern European countries would enjoy self-determination and autonomy. Stalin refused. He signed the Yalta accords, apparently endorsing their idealistic precepts, but they meant nothing; "we'll . . . do it our own way later," he assured Molotov.[3]

Stalin insisted on this security zone because the underlying premise of his diplomacy—rooted in Marxist-Leninist ideology, Russian xenophobia, and his own suspicious personality—was a belief in the unwavering hostility of the Western capitalist world. "I do not believe in the goodness of the bourgeoisie," he had told H. G. Wells in the 1930s. Capitalists were predators. They preyed on one another and would destroy the workers' state if they could. The wartime alliance had been necessary for survival, but the nature of capitalism had not changed; the struggle against it would continue. "The crisis of capitalism found expression in a division of the capitalists into two factions," Stalin explained to Georgi Dimitrov in January 1945, "one fascist, the other democratic. . . . We are now with one faction against the other, but in the future we shall be against that capitalist faction too."[4] Neither a declaration of preference nor a statement of intent, Stalin's prediction reflected fatalistic acceptance of what must be according to the scientific laws of Marxist-Leninist historical materialism. Stalin's perception of the outside world as hostile did not translate to the plotting of revolutions or aggressive wars. Rather, it meant tearing away what he called the false "veil of amity," treating every Western move with suspicion, playing imperialists off against one another, securing buffer zones that rolled back capitalist influence, and insulating Soviet society from contaminating contact. Most of all, it meant making Russia too powerful to be attacked and never giving the slightest hint that it could be intimidated. If the imperialists sensed weakness, they would exploit their advantage to the fullest.[5]

As Gaddis Smith has suggested, the ghost of Adolf Hitler haunted the victors in both East and West.[6] The war left everyone more sensitive about security and possible threats. They looked to the immediate past and drew lessons from the failure to deal with aggressors in the 1930s. "How horrible, fantastic, incredible, it is that we should be digging trenches and trying on gas-masks here," Neville Chamberlain had declared in September 1938, "because of a quarrel in a far-away country between people of whom we know nothing!"[7] The war seemed to prove that what happened in faraway countries mattered to everyone. Security was indivisible; aggression would spread unless confronted early. Weakness, compromise, and concession invited attack; only firmness could assure peace. Just as Poland and Pearl Harbor had driven home these lessons in British and American minds, Operation Barbarossa, Hitler's invasion of the Soviet Union, had seared similar convictions into Soviet consciousness. The psychological effects in Russia far exceeded those in the West because of the horrendous price the Soviet Union paid during the war. One-quarter to one-third of its national wealth was obliterated, a total of $128 billion. The human toll staggers the imagination. At least 25 million Soviets died (some estimates are higher), tens of millions were wounded, and 25 million were left homeless. These losses dwarfed those of the Western powers: as David Reynolds has pointed out, one Russian city, Leningrad, suffered more casualties than the United States, the United Kingdom, and the Commonwealth combined. On the evening of V-E Day, one Russian wrote, "there could not have been a single table in the Soviet Union where those gathering around it were not conscious of an empty place."[8]

This catastrophe reinforced Stalin's sense of insecurity. Victory brought no relief, only renewed calls for more sacrifices from the Soviet peoples. The renewed prominence of ideology in Soviet pronouncements caused Western analysts to revert to older models of Soviet behavior, and the wartime admiration for Russian resistance to the Nazis gave way to new fears of communist subversion. In turn, Western efforts to preserve maneuvering room for noncommunist parties in Poland and eastern Europe in 1945 and opposition to Soviet aspirations in Turkey and northern Iran in 1946 reinforced Stalin's suspicions of the Western powers and intensified the siege mentality in the Kremlin. Although none of the early clashes in this spiral of suspicion made later ones inevitable, the memory of each poisoned the next. By mid-1947, officials East and West were coming to see problems not as isolated incidents but as episodes in a conflict that threatened national survival. Germany was too important to remain an exception.

LIKE THE EMERGING COLD WAR of which it was a part, the collapse of the Grand Alliance in Germany is a complex story of interaction and unintended consequences. Each of the four Allied powers wanted and expected cooperation after the war—cooperation of a kind, on its own terms. Through diplomatic skill, force of personality, or the logic of events, officials from all four powers believed they could induce their partners to accept their definition of the common interest. Four generals bore responsibility for forging common policies in Germany: Lucius D. Clay for the Americans, Brian H. Robertson for the British, Vasily D. Sokolovsky for the Soviets, and Pierre Koenig for the French. The first three initially served as deputy military governors and were later promoted to the top position, while Koenig became French military governor in the summer of 1945 and held the post for the next four years. The organization in which these men and their staffs worked was called the Allied Control Authority (ACA); it was often referred to (incorrectly) as the Allied Control Council, or ACC, which properly referred to the four military governors collectively. The ACC, the senior policy-making body in Germany, met every ten days or so. Below it was the Coordinating Committee, made up of the four deputy military governors. A secretariat handled administrative details and coordinated activities of the staff, divided into about a dozen directorates. A special four-power committee, the Kommandatura, supervised the operations of the Berlin city administration, the Magistrat. Chairmanship at all levels rotated among the four powers monthly.[9]

From the start, Clay made decisions on the American side. As early as October 1945, Eisenhower regarded him as "the only 'indispensable' man in the whole business."[10] Eisenhower and his successor, Joseph McNarney, let Clay handle nearly everything regarding military government and the ACA. That responsibility was some consolation for the intense, brilliant engineer. The assignment to Germany was "the last thing I wanted," Clay recalled. He longed to command troops in battle but had spent nearly the entire war in Washington. His appointment as Eisenhower's deputy in March 1945 meant that others would lead soldiers to victory in the remaining theater of war, the Pacific. He channeled his combative energies into the myriad problems facing him in Germany. Driven and self-assured, Clay thrived on overwork, relished challenges, and insisted on doing things his way. Son of a U.S. senator, he had a strong political sense, honed during years of work in the Corps of Engineers and as Byrnes's right-hand man in the Office of War Mobilization. Clay was smart, and he knew it, and his self-confidence made him impulsive and intolerant of differing views. He could be difficult to work for. Aide Robert Bowie recalled that "the focus of Clay's personality and his intensity when he contested or argued something—it was almost like a physical blow." And Clay loved to argue. He had opinions about everything, and the more evidence marshaled against his views, the more tenaciously he clung to them. He would clash with officials in Washington, particularly foreign service officers in the Department of State, over policy in Germany, making it hard for contemporaries and historians alike to say what U.S. policy was. Clay served as deputy military governor and commanding general of the Office of Military Government (United States) (OMGUS) under Eisenhower and McNarney before becoming theater commander and military governor in March 1947.[11]

Brian Robertson possessed all of Clay's ability. He had served on the western front in the First World War, then campaigned along India's northwest frontier and worked in the War Office before retiring from the army in 1933. The following year he immigrated to South Africa and went into business. Returning to uniform in 1940, he rose to become Montgomery's chief administrative officer in North Africa. That post was more important than it sounds, for Robertson was no mere paper-pusher. Under the British staff system, he was one of Montgomery's top two subordinates, responsible for administration, personnel, and logistics (the G-1 and G-4 functions in the American army). Monty rated Robertson "the best chief of administration in the British army"; British official historians described him as an "administrator of genius." A model staff officer, he had a penetrating, analytical mind. Robertson could be counted on to follow his government's lead in a way that Clay could not, reflecting his more reserved personality and his family history: his father, chief of the imperial general staff during the Great War, had opposed David Lloyd George's "peripheral" strategy and had been sacked in February 1918.[12]

Another superb staff officer, Vasily Sokolovsky had led a company of Red Army troops during the civil war and served in a series of staff and command posts during the Great Patriotic War. Zhukov commandeered him as his second in command for the assault on Berlin, and Sokolovsky took part in the negotiations leading to the city's surrender. Stalin let Zhukov keep him after the war as deputy military governor, and Sokolovsky took the marshal's place in April 1946. Westerners liked and respected this quiet, intelligent soldier. In a memoir written at the height of the Cold War, Canadian General Maurice Pope remembered him as a man of great charm, while Clay found his sense of humor "delightful."[13]

The fourth member of the ACC was a war hero. Pierre M. Koenig had won two medals for bravery during the First World War and fought in Morocco with the Foreign Legion in the 1930s. A member of the ill-fated Allied expedition to Norway in the spring of 1940, he joined de Gaulle's Free French that summer. Posted at the southern end of the British line in the Libyan desert in May 1942, his four battalions fought three divisions of Rommel's Panzerarmee Afrika to a standstill for two weeks at Bir Hacheim. By the spring of 1944, Koenig was commander of the Forces Françaises de l'Intérieur; he then served as military governor of liberated Paris.[14]

The main task facing these men was to reform Germany so that it never again threatened peace. For Clay, Robertson, and Sokolovsky, common policies had been agreed on at Potsdam. The conference protocol confirmed the authority of the ACC, vesting supreme power in the Allied commanders in chief both collectively as the council and singly as zonal commanders. The commanders were to treat the German population uniformly, "so far as is practicable." They were to disarm, demilitarize, and denazify the Reich. No central government would be established "for the time being," although central administrative agencies would be created under Allied supervision in areas such as finance, transportation, communications, foreign trade, and industry.

The protocol's economic provisions formed an intricate web. The three powers agreed to treat Germany as an economic unit, with common policies in all zones regarding industrial production and allocation, agriculture, wages and prices, rationing, currency, reparations, and transport and communications. Application of these common policies might take into account "varying local conditions." The allies were to devise import and export programs for the entire country and achieve a balanced economy; essential commodities were to be distributed equitably among the zones. The ACA was to define a level of industry that would support, without external assistance, a standard of living that was no higher than the European average, excepting the Soviet Union and Great Britain. Excess industrial capacity, plus all war industries and arms production, would be dismantled and made available as reparations. Each occupying power would meet its reparations claims through removals from its own zone, although the Western powers agreed to give the Soviets 10 percent of the capital equipment they dismantled, plus an additional 15 percent in exchange for an equivalent value in food and raw materials from the Soviet zone. Profits and proceeds from current production and stocks would be used "in the first place" to pay for imports.[15]

All this seemed to be a promising start, yet four-power cooperation in Germany failed. One reason, paradoxically, was the Potsdam agreement itself. The product of compromise, it was vague and contradictory. It did not create strong unifying policies or institutions to offset divisive tendencies already making themselves felt. To the contrary, the protocol left the powers free to do as they pleased with regard to reparations and trade. The EAC had intended the zones to have no other purpose than to delimit the areas each army would occupy. Potsdam's reparations clauses gave the zones new life.

A second reason for the collapse of cooperation was the attitude of the French. In working out the Potsdam accords, British, American, and Soviet leaders had taken for granted—as they had throughout the war—that they could make binding decisions for all the Allies. Even though the French would have a seat on the ACC and a zone, the other three powers had excluded them from Potsdam. This proved to be a colossal error. The French felt free to oppose aspects of the Potsdam agreement they did not like—and they did not like most of them. They regarded the central administrative agencies called for in the protocol as "the first sign of a rebirth of the Reich"; Koenig vetoed them. Furthermore, it was axiomatic in Paris that the German desire for power could not be eradicated; therefore, Germany must be deprived of the means to threaten the peace of Europe. The Ruhr must be separated from the rest of the country and put under international control, and its resources must be dedicated to rebuilding the economies of Hitler's victims, France foremost among them. In the French view, Germany should also lose the Rhineland and the Saar. The French were determined to impose this program not simply because they believed it was the only way to prevent another German invasion (and because they feared that a central government in Berlin would be subject to Soviet influence); they had made it the keystone of plans for their country's recovery. The Monnet plan rested on the premise that France could draw freely on German resources and replace Germany as the industrial heart of western Europe. For the French, failure in Germany meant economic and political defeat at home.[16]

The French stance magnified the ACA's two fundamental weaknesses. Like its contemporary, the United Nations Security Council, it operated on the basis of great-power unanimity. As long as the four governments agreed on common policies, the ACA could work effectively. French policy threatened stalemate. Further, the ACA had been intended to oversee the work of a German central administration, not to rule Germany itself. Koenig's vetoes forced the ACA to shoulder those responsibilities, something it was ill-suited to do. The French stance intensified centrifugal forces in postwar Germany.

Yet the main reason cooperation failed was the attitude of the Soviet Union. Norman Naimark has written that "from the onset . . . the Soviets thought of themselves as being in a struggle with the Western Allies for the future of Germany." Soviet words emphasized unity; Soviet actions fostered partition.[17] From the first, the Russians operated their zone as an exclusive preserve, free from the pretense that the ACA or the other Allies had any influence there; at the same time, in the name of unity, they insisted on having a voice in the western zones. Even before the war ended, Stalin had ceded more than a third of his zone to the Poles without consulting or informing his Western partners. In September 1945, Sokolovsky opposed an Anglo-American proposal to centrally finance Germany's railways. It would be better, he thought, to handle the matter "zonally" so that "deficits were not incurred by zones."[18] Later that month, Deputy Foreign Minister Andrei Vyshinsky turned aside a U.S. call for a single plan covering removals for reparations. The idea was contrary to Potsdam, which allowed local variations, he claimed. The Soviet deputy military governor's parroting of this position would lead directly to Clay's May 1946 halt of reparations.[19] In December 1945, the Russians blocked Anglo-American plans for a centralized administration for agriculture; in August 1946, they withdrew their own draft plan for a central agency for industry, fearing it might weaken the autonomy of their zone; a month later, they withdrew from a quadripartite coal pool.[20] Communist officials torpedoed efforts to promote interzonal cooperation that did not hew to their own agenda, most notably an initiative by Western minister-presidents in the summer of 1947. And, as noted earlier, they were slow to open their zone to travel by their allies or by Germans from other zones. When the ACC began discussing a new currency, the Soviets wanted notes for their zone printed (and issued) separately from those for the western zones.[21]

Determined to prevent German aggression by destroying the social roots of fascism, the Russians embarked on a unilateral program of transforming their zone. To break the power of landowners, the Communist Party organized "spontaneous" action by peasants to seize large estates. By mid-September, all five *Länder* (provinces) in the zone had passed land reform laws.[22] Committed to weakening "capitalists as a class," the party denounced big business as an ally of the Nazis, and at the end of October, the Soviet military administration began taking over firms (it had frozen bank accounts in July).[23] It may be, as Naimark has suggested, that the Soviets bolshevized their zone because that was the only way they knew to organize society, yet this "policy of unilateral faits accomplis" tended to divide Germany along the western border of the Soviet zone.[24]

The forced merger of the two Marxist parties, the German Communist Party (*Kommunistische Partei Deutschlands,* or KPD) and the German Social Democratic Party (*Sozialdemocratische Partei Deutschlands,* or SPD), had the same unintended effect of intensifying zonal divisions. The KPD began urging fusion in the winter of 1945. The reason was simple: the SPD had emerged as a serious rival in the eastern zone. Fusion aimed at absorbing the SPD into a communist-controlled movement throughout Germany, if possible, or in the eastern zone alone, if need be. The result was not only to smother political diversity in the eastern zone but also to accentuate differences between the Soviet zone and the rest of the country because, although SPD leaders in the Russian zone accepted the merger idea in February 1946, socialists elsewhere opposed it. The party's leader in the western zones, Kurt Schumacher, would have nothing to do with the proposed Socialist Unity Party (generally known by its German initials SED, for *Sozialistische Einheitspartei Deutschlands,* or, as wags would have it, "so endet Deutschland"). Fusion went ahead in the Russian zone, as the Soviets insisted it must, but not in the other three, creating two distinct party systems.

The SED suffered its most mortifying setback in Berlin. A referendum on the merger in the western sectors of the city (the Russians blocked it in theirs) overwhelmingly rejected fusion. Roughly three-quarters of SPD members voted. Although they endorsed cooperation with the KPD by a margin of nearly three to one, they rejected the merger by more than six to one: 2,940 for, 19,529 against.[25]

The vote was a turning point in Berlin's postwar history. Had it gone the other way, the KPD would have gained a commanding majority in the city assembly and unshakable control of the Magistrat. Under these conditions, contested municipal elections in October 1946 and Western resistance to a blockade in 1948–1949 would have been impossible. Interestingly, Berliners—Marxists, at that—waged and won this battle, while the Western powers largely sat on the sidelines. To Frank Howley, now deputy commandant of the U.S. sector, "The difference between the Communists and the Social Democrats was not easy to see." Politics was "a German question," and whether the merger was "good or bad was beside the point."[26] Officially neutral, Western authorities intervened to ensure a free and fair ballot, pledging publicly to protect voters and arresting eleven KPD members for intimidation.[27] Minimal as these Western actions were, they were important. The vote allowed the SPD to survive as an independent political force and positioned it to challenge communist control of the city government. Western support also signaled the start of a change in the relationship between Berliners and the Western powers. The latter were no longer just occupiers; they were beginning to defend Berliners against Soviet coercion, not because of a conscious decision in London or Washington but in response to events on the ground.[28]

Differences deepened later that spring when Clay suspended the delivery of reparations. For the Russians, obtaining reparations was the key purpose of the occupation. They had a strong moral case, given the destruction inflicted by the Germans on Soviet society during the war. Past wrongs aside, Stalin's suspicions of the outside world spurred him to rebuild Soviet strength as quickly as possible. German resources would help, and reparations would also weaken Germany's ability to threaten its neighbors—even if the dismantled factories merely rusted on railway sidings and were never reassembled in the Soviet Union.

Reparations depended on the level-of-industry plan mandated at Potsdam. War industries and any industrial capacity beyond that needed to sustain a set standard of living would be dismantled and removed as reparations. This approach gave the Soviets a strong incentive to push living standards as low as possible. Clay's stance in the level-of-industry discussions—on instructions from Washington—contradicts the claim that the United States was committed to German economic revival from the start of the occupation. He endorsed the Soviet approach, declaring that the United States would let the German living standard fall to whatever level was necessary to ensure that all German war-making potential was destroyed.[29]

The ACC endorsed a plan in March, only to have it collapse in April. On April 26, the Soviet representative in the Coordinating Committee, General Mikhail Dratvin, insisted there was no connection among reparations, exports and imports, and central agencies, while Koenig reiterated France's opposition to central agencies. Clay countered that all three topics were linked as common policies agreed on at Potsdam. If the ACC did not create central agencies and adopt a common export-import plan, he "might now find it necessary" to stop dismantling factories in his zone. Clay carried out his threat when the Coordinating Committee met again on May 3.[30]

The Russians felt cheated. After nine months of discussion, the West had promised much but delivered little. In Soviet eyes, Clay's stance meant that Washington preferred to let Germany keep resources that would otherwise go to the Soviet Union. Quick to punish the Russians for not treating the Potsdam agreements as a package, the Americans did nothing to compel the French to accept central agencies. At the same time, to the Russians, the Western call for economic unity appeared to be a scheme to bilk them. To Clay and Robertson, asking the Russians to treat Germany as a unit and to pool resources seemed like elementary fairness and a simple adherence to the Potsdam agreements, yet they were asking the Soviets to subsidize Western deficits—a stance that was unrealistic in light of increasing Cold War divisions, hard to justify in light of Russian poverty and Western wealth, and contrary to verbal assurances by Byrnes at Potsdam. The Soviet answer was simple: Germany was a rich country. It had lost the war, its victims were entitled to compensation, and the Western powers could avoid deficits in their zones by curbing consumption.[31] Letting German living standards fall was certainly preferable to shifting the burden onto the Soviet Union. Even in defeat, Germans lived better than Russians. The Soviet insistence on taking reparations out of Germany while the Western powers pumped money into the country made no sense to officials in Washington and London, but the Western notion that Germany could not afford $10 billion in compensation for the tens of billions of dollars in damage it had inflicted on the Soviet Union must have struck Russians as obscene.

When the foreign ministers met in Paris a few weeks later, Bevin warned that zonal autonomy meant a divided Europe. To avoid that, Britain was ready to cooperate with any and all zones. Should this plea go unanswered, however, Britain would have to organize its zone independently. To stave off that prospect, Byrnes offered to merge the American zone with any other "zone or zones" for economic purposes, pending four-power accords.[32] Molotov turned this aside as a departure from Potsdam, and French Foreign Minister Georges Bidault gave no direct answer. After several weeks of hesitation, the British accepted.[33]

London's acceptance deepened the division of Germany and intensified the Cold War. Bevin had resisted such a move for months. He had circulated a paper to the cabinet on May 3, laying out the advantages and disadvantages of an independent policy in the western zones. He concluded that "the general dangers of splitting Germany now are greater than those of continuing our present policy" of trying to make four-power controls work. Bevin took that view despite his belief that the Soviets sought to draw all of Germany into their sphere. On the other side of the ledger were serious financial and political considerations. The British zone could not support itself, so an independent policy would accelerate the drain on an already straitened exchequer. Politically, it meant "an irreparable break with the Russians," the loss of Berlin, and the division of Europe—prospects the Americans were not ready to face, yet "full American support would be essential."[34] Bevin held to his position, telling the cabinet in early June that if Potsdam were to be cast aside, he wanted the Russians to "take the initiative."[35] Finally, in late July, he was willing to act.

Once again we see the ironic interplay between intention and results that bedeviled postwar Allied relations in Germany. As John Gimbel once suggested, "Byrnes neither proposed nor apparently envisioned the division of Germany in July 1946," yet that was where his offer led. When Clay had first conceived the idea of a zonal merger of the willing in April, he thought the British would definitely accept and the Soviets probably would, leaving the French as holdouts. As he explained years later, "We weren't trying to kill quadripartite government—we were trying to find another formula for it." He remained optimistic even after the Russians stayed out. He thought that if the merger worked, the Russians and French would join, although, he confessed, "it may have just the reverse effect."[36]

In some ways, the situation was past retrieving by late 1946. Both sides—and it was increasingly accurate to speak of two sides—saw themselves as acting defensively. Caught in a spiral of mistrust, both of them were. Eisenhower's 1945 expectation that closer contacts would foster cooperation had given way to the notion that close ties were part of the problem: one British official suggested in October 1946 that "in the end we may have smoother relations with the Russians in Germany if we accept the division and cease to quarrel so much about what they do in their zone and what we do in ours, than if we indulge in an internecine war for the body of a unitary Germany."[37] The British and the Americans increasingly interpreted Soviet policy in Germany in light of disputes elsewhere. The Russians did the same. If they had begun the occupation, as Naimark says, with the view that the Western powers were enemies, events of the past year had only strengthened that belief. Western policy seemed to aim at not only undermining the Soviet hold on the eastern zone but also reviving the western zones economically and politically.

ELECTIONS IN THE EASTERN ZONE and in Berlin in the autumn of 1946 added to the Soviets' growing sense of vulnerability. The SED won a bare majority of the vote in the zone, and the balloting in Berlin was a catastrophe. Turnout in the city was high—90 percent of eligible voters—and the SPD just missed an outright majority in a four-way race; it won 48.7 percent of the votes, to the Christian Democratic Union's 22.1 percent and the Liberal Democratic Party's 9.4 percent. The SED ran a poor third with 19.8 percent. It did better in the Soviet sector, with 29.9 percent, but the SPD outpolled it even there, with 43.8 percent of the votes.[38]

The SED found itself trapped in a vicious circle: its closeness to the Russians weakened its popularity, which increased its dependence on the Soviets, which left it even more unpopular. Unable to compete in an open political system, the best the Soviets and the SED could hope for was to preserve their position through coercion and intimidation. They launched a purge of district administrations in the eastern sector, while communist-controlled city police helped abduct opponents in the western ones. According to one account, more than 5,400 Berliners disappeared between May 1945 and November 1947.[39]

Facing the loss of the preeminent position they and their supporters had enjoyed in the city since the summer of 1945, the Russians did all they could to preserve it. They found a weapon in the city's provisional constitution, which stipulated that "resignation of the Magistrat or one of its members, as well as appointment and discharge of leading persons in the city government, may take place only with the permission of the Allied Kommandatura." When the city assembly elected a new Magistrat led by the SPD's Otto Ostrowski, Soviet commandant General Alexander G. Kotikov invoked this clause to insist that the new body could not assume office until the Kommandatura approved each member—by unanimous vote. Western representatives countered that this provision was not intended to apply to elected officials, who should take office unless the Kommandatura unanimously rejected them, but Kotikov would not budge. The deadlock lasted until mid-January 1947, when the Soviets retreated. The price was Western acquiescence in Soviet vetoes of three of Ostrowski's colleagues.[40]

Ostrowski may have thought the crisis over, but his troubles had just begun. When he tried to remove some officials appointed by the old Magistrat, the Soviets set a stiff price: he could fire four of them, but only if the SPD and SED adopted a common program for the next three months. When Ostrowski accepted without consulting his party, SPD members in the city assembly revolted, passing a motion of no confidence in him on April 11.[41]

Ostrowski resigned a week later—or thought he did. His likely replacement was Ernst Reuter, one of the three functionaries Ostrowski and the Western powers had jettisoned in January and a man the Russians bitterly opposed. Kotikov attempted to justify his government's stance by claiming that Reuter's "political past was not clearly known," an assertion Berliners found contemptible.[42] Reuter's record was no secret to the Kremlin. Converted to communism in a Russian prison camp during the First World War, he had returned to Germany in 1918 and helped found the KPD. After leading the party's Berlin branch, he broke with Moscow and joined the Social Democrats. By the early 1930s, Reuter had been chief of transportation and utilities in Berlin, a member of the Reichstag, and mayor of Magdeburg. Twice jailed by the Nazis, he was released and went into exile in Turkey. When he was allowed to return to Berlin in 1946, the SPD promptly put him back in charge of the city's transportation system.[43]

The Russians knew this man only too well. To block Reuter, Kotikov vetoed action on Ostrowski's resignation; he would accede only if the Kommandatura approved the new *Oberbürgermeister* in advance. The issue went to the ACC, which accepted the Soviet position. Action shifted to the city assembly, where the Russians and the SED lobbied energetically but fruitlessly against Reuter. Kotikov, of course, vetoed the selection when it came before the Kommandatura on June 27, and the ACC upheld his position on July 10. The city assembly refused to choose anyone else, so Berlin would be governed for the next year and a half by its first deputy major, Louise Schroeder of the SPD.[44]

Diplomatic relations among the occupying powers paralleled events in Berlin. The foreign ministers gathered in Moscow on March 10 to rehash their differences, adjourning after six weeks of fruitless debate. Europe's economic troubles loomed large in the thinking of the new secretary of state, George C. Marshall, as he returned to Washington. The Americans had assumed Europe would put itself back on its feet relatively soon. Washington had extended $9 billion in aid since the war but had seen only minimal signs of recovery. The immediate worry was Europe's lack of dollars to finance a widening trade deficit with the United States; longer-term problems included the slow pace of recovery, low productivity, and the growing sense that the German economy was holding back the rest of Europe.[45]

As Marshall explored what should be done, the ideas of European economic recovery and German revival blended together in new ways. What Europe needed most was coal, steel, and industrial machinery, and a Germany unshackled from economic restraints might provide all three. Even FDR and the French had talked of using German resources for the benefit of Europe, so in a way, this was an old idea. Yet if the words were similar, the meaning was far different from what the late president and the French had had in mind. They had envisaged giving Germany's neighbors first claim on its resources, not, as Marshall's advisers were saying now, making Germany the "locomotive" of European recovery.[46]

Skeptical of the American initiative and regarding it as a desperate attempt to avert imminent economic collapse, the Soviets denounced it. They feared acceptance would open eastern Europe to Western economic and political influence, and they worried about the Marshall Plan's implications for Germany. Molotov insisted that reparations remain the first claim on German resources, that German industrial capacity not increase (because growth would divert resources otherwise available as reparations), and that German issues continue to fall under the exclusive purview of the ACC and the council of foreign ministers, subject to Soviet vetoes.[47]

The Marshall Plan and the Soviet rejection of it moved the German question to the top of the international agenda, where it would remain for the next two years. On the one hand, Germany's link to the Marshall Plan intensified East-West conflict. As Western officials centered their diplomacy on European economic revival, Germany's potential contribution came to be seen as fundamentally important. Without it, the Marshall Plan and all it represented would fail. Retribution made less and less sense to British and American leaders; Soviet obstruction became less and less acceptable. But Moscow defined German revival under Western sponsorship as an intolerable menace. Western policy in 1945–1946 had denied the Soviets reparations and a share in Ruhr controls. The United States was now reviving German power and directing it against the Soviet state. That the Americans had more than simple economic revival in mind seemed obvious. As Scott Parrish has written, Soviet leaders saw the Marshall Plan as nothing less than a plot to create an anti-Soviet bloc that would serve as "a jumping-off place for attacking Soviet Russia."[48]

On the other hand, deepening East-West conflict had ominous implications for Germany. Neither side could risk allowing that country, perhaps the decisive weight in the balance of power, to come under the control of the other. Thus, the odds greatly increased that Germany would be partitioned along zonal lines. Decisions in 1945 and 1946—confirmation of the EAC zonal plan at Yalta, Byrnes's reparations proposal at Potsdam, the Soviets' independent course in their zone in the summer and autumn of 1945, Clay's reparations halt, and the British, French, and Soviet responses to Byrnes's offer to merge zones—had not aimed to divide the country. Still, they had increased the chances that it would be. The Marshall Plan and Stalin's reaction to it made that outcome all but certain.

Fear and hope drove both sides and made agreement less likely. Hope led each side to expect concessions from the other. Western officials believed the Kremlin would make concessions in order to gain access to the Ruhr, while Soviet diplomats expected that capitalism's inherent contradictions would make the Western powers pliable. Fear made each side unyielding. The Soviets knew they had no popular support in Germany and dreaded further erosion of influence in their zone. "Defensive" motives led them to oppose any arrangements that would not leave them in unchallenged control there. For their part, the Western powers feared that the Soviets' economic program sought to create poverty and economic chaos, in the expectation that the Germans would turn to communism in desperation. The British and the Americans, to say nothing of the French, were not sure the Germans had been cured of their penchant for authoritarian rule. In the remaining months of 1947, whatever hope there was of reversing the trend toward partition flickered and died.

THE FOREIGN MINISTERS GATHERED on November 23 at Lancaster House in London, where the EAC had labored a few years before. They quarreled for two days before agreeing on an agenda, then deadlocked on matters of substance. In the end, the British and Americans orchestrated an adjournment on December 15.[49] The London meeting marked the end of the Yalta-Potsdam system for Germany. The Moscow council of foreign ministers had shown the unlikelihood of four-power agreement, but it took this failure in London for the Western governments to abandon Potsdam and quadripartite rule. Now they turned to new policies—in Germany and in Atlantic security.

Over the next three days, the British and Americans decided to expand the Bizonal Economic Council until it became a provisional government. Clay and Robertson worked out the details; Marshall and Bevin approved them at a working lunch at U.S. Ambassador Lewis W. Douglas's residence in Prince's Gate on December 18. This new policy risked confrontation with the Soviets. Indeed, Clay predicted "difficulties" in Berlin but minimized them. He and Robertson intended to remain in the city as long as possible, he explained. If things became "too tough," they would refer to their governments. In other words, they would raise the question of Berlin's vulnerability only when the city was under attack. This extraordinary suggestion prompted only desultory discussion. Answering a question from Marshall, Clay commented that they—he almost certainly meant the Western garrisons and the ACA staff—had "adequate resources on which to live in Berlin for some time." Just how long that might be was anyone's guess. What would westerners do when resources ran low? What would they do if supplies for the city's population were disrupted? The written record contains no hint that the group explored such issues.[50]

Bevin had raised the question of Atlantic security with Marshall the night before. The West needed "a positive plan for an association of the Western democracies," he argued. This would not be "a formal alliance, but an understanding backed by power, money and resolute action," a "spiritual federation of the West." Marshall was cautious then and again in January, when Bevin revisited the subject.[51] He and Under Secretary of State Robert A. Lovett worried that Congress would reject the European Recovery Program if it discovered that the Europeans wanted not just billions in economic aid but extensive U.S. military and political commitments as well.[52]

There matters stood until events in Prague changed American minds. Facing a political crisis and communist crowds in the streets, President Eduard Beneš appointed a cabinet on February 25 in which communists assumed all key posts. British and American officials had expected the Russians would tighten their grip on Czechoslovakia; still, the speed and thoroughness of the takeover came as a shock.[53] Clay told Douglas that for the first time he thought the Russians wanted war—soon.[54] The coup fueled extravagant fears about Soviet fifth columns in France and especially in Italy, where many observers thought the communists were poised to win elections in April, and it had a "powerful and depressing" effect in Germany. Jean Chauvel of the French Foreign Ministry saw the coup as the first step toward a Soviet invasion of western Europe, and the French stepped up pleas for American military aid.[55]

The coup swept Washington into a "dither," as George Kennan characterized it, fueled by a hair-raising message from Clay. Surprised by the "brazenness" of the Czech coup and a new truculence displayed by the Russians in Berlin, Clay acceded to the urgings of his intelligence chief, Major General Robert Walsh, and visiting army intelligence director Lieutenant General Stephen J. Chamberlin to warn Washington of "a subtle change in Soviet attitude" that raised the possibility that war "may come with dramatic suddenness." Clay's biographer, Jean Edward Smith, has argued that the cable stemmed from Chamberlin's appeal for Clay's help in persuading Congress to reinstate the draft and increase the army's appropriations. In his 1974 edition of Clay's papers, Smith wrote that the cable "was not, in Clay's opinion, related to any change in Soviet strategy," a point he repeated in a 1988 article. His 1990 biography of Clay included a long quotation by the general outlining Chamberlin's request, its rationale, and his response.[56]

The belief that Clay suppressed his real views in order to help the Pentagon frighten money out of Congress has become a staple of Cold War historiography.[57] It is open to serious doubt. We have assumed that Smith's account rests on his interviews with Clay. On file at Columbia and Georgetown Universities, those interviews contain repeated references to a change in Soviet behavior, echoing Clay's earlier remark to Douglas. "I felt that something was taking place," Clay declared. A few lines later, he referred to "a substantial change in attitude on the Russians' part"; "something was really brewing." The "whole atmosphere was just cooling off," Clay continued, and the relationship with Sokolovsky was changing in "unseen ways."[58] Clay, in short, repeatedly told Smith that he *did* sense a change in Soviet strategy, and there is no evidence that he retracted or altered these views later. The long quotation from the biography is nowhere to be found, either in the interview transcripts or in Clay's correspondence with Smith. Queried about the episode, Smith explained that Clay must have made the statements "off the record." In short, his characterization of the general's views has no documentary corroboration whatsoever.[59]

Clay's telegram arrived in Washington with "the force of a blockbuster bomb."[60] Its effects and those of the Prague coup can be seen in the American response to London's new call for discussions about a military pact. In January, Marshall had evaded Bevin's request; now he urged British negotiators to come at once.[61] The French, who were more nervous after Prague than the Americans, were kept in the dark about these "Pentagon talks" because the British and the Americans believed that whatever was known in Paris would soon reach Moscow. The Soviets, ironically, were kept fully informed by their spy in the British embassy, Donald Maclean.

Moscow reacted to the failure of the London foreign ministers' meeting by calling into question Western rights in Berlin. The Soviet-licensed Berlin daily, *Tägliche Rundschau,* ran an editorial on December 19 arguing that quadripartite control of Berlin made sense only as long as Germany remained under four-power rule. After Clay and Robertson announced plans to give the Bizonal Economic Council limited political power, a second, stronger editorial appeared, reiterating the link between moves toward a west German government and a Western presence in Berlin. The newspaper claimed the West had created a west German state and thereby "nullified" Western rights in Berlin, which was part of the Russian zone.[62]

Western officials shrugged off the editorials as crude threats. In late January, Bevin proposed a meeting of the three Western powers and the Benelux countries to discuss the future of the western zones. The Russians were pointedly excluded from this London conference, which ran from February 25 to March 5, recessed, and reconvened from April 20 to June 2. It proved to be "the most important conference on the future of Germany since the end of the war," for it brought the French, British, and Americans together in a common program.[63] The communiqué issued when the conference recessed on March 5 announced agreement on west German participation in the Marshall Plan, a federal form of government, and coordination of the economic policies of the French zone with those of the Bizone. This cluster of initiatives came to be known as the "London program."[64]

The Russians regarded the conference as a threat to the Soviet state, not just to their interests in Germany. The Western powers were bent on German political, economic, and military revival and a separate west German government; something had to be done to deter them from this dangerous course. Stalin expressed his displeasure in several ways, including harassment of Western traffic to Berlin, steps toward an east German regime, and diplomatic maneuvering. The Soviets tried a variety of measures, and as each failed, they saw no choice but to escalate.

Soviet inspectors boarded a U.S. military train at Marienborn on January 6 and demanded to check the papers of German passengers; Russian liaison officers at Clay's headquarters were persuaded to recall the inspectors after a thirty-five-minute standoff.[65] On January 12, the day after the second *Tägliche Rundschau* editorial, Russian officials began requiring Soviet countersignatures on interzonal consignments out of the western sectors. On January 15, they prohibited German vehicles from entering the Soviet zone from west Berlin; drivers were instructed to pass through the Russian sector and obtain a special pass first.[66] Soviets stopped a British passenger train en route to Hamburg on January 23, demanding to inspect two cars filled with Germans. When British officials refused, the Russians held the train at Marienborn for nearly eleven hours before detaching the two cars, sending them back to Berlin, and letting the rest of the train proceed. Two nights later, they stopped another train; this time, the British allowed them aboard. After the Soviets were satisfied that all the Germans had valid interzonal passes, they allowed the train to continue westward.[67]

Americans noted "ever increasing" efforts to curb air travel in January. At a meeting of the Berlin Air Safety Center in February, the Soviet controller proposed changes in the regulations governing the corridors and the Berlin Control Zone. He also wanted civil aircraft to obtain in advance Soviet permission to use what he described as the "air corridors of the Soviet Zone of Occupation."[68]

On March 9, four days after the London session adjourned, Moscow called Sokolovsky and his political adviser, Vladimir S. Semenov, home for consultations. They and their superiors decided to impose an escalating series of restrictions on Western traffic to and from Berlin in order to compel the Western powers to abandon the London program or leave Berlin.[69] Stalin seemed to prefer the latter course in discussions with SED leaders on March 26. Predicting defeat for his party in city elections scheduled for the autumn, Wilhelm Pieck told Stalin that he and his colleagues "would be glad if the [Western] Allies left Berlin," prompting Stalin to reply, "Let's try with all our might, and maybe we'll drive them out."[70]

One can read too much into these words. They do not necessarily include a willingness to use force to expel the Western powers. A better approach was to harass them until they left of their own accord. Furthermore, Stalin's words suggest that he had not thought carefully about his goals. As compatible as they appeared at first glance, they were at odds. In one tactic, Berlin was to function as a hostage: in exchange for the city's safety, the West would drop the London program. Yet if Pieck had his wish and Berlin came under Soviet control—if the hostage died—Moscow would lose leverage over the London program. The paradox that local success might undermine overall Soviet goals would plague Kremlin diplomacy throughout the coming crisis.

Stalin's efforts to derail the London program went beyond the harassment of Western transit. He also took steps toward establishing an east German regime, paralleling Anglo-American initiatives in the Bizone. On February 13, *Tägliche Rundschau* announced that Sokolovsky had given the economic commission of the eastern zone powers comparable to those just given to the Bizone's economic council.[71] A more ominous move followed a month later, when the Soviets began establishing so-called People's Police. Organized and equipped more as military formations than as police, these units gave the SED a private army.[72]

In diplomacy, the Soviets sought to reassert Moscow's voice in German affairs. A single theme united Russian protests over the Bizone and the London conference: these Western actions involved questions that only all four occupying powers could decide. The West, the Soviets contended, was usurping the prerogatives of the ACC and circumventing the Soviet Union.[73] Stalin had accepted the EAC protocols and the Potsdam agreements because they gave him a veto over Germany's future; he was not about to surrender it.

Stalin chose to remind the Western powers of the ACC's value—and the link between it and the continued Western presence in Berlin—by putting the ACC in jeopardy. The break came on March 20. No council meeting had been scheduled, but Sokolovsky suddenly exercised his right as chairman that month to call one. He opened the meeting by demanding full information about the London conference. After Robertson and Clay avoided giving direct answers, Sokolovsky read a long prepared statement denouncing the conference. The Western powers, he concluded, had proved that the ACC "virtually no longer exists as the supreme body of authority in Germany." He declared the meeting adjourned and marched out of the room, his delegation at his heels.[74]

Sokolovsky also began carrying out the instructions he had received in Moscow. Russian troops mobilized and moved to the zonal border on maneuvers. The Soviet-licensed press began to carry stories that "subversive and terrorist elements," bandits, and criminals were taking advantage of lax transit regulations to disturb the tranquility of the eastern zone. To stop such outrages, the Soviets announced on March 30 that "supplementary regulations" covering Western travel to and from Berlin would take effect April 1.[75] Berlin had taken center stage in the East-West conflict.

THE WARTIME AGREEMENTS were preconditions of the blockade, not its cause. That cause can be found in the emergence of Cold War tensions. The Soviets regarded the Western powers as enemies from the start of the occupation, a view that proved self-fulfilling. The West responded by taking steps to contain Soviet influence, such as the Marshall Plan, a North Atlantic security pact, and a west German government. Stalin interpreted these actions as offensive maneuvers aimed at the destruction of his regime. Nikita Khrushchev, no admirer of the Soviet dictator, recalled that the West's actions "represented a direct threat to our national security, a challenge to the impregnability of our borders." As he summed up the view in Moscow in the spring of 1948, "Stalin imposed the blockade as an act of survival."[76] The Western governments, frightened by the Prague coup, were equally convinced that they could neither abandon their risky new initiative nor let their exposed outpost fall. A new and more dangerous phase of the Cold War was about to begin.

CHAPTER 3

"The Danger Point Is Berlin"

The Soviets increased their pressure on Berlin in April, attempting to stop the London program. Analysts have treated this as a case study in the failure of deterrence, in that the Western powers did not dissuade the Soviets from interfering with access to Berlin.[1] There was a second failure: the Soviet attempt to deter the Western powers from going ahead with their London initiative. Stalin gave the West no warning of the price he might impose if it persisted in the London program, and he made no explicit threats. In addition, he failed to grasp the sense of economic and political vulnerability that drove the Marshall Plan and the London program.

Soviet misjudgments of Western resolve were understandable; the Western powers themselves were unsure how important Berlin was to them. The city was not a symbol of Western resolve—that would emerge later. Officials doubted the Soviets would push matters and devised no strategy to respond if they did. The Western powers gave little thought to how their program for western Germany appeared in Soviet eyes and therefore underestimated Stalin's motivation to stop it. With underlying issues unresolved, the conflict in central Europe came to a head in June.

SOKOLOVSKY'S DEPUTY, General Dratvin, advised his Western counterparts on March 30 that new regulations for traffic to and from Berlin would take effect April 1. His "supplementary provisions" afforded endless opportunities for mischief. Westerners crossing the Soviet zone were to carry documents proving their identity and affiliation with the military government. Dratvin asserted a right to inspect freight, exempting only luggage carried in autos or in railway passenger coaches. Military freight leaving Berlin would require Soviet permits. Inbound military cargoes would be cleared "on the basis of the accompanying documents," which could mean anything.[2]

If the Russians could inspect passengers and freight, they could control access, leaving the Western presence in Berlin at their mercy. Robertson's deputy, Major General Nevil C. D. Brownjohn, rejected Dratvin's claim to unilateral control of traffic. Robertson urged Whitehall to explore ways to retaliate against Soviet ships and airplanes outside of Germany and remove any doubts about British determination to stay in Berlin.[3]

Clay wanted to confront the Russians, who, he declared in a high-priority message to army chief of staff General Omar N. Bradley, were determined to "drive us from Berlin." He intended to double the guards on American military trains and order them to shoot Russians trying to board, and he wanted Bradley's approval within two hours. "Unless we take a strong stand now," Clay warned, "our life in Berlin will become impossible. A retreat from Berlin at this moment would . . . have serious if not disastrous political consequences in Europe. I do not believe that the Soviets mean war now. However, if they do, . . . we might as well find out now as later."[4]

Western officials had foreseen something like this since the foreign ministers' meeting had broken up in December. The Central Intelligence Agency (CIA) had warned the president that the Soviets would "probably use every means short of armed force" to eject the Western powers.[5] The acting chief of the State Department's Division of Central European Affairs, E. Allan Lightner Jr., predicted "a determined Soviet effort to get the Western Allies out of Berlin." He recommended "coordinated counter-measures," without specifying what they might be.[6]

The Pentagon had no more success in devising a response. In a hurried answer to a query from army secretary Kenneth C. Royall, the Plans and Operations Division urged making "every effort" to stay in Berlin, including reducing the American presence to a token garrison relying on air supply. Yet it acknowledged that, in the end, the Soviets could compel withdrawal.[7] This rushed analysis omitted consideration of what effects Soviet restrictions might have on Berlin's population, a subject addressed in a revised paper dated January 19. This study predicted that the Kremlin would "probably" feed Berliners so as not to alienate the Germans, even as it was severing supplies for the Western garrisons. Aerial supply of the city would be impossible if ground routes were cut.[8]

Robert Blum, an aide to Secretary of Defense James V. Forrestal, thought the Western powers should stay as long as possible but pick a time to leave rather than have one thrust on them. The problem was that until a crisis emerged, withdrawal seemed unnecessary; once a showdown began, it would appear to be a retreat.[9] This paradox made those who emphasized Berlin's vulnerability look like nervous Nellies. Sir Ivone Kirkpatrick, one of Bevin's deputy under secretaries, described withdrawal under compulsion as "intolerable," but he thought the Western powers should make a "dignified withdrawal" if there was "any doubt" that they could stay. Walter Bedell Smith, the U.S. ambassador in Moscow, denounced Kirkpatrick as an appeaser and doubted the Russians would push matters to a break. "If I am wrong," Smith continued, echoing Clay, "the sooner the issue is joined the better."[10]

Bevin addressed Berlin's vulnerability early in the new year, and like the Americans, he minimized the danger. The Russians wanted to end the Western presence in order to consolidate their grip on their zone, he thought; still, Moscow understood that squeezing the Western powers was "very risky." Thus, his view—"little more than a guess," he confessed—was that the Russians would not resort to extremes. Instead, they would try to undermine Western credibility in German eyes and make the Western powers' position as uncomfortable as possible, in hopes they would abandon the city.[11]

Two points emerge from these assessments. First, no one confronted the extent of Western vulnerability in Berlin. Officials assumed the Russians would not exploit their geographic advantage, limiting themselves to a war of nerves. Planners avoided the hard policy questions: Should the West remain? Why? Why not? Why should the Russians exercise restraint? What were the costs of withdrawal? What risks were involved in staying? Instead, officials preferred to decide only what had to be resolved at the moment. We will see this pattern again.

Second, no action followed. Truman did nothing about the CIA's warning; Lightner's call for interagency consultations fell on deaf ears. Blum had urged discussions with the western Europeans and wanted the National Security Council to consider Berlin "as a matter of urgency"; neither happened. Bevin's report to the cabinet implied that he had the risks under control, forestalling action.[12]

Officials apparently believed the Russians were bluffing. If Moscow halted Western supplies for the city, feeding the German inhabitants "would automatically become a Russian responsibility"—one that officials such as John D. Hickerson, director of the State Department's Office of European Affairs, were certain the Soviets wanted to avoid.[13] Destruction of the ACC or an attack on Berlin's four-power status would mean a break with the West, "virtually an act of war," as one put it. It would end any hope the Soviets entertained of obtaining a foothold in the Ruhr, halt interzonal trade, and partition Germany. Surely the Russians would not take public responsibility for that, having courted German nationalism for a year and a half. Further, what could be done if the Russians defied all logic and cut off supplies for Berliners? No one believed the Western governments could feed the city under those conditions. Countermeasures could not be prepared because none were feasible.[14]

Whatever their reasoning, British and American officials reached the same conclusion: Berlin's vulnerability was more apparent than real. In hindsight, these calculations appear incomprehensible. Officials understood how exposed Berlin was, but they did nothing to reduce the danger, persuading themselves that the Soviets would not exploit the city's vulnerability. Why the Kremlin would exercise such restraint was not a question these men—who believed the worst of all communists—asked. No one looked at how the situation might appear from Moscow's perspective or how Stalin might calculate risks and opportunities. No one considered how the West could maintain its position in Berlin if it allowed economic control of the city to pass to Soviet hands, the inevitable result if the Russians assumed responsibility for feeding Berlin. Determined to break free of four-power rule and pursue an independent policy after years of exasperating deadlock, Western officials wanted no reminders of the risks involved in their new approach. Dratvin had now exposed that as wishful thinking.

Believing that only a strong response would stop Soviet pressure, Clay stated the danger as starkly as he could. That proved to be a mistake. Instead of rallying his superiors in Washington, he frightened them. Bradley put off a decision about armed guards, and Royall was even more cautious. He pressed Clay for information—lots of it: Dratvin's letter verbatim, Robertson's probable action, and details about current road, rail, and air schedules. Clay complied, commenting at the end of his summary that he could feed his soldiers and their families by air, "but not Germans in the city." Moreover, relying on an airlift "would be most damaging to our prestige and would be met by new acts." Betraying irritation at the close supervision, he pleaded to be "permitted to proceed on my judgment."[15]

That was the one thing Royall would not do. Clay had succeeded only too well in alarming Washington—again. His casual talk of shooting Russians convinced Royall and Bradley that he was impulsive and indifferent to risk. No one accepted his claim that the Russians were bluffing. Instead, intelligence reports emphasized extensive Soviet troop movements and a real danger of war.[16] Clay's perceived recklessness would lead officials in Washington to circumscribe his actions now and again in June.

Royall continued to seek information, especially about access rights. Presidential aide George Elsey recalled "mad scrambling" in search of documents supporting Western claims.[17] None could be found, so Royall asked Clay for whatever he might have. Clay mentioned the EAC and his conference with Zhukov in 1945, recalling that General Parks, now on duty in Washington, had taken notes. Clay contended that Zhukov had agreed to "free entry," and he pointed out that since 1946, the Soviets had contented themselves with checking railway passenger lists and freight manifests. Allow Russians on board, he predicted, and "it will be only a day or two until one of our people is pulled off on trumped up charges." He then sent his proposed reply to Dratvin. The United States would permit Soviet officials to check the identity of its citizens in autos, but not on trains, and it rejected any claim to inspect baggage. Train commanders would continue to provide passenger lists and freight manifests, but they would not allow Soviet inspectors aboard.[18]

Royall delayed the next teleconference to allow more time for consultation in

Washington. Bradley, Royall, air force secretary W. Stuart Symington, the chief of naval operations, Lovett and two associates from the State Department, plus Eisenhower and the air force chief of staff conferred with Forrestal about what to do. Two key figures were absent: Marshall was in Bogotá, Colombia, and Truman received recommendations from the group but took no part in its discussions.

The participants considered having the president consult congressional leaders or protest to Stalin. Lovett thought a protest would suggest jittery nerves, prompting the Russians to increase the pressure. When briefed, Truman rejected consulting legislators because word would leak and cause "war hysteria." The group was willing to let Clay's guards shoot in self-defense, but only if the Soviets fired first. A news ticker reported that London intended to continue running trains with armed guards aboard. With British views so closely paralleling their own, the Americans saw no need for formal discussions. No one thought to consult the French, perhaps in the belief—inaccurate, as it turned out—that they did not operate trains to Berlin.[19]

The Pentagon's first impulse was to evacuate. Army Lieutenant General Albert C. Wedemeyer, director of the Plans and Operations Division, asked his staff to find out how many transport planes Clay had, how many passengers they could carry in an emergency, and how many Americans were in Berlin. Staffers at air force headquarters drafted a message to the commander of United States Air Forces in Europe (USAFE), Lieutenant General Curtis E. LeMay, offering armed bombers to move supplies and people in and out of Berlin. Asked whether the United States could use atomic weapons if the crisis escalated, Brigadier General Kenneth Nichols, head of the Armed Forces Special Weapons Project, said no; the only qualified assembly teams were on a Pacific atoll for weapons tests.[20]

Truman's minimal role deserves comment. In one sense, it was not unusual. Truman had taken little interest in the occupation since Potsdam,[21] and that hands-off style continued after the London Council of Foreign Ministers. Marshall made commitments at Prince's Gate on his own. Although Truman stayed informed about developments, he ratified policy; he did not make it. Forrestal discussed the crisis with him by telephone, and Royall sent him Dratvin's letter, Clay's proposed reply, and the transcript of the teleconference with Clay. Truman's preference was to avoid a public role: no consultations with Congress and no public statement. Yet his stance was odd in at least two respects. First, he considered the situation serious—"as serious," he told the Canadian prime minister, "as in 1939"—and his notion of a leader's responsibilities during a crisis did not include inaction. Second, his behavior was inconsistent with the famous Clifford-Rowe memo on election strategy, which called on the president to rally voters by asserting leadership in foreign affairs.[22]

Bradley and Wedemeyer were in the communications center again at 10:00 P.M.

Berlin time on March 31 (4:00 P.M. in Washington). They were ready to approve the reply to Dratvin, subject to a final question: hadn't Soviet officials walked through Western trains as recently as September? It was an important point. If Russians had routinely boarded Western trains in the past, how could Clay's soldiers shoot them now?

Washington's preoccupation with the risk of war—the unintended consequence of his own efforts to dramatize events—infuriated Clay. He mustered all his eloquence for one last plea.

> Legalistic argument no longer has meaning. We are now faced with a realistic and not a legalistic problem. Our reply will not be misunderstood by 42 million Germans and perhaps 200 million Western Europeans. We must say . . . "this far you may go and no further." There is no middle ground which is not appeasement. . . . Please understand we are not carrying a chip on our shoulder and will shoot only for self-protection. We do not believe we will have to do so. We feel the integrity of our trains as a part of our sovereignty is a symbol of our position in Germany and Europe.

When this appeal failed to sway Bradley, Clay was ready to drop the whole business. Bradley approved the reply with minor changes, only to have Clay snap that the reply was unimportant. "Our subsequent action is all that concerns me," he declared. He was so angry that he said he may have erred in referring the crisis to Washington: "I am not too sure I was right in ever bringing it up," he told Bradley in disgust. Bradley ignored this outburst and authorized Clay to move trains, as long as they did not carry additional guards or additional weapons. Guards were to prevent Soviets from boarding, but they could not shoot first. Even after Bradley pointed out that the president had approved these instructions, Clay complained. His soldiers would obey, but the orders were unfair "to a man whose life may be in danger."[23]

With the Russians asserting a right to inspect passenger trains, arguing over how far guards might go to stop them made sense. It was also worth testing the Russians to see whether they would enforce Dratvin's restrictions, rather than just accepting his declaration at face value. Yet the argument between the two generals seems oddly off target. Both seemed to forget that the Russians controlled the railway signals and switches. What could be done if they simply shunted the trains onto a siding?

Six trains approached the Soviet checkpoint at Marienborn after midnight. A French train submitted to inspection and was allowed to proceed. One U.S. commandant allowed Soviet inspectors aboard. After passengers were wakened and their identity cards checked, the Russians sent the train on its way. Clay court-martialed the hapless officer. Commanders of two other American trains denied the Soviets admittance, and the Russians did not try to force entry. After an overnight standoff, the two trains backed out of the Russian zone. Two British trains carrying rations for several days sat on sidings for more than twelve hours before giving up. Rather than submit to Soviet inspection, Robertson and Clay canceled military passenger trains to and from Berlin.[24]

Clay was right about one thing. The reply to Dratvin proved unimportant, for it triggered no change in Soviet policy. The note, signed by Clay's chief of staff, Brigadier General Charles K. Gailey, contended that the "agreement" under which American forces had entered Berlin "clearly provided for our free and unrestricted utilization of the established corridors." Further, this transit agreement had been a precondition of U.S. withdrawal from Saxony and Thuringia. Dratvin airily dismissed Gailey's history lesson. Regulation of transit across the Soviet zone was an "internal matter." There never had been, "and there cannot be, any agreement concerning . . . orderless and uncontrolled traffic" across the zone. Gailey countered by insisting that American representatives in 1945 had understood that their forces would have free and uncontrolled access, a marked retreat from his initial claim. Like Brownjohn, he was ready to discuss new procedures, but no Soviet inspectors would be allowed onto U.S. military trains. Dratvin did not reply.[25]

With surface lines of supply uncertain, Clay organized an airlift. On April 1, he ordered the twenty-five C-47s (military versions of the famous DC-3) at Rhein-Main air base outside Frankfurt to deliver 80 tons of supplies a day to the American garrison. Only 7.5 tons arrived on April 1, but 42.5 tons were delivered on the second, and more than 84 tons on the third.[26] The garrison's logistics staff could specify what it needed because it had begun analyzing requirements in January, after the Soviets interfered with British trains. The Royal Air Force (RAF) also organized an airlift, and the French began one flight a day from their zone.[27]

Clay's mind ran to retaliation. He ordered Howley to blockade the headquarters of the Soviet zone's railway system, located in the American sector, after Kotikov posted armed sentries outside. American soldiers surrounded the building, and Howley cut off utilities and supplies until the Russian guards withdrew on April 4. The head of the Canadian military mission in Berlin, General Maurice A. Pope, recalled a "bellicose spirit" and "much talk of war in local OMGUS circles." Clay's deputy there, Major General George P. Hays, told Pope flatly, "if war was inevitable it would be of advantage to begin it without delay."[28]

War was on the minds of officials in Washington, too, but as a disaster to be avoided, not an opportunity to be welcomed. Wedemeyer warned overseas commands that the United States was "taking a firm stand" in response to Soviet restrictions, and an "incident could result." When the National Security Council met, Lovett stressed that "we must have a very strong case to show publicly that we took every step possible short of shooting" and "make it clear that the Russians are the ones who are breaking the quadripartite agreement."[29]

The situation did not look as dangerous on April 2, strengthening the impression that Clay had overreacted. He reported that things had "settled down considerably" and he faced "no immediate crisis." That was because the Soviets were not enforcing Dratvin's new regulations. Highway traffic in and out of the city was normal, as was German civil freight. A British military freight train arrived following routine clearance at Soviet checkpoints. Russians at Marienborn made no attempt to inspect the train, declaring they did not care about inbound freight. Clay ordered a U.S. military freight train into the city. It arrived without incident on April 3, and another pulled in April 5. The Soviets suspended barge traffic into the city on April 2, but it resumed three days later.[30]

Tension spiked again in the early afternoon of April 5 when a Yak fighter collided with a British European Airways Viking airliner over Berlin. The Yak's movements reminded one eyewitness of wartime fighter attacks on bombers, as it dived on the Viking from above and behind, then pulled up in a steep left turn until it was directly ahead of it and on a collision course. The Russian pilot tried to swerve below the airliner, but the Yak's right wing clipped the Viking. Both planes spiraled to the ground a thousand feet below. The Russian pilot, the Viking's four RAF crew members, and ten passengers all perished.[31]

This was clearly an accident, but the Western powers worried that the Soviets had begun a campaign of aerial harassment to match the one on the ground. Robertson went to Sokolovsky's headquarters at Karlshorst to demand a four-power inquiry and assurances that British aircraft would not be molested. He ordered fighter escorts for all passenger flights. Clay followed suit. Sokolovsky was ill at ease during his meeting with Robertson. He offered regrets and assured his guest that the collision had not been intentional. Having thus tacitly admitted that the Soviet pilot was responsible, he went on to claim that the Viking had rammed the fighter. He insisted that any investigation be bilateral, because only British and Soviet aircraft had been involved, waving aside Robertson's objection that two Americans were among the dead.[32]

Through his anger, Clay saw political advantage. Chairman of the ACC during April, he had resisted British and French suggestions that he call a meeting to discuss Dratvin's demands. Now he told Robertson that he would convene a session if asked, because "we shall never get a break under more favorable conditions." Bevin immediately cabled back, "we do not want . . . a break," and expressed the hope that the disaster would cause the Russians to reconsider.[33]

Like Clay, the Soviets saw political advantage and tried to use the crash to restrict Western access. They revived old demands for stricter flying regulations and circulated new ones. On April 17, with Western nerves taut over the April 5 crash, three Soviet fighters made gunnery passes at a C-47 in the southern corridor but did not fire, and the Russians conducted antiaircraft gunnery practice in the corridor. Soviet fighters conducted exercises in the corridors on May 18 without notifying Western controllers in the Berlin Air Safety Center. Later that month, the Soviets announced vague fighter movements in the corridors, an apparent attempt to preempt Western use of them.[34]

Harassment on the ground continued. On April 9, Soviet officials announced that they would no longer clear outbound German freight on the basis of bills of lading issued by the Magistrat; after April 16, a Soviet stamp would be required. The Russians issued the stamp in limited quantities, threatening the city's trade balance. They no longer allowed U.S. communications teams to inspect repeater stations along the single cable that carried telephone and telegraph circuits between Berlin and the U.S. zone, and they expelled British signals technicians from Magdeburg. Russian officials delayed outbound mail, claiming that parcels contained food, in contravention of an imaginary Allied ban on food shipments from the city. Other officials began requiring individual clearances for barges moving through their zone, overturning the 1946 agreement with the British, whose request for a meeting was ignored. On April 24, the Soviets suspended the last Western rail passenger service to Berlin—two French cars routinely attached to a German train.[35]

The April confrontation over passenger trains came to be known as the "baby blockade," to distinguish it from the more extensive blockade the Soviets would impose in June. The name is misleading, and not just because it was applied in hindsight. This was not a blockade; supplies for the city's residents continued, as did Western highway traffic. The main effect of the so-called baby blockade was the stoppage of Western passenger trains, and they halted because Clay and Robertson refused to submit to Soviet inspection. Although this was understandable from a Western perspective, it was not a reaction Stalin could have counted on. If Stalin had intended a blockade, he would have imposed one, rather than assuming the West would cooperate.

The notion of a baby blockade is also misleading because it implies a brief period of Soviet pressure followed by a pause. The Soviets did not relax their restrictions and allow rail traffic to resume. This puts a different light on the traditional criticism that Western officials ignored the clear warning provided by the baby blockade. The West could not look back on the baby blockade and mull over its "lessons" because it was never history. It was a daily fact of life from April 1 onward. Continuing harassment inclined Western leaders to expect more of the same and to discount the possibility of abrupt changes in the level of Soviet coercion.[36]

Whatever we call it, the Soviets savored what they regarded as success. They had made the Western powers appear weak. Uncertainty and a feeling of powerlessness spread among Berliners, who feared war and Western withdrawal in equal measure.

Still, the Western powers gave no sign of reversing their policies, so the only course seemed to be more pressure. Accordingly, on April 17, Dratvin and Semenov urged new postal procedures, restrictions on Western air traffic, and Soviet control of outbound freight.[37]

Ironically, Western observers drew equally optimistic conclusions from recent events. Two preconceptions guided Western assessments. The first was the shadow of the March war scare, which led analysts to concentrate on whether the Soviets were about to start a war. The CIA thought "devious" maneuvers in Berlin made no sense if the Russians were on the verge of overrunning the Continent. Lovett detected indications that the Kremlin had no desire to push matters to extremes, including "the failure to follow up vigorously" its interference with Western access.[38]

The other preconception was the notion that the Russian objective was local: to compel the Western powers to leave the city. That ruled out broader goals, at least for the moment, and a link to the London program. In the CIA's view, Russian actions were not responses to Western moves; rather, the London program was the "occasion" the Russians had been waiting for to consolidate their position in the east. Reports from Berlin bore out this interpretation. Murphy reported that Soviet and SED officials were predicting the West would leave soon, and intelligence officers collected similar rumors. Clay thought the Soviets were intent on making the Western position "untenable" but would not run great risks "for the time being." Overt aggression was possible only as a "last resort." One other strand of the American analysis is worth emphasizing. Analysts believed the West had to cooperate for the Soviet campaign to succeed. Moscow would not try to eject the Western powers; harassment was aimed at inducing them to withdraw on their own. If the West did not panic, it could stay put.[39]

British analysts reached similar conclusions: the Soviet aim was limited and could be thwarted if they kept their wits. The minister of state at the Foreign Office, Hector McNeil, told Canadian high commissioner Norman Robertson that the Soviets were as anxious to avoid a crisis as the West was. Bevin took a similar line when he summarized developments for the House of Commons on April 6, declaring that Moscow was not prepared to "provoke a real crisis over Berlin."[40]

Not everyone was so optimistic. One senior American in Berlin (probably Howley) believed that although the Russians were bluffing, they would succeed because the Western powers were afraid to call their bluff. He expected the Soviets would escalate restrictions until the West could no longer feed its sectors. "I do not see how we could do it 100% by air," he wrote. In the end, "we will have to go," and U.S. credibility in Europe would go, too.[41] Calvin Hoover, a Duke University economics professor and former member of Clay's staff, urged the president to weigh alternatives. Encouraging European recovery and resisting Soviet expansion were the right policies, yet the West lacked the muscle to back them up. It must avoid a showdown until it had the requisite military strength. Hoover doubted the Russians would back down, and he took it for granted that an airlift could not feed the population. Under what conditions would we evacuate? Under what conditions would we fight?[42]

Similar questions haunted the French, who were torn between recognition that retreat would be a disaster on a par with Munich and fear that American rigidity would pull everyone over the brink. Bidault and Chauvel believed the Russians would not resort to force—nor would they need to. French air force officers echoed this assessment, as did Maurice Couve de Murville, director general for political affairs at the Quai d'Orsay. "The Russians are physically capable of driving us out of Berlin through hunger, thirst, and darkness," he argued, and no airlift could sustain the city if Moscow cut surface communications with the western zones.[43]

The only official to suggest a link between the London program and Soviet pressure was Clay. In an April 10 teleconference with Bradley, he predicted that currency reform and creation of a west German government "will develop the real crisis." Recent Soviet steps were "probably designed . . . to scare us away from those moves," he added. The one man who grasped the connection the Soviets were trying to draw was the one least likely to scare.[44]

THUS, WHILE WESTERN LEADERS considered a variety of responses to Soviet pressure, abandoning the London program was not one of them. Discussion centered on five topics: improving the garrisons' ability to withstand new restrictions, retaliation, evacuation of dependents, a military show of force, and diplomatic protest. As part of the first, authorities increased stockpiles and refined airlift plans. Coal shipments, less than 1,500 tons in March, rose to 12,000 in April and 10,000 in May. The RAF was busy drafting "Knicker," a plan to support the garrison. Not completed until June 19, Knicker called for two "Dakota" (C-47) squadrons (a total of sixteen planes) to move from Britain to Germany and deliver sixty-five tons a day for up to thirty days.[45]

Robertson had suggested on March 31 retaliating against Soviet shipping in other parts of the world, and Clay raised the idea with Washington. Assessments in both capitals were pessimistic. There was no value in "inflicting pinpricks on the Russians," a Whitehall meeting determined, and officials in Washington feared retaliation might lead to "incidents."[46]

General J. Lawton Collins, Bradley's deputy, had broached the issue of evacuating dependents from Berlin on March 17. Clay had responded with arguments he never abandoned: friends and enemies alike would interpret the move as proof of America's intent to "abandon Europe." It would encourage the Russians and cause Europeans to rush "to communism for safety."[47] Clay would allow the fainthearted to leave, was gradually reducing nonessential employees, and would replace married soldiers at the end of their tours with unmarried ones, but any mass exodus was "unthinkable" on the eve of the Italian elections.[48] Washington was thinking the unthinkable. Lovett thought the United States might portray evacuation as a "move to clear decks for action," and a cabinet committee looked into the idea. While ruling out wholesale evacuation, it recommended that Clay quietly reduce numbers.[49]

Robertson thought it "quite wrong" to evacuate families, but he believed it was time to "clear the decks" and limit commitments to the minimal essential garrison and staff. Members of the Foreign Office approved his recommendation that families and staff be reduced gradually, with the timing left in his hands.[50]

Evacuation of dependents inevitably raised the subject of complete withdrawal. No one wanted to do that. Sir Orme Sargent described withdrawal as a "resounding victory" for communism, and the CIA called it a "political defeat of the first magnitude" with "profound effect[s] throughout the world." Yet how could the Western powers stay? Robertson was certain the Soviets did not want war, and he did not expect them to use force. They would not need to. They could easily create conditions that would compel the West, not the Kremlin, to choose between starting a war and backing down.[51]

Bradley made the same point to Clay. He stunned the military governor by remarking that officials in Washington doubted "our people are prepared to start a war in order to maintain our positions in Berlin and Vienna," where the Soviets were also interfering with Western access. He suggested that the Western governments consider under what conditions "we might ourselves announce withdrawal." Clay assured him the West could stay unless and until the Russians started shooting. The one exception would be if the Russians stopped all supplies to the city, but Clay was confident that would not happen; Moscow was too smart to "alienate the Germans." Hickerson sought reassurance from Murphy, asking whether the London program might put Berlin in jeopardy. Murphy assured him it would not, but he added an ominous and contradictory prediction. The Russians, he was sure, would not sever food supplies "until [the] last moment."[52]

Murphy and Clay were telling Washington what they thought it needed to hear. Contrary to claims in their memoirs that they repeatedly warned Washington, it was not in their interest to emphasize Berlin's vulnerability, and they did not. The administration's behavior during the April crisis showed all too clearly that Washington did not share their conviction that the Russians were bluffing. The two men suspected that Berlin was causing the administration to have second thoughts about the London program. Abandoning that initiative would ruin all they had worked for in the last four months, so they resolved to do what they could to stiffen Washington's resolve. That meant minimizing the risks and emphasizing the advantages of the policy adopted at Prince's Gate. Murphy told Hickerson that his only worry was "strength of determination in Washington." But in a private conversation with

British representatives on April 28, Clay admitted that he thought war over Berlin was "inevitable," and the Russians would put the onus for starting it on the West.[53]

That belief made Clay's proposal to challenge the blockade with an armed convoy all the more extraordinary. He first outlined the idea to Bradley on April 1, after the Russians sidetracked his trains. Bradley quickly instructed him not to send convoys unless ordered to do so. Clay responded eleven days later with a more detailed proposal, advertising it as a way to "win the present situation for us." Under his plan, the British, French, and Americans would each assemble a division at Helmstedt and march them to Berlin, after warning the Russians that they were coming. Clay predicted the Soviets would "fold up in [the] face of such a move." There was only a "remote" risk of war, he thought, going on to argue that if he were wrong, the troops could render a better account of themselves in the city than in the western zones, which his move would leave defenseless. Robertson saw "no future in this"; a few Soviet tanks in a defile could stop the column in its tracks. Even if it reached Berlin, there was nothing to prevent the Russians from interfering with later, nonmilitary traffic. Senators Arthur Vandenberg and Tom Connally were horrified when Lovett broached the subject. Bradley diplomatically told Clay the suggestion "might jeopardize our longer range objectives in the Western Zone."[54]

It was no time for a showdown. If Clay was wrong and war broke out, some 6,500 Western soldiers would face 18,000 Russians in Berlin, with 300,000 more in the eastern zone. LeMay thought the Soviets could overrun the western zones in eight hours.[55] Bradley also had to consider public opinion. The administration did not believe the American people understood the situation. A White House consultant complained of "widespread ignorance" of foreign policy, while the cabinet agreed in early March that the country needed guidance. Furthermore, the Europeans would never agree. The French were terrified of provoking the Russians, and Bevin emphasized to Marshall the need for "moderation and patience" and the dangers of "ill-considered action."[56]

With retaliation ineffective, evacuation delicate, and convoys risky, the Department of State decided on a protest. The draft it shared with the British and French embassies asserted that Berlin was an "international zone of occupation" and "not a part of the Soviet zone." U.S. rights were derived from EAC protocols and postwar usage, which guaranteed the West "free access." The United States assumed, the note ended, that the Soviet government would not "authorize or permit" Russian officials to infringe on "unquestioned rights which the US Government is fully determined to maintain."[57]

The draft got a chilly reception. The head of the German Political Department at the Foreign Office, Patrick H. Dean, disliked the American text, but he believed a note should be sent to brace the French and to put a warning on record. Although a restatement of Western rights might be useful, the British preferred to say nothing about what the West might do to enforce them.[58] Bidault worried where the note might lead. What would the Americans do "if things went wrong?" A retreat from Berlin "would be another Munich," but staying might lead to war. Bevin agreed it was essential to pin down the Americans, not just over Berlin but also over "their responsibilities in regard to supporting the Brussels treaty."[59]

In two meetings on April 28, Western officials were unable to agree about the note. Clay, Robertson, Douglas, and Strang met over lunch; Couve, Koenig, René Massigli (French ambassador to the United Kingdom), and Jacques Tarbé de Saint-Hardouin (Koenig's political adviser) joined them later. In the first session, Clay predicted that war over Berlin was "inevitable" within eighteen months. In a rambling discussion, he outlined several ways it might start. He asked Strang and Robertson point-blank whether Britain would stay in Berlin "'come hell or high water,' even if it meant war." They replied they could not commit their government. An overt attack would leave London no choice, but isolated incidents need not lead to hostilities. If the Russians continued to rely on nonviolent measures, the British intended to stay as long as possible. Douglas's interpretation of the British stance was that they would not "take the categorical position that under all circumstances and in all events, they will fight to maintain a position in Berlin." Clay and Douglas believed their government had taken such a stance. They interpreted the last sentence of the draft note as "serving notice on the Soviet Government that the Americans would go to war rather than be forced out of Berlin." Strang and Robertson questioned the wisdom of that position and of stating it so baldly to the Soviets. "It was never wise," they said, "to let diplomacy outrun the forces available to support it." Clay countered that "if the sting were taken out of the tail," the note would be "worse than useless."[60]

During the session with the French, Clay concealed his belief that war was certain. Instead, he contended that the Western powers could stay in Berlin unless the Soviets ejected them "by an act of war," and he expressed his conviction that Moscow would not go so far. Because the Soviets "understood only strong words," a firm Western stand was the only way to induce them to relent. Robertson was more honest. The Soviets, he said, could create a situation in which the West would be forced to make war if it wanted to stay. His government "could not be asked to decide [that question] now, and indeed he doubted whether any democratic government could take this decision now." A restatement of Western rights would be "helpful," but without the "sting" Clay demanded. The French shared Robertson's doubts, wanting to know precisely what actions the United States might take. Massigli "asked how in fact we could . . . maintain our position in Berlin if the Russians were determined to get us out." Robertson dodged the question by suggesting that if the West could stay long enough to build up west Germany, perhaps eighteen to twenty-four months, "the Berlin problem might vanish."[61]

Replying to Douglas's brief report on this conversation, Marshall commented that the British had misinterpreted Washington's intent. His explanation made it clear that Clay and Douglas had misjudged it, too. Marshall's position was that the United States must stay in Berlin and meet force with force. However, it would not "initiate the application of force." Unconsciously echoing Robertson, the secretary of state thought it neither advisable nor necessary to decide at that moment when force might be used.[62]

Bevin passed these exchanges on to Prime Minister Attlee. Dean noted that "Bevin is really waiting until the Americans can be induced to commit themselves more clearly behind the Brussels Treaty and to specify more exactly what they are prepared to do if the Russians do take strong action in Germany." The British foreign secretary thus seemed to see the situation in Berlin as a useful argument in the campaign to obtain the American commitment to European security he had been seeking since December.[63]

Meanwhile, the second session of the London conference was "not going well," in Bevin's opinion, and he blamed French foot-dragging. The British and Americans regarded French opposition as disingenuous, a "facade," as Bevin put it. They attributed the French position to domestic politics and an exaggerated concern over European security, not the merits of the issues under discussion. Bidault faced strong opposition from socialist members of the cabinet, in addition to the predictable stances taken by Gaullists and communists outside it. The French also complained that the United States was "growing cold" about European security, with no action taken since the Brussels treaty. Lovett quickly denied this, but he did not reveal the Pentagon talks, referring instead to a draft resolution being discussed with Senator Vandenberg. Secure in the conviction that French concern was due to ignorance, he was inclined to dismiss it. So when Massigli claimed on May 11 that his government was deeply concerned about the possibility of "unpleasant reactions from the Russians," Strang and Douglas waved such hyperactive imaginings aside. It was too late to turn back. The Russians and Germans would interpret hesitation as "a sign of weakness." Nothing the West did, Douglas lectured, "could either provoke or conciliate the Russians." It could "only arrest or deter them."[64]

Even as Douglas was setting out this line, events in Moscow raised doubts that he represented U.S. policy. Worried that the Russians might underestimate U.S. resolve because of election-year divisions, John P. Davies of the Policy Planning Staff had suggested that Ambassador Smith clearly state both Washington's desire for improved relations and its determination to oppose Soviet expansion. Truman endorsed the plan. Not mentioned in Smith's instructions was the fact that Berlin was one reason for the initiative, which would substitute for the more explicit warning the Europeans had refused to endorse. As Lovett explained, the administration wanted to avoid Soviet miscalculation by making it clear that the United States would insist on its rights "in Berlin and elsewhere."[65]

In his May 4 conversation with Molotov, Smith stressed both points contained in his instructions. Molotov replied on May 9 by blaming the United States for the Cold War. The following day, *Tass* printed carefully edited versions of both statements, giving the impression that the United States had proposed bilateral talks and Molotov had accepted, only to have Smith retreat from his initial offer.[66]

Western Europeans were aghast. How could Washington approach Moscow without consulting them first? How could it consider negotiating with the Soviets behind their backs, especially now, with the Marshall Plan just under way and the London conversations in midstream? Officials in Whitehall feared "a new Yalta." In Washington, Britain's ambassador, Lord Inverchapel, delivered a stern message from Bevin: Britain had endorsed Western Union (the military organization created by the western Europeans in March as part of the Brussels treaty) and the London program because of assurances of U.S. support. Those were now in question, and Bevin wanted new pledges "to restore confidence." The first thoughts in Paris were also about the London talks. Ambassador Henri Bonnet called the Department of State to ask how the discussions in Moscow would affect Western plans in Germany.[67]

The initial reaction by the American public, in contrast, was euphoric: the Cold War was over. Marshall and Truman pricked this balloon to reassure their allies, reinforcing the image of American recalcitrance that Molotov had manufactured. Their statements showed how the Soviet foreign minister had outmaneuvered Smith, but these attempts at damage control merely reinforced the impression that the administration was incompetent. Its fumbling over Palestine in the United Nations that same week added to the image of confusion and ineptitude. In postmortems, Marshall attributed the problem to the public's "susceptibility . . . to propaganda," Lovett blamed "ignorance," and Forrestal pointed to "dangerous complacency" that threatened a renewal of the draft.[68]

Truman's troubles had not ended. Progressive Party leader Henry Wallace sent Stalin an open letter proposing "definitive, decisive" steps on a long list of issues; on May 18 the generalissimo described the list as a "good and fruitful basis" for discussion. Truman's anger and embarrassment deepened. Moscow was not seeking a settlement, he told his staff; it was interfering in a presidential election. There was "nothing to negotiate," he declared, because "Russia has never kept any of the agreements she has made." A State Department press release contended that all these questions were under discussion in the proper diplomatic forums, where Soviet intransigence prevented agreement. As Stalin had intended all along, the impression remained that the Soviet Union wanted peace and the United States did not.[69]

THE NEWS FROM MOSCOW reinforced French doubts about the London program. The day after Stalin's reply to Wallace, Massigli suggested that the program be delayed due to the "softening" in Soviet policy. Douglas refused, reiterating familiar arguments: delay would reveal "weakness," encourage Moscow, and undermine German morale. Lovett fired back a cable endorsing Douglas's stance and indicating Washington's agreement that the "risks of proceeding with establishment of provisional Govt are less than risks of further delay."[70]

As Bidault made clear on May 20, the French believed the exact opposite. A separate west German state meant the partition of Germany, stimulating right-wing nationalism at a time when neo Nazi groups had shown alarming strength in recent elections. More important, it would provoke Russian retaliation "in Berlin and elsewhere." Therefore, they should postpone the London program "until the autumn." Bidault told U.S. Ambassador Jefferson Caffery that the Russians "might actually drive us out of Berlin" in response to it.[71]

Even before diplomats had drafted an initial text for a North Atlantic treaty, one theme in the alliance's history was beginning to emerge. During (and after) the Cold War, Europeans would be quick to criticize the United States for unilateralism and high-handedness—and to complain whenever it failed to lead. (For their part, Americans would press Europeans to show more initiative and energy while expecting them to stay in step.) Now, in May 1948, the French regarded Washington's European policy as too timid and its German policy as too assertive. They not only doubted the United States *could* defend western Europe; they were not sure it *would*. In Washington, Bonnet attributed Bidault's stance to "lack of progress on American support for the Brussels treaty." Marshall had assured Bidault that the London conference would provide an opportunity to discuss security issues, but nothing had happened. Massigli explained to Sargent that the Smith-Molotov affair had made his government wonder whether it could count on the consistency of American policy toward the Soviets; the French were "always afraid" that Washington might strike a deal with Moscow behind Europe's back. Massigli also complained that Douglas had "evaded" his attempts to discuss the consequences of the London program for Berlin. Worse, Douglas had "seriously alarmed" the French by saying the United States would initiate the use of force if necessary to remain there.[72]

The British and the Americans regarded French complaints as an "eleventh-hour" betrayal of the implicit compromise undergirding the London talks: French concessions on a German political structure in exchange for Anglo-American acceptance of economic and military controls over a revived west Germany. Now, with nearly all the major issues resolved, the French wanted to pocket British and American concessions and withdraw their own.[73]

While acknowledging French fears, British and American diplomats believed other motives were more important in shaping French policy. First, no doubt, was France's intense aversion to German revival and the desire to exact as many concessions as it could. Second, Bidault's move seemed rooted in French domestic politics; he was reportedly "in a panic" over charges in the press and parliament that he had conceded too much in London. As for the purported neo-Nazi revival, Strang observed that Paris was disturbed by a 3 percent showing in Hesse for the National Democratic Party, hardly a tidal wave of support for fascism.[74]

It was harder to dismiss French concerns about Berlin. Strang, Douglas, and their colleagues realized that the city was the likely target of Soviet retaliation against the London program—Dean conceded "the danger point is Berlin"—but they preferred not to dwell on its vulnerability. To do so would be to admit that the French had a case and to call into question all that had been achieved since December. It also meant facing some serious questions. As army under secretary William Draper suggested, the discussion of possible Soviet steps meant that "we are dangerously close to being committed to military conversations with the British and French."[75] The British and Americans preferred to emphasize the dangers of delaying the London program. Delay would shatter Western prestige and eliminate the German contribution to European recovery. Dean claimed the Germans were "anxiously awaiting" the Western initiative, but, if faced with any delay, they "will get cold feet and re-insure with the Russians."[76]

Delay would also be a "sign of weakness" that would encourage the Soviets to new aggression. Caffery took this line, turning the French argument about Berlin inside out. So did Bevin. "If the Russians know that the Western powers are afraid of them and are holding up their programme in Germany on that account," the foreign secretary argued, "they will . . . be in a very strong position to intensify the pressure upon the Western Powers in Berlin."[77] Yet that fit poorly with another Anglo-American contention—that Soviet policy was immune to external influences. Dean argued, as had Douglas, that "nothing . . . we do is likely either to deter or provoke them"; "the Russians probably have their plans in Germany more or less ready."[78] Lovett, in a case of obvious prompting, asked Douglas and Clay (in London for the six-power talks) two leading questions: Had they considered that the establishment of a provisional west German government would give the Russians an "excuse to intensify pressure in Berlin"? Did the British and American delegations believe the dangers of delay exceeded those entailed by a Soviet reaction? Douglas quickly cabled back the answers the under secretary wanted.[79]

The London conference adjourned May 31, forwarding its recommendations to the six governments a day later. The heart of the program consisted of proposals for a west German state. The military governors would meet their minister-presidents no later than June 15 and instruct them to convene by September 1 a constituent assembly that would write a constitution for a west German government; that government could become a reality within a year. The military governors would approve the constitution before it was submitted for popular ratification, and occupation authorities would retain power over foreign relations and trade. There would be no territorial separations and no Rhenish state; the Ruhr would remain German. The principal concession to the French was an international authority for the Ruhr that would allocate the region's coal, coke, and steel production between Germany's "essential needs" and those of western Europe. The French also obtained pledges that the Western powers would withdraw occupation troops only after consultation; a Military Security Board would enforce measures to disarm and demilitarize the Reich.[80]

If the London recommendations received prompt approval in Washington and London, they met an unenthusiastic reception in Germany, where they meant partition. Robertson described initial reactions as "unenthusiastic" and "very negative." The two main parties, the Christian Democratic Union (CDU) and the SPD, threatened boycott. Robertson hoped the minister-presidents, who were "always better to deal with than the [political] parties," would be more receptive. In Washington, the CIA described Germans as "apathetic" toward the program and "resentful" of attempts to introduce democratic institutions. An OMGUS poll found, more optimistically, a majority acquiescing in the program, although it noted "widespread ignorance" and apathy.[81]

The London program was no more popular west of the Rhine. Officials in the Quai d'Orsay thought it provided adequate safeguards, preserved French influence over German recovery and Anglo-American policy, and thus served France's interests. Few others did. Cabinet members feared it would provoke the Russians while stimulating German nationalism. Bidault's critics in the cabinet included members of his own party. The divisions were so deep that the cabinet decided to submit the proposals to the National Assembly, where a narrow majority, 300 to 286, passed them with reservations on June 17.[82] Within forty-eight hours of the vote, France's worst fears about Soviet retaliation in Berlin began to come true.

THE RUSSIANS REACTED to the second session of the London conference in three ways, paralleling their response to the first. They increased restrictions on traffic to Berlin, destroyed the Kommandatura, and mounted a propaganda offensive. New restrictions began while the conference was still in session. On May 4, the Soviets began rejecting German freight for "insufficient documentation," announced unilateral regulations for parcel post, and required the re-registration of barges on inland canals. As James Riddleberger summed up matters, Soviet restrictions, though few, were effective. The Russians concentrated at first on outbound traffic, with only minor disruption of movement from the western zones.[83] Officials required lists of railcars' contents, precise destination, and consignees starting June 1. The British commandant, Major General Edwin O. Herbert, thought these requirements might "strangle essential traffic."[84] Over the next few days, Russian soldiers delayed outbound mail trains. On June 9, Soviet officials began turning back Germans trying to enter the eastern zone, alleging that their passes were not in order and that—contrary to ACC directives—officials in the town to be visited had to grant permission.[85] As the British expected, the new Soviet system of issuing permits for interzonal barges broke down. No trains reached Berlin on June 11. Russian officials justified the halt by alleging (falsely) that Berlin's rail yards were congested.[86]

The Soviets let trains resume on June 12 but announced they would close the autobahn bridge over the Elbe on June 15 for "repairs." They diverted traffic over poor secondary roads to a small ferry fifteen miles away. Sokolovsky waited a week before rejecting Robertson's offer to help repair the bridge or install a temporary replacement. With the ferry closed between 10:00 P.M. and 6:00 A.M., a ban on autobahn traffic at night was the next logical step, and it followed on June 16.[87]

The second Soviet response was to destroy the Kommandatura. Since January, the four-power agency had degenerated into a propaganda forum. Customarily, at the end of each month the commandants approved the next month's schedule of meetings, but starting April 20, the Russians would schedule only one meeting at a time. They prolonged meetings at all levels with lengthy prepared statements and quarrels over agendas and minutes.[88] The final blow came June 16. At 11:20 P.M., after thirteen hours of fruitless argument, Colonel Howley asked the chairman, French General Jean Ganeval, for permission to leave. As Ganeval waved Howley's deputy, Colonel William T. Babcock, into his chair, Howley left the room, slamming the door behind him. Following whispered consultations with advisers, the Soviet representative, Colonel A. I. Yelisarov (Kotikov's deputy), denounced Howley's "hooligan manners" and led the Soviet delegation out.[89]

The third Soviet reaction, propaganda, culminated in the Warsaw Declaration of June 24, issued after a meeting of Eastern bloc foreign ministers. Its most startling aspect was ineptness, as it tried to play simultaneously on nationalism in Germany and hatred of the country elsewhere. According to the declaration, a specter was haunting Europe: German aggression. At the same time that it excoriated German "revanchism," it appealed to German sentiment by lamenting the destruction of German unity and subordination of the nation's economy to Anglo-American interests. It concluded by appealing for a return to the Yalta-Potsdam system of four-power control.[90]

Murphy thought the Soviets were either preparing to cut off Berlin or hoping to push one of the Western powers into convening the ACC.[91] Robertson thought the Soviet goal was to "wreck" the Marshall Plan. Moscow intended to undermine German confidence in the Western powers and the German institutions they sought to create. If that failed, the Soviets would turn to sabotage. Barring a Western response, this would lead to "an all-out effort to paralyse the economy of the zone" and expel Western troops. Resolute action, he thought, would forestall further erosion, though he did not spell out what that action should be.[92]

If Western leaders shrugged off dissolution of the Kommandatura and the Soviet propaganda campaign, interference with access to Berlin was another matter. Clay's deputy at European Command, Lieutenant General Clarence R. Huebner, predicted on June 11 that the Soviets intended to stop surface traffic to Berlin. Huebner doubted an airlift could feed the city and expected Berliners to turn against the Western powers, making the latter's position "untenable." If this echoed earlier assessments, it raised eyebrows in Washington. Wedemeyer shot back a cable, asking for information about travel restrictions and the "practicability" of maintaining an American presence. "There is no practicability in maintaining our position in Berlin," Clay replied. He could feed the garrison indefinitely by air, but not the Berliners. He intended to remain "until the German people are threatened with starvation," because an American presence in the city was a symbol of U.S. intent and "essential to our prestige."[93]

The CIA predicted increased efforts to eject the Western powers but was vague on when that would happen and under what conditions. It expected no demand for Western withdrawal until after a west German government had been established and was "successful to a degree dangerous to Soviet objectives." The CIA director, Admiral Roscoe H. Hillenkoetter, repeated this prediction in a paper for the president on June 12. This implied that a showdown was months away. A second paper, examining the effects of Soviet transport restrictions as of June 1, was also unlikely to set off alarm bells. Issued June 14, it contended that Western intelligence activities, the Kommandatura, and the Magistrat had suffered more than travel had. Barges carried most of the city's supplies and had not suffered major hindrance.[94]

The Wedemeyer-Clay exchange bothered Marshall, who asked what the army would do if the Russians cut supplies. The Intelligence Division had studied how to support the garrison by airlift, but it had no other plans. Wedemeyer noted, with some understatement, that "additional planning is indicated." There was no sense of urgency. The staff drafted a paper for Wedemeyer to use in discussions with Clay during a trip to Europe planned for the following week. The paper predicted that Moscow would provide its own stocks of food and fuel for Berliners if it cut off Western supplies. Because Berlin was not worth a war, the paper's authors did not rule out abandoning it "under the most adverse circumstances short of war." Back at the State Department, the Policy Planning Staff was also considering Berlin and its implications. Describing the city as "one of the most dangerous spots in the world," it began exploring ways to bring the subject before the National Security Council. Events had already outstripped these tentative thoughts, however, as a decision by the Western powers to introduce a new currency into their zones brought the crisis to a boiling point.[95]

CURRENCY REFORM HAD BEEN a contentious issue since the war. The Nazis had put some 73 billion reichsmarks into circulation against a need of perhaps 8 billion. Early in 1946, Clay had put a group of experts to work on currency reform, and he submitted the results to the ACC that August. It recommended not merely a tenfold contraction of the money supply, a capital levy, and cancellation of the national debt but also replacement of the reichsmark with a new currency—the deutsche mark—for maximum psychological effect, and a central agency to issue notes and control their circulation. This raised questions that simple revaluation would have avoided—who would print the new notes, and where? On these questions, the ACC could not agree.[96]

Clay proposed that the *Staatsdruckerei* in the American sector print the new notes under quadripartite control and that a central bank issue them. The Soviets insisted on what amounted to parallel procedures. Notes printed in Berlin would be issued in the western zones, while notes for the Soviet zone would be printed in Leipzig. According to Michail Narinskii, Soviet officials interpreted an effective four-power system as giving the Western powers "control" over the Soviet zone's economy and the authority to limit Moscow's ability to "issue banknotes to cover occupation and reparation expenses." So while the Soviets assured Western representatives that a central agency would control both plants, they sought to ensure that its oversight could be easily evaded. They would accept Clay's proposal only if the four powers agreed on reparations and central administrative agencies first, effectively holding currency reform hostage to the two most contentious issues before the ACC.[97]

Months passed. The British expected a breakthrough after the 1947 foreign ministers' meeting in Moscow, but the ACC remained deadlocked. Clay was ready to compromise, but Washington continued to insist that the new notes be printed in Berlin alone or not at all.[98] The American stance rested on a misreading of recent history. In preparing for the occupation, the British and Americans had agreed to use a common occupation currency, printed in Washington and valued at par with the reichsmark. The Soviets agreed to join this arrangement but insisted on printing their own supply of notes. No one bothered to work out any controls beyond a dash inserted in front of the serial number on the Russian bills. At war's end, the presses in Moscow ran off billions of notes, which spread "like fall leaves over the country."[99] These military marks were worthless outside of Germany, and the Soviet government would not allow its soldiers to convert them into rubles. Eager to get rid of this paper money before they demobilized, Russians paid as much as 10,000 military marks for a $4 GI watch. Converted at a ratio of 10 marks to the dollar, this meant a neat $996 profit for the American soldier—and a $1,000 debt for the Treasury. The drain became serious. In July 1945, American soldiers in Berlin drew $1 million in pay but sent home over $4 million, and the Treasury was out the difference.[100] American officials were furious that Moscow never gave the ACC any reckoning of the bills it issued; they alleged that the Russians had cost British and American taxpayers more than $800 million. The experience embittered Clay, Robertson, and their subordinates, who vowed never to be tricked again.[101]

Actually, deficits existed everywhere Americans served overseas. Berlin's deficit was proportional to those in other areas, given the number of soldiers involved, and in Berlin, most of it was due to troops manipulating a twenty-to-one difference in the value of the military mark in the "official" economy versus its value in the black market. Their partners in this currency manipulation were usually Berliners, not Russians. In congressional hearings on the matter, John Hilldring, now assistant secretary of state for occupied areas, testified that the Soviets were "very indirectly if at all connected" with the deficit. Furthermore, the British thought the Americans were barking up the wrong tree. If the Soviets were determined to cheat, controls on printing would not prevent them. The real safeguard was controlling the issuance of notes, not their printing.[102]

Beginning in July 1947, Clay worried over reports that the Russians intended to introduce a separate currency in their zone. This would be a "calamitous" development, according to his financial adviser, Jack Bennett, because holders of reichsmarks would dump them in the western zones, where they remained legal tender. Clay persuaded Washington to print new bills "purely as a defense measure." The air force flew over a thousand tons of them to Germany, and the army distributed them to secret holding areas throughout the Bizone.[103]

Both sides were acting for identical reasons. The Russians had been considering a separate currency reform since January 1947, but only in response to a Western one, and Clay's precautions did not mean that the Western powers had committed themselves to a separate reform. Hilldring's view, shared by Marshall and Lovett, was that the search for quadripartite agreement should continue, if only for "political reasons," the main one being to avoid the blame for Germany's partition. Robertson commented publicly that a separate reform would mean the "division of Germany," a step his government was unwilling to take "unless and until we are forced to do so."[104] Meeting Bevin and Bidault after the Council of Foreign Ministers session in London, Marshall pressed for one more try. Clay also thought one last effort was necessary, if only to justify whatever separate initiatives might be taken later.[105]

When Clay circulated his proposal in the ACC on January 20, 1948, Sokolovsky rejected it. He insisted that a central German finance agency and a central bank of issue be created first. Bennett portrayed this measure as obstructive—and in part it was, because Sokolovsky knew the French had not dropped their opposition to central agencies—but Bennett forgot that both institutions had been part of Clay's plan from the start.[106] At the same time, Sokolovsky dropped his demand that notes be printed in Leipzig. Encouraged, the ACC directed its financial experts to meet in continuous session and report by February 10. When the council considered their report on the eleventh, Sokolovsky proposed starting the presses in Berlin while technical experts worked out other details. Clay was willing to proceed, but he insisted that the United States retain its freedom of action if differences remained after sixty days. The council accepted Sokolovsky's plan on this basis.[107]

Both sides, as historian Jochen Laufer points out, were playing a double game, seeking agreement while maneuvering to pin blame for failure on the other.[108] Everything depended on the technical talks, and progress slowed. In early March, the Soviets resurrected their insistence on central agencies. The talks stalled, and the Americans began having second thoughts.[109] They had continued preparations for a bizonal currency reform in case four-power talks broke down. Clay, Murphy, and Draper now worried that quadripartite currency reform might allow the Russians to disrupt the economic recovery of western Germany and western Europe. On March 11, the Department of State agreed and reversed its policy: Clay was to break off four-power talks as soon as possible.[110]

Sokolovsky's walkout on March 20 thus suited Western officials nicely, for it let them put the onus for the financial talks' failure on the Soviets. But if Clay expected Soviet disagreement to open the way for Western action, he was quickly and unpleasantly surprised. London had authorized Robertson to go ahead on a bilateral basis, but preparations stalled when the British and Americans disagreed over how to handle the Reich debt. In mid-May, the French agreed to join the currency reform, forcing another delay while plans were redrawn on a tripartite basis. On June 15, matters stood about where they had a month before, due to French foot-dragging. Clay was impatient, grumbling, "I thought we had crossed the Rubicon in London but apparently we sat down in the middle of the stream." He won approval to go ahead, with or without the French, on June 18, three days away. Clay and Koenig's deputy conferred until 3:00 A.M. on June 17 without achieving a breakthrough. Then, a few hours after the National Assembly vote in Paris, the French gave in. The three military governors made the announcement after banks closed on Friday, June 18, and the reform took effect on Sunday, June 20.[111]

The eastern and western zones would have separate currencies. Which would circulate in Berlin? Draper had raised the issue as early as February, when he asked Clay for ideas. Clay had none. The difficulty, as Clay and Murphy both observed, was the city's close economic ties with the surrounding Soviet zone; no one believed Berlin could operate independently. A State Department study concluded that, economically, Berlin "belongs to the Soviet zone," and a separate currency would cripple it. The Civil Affairs Division (CAD) took a similar line on April 28. It thought "immediate agreement" with the Russians on a special currency for Berlin, either the reichsmark or a special Berlin mark, would be the best solution, as long as notes circulated under four power control. If the Soviets countered the deutsche mark with a new currency of their own, CAD opposed using the eastern mark in Berlin, because "currency issue is sovereign power." If the Russians introduced their currency in the city, CAD suggested that Clay counter with a version of the deutsche mark and make it work, somehow.[112] Clay favored a "monetary union" between the city and the Soviet zone, with the Kommandatura controlling the notes issued for Berlin. If Sokolovsky refused, Clay agreed that the Western powers would have to issue the deutsche mark in their sectors.[113]

Bevin's assessment for Attlee minimized the odds of a sharp Soviet response. The Russians "no doubt" would react to the deutsche mark by replacing the reichsmark in their zone with a new currency. If they introduced that new currency into Berlin, the Western powers would have no choice but to extend the deutsche mark into their sectors. Beyond that, he could not predict events. Officials had given considerable thought to the subject, and Bevin's soothing conclusion was that the military governors had made "such plans as are possible for dealing with developments."[114]

Once again, Western officials discounted the risks their actions involved. That they understood these risks seems undeniable. Clay had warned Bradley as far back as April 10 that the currency reform and creation of a west German government would trigger "the real crisis"; on June 13, he predicted that the Soviet effort "to force us from Berlin . . . will come when we install separate currency if it is to come at all." Robertson had advised Bevin that currency reform "may well be the signal for any Russian move which is contemplated," and British officials foresaw serious economic and political problems in the city if either side acted unilaterally.[115] Western leaders, in other words, assumed that in the midst of "the real crisis," the Soviets would obligingly cooperate in arranging a new quadripartite currency system for Berlin. Alive to the dangers a Soviet reform entailed for their zones, Western officials ignored the effects their reform would have on the Soviet zone—and their sectors' vulnerability to Soviet counteraction. That a Western currency reform might harm the Soviets, and that they might respond by tightening their grip on Berlin, was a possibility policy makers preferred not to contemplate.

THE WESTERN MILITARY GOVERNORS informed Sokolovsky of the currency reform a few hours before the public announcement.[116] The calamity Bennett had predicted for the western zones now confronted the Soviets, who suspended passenger travel by road, rail, and foot into their zone. Some traffic to and from Berlin continued, but Soviet officials insisted on inspecting all trains and clearing them one at a time at Marienborn. The restrictions did not greatly alarm Western officials, who had expected something of the sort. As Clay remarked to his staff, "If they put in a currency reform and we didn't, it would have been the first move we . . . would have had to take." In London, Patrick Dean said much the same thing, telling a Canadian diplomat that the Soviets' responses to the Western currency reform "were not unexpected and were exactly what Britain would have followed in [the] opposite contingency."[117]

Still, Clay was not one to take these developments lying down, and he pushed back in two ways. The first was to challenge Soviet bans with a train. After giving the Soviets advance notice, he sent a train into the eastern zone. When the Soviets ordered it to stop for inspection, its commander tried to continue to Berlin. The Russians shunted it onto a siding several miles down the line. After a thirty-six-hour standoff, Russian troops overpowered the crew, attached a Soviet locomotive, and dragged the train back to Helmstedt. Clay had resumed airlift flights on June 20; he now told Washington that he was supplying the Berlin garrison by air because he would not submit to Soviet inspection.[118]

Clay also urged Washington to protest to Moscow, but officials thought the Europeans would probably balk again, and a unilateral American protest would reveal Western disunity. Things would be clearer after the Warsaw meeting of communist foreign ministers. In the meantime, the State Department saw the situation as a propaganda opportunity.[119]

While Soviet interference with access was bothersome, the Berlin currency situation was a tangled knot of complications. Ganeval called a meeting of the Kommandatura on June 19 to discuss the Western currency reform. Yelisarov refused to attend, pleading other business. That same day, Sokolovsky forbade circulation of the deutsche mark in the Soviet zone and, in an ominous move, throughout Berlin as well. His order contended that the city was in the Soviet zone and "is economically part of the Soviet zone." Clay and Robertson rejected Sokolovsky's claim, only to have him repeat it the following day.[120]

The Soviets agreed to a meeting of currency experts on June 22. Their first question was whether the Western powers planned to circulate the deutsche mark in Berlin. The Soviets insisted that Berlin formed an integral part of the eastern zone's economy; therefore, their currency must be the sole legal tender in both the zone and the city. Because any currency action in Berlin would affect their zone, "only they . . . could safely be trusted with discretion in this field." This was an understandable position, especially after the June 18 announcement, and one that Soviet officials were under explicit orders from Moscow to uphold, but it offered the Western powers no protection against Soviet abuse. The Americans proposed the establishment of a special Berlin currency, neither the deutsche mark nor the Soviet mark. The British were willing to discuss accepting the Soviet mark if its circulation were under four-power control and if the Russians guaranteed Western access rights. Rejecting both ideas, the Russians threatened "economic and administrative sanctions" to compel acceptance of the new Soviet currency throughout the city. The British and Americans replied that they might have to introduce the deutsche mark. The French made it clear that they were unprepared to go that far.[121]

Both sides sought to protect their positions, but in Berlin, each could protect itself only through action that jeopardized the other. The Russians were not about to give Westerners a veto over the Soviet mark. Even if the Westerners restrained themselves and exercised control over only currency circulation in Berlin, it would affect the Soviet zone. For their part, the Western powers could not allow the Russians to control the city's economic life. Acceptance of the Soviet mark as the city's only currency would have a tremendous psychological effect on Berliners, Russians, and Westerners alike, not to mention the economic and political leverage it would give the Soviet Union. Even a willingness to accept the Soviet mark under four-power control would, as the next few months would show, put the Western powers on a slippery slope.

While these talks were still in session, the Soviets announced their own currency reform effective June 24. Until new notes were available, the Russians attached a gummed stamp to each old reichsmark bill. Although this appeared to be a hasty improvisation, the stamps had been ready since December. By appearing confused and surprised, the Soviets hoped to avoid blame for partition and channel nationalist resentment against the West. Sokolovsky extended the reform throughout Berlin, in keeping with the slogan that the city was "located in the Soviet occupation zone and economically forms part of it." To accept this contention, as Clay put it, would place Berlin in Soviet hands. The suggestion that the Western powers should have waited until the harm was actual, not just anticipated, ignores Narinskii's conclusion that "the Soviet Government was trying to include all Berlin in the financial and economic system of the Soviet zone."[122]

The next day, the Western commandants declared Sokolovsky's order null and void in their sectors and introduced a special version of the deutsche mark. The French agreed only at the last minute, handing Clay and Robertson a statement disclaiming responsibility for the "incalculable consequences" of this latest Anglo-Saxon initiative.[123] There were several indications that the Western powers were still hoping for compromise. Their bills were stamped with a large "B" to distinguish them from currency introduced into the western zones and thus permit their withdrawal from circulation without affecting the zonal reform. And although they nullified the Soviet order, the Western commandants did not ban Soviet currency in their sectors. (The Russians immediately banned the "B-mark," as it was known, in their sector.) Two currencies thus circulated in west Berlin, with no exchange rate between them. To keep up the value of the B-mark, the Western powers issued small quantities. Only a quarter of the western sectors' money was in B-marks; the rest was in Soviet notes.[124]

The city government now had to decide which order to obey. The Magistrat denied that the Soviet order applied to all four sectors, but final action was up to the City Assembly.[125] The SPD's Otto Suhr, assembly chair, called a meeting for 4:00 P.M. on June 23. By 1:00 in the afternoon, several hundred SED demonstrators, some delivered in Soviet army trucks, had filled the galleries and the street outside. Suhr announced that the meeting would not begin until the galleries were cleared, and SED members did not signal their supporters to leave until 6:00 P.M. Over SED opposition, the assembly accepted the Magistrat's recommendations: the Soviet order would apply in the eastern sector, with the Western one taking effect in the remaining three. Legislators then had to run the gauntlet awaiting them outside. Jeanette Wolff, who had survived a Nazi concentration camp, and several of her colleagues endured severe beatings as the eastern sector police pointed out assembly members for attack.[126]

Having failed to cow Berlin's leaders, the Soviets turned to the populace. At 2:00 A.M. on June 24, Soviet officials announced that the rail line from Helmstedt had closed due to "technical difficulties." Traffic could not be rerouted, they claimed, without disrupting the rail network in the eastern zone. Road and barge traffic was also suspended (some trains and barges en route at the time managed to slip into the city over the next few weeks). Citing "shortages of coal," Soviet officers stopped supplying electricity to the western sectors. There was perhaps a ten-day supply of coal at western sector generating plants. Completing west Berlin's isolation, Russian officials prohibited the sale of food and supplies from the Soviet zone, to prevent, they said, circulation of the Western currency in the eastern zone. Meanwhile, eight divisions moved in combat order to assembly areas near the interzonal border.[127]

Berliners thus awoke on Thursday, June 24, to find themselves under Soviet blockade. Howley recalled the shock that swept the city. The Soviets may have calculated that morale was so low, following defeat and years of occupation, that the news would frighten the city's residents into accepting Soviet rule. They tried various measures to spark panic. *Tägliche Rundschau* claimed that the Soviet Military Administration was "the only legitimate occupation authority" in the city. Rumors spread that the Western powers were leaving, and reports hinted at Soviet military maneuvers near the city. An American news agency repeated stories that the Russians had arrayed barrage balloons near Tempelhof airfield, interfering with landings.[128]

The rumor campaign's greatest success was a radio report that the power shortage had shut the city's sewage plants, imperiling the water supply. Frightened people rushed to fill pots, pans, and whatever else was handy, nearly draining the system. Howley went on the radio to assure residents that there was plenty of water, and his gamble paid off: Berliners turned off their taps.[129]

Howley was not the only Western leader trying to counter the Soviet psychological offensive. Herbert assured Berliners that food stocks were adequate and there was no cause for "immediate anxiety." In Heidelberg, Clay told reporters that the Kremlin had launched its "final pressure to drive us out of Berlin," but he was confident it could not succeed "by any action short of war." Despite Clay's brave words, the *New York Times* reported that Berliners had the impression that the Western powers would withdraw if civilian suffering became severe. Another of the general's comments showed that, even on the first day of the blockade, Western leaders could not rid themselves of the notion that the political costs of coercion were too high for the Kremlin. "Do you think," he asked correspondents, "the Russians want to starve 2,000,000 Germans?" In Whitehall, Dean took a similar view, predicting that Moscow's "policy of starving out the German population . . . will be changed as they realise it is not proving good propaganda."[130]

Ernst Reuter and other city leaders worked to rally public opinion. The SPD held a mass meeting that afternoon, with over 80,000 Berliners attending. Louise Schroeder and Jeanette Wolff were greeted by thunderous applause. Reuter gave the main speech. The city hall riot, he claimed, had aimed at seizing control of the city. Having failed, the communists were now trying to win through starvation and economic coercion. Local SPD chairman Franz Neumann closed the meeting with an appeal to the Western powers to rally to Berlin's cause.[131] Would the Western powers respond? Members of Clay's staff shared their doubts with reporters. Officials in Washington, they feared, were "engrossed" by the Republican convention, which nominated Thomas E. Dewey for president on the night of June 23. Having anxiously and minutely followed events in April, Washington now failed to recognize that "we have a problem."[132]

EISENHOWER'S "EXPERIMENTAL LABORATORY" had failed. He and Clay had begun the occupation believing that closer contact with the Russians would promote mutual understanding and cooperation. The opposite had happened. Cooperative institutions rest on shared interests. By early 1948, the only shared interest in Berlin was avoiding another war. No mutually satisfactory system of joint control could be worked out because power sufficient to secure the interests of one side menaced those of the other, and each feared the other would abuse whatever loopholes it could find. The Soviets were convinced the Western powers were intent on reviving Germany and using it to spearhead new aggression against the Soviet Union. They had tried for months, through escalating pressure on Berlin, to compel the Western powers to abandon their plans. Introduction of the deutsche mark was the last straw, and only a sharp response held any hope of derailing the Western program. Berlin still appeared to be the West's most vulnerable spot. If past pressures there had not worked, it was because they had not been intense enough. It was time to bring matters to a head.

CHAPTER 4

Prudence and Resolve

The situation Western leaders faced on June 24 was not as clear and simple as it appears in retrospect; neither were their responses. Looking back, we see a straightforward, unambiguous Soviet challenge—an open-ended blockade—and an equally clear Western response—a decision to resist, uphold rights, and defeat the blockade with the airlift. That is not how things looked at the time. No one could be certain how serious the situation was or how long it might last. There were signs that disruption of access would last only until the Soviets completed their currency reform. Until the situation clarified, the Western governments took things one day at a time, comforted by the knowledge that stocks of food and fuel in Berlin postponed the day of decision. Although flying supplies into the city would help, no one thought it could overcome the blockade. Sooner or later, unless the Soviets relented, the Western powers would face stark choices: withdrawing, acceding to Soviet demands, or risking war by attempting to break the blockade on the ground.

Policies on both sides blended prudence and resolve, typical of crises in an age of weapons of mass destruction (WMD). Governments demonstrate resolve to protect their interests while exercising prudence to control risks. Conciliation can jeopardize interests; rigidity risks plunging over the brink. Achieving a balance is never easy, and maintaining it is difficult; sustaining unity of action with allies is harder still. The West did not adopt a forthright policy of resistance. It struggled over how important Berlin was and what risks might be run. By mid-July, only tentative answers had begun to emerge.

Having expected a quick victory that did not materialize, Stalin also improvised. The best course seemed to be to persevere. The alternatives? Although it might make sense in the abstract to interfere with the airlift or seal off west Berlin, there was no point in backing the West into a corner; the imperialists might do something desperate. To retreat would encourage them and guarantee the success of the London program. So the Soviets were careful not to push matters to extremes, and they constructed a rationale for the blockade based on "technical difficulties." And they kept up the pressure. On July 3, with no sign of Western counteraction, Sokolovsky felt confident enough to scuttle the "technical difficulties" justification and make explicit the link between the blockade and the London program. The Kremlin took the same line on July 14, when it rejected the West's demand for an end to the blockade. Both sides found themselves in a prolonged deadlock that neither had expected.

THE BRITISH WERE THE FIRST to take a position. The cabinet considered the situation on Thursday, June 24. Bevin was on vacation, and without him, the group reached no conclusions. McNeil could not say whether Soviet restrictions were part of a "tactical reply" to the B-mark or "the first move in a major offensive" to expel the Western powers. The cabinet acknowledged that "a very serious situation might develop" and thought the powers "should take their stand on a position which they were confident of being able to sustain." The record is silent on what Attlee and his colleagues thought that position might be. In light of the assumption that the city could not be supplied for long, such a formulation did not point toward firmness.[1]

Robertson reported some hours later that food and gasoline would last twenty-seven days; coal, thirty-five. McNeil therefore saw "no cause for immediate alarm." He expected the Russians would continue their restrictions for a "few days and probably longer." Uncertainty over Soviet intent continued to absorb him. The Russians might be trying "to drive us out of Berlin," he thought, or they might be "establishing a strong negotiating position."[2]

Bevin returned from vacation Thursday night and took charge the following morning. Whereas McNeil puzzled over Soviet purposes, Bevin concentrated on British actions. He thought it "essential" to remain firm, but even more important was to ascertain whether the United States "would be solidly behind us *if* we made a stand in Berlin." Perhaps recalling the Smith-Molotov affair, he wanted assurances from the Americans that "there would be no chance of their wavering." Assuming such a commitment, the foreign secretary described five steps the West should take. First, he wanted the Combined Chiefs of Staff to study military aspects of the crisis as a way of concerting policy and involving the United States. Second, he hoped Washington would give Douglas or some other representative full authority to coordinate Western diplomacy from London. Third, he wanted "a big display" made of flying supplies into Berlin. Fourth, he wanted the RAF to send "a very big bomber force" to the Continent. Fifth, Bevin wanted a careful study of the Warsaw Declaration. In a week or so, the Western powers might have to demand a reopening of the rail lines, and the declaration might give some insight into the Soviet response. There should be no approach to Moscow until the airlift was established and the bombers deployed. Despite his notion of issuing an ultimatum in a week,

Bevin concluded by commenting, "if the Russians failed to get us out of Berlin by the end of August they might give up."[3]

This was a remarkable program, and the Western powers would follow it in nearly every particular. It is even more remarkable, given that Bevin proposed it on his first day back at work following a week's absence and without briefings or consultations with members of the cabinet or the Foreign Office. Alan Bullock's praise for Bevin's "capacity for action" and "firm grasp" of the situation seems fully warranted, especially because the foreign secretary devised his program a full day earlier than Bullock thought.[4]

In the cabinet meeting that followed, Brownjohn outlined the situation. Berliners would resist if they were assured of Western support. Military operations in and around Berlin, such as a relief convoy, were out of the question. The city almost certainly could not be fed by air, even if all those willing to leave were evacuated on return flights. Bevin took a limited role in the discussion and did not outline his five points. If he knew his own mind, he was unsure of what his colleagues were thinking, especially Attlee. For now, he suggested that the cabinet form a select group of ministers to deal with the crisis. Attlee agreed.[5]

Bevin went directly from the cabinet meeting to the House of Commons, where he unwittingly revealed his colleagues' hesitations. He admitted the situation was serious because of Berlin's dependence on the western zones for food and coal. When asked whether His Majesty's Government intended to stay in Berlin, he refused to go beyond his prepared statement. He evaded another questioner who wondered whether an airlift could supply the city, pleading, "I do not think I should be pressed to answer on all these details." It was not a forceful performance, and Bevin no doubt found it frustrating to conceal his own resolve because of his uncertainty about how far his colleagues were willing to go.[6]

By that afternoon, Bevin felt sure enough of his ground to summarize his program for Douglas, and the two men went over it again on Saturday morning. Bevin argued for the deployment of U.S. bombers to Europe to show "we meant business," and he justified London as a diplomatic clearinghouse because of the close contacts developed there during the recent talks on Germany. Bevin confessed he was not so certain about diplomacy. The Russians would probably parry a protest over Berlin with a call for four-power talks on Germany. Douglas thought it best to delay sending any note until the German minister-presidents had met the military governors. The National Assembly debate in Paris had delayed that meeting to July 1, and Douglas wanted the London program "irrevocably commenced" before talking with the Russians about Berlin.[7]

There were signs that the British position was by no means fixed. The *London Times* hinted at compromise, with several reports suggesting that Whitehall was willing to withdraw the B-mark if the Russians would agree to four-power control of the Soviet mark—a return to the British offer of June 22. That such ideas were not merely the idle musings of newspaper editors became clear on Saturday, when Robertson made just such an offer in a letter to Sokolovsky. McNeil echoed Robertson's offer in a speech on Sunday. Although these statements did not depart from existing positions, they were unilateral steps that suggested Western disarray.[8]

Early reports from Paris suggested uncertainty. A Foreign Ministry official told the U.S. embassy that, though France would follow the Anglo-American lead, the Western powers had erred by committing their prestige to an indefensible outpost. Koenig was ready to postpone the London program and the meeting with the minister-presidents. The chargé in London told Kirkpatrick that it was hard to share Anglo-American views when France "could be invaded whilst Britain and America could not," and he predicted the Western powers would be in a "difficult, if not untenable, position" when Berlin's supplies ran out some thirty days hence. He blamed the situation on the London program and currency reform. Bidault took a similar line. In Berlin, Ganeval worried about the situation at the end of July, when the circumstances of the city's residents would become, in his words, "absolutely hopeless." The Western governments had to resolve the crisis one way or another by the middle of the month; any later, and the Soviets would have "a knife at our throat."[9]

Private doubts found public expression. Speaking before the Foreign Affairs Committee of the National Assembly on Saturday, Bidault said that France was willing to discuss not only Berlin but Germany as well. Premier Robert Schuman echoed this in a speech, expressing the hope that the British and Americans would agree to one more try at settling the German question with the Russians. Journalists reported that the French blamed the crisis on Anglo-American actions they had approved only reluctantly—the London program and currency reform—and were now eager to trade both for an end to the blockade. Though Bidault claimed that France would stand by its allies, he excoriated Clay. Other officials denied that the Western powers had met to discuss the crisis, while still others predicted that France would not take part in the meeting with the minister-presidents.[10]

There were countervailing trends. Officials at the Quai d'Orsay blamed the crisis on Russian claims to sovereignty over Berlin, arguing that the Western powers had to insist on their rights. Massigli told the British ambassador, Oliver Harvey, that firmness alone could induce Moscow to negotiate. He doubted the Russians would let Berliners starve; doing so would undermine their efforts to ingratiate themselves with the Germans. Events from a decade earlier obsessed one official in the German affairs section, who predicted that if the West retreated, "the distance in time from Berlin to Paris" would match what it had been "from Munich to Paris," that is, about twenty months.[11]

The French position stiffened on Monday, June 28. Schuman's cabinet concluded that the Western powers must remain in Berlin "at all costs" to prevent a "shattering loss of prestige." The only way to induce the Soviets to relent was "vigilant resistance." Bidault ordered Koenig to participate in the session with the Germans. One of Massigli's assistants told Canadian diplomat Charles Ritchie that the Soviets would realize they could not expel the Western powers and would gradually ease the blockade. Finally, to Caffery's amazement, the Quai d'Orsay urged the American government to speak up in support of Lucius Clay.[12]

British policy also hardened on Monday, when Bevin won cabinet support for his five points. "There could be no question of yielding to Soviet pressure," he insisted in a morning cabinet meeting. If the Western powers left Berlin, "Western Union would be fatally weakened." Firmness would win the day, Bevin told Dominion high commissioners. He was confident that Soviet tactics would change "if we could prove that they could not starve us out."[13]

Officials sought ways to deal with the situation. The chiefs of staff and the special ministers' committee approved Robertson's request to survey quarters for additional troops in the British zone, so the Russians might conclude that London was about to reinforce the British Army of the Rhine. That was a ruse, because Attlee had no troops to send, but it might help induce a Russian retreat.[14]

Britain might outwit the Soviet Union, but frightening it would require American power, as the RAF director of plans, Air Commodore W. A. D. Brook, reminded the chief of the air staff, Sir Arthur Tedder. Brook thought the Americans should threaten the Soviet Union with atomic attack. "Our only advantage is our possession of W.M.D.," Brook argued, *if* Washington was willing to exercise it. The West's lead in atomic weaponry, "which is now absolute, is shortening steadily as time goes on," he continued. "Logically, therefore, the earlier we exercise this threat the more effective it should be." Brook did not intend an actual attack, only the threat of one, and he acknowledged, "There is a very real risk of our bluff being called, in which case we may be worse off."[15]

At a chiefs of staff committee meeting, the first sea lord, Sir John Cunningham, made a similar suggestion. He wanted to leak reports that B-29s visiting Europe were "equipped with atomic bombs." The idea fell flat. Tedder explained that the big bombers could not be escorted deep into the Soviet Union and would be vulnerable to jet fighters. "The Russians would therefore realise that the threat of the B.29s was not very serious," he concluded.[16]

Clearly, as the British groped for a solution, the key consideration was what the United States would do. The view that Monday was unclear, and two visitors from Washington, Draper and Wedemeyer, could shed little light on their government's intentions. Wedemeyer discussed emergency plans and command arrangements with the British chiefs, as well as B-29 movements, a possible airlift, and convoys. Two squadrons of B-29s had flown to Newfoundland and could leave for Germany on three hours' notice, he explained, and the Pentagon was assessing whether an airlift large enough to sustain Berlin was feasible. The joint chiefs regarded Clay's convoy idea as "impracticable," Wedemeyer continued; "entry of armed American Forces into the Russian zone would in fact be an aggressive act."[17]

Bevin could learn little more from Douglas, who reported that his government was committed to a "firm though unprovocative attitude and . . . a strong line of propaganda." Washington was considering a protest but was uncertain of the timing. Bevin wanted to wait until aerial resupply had begun to show results. In the meantime, he pleaded for a firm statement from the Americans; so far, he complained, only the British had spoken publicly. From the first meeting with his advisers on Friday morning, Bevin had insisted on a commitment from the United States; none had been forthcoming.[18] Why the delay, and when would it end? Now that the chips were down, where was Harry Truman's fabled decisiveness?

COMPLAINTS THAT THE AMERICANS were slow to decide were not entirely fair. Washington reached its initial conclusions on Monday, the same day Bevin won approval for his program. The Truman administration was slow, however, in making any public declarations, and when they came, they were not as definite as the British had hoped. Preliminary discussions in the American capital were as tentative as they had been in London during Bevin's absence. On Thursday morning, State Department counselor Charles E. Bohlen presided over the first meeting of U.S. officials to deal with the blockade. Summarizing the meeting for Forrestal, one of his aides noted a growing sense among army and air force leaders that the National Security Council should meet "so that we can come to some conclusions as to exactly what our position is."[19] Reaching those conclusions took longer than anyone would have predicted. In London, Bevin had to win cabinet approval for his plans; in Washington, Truman had to reconcile widely divergent views held by strong-willed advocates.

Lucius Clay once complained that his superiors saw Berlin as a military problem; only he grasped the political essence of the crisis.[20] This characterization highlights the debate within the Truman administration over Berlin in June and July 1948, although its terms are unfair. Differing political assessments and values clashed, not a military analysis versus a political one. The idea of maintaining American prestige dominated one view; avoiding war dominated the other. Advocates of both positions adjusted logic in the name of their particular value: Clay manipulated risk in the name of prestige; his opponents manipulated prestige in the name of peace. Preoccupied with controlling risks of war around the world, the cautious men in Washington seemed to be concerned exclusively with military matters, neglecting what Clay considered the fundamental issues of prestige and politics.

Part of the difference stemmed from perspective, suggesting that there is truth in the adage "where you stand depends on where you sit." Issues appeared differently when viewed from Berlin or the Washington bureaucracy or, for that matter, from the White House. Clay and his opponents looked at the issues in relatively simple terms; the president stood above the debate within his administration, sharing the perspectives of both sides. He did so because he was not the simple man many historians assume he was. Truman was, his naval aide once remarked, "the most complex individual I ever knew."[21] His career reflected some of these complexities. A farm boy taught to trust in his Bible and William Jennings Bryan's brand of populism, he joined a large urban political machine with a national reputation for corruption. A New Dealer, he disliked the words *progressive* and *liberal* and thought Franklin Roosevelt had surrounded himself with "crackpots and the lunatic fringe."[22] Born and raised a southern Democrat, Truman split his party in 1948 over his commitment to civil rights for blacks. As president, he won a reputation as an efficient administrator, whereas in practice, he had "more feel for personalities than jurisdiction."[23] Though we remember him as a decisive leader and initiator of policy, an aide described him as "never afraid to make a decision when someone in whom he had confidence . . . told him . . . what needed to be done."[24] More to the immediate point, Truman had not been involved in decisions about Germany, and he had not expressed clear or firm views on the subject.

With the president's position unclear, both groups marshaled arguments for their views. Both tailored logic to their policy preferences, exaggerating the likelihood that their preferred program would succeed, minimizing risks, depicting alternative courses in apocalyptic terms. Sensitive about prestige, Clay and his supporters saw Berlin as a test of Western steadfastness with worldwide implications. Like all sandlot bullies, their argument ran, the Russians pushed against weakness and recoiled from strength; Moscow was bluffing. Clay's position, reduced to its essentials, was that the West must remain in Berlin; therefore it could.

Clay's most vocal opponents were on the army staff, and a quirk of military organization gave them unusual influence over Berlin policy. The joint staff was not large enough to work out defense policy on its own, so it relied on the various services to act as "executive agents" for specific topics. Because most American troops in Europe belonged to the army, it acted as the National Military Establishment's executive agent for European issues. Thus, throughout the blockade, the army staff weighed options and alternatives, developed recommendations, and shepherded them through the bureaucracy. In other words, the army, not the air force, handled issues relating to Berlin and the airlift and spoke for the Pentagon in interagency discussions. The army's view of the crisis inevitably started with the hopelessness of defending Berlin in any clash with the Russians.

Clay's opponents reversed prestige and risk. With their starting point being the undesirability of war, they concluded the risk was too great. They doubted the

Russians were bluffing, worried that accident or miscalculation might produce a clash neither side intended, and thought the West should prepare to withdraw. They narrowed the issues as much as they could. The United States had only a limited stake in Berlin, prestige was not all-important, and withdrawal, though harmful, need not do fatal damage to the Western cause. Their position was that the Western powers could not remain in Berlin; therefore they need not.[25]

These approaches were displayed in a spirited teleconference between Clay and Royall. The army secretary feared events could not be kept under control and urged caution. His first instructions were to do nothing that might lead to war. Delay introduction of the B-mark if you have to, he told the general, who protested that it was too late; conversion had already begun. Unhappy over a report in that morning's *New York Times* that Clay had claimed the Russians could not force the Western powers out of Berlin short of waging war, Royall ordered him to keep quiet. Possibly at Truman's request, the secretary revived the suggestion that dependents be evacuated; Clay countered the political damage would be prohibitive.

Royall's caution was only half the story, for he saw little value in Berlin. What was at stake was "a minor issue"—Berlin's currency—and this, he told Clay, was "not a good question to go to war on." Faced with a conflict between the value of Berlin and the risk of war, Royall resolved it by emphasizing the danger and reducing the stakes in Berlin to the narrowest possible terms.[26]

Clay later told Jean Edward Smith that the blockade made him "mad as hell," and surely Royall's approach did nothing to soothe him. The stakes were not local. They involved American prestige and the will to resist aggression; "to retreat now is to imply that we are prepared to retreat further," Clay declared. American prestige in Germany, not to mention a moral commitment to anticommunist Berliners, required that the United States enforce its rights. Currency was a pretext; if war came, it would be because the Kremlin had decided to make its bid for world conquest. The secretary's focus on currency so troubled Clay that he went over the ground once more that afternoon. "Please remember, emphasize, and never stop repeating," he implored Major General Daniel Noce, chief of the Civil Affairs Division, that "currency in Berlin is not the issue—the issue is our position in Europe and plans for Western Germany."[27]

Clay thought the Western governments should send a note informing Moscow that if the Soviet Union could not keep supply lines open, they would. Rejection of this note would justify a military convoy to break the blockade. Western governments must decide how far they would go *short of war* to stay in Berlin, and Clay was ready to go far indeed. He recognized that a convoy was dangerous because "once committed we could not withdraw," but he believed the Russians would back down. "I do not expect armed conflict," he assured Royall. The Russians had imposed the blockade to frighten Berliners away from the B-mark, not to starve them, and certainly not to start a war. Clay evidently saw no danger that the Russians might be provoked or that the situation might spin out of control. Moscow's stance, he implied, was not as bellicose as it seemed. He resolved the conflict between the value of Berlin and the risk of war by inflating the former and deflating the latter. With war unlikely and great values at stake, the logical course was to remain. Yet even Clay did not advocate waging war for Berlin. Instead, he proposed taking measures "short of war" and staying "unless German suffering drives us out."[28]

Murphy echoed Clay's analysis: the stakes were great, the risks small. He endorsed the general's call for a note followed by a show of force. Murphy stressed American rights and obligations as an occupying power and the commitment to Berliners. The issue was not local, and it was certainly not a technical one over currency (Murphy's cable came after the Clay-Royall conference; like the general's plea to Noce, he was trying to stiffen backbones in Washington). Berlin was a symbol of U.S. determination and prestige; Europeans, he maintained, would measure America's will to resist communist aggression by what it did now. Withdrawal would be catastrophic, for Europeans would conclude that the United States would surrender them to Stalin one nation at a time. Murphy returned to this point repeatedly, depicting the calamity in lurid colors. Withdrawal would reflect a "lack of courage," reveal weakness, and result in humiliation. In short, he intoned, retreat from Berlin would be the "Munich of 1948." Such a disaster would be doubly tragic because it was unnecessary. There was little danger of war because the Russians would back down if confronted. Like Clay, Murphy was sure the Russians would lift the blockade before things became desperate because letting Berliners starve would undermine "Soviet political aims in Germany." Firmness would preserve the peace and Western rights; Moscow "will bargain in the end." This was an ironic transformation of the notion that the political costs of blockading Berlin were too great for the Russians to bear. If that idea had led Western officials before June 24 to underestimate the likelihood of a blockade, it strengthened their resolve afterward, in that it encouraged them to believe the Soviets would soon retreat.[29]

Draper endorsed these arguments. In a Sunday cable from London, he sought to assure Royall that a firm stance would not trigger war. Draper saw only three options: withdrawing, staying while trying to negotiate an end to the blockade, and challenging the Soviets on the ground. The first would make a U.S. presence in Europe untenable and European recovery impossible; the second would lead to humiliating failure. That left Clay's plan. Draper's premise was that the Soviets did not want war. Therefore, a statement of Western intent to restore access, by force if necessary, would cause them to retreat. "If the Russians have determined on war, which I doubt, our leaving Berlin will not prevent it. If they do not want war our standing firm in Berlin should not bring it on." Like Clay and Murphy, Draper assumed that Stalin had absolute control over every action his subordinates took:

Stalin did not want war; therefore, Russian soldiers confronting Clay's armored column would not resist. Draper made no allowance for chance, panic, or confusion in a delicate and dangerous situation. Further, he urged speed. The United States needed to decide at once "whether we will stay in Berlin to the point of war."[30]

If Royall's preoccupation with risk angered Clay and Murphy, they would have been unnerved had they been aware of the cavalier treatment others in Washington accorded the German crisis. Royall, at least, took the situation seriously. Truman's cabinet met Friday morning and confirmed the suspicion that members of Clay's staff had shared with reporters—that officials back home, distracted by politics, did not understand that they were facing a dangerous foreign crisis. Truman opened the meeting by asking Forrestal for a report on the "German currency squabble with Russia." Forrestal's soothing report that press accounts exaggerated the dangers brought a quick dissent from Royall, who had just gotten off the line with Clay, but the discussion ended there as the president steered the meeting to more interesting topics. He had stayed up the night before to watch on television as Dewey accepted the Republican nomination, and he noted with glee that the convention had given its standard-bearer a chilly reception.[31]

Afterward Truman conferred with Forrestal, Royall, and Lovett. (Marshall was hospitalized at Walter Reed and would not return until July 1.) The president confirmed Royall's instructions to Clay to keep quiet. He shared the army secretary's fear of escalation, with a slight difference. Whereas Royall believed the Russians had deliberately accepted high risks in confronting the West, accidental war haunted Truman. In his memoirs, he wrote that the immediate danger was that a "trigger-happy Russian pilot or hotheaded Communist tank commander" might spark an incident that would spiral out of control.[32] Given Clay's eagerness to force the issue, Truman was no doubt worried as much about American hotheads as Soviet ones. The president's concern contrasted sharply with the simplistic assumption by Clay, Murphy, and Draper that officials in distant capitals controlled events. In the weeks to come, it would prove an insuperable obstacle to Clay's convoy plan.

If the president worried about escalation, as Royall did, he also shared some of Clay's concerns, and there was an intriguing discussion of Western rights. The army had a hazy institutional memory, triggered by events in April, of an exchange of telegrams with the Russians and a Clay-Zhukov meeting. Royall outlined what the army had found in its files. He thought that sometime in 1944, Hopkins had urged FDR to let the Russians capture Berlin, provided the Soviets granted the United States free access to the city after the war. Roosevelt had supposedly discussed these arrangements with Stalin, who had agreed, on the understanding that commanders on the spot would work out the details. Royall doubted this had been done, although Floyd Parks recalled that Zhukov had promised Eisenhower some sort of access for American forces.

This is a fascinating account, because nearly all of it is wrong. Truman, not Roosevelt, had cabled Stalin about access (interestingly, the president had no independent recollection of these events). Neither then nor in subsequent talks had the Soviets recognized (nor the West claimed) an unrestricted Western right of free access to Berlin. It was remarkable that after three months of Soviet harassment, senior leaders of the U.S. government had such a foggy recollection of events—a sign of how unimportant Berlin had been in American eyes before June 24.[33]

As the discussion continued, the four men considered possible responses to the blockade. None were appealing. Clay and Howley had done all they could locally. Retaliation outside Germany, such as closing the Panama Canal to Russian ships, would not harm Stalin's self-sufficient realm. Diplomatic protests were likely to trail off into what Royall styled a futile "typewriter war." None of the participants recorded any discussion of a convoy or an airlift.

The group canvassed the Western obligation to Berliners, but this moral imperative was an ambiguous guide. The West had a responsibility to its friends in the city, and Truman worried about their fate if he ordered Americans out. Equally compelling, though, he realized that if the Western powers stayed, Berliners would endure great privation in the name of Western prestige. Therefore, for Truman, concern for the city's residents did not amount to the clear-cut command to stay that it did for Clay. The president thought the United States should take "determined steps . . . to stay in Berlin," but no one recorded any decision as to what those steps might be. Truman wanted to maintain a presence but was worried about risk, dubious of success, and uncertain of the moral course. Stockpiles of food and coal would last several weeks, so there was no need for a final decision, and he made none. When Leahy checked with him several days later, Truman said he wanted to stay in Berlin "as long as possible" but directed that the joint chiefs could not make any commitments in the military talks Bevin had requested. These instructions neatly summarized Truman's policy of postponement.[34]

Officials worked over the weekend, trying to agree on what to do. Lacking decisions at higher levels, they made little progress. They not only felt adrift without policy guidance; they also suffered from poor information flow. Officers briefing Bradley on Sunday confessed they did not know the results of the president's meeting with Forrestal, Royall, and Lovett two days earlier, and they told the chief of staff that it was "imperative" that top officials decide at once what U.S. policy would be.[35] Army planners endorsed Clay's suggestion that he approach Sokolovsky about the currency dispute, and they thought the State Department should consider four-power talks on Germany. They doubted that either measure would lead anywhere and regarded long-term prospects as bleak. Echoing Clay, they believed the Western powers must withdraw when German suffering became severe. After consulting Lovett, Bohlen reached similar conclusions. The Western powers had "at least 10 days before the situation in Berlin becomes untenable," ten days "before it is necessary for this government to decide the basic question of whether or not to remain in Berlin." How should they use that time? Bohlen agreed that Clay should confer with Sokolovsky and that the Western governments should prepare a diplomatic protest in case, as expected, Clay's initiative failed. If the Russians ignored Clay and the note, Bohlen proposed telling them that all four-power accords on Germany would be "open for reexamination," a veiled threat to accelerate the London program and exclude the Soviets from any accords over the Ruhr.[36]

Forrestal, Lovett, Royall, Bradley, navy secretary John L. Sullivan, and air force deputy chief of staff for operations Lieutenant General Lauris Norstad, flanked by aides and experts, gathered late Sunday afternoon to prepare for a presidential review of the crisis the following day. The group saw three alternatives: decide now to withdraw at an appropriate moment (when developments elsewhere might offset the loss, such as September 1, when the west German constituent assembly was to meet); use "all possible means," including force, to remain in Berlin; or continue the present "unprovocative but firm stand" and negotiate, while postponing the "ultimate decision" between withdrawal and war.

If the alternatives were clear, the choice was not. Discussion went round and round. Bradley recalled the meeting years later with horror: there was no guidance from the White House or the National Security Council, so no one knew what policy was, yet "everybody [was] talking at once." Advocates of withdrawal argued that if the West was unwilling to use force, "we must withdraw"; the humiliation of remaining in Berlin under blockade would be "worse than getting out." If the West withdrew on its own, opponents countered, no one would ever know if retreat had actually been necessary. In any case, withdrawal would have repercussions throughout Europe, so perhaps the Western powers should remain, even if they had to fight. Critics of this choice argued that the United States should not initiate the use of force, Berlin was not worth a war, and the United States was unprepared for one. Moreover, the American public, not understanding the issues, would not support a war. Even if the British and American publics could be "educated," the French would never agree. That left the third option—remain for now, negotiate, and put off a final choice. Royall and Bradley, reflecting briefings from their staffs, opposed this procedure. It avoided the real issue, Royall told the group; "a decision should be reached now concerning our ultimate position." Short-term steps had to be taken soon and should be consistent with long-term policy. Postponement risked having events decide the issue, while making preparation for either war or withdrawal impossible. Inclined toward withdrawal, Royall worried that delay would make it more difficult and more humiliating. Bradley reached the same conclusion by a process of elimination. He rejected war over Berlin and thought that delay amounted to trying "to stand on quicksand." That brought the discussion back to withdrawal, and the debate began again.[37]

After several hours of inconclusive argument, the group could not agree on a recommendation. Everyone ruled out immediate withdrawal and thought the Western powers should do as little as possible to aggravate the situation, yet no one could translate those negative commandments into a positive course of action that promised a solution. The three long-term options remained open. Lovett's interim instructions to American embassies that evening leaned toward the third. It even used the same phrasing: the United States would continue its "unprovocative but firm stand," Clay would approach Sokolovsky, and the governments would prepare a protest while exploiting the "propaganda advantages." Lovett approved London as a diplomatic clearinghouse and told Douglas the Americans were interested in sending B-29s to Europe, but he was silent on Bevin's other proposals. There was no need for drastic action at the moment, because existing food stocks meant that "zero hour" was two or three weeks away. What the United States would do when time ran out remained for Truman to decide.[38]

When the president conferred with Forrestal, Lovett, and Royall, Lovett gave him two papers—one summarizing the Truman-Stalin messages of June 1945, the other analyzing the crisis. Lovett recapped the previous day's discussion; Truman approved sending B-29s to Britain and approaching Sokolovsky on currency. What happened next is not so clear. According to Forrestal, when Lovett raised the question of whether the United States should remain in Berlin, the president interrupted, saying there was no need to discuss it: "We were going to stay period." Yet Royall's account suggests that Truman made no open-ended commitment. After discussion, the president gave "tentative approval" to staying "at all costs" but went on to say that this was not a final decision; he wanted to review the papers Lovett had given him and discuss the situation further on Tuesday.[39]

Truman's decision to rule out immediate withdrawal bothered Royall, who suggested that "we might not fully have thought through our course of action"; Truman did not seem to realize that if Russian pressure continued, we would have to "fight our way into Berlin." If we made a good case before world opinion and then abandoned the city, the army secretary continued, we would have suffered greater loss of face than if we withdrew at once. Royall's position looked soft to a president predisposed against withdrawal under pressure. Truman replied that he "would have to deal with the situation as it developed"; he could make no "black and white decision now," except to say that the United States was in Berlin under international agreements, and the Russians had no right to use force.[40]

It would be easy to exaggerate Truman's decisiveness here, and historians have. This was not a "command decision," a final decision to stay "at all costs," or "an unequivocal intention to stay."[41] The president, in effect, had settled on the third course: remaining in Berlin for the time being and postponing a decision on long-range policy—dealing with the situation as it developed, as he himself phrased it. Staying might lead to war, but if so, that was something to be faced in the future. When zero hour arrived, he would have to decide what to do. Putting off that decision avoided, for the moment at least, the political disaster of withdrawal and the military risks of Clay's convoy.[42]

Lovett's summary of policy, flashed that evening to American embassies, reflected some of these uncertainties. The United States would stay in Berlin and supply it "as a beleaguered garrison," and Clay would try to settle issues. If he failed, the Western powers would protest, mobilize world opinion, and refer the dispute to the United Nations. "We are hopeful that war can be avoided by these means," Lovett wrote. What the president would do if staying in Berlin meant that war became inevitable was left unsaid. We must decide *now,* Royall had insisted. Truman had not done that. Bohlen spoke the truth the next day when he confessed to the French ambassador that "we haven't fully clarified our position."[43]

Truman's indecision over the larger issues of policy was contrary to the typical portrayal of him as uncomplicated and resolute, a man who never put off a decision or worried about one afterward. That typical portrayal is wrong. Truman was not a simple man, and here he faced difficult, uncertain circumstances and divided advisers. Indeed, from another perspective, his hesitancy was not unusual, because crises impose conflicting demands on high officials. An increased risk of war—the essence of crisis—inclines them toward prudence and restraint, while the need to show resolve encourages them to take risks. Presidents take problems, especially those with no clear solutions, day by day, buying time and hoping for the breaks. There are few better examples than Harry Truman's initial response to the Berlin blockade.

WHILE BEVIN, ATTLEE, TRUMAN, and their advisers grappled with the dilemmas of crisis management, other officials sought to devise a diplomatic strategy that would induce the Soviets to lift the blockade. These efforts had started soon after Soviet barriers closed the autobahn. Clay prepared to discuss transport and currency with Sokolovsky, although he had "no real hope" of success. "I do not like my proposal," he confessed to Noce. But his teleconference with Royall had convinced him that "Washington did not want to have an issue now." Royall authorized him to propose exclusive use of the Soviet mark throughout Berlin, provided it was under four-power control and that Moscow guaranteed the Western powers free access to Berlin.[44]

Before Clay attempted to resolve the crisis, however, he felt compelled to see the marshal on another matter. On the twenty-sixth, military police had stopped Sokolovsky's limousine for speeding in the American sector. When an American jeep forced the Russian driver to halt, Soviet bodyguards in a chase car jumped out, guns in hand. American reinforcements—another jeep and an armored car—converged on the scene, and an uneasy standoff ensued until an American officer and an interpreter arrived, identified Sokolovsky, and let him continue. Clay visited Karlshorst two days later to express regrets. It was an awkward meeting. Brushing aside Clay's denials, Sokolovsky claimed the incident had been deliberate. Both promised to avoid steps that might aggravate the situation, then waited for the other to broaden the discussion. Clay sensed that his host "hoped I was bringing some proposal." Clay had decided beforehand to let Sokolovsky make the first move, however, so the two sat in strained silence for several minutes until Clay said his good-byes and left. A sense of personal sadness runs through Clay's account of the meeting, and it must have been a poignant moment as the two men, once friends, faced each other across the chasm of the Cold War.[45]

Sokolovsky broke his silence on June 29 when he answered Robertson's letter of three days earlier. He noted that he had lifted the ban on travel by Germans from the western zones. Unfortunately, his duty to keep the deutsche mark out of Berlin prevented him from lifting the ban on western autobahn traffic. Equally regrettable, continuing "technical defects" made it impossible to reopen the railway. He hoped these problems would be resolved soon. While appreciating the "energetic measures" taken by the Western powers to feed the city by air, he insisted that all safety rules be observed.[46]

Because this was the first official Soviet pronouncement since the blockade, it received close attention. Robertson warned Bevin to treat it with the "utmost reserve" and urged no relaxation in the airlift, yet he saw Sokolovsky's note as "preparation for a Soviet withdrawal from their present position" and abandonment of any intent to starve Berlin's population. The commander of U.S. naval forces in Germany believed the Russians intended to lift the blockade, while Douglas considered the letter a sign of Soviet irresolution. A continuing trickle of barges into Berlin intrigued Wedemeyer's staff. Might the Soviets be retreating? Clay detected no change in Moscow's position, while Murphy dismissed the letter as a "typical Soviet example of vague and implied promises." Bevin agreed, telling Douglas the letter was probably a maneuver to induce the West to let down its guard. He urged the Americans to expand the airlift.[47]

The equivocation of Bevin's earlier statements vanished when he reviewed the situation for the House of Commons on June 30. The powers could not allow Germany to remain a "great human slum," he said, in justifying the London program and currency reform. Wartime agreements made it clear that Berlin was not part of the Soviet zone. The West would defend its rights, protect "those stout-hearted Berlin democrats," and oppose Soviet attempts to absorb the city. Bevin acknowledged that firmness risked war. "His Majesty's Government and our Western Allies can see no other alternative between that and surrender, and none of us can accept surrender." The only bright spot in his ominous report was an offhand remark that the airlift was exceeding expectations.[48]

Marshall, still at Walter Reed, had the State Department issue a statement in his name. The United States was in Berlin under agreements and intended to remain. The blockade raised "basic questions" that the Western powers would deal with promptly. Meanwhile, the United States would rely on the airlift, which had shown greater potential "than had at first been assumed."[49] This was a pale echo of Bevin's words. Political scientists have highlighted the dilemmas inherent in threats: clear, unambiguous statements maximize coercive power yet flirt with disaster; vague ones avoid commitment but risk being "bested in the crisis contest of wills." Judged from this perspective, Marshall's statement falls near the noncommittal end of the scale. This is odd, because political scientists also argue that both sides tend to emphasize coercive behavior in the early stages of a crisis. In this case, though, as Oran Young once noted, there were "clear indications of a desire to avoid becoming too quickly committed to a dangerous and possibly irreversible posture."[50] Marshall's press release showed that this desire shaped Washington's policy much more strongly than it did London's. Observers at the time noted the weakness of the secretary's statement. The British, according to one scholar, were "appalled and concerned by the lack of initiative and determination." Suspicion grew that "Britain could not rely completely upon the Truman administration in an election year." A day later, Douglas was echoing British calls for a statement by the secretary or the president on a par with Bevin's in the House of Commons.[51]

Washington was not yet ready to oblige. Truman refused to comment in his July 1 press conference, referring reporters to Marshall's remarks. Like his silence in April, this contrasted markedly with the Clifford-Rowe memorandum, the supposed blueprint of Truman's election campaign. Truman should speak out often on foreign policy, the two advisers had written, singling out press conferences—a chief executive's "great and useful sounding board"—as a natural forum. The contrast between their advice and Truman's behavior highlights the president's continued uncertainty over Berlin and his unwillingness to commit himself to a policy he doubted he could sustain.[52]

The Western governments continued to debate diplomatic tactics. The British wanted Robertson to reply to Sokolovsky's letter with one of his own, and Clay had prepared an oral approach to the Soviet marshal; Lovett and his aides preferred a protest to Moscow. Officials debated timing, whether to suggest a foreign ministers' meeting or refer the dispute to the United Nations, and whether these steps were complementary or mutually exclusive.[53] Developments in Frankfurt and Berlin soon overshadowed these debates. On July 1 in Frankfurt, the Western military governors met the minister-presidents from their zones and gave them papers outlining the London program. The reception, according to a British report, was "very lukewarm," although the Germans' official response would not come until they had met among themselves on July 8 and 9 in Koblenz. The London program was further along but still not "irrevocably commenced," and the Western position remained vulnerable.[54]

As if in response to the Frankfurt session, half an hour after it began the Soviets announced they would no longer participate in the Kommandatura, which, they claimed, no longer existed. Clay expected the Russians would dissolve the Magistrat next, creating a "puppet" regime claiming authority throughout Greater Berlin. Hermann Matern, chairman of the Berlin SED, announced that the Soviet Military Administration had directed the Magistrat to obey its orders alone, only to retract his statement a few hours later. The incident led Clay to insist that the West could delay no longer. He thought Matern had merely been premature and that a Soviet order was imminent. The Magistrat would reject it, and Sokolovsky would dissolve the Berlin government. The Western military governors could not meet him under these conditions, so an approach, if one were to be made, should be initiated at once. Royall authorized Clay to go ahead.[55]

Clay and Robertson now blended their approaches. In the predawn hours of July 3, Robertson answered Sokolovsky's letter and asked for a meeting. Clay's liaison officer followed up with a telephone call requesting one as well.[56] When Sokolovsky greeted the Westerners that afternoon, Clay sought to limit the discussion to the blockade. He and his colleagues had come to ask when traffic would resume, he said. Robertson chimed in that "technical difficulties" had disrupted rail service for some ten days now; surely Sokolovsky could tell them what the problems were and when they would be corrected. Sokolovsky struggled to evade the limits his guests tried to impose. A shift in rationale from technical problems to politics would be transparent, but that was all to the good; the Westerners could not miss the message. So while the Russian commander referred several times to technical problems, he moved quickly to a discussion of the disruption the London program had caused in his zone. The Western powers "seemed to overlook the fact that the Berlin situation was essentially linked with the London Conference," he scolded. "They should have thought about that before." The disruption caused by the conference prevented him from providing alternative rail service to Berlin. The disruption, and hence the blockade, would continue until the West agreed to four-power talks on Germany. Pressed by Robertson, Sokolovsky denied that the technical difficulties were linked to the London program but insisted that "the situation in Berlin was directly linked." With that, Clay said there was nothing further to discuss. He and his colleagues left.[57]

The complexion of the crisis had changed. Further conversation in Berlin was pointless. Sokolovsky's message had been received: the blockade would not end until the Western powers abandoned their plans for a west German state. Because local approaches had been tried and failed, the next step was a diplomatic protest to Moscow—at least that was the view in Washington. The British and French were inclined to delay, and the Western powers remained divided over mentioning the United Nations. The Americans insisted on it; the French were opposed. In a letter to his father, Douglas hinted at the intensity of the discussions. He complained not about the French but about "a note of arrogance" in Washington's treatment of its allies. "By that I mean the disposition to demand that other countries bow to us and accept, without question, our view, and what is worse, our precise language." In the end, Washington gave way.[58] The notes to the Soviets would call for an immediate end to the blockade, followed by talks among the military governors on "any question in dispute" regarding Berlin, but they would not mention further steps.

The notes were delivered to Soviet embassies in the three Western capitals on July 6 and released to the press three days later. Creditable defenses of Western rights in Berlin, they argued that Allied rights of occupation derived from the defeat of Germany and international agreements. Berlin was not part of the Soviet zone but an international zone of occupation. The British and American version stressed the June 1945 exchanges with Stalin and contended that Stalin's answer had approved free Western access. This idea had a curious history. A long line of Americans, from Draper and Royall to State Department legal adviser Ernest Gross, read confirmation of Western access into Stalin's vague cable. Lovett expressed doubt, and Bohlen declared that Stalin's reply added nothing to the Western legal case. Asked about Stalin's reply to Churchill, Bevin reported that it was "completely noncommittal" and urged that if the generalissimo's cable to Washington paralleled the one to London—as it did—the matter should be dropped. Against his better judgment, the note followed the American draft.[59]

Westerners doubted their protests would sway Stalin. Bohlen expected the Soviets to continue Sokolovsky's approach of blaming technical difficulties while offering to end them in exchange for political concessions. He feared a Russian call for simultaneous suspension of the London program and the blockade, followed by a foreign ministers' meeting, for this would put the West on the spot. Refusal would make the West appear recalcitrant and allow the Russians to continue the blockade, while acceptance meant abandoning the progress made since Prince's Gate. Leahy thought war in the near future was "not unlikely," and Lovett told David E. Lilienthal of the Atomic Energy Commission that matters would come to a head in the next ten days. The under secretary worried that the Russians might feel their prestige was at stake and go too far; "anything could happen," he said.[60]

British officials saw no way out. The minister in the Moscow embassy, Geoffrey Harrison, reported that the Russians "are convinced . . . they hold all the cards." They were waiting for the airlift to fail; when it did, they expected the West to concede Berlin or convene a foreign ministers' meeting rather than fight. Strang thought that *if* the Russians could not compel Western withdrawal short of force, they might relent, advising Bevin, "In this conflict of wills we ought not to yield." The West should stay put, expand the airlift, and continue the London program as a way of strengthening its negotiating position. Yet, like Harrison, he doubted negotiations would lead anywhere because the two sides were committed to irreconcilable policies.[61]

For some, that raised "ultimate" questions. The British chiefs of staff and Minister of Defence A. V. Alexander discussed the situation on July 7. Tedder doubted the airlift could provide enough fuel and coal for the winter, noting that fuel stocks might disappear "within two months." A convoy was impractical. That led Montgomery to declare that the Russians could "squeeze us out of Berlin if they wished to do so." Monty "did not think that all was lost if we had to withdraw from Berlin," but he acknowledged the government's desire to stay. The only way the West could remain, though, was "to start a shooting war." Montgomery bluntly asked Alexander if the British government would go that far. Although he did not really expect an answer, one would be helpful because it affected everything the chiefs did. Tedder and Cunningham chimed in that an answer was "most necessary," adding that the Western position in Berlin was "militarily unsound and could not be maintained by fighting." Because the Russians could squeeze the Western powers out "without themselves firing a shot . . . hostilities would have to be opened by ourselves."[62]

Alexander could only refer to Bevin's public statements that London would not yield to coercion and promised to seek a more precise answer. He arranged a meeting with Bevin and Attlee two days later. The chiefs left the session little wiser, having learned what they already knew: war was possible. Attlee and Bevin judged a decision on Berlin "premature"; in any case, His Majesty's Government "would not take this decision alone. At the same time it would be prudent to plan on the assumption that there might be a war." Britain could not withdraw from the city "without making the most strenuous efforts to stay there," and those steps might lead the West to start a war.[63]

The JCS were just as eager as the British chiefs to find out what their government would do when the airlift failed. Omar Bradley agreed with a June 28 planning paper that argued, "We *must* decide now whether we are willing to fight to stay in Berlin." If so, full-scale preparations for war must begin immediately. If not, the West needed to start doing whatever it could to cushion the disastrous political and psychological effects of Soviet victory in Berlin. Charles E. Saltzman, assistant secretary of state for occupied areas, echoed the army's call. Like the soldiers, he had little faith in an airlift. "We must not contemplate continuing the air supply operation for a long or indefinite time," he thought. It was expensive, "put the

United States in a progressively unsatisfactory and undignified position," and could not solve "the basic problem." Saltzman pleaded with Lovett that the United States "reach a decision promptly as to whether we shall ultimately elect withdrawal or war . . . ; in other words, that the fundamental issue be faced *now*."[64]

Immediate prospects, though, depended on Moscow's reply to the Western notes. Russian diplomats delivered that reply on July 14. The Soviets had tried for three years to keep Germany weak, and now their failure and frustration boiled over. The crisis was the fault of the Western powers. The victors had resolved at Yalta and Potsdam that Germany would be demilitarized, democratized, and transformed into a peace-loving state, and its revival as an aggressor would be prevented. They had agreed that Germany would pay reparations to compensate the victims of Nazi aggression. The Western powers had broken their word at every point. Demilitarization was incomplete, and the Ruhr, the heart of the German war industry, had been removed from the control of the four powers. The Soviet reply was venomous in denouncing Germany's economic recovery, sounding at times as if the wartime Allies had adopted the Morgenthau plan. Yet in an about-face, the Soviets condemned Western dismemberment of the Reich, the London program, and the separate currency reform. Having damned the West for not carrying out a Carthaginian peace, the Russians portrayed themselves as the true friends of the German people. As proof, Moscow now offered to supply all of Berlin's needs, a shrewd ploy that undercut the Western governments' recent attempt to highlight the contrast between their own humanitarian policies and Stalin's ruthlessness.

The Soviet reply claimed that the blockade—an "urgent" and "temporary" measure to defend the Soviet zone—violated no international agreement. It scorned the Western interpretation of the Truman-Stalin messages: the exchange had merely granted Western soldiers the "opportunity" to enter Berlin; it did not create a right. The Soviets reiterated the claim that the entire city was part of their zone and argued that the use of currency in Berlin that had no validity in the surrounding area was contrary to the interests of Berliners. Circulation of such currency in the western sectors threatened the economic life of the Soviet zone, so protective measures must continue. This hint that the Russians might be interested in Robertson's currency compromise was overshadowed by an ominous new contention. Western rights depended on the fulfillment of Allied agreements regarding Germany, and in ignoring their obligations, the Western powers were undermining "their right to participation in the administration of Berlin." The reply concluded by rejecting conditions for negotiation—the blockade would not be lifted prior to discussions—and then established one of its own. The Western powers must agree not to limit talks to Berlin. The dispute over the city could not be severed from the issue of four-power control of Germany.[65]

Western reactions were somber. Sir Maurice Peterson, writing from Britain's embassy in Moscow, called the exchange a "dangerous crystallization," as both sides committed their prestige. Bedell Smith thought the reply more uncompromising than expected. The Soviets "clearly realize they hold all the cards," he thought, and seemed determined to drive the Western powers from Berlin. The risk of war had increased. Bidault saw Moscow's reply as "a pretty blank refusal." Bevin urged the Americans to expand the airlift, send the B-29s to Europe, and avoid a hasty reply to Moscow.[66]

Reaction in the Oval Office was as gloomy as it could be. Truman told Bohlen, who had come to brief him on the note, that it was a "total rejection of everything we had asked for." Truman's daughter Margaret has reported that, as he waited beneath the rostrum in Philadelphia that night to accept his party's nomination for the presidency, he was convinced the world was on the brink of war.[67]

CHAPTER 5

"Doomed to Failure"

Truman's gloom derived in large part from what his advisers were telling him about the prospects of sustaining Berlin by air. Standard accounts discount this pessimism in characterizing early Western policy decisions. They contend that the Western governments quickly decided to counter the blockade with the airlift, a move that turned the tables on the Kremlin, capped risk, and allowed the West to pursue its goals in western Germany. For example, Avi Shlaim argues that Clay improvised an "airlift strategy," intending from the start to rely on an airlift to sustain the city's needs; Truman adopted this strategy as his own and put it on "an organized and full-scale basis." In Gregg Herken's view, the airlift "had effectively broken the blockade" by the end of July, while Ronald Pruessen maintains that Truman's reliance on the airlift and negotiations produced a crisis "that could be kept within manageable proportions. . . . Negotiations could go on indefinitely and in a variety of settings: if they succeeded, all well and good; if they failed, Berlin would continue to be supplied—and 'held.'"[1] These authors take for granted that the airlift would succeed and that decision makers knew so at the time. In fact, no one saw the airlift as a solution; no one had much faith that Berlin could be "held." An airlift might postpone a choice between war and withdrawal; it could not avert one. What the Western powers would do when confronted with the necessity of decision weighed heavily on their leaders, who looked to the future with apprehension, not confidence.

THE AIRLIFT BEGAN before the blockade, not after it. It started as a repetition of the April lift, a short-term measure to feed Westerners. Expecting trouble after the Soviets stopped interzonal travel in response to the Western currency reform, officials began gathering supplies for the garrisons. The U.S. Army set up a traffic control point at Rhein-Main to prepare cargo for airlift on June 18; European Command ordered that supplies be trucked there from the depot in Giessen, north of

Frankfurt. Three C-47s flew 5.9 tons of supplies to Tempelhof on June 21. Forty flights delivered 90 tons on June 22, the same day that Huebner directed LeMay to commit all planes to the effort. USAFE lifted between 80 and 90 tons a day for the next few days.[2]

On Thursday, June 24, the British Air Forces of Occupation (BAFO) ordered Operation Knicker. Eight Dakotas flew the next day from RAF Waterbeach, northeast of Cambridge, to RAF Wunstorf, a few miles west of Hannover in the British zone. Three of them flew into RAF Gatow that night, delivering 6.5 tons. Eight more reached Wunstorf on Monday, June 28.[3]

Bevin's Friday discussion with his staff canvassed the prospects of an expanded airlift. Although he "did not imagine that it would be possible to feed two million Germans," the foreign secretary thought "a big display" would boost German morale and show resolve. The cabinet approached an airlift in similar terms later that day, deciding to launch one to show "strength and determination" and to bring in "at least some supplies for the civil population."[4]

Bevin reiterated these points in discussions with Douglas. He acknowledged that "we could not supply the whole German population by air." Even so, the effort would bolster morale, symbolize Western determination, and be good propaganda: "Such humanitarian action in the face of the ruthless Soviet policy of starving the Germans in order to secure political advantage would show the Russians up in . . . world opinion."[5]

Bevin received a strong second from Reuter, who discussed the situation with Robertson's staff on Friday. Berliners needed "definite action and not mere assurance" from the West. "Time was short," he noted. Food would run out in four weeks, and Berliners needed proof that the West would do something to ease the situation. "An early gesture of support, such as the arrival of some planes carrying food for the Berlin population, would be a great deal better than nothing," Reuter thought, "even if it could have no long term effect on the total food supplies."[6]

Robertson discussed an expanded airlift with Clay that Friday and reported that the Americans were urgently studying what could be done. But getting Clay to take the project seriously was an uphill struggle. Wedemeyer and air force leaders had discussed increasing Clay's air cargo fleet on Wednesday, the twenty-third, and Draper planned to raise the subject with Clay during his visit to Europe. In light of events on Thursday, Draper cabled Royall to recommend moving a transport unit from Hawaii to Germany. Royall passed on the suggestion to Clay. The general, who was still thinking in terms of feeding the garrisons, turned it down, saying he had enough planes. The city had a thirty-day reserve of food and coal, and he doubted the crisis would last that long. The Russians, he thought, were trying to frighten Berliners away from the B-mark, not starve them.[7]

Clay pursued Robertson's suggestion by telephoning LeMay's headquarters on

Friday afternoon to ask how much the air force could bring into Berlin. LeMay was away, and his chief of staff, Brigadier General August W. Kissner, took Clay's call. He estimated 225 tons a day in good weather. Clay next wanted to know how many planes would be needed for a "very big operation," boosting the total to 500 tons and sustaining that level for three to six weeks. Kissner replied that it would require one transport group, that is, thirty planes. Clay set 500 tons as the goal of "our maximum airlift," and LeMay expanded his cargo fleet by scouring European airports for the personal planes of generals and ambassadors and asking the Pentagon for the additional group.[8]

Clay held out little hope. When a reporter asked him if an airlift could supply the entire city, he replied that it was "absolutely impossible." "As matters now stand," he warned Washington on Friday, Berliners "will begin to suffer in a few days and this suffering will become serious in two or three weeks." He reiterated this assessment on Saturday, telling Pentagon officials that an airlift "cannot supply the German civilian population with adequate coal and food."[9]

The same day, RAF Air Commodore Reginald N. Waite called Clay's conclusion into question. That morning, someone asked for "a rush appreciation" of feeding the British sector by air. By 1:00 P.M., Waite had produced what he regarded as a "very rough but . . . fairly good guess." It could be done. Using concentrated or dehydrated foods, all three western sectors could be sustained by a lift of 2,000 tons a day.[10] Waite's staff work would prove important, although the suggestion that he was the "father" of the airlift is exaggerated. Bevin had started the ball rolling in London and wielded much more influence over policy. Still, Waite was the first person to produce data suggesting that support by air was possible. But in fact, his calculations were wrong; they omitted coal, which would make up two-thirds of the tonnage flown into the city. It proved to be a providential error. Waite's estimates of food deliveries indicated a goal that was within reach. A full statement of needs at this stage would have confirmed the conventional wisdom that even an all-out effort could never succeed.

Robertson soon had Waite in Clay's office. Though skeptical, Clay was impressed enough to agree to fly in food for Berliners starting on Monday. LeMay rounded up C-47s scattered across Germany on miscellaneous assignments, plus the 60th Troop Carrier Group in Bavaria, and sent them all to Wiesbaden, with orders to begin flying cargo into Berlin on Monday morning. Clay then doubled LeMay's request for more planes. He asked Washington on Sunday for fifty planes (two groups, not one), describing the need as "urgent." These planes—the most Gatow and Tempelhof could absorb at the moment—would boost U.S. deliveries to 600 or 700 tons a day. The British thought they could deliver 400 tons a day by June 30 and 750 tons by July 3, when a new concrete runway at Gatow would open. Western garrisons needed 50 tons a day, and Clay intended to distribute the rest to Berliners.[11]

In other words, the daily lift fell 600 tons short of meeting demand, but that was not Clay's purpose. Every ton postponed the day when the West would have to face the dilemma Stalin was trying to impose. Bradley, Norstad, and army planner Major General Ray T. Maddocks approved Clay's request immediately, and thirty-nine C-54 Skymasters began to move a few hours later. The air force assigned the code name "Vittles" to the transatlantic flights.[12]

Dispatch of these planes did not mean the United States had embarked on a campaign to break the blockade through airpower. Historians have exaggerated the West's early reliance on an airlift because of a misleading claim in Truman's memoirs. The president wrote that on June 26, he ordered that aerial relief operations "be put on a full-scale organized basis and that every plane available to our European Command be impressed into service." Shlaim has described Truman's step as throwing presidential power behind what he calls Clay's "airlift strategy." Shlaim regards Truman's action as "a prime example of the assertion of presidential leadership in crisis" and a step that "elevated the airlift option to the status of national policy."[13] It was none of those things because it never happened. There is no trace of such an order in the Pentagon's files; nor is there one in the records of either Clay's or LeMay's headquarters. European Command had directed USAFE to use "the maximum number of airplanes" to fly supplies to Berlin four days earlier, making Truman's supposed initiative superfluous.[14] Mobilizing European Command's limited cargo fleet was a far cry from establishing the "full-scale airlift" Shlaim believes Truman set in motion. That airlift, and the indispensable logistical network to support it, did not spring into existence overnight; both grew incrementally over months and months. The C-54s that Bradley, Norstad, and Maddocks sent to Germany—without consulting the White House, incidentally—were the first of many to cross the Atlantic, and the last ones did not arrive until January 1949.

Shlaim also errs in contending that Clay had adopted an "airlift strategy." Robertson explained to Clay that London intended to fly in supplies to "prevent suffering among the German people as long as possible while ways and means are being considered by Governments to break the present blockade." The British also urged the deployment of U.S. bombers to Europe before negotiations with Moscow. "I agree fully with these views," Clay advised Washington on June 27. The airlift would boost German morale and buy time. It was not one of those "ways and means" by which the crisis would be resolved, any more than the bomber deployment was. Clay contended that an airlift would "seriously disturb the Soviet blockade"; he did not claim it would break it. Waite had not convinced him. Even as he ordered planes into the sky, Clay told a German friend with a snap of his fingers, "I wouldn't give you *that* for our chances." Publicizing the gap between requirements and deliveries would have been so demoralizing that Clay banned press releases regarding the operation "in order not to build up German hopes."

Newsweek reported the general as saying that "the Westerners might have to get out to save [Berliners] from starvation," hardly the view of a man who believed he had selected a winning strategy.[15]

William Draper's claim of airlift paternity has about as much basis as Truman's. In a 1972 oral history memoir, Draper recalled that he and Wedemeyer learned of the blockade as they were flying from Washington to Europe on the morning of June 24, when they opened their briefcases and saw the initial reports. Draper knew conditions in Germany, and Wedemeyer had witnessed the "Hump" airlift into China during the war. They compared notes and, in Draper's recollection, "planned the airlift" as they flew across the Atlantic, then persuaded the British and Clay to make the attempt.[16] It's an entertaining but inaccurate story. Although they doubtless discussed the Hump and Berlin en route, Bevin, Robertson, and Clay had begun the airlift before the two travelers reached London or Berlin (they went to Paris first). Draper and Wedemeyer reinforced actions already under way; they did not set them in motion.

Breaking the blockade by airlift did not figure in the discussion when the president's senior advisers gathered on Sunday afternoon, June 27. The only value of an airlift in their eyes was to buy time. Current stocks plus the airlift of dehydrated foods might enable Berlin to hold out for two months. Days after Truman's supposed "command decision" to stay, the army staff remained convinced that withdrawal was inevitable and was exploring ways "to divest our eventual withdrawal of the appearance of a rout."[17]

In London, Bevin was perhaps the airlift's greatest advocate, but he had no illusions about its long-term value. One of his aides talked in terms of feeding *some* Berliners. If the Western powers could feed "the key Germans on whom we depended, i.e., newspaper proprietors and politicians who collaborated with us," Kirkpatrick told the British chiefs of staff, "we should be able to ensure that they were not . . . subject to arrest by the Russians." Others (both Britons and Americans) considered how to evacuate the city's residents.[18]

If Truman thought European Command could feed Berlin unaided, he overestimated its capabilities. There were not enough cargo planes in Germany. The French flew a handful of Ju-52s. BAFO had half a dozen transports to shuttle passengers and mail around the British zone, plus another for its commander, Air Marshal Sir Arthur P. M. Sanders. USAFE had two troop carrier groups, for a total of perhaps seventy operational planes, but they were busy moving people and cargo throughout Europe and the Middle East and training with the army. Both units flew twin-engine C-47s, the military version of the Douglas DC-3. Designed in 1934, the reliable "Gooney Bird," as American pilots called the plane, had become the workhorse of the world's airlines before the war. Then it saw extensive service as a troop carrier. A passenger ship, not a freight hauler, the C-47 could carry 2.5 to 3 tons. These small, aging planes, some bearing faded black and white stripes marking them as veterans of the Normandy invasion, operated from two bases. The 61st Troop Carrier Group, with around twenty-five C-47s at Rhein-Main, was in a good position to support Berlin. The 60th Troop Carrier Group and its forty-five planes were well to the south at Kaufbeuren in Bavaria.[19]

USAFE and BAFO had only a few airfields, none of them suitable for a large airlift. The Americans could use Rhein-Main and nearby Wiesbaden. The former was a fighter base with aircraft hardstands dispersed along both sides of a 6,000-foot runway. The latter, another fighter base, had a 5,500-foot runway. The RAF base at Wunstorf was better, with two concrete runways, taxiways, and concrete aprons. The real bottlenecks were in Berlin. There were two airports in the western sectors, Tempelhof and Gatow, and no one knew if they could handle the necessary traffic, assuming USAFE and BAFO were reinforced. In the heart of the city, Tempelhof could challenge even the bravest pilots, as crews on final approach had to dodge a 400-foot brewery smokestack and skim within 100 feet of the tops of apartment blocks surrounding the airfield. Tempelhof's spectacular curved building and broad parking apron of marble blocks contrasted with its lack of concrete runways. In the summer of 1945, engineers had laid a 5,000-foot pierced-steel plank (PSP) runway that planes used for landings. They took off from sod. Gatow was on the city's western outskirts and was operated by the RAF. Like the Americans, the British had laid a PSP runway, but sandy soil made it unsuitable for even light traffic, so the RAF began constructing a 6,000-foot concrete runway. The work was three-quarters complete when the airlift began. Electricity came from a power station in the Soviet zone.[20] Navigational aids were limited. The three American bases had ground-controlled approach systems. Rhein-Main, Frankfurt, Fulda, and Tempelhof hosted radio ranges, while Tempelhof, Wiesbaden, and Offenbach had beacons. For much of the route over the Soviet zone, planes would be on their own, flying by dead reckoning.[21]

Officials saw only limited potential in an airlift for other reasons as well, such as history, the weather, and possible Soviet interference. Few large-scale efforts at aerial resupply had succeeded. The exception was the Hump operation from India to China during the war. If precedent were not bad enough, there was also weather. If U.S. airports were ranked according to flying weather, Pittsburgh would be at the bottom of the list. But compared with the weather at German airports, Pittsburgh's would win top rank. Put another way, the worst American flying weather was better than the best German weather. And Berlin? It had the worst flying conditions in Germany.[22] Soviet interference was another potential problem. If Moscow were serious about driving out the Western powers, it might disrupt Berlin's aerial lifeline. Soviet interference could take several forms, starting with disruption of Gatow's electricity. No one could rule out attacks on Western aircraft, though they appeared unlikely. Jamming radio traffic and navigational aids or flying barrage balloons in the corridors did not exhaust Soviet opportunities for mischief.

The possibility of Soviet interference led to revealing discussions in Washington on Wednesday, June 30, following wire service reports that there *were* balloons in one corridor and the British intended to shoot them down. That was indeed British policy. The issue had come up during a planning meeting Robertson held with his army and air force commanders on Sunday evening. When Sanders asked what to do if fighters or balloons interfered with British aircraft, Robertson replied that "all risks must be accepted" regarding fighters and to "shoot the balloons at once." The British chiefs endorsed his stance on Monday, Wedemeyer assured them that the joint chiefs agreed, and the special cabinet committee confirmed that balloons obstructing the corridors should be shot down.[23]

Two days later, that hypothetical seemed all too real. Forrestal called an emergency meeting with Royall, the JCS, and other aides. He had talked earlier with Lovett, who urged caution: there should be no military action until the presence of the balloons was confirmed. Lovett said he had talked to Marshall and Senator Vandenberg. Marshall termed the Soviets' move "an overt act"; the senator urged no response stronger than a diplomatic protest. His nephew, General Hoyt S. Vandenberg, was the air force chief of staff; the general worried that shooting down the balloons could lead to an escalation of hostilities and advised, "We've got to decide this thing all the way through." Leahy intervened to summarize a conversation he had had with the president the day before. Leahy had told the president:

> I would like to have some information about our policy, if we have one—I didn't hope that we had any—so that I could talk intelligently to the British. He [Truman] said there wasn't any. He said we were going to try to stay in Berlin for as long as we could, and I asked if that involved shooting down barrage balloons, and he said "Certainly not," that that would start a war and he did not seem to believe that at that time we had enough soldiers in Europe or in the world to start a war, and he was quite positive about that.

Truman's only instructions were to listen to what the British had to say "and make no comments and certainly no commitments whatever. That was the attitude he had yesterday," Leahy concluded. "I have no doubt it is the same unless somebody's talked to him since."[24]

Forrestal worried that "we are going into war backwards"; he wanted the British to rescind their order. Leahy thought the question was a political one, adding, "From the military point of view, what I'd do is get out of Berlin without any delay because we are facing a defeat if we are there if the war comes," although he acknowledged that, "politically, it may be quite important for us to take a defeat there." Royall joined the meeting to say that press stories were exaggerated (Hays reported that the Soviets intended to fly a balloon but had not launched it). If there was no immediate crisis, Forrestal wanted to make it clear to the British that the United States opposed shooting down "even barrage balloons" until the West had lodged "a political protest." It was important that not only the Russians but also the American public understood the issue. General Vandenberg added that not warning off the British would be "leading our Allies, the British and our own public to believe that we mean to stay in Berlin and we're not because we—obviously, it's impossible to stay in there if we don't have some trap [*sic*; traffic?]."[25]

Royall ordered Clay not to destroy any balloons without approval, and Douglas asked Bevin to revoke London's orders to Robertson. Lovett insisted that the West not destroy balloons until "every possible step" had been taken to end the blockade. He feared that Russian fighter planes would defend balloons, leading to "full-scale air action." The American public "does not (repeat not) fully understand [the] situation," Lovett added, and would support force only after all other means had been exhausted. Lovett proposed that neither country take any action that might involve the other in war unless both governments agreed first. The British agreed and revoked Robertson's orders.[26]

The episode reveals much about American thinking at this stage. The president wanted to remain in Berlin "for as long as we could" (a far different formulation from his brave words on Monday), but he would not start a war to stay there. For Forrestal and his associates, this meant withdrawal was inevitable. The airlift offered no way out, and its prospects were not so promising that the U.S. government would use force to keep Berlin's air corridors open. The balloon decision is irreconcilable with the notion that Truman had chosen an "airlift strategy" and undertaken an open-ended commitment to Berlin.

EXPANDING THE AIRLIFT made sense, even if its prospects remained bleak. The purpose of Robertson's June 27 meeting had been to organize a maximum effort. The army would collect food and deliver it to Wunstorf; the RAF would fly it to Berlin. The city needed 1,800 tons a day. BAFO thought it could lift 500; reinforced by four-engine Yorks, it might deliver 1,100. Robertson did not expect to break the blockade. He sought to prolong, as far as possible, a minimum ration scale, support Berliners' morale, and show determination. Like Clay, he was dubious about publicity and ordered that "on no account should detailed figures of the position be given." Number 46 Group convened a meeting on Monday evening in which the commander, Air Commodore J. W. F. Merer, outlined plans to move thirty-eight more Dakotas to Wunstorf on Wednesday. Orders on the thirtieth called for 161 sorties (440 tons) a day until July 4, when forty Yorks could use Gatow's new runway and boost deliveries to 840 tons.[27]

The United States flew eighty-seven C-47 sorties into Berlin on June 28, the first day of Clay's large-scale effort, and delivered over 250 tons. The 60th Troop Carrier Group, which had received its order to deploy from Kaufbeuren at 5:00 the evening before, had a C-47 on its way from Wiesbaden at 7:45 the next morning. The British flew 59 tons in twenty-one missions. Clay's director of logistics, Brigadier General Williston B. Palmer, learned of plans to feed the civilian population that day when he attended a conference at USAFE headquarters. LeMay declared that planes would fly around the clock, seven days a week, "on a wartime basis." USAFE estimated it would be lifting 450 tons a day in forty-eight hours and 1,500 tons a day by July 10. Palmer began organizing deliveries to the airfields. Truck and labor service companies converged on Rhein-Main and Wiesbaden, along with mechanics from the 60th Troop Carrier Group who had been left behind in Bavaria when the C-47s rushed to Wiesbaden. In the northern zone, the British set up an Army Air Transport Organisation. Consisting of Royal Army Service Corps troops, the unit had two components: a Rear Airfield Supply Organisation at Wunstorf collected, stored, and prepared cargoes for shipment and loaded them; a Forward Airfield Supply Organisation at Gatow unloaded cargo and turned it over to military government and Berlin officials. The Army Air Transport Organisation's headquarters first operated from Wunstorf but moved in mid-July to Bückeburg and BAFO headquarters.[28]

By that historic Monday, it was clear the blockade would last more than a few days. To put the operation on a more solid footing, LeMay appointed Brigadier General Joseph Smith commander of an airlift task force on June 29. Smith was no airlift expert. His current assignment was commander of the Wiesbaden military post. He received the new job because he happened to stop by LeMay's office after lunch, just as LeMay was looking for a general to take charge of the operation. Smith's staff was as qualified as he was. Major Edward Willeford confessed that when Smith made him task force air cargo officer, he had no idea how much freight a C-47 could carry.[29] Smith's orders were for forty-five days, the current estimate of Berlin's stockpiles. Expecting that the operation might be shorter, no more than two weeks, Smith asked for a staff of four people: Willeford plus Colonel Carl R. Feldmann (operations), Colonel John W. White Jr. (assisting Feldmann), and Lieutenant Colonel William H. Clark (supply and maintenance). Smith set up shop at Camp Lindsey, a former German caserne on the outskirts of Wiesbaden.[30]

To man the planes, Smith combed the USAFE staff and bases throughout Germany and Austria. The only crews at Wiesbaden, where he concentrated eighty C-47s, had flown the planes there, and some had worked for forty-eight hours straight. Many of the men sent to help them were unfamiliar with heavily loaded Gooney Birds, including "several fighter pilots who had never flown multi-engine aircraft."[31] Although the air force had used Vittles as a code name earlier, the term did not catch on until reporters asked Smith about a name for the U.S. airlift. He suggested they call it "Operation Vittles" because "we're hauling grub." For their airlift, the British eventually chose a play on words: "Operation Plainfare."[32] The mission: deliver 30,000 tons of food to Berlin in July, with Smith's force flying two-thirds of it and the RAF flying the rest.[33]

BAFO was a fighter organization short on airlift expertise. One staff officer recalled that he and his colleagues did not look forward to Plainfare "with any great enthusiasm," expecting "a hell of a bore." They knew little about transports and had no idea of Berlin's requirements. Short of trained people, lacking an operations room (command post), and functioning more as a maker of occupation policy than an operational headquarters, BAFO was "in the worst possible state to take on an operation of which we knew nothing."[34] RAF Transport Command sent Group Captain Noel C. Hyde to Wunstorf on June 30 to command the transport fleet there. Improvisation marked the early days, along with a carefree spirit. One British pilot remembered it best: "Pilots full of doughnuts and tea went forth to seek any aircraft which happened to be fueled, serviced, and loaded. Hot was the competition, and great was the joy when one was found. Soon the summer skies were full of a monstrous gaggle of aircraft headed in the general direction of Berlin."[35]

Arrival of the first C-54s signified a move away from such lighthearted improvisation. Washington announced on June 27 that three squadrons were en route from Panama, Alaska, and Hawaii. A fourth followed two weeks later. The military version of the Douglas DC-4, the C-54 was designed to carry passengers, not freight, but with its seats removed, it could lift 19,600 pounds, over three times the payload of a C-47. The first of these larger planes landed at Rhein-Main on June 29 and flew supplies into Tempelhof before the sun set. By July 11, forty-five of them, along with 1,250 crew members and mechanics, crowded the ramp at Rhein-Main. The planes were from the air force's troop carrier contingent, not the new Military Air Transport Service (MATS). MATS supported the Strategic Air Command, moving atomic bomb components and assembly teams to forward bases, and air force leaders did not want to draw on it except as a last resort. That created a public relations problem. Troop carriers suggested evacuation, so officials stressed that the planes would fly cargo into Berlin, not passengers out.[36]

The British stepped up their airlift, diverting thirty-eight more Dakotas on June 28 and forty Yorks on July 4. Some maintenance in Britain was put on contract so that 300 RAF mechanics could transfer to Germany. The Yorks, roughly equivalent to C-54s, carried around 8.5 tons at a cruising speed of 185 miles an hour and would allow the RAF to double deliveries. In sending them, the British were gambling on a short operation. London stripped Transport Command, not only canceling services to Africa and the Far East but also suspending transport crew training, which it had never done before, even during the war. If the operation lasted longer than a few months, the RAF would face a dilemma: restart training by withdrawing planes and crews from the airlift, which would mean a sharp drop in tonnage, or sustain the lift and watch its crew force erode from lack of replacements.[37]

A colorful British operation began on July 5 when Sunderland flying boats started shuttling between Finkenwerder, the old Blohm and Voss seaplane base on the Elbe River at Hamburg, and Berlin's Havel See. Ten of these planes hauled sixty tons of cargo a day. London sent them largely to show Berliners (and Russians) that it was making every effort to help the city.[38] Starting August 11, the Sunderlands flew salt, which most aircraft could not carry because it leaked out of containers, sifted down into the belly of the airplane, and corroded control cables there. The Sunderlands, with their cables high in the fuselage, could carry salt without risk. As one U.S. observer reported, the operation ran "on a shoestring." Flight controllers directed operations from a tent pitched on the banks of the Elbe, working in knee-deep mud. The planes took off and landed on the river, dodging ships and bombed-out hulks. In Berlin, they transferred their cargoes to "a ramshackle fleet" of boats and barges. Two civilian Hythe flying boats flown by Aquila Airways joined the Sunderlands in August.[39]

The Sunderlands were the first planes to use the northern corridor. Thus far, the British had used the central corridor to fly to and from Wunstorf, and the Americans used the southern corridor on their way into Berlin and the central corridor on their way out. Two-way traffic in the central airway was separated by altitude. The Americans stayed above 8,000 feet, while the British flew at four levels, two inbound and two outbound, ranging from 1,500 to 4,500 feet.[40] At first, the planes flew in daylight only, and Frankfurt air traffic controllers insisted on twenty-five minutes' separation. LeMay overruled them by putting Smith in charge of air traffic control, and within a few weeks, the airlift was running around the clock. Smith ordered planes through the corridors at four-minute intervals separated by 1,000 feet in altitude. At first, the RAF spaced Dakotas six minutes apart by day and fifteen minutes apart at night; it soon shortened the intervals to four minutes by day and ten at night.[41]

Reinforcements led to changes. C-54s cruised ten knots faster than C-47s, and Yorks were fifteen knots faster still. That, plus increased numbers, led Smith and Hyde to introduce a "block" system. Smith introduced it on July 4, and Hyde followed a week later. All Wiesbaden C-47s left at four-minute intervals, followed by Rhein-Main C-47s. The C-54s from Rhein-Main followed, with the first one calculated to reach Berlin four minutes behind the last C-47. The cycle repeated three times a day. Because of their larger payload, C-54s had priority over C-47s. Hyde's system was similar. He launched his Yorks as a group, followed by Dakotas. The first York would return before the last Dakota left the ground. It would then take on another load and launch, timed to reach Gatow a few minutes behind the last Dakota. The cycle repeated every four and a half hours.[42]

Weather interfered with operations throughout early July, with low clouds and rain. Planes encountered ice above 5,000 feet. One report described conditions as the worst July weather in thirty-eight years. Smith recalled two weeks of thick fog, rolling in like pea soup. Half the flights were on instruments. Conditions were so poor that RAF Group Captain Brian C. Yarde told reporters at Gatow that planes normally would have stayed on the ground. On July 2, electrical faults due to heavy rains grounded twenty-six Dakotas at Wunstorf. The base went through a year's supply of windshield wipers in two weeks. It had no concrete parking aprons, so aircraft parked on the grass, and the rains turned Wunstorf into "a sea of mud." Engineers laid 1,700 yards of PSP, only to have its corners buckle under heavy loads, wreaking havoc on tires. The problem was not confined to the British base. One C-54 needed three new tires after just three landings on Tempelhof's PSP runway, while Rhein-Main acquired a new nickname—"Rhein-Mud." Under conditions such as these, everyone welcomed the opening of Gatow's concrete runway on July 17.[43]

General Smith struck an upbeat tone with reporters on July 2, saying that deliveries exceeded 1,000 tons a day. Bevin also emphasized the positive, telling the House of Commons that the "great airlift will grow in strength . . . and the weapon of starvation will not be allowed to succeed."[44] Others were not so sure. From Berlin, Pope assessed the long-term prospects as bleak. The airlift, he commented, was being conducted with an intensity of purpose reminiscent of Dunkirk, hardly an encouraging comparison. Bohlen reached similar conclusions, writing on July 6 that the airlift was "obviously no solution." The Western position in Berlin "could not be maintained indefinitely" because of cost and because the airlift could not deliver "coal and other raw materials necessary for the continuance of economic life." Howley confessed two days later that the airlift could not meet the city's needs. Cutbacks in electricity seemed to bear out these gloomy predictions, limiting domestic use to four hours a day, halting streetcar and subway service between 6:00 P.M. and 6:00 A.M., turning off three-quarters of all street lighting, and pulling the plug on nonessential industry. Even with these cuts, Howley's staff estimated that stocks would run out in October or November. The British air secretary, Arthur Henderson, was also pessimistic, perhaps inspired by a report from Robertson predicting serious problems in a "few weeks." The British military governor reiterated instructions not to put an optimistic spin on reports. "Do not," he ordered, "give [the] impression that we are satisfied with this expedient as a long-term measure or that it can ever fully meet all Berlin's requirements. Beware for instance of conveying the impression that Berlin's coal needs can or will be met by air." Reporters sensed the mood. The *New York Times* predicted that although enough food could be flown in, the airlift could not sustain Berlin's economy and could not continue during the winter. July 8 brought home some of the cost, when the first crash of an airlift plane killed three Americans near Wiesbaden.[45]

The American air force evinced little enthusiasm for the cargo operation in distant Germany. The chief of air force public affairs told a reporter that the airlift was "an Army job" and advised the journalist to contact Royall's office. One reason was the desire not to be involved in what everyone regarded as a doomed effort, but deeper institutional reasons were also at work. The air force had grown up committed to strategic bombing and regarded freight hauling as a peripheral mission. The cargo fleet's main role was to support the atomic strike force. Berlin was a diversion, and a dangerous one at that. Concentrating cargo planes in Germany left them vulnerable to Soviet attack and unavailable to move atomic bombs, technicians, and crews to overseas bases. In short, General Vandenberg and his staff believed in June and early July that assigning C-54s to the Berlin airlift "would deny any atomic capability should the crisis . . . erupt into war."[46]

Another source of pessimism was the belief that the airlift could not deliver coal, which was as necessary to Berlin's survival as food. Not just a source of heat, it powered the city's electrical, sewage, and water systems, and according to one estimate, Berlin had ten days' supply. Clay and LeMay discussed the problem on June 29 when LeMay flew into Tempelhof to see what his crews were up against. Clay reported that coal "rather than food will be our most difficult problem unless surface transport [is] reopened within next month." With all available C-47s flying food, he reasoned that the only choice was to load coal into the bomb bays of B-29s, which were too large to land at Tempelhof anyway, and drop it somewhere in Berlin. LeMay opposed the idea because, as he advised Washington, "bombers would not then be ready for striking mission if needed," but orders were orders. The Tempelhof base commander, Colonel Henry W. Dorr, set to work finding a site. He picked a former training area in the French sector. A demonstration succeeded only in pulverizing the coal when it hit the ground and covering the observing dignitaries with black dust.[47]

A less dramatic means of delivery had to be found. Someone realized that army warehouses held half a million duffel bags left over from the war. They would do. Early on the afternoon of July 7, the first C-54 landed in Berlin loaded with 200 duffel bags filled with coal. Other planes followed, delivering 261 tons that day. Public utilities alone required 1,780 tons daily, and *Newsweek* called the effort "little more than a drop in the scuttle." Food received priority, and in the remaining twenty-four days of July, the airlift provided the same amount of coal that trains had delivered in two days before the blockade.[48] The RAF lifted its first coal on July 19, also in duffels. This system worked, despite problems. Each sack was supposed to weigh 110 pounds (plus or minus 4 pounds), but random samples found a range in weight from 80 to 150 pounds. Despite the packaging, coal dust collected everywhere, sometimes ankle deep, and clogged flight instruments. Oddly, the combination of dust from the airlift's two main cargoes, coal and flour, was even more dangerous than coal dust alone. It was highly combustible and corroded control cables, electrical circuits, switches, and connectors. Covering the floor with tarps or wetting the coal added weight but brought little relief. Sliding one end of a rubber tube out a porthole so the slipstream could suck dust out of the cabin was promising in theory but only partly successful in practice. The RAF coated cabin floors with plastic sealant, which protected the compartments underneath the main cabin but not the cabin or the cockpit. Only constant, thorough sweeping did much good. In Berlin, women swept the cabin as the plane taxied out for departure, climbed down the ladder with their burlap bags of precious coal, and boarded a truck that would take them back to the unloading ramp for a repeat performance. Before the airlift was over, they saved 500 tons of coal that otherwise would have been lost, and for the city, that meant fifty "free" planeloads. Crews eager to cut turnaround times did not let the sweepers linger, however, and the planes showed it.[49]

Tonnage goals proved to be a moving target. On June 29, Clay outlined a target of 20,000 tons for July. That same day, his deputy at OMGUS, General Hays, asked the British-American Bipartite Control Office (BICO), an Anglo-American military government committee coordinating the economies of their zones, for 29,653 *metric* tons, or over 32,600 short tons. Three days later, Clarence L. Adcock at BICO reported plans to deliver 30,000 tons of food in the first fifteen days of July, after which the priority would shift to fuels.[50] With coal deliveries added and other requirements refined, the tonnage goal climbed from 2,000 tons a day to 3,200 tons on July 8 and 4,371 tons five days later. Struggling to cope with the growing demand, USAFE on July 15 diverted to Wiesbaden sixty-six C-47s that had been earmarked for transfer to Turkey. Targets continued to climb. By the end of July, planners had rounded up the total to 4,500 tons, and Howley thought it might go as high as 5,650.[51]

The amounts and the diversity of Berlin's needs stagger the imagination. Coal totaled nearly 2,000 tons a day, and food amounted to over 1,300 tons: 646 tons of flour, 180 tons of dehydrated potatoes, 144 tons of vegetables, 125 tons of cereals, 109 tons of meat and fish, 85 tons of sugar, 64 tons of fat, 19 tons of salt, 11 tons of coffee, 5 tons of dehydrated milk, and 3 tons of yeast. Much of the food came from Germany, but not all of it. Some wheat flour came from the United States, while rye flour came from Denmark and (surprisingly) Hungary. Italy provided rice; Norway, fish. Dehydrated milk came from the Netherlands, Belgium, Denmark, and Switzerland, while Germany, the United States, Britain, and the Netherlands provided dehydrated potatoes. The airlift also shipped 13 tons of newsprint a day so west Berlin newspapers could fight Soviet propaganda.[52] To deliver it all, LeMay asked Washington for fifty more C-54s, only to boost the number to seventy-one on July 15. The big planes were critical because only so many aircraft could land in Berlin each day. Every time a C-47 landed instead of a C-54, the airlift delivered 3 tons but passed up the chance to deliver 10.[53]

Clay energetically supported his air force commander. Meeting LeMay's request would enable the British and Americans to deliver 3,000 tons each day. The airlift was expensive and could not continue indefinitely, but it had to be sustained at maximum tonnage if Moscow were to take seriously Western diplomatic protests. Clay urged haste. With present resources, "we can only hold our own in food." With the airlift now delivering coal as well, stocks were falling. "Each day of delay will make our position more difficult," the general warned. Unwilling to act on its own, the air force contended that the request required a government decision, and Royall put the subject on the National Security Council's agenda for July 15.[54]

EXPANSION OF THE AIRLIFT had already produced problems. Unprepared for the demands placed on them, airfields in Germany lacked everything from runway lights to warehouses. USAFE's aviation fuel consumption for July was three times that of June. BAFO had previously used half a million gallons of fuel a month; now it needed that much every four days. The supply system could not provide enough gas, and storage tanks in western Germany began to run dry. Airlift planes would have been grounded in July if three large oceangoing tankers hadn't been diverted to German ports, their cargoes shipped posthaste to airlift bases.[55]

Yorks, Tudors, C-47s, and C-54s had been designed for long flights; frequent takeoffs and landings under heavy loads subjected the aircraft's structures to unusual stress. Planes landed and took off at five times the expected rate per flying hour. To deliver as much cargo as possible, the British and American air forces allowed planes to land at higher gross weights, up to 5,000 pounds more than normal, adding to the strain on landing gear, brakes, and tires. RAF Transport Command saw the demand for tires and brake assemblies quadruple as soon as the airlift started. Flights to Berlin overworked engines. Given the short time at cruising speed, engines spent an unusually high percentage of operating time at high power settings. Idling on the ground for an average of thirty minutes awaiting takeoff wore out seals, gaskets, and wiring.[56]

Because Dakotas were unfamiliar sights in BAFO and C-54s were an even greater rarity in USAFE, the two commands' mechanics lacked the parts, manuals, equipment, and know-how to keep planes in the air. USAFE had no consumption data on C-54 parts (there were a quarter million of them). The information would have been of little help anyway, because it assumed normal usage of two to three hours a day, not eight to ten. Vittles and Plainfare thus confronted American and British logisticians with unknown and unknowable requirements. Answers could come only through experience. Assuming the airlift would be short, squadrons were told to bring a thirty-day supply of parts, and they tried to make do. To complicate matters, there were several types of C-54s, and many parts were not interchangeable. Skymasters could use one of two types of engines (Pratt and Whitney R-2000–9s and R-2000–11s), and port and starboard power plants differed. For a time, Tempelhof had no spare starters; to get C-54s with defective starters back in the air, mechanics had to start an engine using bungee cord. Shortages of trained supply clerks meant that parts on hand could not be found. In desperation, USAFE bought C-54 parts from the Douglas Aircraft Corporation's office in Brussels or cannibalized planes. It had better luck supporting its C-47s, but still, consumption far exceeded normal. The depot at Erding issued its six-month stock of windshield wipers in twelve days.[57]

The maintenance system faced similar shortages and a lack of trained mechanics, tools, and adequate facilities. Ground crews welded steel bed frames together to make maintenance stands. One plane flew for three days without a door.[58] Aircraft flew around the clock, but poor lighting at Rhein-Main and Wiesbaden hampered night maintenance. Although not a problem in the summer, with its short hours of darkness, lighting became more serious as summer turned to autumn. Floodlights could illuminate Wiesbaden's parking ramp, but no easy solution existed at Rhein-Main, where planes were loaded at dispersed hardstands. Truck drivers jury-rigged lamps atop their cabs and shone them into trailer beds.[59]

To move parts, USAFE ran an express train each night from its depot at Erding to Rhein-Main and Wiesbaden. Return runs brought parts that needed repair from airlift bases to Erding and the other large USAFE depot in Bavaria, Oberpfaffenhofen. When C-54s moved north into the British zone, trains and C-47s shuttled parts between Rhein-Main and Fassberg.[60] Looking beyond these short-term fixes, USAFE considered how to support C-54s in the future. Each Skymaster was supposed to be overhauled every 200 flying hours. USAFE planned to reopen Burtonwood, a wartime depot near Liverpool, to perform this work. Until then, Oberpfaffenhofen had to handle the assignment, with a goal of six planes a day. After 1,000 flying hours, the C-54s would return to the States for a major overhaul.[61]

Smith tried to boost efficiency. On July 9, he centralized C-54 supply support at Rhein-Main. The base would repair C-54 engines and distribute spare parts to other airfields. Four days later, Rhein-Main began sending the Air Materiel Command in Ohio a consolidated daily list of C-54 requisitions that USAFE could not fill. On July 12, Smith decided to make Rhein-Main an all–C-54 base, moving its C-47s to Wiesbaden. Rhein-Main launched its last C-47 Vittles flight on August 3. In another move to standardize, Smith decided on July 26 to have Rhein-Main concentrate on food and coal, while Wiesbaden's C-47s would handle all other cargo, such as supplies for the garrisons and industrial items.[62]

The rapid influx of planes and personnel had implications beyond maintenance and supply. People needed care and support, just as airplanes did. Mess halls were cramped and shorthanded. Post exchanges, laundries, snack bars, and recreational facilities, if they existed, were often closed at the only times men working the night shift could get to them. The biggest problem was housing. Quarters were so crowded that two or three pilots often shared the same bed, sleeping in shifts. With schedules so erratic, crews flying at night could not be segregated from those flying days. People came and went at all hours inside the barracks, and aircraft engines roared around the clock outside, making uninterrupted sleep impossible. Heat, lighting, and furnishings were poor, and there were chronic shortages of hot water. Low water pressure prevented men on the second floor of the barracks at Wiesbaden from flushing their toilets. Some crews arriving in July could not find beds and lived for a while in the loft of a barn. Men billeted off-base escaped the engine noise but had to rely on an overworked transportation system to go to and from the airfield, which stretched their workday even further.[63]

By late July, everyone was exhausted. People put in long hours because the job required it, but they could do that for only so long. For many, airlift duty was in addition to their ordinary jobs. Some flew for nine hours only to face ground duty before they could rest. Because of confused scheduling, bad weather, and other delays, many hours were wasted waiting. Wildly fluctuating workdays were as tiring as long ones; there was no consistent schedule. One pilot remembered that early on, the job was to fly two loads a day into Berlin, no matter how long it took. A flight surgeon thought "a dangerous level" of exhaustion had been reached by mid-July. Some crews reported that "both the pilot and co-pilot had dozed off, only to be awakened by the changing attitude of the plane." RAF crews were in similar straits, often working eighteen-hour days. Ninety percent of York and Dakota crews surveyed in July and August complained of fatigue (as distinguished from simply being tired) due to lack of sleep, wasted time before and between flights, and poor living conditions. Aircrews' lives depended on the alertness and morale of ground crews, so poor conditions for mechanics mattered just as much as conditions affecting the men in the cockpits.[64]

Both armies worked to collect cargoes for the airlift fleets. Through July, the U.S. Army shipped commodities to Rhein-Main and Wiesbaden. The goal was to stay one day ahead of the air force. At first, the Bizonal Economic Council could not keep up, so European Command's Transportation Division took over the job, commandeering cargoes wherever it could find them. The British faced similar problems. The rail line to Wunstorf was single-tracked; only one train could unload at a time. Three trains might arrive one day, none the next.[65]

To provide a single voice defining requirements, the British and American commandants in Berlin established an Air Lift Staff Committee in mid-July. It would pass requirements on to BICO, which would obtain supplies, allocate them, and move them to railheads near the airfields. The two armies moved cargoes from the railheads to the bases, delivered them planeside, and loaded them aboard aircraft (the last under air force supervision). An airman, called the "flight checker" or "traffic technician," directed the truck as it backed up to the plane. He supervised loading and distribution within the cabin, as well as tie-down and manifesting. The pilot cross-checked to ensure the load was properly distributed and secured.[66]

We tend to think of an airlift as a "high-tech" operation, so it helps to recall, as Elizabeth Lay put it, that nearly every pound was moved "part of the way on a man's back."[67] Six-man teams at railheads transferred cargoes from trains to trucks, with a goal of one ton per man per hour. Ten-man crews loaded planes. Unloading crews in Berlin were larger, consisting of twelve men, to do the job faster. Six clambered aboard and slid the bags down chutes, while the others stacked the bags in a truck. The workforce was a mix of Germans and eastern European refugees. By the end of summer, 2,000 men worked at Tempelhof, divided into four shifts, and they were unloading twenty-five to thirty aircraft an hour. At first, loading a C-47 could take up to five hours. Soon the average had dropped to ten minutes. Unloading at Tempelhof took eight to forty-five minutes, with thirty minutes the average. Some cargoes were harder to deal with than others. For instance, the French sent 25 tons of fresh vegetables from Mainz to Wiesbaden each morning, creating "a novel loading problem." Dehydrated potatoes saved 720 tons a day, but "lashing this commodity," one official noted, "is like lashing jelly."[68]

To move cargo, the U.S. Army stationed two truck companies at Rhein-Main and another at Wiesbaden. Drivers worked twelve-hour shifts. Keeping trucks and trailers moving proved to be almost as challenging as keeping planes airborne. Like the C-47s and C-54s they supported, the ten-ton rigs were built for smooth surfaces and long distances. They now faced short hauls with heavy loads over gravel, dirt, and mud. Like the planes, many of the vehicles were worn-out veterans from the war. Wear and tear occurred at twice the normal rate for tractors, four times normal for trailers. Standing gear were designed for solid surfaces, not dirt, and were meant to bear full loads briefly. Now trailers were loaded and parked in reserve until tractors retrieved them and took them to an aircraft. Frequent coupling and uncoupling warped trailer beds. Brakes, axles, and clutches wore out at unprecedented rates. To keep the fleet rolling, the 559th Ordnance Maintenance Company worked seven days a week, repairing trucks and trailers and rebuilding one truck engine a day.[69]

Tempelhof's PSP runway began to come apart, putting this immense effort in jeopardy. LeMay sent Lieutenant Colonel Maceo Falco to the base with orders to keep the runway open, even if it meant putting "German workers one yard apart on both sides of it." That was just about what Falco had to do. Work crews of 225 men swarmed onto the runway after a plane touched down, beating the mats back into place, filling holes with gravel, and scrambling out of the way as the next plane roared in. While C-54s banged down on the fragile PSP, engineers laid out two sod runways for C-47s, one for takeoffs and one for landings. They held up "fairly well" once dry weather set in by late July, until the legendary "Black Friday" storm closed them on August 13. Meanwhile, Falco had recommended construction of a second PSP runway, 5,500 feet long. Work began on July 8 and continued sixteen hours a day, women working alongside men. All materials, except brick rubble from Berlin, had to be flown in, adding seventy-five to eighty tons to tonnage targets. The runway was ready September 12. Then work began on a third strip, which opened in late November.[70]

For all the problems and improvisations, there were signs of progress. Smith and Hyde had begun to impose order and improve efficiency. They streamlined communications procedures. They began experimenting with scheduling and control techniques so that different aircraft types, flying at different speeds, could operate in the corridors. They improved existing navigational aids and installed new ones. They tried to stabilize crew schedules and improve living conditions. They began studying ideas that their successors would receive credit for, such as concentrating C-54s in the British zone, closer to Berlin, so the big planes could make more trips and deliver more tons each day.

Despite these gains, on July 15, the National Security Council postponed action on Clay's call for more aircraft. The decision stemmed from confusion over Berlin's needs and concern about war plans. In the course of a meandering conversation, assistant air force secretary Cornelius Whitney summarized the situation: Smith and the British were delivering 1,750 tons a day, while the air force pegged requirements at 5,300. Recalculations might boost that to 8,000. If the United States sent 180 C-54s and 105 C-47s, "a complete use of everything we have," and the British likewise made a maximum effort, the total might reach 4,000 tons. Thus, Whitney concluded, "the air operation is doomed to failure." The council debated whether the figures were averages, whether they included stockpiles, and whether bad weather had been factored in. No one knew, and Royall suggested they clear up the discrepancies before making a decision. Opposed to giving Clay more planes, Whitney pointed out that the aircraft were "required in emergency war plans"; sending them to Germany risked their destruction if war broke out. Marshall, speaking "as an individual rather than as Secretary of State," found that a compelling argument and expressed concern about putting "our planes in a concentrated area where at least 25% might be destroyed at the first blow." There seemed to be more questions than answers. In the end, the council accepted Marshall's suggestion that it defer a decision on increasing the airlift. The topic would come up again a week later, when the air force would present some surprising answers to the council's questions.[71]

THE DECISION TO UNDERTAKE *an* airlift was not the decision to undertake *the* airlift. No one in June 1948 was thinking of *the airlift*, as we understand the term. No one saw an airlift as the preferred course of action that would resolve the crisis. There was no single decision. The British began flights without reference to the Americans, and vice versa. For many months, there would be no single coordinated and centrally controlled effort. After April, an airlift was a "conspicuous alternative," a step that had been tried before and had been shown to entail little risk, so it is not surprising that the idea occurred to many people simultaneously.[72] But British and American officials were not committing their governments to supply Berlin using whatever resources were required, nor were they trying to break the blockade with airpower. They began *an* airlift to buy time and boost Berliners' morale. Western leaders regarded this airlift as a short-term tactic, not a long-term solution. As they expanded it, they continued to search for ways of balancing prudence and resolve.

CHAPTER 6

"The Next Step"

Tension over Berlin peaked the third week of July. Diplomatic exchanges with Moscow had failed, and the Western powers had to decide what to do next. Clay wanted to send in his armored column. Though no more inclined than Clay to abandon Berlin or the London program, leaders on both sides of the Atlantic thought his tanks were more likely to trigger war than break the blockade. A convoy might be the last step, but for now, Western leaders preferred to concentrate on immediate ones: a new approach to Moscow, followed perhaps by an appeal to the United Nations.

The Western powers did not adopt an *airlift strategy* at this stage. The airlift's purpose remained to buy time; its perceived ability to do so was limited. British and American officials expected that weather would ground it in October, setting a deadline for diplomacy. If the Western governments had not reached agreement with the Soviets by then, the West would face a choice between retreat and Clay's armored column.

Thus, although Western leaders obeyed their first impulse and resisted Soviet pressure, their resolve was not as firm as it appeared in hindsight. Their hesitancy was not unusual, but it runs counter to our traditional view of Harry Truman as well as the image, prevalent among decision-making theorists, of leaders grappling with "strategic" choices. Presidents and prime ministers "do not think or act like . . . game theorists"; their priorities are determined by what must be done next. They take problems, especially those with no obvious solutions, day by day.[1] In July 1948, Western leaders did just that. They expanded an airlift they expected would fail, and they devised a new approach to Stalin they believed he would reject. They concentrated on the next step, not the last one, and they ignored calls from advisers for definitive answers about long-term policy.

ON JULY 17, THE PENTAGON announced it had sent sixty B-29s to Great Britain, describing the missions as training flights. Commentators knew a cover story when they heard one. It was an odd time to send these planes on practice missions, especially to bases within range of Russia. Everyone remembered that less than three years before, this president had sent B-29s to Hiroshima and Nagasaki. Stocks broke on Wall Street, and Harold Nicolson described the City—London's commercial and financial district—as panicky. The *New Republic*'s T. R. B. summed up almost everyone's reaction: "Hold on to your seats, folks; this is the showdown."[2]

No training maneuver, the B-29 deployment was indeed a response to the blockade. The idea had originated with Bevin, who regarded it as "a political gesture," proof of American interest in European defense. The only way to induce the Soviets to retreat was a demonstration of airpower, he told Douglas on June 25. Bevin proposed assembling a large bomber force in western Europe, including British planes from Africa or the Middle East, before any diplomatic approach to Moscow.[3]

Pentagon officials discussed this suggestion on June 27 and sought Clay's views. He thought the move "urgent." The Russians were "definitely afraid of our air might," and the bombers might be decisive in "sustaining Allied firmness." Bradley wanted to know where the bombers should go. Clay answered that while LeMay preferred Britain for "operational reasons"—they would be safe from Russian attack—Clay wanted two squadrons (twenty planes) sent to Germany first to show resolve.[4]

The air force had begun preparations. A squadron of the 301st Bomb Group was in Germany on routine deployment. Strategic Air Command (SAC) ordered the group's other two squadrons to Goose Bay, Labrador. There they waited on three-hour alert. Sixty planes—two bomb groups—were to go later. After conferring with Forrestal, Royall, and Lovett on June 28, Truman approved sending the two squadrons at Goose Bay to Germany. The Pentagon announced the move on June 30.[5]

The 301st's B-29s could not carry atomic bombs, but that did not prevent American and British officials from considering using the deployment to deepen Soviet fears of atomic attack. Wedemeyer, Draper, and Douglas had discussed B-29 deployments on June 26, with some attention to "the various interpretations" that might be attached to them. Draper thought "we should exploit this movement to the utmost" in terms of publicity and propaganda.[6] Meanwhile, Air Commodore Brook's proposal was on its way to Tedder's desk.

Royall and Forrestal told Atomic Energy Commission chairman David Lilienthal that atomic weapons were "the best and almost the only thing we had that could be used quickly." The Soviets had a "healthy respect" for them.[7] When the joint chiefs met Forrestal to deal with rumors about barrage balloons in the air corridors, talk turned to what might happen if things escalated. Leahy remarked that such a situation "could be settled with what we have—we haven't very much but still we could make plans to use what we have. . . . It might be a very good idea to have them over there anyway"—a reference to moving bombs (or bombers) to Britain. Royall thought the crisis made it "all the more imperative" to decide what to do about the custody and use of atomic weapons. General Vandenberg's staff was working on a study of where bombs might have the most effect. Forrestal thought the issue was "whether or not you gamble that a reduction of Moscow and Leningrad would be a powerful enough impact to stop a war."[8]

Preparations for the next B-29 movements continued. Air force headquarters alerted the 307th Bomb Group at MacDill Air Force Base, Florida, and the 28th Bomb Group near Rapid City, South Dakota. The commander of the 28th issued orders over the local radio station for his men to return to base at once. The broadcast sparked "considerable consternation and speculation" as it spread over the airwaves of the upper Midwest. SAC put the rest of its units on alert to deploy on twenty-four hours' notice.[9]

In London, the Berlin committee dropped plans to move British bombers. Bevin won approval to receive the American planes, though, and he informed Douglas. Both sides then had second thoughts. The Americans wanted to see what results might come from Sokolovsky's letter and "whether traffic to and from Berlin was being genuinely resumed."[10] The British thought the bombers should stay in the United States until Generals Robertson and Clay had answered Sokolovsky and, reversing Bevin's earlier suggestion, until *after* the protest notes to Moscow. Otherwise, public opinion might regard the move as provocative.[11]

Marshall agreed with Bevin's last point, telling the cabinet that any effects of deployment on the Russians had to be balanced against reaction in the United States. Days passed. Although support for the Western notes of July 6 was "almost unanimous," Marshall was worried the American people might regard the deployment as bellicose. He had discussed matters with Sam Rayburn, the House minority leader. As Marshall explained to the National Security Council (NSC), Rayburn believed average citizens had "fear of war in the forefront of their minds." People supported a strong policy and rearmament only because they believed these measures would assure peace. They would not support moves that looked toward war.[12]

Marshall waited until July 10. By then, Robertson and Clay had met Sokolovsky, and the Western notes had been sent. Did Bevin want the B-29s? Douglas answered on July 13: yes, and quickly, although the British wanted the move described as a training flight. Douglas seconded Bevin's recommendation, noting it would be harder to send the bombers later. Clay urged that the B-29s go "at once," so they would be in Britain when his convoy moved down the autobahn.[13]

Now Marshall hesitated. He wanted to reexamine the deployment in light of the Soviet note. He outlined the issue for the NSC, which on July 15 decided to send the planes. According to Forrestal's published diaries, there were three reasons: the deployment would show the American people how serious their government was about Berlin, it would give the air force experience and training, and the move would accustom the British to having foreign soldiers on their territory again.

Washington should act while Bevin's offer held. If the crisis escalated, the British might withdraw the option just when the Americans wanted to exercise it.[14]

The decision in fact turned on the first reason. The other two, as one NSC member described them, were less important. Marshall opened the discussion by summarizing Bevin's views, then his own. Although the B-29s would show firmness, the secretary believed that "our position has already been made very clear." The move would stiffen the British and the French, checking "any tendency toward weakness or appeasement." Yet Marshall's main worry was the American public's reaction. He described his discussion with Rayburn and commented that the public's fear of war meant that "we must not adopt too militant a course" or appear to be "trying to put something over on them."

Forrestal also had public opinion foremost on his mind. He doubted the public realized the gravity of the situation. Royall agreed, declaring, "If we have decided to stay in Berlin, we must start conditioning the American people." He pointed out that the State Department was considering an appeal to the United Nations, and the public might regard the B-29 move as undercutting the international organization. It would be better to send the B-29s "when we have reached the convoy stage." Lovett countered that American support of the United Nations should not bar actions "where our vital interests are concerned." A bomber movement now would not rule out an appeal to the Security Council later. Cornelius Whitney added what he regarded as "minor" reasons for sending the B-29s: it would "grease the wheels for this kind of operation with the British," and "we now have permission but if the situation deteriorates we may no longer have it." No one raised a point Douglas had made earlier: canceling the move might raise doubts in London about American determination. The council agreed that Marshall and Forrestal should ask for Truman's approval. The president approved the deployment that afternoon, saying he had concluded on his own that the bombers should go.[15] Aircraft started across the Atlantic that evening, with the first one landing in Britain on July 17.[16]

How the Soviets viewed the move is hard to assess. Thanks to Donald Maclean, they knew the B-29s did not carry atomic weapons.[17] Although this suggests that the deployment had little effect on Stalin, concentrating on the move itself overlooks the broader effects of the U.S. monopoly. *These* planes could not attack Moscow with atomic bombs, but others would if war broke out. The Soviet system might perish. Stalin had seen war topple one Russian regime and nearly destroy another. The bomb was, he had declared earlier in the year, "a powerful thing, pow-er-ful!"[18]

The deployment highlights the problems facing the Western powers and the Soviet Union in the early months of the crisis. The blockade attempted to turn local advantage into strategic gain. The West mobilized its strategic power in the hope of offsetting local weakness. Neither maneuver succeeded. Moscow could not prevent creation of the Federal Republic of Germany, the economic revival of western

Europe, or the movement toward a Western alliance. Nor could SAC frighten the Kremlin into relaxing its grip on Berlin. The city's rescuers would come by air, but not in bombers.

THE B-29 DECISION brought to the fore questions about the custody and use of atomic weapons. Controversy had swirled around custody since creation of the Atomic Energy Commission (AEC) the year before. The commission took control of the stockpile from the military, and it issued officers few "Q" clearances, which granted access to information about atomic weapons and the equipment associated with them—so-called restricted data. Thus, planners and flight crews knew little about the bomb, and the commission knew just as little about military requirements. Officers proposed transferring the stockpile to the air force in 1947, but the commission refused. The Military Liaison Committee, supported by the service secretaries, revived the issue after the Czech coup, and Forrestal raised it with Truman.[19]

The president's first reaction was that Forrestal "had a point." Lilienthal countered that "the decisive question was the policy question"—whether the United States would use atomic weapons in war—and suggested that the military was using custody to prejudge use. Truman wanted to discuss the matter later, remarking, "I certainly don't want to have to use them again, ever."[20] He stuck to that view in May, after Leahy outlined the current war plan, which relied on atomic attacks. The next day, Truman ordered the military to draw up another plan, without atomic bombs. As he explained to Forrestal, "we are preparing for peace and not for war," and he turned aside the secretary's plea for another supplemental defense appropriation. With Truman nodding approval, Marshall told Forrestal that the administration assumed "there would not be war and that we should not plunge into war preparations which would bring about the very thing we were taking steps to prevent."[21]

Truman's stance shocked Royall, who asked the NSC to study whether the United States would use atomic weapons in war. The army had assumed it would, he noted, but now there was doubt "in some quarters."[22] The AEC conferred with Royall and Forrestal at the end of June but failed to find common ground. Lilienthal recalled that Berlin gave the session added urgency. As Royall left time and again to get the latest news about those elusive barrage balloons, "the shadows of the current troubles . . . in Berlin rather followed him around." Royall thought the crisis made decisions imperative: "Will we use this weapon, if we are compelled to use force? Upon what kind of targets? And under what general circumstances?" His approach made it clear to Lilienthal that military leaders "have been *assuming* that they already have the answers to such questions" and that they were the proper ones to answer them. Lilienthal countered that although these were indeed the key questions, they were for the president to decide. Truman agreed, refusing to transfer custody.[23]

Royall continued to urge action, telling the NSC on July 1 that the staff study was needed soon because "we may have another flare-up over Berlin" at any moment. Forrestal wanted to discuss the matter with Truman first and arranged an Oval Office meeting on the subject, but the president hinted that the decision would go against him: "he proposed to keep, in his own hands, the decision as to the use of the bomb." Truman would not, he declared, let "some dashing lieutenant colonel decide when would be the proper time to drop one."[24]

The late-afternoon meeting at the White House on July 21, which lasted fifteen minutes, went badly for Forrestal.[25] He and his aides argued that the military could not use the bomb unless they had "complete familiarity" with it, which could be acquired only by "constant inspection and handling of the weapon itself." The military lacked that. Lilienthal turned this argument inside out. The bomb was no ordinary weapon. Turning it over to organizations that lacked the technical skills and scientific knowledge to handle it would be foolhardy and imperil the nation's safety at a critical moment. Transfer also would weaken the principle of civilian control.

When Symington complained that some scientists at Los Alamos did not think the United States should use the bomb, Truman cut him off. "I don't either," he declared. The United States, he continued, should not "use this thing unless we absolutely have to. It is a terrible thing to order the use of something that . . . is so terribly destructive. . . . You have got to understand that this isn't a military weapon. . . . It is used to wipe out women and children and unarmed people, and not for military uses." Royall would not take the hint. Ninety-eight percent of the atomic energy budget went to weapons, he grumbled; "if we aren't going to use them, that doesn't make any sense." Truman ended the meeting by saying, "I . . . can't make my mind up right off about a thing as important as this. I'll let you know."[26] His decision, announced at a cabinet meeting two days later, left custody with the AEC. The formal notification several weeks later cited "public policy," the efficiency of existing arrangements, and "the general world situation" as reasons for the decision.[27]

The Berlin crisis permeated the atmosphere in which Truman considered this issue. Although the blockade put the question at the top of the Pentagon's agenda, the crisis worked against the military because Truman did not want to take any actions the Soviets might regard as provocative. It was, as he declared at the end of the discussion, "no time to be juggling an atom bomb around."[28] More important, the president opposed transfer in principle. Discussions made it clear that participants could not separate custody and use, so a positive decision on custody would have been interpreted in the Pentagon, if not elsewhere, as a decision on use—and Truman was determined to retain this decision himself.

Forrestal considered resigning but decided against it. Declaration of policy was one thing, implementation another. In a meeting with the JCS a few days later, he reversed, on his own authority, Truman's May 5 directive on war plans. He ordered the joint chiefs to give "top priority" to war plans involving atomic bombs and "low priority" to those that did not.[29]

THE SOVIET NOTE FORCED the United States and its allies to take stock. Arrival of the B-29s in East Anglia was reassuring but offered no solution to the blockade. Nor, in the view of Attlee's cabinet or the American NSC, did the airlift. U.S. and British leaders groped for a policy that would avoid both war and retreat.

Robertson offered a radical proposal in mid-July. To retain Berliners' support, the Western powers must show a "definite prospect of a satisfactory solution." The airlift could not do that. Although it could support Berlin until September, Robertson thought, sustaining the city through the winter was "not practicable." "We are fooling ourselves," he warned, "if we imagine that we can stay in Berlin indefinitely in defiance of the Soviet." He believed Stalin sought to prevent stability in western Europe and would go to "almost any length short of war." The Soviets would lift the blockade if they saw it leading to war or producing sustained anti-Soviet sentiment in Germany. Clay wanted to exploit this Soviet fear of war and challenge the Russians with a convoy; Robertson preferred to take advantage of rising German anger about the blockade. He confessed he had underestimated the likelihood of a blockade because of the reaction it would trigger in Germany. "They have stopped the supplies," he wrote; "the reaction has occurred. Now . . . is the time to cash in" and "take a chance on the Germans." Moscow wanted to force a meeting of the Council of Foreign Ministers. Very well. The Western powers should go beyond the London program, give the Germans "real freedoms to set up their own Government," and, once the council met, propose the withdrawal of occupation forces to "frontier areas," with Berlin and the rest of the country under a central government. There was a chance this regime would fall under Soviet influence, but Robertson doubted it; hatred of the Russians would roll back Soviet influence to the Oder.[30]

This proposal resembled Kennan's later Program A and met the same fate. Roger Makins, one of Bevin's deputy under secretaries, dismissed it as "an economic 'Munich'" and "the end of the Marshall Plan." Dean found it "too dangerous," even as a ploy. Strang agreed but offered no alternative. The problems with Robertson's plan, he confessed to Bevin, "would almost certainly apply equally in any comprehensive discussions with the Russians on Germany as a whole." At a time when the Western governments hoped to offer four-power discussions on Germany in exchange for an end to the blockade, that was a bleak assessment.[31]

Taking a chance on the Germans must have seemed folly at a time when the minister-presidents were dragging their feet over the London program, which the military governors had presented to them on July 1. In a formal reply, the minister-presidents opposed "everything . . . that would give the character of a state" to the new organization and deepen the country's division. Both sides were willing to settle for cosmetic changes in verbiage—substituting "basic law" for "constitution" and "parliamentary council" for "constituent assembly"—so the program lurched forward. Its future remained uncertain, however, especially if the Soviets could find a way to exploit German (and French) coolness toward it. Bevin rejected Robertson's suggestion.[32]

One of Alexander's closest aides, General Sir Leslie Hollis, circulated an even more dramatic proposal: mass evacuation of Berlin by air. The airlift was doomed, he thought, and the Russians could squeeze the Western powers out. The threat to remove Berliners, their belongings, and industry was "our one trump card," Hollis contended; the Russians would negotiate if they saw their leverage being taken away a planeload at a time. The Foreign Office asked Brownjohn to draw up a list of Germans to evacuate, but Strang, Kirkpatrick, and Robertson thought Hollis's idea would panic Berliners.[33]

Dean's views seemed more congenial to senior British leaders. He was sure that, above all, the Soviets wanted a stake in the Ruhr and could obtain it only through negotiation. The Marshall Plan and the London program would bring the Western powers long-term advantages if they could stay in Berlin and give those initiatives time. Bevin professed similar hope in a conversation with Canadian Norman Robertson. Even though "he had not wished to be in Berlin" and had thought "a good deal" about withdrawing over the years, it was "right and wise" to stay. The right course was to "hold firm, make sure the whole weight of world opinion was on our side, avoid any action or words that could be construed as provocative and give the other fellow an opportunity of extricating himself from the position he had taken up."[34]

Avoiding provocation meant opposing Clay's convoy. Jebb relayed to Strang an American paper reiterating the need to take steps at the United Nations that would open the way for Western action. When presenting the case at the United Nations, the paper argued, the Western powers "need to have clearly in mind the ultimate action which they . . . would be prepared to take." To Jebb, it seemed that the Americans looked forward to a Soviet veto and were "determined to have a show down" sometime in the next three weeks.[35]

Bevin shared his aide's concern, and discussions among the Brussels powers at The Hague on July 19–20 reinforced his opposition to drastic steps. Before the meetings began, he cabled Marshall that European opinion would not support "extreme measures in Berlin, involving risk of war, without a further attempt at reopening conversations with the Soviet Union."[36] The meetings in the Dutch capital, Alan Bullock recorded, "made a deep impression on Bevin." French weakness depressed him and reinforced his belief that Britain's security lay in an Atlantic, not a European, framework. The meetings also led him to accept Bidault's idea of holding discussions with the Soviets on Europe instead of Germany. As Bevin explained to Norman Robertson, "It was arguable whether the chance of a German settlement would be enlarged by offering to discuss . . . Austria, Trieste, Greece and Turkey at the same time, but on balance he thought the psychological and political advantage of taking the initiative in the 'peace offensive' away from the Soviet Union was worth some risk." The Americans were unlikely to agree.[37]

The Soviet note prompted no review in Paris, where Schuman remarked that it was "about what we expected." Attention focused on the latest cabinet crisis. Schuman's government fell on July 19 after the socialists, with an eye on the autumn elections, abandoned their partners in a vote on the army budget. The British embassy described Bidault in schizophrenic terms: afraid that American policy would lead to war and worried that the Americans were considering a deal with Moscow. At The Hague, the French foreign minister condemned American policy. At long last, talks about a North Atlantic treaty had opened in Washington on July 6, only to have Lovett declare that the United States "did not contemplate any kind of a guarantee." As Bidault saw it, Washington had "abandoned" the Brussels powers. What would the United States do if war came? When Bevin asked if France would go to the Russians regardless of Moscow's terms, Bidault avoided an answer. France did not want the West to box itself into a choice between war and withdrawal. Bidault seemed convinced that American policy sought just such an outcome.[38]

Washington had not resolved on war. Discussions were intense yet diffuse, occurring in several unconnected forums. The military was studying Clay's call for a convoy, while the State Department was pondering responses to the Soviet note. Although no one had ruled out a resort to arms, Clay's was the only voice calling for an immediate showdown. He was overruled—for the time being.

Military leaders commonly oppose the use of military force for diplomatic coercion, believing it corrupts their function.[39] Clay, however, was an uncommon military man. In April, he had concluded that a convoy was the proper Western response to Soviet interference with access to Berlin. A country that can hold its position unless its adversary is willing to risk war has the advantage. The blockade had given the Soviets such an edge; they could wait while the West searched for a peaceful way to restore access.[40] Clay thought two could play that game. If the West sent a convoy, the decision to resist would be Russia's. Clay's maneuver was an example of what political scientists call *compellence,* or using the mutual fear of war to induce an adversary to *stop* doing something (in contrast to *deterrence,* or dissuading the adversary from starting something).[41] This is not to suggest that Clay had thought this through; his motives were summarized by his comment some months later that "sometime I would like to start trouble instead of having it all started by the other side."[42]

Once the blockade began in earnest, Clay revived his proposal. He picked

Brigadier General Arthur G. Trudeau to lead a convoy of American armored and engineer troops, British infantry, and French armored cars. Trudeau recalled that his soldiers were ready, even eager, to shoot their way into Berlin. And there would have been shooting, all right, far short of Berlin. As Victor Gobarev suggests, Sokolovsky's soldiers regarded the boundaries of their zone as "sacred Soviet borders" to be defended to the last against Western invaders. Such a possibility never occurred to LeMay. Responsible for Trudeau's air support, he expected "no resistance." Just in case, though, he prepared attacks on every Soviet airfield in eastern Germany, on the assumption that if Trudeau encountered opposition, Stalin had decided on war. If a highway shoot-out did not bring on World War III, LeMay's "protective reaction" strikes would. Primed for war, Task Force Trudeau was poorly suited for its mission of reopening the autobahn. Trudeau had so few pontoon bridges that if he had to build a bridge across the Elbe at Magdeburg, he would not have enough remaining pontoons to reach Berlin, unless he picked them up behind him and reused them.[43]

Wedemeyer's planners pressed Clay's staff for details. Their questions were pointed, the answers embarrassing. Clay had little more in mind than a three-nation escort for 200 trucks, with orders not to shoot first. If this convoy reached Berlin, others would follow. Clay assumed the Russians could stop the convoy only by shooting, and because he was sure they would not, Trudeau would reach Berlin. Pentagon planners dealt harshly with these assumptions, pointing out that the Soviets could bottle up the convoy in eastern Germany without firing a shot, by blowing up bridges ahead and behind. Western troops would have to occupy the entire autobahn; did the plan provide for that? Berlin said no; Clay did not have enough soldiers. Washington next wanted to know how European Command would supply Berlin if the convoy worked but the Russians kept other routes closed. When winter came, the airlift would stop, and truck convoys alone could not save Berlin. Clay's staff answered meekly that they would have to ask the general.[44]

Clay returned to the fray after the Soviet note made it clear that no end to the blockade was in sight. He asked Bradley to allow him to test Soviet intentions by sending Trudeau into the Soviet zone. Bradley refused, answering that only the president could make such a decision. Royall ordered Clay home for consultations.[45]

Even this did not deter Clay from making one more effort. Commenting on an analysis of the situation from Douglas, he agreed that the best course was to negotiate but opposed the ambassador's willingness to discuss Germany. Clay feared the effect this would have on the London program and appealed to the wisdom of past decisions. He contended (falsely) that the Western powers had accepted the risks when they resolved to create a west German government. To "throw it away" the moment they encountered the "first major evidence of Soviet resistance" was weakness. Concessions were pointless. The Russians were either bluffing or intent on war. Concessions were unnecessary in the first case, futile in the second. The trouble was that Clay could not make up his mind which interpretation of Soviet behavior was correct. In arguing for a convoy, he admitted there was a risk of war, but because the Russians were bluffing, it was small. He had apparently settled on the first hypothesis, only to shift ground. Rejecting concessions, he insisted, "Retreat will not save us from again and again having to choose between retreat and war." In other words, the Russians were bent on expansion. Here, Clay was advocating his second hypothesis, which he had rejected only moments before. The dance of illogic did not end there, for a few paragraphs later, he shifted again. "Only America can exert the world leadership, and only America can provide the strength to stop this policy of aggression here and now," the general contended. "The next time may be too late. I believe determined action will stop it short of war." Determined action would call the Soviets' bluff, as Clay again embraced his first hypothesis.[46]

How much of this argument Clay believed is difficult to tell.[47] Rather than adjust his recommendations to a deeper interpretation of Soviet motives, he bent the latter to the former. Arguing against retreat, he claimed it was pointless; the Soviets could create pretexts for war, and retreat merely postponed the inevitable. But if the Soviets wanted war, Clay's convoy was the worst possible move, for it would make the West responsible. So in urging the convoy, Clay had to change his position and argue that the Russians were bluffing, not bellicose; they would retreat when confronted by Western resolve.

Murphy supported his chief. His starting point was the belief that the airlift was doomed. It might be "spectacular and dramatic," he admitted, "but everyone recognizes that it is an expedient and not a solution"; it was "a confession of inability or unwillingness to enforce a well-earned right of surface passage." The West should exercise its rights, warning the Soviets first. Murphy claimed the convoy idea had "almost universal" support among British, French, and German opinion in Berlin, which, to be polite, was an exaggeration. Robertson had earlier regarded a show of force as "the only effective solvent" of the crisis, but for some days now, he had dismissed Clay's idea as "militarily unsound and politically unwise."[48]

Desperation, not logic, shaped the outlook of American officials in Berlin, if a July 10 report by one of Murphy's aides is any guide. Perry Laukhuff declared that conditions were deteriorating "with alarming rapidity," and "almost total breakdown" was just around the corner. The dehydrated food being flown in, meager in quantity and poor in quality, barely sustained life and morale. The blockade crippled industry, and Western tolerance of the eastern mark had alienated the city's political leaders. Time was on Moscow's side. Unless the blockade were lifted in the next ten days, Laukhuff predicted, the Western position would become "virtually . . . untenable." His analysis suggests that the convoy appealed to Clay and Murphy because, in their eyes, it offered the only chance of preserving the Western position.

The likelihood that it would fail was something they preferred not to think about. Desperate times justified desperate measures.[49]

Focused on risk, Bradley and his aides did not share Clay's willingness to gamble. While convoys risked catastrophe, the airlift appeared futile. It was not meeting Berlin's needs, and even with additional planes, it never could. At current rates, supplies would run out by October 25. The army pointed out that "no accurate tonnage requirements are available," with LeMay reporting that Clay wanted between 3,351 and 4,411 tons a day against current deliveries of 1,000. Sending LeMay the eighty-five planes he wanted would not close the gap, which would widen after October. Diverting C-54s from MATS could not break the blockade, but it would cripple the air force's ability to carry out war plans, including SAC's atomic offensive.[50]

Bradley presented recommendations to Royall and the JCS on July 17. The United States must reconsider what he termed its decision to remain in Berlin "for the present." Air supply met two-thirds of the city's needs, and because the two air forces could not sustain the current effort, "air supply cannot be a long-term solution." Even so, Bradley recommended sending eighty-five more C-54s, which was all that Berlin's airfields could handle, in order to postpone Stalin's victory. He wanted *planning* for a convoy to begin "as a matter of urgency" (as well as planning for "the orderly evacuation of Berlin"), and war plans adjusted to reflect the diversion of MATS aircraft to Berlin.[51]

Wedemeyer was even more pessimistic. He thought the Western powers must use "all resources . . . short of war" to stay "until and unless our position becomes untenable." At that point, they should withdraw, and he put his staff to work preparing arguments against going to war. Planners advanced several contentions: the airlift could not break the blockade, the American people would not support war for Berlin, and the consequences of withdrawal could be localized. They recommended offsetting withdrawal by measures to assure the world of American determination to "stand fast on tenable (not untenable) lines."[52]

Not everyone shared the army's doubts about Clay's convoy. Marshall commented at the July 15 NSC meeting that his department "felt that *we must pave the way for any possible use of armed convoys* by showing that we have exhausted all other ways of solving the problem." Otherwise, the American people would not support the use of force *when* the time came. This approach, treating a convoy as a last resort, would guide the administration through the rest of the crisis. Forrestal also worried about the need to mobilize public support. "We are facing an October 15 deadline when we will have to face up to the hard decision whether to use convoys," he remarked. If the West intended to attempt a convoy, he and Royall urged, "we must start conditioning the American people." Lovett thought that "opinion seems to be firming up for the use of armed convoys." There seemed to be no alternative. The airlift was "an unsatisfactory expedient" that could not last past October, he commented. The Western powers were facing an autumn deadline, but the airlift gave them two months to find a solution. Thus, Marshall's strategy centered on new approaches to Moscow and obtaining UN sanction for enforcing Western rights.[53]

If war was inevitable, Marshall and his colleagues wanted to postpone it as long as they could and make it clear to their allies and the American public that everything possible had been done to settle the crisis. As Bohlen explained to Bonnet, the airlift bought time, "and during that time we had to use every possible means to bring an end to [the] blockade." That meant exploring intermediate steps. Washington's first impulse was referral to the United Nations, but the British had doubts about this course of action, and the publicity surrounding such a step seemed likely to harden Stalin's position. Bohlen endorsed the idea of private talks, provided the Western powers agreed, the blockade was lifted first, and the United States was resolved to pursue the issue "through to the end." Private talks would let the West convey "a very stern warning" and give the Russians an opportunity to back down.[54]

Cables from Douglas and Smith, as well as private discussions with John Foster Dulles, reinforced such second thoughts. From London, Douglas suggested on July 15 that the West take all measures necessary to uphold its rights, including a convoy. Two days later, he retreated slightly. Although, in the end, the West would probably face a choice between withdrawal and force, negotiations and an appeal to the United Nations remained possible intermediate steps that should be explored. From Moscow, Smith agreed with Murphy's notion that the Russians would not necessarily respond to "a little shooting" by going to war, although he pointed out that Murphy did not seem to realize that the American public would react with fury if American soldiers died under Russian guns. A convoy made sense only after "all other possibilities" had been exhausted and world public opinion had accepted the "rightness of our position."[55]

Four days after stressing the importance of public opinion to the NSC, Marshall called in Dulles, Dewey's foreign policy adviser. The administration would make decisions about Berlin that day, Marshall explained, and he wanted the views of an intelligent outsider before talking to the president. The Western powers would not leave Berlin, because concessions would encourage stepped-up Soviet pressure throughout Europe. These comments suggested a firm stance, yet Marshall confessed that "the question of what next step to take was difficult." Dulles argued against sending another note. It would be published, as the previous notes had been. Publicity would further commit Soviet prestige, which Dulles regarded as the Kremlin's principal motivation. As he saw the situation, the West's proper goal was to find a way for Moscow to back down while saving face. The secretary seemed impressed by Dulles's comments, and after an hour's conversation, he asked Dulles to go into the details with Bohlen, Kennan, and other key officials.

Dulles listened as Marshall's aides outlined the situation. Their starting point was the airlift's inadequacy. It could expand only by taking aircraft away from MATS, which, the group said, the army opposed. Expanded or not, weather would ground the airlift in October. They had to find a solution by then; otherwise, "we would . . . have to try large scale force." Dulles doubted that Berlin's loss would have the dire consequences his hosts took for granted. He endorsed peaceful steps to restore access and believed that force was irrelevant to the task before the Western powers, which was to create conditions that would allow Moscow to relax the blockade without embarrassment. Appeals to the United Nations were unlikely to yield results. At best, the international body "could give moral sanction to a large scale use of force which, however, is not what we want. We want peace, not a legal basis for war." The best approach, Dulles advised, was to offer a foreign ministers' meeting to discuss Berlin and Germany, without making an end to the blockade a precondition. At the same time, the Western governments should let the Russians know that they intended to send an unarmed truck convoy, "which could be stopped only by superior force." The West should also warn the Russians that forcible interference with the convoy would be referred to the United Nations. Dulles did not envisage any use of force; he intended the convoy to be a probe to see whether the Soviets would "block us by deed as distinct from word." He expected that Sokolovsky's "technical difficulties" would disappear before the trucks rolled. Blissfully unaware of LeMay's plans, he assumed there would be time to appeal to the Security Council or arbitration if things went wrong.[56]

This was a different approach from Clay's, yet it ran the same risks. At best, it promised a repeat of Clay's trains of April 1 and June 20; at worst, it would leave "peace at the mercy of a chance shot."[57] Dulles's focus on Soviet prestige led him to conclude that Stalin was entangled in a confrontation he wished to escape. But if that were so, the Soviet leader could have announced at any time that repairs to the autobahn and rail lines were complete. He did not need an elaborate Western charade as cover. Dulles had not "clearly thought the matter through."[58] He simply wished away the problem's core by coming up with a superficial answer—prestige—to the question of why the Soviets had begun and continued the blockade.

Dulles did help. The administration had resolved to keep Clay on a tight leash, and Dulles strengthened that determination. He tempered the State Department's enthusiasm for an appeal to the United Nations and encouraged the administration to think about behind-the-scenes approaches to Stalin and Molotov. In short, he strengthened the administration's interest in pursuing step-by-step, incremental efforts and helped delay a showdown. Dulles had no immediate effect, however, because Marshall had to leave for the White House before talking with him again.

Marshall, Forrestal, and the president met for half an hour to discuss Berlin. The secretary of state thought the United States faced two alternatives—firmness in Berlin, or the collapse of U.S. policy in Europe. Retreat from Berlin would reverse recent momentum in the West's favor, such as the Italian elections and Tito's defection. Forrestal countered Marshall's optimism with a discouraging assessment of the military balance. If firmness led to war, Western forces could not withstand a Soviet attack. Although Forrestal was saying what Truman himself had emphasized to Admiral Leahy on June 30, Truman derided his attempt to highlight the dangers. "Jim wants to hedge," he complained that night in his diary; "he always does." Forrestal recorded that Truman ended the meeting by hedging himself. The president accepted Marshall's policy: the United States would stay in Berlin "until all diplomatic means have been exhausted in order to come to some accommodation to avoid war." As W. Phillips Davison noted long ago, this was not necessarily a strong stand. Nor was it a clear one: was the president's ultimate goal remaining in Berlin, reaching an accommodation, or avoiding war? Truman, characteristically exaggerating his own decisiveness, recorded in his diary a more steadfast statement: "We'll stay in Berlin—come what may."[59]

Marshall's comments to Dulles that morning notwithstanding, this hardly seems like a dramatic crossroads of policy. Neither the Department of State nor the Pentagon had developed specific courses of action and presented them to the president. The sole step endorsed by Truman was renewed diplomacy. No one asked for an open-ended commitment to maintain an American presence in the city even if it meant war, and it is unlikely that Truman gave one. No one settled on a strategy for resolving the crisis. Ends had been articulated, not means.

Marshall understood his president to be speaking in strong terms. He cabled ambassadors that evening that the United States was determined to maintain its position, taking "all measures necessary." The secretary added that "because we are firm in our determination to carry this matter through to the end," the Western powers would explore every possible peaceful solution—specifically, a three-power approach to Stalin.[60]

A second meeting with the president followed, including Forrestal, Royall, Lovett, and Draper. Draper was honoring a request from Averell Harriman, the Marshall Plan representative in Paris, to deliver his personal recommendations to the president. Truman may have regarded Harriman's request as presumptuous. He listened impatiently to Draper's report and dismissed it in his diary as a "rehash of what I know already." Harriman maintained that the Western powers must soon reach an "absolute determination to stay in Berlin"—short of war. Truman snapped that he had already decided to stay, "even at the risk of war." Harriman thought it essential that the president speak to Congress; Truman would show his statesmanship by taking hold of the crisis, Harriman advised, implying that Truman had not yet done so. The president rejected the idea of a speech, fearing it might "unnecessarily disturb the present delicate international situation." Truman liked Harriman's third point—a suggestion that any approach to Moscow be made through

Stalin—but he failed to reveal that he had approved such a demarche half an hour earlier. Harriman's last idea, that the president decide whether the United States would use the atomic bomb in war, met stony silence. Harriman believed "there may not be time to go through the painful process of decision" once war began, so decisions should be made now. If the bomb was to be used, "all details . . . should be worked out and made ready for immediate execution." The president could have turned aside this suggestion by referring to his meeting with Lilienthal and Forrestal, on his schedule for two days hence, or to the NSC study that Royall had requested; instead, he said nothing at all.

Draper's record thus suggests that the president avoided the difficult issues raised by Harriman's unbidden and unwelcome advice. If Truman was willing to run risks, he said nothing about the degree of risk. As in April, he considered the crisis too delicate for him to address Congress or the nation. He avoided any discussion of the bomb. Truman saw the situation differently, or at least he conveyed that impression in his diary. "I don't pass the buck or alibi out of decisions I make," he wrote.[61]

Despite the tough talk in the pages of his diary, Truman again left it to Marshall to explain U.S. policy to the world. The secretary issued a statement on July 21 outlining the position he had presented to the NSC. "We will not be coerced or intimidated," the release vowed. "At the same time we will . . . invoke every possible resource of negotiation and diplomatic procedure to reach an acceptable solution to avoid the tragedy of war for the world. But I repeat again, we are not going to be coerced."[62]

Lovett elaborated the policy in off-the-record talks with the diplomatic corps and the press. Principles were at stake. The blockade was violence directed against former allies and could not be permitted to succeed. The Western powers realized that "appeasement would get them nowhere"; firmness was the only way to peace. Yet firmness did not mean bringing matters to a head. If fighting began, responsibility must rest with the Russians, and Lovett doubted they wanted war. The airlift provided two months to find a solution. The next steps would be diplomatic ones, perhaps high-level exchanges with Stalin. "It was of the greatest importance to exercise restraint" and avoid hysteria, Lovett told reporters, dismissing calls for an armed convoy as "wild talk." He thought the Soviets were on the defensive and might gradually ease the blockade. Berliners' stout resistance and the speed and efficiency with which the West had organized the airlift had surprised the Soviets, while signs of unrest in eastern Europe distracted them. Soviet leaders had not told the Russian people about the crisis, Lovett observed, and their reliance on "technical difficulties" left them a way out.[63]

Policy had a political dimension. Lovett remarked to Sir John Balfour of the British embassy that the administration had to take a "thoroughly firm" line toward the Russians "to retain bipartisan support." He mentioned to reporters a "startlingly revealing" Gallup poll indicating that 92 percent of the American people supported the Western refusal to leave Berlin. The poll actually indicated more. When asked whether the West should use force if necessary to stay, 86 percent of the respondents said yes, 8 percent said no, and 7 percent had no opinion. That could have been interpreted as support for a convoy, but the administration did not believe the poll. Marshall and Lovett in particular thought the public did not grasp the seriousness of the situation; Americans endorsed a firm stance because they expected it to induce Moscow to back down. The two men recalled too well the public's euphoria during the Smith-Molotov affair, and they doubted the American people would, in the end, support a war for Berlin. Instead, their analysis of press commentary mirrored the administration's own ambivalence: a refusal to submit to coercion balanced by a desire to explore every chance to achieve a peaceful settlement. The British embassy, anxiously taking the public's pulse, reached similar conclusions. Although it noted "virtually no disposition to withdraw," it sensed none to force the issue.[64]

Truman, Marshall, and Lovett had chosen a diplomatic strategy; the joint chiefs were trying to devise a military one. They rewrote a pessimistic report by the joint strategic survey committee because its preference for withdrawal was too direct a challenge to Truman's desire to stand firm.[65] The chiefs endorsed expanding the airlift "to the greatest possible extent" to meet Berlin's "minimum requirements." They acknowledged that this crippled MATS's "essential" support if war broke out, but it provided "a cushion of time" in which "some other solution" might be found. They were, in other words, willing to put wartime strategy in jeopardy in the hope that war could be avoided. This shift reflected more optimistic assessments of the airlift from Clay and the air force, as well as a desire to stay in step with the president.[66] Even so, keen awareness of the West's unpreparedness for war left the chiefs uneasy about Truman's apparent determination to keep American forces in Berlin. Though unwilling to endorse their subordinates' call for evacuation, they were reluctant to exclude it. They maintained:

> Some justification might be found for withdrawal of our occupation forces from Berlin without undue loss of prestige. Although this is contrary to the assumption as to maintaining our position in Berlin . . . the possibility remains that reasonable justification, such as humanitarian consideration for the population of the Western sectors of Berlin, might develop. Therefore, subject to unalterable decision that withdrawal in no circumstances will be undertaken unless forced by war action, the withdrawal possibility should at least be borne in mind. The development of plans for such a solution appears desirable, as neither air transport nor armed convoy in themselves offer a long-range solution to the problem.

As the JCS interpreted American policy, no "unalterable decisions" had been made, and their memo closed with a request that one be made at once. They avoided an explicit statement as to what that decision should be, yet one could read between the lines. Given that an airlift "cannot . . . be regarded as a permanent solution" and a convoy involved "major war risk," withdrawal was the only peaceful option. Continuing the existing policy of staying put would sooner or later require that Berlin be supplied "by force." "Full-out preparations" for war should begin "immediately," in that case, because the time available might be "less than needed."[67]

Whether the chiefs' views influenced policy is a matter of dispute. Their official historian says no, based on the formal record: this memo did not reach the NSC until four days after it met on July 22. Nor is there any indication in the summary of that meeting, sent to the Oval Office the next day, that the chiefs informed the NSC of their position. Still, Murphy claims in his memoirs that their opposition to a convoy was decisive. When he and Clay arrived in Washington on July 21, they learned from Marshall and "friends at the Pentagon" that it was pointless to press their case. Truman did not want to do anything that the voters might consider rash. He would order a convoy if the JCS would agree, but they would not. Marshall, an old soldier himself, gave undue weight to the military's point of view, Murphy complained.[68]

One might question Murphy's assessment of the chiefs' influence. Truman and Marshall had already ruled out precipitate steps on July 19, before the chiefs stated their position. Although it may be logical to assume that Marshall and Lovett relied on friends in the Pentagon to stay in touch with military opinion—especially in the army, where opposition to Clay was strongest—there is nothing to confirm that they did. In fact, there is evidence that consultation within the administration left much to be desired, despite the creation of an interagency Berlin group under Bohlen. For example, on July 19, Lovett told Dulles that the army opposed an expanded airlift, even though Bradley had endorsed one just two days before.[69] Notwithstanding this weak coordination, civilian and military leaders reached the same conclusion independently: the convoy was not necessary now. If it ever made sense, it would be the last step, not the next one.

The July 22 NSC meeting in the Cabinet Room of the White House thus did not weigh fundamental choices, although it gave officials an opportunity to talk with Clay and Murphy. The agenda called for a review and assessment of the crisis, from the effects of withdrawal, the possibilities of continued negotiation, and supplying the city by air or convoy to evacuation. Both Truman and the joint chiefs attended, which was unusual.[70]

Taking up the first agenda item, Clay contended that withdrawal meant "the loss of our position in Europe." The British, French, and Berliners were firm; the United States must stand with them. "We should be prepared to go to any lengths to find a peaceful solution . . . but should be determined to remain in Berlin," the general continued. He then turned to the airlift and Berlin's needs. The current effort had reached 2,400 to 2,500 tons a day, which was enough to provide food but not food and coal; that would require seventy-five more C-54s. Raising the lift to 4,500 tons a day, enough to build reserves against winter, would take even more.[71]

Clay's summary gave General Vandenberg an opening. The same day Whitney had told the NSC the airlift was doomed, Vandenberg had asked MATS what tonnage could be flown into Berlin during the winter, assuming the entire command was committed and a third airfield was available there. The answer was 3,000 tons a day.[72] A few days later, the air force director of plans and operations, Major General Samuel E. Anderson, instructed his staff to plan an Anglo American lift of 4,000 tons a day. Officers were to determine how many C-54s, pilots, and support troops would be needed, as well as what airfield improvements and expansions were necessary. A plan was required, the general remarked, because national leaders would almost certainly order a dramatic expansion of the airlift.[73] When Vandenberg put the airlift on the NSC's agenda on July 21, he told Draper that the air force wanted to know "if it is . . . national policy to continue the airlift as a matter of priority for an indefinite period . . . throughout the winter if necessary, and if so at what tonnage level." The air force would need more money, planes, and equipment, not to mention a maintenance depot in Britain and another airfield in Berlin, to support such an effort.[74] The air staff had begun working out the details, and Vandenberg now summarized them. Sending fifty C-54s (Clay's July 10 request) was uneconomical. If the airlift was going to last a long time, Vandenberg declared, the air force preferred "we go in wholeheartedly. If we do, Berlin can be supplied." He pressed for a prompt decision, so the new airfield could be ready before winter.

Marshall reiterated his worry about losing planes to Soviet attack. Vandenberg acknowledged the risk. If war broke out and the Soviets destroyed the transports in Germany, the United States would be hard-pressed to supply its overseas forces and defend outlying bases. The air-atomic offensive might be delayed for months. Clay predicted the Russians would not interfere with the airlift "unless they mean to go to war," and, answering a question from the president, he doubted they meant to do that.

Clay then turned to convoys, offering a halfhearted defense of the idea. He had told Forrestal over dinner the night before that a convoy would have reached Berlin "without difficulty" three weeks earlier. Now he acknowledged that convoys "might lead to war" and therefore should not be attempted "until all other ways have been tried and failed." The British would accept a convoy as a last resort; the French, probably not. If convoys reached Berlin, successive ones would not need to be as heavily armed. In the end, Clay confessed, "we might have to put troops along the corridor." He then declared, "If we move out of Berlin we have lost everything we are fighting for." Truman echoed this view.

Marshall asked about the Ruhr, and Truman and Leahy left to attend a budget meeting. Marshall focused the discussion, which continued for another forty-five minutes, on constructing the third airfield in Berlin. He thought it would have a "good psychological effect," showing that the West was "earnest about staying." The group agreed that work should start at once. The next issue was reinforcing the airlift. Vandenberg said this could be done without disrupting vital peacetime routes. Ignoring Vandenberg's earlier suggestion of a maximum effort, the council decided to add seventy-five C-54s to the fifty now in Germany. More might be sent later, depending on results of the diplomatic approach to Moscow.

Marshall and Lovett outlined the next diplomatic steps. As he had done the week before, Marshall explained that "the major consideration under study by State is to lay the ground for any eventual action we may have to take." Each step also had to be guided by probable reactions in Europe and at home, the latter being "extremely complicated by an election year." The West had to be able to "come before the United Nations with the cleanest possible case so that we will get majority approval here and abroad for our future course."

Lovett repeated the main points of his off-the-record press talks. The West must avoid hysteria, exhaust all peaceful means, and not let itself be "kicked out of Berlin." He outlined "our time schedule" in the same terms as the week before. He began by "working back from a deadline of the first of October. This means that by the 15th of September we must decide whether we are prepared to go ahead regardless of the consequences. By the first of September we must, therefore, convene a special session of the UN General Assembly. To do this we must refer the matter up to the UN Security Council during the first week in August. Therefore, by the first of August we must have completed our initial feeling out maneuvers." When Symington asked about "a decision to increase the air lift to the maximum," Lovett answered that the situation would be clearer in perhaps two weeks; then the Western powers could decide "whether to throw in our whole air lift." With that, the council agreed that Clay could hold a press conference, and it adjourned.[75]

Historians have exaggerated the importance of this meeting in the evolution of American policy toward Berlin. The meeting was not the open forum for debating alternatives that it appeared to be. The president had settled the issue on July 19 by reaffirming the position Marshall had outlined at the NSC four days earlier. There would be no immediate withdrawal from Berlin and no "extreme" or provocative steps, at least for the time being. Thus the president had ruled against Clay before the general even arrived in Washington. The July 22 NSC meeting was held because Royall, contrary to the president's wishes, had summoned Clay home. The meeting gave Clay and Murphy a chance to say their piece—a chance they let pass, knowing it was futile. Indeed, it was. Bohlen cabled Douglas later that day and noted that the two men's reports had done nothing to shake the conviction in Washington that there was "no real need to take hasty action as to the next step."[76]

Though Clay was not given the green light for his convoy, one had not been ruled out. Officials regarded it as a long-term possibility—not the next step, but perhaps the last one. Planning continued. Six days after the NSC meeting, Forrestal asked Marshall to discuss tripartite convoy plans with the British and French. Marshall tossed the ball back to the Pentagon. When approached, the British chiefs of staff would not agree "under any conditions" to plan, much less conduct, such an operation. Under instructions from Washington, Clay continued unilateral planning for a tripartite convoy, without telling Robertson or Koenig. Royall would raise the subject again as late as March 1949.[77]

The NSC thus did not rule out Clay's convoy once and for all and commit the United States to a policy of defeating the blockade by airlift, as Truman suggested in his memoirs. The president did not override a reluctant General Vandenberg and order an increased airlift because the alternative was a war-triggering convoy. Vandenberg was ready to "go in wholeheartedly"; the points he raised were problems to be solved, not objections. By the time the council decided to send more planes, Truman had left the room. He used his memoirs, released in the mid-1950s, to bolster his reputation as a decisive leader and staunch anticommunist.

The council did not select an airlift strategy. Although it agreed to send seventy-five C-54s, LeMay had asked for eighty-five. Nor did it commit the nation to an all-out effort. Vandenberg and Symington had made that suggestion and been ignored. Lovett thought that decision should come later. This stance was perhaps a compromise to limit the effects on wartime capabilities or a recognition that an immediate all-out effort was, as Vandenberg himself had pointed out, impractical until new airfields and depots were ready; or perhaps it reflected a sense that diplomacy might make a maximum effort unnecessary. Whatever it was, it cannot be characterized as a decision to rely on the airlift to defeat the blockade.

No one could have left the meeting with a sense that a solution had been found, that long-term options had been weighed and one chosen. As in June, Truman and his advisers were feeling their way, making incremental decisions. Before the day was over, Lovett began to grasp the implications of the air force's new position; at the meeting, he had preferred not to improvise and abandon the position he and Marshall had worked out beforehand.[78]

The nation's leaders did not commit themselves on July 22 to an airlift strategy they thought would break the blockade; they did not resolve the fundamental dilemma facing them. One analysis of this meeting, cast in terms of the three courses of action discussed in Royall's office on June 27 (withdraw, stay even if it meant war, or postpone a choice between these alternatives), concludes that the NSC chose the second one, "the only viable alternative, given Truman's belief system."[79] At first glance, evidence supports this interpretation. The short record of the council's actions indicates that the group agreed to remain in Berlin "in any event"; Bohlen recalled Truman's "absolute determination" to stay; and Leahy thought the president would not yield until the Soviets attacked Western forces or supply lines—in other words, until war broke out. Terrified, Wedemeyer warned the British that Clay had urged the council to go to war "now rather than later" and that the president's "strong inclination" had been to agree.[80]

As in June, the administration pursued the third option. It dealt with immediate questions: whether to authorize a convoy and whether to send more planes. It set aside broader issues. As Wedemeyer told the British, "No definite decisions were made." On July 22, Truman and the NSC did not have to choose between the stark alternatives historians claim confronted them. That was the fundamental attraction of the airlift. By expanding the airlift, the NSC could postpone the choice between war and withdrawal for as long as possible. Truman as he is usually depicted would have rejected this strategy of delay; the real-life Truman found it irresistible. Like presidents before and since, he would take matters one day at a time and hope for the breaks.

CHAPTER 7

The Moscow Discussions

The Western powers had not adopted an airlift strategy in July, and they did not adopt one in August. Although the British and Americans expanded the airlift, doubt remained that it could sustain the city once bad weather set in. The Western powers relied on negotiation, not airlift, and hopes for a diplomatic breakthrough rose and fell. By the end of August, the two sides had agreed on the outline of an accord and directed the military governors to work out the details. Then it all collapsed.

THE U.S. AIR FORCE REACTED quickly to the decision to expand the airlift. On July 23, General Vandenberg directed MATS to send nine squadrons (81 aircraft and 243 crews) and a headquarters to Germany. If orders flowed quickly, implementation took longer. Vandenberg ordered two squadrons to go at once; the remainder would follow in pairs at seven-day intervals.[1] Even this measured pace compounded the crowding at west German airfields. There were too few bases and not enough pilots, few spare parts and even fewer mechanics to install them. Available men and materials were not put to their best use: cargo loading was haphazard, flying discipline was erratic, and unloading in Berlin was plagued by long delays. Pilots flew twice the number of hours allowed, and desk officers dashed to the flight line for a jaunt to Berlin in whatever airplane happened to be available.[2]

Commanders saw such confusion as unavoidable; by the time it could be corrected, the airlift would be over. Major General William Tunner disagreed. Commander of the Hump airlift during the war and now MATS deputy commander for operations, Tunner had the expertise—and the persistence—to ensure a hearing. Still, it was a struggle, because Tunner's ideas contradicted air force dogma. Since the days of Billy Mitchell, the air force had equated airpower with strategic bombing. Tunner thought transport mattered more than bombardment: the airplane's ability to move people and equipment great distances overnight had revolutionized warfare. Unable to remain on the sidelines, he made a nuisance of himself until he secured appointment as commander of the new airlift headquarters in Germany. He arrived in Wiesbaden on July 29.[3]

Tunner reported to LeMay, who wasted no time on pleasantries or even discussion. "I expect you to produce," he told Tunner. "I intend to," Tunner shot back. He began organizing his headquarters in a rundown apartment house.[4] One of the first tasks was to define the mission and determine how many planes were needed to achieve it. Sometime during Tunner's first week, LeMay called Tunner's chief of staff, Colonel Theodore R. ("Ross") Milton, into his office, handed him a slide rule and a pad, and ordered him to produce the answer. It was all quite casual; Turkish officers dropped by for a chat with LeMay while Milton worked in a corner, the fate of 2 million people resting on his slide rule. Tossing in "some weather factors and various other guesses," he came up with a number: 225 C-54s. Would Washington act on his estimate? That was hardly likely, because it would mean committing its entire air cargo fleet. Furthermore, LeMay had informed Washington that the most he could operate, given the weather and Tempelhof's capacity, was 139 Skymasters.[5]

Tunner believed he had grasped the situation after a few days. He wrote to the MATS commander, Major General Laurence S. Kuter, that "the key to the whole problem is big airplanes and lots of them." Echoing LeMay, he recommended replacing all C-47s with C-54s. Three days later, he reported, "The whole problem is pretty well reducible to certain essential denominators." He singled out three: reducing turnaround time in Berlin, moving C-54s to the British zone, and creating a single Anglo-American airlift command.[6]

Steeped in Frederick Taylor's theories of scientific management, Tunner regarded the derring-do of the stereotypical aviator as the source of the airlift's problems. Reporters might gush about pilots working until they dropped or staff officers taking the afternoon off to fly coal to Berlin, but to Tunner, these were signs of ineptitude and inevitable failure.[7] He seemed to believe that LeMay and Smith had chosen such techniques—dismissing them as "bomber generals" who did not understand airlift—when in truth, they had been driven by necessity. Facing unprecedented demands, they had done what they could with inadequate resources. Tunner had the advantage of building on what they had accomplished. He brought to the task a belief in regimentation and attention to detail. Motion-study engineers analyzed every aspect of the airlift, from the army's gathering of supplies in western Germany to their distribution in Berlin, and once these experts found the most efficient way, Tunner imposed it everywhere. If the airlift's goals were humanitarian, his methods were ruthlessly mechanical. He hoped to produce a "steady, even rhythm with hundreds of airplanes doing exactly the same thing every hour, day and night, at the same persistent beat."[8]

Tunner tackled the first of the three bottlenecks, the long turnaround at

Tempelhof, which he called "*the* most vital factor."[9] On average, planes took off from Berlin seventy-five minutes after landing, even though it took less than twenty minutes to unload them. Crews had to obtain clearance and weather information for their return flights, and then they adjourned to a snack bar. Tunner changed that procedure on his third day. He ordered pilots to stay with their planes. An operations officer would bring them their clearances, followed by a weather officer; then a jeep would pull up, equipped as a snack bar. Turnaround dropped to thirty minutes.[10] Nothing was too small to escape his attention. On August 9, Tunner directed that crews leave planes by a forward hatch so as not to interfere with unloading. Pilots were instructed to ensure that the cargo door was open by the time the plane parked. Loading cargo for shipment out of Berlin (which airlifters called "backloading") delayed departures, so Tunner restricted it to daylight and used C-47s to avoid delaying the large-payload C-54s. Loading crews in Berlin put awkward freight in aircraft that needed minor repairs because those planes would be delayed anyway. Color-coded panels told ground crews whether returning planes needed fuel or oil, whether they were empty or carried cargo.[11]

Haste sometimes made waste. One crew slammed the doors and taxied out to the end of the runway at Rhein-Main with the loading crew on board. (In another version of this story, a plane actually took off from Tempelhof with the unloading crew aboard.) Late that summer, an American diplomat's plane landed at Wiesbaden to refuel, and when he and the crew returned half an hour later, they found their C-47 loaded with three tons of flour.[12]

The effort to save time produced one of Tunner's best-known changes: the ban on "stacking" planes in bad weather. If a plane missed its approach into Berlin, it did not circle and try again. That would delay the aircraft behind it. Instead, it flew out the central corridor and started over. The change resulted from one of the airlift's most famous episodes, Black Friday, the thirteenth of August. The weather that day was bad. Radar could not penetrate the rain that swept Tempelhof, and controllers in the tower could not see the runway. A C-54 overshot the strip of pierced-steel planking and crashed, "exploding into a fireball as the crew scrambled clear." The next Skymaster landed long and braked so hard it blew two tires. Another dropped out of the clouds onto the concrete runway, which was still under construction, and ground-looped, damaging its landing gear and a wing. Controllers started stacking planes. Soon two dozen were circling in thick clouds, with more arriving. Controllers would not let unloaded C-54s take off because it would increase the risk of midair collisions. The airlift stumbled to a halt before Tunner's eyes because he was in the midst of the stack, on his way to a small ceremony touting how efficient Vittles had become. As he listened to radio calls from anxious pilots trying to find out what was going on, he could hear the airlift disintegrating around him. At that moment, he confessed, "I'd have snapped my grandmother's head off." He ordered all planes but his to return to the western zones, then landed at Tempelhof and set to work to ensure this never happened again. He banned stacks and pressed Washington to send him the best controllers it could find.[13]

The heart of Tunner's plan was rigid air traffic control. Each flight was prescribed in detail, and pilots who deviated learned why Tunner's nickname was "Willy the Whip." The traffic control center at Rhein-Main controlled all flights from Wiesbaden and Rhein-Main. Assigned to the task force, the center operated under Tunner's rules and gave priority to his planes. Each pilot knew the numbers of the three airplanes ahead of him and the two behind him, so he was aware of his exact location in the flow. Aircraft took off at precise times and flew a set pattern at fixed altitudes and speeds. Planes flew under instrument flight rules at all times. Tunner changed Smith's procedure of flying planes at five different altitudes, reducing it to three and eventually two, simplifying approaches and descents. The first way station for both American bases was the beacon at Darmstadt. Planes from Rhein-Main passed it at 900 feet, turned left, and began climbing to their assigned altitude. Planes from Wiesbaden passed Darmstadt above the Rhein-Main flow at 4,000 feet. The stream flew to Aschaffenburg, turning at the beacon for the Fulda range at the mouth of the south corridor. Each pilot listened to planes ahead as they reported the time they passed Fulda. If a pilot reached Fulda less than three minutes after the plane ahead of him, he slowed. If he took longer, he accelerated. Planes thus entered the corridor at three-minute intervals. This timing system was not Tunner's brainchild. Pilots had suggested it in a "gripe session."[14]

The planes went up the corridor, steering by dead reckoning. Forty minutes past Fulda, the pilot tuned his radio to the Tempelhof frequency. The controller guided the plane to the Tempelhof range, where it turned left and descended to 2,000 feet, en route to the Wedding beacon. From there, it turned onto the downwind leg and dropped another 500 feet. After two more turns, the pilot was lined up with the runway, six miles out. If the ceiling was over 400 feet and visibility was a mile or better, he would land. If the weather was worse, he would fly out the center corridor. All Berlin airfields changed their landing direction simultaneously to reduce the risk of midair collisions.[15]

Procedures in the northern corridor were similar, if more complicated. Eventually, planes from eight bases had to be integrated. The beacon at Dannenberg served the same purpose as the range at Fulda. At the other end of the corridor, the key landmark was the beacon at Frohnau. Planes were supposed to pass it within thirty seconds of their scheduled time. Unlike the Americans, British pilots in the corridor did not rely on dead reckoning, their planes being equipped with navigational aids such as Gee, Eureka, and Rebecca, which allowed them to pinpoint their location and adjust their speed. But it took time to install beacons. Until then, pilots could not guarantee they would arrive at a given point on time. Two South African pilots recalled that no one worried about timing in good weather. "It was generally possible to see at least two of the aircraft ahead, but when flying on instruments it came as something of a shock when the aircraft just ahead of you called up at . . . [Frohnau] and nearly took the words out of your mouth, while your peace of mind was in no way set at rest by the following aircraft calling up a few seconds later."[16] Another complication in the northern corridor was that it remained a two-way air lane, with traffic separated by altitude.[17]

Schedulers relied on the block system, even as its drawbacks became evident. Up to thirty planes might be lined up to take off, wasting time and fuel. Ground crews faced surges and slack periods. The four-hour cycle that was standard for much of the airlift in the northern corridor posed problems for the British. It had been calculated for the convenience of the American C-54s at Fassberg and Celle, because they lifted the most tonnage. Yorks and Dakotas usually took more than four hours for a round-trip. Having missed one block, planes sat idle until the next. Tunner would tinker with the block system into 1949.[18]

He also experimented with larger craft, C-74s and C-82s, but found they disrupted the rhythm he wanted, so he reserved them for specialized cargoes the Skymasters could not handle. A C-74 arrived at Rhein-Main on August 14 carrying eighteen precious C-54 engines. The huge plane flew 20 tons of flour to Gatow three days later. It returned to the States on September 21, having made twenty-five trips to Berlin and delivered 445.6 tons.[19]

Tunner's air traffic flow depended on good radio communications and modern navigational aids. USAFE and the units of the Airways and Air Communications Service (AACS) began expanding the network when the blockade began. On July 2, Berlin AACS requested the installation of a beacon at Braunschweig (Brunswick) to mark the western mouth of the central corridor; it went up the following day. The key Darmstadt and Frohnau beacons did not exist when the airlift began and were installed in August. As they expanded the airways network, communications units faced staggering demands for Teletype and telephone circuits to link offices and bases, and they struggled with shortages of equipment, parts, and experienced technicians. They installed direct "hot lines" for voice and data traffic, connecting airlift headquarters with its operating bases, and Teletype links to USAFE depots. Base telephone systems were manual; operators placed all calls. At one base, the average wait for an operator was four minutes.[20]

The volume of traffic was equally high in the corridors, where such communications delays were dangerous.[21] Both air forces found standard four-channel radios inadequate. The USAFE depot at Oberpfaffenhofen began installing eight-channel AN/ARC-3 radios as early as mid-August. Eventually, each C-54 carried two of them.[22]

Weight could be as important as time, so dehydrated food was used when possible. Flying ingredients often proved smarter than sending finished products. For example, airlifting bread was less efficient than sending the flour, yeast, and coal used to make it; furthermore, keeping Berlin's bakers at work slowed the rise in the city's unemployment rate. Replacing the ersatz coffee Berliners drank with real coffee saved the fuel used to make the substitute. Packaging was dead weight. Any spillage from lightweight paper bags, cloth sacks, or cardboard boxes was more than offset by the weight they saved. Cutting the aircraft's tare weight allowed heavier payloads. Tunner stripped his C-54s of unnecessary long-range navigation and communications gear. Planes flying below 10,000 feet did not need oxygen tanks; removing them saved another 500 pounds. Short round-trips to and from Berlin did not require full fuel tanks. Efforts to improve efficiency continued throughout the blockade: in May 1949, the Burtonwood depot boosted the payload of three C-54s by an average of 2,500 pounds.[23]

Tunner's second major initiative was opening Fassberg to C-54s. The base was in an ideal location, just west of the Soviet zone and near the entrances to the northern and central corridors. Shorter flying times to Berlin meant that each plane could make more trips each day. British Dakotas had moved in during July, but it made sense to station as many C-54s at Fassberg as possible. Smith and the British had sketched out this idea in July, and Tunner embraced it. "That operation would be about perfect for us," he advised Kuter. Americans began arriving on August 13. Three squadrons of C-54s followed, with the first flight into Berlin on the twenty-first.[24] The base worked under BAFO's operational control, with the RAF assigning it intervals and block times.[25]

Fassberg was unique: although it was a British base, an American was in overall command. At first, an RAF station commander and his administrative (base support) staff ran the base, while operations and maintenance were under American control. But dividing authority between two senior officers from different nations—neither one responsible to the other, and neither having a clear idea where his responsibilities ended—did not work. Tunner's solution was to transfer the American officer, bring in another, and put him in charge. It worked because of the personality and hard work of the new American commander, Colonel Theron ("Jack") Coulter.[26]

The base quickly proved its worth. It specialized in one cargo: coal. Analysts calculated that one C-54 at Fassberg did the work of 1.6 C-54s at Rhein-Main or Wiesbaden, and Tunner attributed a fleet-wide jump in utilization in September to the new base. In mid-July, Skymasters were averaging 1.9 trips and delivering 18.1 tons to Berlin each day; by September 9, the averages were 2.7 trips and 25.6 tons. The advantages were so apparent that the force at Fassberg, initially twenty-seven C-54s, eventually grew to over sixty.[27]

As popular as Fassberg was with commanders, GIs hated it. Surveys found that morale there was the lowest of any airlift base. Americans griped about meals, quarters, mail service, recreational facilities, shortages of tools, and lack of information about the operation and how long it might last. Food and living conditions sparked the most complaints. A visiting USAFE flight surgeon sympathized, criticizing the mess hall as "poor" and unsanitary. Two years later, his memories of Fassberg remained vivid: "When conditions were at their worst, such as at Fassberg in the winter," people lived in overcrowded rooms "similar to those found in concentration camps." Some took pleasure in writing the notorious "Fassberg Diary," an imaginary chronicle of bearded, ancient aviators who had been on continuous ninety-day temporary duty for over 230 years. When visited by a reporter, the aged fliers shanghaied him into service as the first replacement they had ever seen.[28]

Fassberg boosted tonnage so much that Tunner wanted two of them. He found the other at nearby Celle. Although Celle had been a Luftwaffe transport base, its runway could not support C-54s. A new one was ready December 15, and the first Skymaster lifted off for Berlin the next day. Engineers incorporated lessons learned at other bases, making Celle the airlift base with the best physical layout. Unlike Fassberg, the British remained in charge of base administration.[29] Like Fassberg, Celle was not a hit with the Americans stationed there, for many of the same reasons. Quarters were scarce and mediocre. Family separation was a significant issue, too. The three squadrons of the 317th Troop Carrier Group had left their families in Japan, and word soon reached them that General Douglas MacArthur wanted to evict their loved ones from government quarters because the unit was no longer part of his command.[30]

USAFE and BAFO struggled to cope with the influx of planes, pilots, and mechanics. "The number of C-54s . . . was increased to 160 before adequate support was available for more than 50," one after-action report commented. After Washington sent 225 Skymasters, "support was available for approximately 100."[31] USAFE reported that personnel shortages were "perhaps the most serious foreseeable problem." The command curtailed the transfer of officers on July 1 and the transfer of enlisted people on August 15 to retain the pilots and maintenance specialists Tunner needed. Communications units were 60 percent manned; civil engineers faced the loss of half their experienced people by year's end. USAFE estimated it needed 4,000 more people by October. Managing a rapidly expanding temporary-duty force was a challenge. Shorthanded itself, the USAFE personnel office did not know who had arrived or what their specialties were. Accountability was so poor on the British side that the RAF sent an officer from England to do a head count. In August, with no end to the blockade in sight, USAFE extended all temporary tours to 180 days.[32]

Oberpfaffenhofen struggled to perform the 200-hour inspections and overhauls of C-54s. (GIs, incidentally, struggled with the depot's name, calling it "Obie" or "Oberhuffinpuffin.") Work began on August 7 on an interim basis until the large wartime depot at Burtonwood reopened. Tunner set a goal of six C-54s a day for Obie. In August, the average was four, even though USAFE transferred 100 mechanics from Rhein-Main to help. Aircraft tended to arrive in groups rather than in a steady flow, causing congestion and delays. The amount of work each Skymaster needed varied, further disrupting the schedule. By late September, 450 mechanics were working at the depot, 395 of them on loan from airlift squadrons. Despite an erratic flow of spare parts, they completed 45 planes in August, 108 in September, 139 in October, and 96 in November, when Obie handed the job over to Burtonwood.[33]

Tunner made considerable progress in August. Deliveries for the month averaged just over 3,800 tons a day—a gratifying increase over July's 2,226, but well below Clay's target of 4,500. The airlift showed promise, but it could not be relied on to defeat Stalin, and it was costing the U.S. Treasury more than a quarter-million dollars a day. In Washington, Marshall briefed the National Security Council that the airlift had been more successful than expected, but "in many respects time was on the side of the Soviets."[34] A solution would have to be found through diplomacy.

AS LUCIUS CLAY'S PLANE droned eastward across the Atlantic on July 24, it carried an extra passenger. Charles Bohlen was on his way to Europe to draw up a new approach to the Soviets. After discussions with Smith, Clay, and Douglas in Berlin, he flew to London for talks with Bevin, Strang, and Massigli.[35] Bohlen expected a chilly welcome, because the Western governments were at odds. The Americans wanted an oral approach to Stalin. A note, they thought, would fall between two extremes: one that accurately reflected Western resolve would be so stiff that, as Inverchapel's successor, Oliver Franks, reported, it might trigger "that final crisis . . . they were so anxious to avoid"; one that failed to rebut Moscow's contentions would suggest irresolution. Publicity surrounding a note would further commit both sides' prestige. Instead, the Americans thought Smith should be empowered to speak to Stalin on behalf of all three nations.[36]

Bevin rejected this procedure. An oral presentation risked distortion, he thought, grumbling that "the Bedell-Smith–Molotov episode was not a happy precedent." British objections were not aimed at Smith personally; they went to the purpose and nature of the American proposal. The Americans seemed determined to meet Stalin "without any clear idea of what they hoped to achieve." They seemed no clearer about what would happen if the talks failed and the West appealed to the United Nations. What did they hope to achieve at the United Nations, and what would follow? Bevin suspected that Washington's fuzzy answers concealed a desire to bring the crisis to a head. Moscow might interpret a strong protest as an ultimatum, and approaching Stalin foreclosed discussions at lower levels, bringing a showdown nearer.[37] The foreign secretary therefore reserved his strongest fire for the approach to Stalin. Involving the Russian leader at this point would prematurely elevate the issue to the level of heads of state. It would restore Stalin's prestige, dented so badly in recent months by the Italians and Yugoslavs, and make him "the final arbiter of peace and war." Bevin also feared that bypassing Molotov would make the Soviet foreign minister even more difficult to deal with. Bevin's alternative was to send a note to Molotov.[38]

Tempers began to flare, as neither side budged. British-inspired leaks to the press fueled American frustration, while Strang complained that Washington's draft contained too many references to war. The disagreement led both sides to consider unilateral approaches to the Russians. Bevin's special Berlin committee reconvened on July 21 and would meet three times over the next week—more than it had in the last month.[39]

Bevin fulfilled Bohlen's worst expectations. Angry and petulant, he waved aside Douglas's contention that they should go to Stalin because otherwise the American public would not believe that all possible steps had been taken to settle the crisis. Bevin turned on Bohlen at one point and made an awkward attempt to joke about his deepest fears. "I know all of you Americans want a war," he said, "but I'm not going to let you 'ave it." He was not about to yield in Berlin, arguing, "If we left Berlin the Slavs would settle on the Rhine, and that would be the end of Western Europe. We must therefore hang on to Berlin at all costs." Yet he urged the Americans to consider the European viewpoint. "We were in the front line," Bevin pleaded, reminding Bohlen and Douglas that he and Bidault had no commitment from the United States if "trouble" broke out. The Washington "exploratory" talks on North Atlantic security offered Europeans scant reassurance, as it was becoming clear that the Americans would not assume binding obligations until after the November elections. What would the Americans do if talks with the Russians failed and the United Nations could not resolve the crisis? Economic sanctions and pressure elsewhere in the world would be ineffective, while an armed convoy risked "real trouble."[40]

At a cabinet meeting on July 26, Bevin contended that yielding to the Russians would lead to "further withdrawals . . . and in the end to war. On the other hand, if we maintained a firm attitude, we might reckon on ten years of peace during which the defences of Western Europe might be consolidated" before war broke out. Bevin's worries thus seemed to be more long term than immediate. Others were not so confident. When the foreign secretary professed optimism about the airlift's chances in the winter, the chiefs of staff entered a quick dissent. They doubted the operation, requiring "practically the whole of the transport resources of the Royal Air Force," could continue so long.[41]

Bevin reported the following day that he had reached a compromise, dropping his insistence on a note. Western representatives would seek talks with Stalin; in exchange, Bohlen agreed to approach Molotov first. The British ambassador, Sir Maurice Peterson, was ill, so Bevin's private secretary, Frank Roberts, would join Smith and the French ambassador, Yves Jean Joseph Chataigneau. They would ask Molotov to arrange a meeting with Stalin. The West was ready to discuss a "practical arrangement" to end the crisis if Stalin showed "a disposition to find a reasonable way out." If he remained obdurate, the West would refer the dispute to the United Nations.[42]

The British remained uneasy. Montgomery wrote to Bevin that it was too late to leave Berlin voluntarily; the choice was negotiate or fight. Tedder told the Berlin committee that putting Moscow on notice that coercion would not succeed, as the American drafts required, implied the Western powers' determination to "maintain their position in Berlin by force of arms" and "a readiness to go to war, if necessary." The Americans were insistent, however, and the "ministers felt therefore that the risk must be accepted." If the Moscow talks and the United Nations could not break the impasse, "a most serious situation would arise towards the end of September." In the meantime, the Americans had to step up to their responsibilities to "meet the situation" and give western Europe the assistance it needed.[43]

Bevin wrote to Attlee that the West could not retreat from Berlin, and it could not buy a settlement with concessions in western Germany. Because the Soviets would not lift the blockade "for anything less," the world faced a prolonged stalemate. The only course open to the Western powers was to "stick it out," make Stalin realize he could not prevail in Berlin without going to war, and keep the doors open for a Soviet change of heart. The foreign secretary's message to Massigli two days later was much the same. He thought the West would surmount "the present Berlin hurdle" because the Russians wanted war no more than the West did. The real trouble would begin once talks began, because any serious conversation with the Russians would show that the West was "not prepared to make any concession of substance." Therefore, Bevin expected the world would face an even more severe crisis in the spring, when talks reached their inevitable end. By then, the Europeans had to have firm treaty commitments and practical aid from the United States.[44]

Privately, Truman had doubts, too. Though he blithely assured a press conference that prospects for peace were "excellent," he confessed to his sister, "It's all so futile. . . . If I win [the election] I'll probably have a Russian war on my hands."[45] His military advisers were also taking precautions. Concerned that the B-29 group in Germany was vulnerable, they ordered it withdrawn. It returned to the United States, while another crossed the Atlantic to Britain. The U.S. Air Force commander there, Major General Leon W. Johnson, visited Germany in early August with the air force secretary and chief of staff. Symington startled Johnson by relaying Clay's prediction that the airlift "will not carry the load" and declaring, "We'll have to fight our way into Berlin by October." The secretary told Johnson "to go back to England and get ready to go to war."[46]

On July 30, the three Western emissaries requested a meeting with Molotov. But Molotov was "on vacation," and his deputy, Andrei Y. Vyshinsky, was away as well. Junior Deputy Foreign Minister Valerian A. Zorin, however, would be happy to receive them.[47] Zorin insisted on meeting each one separately, and Smith's session was frigid. The aide-mémoire Smith handed to Zorin reaffirmed Western rights while expressing a belief that a "frank discussion" among Stalin, Molotov, and the three Westerners might break the deadlock. Smith tried to arouse Zorin's curiosity by indicating that the talks would redefine and amplify the American position. (Roberts would offer similar bait a few hours later, suggesting a "progressive approach" through private conversations.) Smith asked for a meeting with Molotov to discuss Berlin and "its wider implications"; Zorin refused, citing his weary superior's need for rest, and he scorned the aide-mémoire as a vague repetition of old positions.[48]

One can imagine the impression this approach made in the Kremlin. The British, French, and Americans were ready to deal not only over Berlin but also over "its wider implications," which could only mean Germany. The West had taken two weeks to produce not an ultimatum but a call for informal secret talks that might destroy the London program and, through some face-saving formula, ease the West out of Berlin. Surely such possibilities could not be excluded; word began to circulate in European communist circles that a major triumph was around the corner.[49] Molotov decided he could forgo his much-needed vacation, and before another day had passed, Smith, Roberts, and Chataigneau were ushered into his office for separate appointments.

To Smith and Roberts, it seemed obvious that Molotov's purpose was to find out what the West would offer to escape from its predicament in Berlin. He hinted that the London decisions were the source of all recent difficulties and insisted that conversations on Berlin made sense only as part of conversations on Germany as a whole. Smith replied that the American position was on the record but indicated there was room for private maneuver. Roberts and Harrison, the minister at the Moscow embassy, left similar hints.[50]

The Western initiative intrigued the Soviets enough to draw Stalin into the discussion. This was an important sign, for as Philip Mosely once observed, the Soviet leader did not involve his personal prestige in negotiations unless he held a strong hand.[51] That certainly seemed to be the case now. According to the chief of the State Department's Office of Central European Affairs, Jacob Beam, the blockade was having a "cumulative effect"; it had closed nearly 900 factories and thrown some 17,000 workers onto the street. The currency situation was "unsettling" because the Soviet mark was "becoming the main currency." Berliners could not be expected to endure this "nearly intolerable situation." Unsure of the airlift and dubious of the city's residents, Beam felt the Western governments had few cards to play. Smith shared both anxieties. He had "serious doubts" about the airlift and was unsure Berliners could "stand the strain." He was under stress himself, reporting that since neither of his colleagues had had previous dealings with Stalin or Molotov, they relied on him for tactical guidance. He thus bore the burden of the talks, and all they portended, alone. "I am rather on my own here," he cabled forlornly in early August.[52]

Such were the circumstances surrounding the first conversation with Stalin at 9:00 P.M. on August 2. For much of the meeting, the two sides talked past each other. Smith opened by reaffirming Western rights in Berlin, while Stalin was eager to talk about Germany. The Soviet leader contended that the joint occupation of Berlin made sense only as long as Germany was treated as a unit, but, "as a result of the London Conference, a separate state had been created in western Germany." The West had therefore given up its legal right to be in Berlin. This did not mean, however, that the Soviet Union intended to force the Western powers from the city; "after all," Smith remembered Stalin saying, "we are still allies."[53]

The conversation continued along these lines for over two hours. Stalin said he thought the purpose of the meeting was to arrange discussions about Germany. He shrugged aside issues relating to Berlin as "insignificant"; "the only real issue" was creation of a separate regime in the western zones. Stalin seemed to regard Western preparations as leading to the prompt creation of a government claiming to represent all Germans, referring repeatedly to the London program as an effort to create a "government for Germany." The west Germans would meet September 1 and "set up a government," he said; after that, "there would be nothing to discuss." The West's narrow approach would not do, for Berlin and Germany were linked. According to Stalin, "There would have been no restrictions if it had not been for the London decisions." The blockade had been imposed to protect the Soviet zone from the effects of the London program, currency reform, and introduction of the B-mark. Did that mean, Smith asked, that the blockade could be lifted if the western mark was withdrawn from the city and talks on Germany were promised? No, Stalin countered, that was not enough; the London program must be delayed until the four powers met to discuss Germany. He had no wish to embarrass anyone, he said, suggesting that Western surrender of the London program be incorporated in an unpublished accord. His guests turned that idea aside. Stalin's formal proposal was that the B-mark be withdrawn and the blockade lifted simultaneously, but only if the London program were suspended while representatives of the occupying powers met to discuss a common program for Germany. Perhaps they would reach an agreement, Stalin mused, but if the West wanted negotiations, it must postpone the London program.[54]

Smith doubted his government would accept that proposal, and the discussion continued. Finally, the three Westerners took Molotov aside and told him they were getting nowhere. At that point, Smith was ready to give up; it was well after eleven. Stalin suddenly leaned back, lit a cigarette, and asked with a smile, "Would you like to settle the matter tonight?" Smith quickly replied that he would like nothing better. Stalin then amended his proposal. As before, there would be simultaneous removal of the western mark from Berlin and lifting of the blockade. The four powers would meet to discuss Germany, but instead of insisting on postponement of the London program as a precondition, Stalin simply wanted this recorded as the "insistent wish" of the Soviet Union. Chataigneau, Roberts, and Smith agreed to present the proposal to their governments.[55]

Meeting afterward in Smith's office, the three men were pleased with the evening's work. An immediate settlement seemed possible. Once the minor matter of the currency changeover was worked out, the blockade would be lifted. The West would be committed only to discuss German issues; if talks failed, the London program could continue. In a report to Marshall drafted the following morning, Smith remained confident. Stalin and Molotov were so eager for an agreement, he thought, that he might have missed the opportunity to win even further concessions. Yet Stalin's blandishments seem to have had an effect, for Smith suggested it might be wise to "suspend" parts of the London program if it could be done "without undue complications or loss of prestige." Merely the threat to create a west German regime, he argued, would restrain Moscow; once that regime was established, "we will have fired one of the last shots in our political locker." Roberts's private assessment for Bevin avoided such recommendations but took the same view of Soviet purposes. When Stalin passed up the opportunity to counter Smith's opening statement with an equally firm exposition of the Soviet view, he had sensed that the two Russians wanted an agreement. He acknowledged that Stalin's proposal "in fact settles nothing," leaving the "real problems" still ahead. Even so, Roberts saw as good portents Stalin's businesslike approach and his comment that fusion of three western zones constituted "progress." All that remained, it seemed, was to work out the details with Molotov.[56]

FROM HIS BERLIN VANTAGE POINT, Clay saw at once the danger in Stalin's proposal. What the Moscow negotiators viewed as the minor matter of a currency changeover could be disastrous if mishandled. Unless four-power control of currency and credit was guaranteed, the Soviets could use their mark to squeeze the Western powers out of Berlin—which, Michail Narinskii tells us, was indeed their intent. City leaders told Clay that without such protections, they would be at the mercy of the Soviets and the SED. On July 30, the Soviets had frozen the Magistrat's accounts in the city's central bank (located in the Soviet sector), as well as those of all western sector enterprises and organizations. Western help in meeting the city's payroll dealt with the immediate problem, but the Soviet action did not incline Clay to believe that the Russians would forgo using economic leverage for political purposes.[57]

Clay's concern extended beyond the city. He feared that Stalin's maneuver might divide the Western powers and weaken their resolve, as well as increase German uncertainty. Few Germans were enthusiastic about the London program, and any sign that the West was having second thoughts might lead them to reject it.[58]

Marshall's advisers were thinking along similar lines and incorporated their reservations in new instructions to Smith. Four-power control of Berlin's currency was essential to maintain the West's position in the city, and the powers could make no promises regarding the London program. In advancing these views, they expected little difficulty in winning Soviet agreement. Bohlen thought the currency matter was just a detail, advising Douglas that Stalin's points, once clarified, were "exactly what we hoped to obtain." Wedemeyer's staff began to work on position papers for a council of foreign ministers (CFM). So did Kennan's Policy Planning Staff. With a solution so close, it was no time for a slip, and secrecy was intense. Roberts apologized to the Canadians for his inability to go into detail, confessing that he and his colleagues were "very nervous of some leakage which would spoil everything." In Washington, Truman and Marshall warned the cabinet against doing or saying anything that might upset the "delicate negotiation with Russia." No one had forgotten the effects of the publicity surrounding Smith's meetings with Molotov in May.[59]

Whitehall reacted cautiously. An anonymous British diplomat told *Newsweek*, "When I hear that Uncle Joe is in an expansive, friendly mood, my heart sinks." Bevin admitted he was confused. He reminded Roberts that there were to be no negotiations under duress. He had several questions: How could the blockade be lifted and the currency transfer completed simultaneously? Wouldn't negotiations over currency have to occur first—that is, while the blockade continued? Or did Stalin mean that the currency dispute would be discussed at a CFM after the blockade was over? Would the currency be under effective quadripartite control, or have we "handed the whole currency of Berlin over to the Russians?"[60]

With their new instructions in hand, the three Westerners met Molotov on August 6. They presented a draft communiqué calling for an end to "all restrictions" on transportation and communications, detailing safeguards over use of the Soviet mark in Berlin, and promising four-power meetings to consider unresolved issues affecting Germany. Molotov rejected the document. His first comment was that it contained nothing about Stalin's "insistent wish," and he returned to that point again and again. Smith answered that no date had been set for a government in western Germany; the Germans would meet September 1 and begin studying the problem, and their work would take considerable time. In any case, their decisions "shall in [no] way preclude or contravene" agreements reached by the powers.

Molotov remained dissatisfied and, turning to the Western proposal on currency controls, denied that the West could have any power over Berlin's currency once the Soviet mark became the sole legal tender.[61]

With the initial sparring over, the Americans and British took stock. The CIA's opinion was that Moscow wanted a CFM to reduce tension and to trade concessions on Berlin for gains on other issues. The Kremlin's minimal terms were probably suspension of plans for a west German government, resumption of reparations, and "some voice" in the Ruhr. Accepting such terms meant "gambling that the cumulative effects of the ERP [European Recovery Program] and other [Western] measures" would outweigh the advantages the Russians would gain. Hillenkoetter thought that, "weighed against a continuation of our present dilemma," the gamble appeared "worthwhile."[62]

British assessments concentrated on Berlin and the matters at hand. Roberts and Harrison thought the Russians wanted four-power talks in the hope of disrupting the London program, although they judged that Moscow was not optimistic on this score and that its immediate aim was reducing the Western presence in Berlin to a "token affair" or expelling it altogether. Stalin and Molotov expected to use currency arrangements to accomplish this. With this shift in Soviet emphasis, the currency issue was "far more than a technical one," and the danger it posed to the West was even more serious than the blockade. After all, Harrison observed, the airlift "would be of no help in solving it." Bevin agreed that currency lay "at the very heart of our difference with the Russians." To help Roberts through the maze of technical details, he sent comments from the Treasury, the premise of which was that four-power control of Berlin's currency was a matter of principle. Control over issuing marks in Berlin had "limited practical value" without similar measures in the eastern zone, which the West did not claim, but letting the Russians monopolize control was to accept their thesis that Berlin was part of the Soviet zone. Robertson seconded these views in the strongest terms. "If we withdraw our currency . . . without any agreement on quadripartite control, we shall have lost Berlin and the air-lift will have been in vain."[63]

Stalin and Molotov were making their own reassessments. The Soviet leaders had confronted the West with a choice between the London program and an end to the blockade. On August 2, the three powers had seemed so eager to end the blockade that they were willing to remain in a Berlin under Soviet financial control and were irresolute about their plans for western Germany. Now they were demanding power over the Soviet mark and evading any commitment about Germany.

The Soviets dug in. Molotov's counterdraft, offered on August 9, proved to be far from the West's proposal on the three major issues—blockade restrictions, currency control, and the London program—establishing the framework for subsequent discussion. His proposal on the blockade was a retreat from Stalin's formula.

Whereas the Soviet dictator had spoken of lifting all restrictions, Molotov offered to end only those imposed after June 18, when the West had announced its currency reform. Earlier restrictions would remain, and under Molotov's plan, Western rights of access would rest on the "present agreement"—by implication, nullifying rights derived from earlier agreements. Because Molotov's paper did not set forth what those rights were, the Western diplomats suspected a trap. On the currency issue, Molotov wanted to entrust control of Berlin's currency to the Bank of Emission of the Soviet zone and rejected Smith's plea for quadripartite control. The West, he said, had ended four-power control of Germany through the London decisions; if it were resurrected nationwide, "it might also be restored in Berlin." On the London program, the Soviet draft noted that "consideration was given" to the Soviets' wish for delay. Worse, Molotov had transformed Smith's explanation that a government would emerge only after lengthy discussion into a bald statement that the Western governments "did not propose for the time being to deal with the question of the formation of a government for Western Germany." This, he claimed, merely summarized the earlier conversation.[64]

Clay called Molotov's terms "absolutely impossible . . . unthinkable . . . disastrous." He thought the West should demand immediate clarification from Stalin. If he retreated from his position of August 2, the West should go to the United Nations. Marshall was unwilling to go that far, although he did reject Molotov's paper. The secretary had not expected to end all traffic restrictions, for some controls were legitimate, but the June date implied acceptance of the Soviet view that the blockade had been defensive. Furthermore, many of the restrictions imposed between April and June were onerous. Marshall suggested the substitution of a date that implicated no one. And Molotov's reference to "the present agreement," with all its dangers, had to go.[65]

Marshall then turned to the Russian currency proposal. Perhaps the Soviets misunderstood the Western position. While the Western powers had no desire to interfere with the economy of the Soviet zone, they must share in control of the issue and circulation of the Soviet mark in Berlin. Like the British Treasury, Marshall was trying to make an impossible distinction, for power over the Soviet mark in the city inevitably included the ability to influence the Soviet zone. Western officials had to insist on joint regulation of the Soviet mark in the city, but they erred in believing that this need not affect Russian interests elsewhere; their careful but impossible distinction assumed an underlying compatibility of interests that did not exist. Finding common ground regarding the blockade and the London program was difficult enough; linking a settlement to resolution of the currency question made the crisis all but impossible to resolve.[66]

The British were convinced the Russians were up to their old tricks. Bevin thought they were behaving as they had over Iran in 1945: Stalin was affable, while

Molotov waited in the wings with impossible demands.[67] Roberts and Harrison would later comment that the Soviets began the discussions believing that the West wanted to avoid war and would let itself be maneuvered out of Berlin under some face-saving formula. Western refusal to yield on the London program called that calculation into question, so the Soviets stepped up pressure in the expectation that the West would withdraw rather than fight. There was another source of Soviet confidence: we can assume that Donald Maclean shared Western doubts about the airlift with his Soviet handlers, giving Moscow a unique advantage in these negotiations.[68]

As Bevin's optimism faded, he considered what to do next. He could not accept a deeply pessimistic report from Robertson arguing that the airlift was doomed. Deliveries were well below the levels needed to stockpile supplies for the winter, even measured against amounts that provided a bare minimum of existence. "The resistance of the people depends upon their faith in an ultimate favourable solution. As the weeks go by this faith will fail." Nor could the West do much to protect Berliners from strong-arm measures by the Russians and their henchmen. Under the circumstances, Robertson thought some compromise that protected four-power control in Berlin and led to a CFM was the best the West could obtain. His assessment of long-term prospects was so gloomy that Bevin forbade its circulation within Whitehall.[69]

Bevin once more looked to the airlift to buy time. He pressed the point when Symington and General Vandenberg visited London on August 9, and he urged it on Douglas. The next two months would be vital, he declared. If the Americans could boost deliveries to 7,000 or 8,000 tons a day, they might "save the world." He also thought the West should prepare a white paper to counter Soviet propaganda if the talks broke down, as well as continue preparations to refer the dispute to the United Nations.[70]

Royall and his staff were considering more drastic steps. Army planners were unsure which was worse: success in Moscow or failure. Success meant a foreign ministers' meeting. Wedemeyer's staff thought the Russians had everything to gain and nothing to lose at a CFM; the conference "might well be dangerous." The West must not make concessions that hampered western Europe's recovery. Royall declared that if the talks failed, the United States should consider giving the Russians fair warning before closing the Baltic and Dardanelles with mines and denying Soviet ships access to the Suez and Panama Canals. In late July, he had considered convoys a last resort; now he was prepared to tell Moscow that the West might send armed convoys to Berlin whenever it chose. Royall may not have wanted his ideas raised with the State Department, but he was serious. Clay received orders to plan such a convoy shortly thereafter.[71]

Smith and his colleagues presented their governments' objections to Molotov's plan on August 12 and offered new proposals of their own four days later. They rebuffed Molotov's proposal to lift only those restrictions imposed after June 18, so he thought it best to leave out any date, with the understanding that his government would remove restrictions imposed after the Western currency reform. None of the Westerners challenged this phrasing, which merely restated Molotov's earlier position, and the omission would haunt them later. Molotov was equally inflexible regarding currency controls, categorically rejecting quadripartite authority over the Soviet mark. His only suggestion was that the discussion be referred to Berlin—a position he had earlier rejected—but lacking an agreement on principles, this would have led nowhere. It was the first indication the Soviets were losing interest in resolving the crisis.[72]

Smith sensed this shift and expected Molotov to drag out the talks, extracting whatever concessions he could, while the Soviets in Berlin stepped up their pressure.[73] It was an accurate prediction, and during August, Soviet officials increased their harassment of the Magistrat, insisting on interminable meetings at odd hours, paying long visits to city offices, and making work impossible. City officials could not refuse the demands of an occupying power, especially when most city offices were located in the eastern sector. When the Magistrat suspended police president Paul Markgraf on July 26, the Soviets refused to recognize the firing of their handpicked functionary; he and officers loyal to him were the only police the Russians allowed to operate in east Berlin.[74] When policemen acting under the orders of the new police president, Dr. Johannes Stumm, entered the Soviet sector, Markgraf's men rounded them up. Within days, there were two police forces. The pattern repeated itself in other branches of government.

A virulent campaign of propaganda and coercion accompanied these measures. *Neues Deutschland*, the SED paper, reported that the noncommunist parties were planning to force the vanguard of the proletariat from the city assembly. It demanded that the existing "reactionary" Magistrat be replaced by a truly "democratic and progressive" administration. The SED tried to carry out this demand on August 26. As the assembly prepared to meet, about 6,000 SED supporters gathered outside city hall. Some forced their way inside. One SED delegate announced that he would demand replacement of the Magistrat by an "action committee." When city officials canceled the assembly session to avoid a repetition of the June 23 riot, the SED coup (if such it was) fizzled "like [a] defective firecracker," and the crowd went home. The SED had been unable to proclaim its "action committee" on the floor of the assembly that day, but Karl Maron of the SED warned that over the next few days, "decisive things must and will occur in Berlin." When the assembly tried to meet the following day, Magistrat employees locked the doors after the members arrived, only to have 2,000 SED supporters break through an iron gate and force open two doors. After the demonstrators swept in, the assembly speaker adjourned the meeting until September 3. Elsewhere in the city, a jeep full of Soviet soldiers careened along streets in the American sector, knocked over a U.S. military policeman who tried to stop them, and traded shots with other MPs before escaping into the Russian sector. Clay worried that the "unbelievably vicious and malignant" campaign against the Western powers and noncommunist politicians, as well as the petty harassment of Western citizens, would result in an incident the Soviets might exploit.[75]

Bohlen thought the negotiations had reached "the crucial phase." Both sides were sparring over details, when the core issue was Western rights in Berlin. He expected Molotov to continue insisting that the West had forfeited those rights, and the talks would deadlock. Smith wondered how long the West was "prepared to stick it out in Berlin under present conditions." Berliners were valiantly resisting, but "it may be another matter when they really get cold and hungry." The CIA's summary of the situation, prepared for an August 19 NSC meeting, took an equally pessimistic tone. Unless the Western powers achieved their goals in Moscow, their position in Berlin was "untenable in the long run." Failure would "bring the Western Powers closer to the ultimate choices that appear to face them there—resort to force or planned withdrawal."[76]

The NSC, with Truman presiding, did not grapple with these alternatives because Marshall's report on the situation was not so grim. It was too early to know how the talks would turn out, he thought; for the moment, they focused on "highly technical matters" that represented Soviet attempts to "transform the physical blockade into an economic blockade." His worries about American public opinion remained strong. If the talks broke down, "it might be difficult to explain to the American public that they had not broken down because of our insistence on technicalities, but . . . on issues of major importance." At the same time, "there were already signs of public restlessness at the apparent slowness at arriving at an agreement."[77]

The other important development Marshall discussed was the position of France. He did not say so, but this was a critical aspect of the crisis. Moscow had aimed squarely at the London program, and French reluctance to proceed with it was an open secret. The Soviets could win great advantage if France wavered. Rumors spread that this had already happened, but they were untrue. Marshall praised French support in Moscow as unstinting, and he noted that Bonnet had recently asked for closer military ties with Britain and the United States. There was no doubt that one French motive was to prevent unilateral acts by the United States that might drag France into war, but the French were determined not to leave Berlin under Soviet pressure, and they had given no sign that they were interested in taking the Soviet bait over the London program.[78]

Truman left the meeting just as Royall began a report on the airlift. Totals had reached 3,300 tons a day. Berlin had a twenty-five-day reserve of coal and a thirty-two-day supply of food, the latter being "slowly increased." The Magistrat was working "after a fashion." No solution to the currency dispute was likely. Abandoning the fire-eating rhetoric he had shared with his staff the week before, Royall now commented that the West would have to content itself with whatever negotiated solution "seemed to cause the least worry."[79]

With the talks in Moscow going poorly and the situation in Berlin becoming more precarious each day, the Western governments decided on a final appeal to Stalin. The mood was summed up by the caution of two of the military men involved. Marshall would not go to the White House because, he wrote to the president, his visit might be reported and encourage speculation. Meanwhile, the new American military attaché in Moscow, Major General John W. "Iron Mike" O'Daniel—a man, as his nickname suggested, not easily alarmed—spent August 22 cleaning out his files, "just in case."[80]

AFTER THE WRANGLES WITH MOLOTOV, Stalin appeared to be a genial host as he welcomed the three Western diplomats on August 23. Both sides offered new proposals, but again, the five-hour discussion dealt with the three now-familiar issues: the blockade, the London program, and Berlin's currency.

The negotiators quickly—too quickly, perhaps—disposed of the first. Molotov's refusal to lift restrictions imposed before June 18 worried Smith, who tried to move the Soviet foreign minister, who was present at the meeting, back to Stalin's original offer. Stalin offered a compromise, suggesting it would be better to say that "recently imposed" restrictions would end. If any had been imposed before June 18, they would be lifted too. The final draft composed that evening included Stalin's suggestion but omitted the crucial clarification.

The second issue, the London program, was harder to deal with, and the negotiators reached no agreement. Stalin continued to press for delay, trying to insert a statement into the communiqué that Western policy had been discussed "in an atmosphere of mutual understanding" and that a decision had been postponed until the foreign ministers met. In 1942, Molotov had secured Roosevelt's endorsement of similar wording about creating a second front that year, and ever since, the Kremlin had treated the "understanding" as a binding commitment and a broken promise. Roberts realized that western Europeans would conclude that there could be no "atmosphere of mutual understanding" unless the Russians had compelled the West to abandon the London program as their price for ending the blockade. With the Parliamentary Council meeting in Bonn just a week away, Stalin's innocent-sounding suggestion could destroy Western credibility in Germany. Vague statements, Roberts said suavely, were liable to misinterpretation. Stalin was not pleased.

The last issue, Berlin's currency, took up much of the discussion. Stalin proposed that the Soviet mark replace the B-mark the day the blockade was lifted. This changeover would be subject to procedures and safeguards worked out in advance by the military governors. He suggested that a four-power financial commission handle practical measures involved in introducing the Soviet mark, but when Smith insisted that all four powers have equal control, Stalin and Molotov revived their contention that the Western powers derived their rights in the city from its status as the capital of a united Germany—a status the West had undermined. Talk then turned to the commission's powers. Stalin said that the Soviet bank would regulate the flow of currency in the Soviet zone and in Berlin, but the Berlin commandants and the commission would supervise what the bank did in the city and prevent any abuse of its power. According to British and American accounts of the meeting, he was "quite categorical that this commission would be the controlling body and said he did not mind using the word control."[81]

As attention shifted to the wording of a draft directive to the military governors to work out detailed provisions along these lines, the three Western representatives forgot Stalin's discussion of the status of Berlin. Had they remembered it, they would have been struck by how poorly it accorded with the broad supervisory power Stalin seemed to be granting the commission. Suddenly, Stalin had accepted the Western legal position and more. He was proposing a quadripartite agency to control activity in Berlin by the Soviet zone's central bank. Given Stalin's denial of Western rights in west Berlin moments before, he surely had no intention of allowing that. The proposal—like Stalin's wording on the blockade—was meant to fool the Western emissaries into thinking that agreement was near.

Such deception was both a means of controlling risks and a bargaining tactic. With the issues narrowed, the talks would continue, sustaining Western hope for agreement and restraining the Americans from impetuous action. Because agreement on Soviet terms was impossible, Molotov intended to drag out the talks and put the onus for failure on the West. The commission plan was well suited for this purpose: it was an intricate but vague technical proposal that invited endless debate over minor points, none of which the West could elevate into a convincing casus belli. It was a shrewd diplomatic move, an apparent concession so vague that its substance could be quietly withdrawn or, better, interpreted out of existence—a task for which Molotov possessed formidable skills. The four-power commission was not dangerous because it would never meet, and while talks diverted the Western powers, the SED would step up its pressure.

If Smith and his colleagues overlooked the implications of Stalin's comments about Western rights, officials in Washington and London did not. Lovett feared the Soviets would substitute a "financial blockade" for the "present physical blockade," while Marshall complained that the latest Soviet proposals did not reaffirm quadripartite rule and Western rights in Berlin. He and Bevin wanted a clear statement that the West would not delay the London program.[82]

Smith thought Marshall was asking the impossible. Moscow would not acknowledge Western rights, and the unilateral Western statement the secretary desired would not bind the Soviets. Smith was ready to break off the talks over the issue of quadripartite control of Berlin, if that was what Marshall wanted, although he agreed with Bevin that the differences between the two sides were so small that the Western public would not understand Marshall's stance. Smith's view was that the Russians would make some concessions on currency controls and lift the blockade in exchange for withdrawal of the B-mark, because they thought that would give them the upper hand. Thus, the West faced a choice: break off the talks, which meant perpetual blockade and endless airlift, or make an agreement that lifted the blockade but left the West with only partial control over its sectors of the city.[83]

The three Westerners continued their search for agreement. On August 27, they offered a new paragraph on the London program that included both the Soviet desire that no west German government be formed before the foreign ministers could meet and the Western hope that the ministers would agree on Germany. The draft added, however, that the Western partners would not postpone the London program. Such clarity would not do, and Molotov demanded that it be deleted as "unnecessary." When Smith stood firm, Molotov refused to approve the communiqué.[84]

The Soviet diplomat proved more amenable in discussing the directive to the military governors. It provided that transport restrictions "recently" imposed would be lifted, in accordance with Stalin's formula, and Molotov confirmed that this included restrictions imposed before June 18. The directive also instructed the military governors to work out details of the changeover to the Soviet mark, outlining general procedures and safeguards in four lettered paragraphs. They would then report back to their governments, and final arrangements would be worked out. The next paragraph made the Soviet bank responsible for the "regulation of currency circulation." The one after that established a four-power financial commission "to control the practical implementation of the financial arrangements indicated above, involved in the introduction and continued circulation of a single currency in Berlin." This seemed to say that the commission had power over the bank, as Stalin had acknowledged, but when Smith tried to make the directive explicit on that point, Molotov balked, insisting that the directive was clear. He denounced the Westerners' minutes detailing Stalin's comments of seven days before, calling it a "new document" that he would not consider. While refusing to confirm Stalin's statement about the commission's power over the bank—he had not, he fumed, committed the generalissimo's words to memory—Molotov did confirm the thrust of Stalin's remarks.[85]

The ambiguity remained. The bank would regulate the introduction and circulation of the Soviet mark, and the commission would supervise the practical arrangements. Did the commission control the bank? As the discussion droned on, Molotov agreed that the commission's authority ran to the four lettered paragraphs. No one thought to ask whether the commission's control over the "financial arrangements indicated above" included the bank's operations, mentioned in the immediately preceding paragraph. No other reading seemed possible. Smith thought he had obtained confirmation of the Western interpretation of the directive. Once the military governors reported back, he and his colleagues would wrap up the remaining details with Molotov and announce the end of the blockade.[86]

Western leaders, suspicious before, were now euphoric. Bevin expected Sokolovsky to seek maximum advantage but believed that Stalin would not let the talks fail; the military governors would reach agreement quickly. American officials regarded this prospect with even greater satisfaction. In a few more days, the most dangerous confrontation since the war would be history—just in time for the November elections. The Democratic Party and White House staff mobilized to ensure that Truman, far behind in the polls, would derive maximum advantage. Clark Clifford ensured that the president would announce the news; otherwise, as George Elsey put it, he would be "lost on the public relations angle." With the president's approval, staff members polished up a short speech assuring Americans that the administration had skillfully avoided both global war and appeasement. A "long hard road" remained, Truman would say, and "our goal must be—not peace in our time—but peace for all time." Other preparations began in the Department of State. Kennan and his staff stepped up their work in anticipation of a CFM; Byrnes had already accepted Marshall's invitation to serve on the delegation. And in Berlin, rumors spread that coal trains were lined up at Helmstedt waiting for the barriers to be lifted.[87]

Optimism was not universal. Douglas commented that when the West decided to accept the Soviet mark, even under effective quadripartite control, "we implicitly reduced our status . . . to that of a junior partner." He had no doubt that serious trouble lay ahead.[88] Clay, whom Lovett described as being "drawn as tight as a steel spring," agreed. Throughout August he had hoped that the remnants of the talks would not be dumped in his lap; now he faced the prospect of complex, technical discussions under a directive that he regarded as a Western defeat. The United States, he undiplomatically reminded his superiors, had abandoned its own definition of the issue. Four-power control had not been restored in Berlin, and the Soviets had won a preferred position. In Clay's opinion, agreement based on the directive "will render our position difficult if not impossible." He repeated these views when the three Western military governors met to prepare for their sessions with Sokolovsky, and he gave his feelings freer rein in a note to a close adviser.

He had to devise some compromise, he wrote, because the Western governments would not confront the Soviet Union. "You and I both know what that means in loss of prestige alone." As a soldier, he continued, he must obey orders, but, he added, "I have never felt so discouraged and hopeless."[89]

Clay had every reason to be anxious, for he was right—the directive settled nothing. Cast in the form of an agreement, it was merely the framework for one. Crucial Soviet concessions on which hope for a settlement rested had not found their way into the text. As the Western governments interpreted this "Moscow agreement," the Soviet Union would lift all blockade measures imposed since March and agreed that the commission would control the Berlin operations of the Soviet bank. Yet the directive was silent on both points. The West thought it had achieved one agreement, embodied in the directive and based on assurances by Stalin and Molotov. The Soviets would soon claim that the West had agreed to a less advantageous settlement—the directive and nothing more.

CHAPTER 8

The September Crisis

September brought intensified crisis, not agreement, to Berlin. Sokolovsky dashed Western hopes by exploiting the ambiguities in Stalin's promises and destroying the military governors' talks. Britain and France resisted American efforts to refer the dispute to the United Nations, fearing a prelude to force. They acquiesced in the end, after the situation put immense strain on leaders in all three countries. Bevin revived pleas that Britain was in the "front line." Schuman replaced Bidault as foreign minister in the latest French cabinet shake-up, and while the French remained anxious, they saw no choice but to stand with the Anglo-Americans. Truman faced new calls for a decision on whether to use atomic bombs. Meanwhile, the Soviets were no closer to their goals: the London program continued, the Parliamentary Council convened, and the airlift showed no signs of faltering.

THE ATMOSPHERE WAS STRAINED at 5:00 P.M. on August 31, when the military governors met for the first time since July 3. Clay arrived late, refused to shake hands with Sokolovsky, and was cold and taciturn throughout the meeting. The four adjourned after appointing committees on transport, trade, and finance. Committee work stalled immediately. Soviet experts in the transport committee claimed that unregulated air traffic in and out of Berlin circumvented protections afforded the Soviet mark; they demanded restrictions on air travel and refused to discuss the blockade unless Western officials agreed. Western arguments that the directive called for the removal of restrictions, not the imposition of new ones, fell on deaf ears.[1]

Sokolovsky shocked his colleagues by announcing that, contrary to Stalin's assurances of August 23, his government would remove only those restrictions imposed after June 18. He claimed that Moscow had imposed the March restrictions in response to the London conference and the June restrictions in response to currency reform in Berlin. Because the West was reversing only the latter, his government would lift only the June restrictions. Furthermore, air traffic must be limited to support of the occupation forces. His other demands—that military surface transport submit to Soviet inspection and that military trains carry only military personnel (which would, for the first time, exclude soldiers' families and civilians employed by the military government)—seemed minor in comparison to his astounding reversal of Stalin's promises and this blatant attempt to outlaw the airlift. In two days of intense discussion, the generals and their staffs went over the same ground again and again, neither side yielding an inch. Sokolovsky stepped up pressure on September 4, announcing aerial exercises in the corridors and over Berlin and shrugging off Clay's objection that maneuvers were prohibited in the air lanes.[2]

In the committee on trade, the Russians asserted an exclusive right to license Berlin's imports and exports and wanted to exclude food and fuel from calculations of the city's balance of trade. Westerners refused to discuss the resumption of interzonal trade without the inclusion of food and fuel for Berlin and rejected Sokolovsky's claim of a monopoly on licensing external trade.[3]

While debates on transportation and trade went nowhere, discussions of finance proved unprofitable. To Western amazement, Soviet representatives denied that the financial commission would have power over the bank. The commission's powers applied to the four lettered paragraphs in the directive, they said, not the unnumbered paragraph about the bank. Robertson and Clay quoted contrary assurances by Stalin, to no avail; an impassive Sokolovsky declared that the directive was the only document he would discuss. It did not provide for such control, so he could not consider the West's "new interpretation."[4]

Robertson termed the marshal's position "fantastic," while Clay considered it a more serious threat to the Western position than the blockade, in part because Royall seemed receptive. Shaken, Clay feared that Washington would accept any agreement that involved lifting the blockade, no matter how prejudicial to America's rights. He turned to his friend Bill Draper. "I need very much to know what our real desires are," he cabled on September 3. Did Washington want an agreement that ended the blockade or one that enabled the United States to remain an occupying power in Berlin? Royall replied that the United States would not jeopardize its rights to win a quick end to the blockade; still, it was a striking sign of the vagueness of Truman's policy that after ten weeks of discussion, the man on the spot felt compelled to ask what U.S. policy was.[5]

Marshall emphasized the currency issue to Truman on September 2, predicting it could be "the breaking point of the discussions." Should the talks collapse, Marshall wanted them to fail in Moscow on "the basic issue" of Western rights, not over apparent technicalities. He briefed the cabinet the following day, saying there could be no retreat over principles. Kennan was talking in even tougher terms, telling

Canadian ambassador Hume Wrong that "the Russians would have to be 'kicked in the teeth' before the deadlock could be broken," although, Wrong added dryly, Kennan "did not suggest how."[6]

As the talks continued, events in the streets outside took a serious turn. On September 3, the city assembly tried to hold the meeting it had postponed on August 27. SED mobs broke up the session and a similar attempt three days later. Rioters beat up two reporters from RIAS (Radio in the American Sector) who were covering the September 6 meeting "live" while the city listened. Markgraf's police on the scene were reinforced—and joined the mob. Without telling Western officials, Deputy Mayor Ferdinand Friedensburg had asked four dozen plainclothesmen from the western sectors to help keep order; Markgraf's men began rounding them up. Stumm's officers found temporary sanctuary in the western liaison offices in city hall. Soviet soldiers entered the American office at gunpoint and, as Clay described it, "led twenty of the poor devils off to death or worse." Two dozen others barricaded themselves in the French office and held out for two days, until Kotikov promised Ganeval they could leave unmolested. But before they had gone two blocks, Russian troops arrested the lot. Furious, Clay vented his anger to Draper. The United States was "being pushed around . . . like a fourth class nation," he fumed. Unless the administration acted soon, it would lose its prestige *and* Berlin. He considered sending MPs to city hall to preserve order, even though the building was in the Soviet sector; Bradley and Draper dissuaded him.[7]

If events at city hall infuriated Clay, they hardened Berliners' determination to resist. Over a quarter million of them rallied in the Platz der Republik on September 9, with the Brandenburg Gate and the ruined Reichstag in the background, to hear Ernst Reuter, Franz Neumann, Otto Suhr, and others denounce the Soviet Union. Tempers were high as the crowd dispersed, and fisticuffs broke out when Markgraf's police tried to prevent people from passing through the Brandenburg Gate. The crowd pushed back the officers, and more police arrived, weapons drawn. Showered with stones, they fired into the crowd and wounded several people, one of them mortally. Several youths climbed the gate, hurling the Soviet flag to the ground. The crowd below tore it to shreds and began burning the pieces. Soldiers at the nearby Soviet War Memorial (which Berliners called the "Monument to the Unknown Looter") rushed over but could not rescue their banner. One soldier fired his machine gun over the heads of the crowd. The British assistant provost marshal, Major Frank Stokes, dispersed the crowd and ordered the Russians into their own sector. Trouble continued elsewhere. Rioters threw stones at a Russian jeep on its way to the Soviet memorial, overturned several eastern sector police cars, and beat up their occupants.[8]

Clay and Murphy watched with mixed emotions. They did not want to discourage German opposition to the Soviets, but Murphy worried that Berlin's leaders were becoming impatient with the West. That impatience stemmed from two concerns, argued Louis Glaser, one of Howley's top aides. First, Berliners and their leaders thought Western diplomacy was too passive. The Russians had been trying to seize control of the city for more than two years, and even now the West had not weighed in wholeheartedly on the other side. There had been no official statements about the Moscow talks since they began, and rumors of a Western retreat swept Berlin. Reports that the military governors were discussing withdrawal of the B-mark depressed its value—and Berlin morale. The second concern was uncertainty about the airlift. As buoyed as Berliners were by its past performance, doubt about how it would fare during the winter was never far from anyone's mind. Angry and frightened, Berliners had been pushed near their limits; the result was a "volcanic outburst of temper" and a demand for action against the Russians. Clay's misgivings were more fundamental. He mistrusted the Germans. Mass protests against one occupier might lead to protests against others. "We are in the midst of a dangerous game," he warned Draper, because the demonstrations gave free rein to Germans' weakness for chauvinist demagoguery. In the revival of mass politics in Berlin, Clay saw the ghost of Adolf Hitler.[9]

With all this commotion around them, the military governors tried to complete their work by the deadline set in the directive, September 7. They met that afternoon for six hours. Sokolovsky offered tempting concessions, such as lifting all restrictions imposed since March 30 and withdrawing his demand that families and civilians be banned from military trains. But he reiterated his claim that the 1945 corridor agreement limited traffic to that needed to support the garrisons and would not consider allowing the commission any control over the Soviet bank. Clay and his colleagues rejected new restrictions on air traffic and insisted on the commission's powers. The meeting adjourned without a joint report to the governments.[10]

Western analysts found the affair perplexing and frustrating. Apparent agreement had vanished; Stalin's assurances had been disavowed. What had gone wrong? In the daily search for a settlement, Western diplomats had lost sight of the London program's effects on Soviet policy. Worried by the blockade, they tended to see time as being on the side of the Soviet Union, but the Russians had been working against time, too. Stalin knew that on September 1 the Parliamentary Council would convene and begin drafting a constitution. His calls for delaying the London program were, in concrete terms, demands that the council be postponed. The Russians had responded to Western overtures early in August when there seemed to be a chance to disrupt Western plans. When the Parliamentary Council met in Bonn as scheduled, that possibility disappeared, and so did Soviet interest in negotiation.

As for Stalin's assurances, although they were precise, the directive was not, nor did it contain all his concessions. For Western officials, those assurances were the heart of the "Moscow agreement." It was understandable that they would interpret the directive in light of Stalin's statements, but the document itself was so poorly drawn that the State Department's legal adviser told Bohlen that Sokolovsky was "standing on the legal limits of the directive." For the Soviets, the "Moscow agreement" meant the directive and nothing more.[11] When the West went ahead with the Parliamentary Council, there was, as Stalin had said, nothing to discuss, and Sokolovsky used these differences over what constituted the agreement to break up the talks. It was a risky move, but sloppy Western diplomacy allowed the Soviet Union to carry it off and pose as the injured party as well.

COLLAPSE OF THE MILITARY GOVERNORS' conference was galling to the Americans, who were finding global diplomacy an exhausting business. The teleprinter was proving to be a mixed blessing: instantaneous exchange of views was essential, but with a five-hour time difference between Washington and London (and six between Washington and Berlin), teleconferences usually meant that someone was working in the middle of the night. Transatlantic conferences often went on for hours; a friend of Kennan's started one in Washington, and before it was over, he was at the other end in London. Douglas found it the most arduous work of his career; so did Kennan. Marshall told the cabinet on September 10 that everyone was close to exhaustion.[12]

Tired and perplexed by Soviet behavior, Americans groped for explanations. Forrestal talked matters over with Lovett, who thought Sokolovsky was following orders. The Politburo told Molotov and Vyshinsky that they had "lost their shirts" to Smith; Sokolovsky thus had to torpedo the talks when he could not obtain the concessions Molotov had let slip through his fingers. Soviet contempt for the truth astounded Forrestal; the Russians lied even when the West clearly knew they were lying. Truman agreed, writing matter-of-factly to Eleanor Roosevelt that Russia betrayed "every nation that trusted her," defaulting on "practically all of her commitments." If this analysis was correct, the outlook was grim. If the Soviets could not be trusted, even written Soviet recognition of Western rights would be meaningless.[13]

Faced with an imminent collapse of the negotiations, the NSC convened on September 7, a Tuesday rather than the council's usual meeting day, Thursday. Draper had dictated a series of points to guide the discussion. If direct talks with the Russians failed, the next step should be referral to the United Nations. Although Moscow would veto any action in the Security Council, a favorable vote in the General Assembly would mobilize world opinion "for whatever further action is necessary." That implied force, but Draper turned aside from that prospect. Instead, he thought the United States should consider evacuating dependents and Berliners who wanted to leave, "after which we might withdraw our own forces from Berlin as an untenable military outpost."[14]

The State Department controlled the meeting, not Draper. Marshall opened with a brief overview before giving the floor to Lovett, who covered many of the same points he had made to Forrestal the day before. The Western powers had sought two goals during the Moscow talks: ending the blockade and accepting the ostmark in Berlin. Measured against these objectives, the directive "seemed almost too good to be true," if it were carried out in good faith. The problem, Lovett continued, was Soviet bad faith. Repeating Marshall's point to Truman, Lovett emphasized that if the talks failed, they should fail in Moscow over principle, not in Berlin over technicalities the Western publics might not understand. The Western powers should demand a clear answer from Molotov whether his government would honor the Moscow agreement. If he said no or evaded the question, it was time to refer the dispute to the United Nations under chapter 7 of the charter, which covered threats to peace. The British and French were unwilling, however. Lovett mentioned Sokolovsky's air maneuvers and the United States' warning to the Russians that the airlift would continue and Soviet interference would be at their own risk. Truman, silent thus far, commented that this was "the proper line to take." He also agreed with Lovett's summation: "We could not continue to do business this way, . . . and we had to find out what their [the Soviets'] real intentions were."

Symington surveyed the airlift's progress. It had recently averaged 4,000 tons a day; fifty more C-54s would boost the figure to 5,000. The NSC made no decision on committing additional planes, deferring to the JCS. Records of the meeting do not indicate why, but the issue was apparently the balance between the airlift and the need for air transport if war broke out. In July, the NSC had weighed the two and decided to send seventy-five C-54s, accepting the possibility that they might be lost in war. Every call for reinforcements in Germany meant a new weighing of the balance, a reduction in the nation's ability to move troops and atomic bombs to advance bases if war came, and a growing reluctance in the Pentagon to commit more planes.

Marshall then returned to timing. He recalled that the United States had wanted to complete talks with the Russians, one way or another, by August 10 so that the Western powers could raise the issue with the General Assembly on September 1. It was now mid-September, and they were still talking to the Soviets. "Although the air-lift had been more successful than we had expected, we have been losing time," the secretary observed, "and in many respects time was on the side of the Soviets." Lovett noted that the rioting in Berlin made the situation even more delicate, and he wondered what would happen to pro-Western Berliners "if the going continued rough in Berlin. He suggested that they might be helped to defend themselves through the provision of small arms." Royall's mind was on withdrawal. U.S. evacuation plans, he said, gave "loyal Germans" priority right behind American dependents.[15]

Marshall and Lovett tried the next day to convince the Europeans that it was time to "get back to fundamentals." Chataigneau, Roberts, and Smith should demand that Stalin reaffirm his verbal assurances and recognize Western rights. Furthermore, the rioting had assumed large proportions in American eyes; it was a form of duress as serious as the blockade, and it had to stop. If the Soviets refused or equivocated, the West should refer the dispute to the United Nations. Diplomacy would be at an end, because the Americans intended to use the international forum to put the Soviet Union on trial before world opinion.[16]

Before the Europeans could reply, Marshall had to deal with objections from Smith. He was sure the Soviets were not going to confirm Western rights, but what bothered Smith most was the uncertainty at the heart of Western policy—the same ambiguity that troubled Clay. Here was another man on the spot who did not know what his government intended. As he had in August, the ambassador thought the question was whether the Western powers were prepared to live with the status quo in Berlin indefinitely, and if not, what concessions they were willing to make to end it. Those concessions might be substantial. None of Washington's replies gave even a hint that "this basic strategic question had been considered and a definite line of action, beyond immediate reference to UNO [United Nations Organization], decided upon. I do not ask to know what this decision is," Smith added, "but it would certainly help my digestion if I knew that it had been taken." Marshall defended his insistence on reasserting Western rights before turning to Smith's concerns about strategy. The ambassador found little reassurance as he read, "As to the more fundamental questions raised in your telegram . . . , you may be sure that the major consideration of our future course of action has been under constant study here, the Defense establishment and the National Security Council."[17]

Smith's reaction was mild compared with those in London and Paris. American willingness to abandon diplomacy horrified the British and French. This was what they had feared since July, and once more, the Western partnership nearly disintegrated. Bevin thought the Soviets would welcome a settlement in order to end the alienation of German opinion and the harm done to their zone's trade by the counterblockade. The mobs did not bother him enough to make ending them a condition of negotiation. He would not commit his government to a course that might lead to war, and he repeated his reminder that Britain was "in the front line." American insistence filled him with "deepest misgivings," and he warned Douglas of a "very strong feeling, deeply resented here, that the United States were trying to boss us." Sorely troubled, he confessed to Strang that he understood Neville Chamberlain's anguish in 1938. He would not yield; still, the consequences weighed on him. From Paris, Schuman supported Bevin against the Americans.[18]

Now the alternatives had to be phrased differently: pursue the policy the United States thought wise, at the cost of Western unity, or accept one more spin of what

Marshall derisively termed the "Berlin Merry-Go-Round." After consulting Royall, Draper, and Senator Vandenberg (but apparently not the president), Marshall and Lovett decided on one more attempt to reach an agreement.[19]

Seeing this as merely postponing the inevitable, Forrestal was studying war plans. He invited Marshall to the Pentagon for a meeting with the JCS, the service secretaries, and the heads of the Armed Forces Special Weapons Project and the AEC's Military Liaison Committee. His diary noted that the subject was the "use of A." Specifically, the group wanted to send Lauris Norstad, the chief air force planner, to London to discuss constructing "huts" at B-29 bases in Britain. The huts would store bomb components, saving time in an emergency. Forrestal thought the British response to this request would show "whether they really meant to fight": allowing the huts implied allowing the atomic bomb—and its use from British bases. General Vandenberg outlined for Marshall the current war plan, which envisaged an immediate air offensive using both conventional and atomic weapons against more than 100 cities in the Soviet Union. The secretary of state suggested that Forrestal raise the Norstad mission with the president.

Accompanied by Forrestal, Symington, Royall, and Bradley, the air force chief of staff repeated his presentation in the Oval Office in a half-hour meeting on September 13. After listening to the briefing, which the president recalled as a discussion of "bases, bombs, Moscow, Leningrad, etc.," Truman said that although he prayed he would never again have to order atomic attacks, he would do so "if necessary." Repugnant as the last step might be, the president was willing to take the next one; four days later, he approved Norstad's trip.[20]

As in June and July, the president's tough talk was superficially impressive. He had come a long way from his May instructions to the joint chiefs to assume that no atomic weapons would be used. Yet he continued to avoid deeper issues. What did "if necessary" mean? Under what circumstances would Truman again order the destruction of cities by atomic bombs? These and other questions poured in on the president after his visitors left. Alone at his desk, he had a "terrible feeling . . . that we are very close to war." Budget director James Webb told Lilienthal that no one knew what the Russians might do next. "They might walk in tomorrow and shoot General Clay." While Truman had always been optimistic, Webb saw that he was "blue now, mighty blue."[21] The CIA provided slight reassurance by week's end, updating its famous April assessment of the likelihood of war. Its analysts thought a deliberate Kremlin decision for war was improbable; however, the risks of miscalculation and accidental war were greater than they had been in the spring.[22]

Spurred by the sense of crisis, the NSC staff completed the study on atomic weapons that Royall had asked for in July. The question, according to the staff, was whether the United States should now formulate policies regarding use of the bomb in war. The short answer was no. The paper, NSC 30, concluded that the military must prepare to use all available weapons, but any decision would be made by the president "when he considers such decision to be required." The council should not ask Truman to make decisions now about hypothetical cases. Forrestal thought the paper's conclusions "significant." Royall, who had waited months for this day, was disappointed, complaining that the paper did not say whether the bomb would be used or not. The rest of the NSC was not so picky and approved the paper, leaving the issue where it had been and where Truman wanted it: in his hands alone.[23]

Truman also turned back a halfhearted effort by Forrestal to reopen the custody issue. Marshall brought up the subject during a meeting about Norstad's trip. Truman replied that he was "most anxious" to avoid any decision until after the election, only to have Forrestal reiterate his conviction that the military should possess the bomb for training purposes, if for no other reason. He said he hoped Truman would allow him to revisit the issue if "those responsible felt it should be opened." That proved unnecessary, but over the next two weeks, Forrestal and the joint chiefs worked on detailed procedures for the emergency transfer of weapons from the Atomic Energy Commission. The Pentagon and the AEC tested these procedures in December. Meanwhile, Norstad had reported from London that Tedder accepted U.S. views regarding the "immediate use of the A-Bomb," and members of the Armed Forces Special Weapons Project—the Pentagon's nuclear experts—left for England.[24]

In the meantime, the "Berlin Merry-Go-Round" had begun to spin once more, with the protagonists talking for the record. When Smith, Roberts, and Chataigneau asked for an appointment with Stalin on September 14, they were told that he was away on vacation and could not be recalled (déjà vu), but Molotov would see them. The three men presented an aide-mémoire asking the Soviet government to instruct Sokolovsky to honor the Moscow agreement. Molotov replied four days later that Sokolovsky had followed the directive, whereas the three Westerners had tried to twist the agreement to suit themselves. The marshal had not tried to introduce new restrictions but merely insisted that the West live up to the 1945 air accord. The Western military governors had sabotaged the agreement by trying to extend the power of the financial commission "over the whole activity of the German Bank of Emission in Berlin."[25]

Although the carousel might spin a few more times, no one doubted that the ride would end soon and the Western powers would take the dispute to the United Nations. The British and French were convinced that the Americans wanted moral sanction from the United Nations to break the blockade or, failing that, a clear record for domestic consumption showing that it had tried every available avenue before resorting to force. There seemed to be no other explanation for Washington's desire to go to the Security Council rather than the General Assembly and to invoke chapter 7 of the charter rather than chapter 6, which provided for the peaceful settlement of disputes. The Security Council could not find a "threat to peace" and then do nothing about it.

Jebb received scant reassurance when he and Strang raised these points with Samuel Reber, Hickerson's deputy, and with Philip C. Jessup, the deputy U.S. representative and the man who would present the American case. Jebb argued that referral to the Security Council implied that the West had decided "ultimately to use force." Unless such a decision had been made—and he thought the governments should settle that issue "here and now"—referral to the Security Council would be a mistake. The Americans countered that the Western powers "must have the protection of referral to the Security Council *if* they had to resort to force." The General Assembly was "not serious enough." Besides, U.S. public opinion required the West to explore all possibilities for settlement. Jebb countered that there were none; "the only point in reference to the United Nations was to line the nations up behind us."[26]

The Americans urged another line of argument, one their allies disbelieved. Referring the matter to the United Nations was not a ploy to force a showdown; rather, it was the "only way," in Marshall's words, "to get more time without paying for it by appeasement." If the secretary meant what he said, this was a change from the summer, when, as Kennan observed, U.S. officials had talked "as though the appeal to the United Nations was merely a last clearance before we ourselves would take strong measures."[27] The British and French were convinced that the Americans remained bellicose. The notion that the Truman administration—tough, crisp, decisive—had no idea what to do next was too far-fetched to be taken seriously. Yet there was something to it. In discussions among themselves, the Americans agreed that the United Nations was perhaps the only way to avoid "a brutal choice between war or submission."[28] Marshall faced uncertainty within his UN delegation. One of the doubters—but not the only one—was Dulles, serving on the delegation to show the world that American policy had bipartisan backing. He assured Senator Vandenberg that he "went along . . . with the understanding that our initial submission would not call for any concrete action" and that debate would postpone a showdown rather than trigger one.[29] It had been easy for Lovett and others to talk tough in July, with a showdown months away; now they were more cautious. The Americans were unwilling to exclude force, but the Europeans were mistaken when they assumed force was the only option Washington would consider if referral to the United Nations failed. It was an understandable mistake, given what the Americans had been saying for months, and one they could not correct in the absence of a clear decision about what their government would do.

With this and other problems confronting them, Western diplomats hardly cared that September 18, the day Molotov defended Sokolovsky, was also "Air Force Day," the first anniversary of U.S. airmen's long-sought independence from the army. To honor the occasion, the two air forces made a maximum effort, delivering nearly 7,000 tons. A plane landed in Berlin every ninety-six seconds. Vittles and Plainfare were evolving into something more than efforts to buy time.

AIR FORCE DAY CAPPED a month of struggle and improvement by the two air forces. The RAF was approaching the limits of its strength. Though enjoying the advantage of working closer to home than the Americans, the RAF faced its own set of challenges. Instead of inspections after 200 flying hours, RAF planes underwent checks back home every 100, so there was a nearly constant stream of planes crossing the English Channel. The RAF did not move its inspection depots to Germany for two reasons: there was no room, and the steady rotation would give its crews welcome time at home. The preferred aircrew cycle lasted twenty-four days. Crews traveled from the United Kingdom and had the next day off, then flew daylight missions for five days. A thirty-six-hour stand-down prepared them for five nights of flying. After another thirty-six-hour transition, five days of afternoon operations followed, then up to six days in Britain. Ground crews rotated every ninety days, starting in August. As one British after-action report explained, "Fresh energy and vigour was, in those days, almost of equal value with experience in the operation."[30]

When the airlift began, RAF leaders had predicted they could deliver up to 750 tons a day for a month, after which deliveries would decrease. Instead, they delivered a daily average of 1,463 tons in August and 1,259 in September. These achievements were the result of extraordinary measures, and they took a toll. Skilled mechanics were in such short supply that the RAF froze discharges; the ban was then expanded to include cooks, drivers, radar and radio fitters, clerks, and aircrew members.[31] The RAF, gambling on a short airlift, had suspended transport aircrew training in order to send the maximum number of planes and crews to Germany. Transport Command began urging in mid-August that some crews be withdrawn so training could resume, but that meant a drop in British tonnage of 385 tons a day. With no end to the crisis in sight and winter approaching, Robertson reminded London that Britain should be increasing its lift, not reducing it. Bevin used the possible effect on the Moscow talks to stall the move in August, but twenty Dakotas and ten Yorks went home in September, along with thirty-six instructor crews.[32]

London offset these withdrawals by accepting help from the Dominions and chartering commercial aircraft. Australia offered ten Dakotas and crews on August 3; South Africa and New Zealand followed. London was "most grateful." Citing limited airfield capacity, it declined the offers of airplanes but accepted the crews "as soon as they could get here." Tedder thanked the Australians, remarking that "the strain on our crews has been severe."[33] Ten Australian crews arrived at Lübeck in mid-September, followed by ten South African crews a month later and three New Zealand crews in November. Opposition by Prime Minister William L. Mackenzie

King and Defence Minister Brooke Claxton prevented Canadian participation.[34] The Dominion crews rotated after six months, and their replacements were released in August 1949. The British considered asking for ground staff, but because the Dominions would probably want to send entire units in order to maintain unit integrity, and the RAF's shortages were in particular trades (specialties), not across the board, manpower would have been wasted.[35]

The other way to boost British tonnage was to hire contract carriers. The idea had been under consideration since the first of July. BAFO was reluctant, but there was no other way to increase deliveries. From Berlin, Air Commodore Waite emphasized that Gatow was not operating at full capacity and additional planes would be welcome. By late July, the Air Ministry was negotiating contracts for thirty-two land planes and two flying boats that would deliver around 400 tons a day.[36] Three Lancastrians of Flight Refueling, Limited, attracted special notice because they were modified to carry liquid fuels. No one had discovered a practical way to deliver fuel to Berlin. One could drain surplus aviation fuel from the tanks on airlift planes, but this prolonged turnaround times. In addition, the city needed diesel fuel and kerosene, not just aviation gasoline. The Americans loaded fifty-five-gallon drums of fuel onto their planes, but this did not work well. The empty drums had to be steam-cleaned before they could be flown out of Berlin for reuse; otherwise, the fumes made them more dangerous empty than full. The Lancastrians seemed to be the only solution, and they began flying on July 27. The first sortie to Berlin was direct from Tarrant Rushton in Britain; thereafter, the three planes operated from Bückeburg. On August 4, the full civil lift started from Wunstorf and Fassberg. Two chartered Hythe flying boats also operated with the RAF Sunderlands from Finkenwerder.[37]

Although the commercial companies provided additional lift, they were expensive; the Air Ministry estimated the initial cost as £112,000 a week. Coordinating their work proved to be one of BAFO's biggest problems. Companies were short of experienced flight crews, mechanics, spare parts, and maintenance equipment. Planes tended to be small, uneconomical, and without navigational aids; at first, their radios operated on different frequencies from those carried by RAF planes. Because the blockade might end at any moment, early contracts were for only a month at a time (in September, they were weekly), giving the companies no incentive to invest in long-term improvements. Up to fifteen companies operated at a time, each with its own maintenance procedures, standards, and crews. Commercial rivals, they had little incentive to pool ground staff, spare parts, tools, or experience. The companies were supposed to be self-supporting, with the host RAF station providing minimal assistance. In practice, they relied on the military for tools, parts, and advice. During their first four months, the companies planned their own operations and flew mostly in daylight, leaving night missions to the

RAF. They were paid by the flying hour, not by the tonnage delivered, so they had no incentive to increase their load capacity. Originally, British European Airways Corporation was supposed to act as liaison with the RAF and coordinate the charter carriers, but that could not be arranged until mid-December. In the meantime, Air Marshal Sanders complained, he had his hands full with "a heterogeneous and unorganised collection of individual aircraft chartered from many different private companies . . . without adequate backing or servicing arrangements"; he could not rely on them for consistent daily deliveries. Charter performance remained well below the expected 400 tons a day, amounting to only 122 in August, 178 in September, and 258 in October.[38]

Although it is hard to avoid John Tusa's conclusion that managing this group was "one of the most aggravating parts of the entire lift" for the RAF, some companies performed well. RAF officers singled out Flight Refueling and Skyways as particularly efficient and well run. D. C. T. Bennett, who had led Bomber Command's pathfinder force during the war, was the only pilot qualified to fly his company's four-engine Avro Tudor at night. He made two or three trips into Berlin night after night, virtually without a break, for two months.[39]

The RAF also sought improved performance through better organization. Group Captain Hyde's transport wing had dissolved in mid-July, when Plainfare expanded beyond Wunstorf. Since then, a small transport operations branch of the BAFO air staff had directed Plainfare through BAFO station commanders. By September, the operation had grown too large, and BAFO staff and station commanders remained unfamiliar with transport operations. On September 22, BAFO placed the operation in the hands of a newly created advance headquarters, No. 46 Group, at Bückeburg. The new organization absorbed the old transport branch, but its core comprised a group from Transport Command's No. 46 Group: its commander, Air Commodore John W. F. Merer; key officers from his operations staff; and a handful of technical and administrative officers. Merer's new headquarters remained small, twenty-one people. This was spartan, considering the job, which was to control and execute all RAF transport operations and coordinate them with those of the United States and the charter carriers. BAFO exercised administrative control of Plainfare stations, the idea being to allow Merer to concentrate on flying. This was an improvement, but it was still an awkward compromise. No. 46 Group's main headquarters remained at Bushey Hall in Hertfordshire. As group commander, Merer was responsible for five stations and two other organizations back home in addition to his duties in Germany.[40]

British tonnage sagged from 45,000 tons in August to just under 38,000 in September and less than 32,000 in October. Analysts could point to plenty of causes: the withdrawal of planes and crews to restart Transport Command training, mechanical problems with Yorks, a shortage of crews, fatigue, and the effects of being displaced from Fassberg by the Americans. Solutions were harder to find. Using Bomber Command to drop coal might add 120 tons a day but would destroy it "as a potential striking force." Mechanics had been pooled in the name of efficiency, but that had not worked well. Merer restored squadron integrity, fostering esprit de corps and a healthy sense of competition. With winter closing in, Robertson was "most anxious" lest the Americans "accuse us of failing to carry out our share of this operation."[41]

The Americans, whose own effort was gathering momentum, were not interested in finger-pointing. Their gains more than offset British losses. In July, the airlift delivered 2,185 tons a day; the August figure was 3,835. The maximum effort on September 18, Air Force Day, helped push that month's average to 4,593 tons, just above Clay's target. He was ecstatic, telling Washington, "We can last indefinitely in Berlin" and, "except possibly for two or three winter months, we can support Berlin better than ever." It would be expensive, but the cost was "only a fraction of what we are now spending to aid Europe and to re-arm to stop Soviet expansion. Let's do it."[42]

Washington was reluctant. On July 22, the NSC had agreed to send seventy-five more C-54s. Clay complained on August 7 that only thirty-five had arrived. The conflict between the airlift and wartime commitments continued to haunt planners. The NSC had approved the July 22 increase only after Bradley had assured the group that the joint chiefs "could go that far." In August, with Bevin and others urging new increases, the army tried to draw a line in the sand. A Plans and Operations (P&O) memo argued that the current effort had "seriously impaired our capability to execute current emergency war plans." Every plane sent to Germany made the problem worse. P&O wanted to cap the airlift and "not supplement it with additional C-54s."[43]

With diplomacy faltering and winter drawing closer, advocates began to mobilize on the other side. LeMay completed plans for a protracted airlift that would require between forty-one and sixty-nine additional C-54s, depending on whether the C-47s stayed in service. Clay thought the estimate was low because LeMay had exaggerated British capabilities, and he promised Draper firm figures in a few days. Meanwhile, Symington was considering LeMay's report and had raised similar numbers at the NSC. The council endorsed an increase, leaving it to the joint chiefs to strike a new balance between the airlift and wartime commitments.[44]

Clay provided firm estimates on September 10: he needed sixty-nine more C-54s by October 1 and forty-seven more by December 1, "if [the] lift is still continuing at that time." The joint chiefs' initial response was to send forty, ten less than the minimum number considered by the NSC; on September 17, they released the other ten. Available records do not detail the chiefs' rationale, although it seems certain they were worried about wartime requirements.[45]

Air Force Day convinced Clay that the airlift could defeat the blockade, and he lobbied energetically to break though the chiefs' latest ceiling. He told Royall the Western powers could stay indefinitely—*if* he had the planes. Without them, the West would have to take a chance on diplomacy. If the United Nations failed, he continued, "it truly becomes a struggle of nerves until someone folds." The airlift could allow the West to hold its position without resorting to force; that shifted the onus for violence onto the Soviets, and Clay remained convinced that they did not want war. He repeated these arguments before the three foreign ministers in Paris on September 21; two days later, he called on Washington to send him the 116 planes he had asked for on September 10. As dramatic as the airlift's potential was, the current effort was not quite holding its own, he confessed, and he had been unable to stockpile reserves against the winter. He asked for a prompt decision. A week later, Bradley replied that the joint chiefs would study his request.[46]

THIS TEPID RESPONSE was a dash of cold water following the positive reaction Clay had received in Paris, where Marshall, Bevin, and Schuman had assembled for the UN meeting and to weigh alternatives over Berlin. Marshall argued it was time to tell the Russians the West was referring the dispute to the Security Council, but Bevin and Schuman wanted an "intermediate" note. The Americans suspected the Europeans were using doubts about the airlift to support their case, and Clay's presentation had been designed with that in mind. Marshall also tried to reassure the Europeans by urging them to take a broader view. Moscow's "only strong card" was the blockade, and the airlift could trump it. "Everywhere else the Russians were losing the battle." He told Bevin "in confidence" that "the one thing which had *so far* prevented his Government from placing more aircraft at the disposal of the air-lift was the fear that in the event of a sudden Soviet attack the inevitable loss of a large proportion of these aircraft would be a crippling blow to their air transport situation." Based on that, Marshall said, the United States had limited the airlift to 30 percent of its total air cargo fleet. He did not say so, but that limit was now a thing of the past. The mid-September increase boosted the airlift's total to 50 percent of available aircraft, and honoring Clay's latest requests would add 10 percent more.[47]

Encouraging as the American reports were, Bevin and Schuman continued to insist on their intermediate note. Marshall gave in, provided the British and French agreed then and there that this would be the last spin of the merry-go-round: if Molotov's reply was unsatisfactory, the West would go to the Security Council. Schuman and Bevin agreed.[48]

On September 22, the Western governments tried to cut free from the "coils of technical argument" and get back to fundamentals. Their reply to Molotov outlined a "final position": no restrictions on air traffic; commission control over those activities of the bank that related to the introduction and continued use of Soviet currency in the city; and trade, including licensing, under four-power control. Six weeks of disagreement over technical matters had revealed a "fundamental difference of views . . . as to the rights and obligations of the occupying powers in Berlin." The note asked if the Soviet government was ready to lift the blockade and said that the Western foreign ministers, who would be meeting soon in Paris, expected a prompt reply. There was no mention of referral to the United Nations.[49]

Bevin took a strong line in that day's debate in the House of Commons. Concessions would weaken the West without satisfying the Kremlin, he stated, for its appetite was insatiable. When the blockade began, a "great choice had to be made," he declared, Chamberlain's dilemma still on his mind. "We made it. It was either to stand firm there [in Berlin] or . . . go to another Munich." It was easier to stand firm now than it had been ten years before, because of the airlift. Bevin claimed that stocks were higher now than in June and expressed confidence that "we shall be able to see the winter through."[50]

In private, he was less sure. Conferring with Robertson, Strang, and other advisers the following day, Bevin wanted them to plan for every eventuality. "If we were forced out of Berlin," he told Robertson, "we should have to get our friends out." He added that he would not sign anything that appeased the Russians or looked like surrender. When Strang commented that the airlift was a "palliative and not a final solution," Robertson agreed, offering a detailed assessment that challenged Marshall's optimistic predictions. American estimates were based on subsistence-level calculations of need; realistic estimates were much higher. The airlift "must fail in the end," Robertson insisted, because eventually, Berliners' morale would crack. With withdrawal inevitable, Robertson wanted to arrange it so that it appeared to be the "dignified and orderly conclusion to a well-thought out policy" and timed so that the damage could be offset by the creation of a west German government. The worst course would be continually to repeat that the West would not withdraw, then "scuttle out" suddenly. That would shatter Western prestige and abandon thousands of pro-Western Germans, "a stain we should never wipe out." With the Russians determined to expel the West from Berlin, the danger was that they might push the Americans too far. Bevin finished the thought: an armed clash might follow. He was angry with the Russians. They had "played their cards very badly and had forced us into a closer association with the Americans in Germany than we had wished," he complained.[51]

The Russians were quick to offer their version of events. On September 25, they defended the blockade as a measure to protect "the interests of the German population" as well as the economies of Berlin and the Soviet zone. The Western governments had tried to control the economy of eastern Germany by introducing their currency into Berlin, but their scheming did not end there. The ultimate goal was to force the Soviets out of the eastern zone. Against this campaign, the Soviet government had advanced moderate, reasonable proposals, and Sokolovsky had fulfilled the terms of the directive. Moscow followed this private attack with a public blast on September 26, when *Tass* denounced what it termed Western distortions and blamed the military governors, who, instead of settling matters on the spot, as instructed, had referred matters back to their governments.[52]

Marshall, Bevin, and Schuman met in Paris that afternoon. They agreed that further discussion was pointless. The three issued a terse communiqué, followed a day later by a long note addressed to the Soviet government and released to the press half an hour after its delivery.[53] After summarizing the talks from the Western viewpoint, the note contended that the Soviet purpose all along had been to destroy Western rights in Berlin. Technical difficulties in transport and currency controls were pretexts: "The issue is that the Soviet Government . . . is attempting by illegal and coercive measures in disregard of its obligations to secure political objectives to which it is not entitled and which it could not achieve by peaceful means."[54] Washington released a white paper on the Moscow and Berlin talks on September 26; the report had been updated daily so that it could be published at once to counter Soviet propaganda. Three days later, the Western governments referred the dispute to the Security Council, bringing efforts to reach a resolution through direct negotiation to an end.

NEITHER SIDE COULD BE HAPPY about the talks in Moscow and Berlin. The West had come to the Soviet government seeking an agreement and had seemed receptive to Russian terms, but the Soviets had been unable to exploit the situation. The London program continued, and the West remained in Berlin. In Western eyes, these were not successes, for the future remained bleak. Although the airlift exceeded expectations, few shared Clay's belief that it could circumvent the blockade, and the collapse of negotiations dashed hopes for a quick end to Soviet restrictions.

Americans blamed the disappointing turn of events on Soviet duplicity, unaware of the obstacles to settlement caused by the structure of the Berlin situation itself. The Moscow discussions rested on two false assumptions: that settlement depended on a revival of quadripartite agencies, and that settlement must involve a compromise on currency. In 1945, Dwight Eisenhower had seen Berlin as an "experimental laboratory" in which the four powers would learn to trust one another and work together. In 1948, with similar views in mind, diplomats tried to broaden common ground and bring East and West back together. But this approach could no longer work; cooperative institutions rest on shared interests, and in Cold War Berlin, the only shared interest was negative—avoiding another war. No mutually satisfactory system of joint control could be resurrected because power sufficient to secure the interests of one side menaced those of the other; each feared the other would abuse whatever loopholes it could find. Rather than reconciling differences, quadripartite arrangements deepened suspicion and insecurity. Attempts to devise a solution to the crisis based on such arrangements were futile. Robertson had begun to grasp this in late July, warning Strang that there was no going back to Potsdam, the ACC, and quadripartite rule, "no future in [the] resumption of old arguments."[55]

That East-West differences in the city centered on money and finance greatly increased the odds against success, for the two sides' notions about the functions of banks, credit, and money were far apart. Banks in the Stalinist system were state agencies, not a special kind of private firm, as they were in the West. They existed to monitor and enforce the economic and financial plans of the state. In theory, banks extended credit only in accordance with the state's plan; in practice, the Soviets used banks' power over credit to destroy the private sector in eastern Europe after 1945, which suggests west Berlin's fate if Molotov had had his way.[56] Soviet authorities sought to prevent fiscal forces from exercising any influence over the economy that was at variance with the plan: internally, officials in Soviet-style economies restricted the amount of currency in circulation to limit liquidity and prevent unplanned spending; internationally, they imposed a strict separation between the domestic economy and foreign trade, and no eastern currency was freely convertible into any other.[57]

Such differences put insurmountable obstacles in the way of mutually acceptable currency arrangements in Berlin. Even if both sides acted in good faith, the demands of the free-market western sectors of the city for credit and currency would have been irreconcilable with Soviet economic planning. If those sectors could divert money, credit, and resources away from the planned economy at any time—as the Western powers, in order to protect themselves, were bound to insist—planning was meaningless. The plan had to be all-inclusive, or it could not operate at all. That is what the Soviets had in mind when they denounced quadripartite control of the Soviet mark as a threat to the stability of their zone. Similar logic led them to insist on regulating traffic into and out of Berlin; otherwise, unplanned and uncontrolled trade would undermine the regime's hold over the economy. Satisfying Soviet defensive interests through joint economic arrangements thus meant the absorption of west Berlin into the Soviet bloc; satisfying Western interests through such arrangements threatened Soviet interests in the east. Instead of the symbol of cooperation Eisenhower had hoped for, by the autumn of 1948 Berlin had taken on the perverse and dangerous aspects of the "security dilemma": actions to protect one side's interests appeared threatening to the other, triggering a vicious circle of action, reaction, and deepening hostility.

Understandably, observers at the time concentrated on more immediate prospects. Morale in Paris, according to Caffery, was at its lowest point in the last two years, and the French saw themselves as pawns in an impending conflict between

Enemies: An Eighth Air Force B-17 flies over Tempelhof airfield during a March 1944 air raid. Just over four years later, the airfield would serve as the linchpin of the U.S. Air Force's airlift into the city. (U.S. Air Force photograph, courtesy of History Office, U.S. Air Forces in Europe)

Friends: Presidential aide Harry Hopkins (*civilian at right*) and his wife Louise (*center*) tour Hitler's ruined capital, June 7, 1945. Their guide, Soviet General Vasily Sokolovsky (*arm in arm with Louise*), would impose the Berlin blockade in June 1948. (Courtesy of Franklin D. Roosevelt Library)

Berliners on the Potsdamer Platz, July 1945. (Courtesy of Harry S. Truman Library)

The victors at Potsdam, August 1, 1945. *Seated, left to right:* British Prime Minister Clement R. Attlee, U.S. President Harry S. Truman, and chairman of the Council of People's Commissars Joseph V. Stalin. *Standing, left to right:* U.S. Fleet Admiral William D. Leahy, British Foreign Secretary Ernest Bevin, U.S. Secretary of State James F. Byrnes, and People's Commissar for Foreign Affairs Vyacheslav M. Molotov. (U.S. Army photograph, courtesy of Harry S. Truman Library)

Chief Justice Fred M. Vinson (*right*) swears in George C. Marshall (*left*) as secretary of state, January 20, 1947. President Truman and members of his cabinet look on. Nearly two years later, some expected Vinson to be Marshall's successor. (National Park Service photograph, courtesy of Harry S. Truman Library)

This photograph of U.S. Military Governor General Lucius D. Clay conveys some of his intensity. (U.S. Army photograph, courtesy of History Office, U.S. Air Forces in Europe)

Tempelhof from the air. (U.S. Air Force photograph, courtesy of USAF History Support Office)

(Above) By July 1, when this photo was taken at Tempelhof, the airlift was operating around the clock. (U.S. Air Force photograph, courtesy of Library of Congress) *(Below)* Air Commodore Reginald Waite (*left*) explains airlift operations at RAF Gatow to British Military Governor Sir Brian H. Robertson, July 6, 1948. (Courtesy of Alliierten Museum, Berlin)

RAF Yorks deliver their cargoes at RAF Gatow in assembly-line fashion. (Courtesy of USAF History Support Office)

A Coastal Command Short Sunderland flying boat takes on cargo at Berlin's Havel See. (Courtesy of History Office, U.S. Air Forces in Europe)

An Avro Lancastrian operated by Flight Refueling, Limited, discharges fuel at RAF Gatow. Aircraft like this one delivered liquid fuels for civilian use in Berlin from July 1948 to August 1949. (Courtesy of USAF History Support Office)

A C-54 on final approach at Tempelhof airfield. (U.S. Air Force photograph, courtesy of History Office, U.S. Air Forces in Europe)

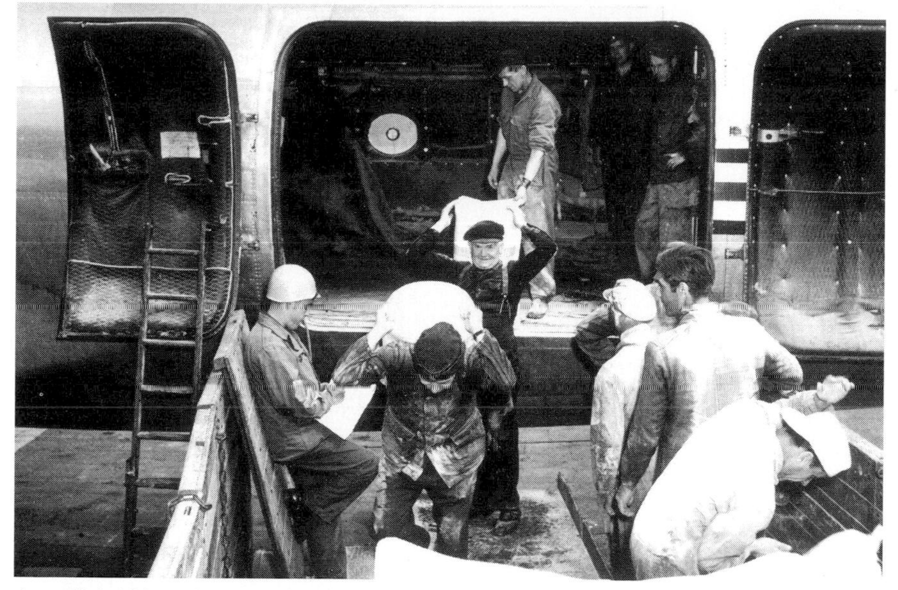

As official historian Elizabeth Lay points out, nearly every pound of cargo delivered during the Berlin airlift traveled part of the way on a man's back. Here, an unloading crew manhandles bags of flour from a C-54 while a U.S. soldier inventories the cargo. (U.S. Air Force photograph, courtesy of History Office, U.S. Air Forces in Europe)

The spirit of blockaded Berlin can be seen in the faces of this crew, which held the record for the fastest unloading time. (U.S. Air Force photograph, courtesy of History Office, U.S. Air Forces in Europe)

(Above left) USAF Lieutenant Gail S. Halvorsen, the “Candy Bomber.” (U.S. Air Force photograph, courtesy of History Office, U.S. Air Forces in Europe) *(Above right)* Airlift commander Major General William H. Tunner. (U.S. Air Force photograph, courtesy of USAF History Support Office)

Jake Schuffert’s cartoon in the February 24, 1949, issue of *Task Force Times* would come to life during the “Easter Parade,” when airlift commander William Tunner goaded competing commanders to greater efforts. (Courtesy of Berlin Airlift Veterans Association)

Russian and American juggernauts. Bevin may have put on a brave face for Schuman in Paris on October 4, but it is unlikely he had changed his views since September 23, when he had worried about evacuation and complained about being dragged along behind the Americans.[58]

The CIA expected the Soviets to mount "unlimited pressure" to compel withdrawal, including interference with the airlift, and intensified political and economic coercion of Berliners. The agency predicted this program would succeed. Any Western course of action predicated on staying in Berlin "is likely in the long run to prove ineffective. The Western position in the city would increasingly deteriorate, and ultimate Western withdrawal would probably become necessary," damaging U.S. prestige "throughout the world."[59]

And what of Eisenhower, the optimist of 1945? He sent Forrestal a long, sad letter on September 27. He had believed the Soviets would concede in the end, but now they seemed so smug and arrogant that "they may push the rest of the world beyond endurance." It was time for everyone to "think in terms of his future duty" and for the nation to go on a war footing. He added, in a handwritten note, that he prayed that Forrestal, with his closer view, saw "some light in what I think a very dark sky."[60]

CHAPTER 9

A Necessary Failure

Tired of complicated arguments with the Soviet Union over ambiguous accords and unwritten understandings, Western officials hoped to break free from these complexities when they took the Berlin dispute to the United Nations Security Council. Americans looked forward to putting the Kremlin on trial before world opinion and, certain their cause was just, expected a conviction. Either the criminal would make restitution and lift the blockade or the way would be open for Western action to break it in the name of the international organization.

Events at the United Nations disappointed the West. The neutral powers sought to mediate rather than adjudicate, and their efforts led Westerners back into the morass they had sought to escape. At first, the Soviets took an antagonistic stance toward the neutrals that played into Western hands; then they exploited the gap between the Western quest for vindication and the neutrals' pursuit of peace. The British and French, dubious about the airlift's long-term prospects and keenly aware they faced disaster if war broke out, put more faith in the neutrals' prospects (or professed to) than the Americans did. At no other stage in the crisis was maintaining Western unity more difficult.

Despite the frustration felt by American officials, recourse to the United Nations served Western interests. In postponing a showdown with the Soviet Union, the UN debate gave the airlift time to prove that it could supply Berlin, even in winter. This unexpected success transformed the structure of the crisis. The blockade had given Stalin a great advantage because it put the choice between submission and escalation on the West. Now the Soviets had to decide whether to interfere forcibly with the airlift or abandon their objectives.

The international organization also served Western interests by showing that previous talks had rested on false assumptions. Recognition that the powers had been pursuing an unworkable line was the first step toward successful diplomacy. With the airlift strengthening the Western bargaining position and the failure of

UN mediation opening the way for negotiation on a more realistic basis, the Western powers emerged from the frustrating and apparently futile discussions at the United Nations in a better position than before.

A NEW ROUND OF diplomatic activity began on September 29, when Western representatives asked UN Secretary-General Trygve Lie to put the Soviet blockade on the Security Council's agenda as a threat to peace. The request took high moral ground. This was no ordinary dispute; it involved neither difficulties in transport nor details of currency control in Berlin. The Soviet Union was disregarding its obligations under the UN charter and using improper measures to pursue illegitimate political aims. The issue before the United Nations was whether it would allow one of its members to coerce others.[1]

The move, Americans hoped, would mark an important shift in the diplomacy of the crisis. Negotiations in Moscow and Berlin had led into a "labyrinth of disagreements"; the appeal to the United Nations sidestepped the tangle of technical details and narrowed the dispute to the issue of the blockade. Here the Soviets were clearly in the wrong, and the West could contrast its own restraint with Russian behavior. The Western powers had not used force to challenge the blockade; they had followed the charter by seeking to negotiate. Now they hoped to be rewarded for their exemplary behavior.[2] The United States in particular was not interested in mediation. When it brought the Soviets "before the bar of the Security Council," Bohlen wrote, it sought moral condemnation. In that effort, a majority vote would not do. As the CIA's monthly review for October noted, American policy increasingly depended on "an unconditional expression of support from world opinion."[3]

Because every abstention would be a defeat, Americans paid special attention to the neutrals, the nonaligned council members. Jessup recalled putting in an average of eighty to ninety hours a week, consulting delegations, explaining policy. He used to good effect the State Department's report on the Moscow talks, released September 26; a British white paper followed two weeks later. The two reports surveyed events since 1945, defended Western rights and policies, and blamed Soviet duplicity for the impasse. Western diplomats ensured that copies circulated through the halls of the Palais de Chaillot in Paris, where the United Nations was meeting.[4]

The Western move put conflicting pressures on at least one nonpermanent member of the Security Council. Canada's view reflected, on the one hand, a desire to arrange a peaceful solution and, on the other, a wish to protect Western interests. Seeking a settlement was imperative, given Canada's self-image as a "helpful fixer." It was especially important because the confrontation threatened the United Nations, an organization the Department of External Affairs valued as both a means of preserving peace and an arena where "skill count[ed] for more than muscle."[5] The United Nations had never before tried to settle a dispute among permanent members of the council, and there was considerable doubt that it would be equal to the test.[6] Russian assertions that the United Nations lacked jurisdiction only strengthened Canadian concern.

For all their desire to mediate, Canadian diplomats sympathized with the Western powers. Western goals were defensive, according to an External Affairs paper. The three powers were trying to maintain their rights in Berlin and Germany in the face of Soviet attempts to spread communism throughout the country.[7] John Holmes recalled that he and other members of the Canadian delegation thought Canada could help by restraining "well-meaning lesser power[s]" that might "unwittingly play the Soviet hand by producing a formula which only seemed reasonable."[8]

Trying to stay in step with the Western powers proved difficult, because Canadian officials were unsure what Western goals were. Did the Western governments want the Security Council to arrange a settlement, or were they simply putting Moscow on trial before world opinion as a prelude to military action? Obtaining an answer was not easy, because the three powers were no clearer on this point than they had been when Reber, Jessup, Strang, and Jebb had argued it three weeks before. As Jessup would write later, they had referred the dispute to the council *faute de mieux*, "since we were determined not to withdraw, not to fight . . . , and not to negotiate under duress."[9] A consensus on what to avoid did not extend to a determination of what should be done. Clay's preference for a convoy was an open secret, and British and French officials worried that the Americans regarded appeal to the United Nations as "the end of the road," after which the West would turn to force.[10] Since early August, Clay and Murphy had favored making the deutsche mark the sole legal tender in the western sectors, which meant repudiating the Moscow directive, and there was support for this step in Washington. Yet other indications pointed in the opposite direction. Marshall told Bevin and Schuman that a convoy was "quite impracticable," and Lovett put the Western currency maneuver on hold due to French resistance, British doubts, and the desire not to undermine the Western case in the Security Council. Holmes recalled a "senior member" of the American delegation (probably Dulles) suggesting that Canada put forward a substantive solution, including perhaps the withdrawal of all four powers from Berlin.[11] At some point in the crisis, Marshall considered turning the city's security over to the United Nations. He discussed the idea with Dean Rusk, director of the Office of UN Affairs, who was opposed. On Marshall's instructions, Rusk broached the possibility to the Canadian secretary of state for external affairs, Lester B. Pearson, whose reaction was "very strong and very negative," and Marshall dropped the idea. Now, on September 27, Marshall told Jessup and other close advisers that, having turned to the United Nations, the West "had to be prepared to carry through," even if the decision harmed Western interests.[12]

The airlift had little effect on these studies of future possibilities. It had exceeded expectations, but no one was sure it could continue in the face of winter weather.

Bevin was hopeful, telling Commonwealth prime ministers in mid-October that it could probably continue "indefinitely." Clay and Marshall also professed optimism, assuming the joint chiefs' reluctance to send more planes could be overcome. Yet Marshall contended that the most compelling argument in favor of using the airlift was not that it might actually break the Soviet hold on the city but that "no alternative had been proposed." Two days later, he reminded Schuman and Bevin that "the procedure we were following was merely a purchase of time."[13]

For the moment, the West seemed to have a sympathetic audience. Over the summer, Jessup had kept Lie informed of developments. The secretary-general regarded the blockade as illegal and a threat to peace, and he believed the West had acted in good faith. Canada and the other noncommunist members of the Security Council—Argentina, Belgium, China, Colombia, and Syria—tended to see the crisis through Western eyes. That said, there was an element of tension and a divergence of views about what should be done. Lie saw the United Nations' role as a mediator, while the Western powers wanted to use the organization to indict the Soviet Union. The secretary-general had considered bringing the dispute before the Security Council during the early days of the crisis, only to be dissuaded by Jessup and British representative Alexander Cadogan, who made it clear that the Western powers preferred to deal directly with Moscow. Throughout the United Nation's consideration of Berlin, the Western governments remained leery of independent initiatives by the secretary-general or his staff.[14]

The Russians recognized a show trial when they saw one. Realizing the advantages the Western powers enjoyed at the United Nations (Stalin complained about the West's "guaranteed majority" on the Security Council), they condemned the Western initiative.[15] In an October 2 press statement, Sokolovsky asserted that because "no blockade exists or has existed," neither did any threat to peace. He blamed Western negotiators for the stalemate, claiming they had demanded that the commission control the Soviet bank, a transparent maneuver to dominate the eastern zone's economy and one he had dutifully rejected. Molotov echoed him in a rambling note the following day. Because the Western powers had divided Germany, he claimed, they had lost their rights in Berlin; still, the situation did not threaten peace. According to Molotov, Stalin had never said anything about four-power supervision of the bank, and in any case, the directive was silent on that point. Molotov called on the West to accept the directive as the basis for negotiation in a CFM, which, he claimed, was the only legal forum for the discussion of German issues. As for the United Nations, under article 107 of its charter, the international organization could not interfere with actions by the occupying powers "in relation to" a former Axis state "taken or authorized as a result" of the Second World War. This meant, Molotov argued, that the United Nations could not consider any question concerning Germany.[16]

When the Security Council met on October 4, Vyshinsky reiterated these assertions and contended that the Western appeal could not be placed on the agenda, much less debated. The council must first decide whether it was competent to act on the complaint, and Vyshinsky was sure it was not. In arguing this procedural point, he outlined the substantive Soviet case: his government was willing to continue talks on Berlin, an issue "closely bound up with the question of Germany as a whole," in the CFM; there was no threat to peace in Berlin, but even if there were, article 107 prevented the Security Council from dealing with it. The West had ignored the CFM—"the only legal way" to deal with Berlin—and was using the United Nations to "further its own aggressive ends."

Telling the delegates they had no authority to consider the issue was bad tactics, and Jessup played on the pride of his audience to exploit Vyshinsky's error. The Soviet stance, the American suggested, raised the question whether "the only existing general international machinery for the preservation of peace can be used to remove a threat to the peace." The issue was not Berlin, not Germany, and not even the blockade; what was at stake was the future of the United Nations.

Jessup, Cadogan, and their French colleague, Alexandre Parodi, left Vyshinsky's contentions about article 107 in ruins. The authors of the charter had included the article as a barrier against protests by former Axis states regarding UN occupation practices; it was irrelevant to disputes among victors that happened to involve occupied territory. Further, the blockade was neither authorized nor imposed as a result of the war. Cadogan noted that while the CFM was a proper forum for the discussion of Germany, Vyshinsky's claim that it was the only proper forum was inadmissible. The Western representatives stressed that their governments were ready to convene a CFM—but only after the blockade was lifted. They would not negotiate under duress.[17]

After two days of debate over whether to put Berlin on the agenda, Security Council president Juan Atilio Bramuglia of Argentina called for the yeas and nays. When the balloting was over, Western victory seemed complete, because no neutral country had abstained or voted with the Soviet Union. The lone dissenters, Vyshinsky and the head of the Ukrainian delegation, Dmitri Z. Manuilsky, announced that they would not participate in any further discussion of Berlin. Yet both were in their places the next day to hear Cadogan, Jessup, and Parodi present the Western version of recent events.[18] This was inept diplomacy, because it forfeited an opportunity to rebut Western charges, elaborate the position taken in Molotov's notes, or introduce counterproposals that might shift the onus for continued deadlock onto the West. Through their silence, Vyshinsky and Manuilsky allowed the West to define the issue, expand its critique of Soviet policy, and avoid ambiguous and complicated technical points.

As the debate in the Security Council continued, Dulles flew to Albany, New

York, to brief Dewey. After a three-and-a-half-hour meeting with the Republican standard-bearer, Dulles told reporters that East-West relations were at their lowest ebb since the war. "The whole situation is very delicate right now, and I wouldn't want to do anything to rock the boat."[19] Worried that some "American hothead in Germany might do something rash," Bohlen cautioned Murphy not to aggravate the situation.[20] As wise as these precautions were, they were incomplete. In the next few days, the American boat would be rocked by none other than the president of the United States.

ON FRIDAY, OCTOBER 8, the *Chicago Tribune* broke a startling story. According to reporter Walter Trohan, President Truman had decided to send Chief Justice Frederick M. Vinson to Moscow for talks with Stalin. The *Tribune* reported that Truman had been making arrangements with the radio networks to announce the trip when Marshall, in Paris for the UN meeting, and Lovett, acting secretary in his absence, learned of the plan. Both threatened to resign, whereupon Truman dropped the scheme.[21] Not all these details were true; still, the leak was a serious setback for the administration.

The Vinson mission was the latest of many efforts by the White House and the Democratic Party to exploit diplomacy for electoral advantage. In August, William Batt of the Democratic National Committee, George Elsey, and Clark Clifford had sought to assure that any announcement of an agreement on Berlin would be made by Truman himself. As the "Berlin Merry-Go-Round" spun down in September, consultant and speechwriter Jonathan Daniels and assistant press secretary Eben A. Ayers were busy trying to show that the president was directing American diplomacy—from his campaign train. Ayers took seriously columnists' complaints that Truman should not be away from Washington when the foreign situation was so precarious. On September 21, Daniels called Assistant Secretary of State John Peurifoy, "as one Democrat to another," and asked him to arrange to have Marshall phone Truman from Paris. The ostensible motive was to keep the president informed about foreign affairs during his campaign trips, but what was really at stake, Ayers acknowledged, was "the public relations aspect of the matter." Even if Marshall "did no more than ask for the President's health, it would be helpful."[22] That same day, Truman's appointments secretary, Matthew Connelly, rejected Lovett's suggestion that the president's staff announce that Marshall had informed Truman of the latest diplomatic moves. Earlier in the day, the State Department had announced the Western powers' reply to the latest Soviet note, under arrangements worked out with Britain and France. Connelly scoffed that, under the circumstances, Lovett's proposed release would not qualify as news. Why had the State Department announced the Western reply? he bristled; that was Truman's prerogative.[23]

On Friday the twenty-fourth, Ayers thought he had found a sure way to "get a smash play in the papers." Bedell Smith was in Washington, and Ayers thought he should meet Truman's train to "report on the Moscow talks" (which had ended three weeks before). He mentioned the idea on the phone to Connelly, who was accompanying the president. Connelly called back minutes later. Truman had approved the plan and wanted Smith in San Antonio when the train arrived there Sunday morning. Ayers relayed this to Lovett, who was horrified. He and Ayers had discussed having Smith meet the president after Truman returned to Washington on October 2, and in the meantime, Lovett had approved a leave of absence for Smith. No one knew where the ambassador was. Frantic calls and a search by the Secret Service failed to find him. Saturday came and went; Smith was still missing. Shortly after Truman's train pulled into San Antonio on Sunday morning, Ayers's phone rang. It was Smith! Omar Bradley, the ambassador explained, had mentioned that the White House was looking for him. Ayers outlined the scheme; Smith agreed and flew to Dallas on the president's plane. Ayers recalled with some pride that the stunt received "pretty good play" in the press.[24]

Given such a background of political exploitation of foreign affairs, the notion of a special emissary to Moscow did not seem out of bounds. Indeed, various people had suggested the idea earlier in the year. In March, for example, Eleanor Roosevelt proposed sending a "picked group"; in July, Batt suggested that Eisenhower go to Berlin as Truman's personal emissary; in mid-September, Royall suggested a private and informal warning to the Russians that they faced either settlement on Western terms or a break in relations. The army secretary thought Marshall should deliver the warning in Paris to Molotov—who would not be there—or someone not connected with the Moscow talks could deliver the demarche to Stalin.[25]

Two speechwriters, David Noyes and Albert Z. Carr, revived the Eisenhower-as-emissary idea in late September and won Truman's approval, although the president insisted that Vinson go instead of the retired general and potential presidential candidate. The change suggested that Truman's calculations were not solely political, because he had enormous respect for Vinson. The tall Kentuckian had been elected to seven terms in the House and had also served as circuit court judge and federal loan administrator. When FDR died, Vinson had just moved into Byrnes's old job as "assistant president," director of mobilization and reconversion. Truman took to him at once and appointed him to take Henry Morgenthau's place at Treasury. The two had similar border-state backgrounds and middle-class outlooks, a buff's interest in history, and more than a passing fondness for poker. Both reveled in hard-nosed practical politics and were avid Democratic partisans. These affinities, plus Vinson's loyalty, skill as a conciliator and administrator, and mastery of tax and fiscal policy, made him one of Truman's closest advisers and perhaps the most influential member of the cabinet, until the president nominated him to be chief justice in the spring of 1946. In 1950 and 1951, Truman would try to persuade Vinson to run as his successor; now he wanted to send the Kentuckian to confer with Stalin and save the peace.[26]

Truman's clear notion of who his emissary should be did not extend to what his envoy should do. According to a draft presidential speech, Vinson was not to seek detailed arrangements but was to deal with the "larger issue of the moral relationship" with Russia and test Stalin's willingness to "work with us in arresting the trend toward war." Truman claimed to believe that, despite his best efforts, the Russians simply did not understand his sincerity and his desire for peace. The Russians were intransigent because the West had not made its intentions clear. The president also pursued a parallel and unrelated line of argument: the problem was not clarity of Western exposition; it was Stalin's paranoia. The Soviet dictator needed "an opportunity to open up," "get over some of his inhibitions," and "unburden himself to someone on our side he felt he could trust fully." If that happened, Truman thought, "perhaps we could get somewhere." As Carr understood the "intellectual core" of the mission, communist doctrine held that war between socialist and capitalist states was inevitable. If Stalin would disavow this "threat of eventual war" implicit in Marxist theory, he would do much to dispel the distrust that poisoned relations. Of course, Truman admitted, if the Russians were "hell-bent" on world conquest, war was inevitable.[27]

This rationale—much of it devised after the fact—does Truman little credit. Someone as close to him as Dean Acheson found it unpersuasive years later.[28] The man who had insisted in March 1947 that the world faced a choice between "alternative ways of life" was now reducing the Cold War to a misunderstanding that could be cleared up by a heart-to-heart chat. As excessive as the rhetoric of the Truman Doctrine had been, the president's current approach trivialized East-West differences. There were difficulties with this approach even if it were taken on its own terms. If the problem was Soviet doubt about American sincerity, one wonders how giving the uptight Russian dictator a chance to get over his inhibitions would improve matters. For all Truman's respect for Vinson, why he thought Stalin would pour out his heart to the American jurist is a mystery. Perhaps Truman was projecting onto international affairs his tendency to see domestic politics in personal terms, which would reduce the Cold War to a matter of personalities, not a clash between differing ways of life. If so, it was an approach filled with pitfalls, because the president was not the best judge of character. He "liked old Joe" Stalin and thought him a "decent fellow," he had remarked casually in June. Truman shared a common illusion of the time—that Molotov systematically misled Stalin about Western policies and purposes. It followed that if someone could get through to the Soviet dictator, problems might be settled. Yet Truman also believed that Stalin was a figurehead, "a prisoner of the Politburo"; "the people who run the government" would not let him honor the agreements he made. Furthermore, the president was convinced that the Soviets *were* hell-bent on the expansionist course outlined in Peter the Great's (bogus) will. It is impossible to boil down Truman's views into something coherent. When all is said and done, the Vinson mission suggests that in 1948 Harry Truman had no clear or consistent view of Stalin, the Soviet leadership, or its foreign policy.[29]

Trying to understand the Vinson mission in terms of what the chief justice was supposed to achieve misses the point; the mission made sense only in terms of what Truman was trying to avoid. It was a sign of political and diplomatic desperation. In recent weeks, he had been forced to look over the brink and begin preparations for the possible use of atomic weapons. Truman believed in action. He was sure something must be done, and therefore could be done, to avert a slide to world war. Details did not matter. A leader created his own opportunities through decisive action.

As important as diplomatic considerations may have been, Truman's central motivation was domestic and political. Far behind in the polls, he knew he needed a dramatic gesture to seize the initiative and capture the public's imagination. Truman's denial in his memoirs that Henry Wallace's campaign influenced him strains credulity. Such a close student of history could not have forgotten 1912, when an incumbent chief executive lost reelection because his party was divided. Now Truman faced defections by Strom Thurmond's "Dixiecrats" and Wallace liberals. The Dixiecrats were a regional problem, but Wallace's Progressives posed a national threat. Wallace claimed the administration was leading the country into needless war with Russia, and Truman and his advisers worried that he might be striking a responsive chord among voters. Although popular dislike of the Soviet Union was strong, "no other subject brought such spontaneous and warm applause" as pledges to work for peace. Batt suggested early in the campaign that one reason voters were critical of American foreign policy was concern that the world was drifting toward war. He repeated the point early in August, writing to Clifford, "Fear of war is unquestionably the major concern of the American people."[30] As we have seen, Marshall had taken to heart similar warnings from Rayburn.

More scientific measures of public attitudes bore out Truman's sense of audience reaction. A Gallup poll in April indicated that 65 percent of the public believed preventing war was the country's most important problem; a month later, on the eve of the Smith-Molotov exchange, 63 percent supported a Truman-Stalin summit, with only 28 percent opposed. A State Department report in late July indicated that, while an "overwhelming majority" supported the administration's determination to remain in Berlin, there was "very strong sentiment" that the Western powers must explore "every possibility of a negotiated solution." Forrestal observed in his diary—two weeks *after* the Vinson episode, interestingly enough—that the most dangerous spot in the world was the United States, because "people are so eager for peace and have such a distaste for war that they will grasp for any sign of a solution." As if to bear him out, White House mail on the Vinson mission ran more than four to one in favor.[31]

Thus, for Truman, the details of what Vinson might achieve hardly mattered; the important point was that voters saw the president trying to reduce the risk of war. Whatever his motives and calculations, he persuaded Vinson in two talks, probably on Monday, October 4, to undertake the trip. The two apparently found time in the midst of weighing grave matters of war and peace to admire a wooden gavel Truman had received from a constituent. It had been made from the "Jefferson Davis" tree in Fulton, Missouri, where the former Confederate president supposedly appealed for sectional reconciliation in 1875. Perhaps the old rebel's call stirred the hearts of the two border-state Democrats as they groped for an end to East-West schisms.[32]

Press secretary Charles Ross called in representatives of the radio networks on Tuesday morning and asked for airtime that evening for a speech by the president. When the journalists pressed for details, Ross revealed Truman's plan. Meanwhile, the White House invited Senators Connally and Vandenberg to meet the president that afternoon. Truman planned to give them an advance briefing—a courtesy no one thought to extend to Oliver Franks or Henri Bonnet. The last detail was to let Marshall in on the secret. Truman called Lovett and told him what was afoot. As the under secretary recalled later, it was the first time he had ever told his driver to "turn on the red light and siren and race for the White House." Ushered into the Oval Office, Lovett told Truman the idea was impossible; if he went ahead, Marshall would resign. The two men went to the communications center in the basement for a teleconference with the secretary of state. As Bohlen recalled, Marshall exploded and began dictating a reply: "Never in the history of diplomatic bungling. . . ." Regaining his self-control, he stopped. "I cannot send a message like that. I am talking to my President." Instead, he told Truman that Vinson's trip would be misunderstood, making the delegation's work in Paris more difficult. He proposed to fly home that weekend for face-to-face meetings, and Truman agreed to postpone a decision until then.[33]

Truman emerged from the teleconference depressed and shaken. Over the objections of some staff members, he canceled the request for airtime and the meeting with Vandenberg and Connally. Yet the Vinson mission was not dead, for Truman continued to toy with the idea. He telephoned the two senators later in the day and asked them to drop by that evening for a private chat. Connally arrived first, and Truman outlined Vinson's mission. Connally opposed the idea so vigorously that Truman did not raise it directly with Vandenberg. Instead, he tossed out trial balloons about a personal approach to Stalin. What about a presidential phone call to the Kremlin leader, for example? Impractical, his guests thought. Truman did not speak Russian; Stalin spoke no English. Even if they could make themselves understood and reached an accord, how could it be enforced? There would be no witnesses or documents detailing what had been agreed on. "He must be feeling desperate about the campaign," Vandenberg remarked as the two legislators left the White House.[34]

Truman resumed campaigning on Wednesday. As if laying the groundwork for Vinson's trip, everywhere he went he stressed peace. Crowds were enthusiastic. Philadelphians cheered when he claimed that peace was "the goal of my public life"; they roared and stamped their feet when he ad-libbed, "I wish for peace, I work for peace, and I pray for peace continually." Throughout the northeastern states, he made the same point again and again, claiming, "I would rather have peace in the world than to be President of the United States."[35]

That was where matters stood when Trohan broke the story on Friday night. Ayers dodged reporters' questions with a terse "no comment," but they found other sources. To Ayers's dismay, the Saturday morning editions reported the story in considerable and accurate detail. Truman's train pulled into Washington at about 9:30, and the president went immediately to National Airport to meet Marshall's plane. Instead of a private meeting on a quiet Saturday, the two men faced a political maelstrom. There could be no question of going ahead; Trohan had accomplished what Marshall had returned to do.

The president and secretary of state, along with Lovett, were closeted most of the day, seeking ways to control the damage. Marshall cabled Marshall Carter, his aide in Paris, asking for an estimate of reactions there. He also outlined a cover story concocted in the White House meetings. "Tell Bohlen," he wrote, "the line we expect to take will be that the President's concern over [the] Soviet attitude regarding [the] Atomic Energy Commission led him to discuss with me the advisability of having Vinson carry [a] message direct to Stalin. We will disassociate his suggested action with the blockade of Berlin and endeavor to confine it entirely to his concern over [the] atomic issue."[36]

There were also personal matters to settle. According to Bohlen, Marshall threatened to resign if Truman went ahead. Forrest Pogue disputes that claim (Bohlen was in Paris, not the White House, after all) but concedes that the secretary almost certainly "made plain that he would leave the Cabinet shortly after the election." Marshall's health was bad, but it was no worse than it had been. The timing of his decision made it tantamount to resignation over Truman's repeated manipulation of foreign affairs for partisan advantage. In the spring, Marshall had resisted Truman's political approach to the Palestine issue; the Vinson mission was the last straw.[37]

Marshall's sense of duty would not let him contradict his president in public. In parallel press releases issued late Saturday afternoon, the two men followed the line

Marshall had outlined for Carter and Bohlen. Truman alleged that he and Marshall had talked by Teletype on Tuesday about Soviet obstruction, particularly over "the atomic problem." He had suggested an effort to remove Soviet misunderstanding of the West's position. But when Marshall described the situation at the United Nations and the risks inherent in "any unilateral action" by the United States, the president claimed, he dropped the idea. For his part, Marshall confirmed that he and Truman had discussed the possibility of Vinson's trip four days before, citing the president's supposed concern over Moscow's "intransigent attitude" over "the atomic problem." He denied reports he and the president disagreed over "important matters of foreign relations" and told reporters the United States was ready to convene a foreign ministers' meeting, provided the Soviets lifted the blockade first.[38]

If the Vinson mission cost Truman his secretary of state, it helped the president politically, for it appealed to the concerns of American voters. This trend in public opinion was more than a residual belief in the need to negotiate. The American people were of two minds: while they favored a hard line, they hoped for a bold diplomatic move that would end the Cold War. The combination of Truman's actions in Berlin and the Vinson mission suited this mood perfectly. Resistance to Soviet coercion in Germany showed Truman to be a resourceful leader who rejected appeasement, while the chief justice's abortive trip showed voters that the former captain of artillery understood war and would do whatever he could to avert it. Issues of war and peace, as represented by Berlin and Vinson, may not have been the critical margin when weighed against the weakness of the GOP, the complacent campaign tactics of its candidate, and the continued cohesion and strength of the New Deal coalition, but they did help Truman win a close race.[39]

Politics may stop at the water's edge, but its effects rarely do. The Vinson mission harmed the nation diplomatically. In September, the Americans had opposed continuing four-power discussions with the Soviet Union; in October, without a word of warning to its allies, the White House was ready to open bilateral talks. In September, the Europeans had been convinced that the Americans were pushing toward a showdown; now Truman had retreated. A bellicose ally is a known quantity, as is a timid one; one that is both makes coalition diplomacy nearly impossible. Bevin had long worried about "the danger of the two big powers joining up," and memories of Smith-Molotov were still fresh. Truman had not only revived Europeans' fear that, in a crisis, the United States would negotiate with the Kremlin behind their backs; he had also reinforced their worry that they were allied with a power unable to make up its mind about world affairs. At American urging, western Europeans had pursued policies that antagonized the Soviet Union, such as the Marshall Plan, the Brussels treaty, and the London program. They expected American protection, but thus far, the United States had evaded commitment. This unwillingness to face the costs of a risky policy upset the Europeans, who, as Bevin was fond of reminding Marshall, were "in the front line."[40] Cadogan's estimate was that Moscow saw the episode as proof that U.S. policy was not as firm as it seemed. From Stalin's perspective, there was no need to negotiate; he could simply wait until Vinson or some other American emissary arrived with a pocketful of concessions.[41]

The Soviets were, according to one close student of their diplomacy, "obviously fascinated" by the prospects. Rumors that Truman might send Vinson after all dogged the president again and again over the next few months. Moscow's first reaction to Trohan's story had been to see a connection between Vinson and Berlin. *Pravda* reported on October 11 that Truman had decided on the move out of dissatisfaction with Marshall's handling of the dispute at the United Nations, while headlines in *Tägliche Rundschau* read: "Retreat on Berlin Question—Security Council to Give Up Debate on Berlin."[42] The Western powers had maintained they would not negotiate until the blockade was lifted; Truman's action demolished that position, encouraged the Soviets to hold out for bilateral talks, and contributed to Stalin's judgment that he need make no concessions. Not surprisingly, Vyshinsky's stance at the United Nations hardened, as a new initiative by the neutrals soon made clear.

THE SAME DAY TRUMAN raised the Vinson mission with Marshall, Bramuglia called together representatives of the six neutral nations to see if they might explore grounds for a settlement.[43] Soviet claims that the Security Council lacked jurisdiction suggested that the best hope for agreement lay in private diplomacy, not plenary debate. The six agreed they should seek information and explore positions. The Canadians reported that the British and Americans supported Bramuglia's initiative, although both showed anxiety and "considerable . . . nervous interest."[44]

There were two grounds for Anglo-American concern. The first was a paradox that weakened the Western position. The stronger the Western legal case, the more the neutrals would press the West for concessions. Knowing the Soviets would not be swayed by world opinion or appeals to morality, the six would turn to the Western powers for the compromises necessary to avert war. Given the precariousness of the West's position in Berlin, that risked disaster. The second ground for worry was that the neutrals' campaign for Western concessions was likely to start where direct East-West discussions had ended—that is, with the August 30 directive. That would reimmerse the West in the technicalities it had turned to the United Nations to escape. Americans feared that if the neutrals took this dangerously ambiguous document as their starting point, they might destroy Western rights in Berlin.[45]

The Western delegations relied on the Canadians to "understand their point of view and forestall unwise actions," and the Canadians did not disappoint them.[46] "By sheer force of personality," the head of the Canadian delegation, Andrew G. L. McNaughton, exercised considerable influence within the group, steering it in ways that kept the reins in Western hands.[47] Throughout, the Canadians stayed in close touch with the Americans and the British, providing daily reports on the neutrals' progress. Jessup and members of the British delegation made a habit of stopping by the Canadian delegation minutes after meetings of the six adjourned. McNaughton assured Cadogan over dinner on October 11 that he would warn of any development that might embarrass the West. When the neutrals began drafting a resolution, the Canadians matter-of-factly asked the British and Americans for suggestions. Holmes recalled stalling work on the draft for a few days while Britain and the United States patched up differences with France.[48]

Bramuglia began by submitting to the Western powers a list of questions dealing with possible settlements. The list annoyed the Americans. A strong stand by the Security Council might improve chances for a settlement, Bohlen contended, but Bramuglia's search for a middle ground might stiffen Soviet resolve and "place the Western powers progressively in a worse position." Therefore, the U.S. answer suggested that the council call on the Soviet Union to lift the blockade.[49]

Bramuglia next approached Vyshinsky, proposing a simultaneous end to the blockade and the Western counterblockade. The foreign ministers would meet—although whether this too would be simultaneous with the lifting of restrictions or occur at some later date was not clear. After checking with Moscow, Vyshinsky refused; after all, this was the week Trohan had broken the Vinson story. He demanded that the Security Council remove the Berlin dispute from its agenda and that the CFM deal with the controversy according to the directive and the Potsdam accords. As for Bramuglia's plan, Vyshinsky would not discuss it. Under the August 30 directive, the Soviet mark was to be introduced throughout Berlin the day the blockade ended; because Bramuglia said nothing about this, Vyshinsky could not consider his proposal.[50]

While this brusque rejection surprised the neutrals, it did not discourage them, and when the Security Council reconvened, Bramuglia submitted new questions. This time, he wanted to know about the origins of the blockade, methods of enforcement, and current conditions, as well as details of the August directive and why it had not been implemented. The Western powers, despite misgivings about the unwelcome attention accorded the directive, promised prompt replies. Vyshinsky refused to answer, denouncing the request as a plot by the West and the neutrals to trick him into participating in the council's illegal debate.[51]

The issue narrowed to one of timing. The Western delegations insisted that the directive needed clarifications and safeguards. Unwilling to negotiate these supplemental agreements under duress, they were willing to begin talks the day the blockade ended. Vyshinsky, however, stood on his statement that the directive required the lifting of the blockade and the currency changeover to occur simultaneously.[52]

China drafted a resolution on this point that sided with the West, only to have Jessup complain that it did not go far enough in condemning the Soviets.

McNaughton and the Canadians warned that the choice was between a resolution along American lines, which would alienate some of the neutrals, and one like China's, which would isolate the Soviet Union.[53] Although representatives of the Western powers worked out revisions with Bramuglia on the evening of October 19, the British reported that the Argentinean was "very irritated" by American pressure the next day for more changes. Cadogan advised London that "tempers were very strained . . . [by] this American attempt at perfectionism."[54] In the end, the Western powers accepted the resolution during council debate on October 25. Vyshinsky spoke last and maintained the uncompromising line he had taken since the Vinson story had appeared. Denouncing the resolution as a Western attempt to dictate to the Soviet Union, he vetoed it.[55]

Canadian diplomats looked back on their efforts with mixed feelings. Though the Security Council had not vindicated the hopes of 1945, it had not collapsed under the weight of superpower confrontation—at least not yet. Canada had worked closely with the British and Americans to protect the Western stake in Berlin without compromising its efforts to arrange a settlement. Yet what Cadogan termed American perfectionism seemed likely to continue to threaten Canada's two-track policy. In a postmortem, Holmes noted growing U.S. ambivalence toward the neutrals. A split was developing within the American delegation between those like Jessup, who encouraged the neutrals, and those like Bohlen, who were ready to repudiate the August directive and make the deutsche mark the sole legal tender in Berlin.[56] During a second round of talks, Canada's position would become increasingly precarious as Bohlen's group gained ascendancy.

Early Western reactions, though, were positive. Meeting two days after the Russian veto, Western foreign ministers reaffirmed their support of the six. There seemed little alternative. Raising the issue in the General Assembly would be pointless. The Russians could ignore even a strong resolution, and Western leaders doubted they could obtain more than a mild appeal to both sides to compose their differences. Trying to carry out the Security Council's resolution against Soviet opposition risked a showdown or rebuff. The best course seemed to be to leave the issue on the agenda without offering any new proposal. Marshall reflected the crosscurrents within his delegation. On the one hand, he worried that the neutrals might put the West in a "bad position" by taking the October 25 resolution as the starting point for the next round, when he and his colleagues had already gone "to the absolute limit" in supporting it. On the other hand, the West could not oppose any effort by the six that promised results and did not prejudice Western rights in the blockaded city.[57]

WESTERN DIPLOMATS LEFT the initiative with the six neutrals. The Americans preferred to have an intermediary work out detailed four-power arrangements governing use of the Soviet mark in Berlin.[58] They had been considering this idea for several weeks and found it attractive. With supplemental safeguards, even the August directive might be acceptable. Dulles reflected this trend of thought in a letter to Vandenberg. Experience indicated there was "little value in agreeing with the Soviets in terms of *generalities,*" he wrote; only an agreement that is "specific as to every significant practical detail" could work. Unless all loopholes were closed, any accord would prove illusory. There were several possible intermediaries: Dutch, Swedish, or Swiss central bankers; the secretary-general's staff; or technical experts from the six neutral nations.[59]

Events over the next few weeks gave the last group the nod. Turning to European central bankers, unfamiliar with conditions in Berlin, seemed unwise. Two attempts by the secretary general had encountered Western resistance. Lie had kept aloof from Bramuglia's efforts so he might offer himself as a mediator should the Argentinean fail. He suggested on October 26 that currency experts from both sides meet under neutral auspices, and Stalin lifted Lie's hopes in a *Pravda* interview on October 29. Attempting to shift attention from Vyshinsky's veto, the Soviet leader claimed that the Western powers had thwarted attempts at compromise; his government desired peace.[60] The next day, Vyshinsky surprised Lie by seeking him out and listening attentively as the secretary-general outlined a plan for currency talks; Vyshinsky authorized Lie to explore the possibilities. Though dubious, Jessup felt compelled to go along. He asked only that the British and French be informed, and there Lie's attempt foundered. London would not agree, preferring a new effort by Bramuglia and a committee of currency experts from the neutral countries in the Security Council. Here, both sides would provide information but not participate in direct talks.[61]

Lie would not be put off. On November 13, he and the president of the General Assembly, Herbert Evatt of Australia, made a public appeal to both sides, calling on them to open "immediate conversations." Moscow's answer was noncommittal, agreeing to talks on Berlin if they were based on the directive and, in a hint that a Western emissary would be welcome, acknowledging that contacts among heads of state were valuable in the search for peace.[62]

The Western answer took more time because, as Jessup recalled, the Evatt-Lie letter "very much annoyed" the Americans. It seemed to apportion blame equally, and it undercut the Western refusal to negotiate under duress. Instead of pressing the Soviets to end the blockade, the neutrals took for granted (or seemed to) that the Soviets would be indifferent to appeals to morality, world opinion, or common interest, so they urged the democracies to retreat instead. Bohlen found the double standard galling. He and Jessup remarked later on how often they had been challenged to prove that America's intentions were peaceful, as if the United States, not the Soviet Union, were the one on trial. Evatt had long been unpopular with American officials, who disliked his personality, his stances in Australian politics, and his foreign policy inclinations. Evatt had "a remarkable ability to alienate people," and he displayed it to the full that autumn. At a reception, Jessup recalled, Evatt turned on him and snarled, "So you want to start another war, do you? Well, we're not going to let you do it!" Marshall attributed the Evatt-Lie initiative to self-seeking: the belief in Paris, he advised Lovett, was that Evatt, ever eager for headlines, had duped Lie, anxious to inject the office of the secretary-general into the dispute, into sending the letter. Evatt's explanation, naturally enough, was different and invoked Truman's recent foray into personal diplomacy. He told Walter Lippmann, then touring Europe, that he had issued the appeal "to give President Truman a chance to act on the impulse . . . illustrated by the Vinson affair."[63]

Marshall's answer reflected growing irritation. Once more he tried to induce the neutrals to accept the West's definition of the issue. He stressed that the October 25 resolution had been a "sincere and statesmanlike" initiative defeated by Soviet intransigence. The Western powers had referred the blockade to the Security Council because it was a threat to peace. It remained a threat, and the moral choice confronting the United Nations also remained. The secretary barely concealed his displeasure with the neutrals' failure to oppose aggression, as he called on them to abandon mediation: "To compromise the principle of the Charter that force shall not be used for the attainment of national objectives would endanger the peace of the world."[64]

To shift attention away from Evatt and Lie, the Western governments welcomed a new initiative by Bramuglia, a series of questions about the proposed four-power financial commission and its authority. The Western reply envisaged this commission as "the controlling authority in Berlin" regarding money, credit, and banking. It would control those activities of the German Bank of Emission that affected the introduction and use of the Soviet mark in the city, and its mandate would go beyond that proposed in the directive to include supervision of the city budget, control of the *Stadtkontor* and other banking and credit institutions, prevention of discrimination against any of the four occupied sectors, and supervision of the Magistrat's licensing of imports and exports. Bramuglia had asked for a draft directive that could be issued to inaugurate this system of financial controls; the Western governments replied that the military governors had been unable to draft such legislation because of Soviet obstruction.[65]

The Soviet reply stood on the August directive. The Russian government agreed that quadripartite control of financial arrangements should be vested in a commission but claimed that the directive described its functions and authority in adequate detail. In answer to Bramuglia's request for the exact wording of an order by the military governors to institute four-power controls, the Russians suggested that the wording "correspond to the agreed directive." A second round of activity by the six seemed imminent, and Marshall and Jessup assured Pearson that the United States would cooperate "fully and loyally."[66]

With the ground prepared, on November 30, Bramuglia proposed that the six neutral nations form a technical committee of experts. Taking into account events since August, the group would attempt to find a way to put the directive into practice. Representatives from Lie's office would assist, and Bramuglia appealed to the four powers to send technical representatives to provide information and advice; they would not negotiate. If the neutrals could not find a solution, they would explain why in a report to the Security Council.[67]

The Western powers reserved their position; the Soviets couched their acceptance in vague terms. Norman Robertson, who would represent Canada, also had mixed feelings. Although he considered the plan "the most feasible approach . . . yet," he regarded the committee's terms of reference as "somewhat wooly" and was worried about the situation in Berlin. A technical solution would be meaningless if "all basis of common action" were destroyed in the blockaded city. The prospects for success were "dubious," he thought. Even so, Canada had a duty as a member of the Security Council to take part if the four powers were willing to make this "final effort."[68]

Robertson's concern stemmed from recent events in Berlin. Even as Bramuglia was pulling together the committee, Berlin's city government split apart. Elections required by the city's 1946 provisional constitution had been scheduled for December 5. The SED had approved plans for the vote in June—a step it immediately regretted, as Berliners' mood made it clear that the party would lose even more badly than it had in October 1946. Faced with the prospect of being swept from power, even in the eastern sector, SED leaders declared the balloting unnecessary. To help, Kotikov set impossible terms; when, as expected, the Western commanders rejected them, he banned the election in his sector.[69] This posed a dilemma for the West, as Marshall and Royall explained to the NSC on November 26. Going ahead with the vote would "irrevocably" split Berlin and destroy "any hope of compromise," while delaying the election "would be interpreted as retreat." Royall thought the only solution was for Bramuglia and his colleagues to request a delay. Four days later, however, the Soviets "deposed" the Magistrat and proclaimed a regime of their own. The SED's Ottomar Greschke, deputy speaker of the city assembly, called an "extraordinary meeting" for the evening of the thirtieth. Greschke lacked the authority to convene such a session, but SED leaders went ahead with their effort, as one of them cynically put it, to "end the division of Berlin." It proved to be an extraordinary meeting indeed. Of the 130-odd members of the assembly, only 26 attended, and they were submerged by some 1,360 other delegates, SED members, and representatives of front organizations in east Berlin. The gathering "dismissed" the Magistrat and elected another under Fritz Ebert, son of the first president of the Weimar Republic and, in Howley's description, a "fat, repulsive . . . opportunist."[70]

Although Western officials denounced the move, some privately welcomed it. Bohlen, for example, called it a "stroke of luck" that saddled the Russians with responsibility for the split, opened the way for the election, and made the August 30 directive irrelevant as a basis for diplomacy. Lovett took it as "final proof" that the Russians "never wanted an agreement," while the CIA interpreted it to mean that Moscow realized western Germany and the Ruhr were beyond its reach and had settled on Berlin as a consolation prize. As a consequence, the agency expected the Soviets to intensify the blockade.[71]

General Pope reported that the elections, held on schedule, were an "eloquent expression of anti-Soviet feeling." Nothing deterred Berliners from voting: not the Ebert government, not banner headlines in the December 4 edition of *Tägliche Rundschau* that the West would abandon Berlin in January, and not the scheduling of a normal workday in east Berlin. Turnout was 86.2 percent, with the leading anti-Soviet party, the SPD, garnering 64.5 percent of the ballots cast in a three-way race.[72]

Installation of the Ebert regime, the subsequent purge of borough administrations in east Berlin, and the vote in the western sectors strengthened the hand of those who opposed further compromise on the currency issue, including Clay and Murphy in Berlin and Bohlen in Paris. They revived the notion of making the deutsche mark the sole legal tender in the western sectors. This threatened to overturn the diplomacy of the last four months. All negotiations since August had rested on the assumption that the price for ending the blockade was withdrawal of the B-mark and Western acceptance of the Soviet mark as the only currency in Berlin. The stumbling blocks in the Moscow talks, the military governors' discussions, and the United Nations debates had centered on how to arrange that currency changeover and how to devise effective four-power controls over the Soviet mark. Banning the Soviet mark would mean explicit rejection of the August directive—and prolonged stalemate. But now the onus for the city's division was on the Soviet Union, Bohlen argued; the West should act.[73] Clay agreed. He thought the only course was to continue the airlift and introduce the deutsche mark, although he acknowledged that it "would of course provide no long term solution" and deepen Berliners' sense of isolation.[74]

The odds against the technical committee thus increased before it ever convened. At its first session, the group elected Norman Robertson chairman. Despite his early doubts, Robertson, one of Canada's ablest civil servants, soon warmed to the work.[75] He may have been encouraged by a new Soviet negotiating position, adopted December 4. The Soviets presented "clarifications" of their November 20 answers to Bramuglia's questions. Actually, these were commentaries on the West's replies, ones that revealed a shift in position. They proposed that a Berlin branch of the Soviet bank be created to carry out, under commission control, financial and credit policy in Berlin. The commission would supervise the city's fiscal policies and financial activities, monitor the currency conversion, and license the city's external trade. Instead of insisting on following the letter of the directive, Moscow now had no objection if the military governors put "the agreement" into effect through joint orders—a procedure suggested by the West. Important differences over external trade and the scope of the commission's power remained, however, and the Soviet wording may have appeared to concede more than it actually did. When accepting a Western point, the Soviets invariably phrased it differently, and the differences may have been designed to serve as breaking points later. For example, the Western powers proposed that the commission supervise and control the currency changeover; the Soviets did not object to commission control over "*the agreement on* the introduction of the German mark of the Soviet zone"—perhaps an important difference, perhaps not. When the Western powers argued that the military governors must issue detailed legislation to create the commission and define its powers, the Russians answered that they had no objection to the military governors putting "the agreement" into effect by order. Did "the agreement" mean a future accord or the August 30 directive?[76]

Robertson and his colleagues completed a draft agreement and sent it to the four powers on December 22. Under its terms, a four-power financial commission, operating by unanimous vote, would control Berlin's finance, credit, and banking. Instead of making the Soviet bank or the *Stadtkontor* the city's central bank, a Berlin branch of the Soviet bank would be established and would operate under four-power control. The branch bank's eight directors would consist of four representatives of the parent Soviet bank and one from each of the occupying powers. Decisions would be by majority vote. This bank would "control" and the commission would "supervise" the city's conversion to the Soviet mark. Berlin's money supply would be linked to that of the surrounding zone: the ratio between the initial issue of Soviet marks in the city and the amount circulating in the zone at the time of conversion would be maintained. The Russians would be obliged to report each month on currency circulation in their zone as well as on similar topics, so that Berlin's wages, prices, taxes, and banking practices could conform to those in the zone. Trade with the western zones and third countries would be under the control of a quadripartite board of trade that would issue licenses; the Soviets would "automatically" grant transit to shipments approved by the board. Imports of food, fuel, and power would be provided under quarterly agreements by the occupying powers; if they reached no agreement, the previous one would continue. Traffic would be controlled at quadripartite checkpoints at ports of entry.[77]

Robertson had already advised Ottawa that such a plan was the only way to maintain a "tolerable political position" for the Western powers in the city. The symbolism of making the Soviet mark the city's only currency was unfortunate, but the Western powers had already restricted circulation of the B-mark (three-quarters of the notes used in the western sectors were Russian), and they had agreed during the Moscow talks to accept the ostmark. Robertson saw the technical committee's function as arranging the introduction of the Soviet mark without increasing Russian influence in the western sectors, and he thought the draft report left the West with "as large a degree of independence as could reasonably be hoped for in the extraordinary position of Berlin."[78]

The Americans disagreed. For days, they had been displeased with the committee's line of thought, and it took less than forty-eight hours for Lovett, Royall, and Draper to decide to reject Robertson's plan.[79] They disliked decision by majority vote on the bank board because the Soviets could outvote the West; they opposed decision by unanimous vote on the commission because the Soviets might use their veto to block attempts to police the bank or protect Western interests. Draper denounced the proviso requiring the city's price, wage, tax, and credit policies to follow those of the surrounding zone as a maneuver to "make the Western Sectors part of the Soviet zone." Army planners did not want to give the Russians any power over Berlin's external trade, even in a quadripartite setting, fearing abuse. They doubted the Russians would provide the economic data needed to make the system work and pointed out that verification of whatever data were provided would be impossible. The underlying argument behind American objections was that the committee assumed cooperation and good faith, while confrontation and mistrust were the governing realities in Berlin. The plan might be reasonable if all four powers desired a return to the quadripartite system devised by the EAC protocols and the Potsdam accords. The trouble was that neither the Soviets nor the Americans were comfortable with that system. Forcing the two together increased opportunities for conflict, not concord. As far as the Americans were concerned, the committee had solved the problem by wishing away its core; it was time to make the deutsche mark Berlin's sole legal tender.[80]

At the same time Lovett and Royall were taking such a stiff line, Truman seemed headed in another direction. At a testimonial lunch for his friend Eddie Jacobsen two days after Christmas, the president commented that "certain leaders" in the Kremlin were "exceedingly anxious" to reach an accord with the West. The president expressed confidence that the Cold War would end during his second term, and he called on all Americans to help him persuade the Soviets that "peace is all we want." Yet he went on to complain that Moscow had broken all its agreements. His remarks raised eyebrows in Europe, where rumors spread of a new Vinson mission and a split between the White House and the Department of State. Bevin was prompted to ask Franks "whether the Administration have got a firm policy, and if so, what it is." The Americans gave reassuring answers, but the British were unsure where Washington was leading them.[81]

Brushing aside opposition from the Treasury and the Bank of England, Bevin welcomed Robertson's plan.[82] He explained his reasons to the American chargé. Echoing Marshall's private comment of three months earlier, he contended that, having brought the dispute to the Security Council, the Western powers could not reject out of hand a solution the United Nations suggested. The committee's plan could be improved and made to work, and he thought it might be more suitable in a divided Berlin than in a united one. Finally, if the United States did not like the committee's plan, it was obliged to provide a better one.[83]

Meeting during the first week of January, Western finance experts could not resolve these differences. Instead of the committee's plan, the U.S. representative wanted to substitute a counterproposal. Under this approach, the Soviet bank would provide the western sectors with an initial supply of marks. Thereafter, the two halves of the city would operate independently.[84]

The American stance raised doubt in London and Ottawa about U.S. intentions. For their part, the Americans found their allies' attitudes "incomprehensible."[85] Bevin interpreted the American position as proof that the United States did not want an agreement and preferred to have the blockade and the airlift continue indefinitely. He resented pressure to introduce the deutsche mark. From Berlin, General Robertson suspected the Americans had devised their counterproposal "deliberately with a view to torpedoing the neutral experts' efforts."[86]

If the American position troubled the British, it caused enormous problems for the Canadians. Norman Robertson admitted being "increasingly puzzled and disturbed" by Washington's attitude, and he asked that Wrong seek an authoritative statement of U.S. policy. Did the Americans want an agreement that lifted the blockade, or did they want the stalemate to continue?[87] Pearson's deputy, Escott Reid, passed the request on to Wrong, along with comments by R. G. Riddell of the UN Division of External Affairs. Since the Security Council debates began, Riddell observed, the question of American intentions had "perplexed" Canadians. Jessup and Marshall had assured them that the United States wanted the council to arrange an end to the dispute, but Bohlen and others had repeatedly suggested that the Americans saw the debates as a prelude to more drastic action. Riddell believed that "either one policy or the other would be understandable, and that we should support it, but we had a right to expect from the Americans that they should tell us which line they wished to take, and that they should not leave us constantly in danger of advocating in the Security Council policies which they might abandon themselves."[88]

When Wrong raised the issue, he was ushered in to see Bohlen, now back in Washington. The American insisted that Marshall's assurances to Pearson remained valid, but once that pro forma protestation of good intentions was out of the way, Bohlen confirmed Robertson's worst fears. The division of Berlin, he argued, rendered any settlement based on the August directive obsolete; anything less than the

U.S. counterproposal was "surrender to the Russians." Rather than accept the committee's plan, the American government preferred that Berlin remain blockaded. What was more, the time had come to make the deutsche mark the sole legal tender in Berlin.[89]

When the committee reconvened on January 14 and the Western governments submitted comments on its draft plan, American isolation deepened. The United States rejected the draft. Robertson's group had tried to lay down precise operating rules in advance, but instead of being a virtue, the plan's complexity was a drawback that created "innumerable" opportunities for "obstructionist tactics." Dulles had written to Vandenberg that the United States would insist on an agreement so detailed that it closed all possible loopholes, but American mistrust of the Soviet Union was now so great that no accord could be detailed enough. Instead of the committee's plan, the Americans recommended their counterproposal. The British and French submitted a separate statement that expressed sympathy for the American plan but did not endorse it, accepting instead the committee's draft as a basis for discussion.[90]

For the rest of January, the committee lapsed into what Charles Ritchie called an "advanced state of paralysis," unable to decide what to do in the face of American opposition.[91] There was a flurry of movement at the end of the month, when the United States moderated its position. It now proposed that the Western powers urge the committee to recommend the American plan to the Security Council as an interim measure until the military governors could devise some way to reunify Berlin. Once that was accomplished, the four powers would consider the neutrals' original recommendations.[92]

This minuscule shift and the belief that withdrawal of the B-mark in postelection Berlin would be politically disastrous persuaded the British to join the Americans. But first, Bevin was careful to secure an assurance from General Robertson regarding the airlift.[93] In Whitehall to discuss a draft cabinet paper, the British military governor had reservations about the new course, complaining that the draft "put forward a new idea, namely that we must have a division of Germany." This is a striking comment that calls into question the assumption by some historians that Western officials aimed at and desired partition from mid-1947, if not earlier. Robertson could accept a temporary split but "could not agree" to a long-term one. "The division of Germany over a period of years would be very dangerous," he thought. "The Germans would never accept it" and "would fail to play their proper part in Western Union." Bevin's aides acknowledged that creating the Federal Republic of Germany would "accentuate and to some extent perpetuate the division of Germany," while arguing that eventual reunification remained possible. Of more immediate consequence, introducing the deutsche mark in Berlin would be "irrevocable": once the Western powers took that step, they could not replace it with the

Soviet mark. That meant scuttling the technical committee and the neutrals—and with them, the only active diplomatic venue—and relying exclusively on the airlift. Despite his doubts, Robertson insisted they must go ahead. Germans (Berliners, really) wanted it, and "above all," so did the Americans. He informed Clay of London's decision, and the two men began planning to introduce the deutsche mark, with a target date of March 10.[94]

There remained the delicate problem of explaining the shift to the Canadians. As the Berlin committee saw the situation, the Americans had gone as far as they could, and Stalin's recent answers to a journalist's questions had added a new condition by demanding that any west German government be delayed until after the CFM had met. Thus, the gap remained unbridgeable and, as Dean explained to Norman Robertson's staff, the West needed to strengthen its bargaining position. That meant relying on the airlift, perhaps for years; introducing the deutsche mark; and scuttling the committee. Dean did not say so, but the cabinet had also decided that western Germany should be made an integral part of "our Western European system." A unified Germany was too great a threat to that system, so "the division of Germany, at all events for the present, is essential for our plans," Bevin had concluded. Wearied by deadlock, Norman Robertson welcomed the shift. The U.S. plan was a "considerable advance," he thought, if only because Soviet rejection of it would leave the Russians in a more difficult position in the Security Council.[95]

On February 5, the Americans won the tripartite statement that had eluded them since early January. Contending the committee's plan could not reconcile the remaining differences, the three powers called on the neutrals to draw up an interim solution along American lines. The Western shift left the committee "puzzled and resentful," and as Norman Robertson expected, it allowed the Soviets to pose as cooperative and eager for agreement. The Russian technical expert summarily dismissed the Western proposal as beyond the committee's terms of reference. The West having rejected the committee's work, he now endorsed it. Differences between East and West were negotiable, he claimed, and surely the gap between his position and that of the neutrals could be reconciled. By the time he had finished, Robertson reported, there was not a "dry eye in [the] house."[96]

Having failed to solve the crisis through diplomacy, the Canadians now employed their skills to shield the Western powers in the committee report. Although the group's charter required an explanation of failure, Robertson feared that a detailed treatment would create "all sorts of mischief" because it would highlight Washington's "unfortunate" attitude. Committee discussion of Robertson's draft report led him to warn Ottawa that the document needed careful handling to avoid "serious damage," and by his own admission, he made "every effort . . . to render the report innocuous."[97]

Even so, the final report, sent to the council president on February 12, left British officials uneasy. They had hoped to forgo making any statement, "because we could not avoid confirming that it was the United States expert, and not the Soviet expert, who found the Committee's draft proposals unacceptable." Agreeing that council debate on the document would yield, as they disingenuously put it, "no positive results," the British and Americans moved to bury it.[98] As the State Department summarized the situation for the White House, that would open the way for introduction of the deutsche mark. The two powers dissuaded the Chinese representative, who was the council president for February, from referring the report to the council, and they had even greater success with his successor, Alberto I. Alvarez of Cuba, who was ignorant of the issues and, in Jessup's characterization, "violently anti-Soviet." He readily accepted Western suggestions not to circulate the report or even publish it as an official council document. Instead, he issued it as a routine press release. After its appearance on March 15, a carefully orchestrated Western public relations campaign explained it away and blamed the Russians for the committee's failure.[99]

The way was now open, as the Americans intended, to introduce the deutsche mark into west Berlin. On March 20, the Soviet mark ceased to be legal tender in west Berlin, but the Americans had given little thought about what to do next. They envisaged new talks with the neutrals and perhaps a special currency for Berlin, neither eastern nor western, circulating under four-power controls. Marshall's successor, Dean Acheson, thought this was the "only rational arrangement"—an odd assessment when his government had just rejected four-power controls as unworkable.[100]

WITH PUBLICATION OF the technical committee's report and Western action on currency, efforts in the United Nations to mediate the Berlin crisis came to an end. Rather than bringing the two sides together, diplomacy seemed to push them apart. Months of hard work had apparently been wasted: the neutrals were unable to mediate East-West differences, the Russians were unable to turn the blockade to diplomatic advantage, and the West was unable to end Soviet coercion. The Americans were perhaps the most disappointed, because their expectations had been so high. Despite this failure, or rather because of it, discussion at the United Nations helped clear the way for resolution of the crisis.

Like the Moscow discussions, diplomacy at the United Nations rested on the mistaken assumptions that agreement must involve the restoration of joint agencies and that the basis of settlement would be a common currency for Berlin. The Western stance on currency presented the Soviets with tantalizing possibilities. Imposing their currency on the city under weak or ineffective quadripartite controls offered a low-risk way of making a Western presence in the city impossible. A dogged Molotov did his best to bring that about in August, Sokolovsky tried again in September, and the Russians did all they could to steer Bramuglia and the technical committee in that direction in the months that followed. In retrospect, the Western powers suffered a narrow escape. Although their willingness to accept the ostmark under four-power controls appears unrealistic, it was an understandable relic of the era of quadripartite rule. Clay's planning for currency reform in the spring had included it, the British had suggested it in the June 22–23 experts' discussions, and Clay had been willing to proceed on that basis. Robertson had suggested it to Sokolovsky on June 26 and again on July 3. The Moscow talks moved it to the top of the diplomatic agenda, where it remained through the UN deliberations. Only when the technical committee tried to reconcile conflicting interests did officials begin to realize that joint agencies—especially ones involving control of currency—carried unacceptable risks and made matters worse. The U.S. government rejected the committee's draft on January 15 on just such grounds. Dulles had wanted a long, detailed document; when the neutrals produced one, the Americans realized that no matter how detailed an accord was, it could not guarantee against Soviet abuse. As Truman would write in his memoirs, "Our experience with the Russians impelled us to reject *any* plan which provided for a four-power operation."[101] The United States thus abandoned the search for a solution based on diplomacy and quadripartite agencies, preferring to consolidate its position through independent action on March 20. Just as the Americans had come to see the financial commission as a threat, the Soviets viewed city-wide elections as a danger, and they too preferred consolidation. If the Americans abandoned the pretense of sharing in the administration of east Berlin when they rejected the technical committee's plan on January 15, the Soviets tacitly admitted that west Berlin was beyond their grasp when they created the Ebert regime on November 30.

Rather than reconciling differences, quadripartite agreements deepened insecurity, and attempts to devise solutions based on them were doomed. This became clear only when the technical committee tried to devise a detailed accord. The cooperative channel had to be pursued to the end before diplomats would abandon it and look elsewhere for a solution. When close relations aggravate, it is best to separate, and the talks at the United Nations helped move leaders on both sides toward this conclusion, if only in response to their own interests. By dispelling the twin illusions that had shaped negotiations since August, the committee's failure was the necessary first step toward a realistic resolution of the crisis, a resolution that would be found not in joint action or joint institutions but in separation.

This is easier to see in retrospect. At the time, both sides seemed to face prolonged deadlock without a strategy for ending the crisis on favorable terms, other than doggedly waiting for the other to give in. Rejecting the technical committee's plan was a major decision that reoriented American policy away from the course it had followed since June. Abandoning a compromise four-power arrangement over currency meant giving up hope for a four-power accord in Germany. It also meant forgoing diplomacy in favor of exclusive reliance on the airlift and accepting, as Clay had put it in September, "a struggle of nerves until someone folds."

The prospect of unending confrontation posed more problems for the Western powers than it did for the Soviet Union, because they were a coalition dealing with a single power. It was easier for the Americans to accept deadlock than it was for their partners. In Canada's case, this might be accounted for by the different status of the two powers: one a global power concerned about its credibility and prestige and a party to the dispute, the other a "middle power" with little direct stake in the crisis. But U.S. differences with Britain were just as serious as those with Canada; French and American policies diverged even further. The British and French delayed referral to the United Nations, were dismayed by the Vinson mission, and resisted American pressure to introduce the deutsche mark and undermine the technical committee. The Americans found it easier to turn their backs on Norman Robertson and his colleagues than the Europeans did because of Washington's greater faith in the airlift and a greater sense of power. British and French pessimism about the airlift was only part of the story. Recognition that they were "in the front line" and much more exposed to the consequences of failure instilled a sense of caution that the less vulnerable Americans could neither share nor understand.

Alliances rest on common interests, so it is natural to assume that something is wrong when allies disagree. Yet interests overlap, they do not coincide, and unrealistic expectations may do more to weaken alliances than quarrels among partners. Alliance members naturally prefer to maximize their partners' obligations while minimizing their own. Alliances bring security—the support of allies when one needs them—at the risk of being dragged into another's quarrels. Wide imbalances in power can intensify this tension, fostering a resentful dependence among the weak and a resentful impatience among the strong. So it was here. That "note of arrogance" in U.S. policy that Lewis Douglas noticed reasserted itself. U.S. officials took for granted their right to set policy for the Western powers, and they expected the Europeans to stay in step. Western Europeans depended on American power to protect them from the Soviet Union, and they relied on American wisdom to do so without plunging them all into another war, but at the time, Europeans saw both as uncertain quantities. Even before the Western nations had agreed on the text of a North Atlantic security pact, we can see the beginning of a pattern in U.S.-European relations that would extend through the Cold War and into the twenty-first century, in which allies bickered over risks, duties, burdens, and burden sharing.

If, in this particular case, the Americans were correct to see the futility of continued efforts to revive unworkable quadripartite arrangements, that does not necessarily mean they were wise in pushing for an early break. Timing was important. There is a strong case to be made that by postponing introduction of the deutsche mark until March 1949, the British and French saved Berlin. To understand that requires an examination of conditions in the city during the blockade and the effects of the Western currency initiative.

CHAPTER 10

"Lieber Pomm als 'Frau Komm!'"

In addition to being a diplomatic struggle between East and West, the Berlin blockade was a political competition conducted in the streets of a proud but ruined city. Berlin's residents were not spectators at a contest among foreign occupiers; they were participants. As Brian Robertson noted at the time, and as others have emphasized since, the West's ability to stay in Berlin "depends in the final issue upon the morale of the population."[1]

Myth and legend overlay our image of the blockade, making it difficult to see the city's residents accurately. When we hear the word *Berliners,* we imagine an undifferentiated mass, solidly pro-Western, stoically enduring unprecedented hardship. The most familiar names are Ernst Reuter, Franz Neumann, Otto Suhr, and Ferdinand Friedensburg. Louise Schroeder would be a better choice, because the average Berliner was a woman.[2] Economic and class differences mattered. Political opinions and intensity of commitment varied. The demands of daily life left little time for politics. And as one author suggested, "There was very little love for any foreigners in Berlin," which was certainly true at the blockade's beginning.[3] Defeat and its aftermath had given Berliners little reason to be enthusiastic about anything. Wartime destruction and postwar dismantling had stripped the city of much of its industry, depriving thousands of their livelihood. Having requisitioned the best housing, the occupiers lived comfortably amid the city's rubble. Violence and intimidation were not restricted to Red Army soldiers and the eastern sector, especially in the early years of the occupation. Anger and resentment over German women's sexual relations with occupation soldiers were widespread.[4]

We tend to see conditions during the blockade as static, but in reality, they (and Berliners' perceptions of them) fluctuated. Circumstances were easier at first—that is, when the blockade was not tightly enforced, gardens could supplement supplies, and people expected the crisis would soon end. Berliners tried to maintain a semblance of ordinary life, which was easier when unemployment remained near preblockade levels. Life became harsher as winter approached, darkness lengthened, unemployment rose, and the end of the crisis receded into the distant future. Anticipation made the autumn a more anxious time than winter itself, which proved unusually mild.

WHAT WERE CONDITIONS LIKE, and how did Berliners cope? Life during the blockade was hard, as it had been for years. By May 1945, after months of bombing and weeks of street fighting, Berlin was a "cemetery of ruins." By one account, it had absorbed more bombs and shells than any other city on the planet and contained one-sixth of all the rubble in Germany. Estimates were that clearing the debris at a rate of 500 railway cars a day would take sixteen years—once trains began to move. So many landmarks had vanished that an American who had lived in prewar Berlin had trouble finding his way. Some thought the city must be rebuilt elsewhere, if it were rebuilt at all.[5] Shattered buildings swayed ominously. Only a quarter of prewar dwellings were habitable. Debris choked bomb- and shell-cratered streets; rubble and sewage clogged rivers and canals; muck filled the subway. Natural gas flared from mains; smoke, dust, and the smell of the unburied dead filled the air. Survivors looked more dead than alive, and many of them would die—4,000 a day in August, twenty-six times the prewar rate.[6]

What the war left untouched fell prey to the victors. Western officials estimated that the Soviets removed 53 percent of Berlin's prewar industrial capacity, more than double the 23 percent destroyed during the war. Some 80 percent of Berlin's surviving machine-tool production, 70 percent of raw materials, 60 percent of light industry, and much of its electrical generating capacity went east.[7]

To support a population of about 3.2 million, the city possessed about a million habitable housing units in 1945.[8] *Habitable* was loosely defined. Several families might share a room, especially in working-class areas. Workers lived in vast tenement blocks that Berliners nicknamed *Mietskasernen* ("rent barracks"). Built in the late nineteenth century, these five-story structures were subdivided into one- and two-room apartments. Small interior courtyards admitted vague hints of light and air to rooms that did not face the street. Built side-by-side and back-to-back, these tenements stretched for kilometer after dreary kilometer, encircling the inner city. Population densities stagger the imagination: a 1925 census reported more than 1,000 people per hectare in some areas, even though space in these buildings was often devoted to small shops and businesses and the occasional school. A survey of a 107-hectare area in Kreuzberg found some 37,000 people living in 16,000 dwellings, 91 percent of which had been built before 1918. Fewer than one in five of these apartments had a toilet. Less than one in six had a toilet plus a bath or a shower. Occupants of the remaining two-thirds shared common toilets in stairwells or courtyards. Central heating was unknown. A coal-burning stove warmed each apartment (and polluted the air outside). That survey, incidentally, dated from 1962, so one can only imagine what conditions were like in 1948.[9]

Reconstruction after the war had gotten off to a slow start, slower than elsewhere in Germany, and businesses received priority over housing. Renovation by the end of 1947 added less than 160,000 dwellings to the market—70,000 of them in the eastern sector. Material for repairs, especially glass, was scarce before the blockade and all but disappeared once it began. Allen Fuller, head of housing in the U.S. sector, noted a "sudden drop" in building work in July. Explosives for demolition and materials for construction came from the Soviet zone; supplies dried up.[10]

Other factors complicated Berlin's housing situation. Some housing was off the market, expropriated by the Western powers. As apartments and houses became available, authorities set some aside for officials purged in east Berlin, such as Stumm's police. Holding rooms in reserve for emergencies made little sense to those without a roof over their heads. Owners found it hard to finance repairs when contractors wanted payment in B-marks and tenants paid rent in eastern marks. The powers pledged to fly in supplies starting in December, but their performance fell short. Improvement in November resulted from a loss in population, not an expanded supply.[11]

Nearly all families cooked with natural gas, and supplies were less than half of normal. Low pressure made cooking a trial. The intermittent supply of gas was dangerous: people who forgot to close the valves after the gas went off could be asphyxiated when it resumed. Power shortages forced sewage disposal and water purification plants to keep short hours. Tons of sewage polluted the rivers each day, and the need to boil water boosted households' demands for fuel. Rationed food was distributed in ten-day blocks, so people queued three times a month. Meals were monotonous and unappetizing: dark bread and coffee for breakfast; pork or canned meat, cabbage, and soup based on dehydrated peas for dinner. Much of the dehydrated food was left over from the war and in poor condition, barely edible. Portions were small, with the average official daily ration through the winter being 1,600 to 1,880 calories, and residents took it for granted that grocers weighed short to set aside a little extra for their own families. Berliners missed fresh potatoes, vegetables, and milk; complaints about the quality and monotony of airlifted food continued throughout the blockade.[12] Hospitals were allowed to heat rooms during the winter, but factories, offices, schools, and other public buildings went without. New clothes were available only on the black market. Some people had to borrow clothes just to leave their houses. Simple necessities became hard to find, with children's shoes leading the list. Some children went barefoot. Food and shoes were the items most frequently pilfered by laborers on the airlift.[13] Getting around was also a chore. Buses and streetcars operated intermittently, during daylight hours only. Cars on the Soviet-operated Schnell- or S-bahn, the elevated railway, were crowded at all times and barely lit at night. Soviet-backed railway police prowled the cars, looking for "contraband." Bicycles became the mode of transportation for many (and the targets of thieves). Others walked.[14]

Berliners worried most about fuel because it affected all aspects of life. Coal generated electricity for homes and businesses; natural gas derived from coal cooked meals in nine out of ten homes. The blockade forced drastic cuts. On June 24, Western officials ordered industries, schools, hospitals, and city offices to reduce their consumption of electricity by a quarter. They curbed gas use for domestic cooking by a similar amount and slashed all other household consumption by half. Consumers exceeding these quotas lost their supply for a month.[15] The commandants imposed further reductions on July 10, cutting street lighting by three-quarters and allocating no current at all to "nonessential" industries.[16] As a result, 3,000 firms closed, and 4,000 shortened their hours. Natural gas use was halved.[17] The Western powers cut electricity to the S-bahn. Faced with the prospect of shutting down the system and disrupting life in their sector, the Russians provided enough current to keep the network running sporadically.[18]

Berliners were hurt the most by cuts in gas and electricity for home use. Electricity for domestic users was limited to four hours a day (two hours between 6:00 A.M. and 8:00 P.M., and another two between 8:00 P.M. and 6:00 A.M.). Current rotated around neighborhoods: one district might have power from 6:00 to 8:00 A.M. one week, 10:00 to noon the next, and 4:00 to 6:00 P.M. after that. Working women complained that having the power on during the day was a waste because they were not at home, and no one enjoyed getting up in the middle of the night to cook or iron clothes and then put in a full day on the job.[19] Many worried how long the supplies might last. Shortages at the end of July caused "grave fears" and frequent complaints. "Confidence in the 'flying coal men' is not very great," a British survey noted in September; "allocations of coal via the air-bridge are not expected."[20] It proved to be an accurate prediction. When the Magistrat asked for 750 pounds of coal per household for winter, the British thought the Western powers could provide 300 at best, while Clay considered any allocation "beyond our ability." Experts debated whether lifting food or coal would keep Berliners warmer. A ton of fat generates more heat than a ton of coal, so the answer seemed to be a priority for food (and perhaps warm clothing), yet everyone knew there had to be a mix—some lift had to be set aside for coal to heat rooms to meet people's psychological if not physiological needs. Robertson feared Berliners might crack. "Berlin winters are cold and the houses bad," he wrote. "To ask the people to go through the winter without any heating in their houses is clearly to put an inhuman strain upon them." Clay believed Berliners would endure; "if they cannot they will deserve the fate awaiting them at the hands of the Russians" was Robertson's summation of Clay's stance.[21] In the end, families had to make do with an official winter ration of twenty-five pounds of coal distributed at the end of November; families with small children or the elderly received slightly more. A limited cutting of trees supplemented this supply, so residents turned to the black market and eastern sources. Clay was proved right on both counts. Berliners endured, and a larger ration would have exhausted supplies.[22]

In an October poll, almost one-third of respondents reported having no lights at home when the electricity was off; about a quarter had neither heat nor lights. An empathetic British official warned London not to underestimate "the depressing effect of . . . having to spend every evening in the dark." Candles and paraffin were in such demand on the black market that the poor could afford neither. No electricity meant not just darkness and cold; it also meant no radio, deepening the sense of isolation.[23] Fuel continued to top the list of worries in November and December as apartments went without heat and families lacked fuel to cook even one meal a day or give children warm baths. Looking ahead, respondents in one poll dismissed the prospect of the airlift delivering enough fuel for the winter as "impossible."[24] Although everyone welcomed an increase in the natural gas quota from 50 to 75 percent of pre-blockade levels on December 1, they ridiculed the offer of twenty-five pounds of coal, which hardly filled an average shopping bag. "Even though people say that they would rather starve and freeze for a time than fall victims to communism," one report concluded, "they await the winter with the gravest forebodings." After all, two winters before, several hundred of their neighbors had frozen to death.[25]

Fears turned out to be exaggerated. Authorities eased the ban on space heating in October, allowing it in hospitals. As they had done in past years, they established heating halls, public areas where people could sit and stay warm. Most of the patrons were working class and elderly; the majority were incapacitated. Pensioners reported that these heating halls offered their only escape from the cold.[26] The electric grid did not follow sector boundaries. A few western neighborhoods found themselves on the "eastern side," as it were, and could draw on Soviet generating plants, which may have accounted for up to 25 percent of west Berlin's consumption.[27] People traded down to smaller apartments, which were easier to heat and cheaper to rent.[28] The most important factor, though, was mild weather. Average temperatures from December through February were more typical of late autumn or early spring.[29]

It seems surprising that concern over food was not greater. It had topped the list of worries in an August 1947 poll, ranked first by two-thirds of respondents. Soviet interference with deliveries in the spring hampered stockpiling, and perishables had reached low levels even before the blockade began. A U.S. Public Health Service group judged official rations inadequate in May, recommending an increase of 300 calories a day. According to reports, suppliers held back food in the first days of the blockade, waiting for prices to rise or hoping to be paid in B-marks.[30] Yet, even with supplies uncertain, Berliners spurned the offer of Soviet food. Moscow offered to supply Berlin's needs in its July 14 note, and over the next two weeks, the Soviet-licensed press touted stories about commodities being gathered and published instructions on how western sector residents could register for them in east Berlin. Just over 20,000 people responded. By September, the total had risen to 56,000. It would peak in March 1949 at 103,000, 5 percent of the western sectors' population.[31]

Scholars' warnings against taking this rejection as an index of anti-Soviet sentiment seem overdone. Contemporaries on both sides saw it that way. The SED's Hermann Matern referred to the political significance of registration, while Magistrat economics chief Gustav Klingelhöfer (of the SPD) declared that signing up for Russian food was tantamount to "political support."[32] Western sector opinion surveys indicated that nearly nine out of ten residents regarded the offer as a maneuver; only 3 percent saw it as genuine. Social pressure ran high against acceptance, as did opposition to allowing those who had accepted Soviet commodities to re-register in the western sectors once the crisis was past. These are all signs that Berliners saw acceptance—and rejection—as a political choice. What might be considered "practical" reasons reflected a mistrust of Moscow and thus had a political dimension. Some western sector residents were afraid to enter the Russian sector. Some rejected the offer as "pure propaganda" or a "gigantic swindle," convinced the Russians could not deliver. Few gave credence to Soviet propaganda claims in general—the Soviet-sponsored *Tägliche Rundschau* (Daily Review) was derided as the *Klägiche Rundschau* (Pitiable Review)—and people scoffed at this one. Berliners knew that stocks in the eastern zone were of such poor quality and so limited that the offer would collapse if more than 10 percent of west Berliners signed up. Obstructing shipments of potatoes ordered by the Western powers from Poland and Czechoslovakia called Russian sincerity into question. So did the Soviet refusal to provide coal. Although travel to east Berlin could be inconvenient and time-consuming, it is odd that scholars who emphasize how extensively Berliners roamed around the Soviet zone attribute residents' tepid response to the Soviet offer to restricted mobility.[33]

Worry about food fluctuated. Distribution delays in late September prompted rumors that the city was living hand to mouth. The onset of frost a few weeks later curtailed supplies of fresh vegetables. To ease these worries, Western officials boosted the ration by a tenth in November—ironically, just as airlift deliveries nose-dived due to bad weather.[34] If one person deserves credit for this increase in rations, it was Dr. F. E. Magee, a nutritionist with the Ministry of Health in London. Western and Magistrat officials began tinkering with the ration in the earliest days of the blockade, seeking to extract the highest possible caloric value from each pound of airlifted cargo. The ration had to take into account more than pure science. Psychological and political considerations weighed heavily. For example, the British devised a ration of dehydrated foods that did not have to be cooked, saving both weight and coal, but Robertson rejected it as impractical. Berliners needed at least one hot meal a day; if the West did not provide one, Soviet propagandists would have a field day. As it was, bread and potatoes were staples in the German diet, with potatoes forming the main part of every hot meal. For Berliners, a meal was not a meal without both, no matter what nutritionists said.[35]

Trying to balance such considerations, and fearing a collapse in the "nutritional state of the population," the British called in Magee. He and his assistants visited Berlin several times. Magee judged a "significant proportion" of the population undernourished and condemned the ration as "incompatible with full health." For purposes of determining rations, the Soviets had divided adults into four groups in 1945; the Kommandatura changed that to three in 1947. Group I, those performing heavy manual labor, received the largest ration, 2,498 calories a day. Other manual workers, pregnant women, and nursing mothers formed group II and were entitled to 1,999 calories. Everyone else fell into group III and made do on 1,608. Children constituted group IV, with three subcategories: IVa, those five years old or younger (between 1,653 and 1,786 calories); IVb, those between six and eight (1,619 calories); and IVc, those between nine and thirteen (1,559 calories). The disparity between these figures and the population's needs, as defined by scientists and researchers, startled Magee. For example, workers' and adolescents' daily rations were 500 to 1,000 calories too little, while infants got 500 to 800 calories too much. The groups did not make sense. Members of group I supposedly deserved a high ration because of the demands of heavy physical labor, but many of them held sedentary jobs such as party, church, and union leaders; judges; senior civil servants; and those prominent in the arts. Composition of the ration was also flawed. It contained only small amounts of meat, fat, and sugar and no cheese or fresh vegetables; the main energy sources were bread and potatoes. Only infants received fresh milk. "For a European accustomed to a varied, mixed diet," Magee commented, "one more drab and uninteresting would be difficult to imagine." Magee understood that the official ration was what people were *entitled to,* not necessarily what they *received.* He also knew that Berliners supplemented their official rations whenever they could. But even if that added 200 calories a day across the board, it did not change the basic picture, and in any case, he could not consider it when adjusting the official ration. He recommended dietary changes (more fats and sugar) plus a 200-calorie increase for groups I and II, a 300-calorie increase for group III, and a 400-calorie increase for adolescents. He proposed shifting people from one group to another (controversially, all teenage boys into group I and all teenage girls into group II), providing vitamin supplements, and evacuating all undernourished children and adolescents. Magee's program would require the airlift to deliver 175 tons more each day. This 8 percent increase in tonnage would boost caloric value 15 percent.[36]

The British had been urging higher rations since June, but the Americans had resisted, citing the airlift's limitations. Magee's report helped break the logjam. In mid-October, Howley's staff agreed to a 200-calorie increase as of November 1. The new ration incorporated some, but not all, of Magee's recommendations. In subsequent visits, he reiterated calls for more calcium and vitamins, dried skim milk for everyone, and group I status for teenage boys. The Americans were opposed to any more increases, and as Brownjohn confessed, they had the final word because they paid the bulk of the airlift's costs. He noted that Howley had a veto, "does not hesitate to use it," and loyally upheld "Clay's point of view" when doing so. Magee regarded his proposals as a stopgap that would allow the population to "tick over"; these rations could not sustain Berliners indefinitely. With that in mind, the British and French urged new increases in March and April, only to have the Americans oppose them. The airlift was not assured, Howley explained to Herbert's replacement, Major General Geoffrey K. Bourne; Berliners' weights had risen; and banning the eastern mark in the western sectors would, according to the American commandant, mean more fresh vegetables from the Soviet zone. Howley saw no need to increase the ration absent convincing evidence of a deterioration in public health.[37]

Indeed, the numbers pointed in the opposite direction; health generally improved. The incidence of infectious diseases, for example, dropped below that of previous years. The death rate in the western sectors, 12.3 per 1,000 in 1938, had nearly doubled in 1946 to 23.1. It dropped to 14.0 in 1948 before rising to 17.0 for the first four months of 1949. The death rate in the U.S. sector fluctuated seasonally: 15.1 in the preblockade months of January to June 1948, 12.9 in the remaining six months of the year. It climbed to 15.7 in the first six months of 1949 before falling to 10.2 in July, August, and September.[38] The death rate in the British sector in the third quarter of 1948 was 11.4 per 1,000 people, down from 14.9 two years earlier. Average weights of adult men and women in the U.S. sector *increased* during the blockade for all age groups, although weight fluctuated seasonally, and gains over the winter of 1948–1949 were less than usual. While children remained underweight, their weights were closer to normal in March 1949 than they had been in July 1948.[39]

The low mortality rate reflected improving conditions—and a statistical quirk. Death rates in 1948 dropped 25 percent from those of the year before; they were so low that, had the age distribution been the same as in 1938, the total and female death rates in 1948 would have been lower than ten years earlier. Yet the main reason for the sharp drop, according to one American report, was the "extremely low number of deaths among people over 60 years, especially female." That, in turn, stemmed from the harsh years of 1946 and 1947, which had carried off so many of the elderly and weak that few were left to die in 1948. Infant mortality showed a similar trend—down from previous years, though not as low as before the war. Berlin's infant mortality rate in 1938 was 58 per 1,000 live births. Nearly constant in 1946 and 1947—123 and 121, respectively—it dropped to 85.5 in 1948. Infant mortality in the British sector dropped from 81 per 1,000 live births to 62 over the same two-year span.[40]

Deaths might have been higher if the British had not evacuated some of those who were most susceptible to cold—the young, the sick, and the elderly. From September 1948 through March 1949, they flew out 50,000 people, including 15,500 children between the ages of six and sixteen.[41] As large as those figures were, the target had been as high as 260,000, mostly children. As General Herbert explained, the purpose was to remove them from the siege, which would not only spare them but also make it easier for their parents to endure harsh conditions. The British argued that children were among the worst fed and would suffer the most. Hospital occupancies were high, leading to doubt that the medical community could cope with sharp increases in patient loads. Howley's staff and Berlin welfare officials thought Herbert's fear was exaggerated. Current efforts, which flew out about 400 children a week on a voluntary basis to join relatives or friends in the western zones, made sense, but nothing more. A big program would spark rumors of wholesale evacuation, with catastrophic effects on morale. In addition, accommodations were scarce in the western zones, and someone would have to pay for the children's upkeep. Challenging Herbert's main premise, American and German officials contended that the truly undernourished were the elderly and teenagers, not school-age children. The British had to settle for a much smaller plan.[42]

As doctors and nurses struggled to care for their patients, politics intruded. Was it ethical to deny medical supplies and treatment to "the other side"? The Russians did not hesitate, blocking Western access to medical supplies in their sector on June 24 and banning deliveries of ether, alcohol, x-ray film, plaster of Paris, pharmaceuticals, and the like to the western sectors on July 1. Western officials responded with a similar ban at the end of July but then reconsidered. Exchange or barter would reduce demands on the airlift, and there was a humanitarian angle: could they deny east Germans the medicines they needed to survive? Colonel Babcock had no qualms. He would trade drugs for coal if the Soviets made the request, but he was "very happy" if their inability to provide proper medical care embarrassed the Kremlin.[43]

The question reappeared in January 1949. Medical care was generally better in the western sectors, home to most of the city's specialized hospitals. Occupancy rates had climbed, and patients from Soviet-occupied areas accounted for a "large proportion of the present strain," filling one-sixth of hospital beds in the western sectors. In certain specialties, the proportions were higher: tuberculosis, 29 percent; mental health, 35 percent; orthopedics, 49 percent. The Kommandatura's public health committee recommended admitting only emergency cases from the Soviet areas. Current patients could remain. The move would reduce occupancy, conserve food and medical supplies, and save money—eastern patients paid into their own medical system, which refused to reimburse hospitals in the western sectors. The drain was more than 1 million B-marks a month. There were drawbacks—Soviet propagandists could exploit the ban, and Soviet officials might retaliate by banning western sector patients from their hospitals—but the committee thought the advantages outweighed the disadvantages, and the commandants agreed.[44]

Accounts have neglected women's roles during the blockade. Women made up 59 percent of the adult population and 46 percent of the workforce, and they were often heads of households.[45] Conditions in wartime Germany had given them unprecedented responsibilities, which continued afterward. They had kept their families fed, housed, and clothed; made the most of networks of family and friends; and learned their way around the black market. Untold thousands of male Berliners did not return from the war. Among those who did, many came home late—1948, 1949, or later—and some could no longer function as breadwinners. Many were weak or sick, under denazification bans, or demoralized by defeat. Norman Naimark notes that roughly 40 percent of returning prisoners of war were unable to work.[46] Men came back to a Germany they did not recognize, one that was difficult for them to understand. Women, who had lived through and adjusted to all the upheavals, knew how to get things done; they now applied what they had learned during the war to this new crisis. Thus, families' needs were often met by "nonworking" wives and mothers who stood in long lines for rationed goods, roamed farms and woods looking for food, and scrounged whatever they needed from wherever they could find it. The author of a study of 498 postwar Berlin families devoted scant attention to males because "in these families women have moved into the central position as providers."[47]

Writers may have gone too far in turning all Berlin women into *Trümmerfrauen* ("rubble women"), steadfast, heroic, self-sacrificing, and able to cope with anything fate sent their way. Not all men went to war, and not all ex-soldiers were incapable of productive lives; meanwhile, years of danger and responsibility had worn down many women.[48] Still, women's actions and attitudes were of central importance. A November 1948 British survey described a representative sample of Berlin's women as consisting of 22 percent single women, 45 percent married, 25 percent widowed, and 8 percent divorced; the survey described 4 percent as upper class, 48 percent as middle class, and 48 percent as lower class. Women's chief worry was obtaining fuel for the winter. Many had little or no stocks, and their homes lacked heat. In summer, many went to the Soviet zone two or three times a week to gather wood for cooking and brought back "astonishing" loads. Elderly women with large sacks of wood were "part of the daily picture on the Berlin transport system." These trips decreased sharply as the Soviets tightened controls, and "all such 'harvests'" were confiscated. For some, gas supplies were sufficient to make hot soup or coffee once a day, but there was no gas between 9:00 P.M. and 5:00 A.M. Many cooked three days' meals at once. Many women complained they could not give their children hot baths because of the lack of fuel; others struggled against depression caused by sitting in darkness night after night. The aged poor, who could not afford to buy wood and coal on the black market, feared winter. But for the better off, heat was "merely a question of money." Those with plenty of B-marks did well because they could buy food, clothes, fuel, and medicine on the black market.[49]

AVERAGES ARE AVERAGES; conditions were not the same for everyone. Where people lived and worked shaped the hardships they faced and their ability to cope. Although the Soviets had little direct leverage over western sector residents, sizable numbers of Berliners commuted back and forth, either living or working in Soviet-controlled areas. One contemporary estimate was that 111,000 west Berliners worked in the eastern sector, while western sector businesses employed 106,000 east Berliners. Economics may have mattered even more than residential patterns. How much one earned (and in what currency) could make the difference between a comfortable life and real privation. The well-to-do had little trouble finding whatever they needed on the black market; the less fortunate struggled. Pensioners and those on relief endured many miseries. Payments, always small, were often late. Unemployment checks in January 1949 were four to six weeks in arrears and five to six weeks behind in April.[50] Whereas 52 percent of respondents from a working-class area in January 1949 were unhappy with their dwellings, 19 percent in an upper-middle-class district complained about theirs.[51]

The dual currencies—and the black market exchange rate of four to one or more—magnified differences. A family's purchasing power depended not on the breadwinner's ability or hard work but on the percentage of B-marks in his or her pay envelope. Officially, everyone in west Berlin was supposed to receive a quarter of their earnings in western marks, but only about one-third did. Some, perhaps one in ten, got a higher percentage, and a fortunate 3 percent received all their pay in the stronger currency. The Siemens factory in the British sector could send much of its output to western Germany by the airlift, so it paid more than half its wages in B-marks. Between a third and half of the population, mainly lower-income groups, had no B-mark earnings. The unemployed and pensioners received 10 percent or less in B-marks, and for long stretches of the crisis, they received none.[52] Officially, rent, food, fuel, transport fares, utility bills, and taxes could be paid in eastern marks, but many landlords and shopkeepers would not accept them. Vendors offered such daily necessities as soap, razor blades, cigarettes, shoe and clothing repair, and medicine only in exchange for B-marks, and black marketeers would take nothing else. "In Berlin," as one British report put it, "nearly everything that makes life pleasant and worthwhile" carried a price tag in B-marks.[53]

The Soviets and SED could not exploit this situation. The first and main reason was Berliners' acquaintance with the day-to-day effects of Soviet power. Admittedly, the Germans were predisposed to resent Soviet rule. No one reacts well to being conquered and occupied, and a dislike of Russians stretched far back in German history, as did a sense of superiority over Slavs. At root, the Russians had themselves to blame. The murders, rapes, thefts, and confiscations that accompanied their victory in 1945 fanned a flame of hatred that touched all segments of the population. The postwar political competition in the city kept that flame alive. So did knowledge that the eastern zone resembled nothing so much as Joseph Conrad's Costaguana, with its "nightmarish parody of administration without law, without security, and without justice."[54] Refugees from the zone, who continued to arrive in the western sectors by the hundreds even during the blockade, brought word of how bad things were.[55] As harsh as conditions in the western sectors might be (and they were not as harsh as conditions recently experienced in some cities at German hands), they were never bad enough to push the population to the breaking point or induce it to submit to Soviet rule. An overwhelming 88 percent of west Berliners in an October 1948 survey preferred the current situation, with all its privations and uncertainties, over Soviet control. Even if some of this consensus was coerced, with waverers kept in line by the fear of ostracism, it seems clear that the quip "Lieber pomm als 'frau komm!'" summed up the attitude of the vast majority of west Berliners. Loosely translated, it meant: better the dehydrated potatoes flown in by the airlift than Soviet rule and a repeat of the summer of 1945.[56]

Second, hard times were not new. Although we tend to assume that the blockade's imposition was a transforming event, daily life went on much as before. Berliners had queued for food since 1941 and had faced shortages of all kinds even before Bomber Command tried to burn their city to the ground. Peace had brought scant improvement. Some Berliners suggested how little times had changed by describing the winter of 1946–1947 as "the eighth winter of the war."[57] The meager diet left people tired and listless, indifferent to their surroundings. "Our hunger was cumulative," one Berliner recalled. Visitors were struck by how slowly people walked, how pedestrians appeared to cross streets in a trance, unaware of cars bearing down on them. Children seemed subdued. Everyone had learned "the art of restricting activity according to intake."[58] Electricity shortages and rotating allocations had become normal aspects of daily life.

In some ways, the blockade was not as bad as what Berliners had already endured. Disease and mortality rates had fallen from postwar highs; weights were closer to prewar norms. The 1948 ration, slim as it was, was double what Berliners had received in October 1945. During the war, they had been bombed day and night and compelled to serve a regime that most of them despised. Now the sound of aircraft engines aroused hope, not dread, and the Magistrat enjoyed a legitimacy the Nazis could never claim. After twelve years of feigned enthusiasm for a system of lies, most Berliners had come to treasure the free expression made possible by the Western powers—a freedom the Soviets were bent on eliminating. Wartime shortages, Allied bombing, conquest, and occupation had inured Berliners to privation and taught them ways to cope that would serve them well in the weeks ahead.[59]

Third, people expected a short crisis. They could not know that the ordeal would last nearly a year. In mid-July, nearly nine out of ten people thought the crisis would not last through the winter. Many shared Friedensburg's belief that the Russians would relent before residents began to starve.[60] They could interpret the Soviet offer of food and the many loopholes in the blockade as proof that the Soviets were not pursuing a total hunger blockade. Others expected the occupiers to reach a quick agreement. It would be easy to hold on for a few more days if doing so would get them through the emergency. Like the Western governments, Berliners tended to take things one day at a time.

Apathy and the demands of daily life worked against Russian attempts to panic the population. During the first few days of the crisis, Berliners were busy with other things, such as the currency conversion, and they paid scant attention to Soviet maneuvers. As weeks passed, many grew apathetic and indifferent to the political fine points. A January 1949 report detected no interest in politics beyond whether a party supported or opposed communism. For most people, "this is where their interest in German politics ends."[61]

The gender imbalance in the city also worked against the Russians. Few of Berlin's women were political, but all remembered 1945, when (according to public health officials) Soviet soldiers had raped half of them in "an unrestrained explosion of sexual violence."[62] Stalin had waved aside Milovan Djilas's complaints of similar behavior in Yugoslavia—what did it matter if "a soldier who has crossed thousands of kilometers through blood and fire and death has fun with a woman or takes some trifle?"[63] Russia now paid the political price for such callousness. Nine percent of male Berliners polled by OMGUS in the spring of 1948 supported the SED, but only 5 percent of females did, and in October, women were twice as likely as men to want the crisis to end with the departure of Soviet forces.[64]

Last, the airlift represented a bond, a commitment to the city by outsiders that lifted residents' hearts and deepened their resolve. It held out the hope that resistance rested on something more substantial than wishful thinking. The psychological effects of the airlift probably mattered more in the early months than the logistical ones. Even those who questioned its prospects could draw inspiration from it, for it assured them that they were not alone. Reuter's call to the outside world to "look to this city" reflected a deep psychological need to be linked with a larger community. The noise of engines overhead, at first annoying, became reassuring, and silent skies became worrisome.

The airlift made it possible to identify with a wider world. Berliners came to see themselves as partners with the Western powers, personified by leaders such as Clay, Robertson, and Howley and by the pilots participating in the airlift. Among the latter, the best known was a young American lieutenant, Gail S. Halvorsen. Halvorsen's story is a familiar symbol of American generosity, but there is more to it than that, for it epitomized the deepening bonds between Berliners and the Western powers. Halvorsen hitched a ride into the city one summer afternoon to see the sights, and he walked out to the end of the runway to take pictures of the planes landing. Some children were standing on the other side of a barbed-wire fence, and those who spoke English began asking him questions. What amazed him, though, was their spirit: "They were more concerned about their freedom than they were the flour" on the planes. "They said they could get along on very little food," he recalled for an interviewer years later, and would do "anything to preserve their freedom." The children knew their friends and relatives in east Berlin could not say what they thought or do what they wanted. "They told me that freedom was the most important thing. Sometimes they didn't get enough to eat, they said, but if they lost their freedom they knew they would never get it back." As Halvorsen turned to leave, he realized that something was different: everywhere he had gone overseas during the war, children had begged him for candy, but these children, who lacked so much, had not. He wanted to give them something, but all he had was two sticks of chewing gum. At first, he thought it might cause a riot if he handed out so little, but he went ahead anyway, breaking each piece in two and passing them through the wire. "The looks on their faces were unbelievable," he remembered, and no riot broke out. "I just stood there with my mouth open." On impulse, he promised to drop enough candy and gum from his plane for all of them the next day. They asked how they could recognize his plane among the dozens in the sky. He said he would wiggle his wings on final approach. Back at Rhein-Main that night, he gathered his weekly candy ration, talked his copilot and engineer out of theirs, and fashioned three makeshift parachutes out of handkerchiefs.

As Halvorsen's C-54 approached Tempelhof the next day, he could see a small cluster of expectant children by the fence. He rocked his wings. He got a quick glimpse of the children jumping and cheering as the plane flashed by and the engineer pushed the tiny parcels out the flare chute. After unloading, Halvorsen and his crew taxied out for takeoff. The children were there, "waving three handkerchiefs through the barbed wire. Kids were jumping up and down and waving like mad. I wished they wouldn't do that," he recalled, worried that it would attract too much attention and he would get in trouble for breaking the rules. But he kept it up for two more weeks, until his squadron commander called him on the carpet. By then, Tunner had taken over as commander, and given his reputation as a stern, no-nonsense perfectionist, Halvorsen was sure he was in hot water. But Tunner, who had seen German newspaper accounts of the story, thought it was marvelous publicity and gave Halvorsen permission to go "full speed ahead." He and his fellow pilots did just that, and Operation "Little Vittles" was born. When the crowds at Tempelhof grew too large, pilots began dropping candy all across Berlin, east as well as west. Back in the States, scout troops and wives' clubs collected money to buy candy and handkerchiefs, and candy companies made bulk donations, one contributing ten tons. Halvorsen, known variously as the "Candy Bomber," *der Schokoladen-flieger*, or "Uncle Wiggly Wings," became a world-famous symbol of the humanitarian essence of the airlift.[65]

Tragedy formed a more solid link than chewing gum. Just before 1:00 A.M. on July 25, a C-47 crashed on approach to Tempelhof, killing the two men on board. Berliners were deeply touched. Men who had been their enemies three short years ago had died trying to help them. Their sacrifice must not be wasted; determination not to give in to Soviet pressure increased. The more Berliners resisted, the more the aircrews were convinced that such people must not be abandoned. Halvorsen denied that he and his fellow pilots were heroes. They were just doing their jobs. Berliners were the true heroes. "They were the ones who went home at night to bombed-out places," he explained, "who went home without enough to eat," surrounded by Russian armies and living "in the jaws of the tiger all the time."[66] Halvorsen's experience is just one example of Charles Pennacchio's point that American influence in postwar Berlin spread best through informal personal contact, not formal channels.[67] The crisis, the shared sense of sacrifice, and the growing sense of mutual obligation and admiration eroded the earlier distance between victor and vanquished. While there had been little love lost between Berliners and Westerners at the start of the blockade, the relationship was dramatically different at its end.

AS PEOPLE TRIED TO MAINTAIN a semblance of normal life, Berlin's political and business leaders sought to sustain the economy. Berlin's economic troubles did not stem solely from the blockade. Even before the war, the city had consumed more than it produced, making up the difference in banking, insurance, tourism, and central government services. Defeat and occupation erased these sources of revenue while adding new problems. Howley had diagnosed the situation in February 1947, complaining that failure to treat Germany as an economic unit had hurt Berlin by disrupting trade and closing off traditional sources of raw materials. Underlying most problems, he thought, was that each sector was supplied from its corresponding zone. In the past, the entire city had drawn from the surrounding territory; now only east Berlin could do so. Soviet barriers against zonal trade compelled the western sectors to rely on "precarious and inadequate" links with the western zones. Within the city, sector boundaries were largely economic frontiers due to different policies regarding supply and trade, different links with the zones, and different administrative procedures. Consumer goods could be traded between sectors only with approval of the local military governments, so there was little movement of goods or raw materials.[68]

Three 1949 reports echoed Howley's views, contending that the problems facing Berlin's industry had been aggravated by the blockade, not caused by it. Wartime damage, dismantling, and reparations had stripped the city's industrial base. Production costs for what remained were 20 percent higher than those in the western zones. The Soviets had seized industries' bank accounts; the city's isolated location made it hard to find western zone customers or understand their needs; and investors were reluctant to rebuild in a city that might slip into Soviet hands.[69] The labor force reflected Berlin's former status as the national capital, with too few blue-collar workers and too many white-collar ones. The thousands of functionaries thrown out of work when the national, state, and party bureaucracies in the city collapsed were a drag on the economy.[70]

Soviet restrictions before the blockade had their effects. Herbert's economic adviser, J. A. N. McEwan, pointed out in early June that the economy was in a precarious state. Goods were piled up, unable to be exported. Some western zone suppliers had stopped making deliveries, uncertain they would ever be paid. Under present conditions, McEwan predicted, small companies would start going under in another month or two.[71] The blockade added to these woes. Berlin had traditionally exported industrial products: how could it obtain raw materials now, and how would it reach markets? "Within a month or so, industrial production will have come almost to a halt because of lack of electricity, coal, and raw materials," one journalist thought.[72] It was a view widely shared. Murphy echoed it, as did Bohlen, and a summary of Murphy's report reached the president.[73]

At first, such frightful forecasts seemed accurate. One industrial association noted that costs had risen 25 to 35 percent due to cuts in power, irregular supplies of raw materials, reduced working time, and lower productivity.[74] The Magistrat and the Western powers had marginal success in coping with the situation. An emergency economic committee set up in July made little progress. Magistrat representatives, who regarded the committee almost as a Western high command in the economic battle for the city, pressed for a variety of steps. They wanted to discuss production, trade, export, wages, the dual currency system, and energy; they proposed shipping goods out by air and opening currency exchanges so people could convert eastern and western marks. The British, who had organized the group, were taken aback and reined it in: such decisions were premature or reserved to the occupying powers. Another project that involved putting the unemployed to work clearing rubble dragged due to bureaucratic haggling over funds.[75] The airlift provided some 15,000 jobs, not including temporary ones connected with airfield construction; tree cutting in the autumn created a few more.[76]

Budgetary problems hampered the Magistrat. With industry at one-half to one-quarter of normal volume, tax receipts plummeted. Income taxes, sales taxes, and luxury taxes also fell. On the other side of the ledger, unemployment payments mushroomed. The budget deficit was soon up to about 100 million B-marks a month. West German *Länder* agreed to provide 40 million marks each month, and Clay got 60 million from Washington.[77]

The Soviets did their best to make matters worse. On July 30, they ordered the central bank to block the Magistrat's accounts, as well as those of enterprises in the western sectors. They lifted the ban on August 5, only to reimpose it a day later. They released 25 million of the city's 350 million ostmark balance to meet the August 6 payroll and demanded that companies transact all future business in the eastern currency if they wanted to get their accounts unblocked.[78] Western officials offered to meet payrolls—not just that of the Magistrat but of all industry and commerce in west Berlin. They ordered the Magistrat to stop fund transfers from western sector banks to the central bank in the Soviet sector and directed it to set up a new city treasury in west Berlin.[79] Despite such steps, the city lived hand to mouth. Municipal authorities had to plead with Soviet officials nearly every week to release enough eastern marks to meet payrolls and pensions, and from time to time, the pay of city workers fell far into arrears.[80]

Private initiatives were more effective. To curb unemployment, companies shortened hours and kept employees on maintenance or make-work—and still made profits by manipulating Berlin's two currencies. Receiving payment in B-marks and paying expenses (wages, rent, fuel, and insurance) in eastern marks more than offset the lower productivity and higher production costs.[81] Firms also sought business in Soviet-controlled areas, with or without the approval of officials from either side. From a wage standpoint, employees who kept their jobs were nearly as well off as they had been before the blockade, because most received 85 percent or more of their preblockade gross income.[82] Still, those forced onto the unemployment rolls stayed there, and young men and women trying to enter the workforce faced long odds.[83]

At the start of the blockade, nearly 47,000 Berliners out of a labor force of 890,000 were without jobs, about 5 percent. By the end of October, probably 300,000 were working shortened hours, and 90,000 were receiving full or partial unemployment compensation. By April 1949, the latter figure had risen to 156,000, more than tripling the jobless rate to 17 percent.[84] By mid-March 1949, some 6,000 firms in the U.S. sector had closed, and another 12,000 had shortened their hours.

Together, they constituted half the industries and shops in the sector.[85] By the end of the blockade, American officials calculated that almost a quarter of the population received some form of public relief.[86]

Effects were not uniform. "Nonessential" businesses went under right away when they were denied electricity. Small firms were hit harder than large ones, and handicrafts suffered more than industry. Over 80 percent of those unemployed or on short hours in the U.S. sector had worked in industry or handicrafts, which constituted 48 percent of the workforce; 11 percent had been employed in commerce, and 4 percent in services. In other words, those affected were disproportionately blue-collar workers, whereas the white-collar commercial and service sectors were only slightly disrupted.[87] Some industries suffered more than others. In November 1948, chemical production was only 53 percent of what it had been a year earlier, while machinery production stood at 75 percent and fine mechanics and optics were nearly untouched at 96 percent.[88]

Nor did the blockade affect all the western sectors alike. About 48 percent of the west Berlin workforce worked in the U.S. sector, 32 percent in the British, and 20 percent in the French. Small firms dominated the French and American sectors, whereas larger ones prevailed in the British. Economies of scale allowed large firms to ride out the blockade more easily than small ones. Arguing that the city's economy depended on the large companies (Siemens and AEG) in their sector, the British allocated them more than two-thirds of the sector's industrial electricity quota. The Americans complained that the British did not control consumption as carefully as they should; as a result, the British sector consumed more electricity and coal than its share of the workforce warranted (36 percent of electricity and 37 percent of coal). Not surprisingly, overall unemployment in the American sector was half again as high as it was in the British sector, and the difference in industrial unemployment rates was even greater.[89]

Berliners endured because they had little choice and because most refused to bow to Soviet coercion. A sense of humor helped. Berliners are known for their mordant wit, and it did not fail them during the blockade. For example, one wisecrack making the rounds noted, "If there must be a blockade, then it's better to be blockaded by the Soviets and fed by the Americans. Just imagine if it were the other way round!"[90]

There was more substance to this jest than one might think. William Stivers has shown that the blockade was less complete than once believed. Smuggling, plus trade authorized by the Soviets, went on between the eastern and western zones and between the western sectors and the Soviet zone. Opportunities to circumvent the blockade abounded in its early stages. As noted, hundreds of thousands of people went back and forth between east and west Berlin daily. More than 400 streets connected the western sectors with Soviet-controlled territory, and Markgraf's police could not be everywhere. If the streets became too risky, apartment blocks sprawling across sector boundaries afforded attractive alternatives: one could enter them in the east and walk out the other side in the west. Berliners could visit the eastern zone and barter with farmers for food, coal, firewood, and other necessities. Border crossings between the eastern and western zones remained open. Trucks with bills of lading listing destinations in the Soviet zone or even the eastern sector could pass through and then slip into west Berlin, their way eased by bribes to border guards and officials. For several months, the postal service delivered tens of thousands of gift parcels to the western sectors. Shady characters and respectable burghers alike took advantage of these opportunities. Motives varied. Black marketers sought profit; the young relished adventure. East Berliners shared with relatives and friends in the western sectors. Stivers believes that one-third of all the food in the first 100 days and nearly one-quarter of all goods reaching west Berlin during the blockade originated in Soviet-controlled areas. According to one contemporary estimate, smuggling and trade with such areas met half the city's needs, with the significant exception of food. Another rated trade with eastern areas as important as the airlift, providing perhaps 1,000 tons of coal a day before October.[91]

The Russians were willing to condone trade with the city they were blockading—if they controlled it.[92] From a Western perspective, this trade kept businesses open and unemployment low. West Berlin companies sought coal, electricity, and raw materials wherever they could find them. Exchange with the eastern zone had dwindled in the months before the blockade; now, ironically, west Berlin businessmen relied on it more than ever, as one of Murphy's assistants learned during a talk with a German factory owner in November. Before the blockade, this entrepreneur had obtained his raw materials from the Russian zone and sold industrial glass in the British zone. Now he traded mostly with easterners. He had no choice and few regrets, because he was better off than before. His new trading partners paid in deutsche marks or dollars. As far as he and his fellow businessmen were concerned, the airlift was "an empty gesture."[93] More than one-fifth of British sector exports in the last six months of 1948 went to eastern areas. A British report concluded that, on balance, western sector companies involved in barter trade with Soviet areas received more value in raw materials than they sent east in finished goods, and Clay's staff professed unconcern as long as the western sectors received a fair return. Trade offered the additional advantage of lessening the demand on the airlift. An airtight blockade would have forced a dramatic expansion in aerial supplies.[94]

We should not conclude from the existence of loopholes that the Soviets were not in earnest. The blockade did not have to be 100 percent efficient to be effective. It was only necessary for consumption to exceed deliveries—or, at another level, for Berliners and Western officials to believe that it did. In the early days, both seemed true. As Soviet and Western officials saw the situation, sooner or later, Berlin's stocks would run out. The airlift could never deliver enough, and whatever leaked through holes in the blockade would be too small to matter. Comments by two SED officials in the first days of the crisis reflected this optimism. Walter Ulbricht suggested euphemistically that the Western powers could no longer "assist" in supplying the entire city. Communist trade union leader Roman Chwalek was more forthright, noting on June 25 that "all links to the West" had been cut; therefore, "all Berliners" would accept the ostmark "in order to guarantee their existence."[95]

When that did not happen, prospects still looked good. In mid-July, Sokolovsky and SED officials discussed steps to absorb the city into the Soviet zone, control its trade, and eliminate the Magistrat. According to a British intelligence report a few weeks later, Ulbricht acknowledged that the airlift had astonished the Soviets, but their assessment of its long-term prospects remained unshaken. "The Russians believed that the Western Powers would have to give up Berlin," the SED leader supposedly continued, "because they could not feed the population . . . owing to the cost and impracticability of the airlift."[96] That was not wishful thinking based on the Luftwaffe's failure at Stalingrad and ignorance of aviation's potential, as General Tunner once suggested.[97] As we have seen, it was a conclusion shared by top Western officials. Everyone agreed that time favored the Soviets. Stocks would dwindle, and the West would eventually face a choice: abandon the city, start a war, or come to terms with Moscow about Germany.

It is notable that the Russians worked hard to plug leaks in the blockade starting in September, a move that says much about their intentions. They "cut the supply line" of trucks circumventing the blockade on September 1.[98] Police set up roadblocks around the western sectors on October 18, as well as checkpoints at west Berlin S-bahn stations. Zonal traffic was diverted around the city, and the Russians imposed new regulations to prevent "looting" of their zone. Foraging trips outside the city dropped sharply as police confiscated wood, food, and whatever else Berliners had collected. American analysts estimated that the restrictions curbed smuggling by as much as 80 percent, so black market prices for potatoes and coal jumped. All goods crossing sector boundaries required permits starting in November. Soviet technicians undertook "feverish plans" to make the electric grid match sector boundaries. The Russians began re-registering vehicles and issuing new identity cards in order to control traffic. In December, Markgraf's police began searching the briefcases and purses of passengers on public transportation leaving east Berlin, and Howley told Royall that the blockade was "about as complete as the Russians are able to make it." Semipermanent barriers and roadblocks went up at sector crossing points in mid-February.[99]

It seems safe to conclude that implementation fell short of intention, as it often does. The Soviets did what they could to plug loopholes, and they were indifferent about those that remained. That indifference rested on confidence that the airlift would fail and the conviction that Berliners' morale would crack. Both proved wrong.

STATISTICS MIGHT INDICATE that life was not as hard as in previous years, but what mattered was how conditions appeared to Berliners. British and American officials understood the importance of morale and watched it closely. Robertson's Public Opinion Research Office (PORO) reported on morale every two weeks and turned out special assessments. The Military Government Liaison Section (MGLS), an intelligence unit, drafted a weekly report for the Foreign Office's German department. OMGUS conducted polls and opinion surveys, while Howley's headquarters circulated a weekly report. The Canadian military mission began reporting weekly in September.[100]

These reports raise questions. It is unclear to whom MGLS talked and on what it based its assessments of opinion, and we know nothing about how representative the sampling by OMGUS and PORO was. Nor is it easy to establish to what extent these reports affected policy. What they do show is how carefully the powers monitored opinion and how nervous they were about it.

The first MGLS report following imposition of the blockade predicted that resistance would depend on how the Western powers dealt with disorder and riots and whether they could "convince the population that they are doing all that is humanly possible to bring in supplies."[101] In an American poll of 300 west Berliners in mid-July, 98 percent thought the West was right to stay, although more thought it was acting out of self-interest than concern for Berliners.[102] In another July survey, only 13 percent of respondents thought Berlin could hold out forever, and 12 percent thought it might hold out for "a long time." About one-third expected that the city could withstand a blockade for at least two months or until the winter, while another one-third thought one month was the limit. Men were more optimistic than women. Forty-one percent of men thought the city could resist for a long or unlimited time, while only 16 percent of females agreed. Thirty-nine percent of women expected collapse within a month, compared with 22 percent of men. Though pessimistic about how well the population as a whole might cope, most were ready to face greater personal privation themselves—just under two-thirds said they could deal with further reductions.[103]

Berliners hoped the Western powers would take strong action (according to these reports, at least). Many favored convoys, announced in advance. A survey of 100 people in the British and American sectors in mid-July found that 79 thought the Western powers should break the blockade, but only 16 thought they would. Dissatisfaction over Western tolerance of the eastern mark was widespread. In addition to the many practical problems of having two currencies circulating in the city, politically active Berliners feared that Western financial concessions would lead to the city's absorption by the Soviets.[104] Lawyers polled by OMGUS urged tough action, including an economic blockade of global Soviet trade. Though they called the airlift "magnificent," it was "purely defensive" and a "surrender" of Western rights.[105] Given the stiff line favored by Clay and Howley, political leaders found the Americans more sympathetic than the French, who seemed all too ready to abandon the city, or the British, who appeared aloof and uncooperative. The British resented the closeness between the Germans and the Americans. After any conversation, one Briton complained, Berliners "fly to the Americans," who seemed "prepared to agree to the most outrageous suggestions without adequate thought" and regarded the Germans "as Allies."[106]

Alarmed by the West's willingness to accept the eastern mark under four-power control, Berliners watched the Moscow talks with dread. Before June 24, the great fear had been that the Western powers would abandon the city. Now that anxiety was replaced by worry that the powers would let it slide under Soviet control. As one British report put it, "It is widely felt that the brilliant achievement of the air lift is being negatived by a politically disastrous economic policy." Residents' "one fear is that the Western Allies may compromise with the Russians." Political leaders expressed "alarm" over reports that the Western powers would accept the eastern mark under four-power control, an arrangement they dismissed as "utopian and unworkable." They wanted the deutsche mark to be the western sectors' sole currency. Furthermore, they opposed a simple return to pre-June conditions. Their "reward" for resisting the Soviets must be a lasting solution to the Berlin problem: firm links with the West, political freedom, and economic independence for the city.[107]

In the first weeks of the crisis, Berliners hoped for a strong sign from the Western powers, "some positive action in the near future." The British detected considerable support for a convoy among Berliners and widespread conviction that the Russians "will not shoot."[108] Robertson saw morale starting to slip by mid-August: the initial enthusiasm of standing up to the Russians began to fade, doubts grew about the line the West was pursuing in Moscow, and realization spread that the crisis would not end soon.[109] The gloom continued into September, after the talks moved to Berlin. "Rarely has the atmosphere in Berlin been more despondent," PORO reported in mid-September. The Americans reported anxiety, disbelief, and bewilderment as the Western powers seemed close to accepting the eastern mark, a step SPD leader Franz Neumann compared with Munich. Berliners saw no prospect of success at the United Nations, where the Soviets could veto any action, and they attributed Western softness to the U.S. presidential election, domestic political instability in France, and the airlift's high cost.[110] Worry about a weak Western position continued into November. PORO detected "disappointment" at Truman's victory. Berliners had hoped Dewey would take a stronger line, and they feared Truman might compromise with Stalin at their expense.[111]

As early as August, Americans feared morale might collapse. Berliners had been under a strain since 1942 and might be reaching the breaking point. Further deterioration in food supplies, coal stocks, or employment might "blow off the lid." Western sector residents identified with the Western powers and were "probably" willing to endure more, "but in view of the past stresses to which the population has been subjected it is reasonable to consider the possibilities of a breakdown in public morale."[112] Opinion remained mixed. A report by Howley's staff noted that conditions were better than a year before. Residents were better nourished and healthier; housing and clothing had improved. Berliners had adjusted to disruptions in the electrical supply, and unemployment was lower than expected. Objectively, the city should pull through; whether it would was a matter of will. If Howley's staff were optimistic, Murphy's aides were not so sure, calling Howley's report overly upbeat and unsupported by hard evidence.[113]

In Washington, Kennan shared Murphy's view that psychology outweighed statistics. He warned that "the population of a great city, particularly one which is in dire need of reconstruction on a grand scale, cannot get along indefinitely with just the absolute minimum of food and fuel." If the airlift could provide those minimums through the winter, it would give the Western powers "a brief respite in which to find a solution to the problem; but it is not itself a solution." Eventually, hardship and uncertainty would break the city's spirit.[114] Clay's thinking apparently ran along similar lines, for he told visiting reporter James Reston that if Berliners came to see the airlift as a way of avoiding an agreement, they "may very well turn against us."[115] Many Berliners preferred a prompt showdown to a prolonged deadlock. American intelligence predicted that an "instinctive repugnance" to endure another winter of privation would cause morale to slump if the situation dragged into autumn.[116]

Pessimists and optimists continued their debate into the fall of 1948 because Berliners' attitudes remained hard to gauge. An American poll indicated that 85 percent were confident the airlift would provide enough supplies for the winter (up from 45 percent in July and 77 percent in August), while British pollsters reported the widespread belief that "catastrophic" conditions were inevitable.[117] Friedensburg was outspoken, declaring in mid-November that because the airlift could not continue, there were only two ways out of the crisis: compromise or war.[118]

Herbert told Kirkpatrick at the end of January that the corner had been turned. Morale was good, Berliners were determined to hang on, and the danger had passed. There might be trouble next winter, Herbert thought, but not now.[119] Morale plummeted in early March, when the weather worsened briefly. Even as the clouds cleared, the sense that the worst was behind them competed with the belief that the blockade would become a permanent feature of the international scene and interest in Berlin would wane. Fear of abandonment was never far from people's minds.[120]

That anxiety contributed to a drumbeat of complaints about currency and support for making the deutsche mark Berlin's sole legal tender. That step would achieve Berliners' main goal—linking themselves with the West and with the new Federal Republic of Germany—though even advocates of such a course recognized that it meant the city's isolation from the Soviet zone and sole reliance on the airlift for the foreseeable future.[121] Converting to a single currency would mean that routine expenses previously paid in eastern marks would be paid in the more valuable deutsche mark, so the cost of living would go up, and with it, production costs and unemployment. Even so, noncommunist political leaders pressed hard for the change because politics outweighed economics: the currency represented a link to the West. There was much "relief" among the pro-Western parties when Norman Robertson's technical committee failed.[122] At various times, introduction of the deutsche mark had seemed imminent, and when it came at last, in March 1949, Berliners took it as a welcome sign of Western resolve.

As Stivers has noted, the economic costs were sudden and dramatic. Unemployment soared. Businesses trading with the Soviet zone did not earn western marks and could not meet their obligations. Firms cut wages and salaries by 10 to 20 percent. Ironically, this Western initiative isolated Berlin more effectively than the Soviet blockade had. If this had occurred in the depths of winter, when Clay had been pressing so strongly for it, the effect on the city might have been disastrous. Berlin may well have survived due to British and French foot-dragging.[123]

BERLINERS ENDURED and life went on, despite the crisis. In some ways, stress promoted cooperation, not division. A small sign emerged in British public opinion polls. One might have thought that those who found no pleasure in life would have been more numerous during the blockade than before it, but the reverse was true. Those who said life held no joy for them in August 1947 totaled 29 percent of respondents; those who felt that way in September 1948 numbered just 10 percent. The explanation can be found in answers to another pollster's question. The proportion of people who listed family and friends as their greatest pleasure in life tripled in that same period, from 5 to 15 percent. As the blockade narrowed life to essentials, Berliners found those essentials in one another. As they had during the war, "cellar communities" became the center of daily life, the hub of local, interlocking social networks. Social acceptance and ostracism could be powerful forces in these small, face-to-face groups of friends and neighbors.[124] From Louise Schroeder, Franz Neumann, and Ernst Reuter to the nameless men and women who built the Tegel airfield, a sense of community, commitment, and sacrifice bound Berliners together. From this came the legend of heroic, pro-Western Berliners that constitutes our image of the blockade. Stalin had no answer to such solidarity, and it set Moscow on the path to defeat.

CHAPTER 11

An Unexpected Success

If Stalin's plans foundered on Berliners' toughness and sense of community, his defeat had additional causes, the airlift ranking high among them. Makeshift in September, it evolved over the winter into an efficient, effective operation. While it did not deliver everything the city needed, it did provide much of the food and nearly all the coal Berliners consumed. Equally important—if not more so—the heavily laden planes were a constant reminder of Western support.

In September, the airlift's purpose remained buying time for diplomacy. Over the next few weeks, Washington redefined the mission in more expansive terms and committed itself to an all-out airlift. The decision was controversial. Concerned over what they regarded as a continuing disparity between the nation's foreign policy and the military means to support it, the joint chiefs challenged the administration's reliance on economic and political measures to contain the Soviet Union. Truman and his advisers rejected their arguments.

Meanwhile, Tunner pushed to get the most out of his people and planes. He combined the British and American lifts under a single headquarters, opened a new airfield in Berlin, overcame logistical bottlenecks, and dealt with morale problems. By late February and early March, with the worst of the winter behind him, he set increasingly ambitious goals. The famous "Easter Parade" was perhaps his finest hour, and by then, his success had transformed the diplomatic calculations of both sides.

THOUGH BUOYED BY the airlift's performance on Air Force Day, no one knew how it might fare in winter. Studying the data, Air Commodore Waite emphasized that German winters "vary amazingly." The only safe thing to do was assume the worst and stockpile as much as possible. The airlift had not outpaced consumption since June, and General Herbert declared in mid-September that the "present lift is something like 40 percent short of the minimum required" through the winter. Clay acknowledged that "our average airlift capacity to date has not sufficed to stockpile for the winter months and in fact we are not quite holding our own."[1]

The only solution seemed to be more planes. The airlift must be "stepped up right now," Waite insisted. If it was not, "we have, in my opinion, 'had it.'" At current rates, Berlin would run out of supplies at the end of January. And it might happen sooner because the city needed more coal during the winter. By mid-September, planners estimated the overall target at over 5,000 tons a day, up from the earlier figure of 4,500. On October 20, they raised it to 5,620 tons. Robertson dismissed all such estimates. "There is no good purpose served by talking about targets," he declared. "The only target is the maximum possible."[2]

Waite urged London to charter "every available aircraft that can carry a cargo, regardless of expense," while Clay sought to overcome Washington's reluctance to commit additional planes.[3] On July 22, the National Security Council had raised the total number of C-54s to 125, 100 below Milton's estimate. In August, the army tried to draw a line against further increases, which would concentrate the U.S. air transport fleet on a few vulnerable and unprotected airfields, "placing all [our] eggs in one basket." Even if war were avoided, the transfers would have "profound" effects on the Military Air Transport Service, shutting down virtually all its overseas routes. Clay conceded these points but insisted that the West's stake in Berlin outweighed them. He wanted 69 additional C-54s by October 1, plus 47 more by December 1. With these planes, he was convinced, the airlift could continue through the winter. Without them, it would fail.[4]

Kuter had no objection to more aircraft, as long as he did not have to provide them. "MATS may either be made or destroyed," depending on who provided the planes, he advised Tunner. "MATS will wind up in a very strong position if you have . . . all troop carrier C-54s when VITTLES terminates. On the other hand, as a global air transport agency, MATS will have in fact been destroyed if we wind up with our resources in VITTLES and the troop carriers doing the global job."[5]

The joint chiefs agreed in mid-September to send fifty C-54s, and discussion shifted to whether to send the remaining sixty-six. Clay reminded Washington on October 4 that his deadline had come and gone and the fifty planes promised in mid-September had yet to arrive. With winter around the corner, there was no time to lose.[6]

In retrospect, the wisest course would have been to use good summer weather to build up large surpluses and offset reduced deliveries during winter. Though Tedder had urged such a course at an Air Ministry meeting in July, it had not happened.[7] Facilities in western Germany could not support an all-out effort. Even if they could, Gatow and Tempelhof could not, so it made no sense to send a large fleet of planes to Germany until Tegel, the airfield under construction in Berlin, was ready. Effects on America's ability to fight if war broke out loomed large in the army's calculations—and in George Marshall's. In July, Lovett had urged delay because of the Moscow talks. It made little sense to launch an all-out effort only to have diplomacy resolve the crisis. In short, throughout the summer, the Western powers did not pursue an airlift strategy but took the situation one day at a time. Officials realized that they might confront that "brutal choice between war and submission" if the blockade continued into October, but they would face it when the time came, not before.

Draper again proved to be Clay's greatest ally in Washington. He had asked P&O to study Clay's requests. The resulting staff study was a curious mixture of Wedemeyer's doubts and Draper's desires. It noted that honoring Clay's calls would shut down nearly all of MATS's overseas schedules, concentrate 45 percent of the C-54 fleet on a few vulnerable bases in Germany (which lacked antiaircraft guns to protect them), and cripple the nation's ability to fight if war came. P&O also argued that there were larger issues at stake. The nation's foreign policy had outstripped the military's ability to support it; the administration must decide whether to "enlarge the military immediately or to slow up our foreign policy" until the balance between ends and means was restored. P&O barely concealed its preference for withdrawal, but Draper controlled the conclusions. As long as the U.S. government was determined to remain in Berlin, every effort should be made to support the airlift. Clay should get his planes.[8]

The paper went to the joint chiefs. Meanwhile, Lovett had asked Forrestal for a study of the military implications of continuing the airlift through the winter, a request the defense secretary passed to the chiefs on October 4. That same day, responding to Clay's plea for speed, Wedemeyer suggested that Bradley ask the chiefs to approve the P&O paper immediately. That did not happen, and the chiefs did not send their recommendations to Forrestal for another nine days.[9]

The chiefs sensed that policy was shifting in a direction they did not like. Thus far, the Western powers had relied on the airlift to maintain their position in Berlin while seeking a negotiated solution. In a sense, diplomacy and the airlift had combined into a surprisingly effective approach. With direct negotiations at an end and no one expecting a favorable outcome at the United Nations, the Western powers were jettisoning that approach and relying on the airlift alone. The consensus in the Pentagon was that this was a mistake. Although General Vandenberg had spoken optimistically at the July 22 NSC meeting, the air force was not the Pentagon's executive agent for Berlin. The army was, and it remained convinced that the airlift would fail. At best, the new policy promised an endless blockade offset by an everlasting airlift; at worst, there would be economic collapse in Berlin or an incident in the corridors that spiraled out of control.

In an October 13 memo to Forrestal, the chiefs argued that the U.S. military could not supply Berlin by air indefinitely without jeopardizing "its primary national security responsibilities." The airlift "cannot be a permanent solution," and Soviet disruption would force Western governments to decide whether "we shall remain not merely at the risk of war but even if war itself be the only alternative to withdrawal." They challenged the view that the NSC had decided that question on July 22, and they asked that it be clarified *now* "beyond all doubt." If the West would fight for Berlin, "full-out preparations" for war should be made "immediately"; if it would not, the Western garrisons should prepare to withdraw. The JCS expressed no preference but made it clear that they thought war "neither militarily prudent nor strategically sound." On the immediate question of the sixty-six planes, the chiefs reluctantly endorsed Clay's request.[10]

As U.S. reliance on the airlift grew, the risk that an incident would trigger escalation increased as well. Bohlen had worried in July that Soviet maneuvers presaged more pressure, and Bradley had asked for a study.[11] Because there had been no significant harassment, the issue had lain dormant; Forrestal now revived it. Kennan replied that the State Department had been considering the problem. The Policy Planning Staff completed a paper but provided few answers. It recommended diplomatic protests in response to buzzings, interference with navigation, or shooting incidents. If the Soviets admitted to deliberate acts, Clay should advise Washington immediately.[12] How he might do that was uncertain. Briefed on the possible disruption of communications from Berlin, Draper had little to suggest beyond using carrier pigeons.[13]

The NSC considered the planners' paper briefly and then referred it to the JCS, asking them to recommend military measures to stop Soviet interference. The chiefs had little to suggest. There were not enough fighters to patrol the corridors; other steps, such as warning the Soviets against interference, were more likely to "incite" war than deter it. The chiefs opposed any military steps unless the United States had decided to fight for Berlin.[14]

While officials in Washington grappled with these potential disasters, Clay's attention remained focused on reinforcement. He pressed Wedemeyer for action. Fog was grounding planes six to eight hours a day. Stockpiles were shrinking. "We need [an] urgent decision and prompt movement of additional airlift," he pleaded. "Please send us the right airplanes now."[15]

When the NSC met on October 14 to consider the situation, Lovett lectured the chiefs like errant schoolboys. The council had made its decision in July fully understanding its implications, he contended, and the United States would stay in Berlin in "any event." He went on to accuse them of having a "case of the jitters" and using Berlin as a ploy to get larger appropriations. Royall chimed in, saying the chiefs were trying to "pass the buck." Lovett then softened his tone. The JCS had supported Clay's call for more aircraft, with conditions. They wanted steps taken to offset the airlift's drain on petroleum reserves, more money for spare parts, and increases in the air force budget and personnel ceilings. Lovett endorsed these "excellent" recommendations. When Symington put the proposal to a vote, there was no dissent.

Lovett then summarized his view of policy, declaring, "It is not necessarily our position to stay in Berlin forever, but rather that we want to be sure that *when* we do get out it will be under favorable circumstances." The country faced two immediate problems: the danger of Soviet disruption of the airlift, and the creation of an overall policy for Germany. Kennan was at work on the second, and Royall suggested delaying discussion of the first until the following week, when Clay would be in the United States to give a speech and could attend the next council meeting. Lovett thought that was a good idea. Almost as an aside, he said the airlift should continue and be increased "as required"; his colleagues readily assented. He added, as if to soothe the chiefs' feelings, that "everything we have done has been designed to avoid war."[16]

As Kenneth Condit has noted, neither Lovett nor Royall answered the "central question" raised by the chiefs: "Would the United States go to war to remain in Berlin? Their evasion suggested a policy of postponing a decision until faced with [the] necessity to fight or get out."[17] That was true; U.S. policy was contingent and uncertain, as Lovett's divergent comments suggested. But Condit and the chiefs overlooked what Brian Robertson had seen so clearly in April: that a democratic nation cannot make such decisions in advance. The military was trying to impose a false clarity on events, one that was symptomatic of its general approach to "national security" issues. The joint chiefs' tolerance for ambiguity was so low as to be nearly nonexistent. For them, the issue was simple: would the West fight or not? If so, it should mobilize; if not, it should get out. The administration's practice of avoiding that question, of running risks for interests it might not be willing to fight for, seemed dangerous and irresponsible. So did the administration's "strategy of containment," which relied on political and economic measures, not military muscle, to curb Soviet expansion. Strategy balances ends and means. The chiefs defined that balance in exclusively military terms. At one level, that was understandable; it was their job. At another, it is amazing that the country's military leaders had not grasped the basic tenets of the administration's foreign policy and national security strategy.[18]

In an unusual move, the chiefs' memos were recalled and destroyed. New drafts were ready October 20, and Forrestal forwarded them to the NSC. The chiefs omitted their call for immediate decisions on ultimate questions, but they would retreat only so far. They reiterated their claims that the airlift was no solution, that it risked war and left the military unable to fight if war came, and that increased military strength was needed to balance foreign policy ends and means. While they agreed to give Clay sixty-six C-54s, he should receive no more. This ran counter to the council's decision to increase the airlift "as required," so the debate seemed certain to continue.[19]

Meanwhile, Admiral Sidney W. Souers, the NSC's executive secretary, had referred the papers to the president, who passed them on to Frank Pace, acting director of the Bureau of the Budget, for review. Pace opposed the call for more funds and manpower; the Pentagon should shift resources from other programs. He had no objection to sending more planes. On that issue, however, Forrestal had been unwilling to wait. Two days earlier, he had told Symington that Clay's need was too urgent; he should go ahead without waiting for the president to act.[20]

Clay and Murphy returned to Washington on October 20 and had breakfast with Forrestal, Draper, Royall, and Saltzman the next morning. Reports from Paris that Vyshinsky had accepted the neutrals' resolution upset Clay, who was wary of any sudden Soviet amiability. If the Russians proposed a neutralized Germany, with the occupation armies pulled back to peripheral areas, the eastern zone police might overrun the country before anyone could react. The only barriers between the Kremlin and western Europe were the U.S. Army and the airlift. Remove them, and the gains of the last year would be swept away. Forrestal thought they could deal with these issues when they saw the president later that morning. He and Royall would convince Truman to ignore the neutrals, while Clay should warn the president that withdrawal from Germany meant abandoning Europe and inviting a third world war.[21]

The NSC agenda called for a discussion of responses to Soviet disruption of the airlift. Forrestal had raised the subject three weeks before as an urgent matter, but he now said there was no need for council action. Souers noted that the president was considering last week's recommendations regarding the airlift, so the council could not act there, either. No one mentioned the chiefs' call for a cap on additional planes for Clay, effectively sidetracking it. With nothing to decide, the discussion rambled, touching on the airlift, elections in the Ruhr, morale in Berlin, slave labor in eastern Germany, the suitability of the August 30 directive as a basis for agreement, and the number of dependents still in Berlin. Clay summarized developments since July, noting that the airlift's success had made Germany "one of the most anti-Communist countries in the world." Unless the winter was unusually severe, he expected the airlift would continue to supply Berlin. He expressed two worries, following Forrestal's cues at breakfast. He warned about the People's Police in the eastern zone, and when Royall prompted him about the risks of withdrawing occupation forces to "selected points," Clay contended that was "substantially our present disposition," noting later that "the line between the communists and noncommunists was really along the frontiers of the U.S. Army." Royall worried that a settlement might lure the United States into a "false sense of security"; Lovett countered that the diplomatic corps understood that an end to the blockade was nothing more than "a transient matter, and not the root of the difficulty." Because "the

Soviets can agree on something Friday and deny it on Saturday, the situation was pretty bad," he added.[22]

After the council adjourned, Clay and Murphy went to the Oval Office, accompanied by Forrestal, Royall, and Leahy. Truman had not attended the meeting, so Clay repeated the high points of his presentation. He assured the president that the airlift could supply Berlin indefinitely unless the Soviets interfered with it. Leahy recorded no estimate of how likely that was, and no discussion of a U.S. response. Truman told the group that the Western powers would stay "unless we are driven out by superior force." Leahy's diary gives no hint whether this provided the answer to the question he and the chiefs had been trying to extract from the administration. Clay apparently came away satisfied. Truman assured him that he would authorize dispatch of the C-54s. He was as good as his word, approving the next day a letter Pace had drafted that went on to rule out the increases in budget and manpower the NSC had proposed.[23] There was no "impassioned plea" from Clay for planes, no president who "tipped the balance in favor of a large and well-supported airlift." Since October 5, when P&O had endorsed sending the planes, there had been no dissent regarding the C-54s, and no balance to be tipped.[24] In any case, the issue was moot, given Forrestal's green light two days before.

There are two noteworthy aspects to these October deliberations. One, noted earlier, was the lateness of the decision. Truman and his advisers passed up the opportunity to stockpile food and coal during good summer flying weather and waited until winter was upon them before raising the airlift to the level Colonel Milton had calculated months earlier. A curious blend of optimism and pessimism shaped this wait-and-see approach. Officials saw little point in reinforcing Tunner's aerial armada when it appeared that negotiations might break the deadlock and the airlift could not succeed anyway. As prospects for an early resolution dwindled and the airlift showed greater potential, Western leaders began to see it as a way of remaining in Berlin, without resorting to force, until the Soviets gave up. If that were possible, the United States and its allies could continue the London program, pursue the North Atlantic treaty, and avoid war; there would be no need to choose among these goals. Not reinforcing the airlift meant sacrificing that possibility and facing, sooner or later, the "brutal choice between war or submission" that the Western powers had avoided since the crisis began.

Also noteworthy is that the October decisions did not clarify U.S. policy regarding that choice. Lovett contended that the NSC had settled the issue in July, but other men who had been in the room said otherwise. It was easy to say that U.S. policy was to remain in Berlin, but when that policy was also to avoid war, how was the balance to be struck? The JCS complaint that U.S. policy was ambiguous was an accurate one, and the October decisions did little to remove the ambiguities. The attraction of the airlift was, after all, that it postponed the need to make decisions.

The chiefs, treating clarity and decisiveness as absolutes, could not understand that. On the other side, no one felt comfortable defending indecision and drift; both were contrary to Lovett's code of statecraft and Truman's notions of presidential leadership. Both men talked one way and behaved another. In later years, the talk would obscure their actual behavior and put an unjustified premium on "toughness" in dealing with the Soviets.

AS THESE HIGH-LEVEL DELIBERATIONS unfolded, Tunner continued to refine the airlift. By late September, he had improved efficiency and arranged with the British to base U.S. planes in the northern zone. He had nearly reached his third initial goal as well—a combined Anglo-American command. With the Americans using the southern corridor and Tempelhof while the British used the northern corridor and Gatow, one could argue that coordination and cooperation were all that were needed. The American move to Fassberg made such an approach obsolete, and it was clearly the first step toward a growing U.S. presence in the British zone. Tunner and LeMay began discussing a combined command with the British in August. The BAFO commander, Air Marshal Sanders, was ready to accept unified air traffic control in the Berlin area, but the Americans seemed to want "full integration," which he thought went too far and stemmed from the Yankees' presumption that everything would somehow work better if they were in charge. Existing arrangements worked "pretty well," Sanders believed, and he saw "nothing to be gained" by adding another layer of command. Unable to sway him, LeMay asked Vandenberg to raise the issue with Tedder. Echoing Tunner, LeMay insisted that cutting "minutes and even seconds" from each function was the "key to the ultimate tonnage which could be sent to Berlin safely," and he was certain unified command would boost tonnage. The new commander would not need control over administration, logistics, or maintenance, just over what units were doing when they were actively supporting the airlift. LeMay thought Tunner's current headquarters plus half a dozen British officers would do. The commander, of course, must be American because of the greater U.S. role in the airlift.[25]

The British gave way, and discussion shifted to details. The main sticking point was the location of the new headquarters. The Americans insisted on Wiesbaden because, as LeMay had suggested, they intended to augment Tunner's existing headquarters with a handful of Britons. Sanders and his staff wanted the headquarters at Bückeburg, arguing that the main effort in the future would be from northern bases. The Americans argued that "dual-hatting" in Wiesbaden was necessary because there were not enough senior U.S. and British officers available to create a separate headquarters. The British yielded "for the time being," reserving the right to reopen the question.[26] They never did.

On October 15, USAFE and BAFO created a Combined Airlift Task Force

(CALTF) with Tunner in charge. Merer served as deputy commander while retaining command of No. 46 Group, and Tunner retained command of the U.S. airlift task force. Milton doubled as chief of staff of CALTF and of the U.S. organization. Tunner's mission as CALTF commander was "to deliver to Berlin, in a safe and efficient manner, the maximum tonnage possible." He had command of assigned U.S. units and operational control of No. 46 Group.[27]

Britons regarded CALTF as a combined headquarters "in name only." The reality was that CALTF and Tunner's U.S. headquarters were one and the same. Merer's appointment as deputy commander was "not really satisfactory," as BAFO's official after-action report noted, because his primary duty remained command of No. 46 Group. At best, he could make the 400-mile round-trip to Wiesbaden about once a week. The British contingent at CALTF remained small, as LeMay expected: two or three operations officers, a communications officer, and an air traffic control specialist. In addition, Group Captain Hyde, who had led the initial RAF force at Wunstorf, returned to the airlift as CALTF director of plans.[28] Personnel aside, the RAF judged that CALTF "did not develop much beyond regulating the traffic flow into the Berlin airfields and co-ordinating the air traffic pattern." No. 46 Group remained responsible for coordinating the flow from fields in the British zone within overall block timings set by CALTF. U.S. operations officers at group headquarters coordinated U.S. flights from Fassberg and Celle, an arrangement that worked smoothly.[29]

The British, already sensitive about their relative contribution to the airlift, worried that the combined task force meant a diminution of their role. As Strang pointed out, Tunner intended to lift the maximum possible tonnage "regardless of flag." While applauding that, Strang noted that it implied the British would be relegated to junior partner status: "Logically, a truly combined operation would . . . mean that all the nearby airfields in the British zone were used almost exclusively by Skymasters." If that happened, "it seems likely that the whole job could be undertaken by Skymasters," with the British contribution limited to "special types (tankers, etc.)." Yet to run the operation on a "national basis" meant lost tonnage. There was no question in Robertson's mind about priorities: "efficiency must come before national prestige." Tedder agreed.[30]

Tunner could look forward to increased deliveries because the new airfield in Berlin was nearing completion. Known as Tegel, it had been the site of Colonel Dorr's abortive coal drops. Work had begun on August 5. Up to 17,000 Berliners helped build the new airfield, more than half of them women, working alongside U.S. military engineers. In ninety-three days, they built a 5,500-foot runway with 500-foot overruns on each end, plus a 2,200- by 400-foot apron, using tons of rubble left from wartime air raids. Engineers needed heavy earthmoving equipment, and there was not enough in the city. Eighty-one rock crushers, rollers, and tractors were cut apart by soldiers at the Hanau Engineer Depot, flown to Berlin, welded back together, and put to work. Tunner, as exacting as ever, insisted that the runway be built parallel with those at Tempelhof and Gatow; otherwise, the paths of planes landing at different airports might intersect. The first plane to land at the new base arrived November 5. Regular operations began November 18.[31] The French unloaded cargoes, using labor provided by the Magistrat, and provided all ground support such as security and administration. A small American detachment from Tempelhof ran the tower and base operations. Tegel became Berlin's main source of liquid fuels. Engineers built ten hydrants on the ramp that drained fuel directly from the planes into four large underground tanks. A pipeline then ran to storage tanks near the Plötzensee.[32]

The field became fully operational on December 16, when Ganeval took action to remove a hazard to flight. Two radio towers for Soviet-controlled Radio Berlin, one of them 200 feet high, were near the field in the instrument approach, posing a danger to planes landing in fog. Ganeval had asked the Russians to remove them; they refused. On the morning of the sixteenth, French military police cordoned off the transmitter. Russian technicians at the site tried to telephone for help, only to find the lines cut. Meanwhile, Ganeval invited the small American detachment at Tegel to his office and, without explanation, began serving refreshments. As his guests tried to figure out what they were celebrating, French sappers planted their charges at the base of the towers. Aircrews were warned to take cover, and just before noon, both towers collapsed in clouds of smoke. "You'll have no more trouble," Ganeval told his guests with a smile.[33]

There was little trouble with the Russians in the corridors, either, which surprised many. Ross Milton and his colleagues wondered when (not if) the Soviets would start interfering with the airlift, a move they were certain would trigger war. "Most of us in those days . . . thought we were simply on the verge of World War III," Milton told an interviewer years later. Everyone believed the two air forces were "buying time for World War III," he continued, "and that had a very distinct effect over the whole atmosphere of this operation."[34]

The Kremlin shared Milton's worry about an incident, according to a CDU official from the eastern zone, who reported that the Russians judged any move to close the corridors "extremely risky." Furthermore, running such risks seemed unnecessary. As late as November, Soviet diplomats were eagerly collecting, for Stalin's edification, reports that Western officials doubted the airlift could succeed.[35] Soviet interference with the airlift thus remained a potential problem, not an actual one: American pilots reported two deliberate buzzings in August, seven in September, and one in October, with one instance of close flying (within 500 feet) each month. The British noticed a rise in Soviet activity but no attempts to interfere with their planes, which, Robertson confessed, were violating the control zone around the Soviet airfield at Dallgow, three miles north of Gatow, "up to seventy times a day."[36]

While attention centered on possible violent incidents in the corridors, everyone recognized that the Soviets need not go to such extremes. The airlift depended on radio communications and navigational aids, and both were susceptible to disruption. LeMay thought jamming would create "an extremely serious problem." Clay told the NSC that jamming ground-controlled approach (GCA) systems could reduce airlift deliveries by 25 to 30 percent. Such a reduction might mean the difference between success and failure, so both air forces hurriedly devised countermeasures. Meanwhile, the Soviets sought to impose new restrictions. They demanded that their representative in the Berlin Air Safety Center receive full information on all flights an hour before takeoff. At about the same time, they contended that *they alone* had created the corridors, not the four powers jointly, and they revived their claim that the corridors were intended to support the garrisons, not the city. Such demands and contentions were brushed aside, and the airlift continued.[37]

Weather was a more serious problem than the Russians, as low visibility and morning fog hampered operations.[38] Tunner took a variety of steps to improve weather reports. Smith had begun B-17 weather flights in the southern corridor on July 9. In August, two aircraft in each block started sending reports from Tempelhof on conditions they had encountered en route. On August 26, Berlin and Frankfurt began issuing hourly forecasts instead of one every six hours. USAFE activated the 7169th Weather Reconnaissance Squadron in November; its C-47s joined weather ships in the North Atlantic and British and American aircraft patrolling the North Sea.[39]

Overhauls of C-54s remained a bottleneck. Planes were serviced every 200 flying hours, then returned to depots in the United States every 1,000 flying hours. The American depot at Oberpfaffenhofen began performing the 200-hour checks in August, an interim step until Burtonwood, a large wartime depot near Liverpool, could reopen. "Obie," as GIs called the Bavarian base, never met Tunner's goal of 6 planes a day; during October, its best month, the average was only 4.5. But its performance was sterling compared with the 1,000-hour inspections being done in the States. Tunner outlined the situation for LeMay's replacement, Lieutenant General John K. Cannon, at the end of November. Planes were not returning on a regular basis: of the 67 sent, only 18 had returned. They had been gone an average of fifty-seven days, with a range of forty-four to eighty-eight. The goal was a twenty-two-day turnaround. Based on usage, Tunner continued, he should have sent 126 planes back, but that would have left only a handful to fly the corridors. He had been able to cope only due to 50 recent arrivals, many of which had flown more than 700 hours since their last overhaul.[40]

Other transatlantic traffic moved more expeditiously. Westbound planes flew parts to depots for repair. Kuter assured Tunner that Air Materiel Command did not "touch any other business each morning" until it had acted on Rhein-Main's daily requisition. In addition to air force planes crisscrossing the Atlantic, commercial airlines moved people, parts, and equipment. Planes moved high-priority parts, but starting in September, less critical ones moved on a special fleet of ships called "Marinex," consisting of U.S. Army and commercial freighters. Marinex ships were loaded so that priority cargo could be unloaded first and rushed to airlift bases.[41]

To deal with the shortage of aircrews, another airlift operation took shape 6,000 miles from Berlin. In October, the air force recalled 10,000 pilots, radio operators, and flight engineers to active duty. Over the next few months, they were sent to Great Falls, Montana, where they spent three weeks flying C-54s loaded with ten tons of sand through a duplicate of the Berlin corridor system. Everything duplicated conditions in Germany—location and radio frequency of the beacons, layout of the glide paths, and runway alignments. Nature cooperated by providing identical magnetic headings and bad weather. The school sought to graduate twenty-seven crews a week. Sent to Germany for 180-day tours with the airlift, the first eleven graduates arrived November 4.[42]

There were other noteworthy organizational changes in October and November. In a paper change, the provisional U.S. task force Tunner had commanded since late July was inactivated on November 4, and USAFE activated a permanent unit, the 1st Airlift Task Force.[43] The change reflected the shift in the airlift from an ad hoc operation to a long-term one. Another change had important and unpleasant consequences for Tunner. He was now a combined commander, and both his bosses left for new assignments. Air Marshal T. M. Williams replaced Sanders as BAFO commander on October 30. LeMay left USAFE to take the helm at Strategic Air Command on October 16, and Cannon took his place.

Milton recalled that Cannon "had an intensely personal approach to command. It was an approach that included a love of detail . . . and a desire to know everything that was going on. It was also an approach that caused an immediate clash with Tunner," who resented interference with *his* airlift. For all his gruffness, LeMay had given his independent-minded subordinate free rein, and Tunner had kept his promise and *produced*. Cannon was determined to put his stamp on the operation, which was *his* airlift, too. Tunner did not like this and seemed to forget that Cannon was his boss. As he explained in his memoirs, "All I wanted was to be allowed to carry out my mission as I saw it should be done. . . . I wanted to be left alone—I knew best how the job should be done." He never saw the airlift as an operation occurring within a theater command. He believed MATS should manage all airlifts, wherever and whenever they occurred. When Operation Vittles began, he had wanted a MATS task force to deploy to Europe and execute the mission under MATS control. It came as a "shock" to some members of his staff to find themselves working for USAFE. He wanted and needed Cannon's "help," as he put it, but resented his supervision.[44]

Poor command arrangements compounded the situation. To keep Tunner's staff small and focused on operations, USAFE retained responsibility for other staff functions. Thus, neither Tunner's combined headquarters nor his U.S. task force controlled U.S. airlift bases; USAFE did. (The RAF operated until December under a similar arrangement, with BAFO exercising administrative control of RAF stations while No. 46 Group had operational control of flying units.) In practice, this meant there was no clear line separating USAFE's responsibilities from those of the task force. A vague division of responsibility between two strong-willed commanders was a recipe for trouble, and Milton later described his role as intermediary between Tunner and Cannon as "the toughest assignment of my Air Force career."[45] That was undoubtedly true. Yet one can make too much of this personality conflict. After all, Tunner's greatest adversary was not General Cannon but Russia's great ally against Napoleon and Hitler, "General Winter." Their great duel was about to begin.

WINTER: the very word gave Russians hope and chilled the hearts of Berliners and those trying to keep them free. Moscow's great hope and the West's great fear was that winter would ground the airlift. Moscow's hopes went unfulfilled, but that outcome was not preordained. Unusually mild weather, coupled with Tunner's unceasing search for greater efficiency and Berliners' ingenuity and determination, allowed the airlift to eke out a narrow success.

The Americans waited until almost the last possible moment to provide the necessary aircraft. Whereas Milton had defined the need in early August, it was not until late October that Truman ordered them to Germany. The planes, including two U.S. Navy squadrons (VR-6 and VR-8), began deploying on October 27, and the last one arrived January 12. The first R5D (the navy's version of the C-54) arrived at Rhein-Main on November 9 and flew its first Vittles mission later that day.[46]

London also sent reinforcements. Two squadrons of its new transport, the Handley Page Hastings, arrived at Schleswigland in November and December. This was the first operational use of the Hastings, which had its share of teething problems, but its eight-ton payload was a welcome addition to the airlift. Ultimately, Schleswigland hosted about sixty planes, including thirty-two Hastings and aircraft from four charter companies, flying coal, food, and liquid fuel.[47] The Hastings more than offset the loss of the Sunderland and Hythe flying boats, withdrawn on December 14 when Berlin's lakes froze for the winter. (Chartered Handley Page Haltons replaced the Sunderlands in delivering salt, carrying it in panniers beneath their fuselages.)[48]

These reinforcements arrived to face the worst weather of the entire blockade.

Thick fog settled over Germany. When the weather broke briefly on November 6, Tunner telephoned Merer and every U.S. base commander to urge a maximum effort. One clear day simply added to the frustration from many bad ones. Only ten U.S. planes reached Berlin on November 30, delivering 83 tons, the worst day of the entire operation. As Kuter summed it up, "November was a black and heart-breaking month." U.S. deliveries fell to just under 88,000 tons, while the British slumped to 25,600.[49]

The fog persisted into December. By midmonth, German meteorologists were reporting that it was the foggiest winter in eighty years. Operations analysts at BAFO, who had predicted in September that the airlift would fail, repeated their gloomy forecast on December 10. As they saw the trends, "an extremely serious situation will develop about mid-February," when coal would dwindle to a few days' supply. Past estimates of the lift had been high and requirements low, they added, which had produced "an undue sense of optimism in many high quarters."[50]

Both air forces sought ways to offset winter's effects. Tunner had won approval for high-intensity approach lighting during a trip to Washington in October, and installation was soon under way. Tempelhof had priority, and the lights were installed at the eastern end of its southern runway by November 25. The lights had to be installed on a row of towers about 100 feet apart, gradually increasing in height until the farthest tower was 75 feet tall. Berlin lacked material suitable for constructing the towers, so engineers cut PSP mats into strips and welded them together. The Soviets saw the project as a propaganda windfall because the towers and the underground electrical cables connecting them ran through a cemetery. With the Magistrat's permission, several graves had been moved, and a church spire blocking one light had been taken down. Soviet-sponsored papers condemned the Americans for desecrating graves. Over the next few months, other airlift bases received the lights. At the same time, ramp lighting at most bases improved, making operations at night faster and safer.[51]

Another key ally against the winter appeared atop Tempelhof: a CPS-5 radar. Installation was completed December 27. Addition of a moving target indicator in January improved performance by eliminating returns from the city's buildings. The new radar could detect planes up to eighty-five miles away. This allowed controllers to space planes at ten-mile intervals by the time they were fifty miles from the city. The CPS-5 lacked IFF—the common "identification friend or foe" system used to recognize specific aircraft being displayed on a radar screen—so controllers distinguished planes by ordering forty-five-degree turns and then adjusted spacing. These teams relieved much of the workload previously shouldered by GCA controllers, who were now free to concentrate on final approaches. Initially, the CPS-5 section controlled traffic moving to and from Tempelhof and Tegel. On March 13, ten controllers from Gatow joined the group. Thereafter, it controlled all Berlin traffic.

Operating in three sections, one for each airfield, this Berlin Approach Control Center was a major advance. Radarscopes were arranged in pairs, one for each airfield. The first controller tracked planes in the corridors, spaced them, and guided them to a certain point, where he handed them over to his partner, who manned the "feeder scope." This individual vectored the plane through the local pattern into the final approach, where the GCA controller took over. As one commercial pilot, Jack O. Bennett, recalled, "the radar coverage from the ground was incredibly accurate. If our plane crept up or fell back, even a few feet, on the aircraft preceding us, radar would warn us to adjust our airspeed by a minuscule knot. We couldn't believe it was possible to fly this accurately." Two South African pilots had similar recollections. One day they "were a bit behind time and so turned a few miles short of [Frohnau] meanwhile calling 'Beacons.' A voice came back, 'Oh no you are not! You have a further 2 miles to go so please continue on your original course.'"[52]

The combination of CPS-5, GCA, the new lighting, and airborne radar (installation of which started in the autumn and was completed in half the C-54s by January) was critical in defeating the bad weather. Because of the buildings around Tempelhof, 400-foot ceilings and one-mile visibility remained the minimums there; however, at Tegel and Gatow, planes could land with 200-foot ceilings and visibility of a quarter mile. Generally, an experienced GCA crew could talk down one plane every five minutes; for periods up to an hour, they could handle one every three minutes. Missed approaches were rare. As the South Africans recalled, "it was very convincing to come out of the cloud . . . [and] find the runway straight ahead." By the end of February, every U.S. airlift base had two GCA sets. In its after-action report, USAFE judged GCA as "perhaps the greatest contributing factor to the success of the airlift." BAFO agreed.[53]

Tunner introduced other improvements during the winter. In December, crews started radioing ahead to their home bases after leaving Berlin, reporting whether their planes needed repairs and whether they carried cargo, so the base could give them a proper reception. Some bases stationed weather observers at the end of runways. By counting the number of approach lights they could see, these observers provided a more accurate estimate of visibility than people in the tower could, and the field would continue operations until weather reached exact minimums. Rhein-Main started matching each hardstand by number to an aircraft. When a plane was inbound, the load was driven out to the hardstand and would be there, waiting, when the plane taxied in. Three RAF stations started plotting what each aircraft was doing minute by minute, which highlighted the causes of excessive time on the ground. Analysis showed that maintenance problems varied according to the number of sorties, not hours flown. Quick inspections between flights cut the abort rate for Yorks in half.[54]

Tunner made a variety of changes in flight operations that boosted tonnage.

Celle opened on December 15, and CALTF soon planned to station up to fifty-seven Skymasters there. To make room at Gatow for Celle's planes, Fassberg now sent its planes to Tegel. A new runway also opened at Fuhlsbüttel on December 15. Fully equipped for night landings, the new strip promised to boost productivity of the charter companies, many of which had moved there from Lübeck on October 5. In January, British and American officials revised the block system for the northern corridor to accommodate increased traffic. Instead of each base launching planes in four-hour blocks, they now used blocks of two hours. Under the four-hour system, planes had wasted time on the ground waiting for their block to start. The change helped smooth out the maintenance workload and ensured that if a plane missed its block, it would not have to sit idle for four hours until the next one.[55]

Supply was the biggest problem at the end of December, to the extent that one analyst spoke of a "supply and maintenance crisis." There were a number of causes. The logistical support needed by the new wave of C-54s lagged the planes by about a month. The effects could be seen at Fassberg, where utilization dropped by 30 percent, from 7.3 to 5.1 hours a day. There were continuing shortages of skilled mechanics and spare parts. Engines remained in short supply. Delays in opening the 200-hour inspections at Burtonwood added to Tunner's headaches. The buildings had deteriorated since the war, and much of the workforce was busy with repairs, renovations, or new construction. Also, airlift support was not Burtonwood's main mission. The depot's chief customer was the B-29 force in Britain. Until January 1949, Burtonwood was part of USAFE, which meant that airlift work received some priority; that month, however, Third Air Division was reassigned directly to the Air Staff, and Burtonwood went with it. Tunner was reluctant to send planes to the depot because they were so slow to return, and Burtonwood complained that the erratic flow of C-54s into the depot was one reason the turnaround time was so long. To speed things along, Washington sent 2,100 people to Burtonwood in the first three months of 1949. By April, the depot was averaging seven planes a day against a target of eight, and by mid-April it was averaging nine.[56]

Commanders worried that the average GI's morale and commitment were waning as autumn turned to winter. Flight surgeons reported "very large" numbers of crew members asking to be taken off flying status. The venereal disease rate, a traditional indicator of poor morale, was "excessive."[57] USAFE considered the issue important enough to request a morale survey in November, and a team from European Command interviewed over 1,400 officers and enlisted men at Fassberg, Rhein-Main, Tempelhof, and Wiesbaden in December. To no one's surprise, morale was lowest at Fassberg, best at Tempelhof and Wiesbaden. More than 80 percent of those interviewed at Fassberg rated the bus service, mail, movie theaters, club facilities, recreational facilities, and supplies of tools and equipment worse than at other bases where they had served. Reflecting the congestion at Rhein-Main, complaints there centered on quarters, meals, transportation, and supplies; two-thirds of respondents rated these as worse than elsewhere. Separation from their families and worries about how loved ones were coping bothered more than 90 percent of married men at all four bases. The survey team found morale highest among men who felt informed about the mission and thought it important, lowest among the ill informed. It was hard to expect 110 percent from men who did not understand why they were in Germany or what was at stake. The biggest source of dissatisfaction, as everyone knew, was the indefinite length of tours of duty with the airlift. Crews and mechanics had deployed in July for 45 days, only to have their tours extended to 90 and then 180 days. As the 180-day mark loomed, many expected to be extended again. Even the hard-nosed LeMay thought this was unfair.[58]

Morale was not as serious a problem in the RAF because most of the men could make brief trips home. Even so, the RAF learned a valuable lesson regarding morale and esprit de corps. During their autumn manning crisis, the British pooled air and ground crews, and it had not worked well. John Dowling, a York pilot, recalled, "We never knew the ground crew, we didn't even know what squadron they were on. . . . I didn't know what squadron I was on." The RAF stopped pooling York mechanics at Wunstorf in December, dividing them instead into sections responsible for twelve or thirteen aircraft. The planes had been so dispersed that under the previous centralized system, mechanics had wasted considerable time going back and forth; also, creating different sections fostered a spirit of healthy competition. Schleswigland and Lübeck copied Wunstorf's example in January. All in all, BAFO concluded, squadron integrity "was a potent factor in the maintenance of a high morale."[59]

The Americans pursued various solutions. USAFE started a troop education program that emphasized the importance of saving Berlin as a U.S. national goal. Tunner worked tirelessly to improve working and living conditions. He set up "ham" radio links so airmen could talk to their families. He worked with the British Navy, Army, and Air Force Institute and the U.S. exchange services to establish snack bars at airlift bases and keep them open around the clock. He arranged for Bob Hope, Garry Moore, and other Hollywood stars to bring touring shows to Germany. Movies started running at Fassberg three times a week in January, to packed houses. In another step to boost morale, USAFE authorized the award of the Air Medal for 100 Vittles missions.[60] Most important of all, in January 1949, it set a firm limit of 180 days for a Vittles tour.

Although setting a definite limit on tours of duty boosted morale, it meant serious shortages of experienced people in January and February as those who had arrived in July and August went home. Departures began January 3, when the first 6 aircrew members left. A total of 402 were due to go that month. Departures exceeded replacements in February, leading to an almost complete turnover of air and ground crews and "serious shortages" in mechanics. One solution was to delay departures. In February, USAFE held 275 officers and 1,425 enlisted members in critical specialties for an extra two months. Another solution was to ask people on temporary duty to accept permanent assignments. USAFE began this program on January 18 but found few takers. By the end of the month, of 1,100 officers and 6,100 enlisted men eligible to convert to permanent assignments, only 28 officers and 19 enlisted had done so. Another remedy was help from the States. In March, USAFE received more than 3,000 additional mechanics.[61]

Another measure that worked well and strengthened the growing sense of partnership with the Germans was to hire German mechanics. Tunner had obtained Clay's permission in the autumn to hire 500, and the program shifted into high gear early in the new year to offset the American exodus. In February, USAFE authorized up to 80 German mechanics in each troop carrier group. Language problems and unfamiliarity with U.S. equipment were early problems, but they did not last long. Many former Luftwaffe pilots and ground crew came forward, among them Major General Hans-Detlef Herhudt von Rohden. He was instrumental in making this program a success, helping to recruit excellent, experienced people and arranging to have U.S. maintenance manuals translated into German. Mobile U.S. training units soon familiarized the new employees with Skymasters and their support equipment. German-speaking U.S. maintenance officers selected and trained German supervisors, and bilingual Germans were found to fill key positions. The RAF used German mechanics too, but to a lesser extent than the Americans.[62]

Last but not least, to everyone's relief, storms moved across Europe in late December, taking the fog with them. For once, Kuter remarked, "we welcome storms as friends."[63] The break in the weather came just in time. Coal was the critical cargo, and by the end of December, stocks were down to nineteen days' supply, two days less than the minimum planners wanted to have on hand at the end of February. Officials took a calculated risk and cut back deliveries of food for ten days to send more coal. That, plus the extra Hastings and C-54s and the discovery of additional coal stocks in the city, provided the critical margin.[64] By January 11, the pessimists on BAFO's operations analysis staff had turned into optimists. "Short of abnormal weather and other factors interfering with the airlift, there is no reason for doubting that stocks will remain adequate," they predicted. Weather, for once, cooperated. Temperatures in Berlin remained unusually mild throughout the winter.[65]

February was the last critical month. Soviet hopes rose as the fog returned, but Berlin ended the month with the twenty-one-day stocks planners had called for.[66] It had been a close call. Without the extra aircraft, CPS-5 radar and GCA system, measures to boost morale, added coal shipments in early January, Herhudt von Rohden and his German mechanics, the mild winter, or Berliners' belt-tightening,

Stalin might have won. Instead, all these things allowed Tunner to achieve a narrow victory. With spring just around the corner, he was about to go on the offensive.

WINTER MADE ONE LAST TRY to disrupt the airlift. March came in like a lion, with snow and gale-force winds followed by a cold snap. The airlift hardly missed a beat, averaging over 6,300 tons a day for the month, more than 1,500 tons higher than forecast. The rise owed much to better weather later in the month, but that was not the only explanation. Increased stocks of spare parts, a rise in Burtonwood's productivity, better manning levels, and the rising experience level among replacement pilots all contributed. The supply situation was so much better that Rhein-Main stopped sending its daily requisition to Air Materiel Command on February 1. Burtonwood inspected an average of 6.3 Skymasters a day in March, up from 2.9 in February. Arrival of the last contingent of Skymasters also boosted deliveries to Berlin. Clay had asked for 66; he received 78 when Washington stopped counting planes undergoing 1,000-hour overhauls against Milton's quota of 225 planes. By April, of the 444 C-54s in the U.S. Navy and U.S. Air Force, 312 were committed to Vittles one way or another: 225 in Europe, 19 at Great Falls, and 68 in the maintenance pipeline. In another welcome trend, more C-54s returned from 1,000-hour inspections in the States during March and April (119) than flew west (109).[67]

There were two positive developments on the British side. In the first, the charter carriers came into their own. One reason was that the British government started awarding ninety-day contracts on March 5. On April 1, British European Airways Corporation formed an Airlift Division under Edwin P. Whitfield to coordinate the charter carriers. Whitfield's office was initially located in Berlin, and he relied on a small staff at each base to schedule flights. On May 1, he moved to Lüneburg, alongside Merer's headquarters. This resulted in increased deliveries: the companies lifted 9,200 tons in January, 10,500 in February, nearly 15,000 in March, over 16,000 in April, and nearly 23,000 in May.[68]

Delivering liquid fuel remained the companies' most important contribution. Tanker aircraft flew from Wunstorf, Schleswigland, and Fuhlsbüttel in the British zone to Gatow and Tegel. Initial operations at Wunstorf were makeshift. Railcars transferred their cargo to fuel trucks, which then pumped it into aircraft. Complicated and time-consuming, the procedure was imprecise and marred by spills. Once underground tanks were ready in April 1949, fuel could be drained into them from railcars and then pumped aboard planes. Schleswigland and Fuhlsbüttel had underground tanks when their operations began, and such a system was included in the blueprints for Tegel. In February, the fuel system at Gatow was streamlined when a pipeline opened between the airfield and Havel See. Until then, fuel had been pumped out of the airfield's underground tanks into trucks, driven to the lake, and transferred to barges.[69]

By the end of the airlift, twenty-five companies had taken part. They flew a total of 103 planes, with a maximum of 52 aircraft in use at any one time. For all the headaches they caused BAFO, the contract carriers made a vital contribution, completing nearly 22,000 trips to Berlin and delivering nearly 148,000 tons of coal, flour, and liquid fuel. That was twice the weight of the mail and cargo carried by all British civil aircraft on scheduled service between 1924 and 1947.[70]

Improved command relationships were the other positive development in Plainfare. As noted earlier, Merer had established an advance headquarters of No. 46 Group in Germany in September. As group commander, he remained responsible for several stations in Britain, an awkward distraction. In December, the Air Ministry transferred those stations to No. 47 Group, allowing Merer to concentrate on the airlift, and it expanded his advance headquarters to a full group staff. Authority over the group remained divided. It was assigned to Transport Command, but BAFO had control, at least for the next few months. The ministry gave BAFO administrative as well as operational control on April 1, and on May 1, it transferred the group to BAFO outright.[71]

Tunner continued to adjust operations and increase efficiency. By the end of April, Fassberg, Celle, and Wunstorf were sending planes to Berlin using consolidated one-hour blocks. This was close to a "continuous flow," which everyone regarded as the ideal. It meant that loaded planes wasted less time waiting for their next block to start. Yet British pilots quickly learned that the new system put a premium on careful scheduling and top-notch maintenance. Under the previous two-hour system, Wunstorf had launched twelve planes in thirty-three minutes. Now it launched eight planes in twenty-one minutes in the first hour and four planes in nine minutes in the second hour. Although a last-minute mechanical problem would probably not affect the first wave of eight planes, there was no longer time for a crew in the second wave to transfer to a ground spare. Perhaps issues such as these led Milton to declare at the beginning of April, "We are now more concerned with maintenance than operations."[72]

By early 1949, the organizations contributing to the operation functioned as a well-coordinated team, and not only in the air. By the twenty-fifth of each month, CALTF's traffic section forecast its tonnage capacity for the following month. An airlift staff committee in Berlin consisting of representatives of the three Western commandants then set priorities and quantities for shipments into the city. An airlift coordinating committee in Frankfurt then allocated to individual air bases the cargoes and tonnage to be lifted over the next two to four weeks. The Anglo-American Bipartite Control Office, also in Frankfurt, coordinated the gathering of supplies and their transportation to railheads near the airfields. At that point, the British and American armies took over, delivering cargoes planeside. By spring, the airlift was operating at close to Tunner's ideal rhythm. In March, it delivered 93 percent of its food goal and 116 percent of its coal target. In April, the figures were 105 and 149 percent, respectively.[73]

Attention could now shift to lesser problems, such as pilferage. Although theft was never extensive enough to affect the airlift, it did occur. Americans as well as Europeans were involved, in the western zones as well as in Berlin. Counterintelligence agents recovered truckloads of goods hidden in the woods near Rhein-Main and Wiesbaden. Delivering cargoes to airlift bases and warehouses around the clock rather than storing them overnight curbed pilfering while reducing the need for guards and vehicles. Theft was more serious in Berlin, where the need was greater and supervision by Western soldiers was apparently not as stringent. About 100 workers at Tempelhof were fired during the airlift for pilfering.[74]

There was a small crisis in February when coal sacks ran short. Until then, the airlift had used duffel bags or British jute sacks. The duffels had been reused up to thirty times each, and when the supply was exhausted, Tunner experimented with four-ply paper sacks. These held fifty pounds of coal and could be used up to three times. Costing less than a penny apiece, they were cheaper than duffels or jute bags, even considering the latter's longer life, and they cut the cost of coal containers from $250,000 a month to $12,000. Sealed with wire, they also helped reduce coal dust.[75]

As spring approached, the two air forces set ever-larger goals. Between noon Saturday, April 15, and noon Sunday, they staged what came to be known as the "Easter Parade." Things were going too smoothly, Tunner recalled, and he wanted to do something to keep people from becoming complacent. His answer was competition. He would schedule a maximum effort, with each unit lifting a load well beyond its previous record. He settled on an overall target of 10,000 tons, about 50 percent higher than the airlift's best day so far. As on Air Force Day in September, it would be easiest to carry only one cargo: coal. The chief of staff at USAFE headquarters, Major General Robert W. Douglass Jr., worried that the all-out effort would exhaust everyone and, in the long run, tonnage would drop. Tunner assured him that deliveries would settle at a plateau above the previous average. Tunner made no announcement in advance, to avoid embarrassment if he missed his target. On Saturday morning, when each squadron's daily schedule was posted, everyone realized something big was happening. As word of the unusually high quotas spread, the race was on.

Tunner visited every base he could, spurring on his subordinates. In one classic story, life imitated art. The two C-54 bases in the British zone, Fassberg and Celle, were rivals. In February, Jake Schuffert, the talented cartoonist for the *Task Force Times,* had drawn a cartoon of an airlift "efficiency expert" telling the two base commanders that the other was outperforming him. The caption read, "Airlift Intrigue, or How Records Are Broken." Now Tunner brought the cartoon to life. He stopped at Celle and was pleased to find that it was 12 percent ahead of its quota. When he reached Fassberg, Colonel Coulter greeted him with a huge grin and proudly announced that his base was 10 percent ahead of its target. "That's fine," Tunner replied, "but of course it's not up to what they're doing over at Celle. They're really on the ball over there." Coulter's smile vanished, and he raced back to the flight line to goad his crews to greater effort. The spirit of competition and enthusiasm spread. The army contingent at Tempelhof was proud that its crews unloaded planes faster than air traffic control could launch them back to western Germany—on a day when a plane landed at one of Berlin's three airfields every sixty-two seconds. By noon Sunday, when the last plane touched down, 12,941 tons had been delivered in 1,398 flights, a truly phenomenal achievement.[76] What was more, as Tunner had assured Douglass, the daily average did not drop to its previous level. It climbed from 6,300 in March to 7,850 in April and over 8,000 in May and June.

As the task force hummed along, its leaders laid plans for an open-ended operation. A mid-February forecast set targets of 7,824 tons a day in the second half of 1949, 7,769 tons a day between January and June 1950, and 7,798 tons a day thereafter. Lifting 8,000 tons a day would take 372 aircraft (including 52 Dakotas). With 475 heavy aircraft and a new C-54 base in the British zone, CALTF could lift over 11,000 tons daily. BAFO and USAFE asked for the new airfield, a second runway at Tegel, and more planes, people, and spare parts. Three weeks later, even larger numbers were under discussion, with the goal for July 1949 through June 1950 set at 8,944 tons a day.[77]

Too few large planes existed to carry out these plans. Keeping the force at current levels would be challenging enough. C-54 production had ended during the war, and planners estimated worldwide attrition at two aircraft a month. Eventually, there would not be enough C-54s left. Indeed, in mid-March, Tunner's fleet in Germany dropped below 225 planes when a C-54 crashed (with no fatalities, fortunately) and another left for maintenance. The Air Staff asked the joint chiefs to start diverting two planes a month from the Pacific.[78]

In April, Royall advised the new secretary of defense, Louis Johnson, that "considerable increase in the size and efficiency of the airlift during the next two years will be necessary." By 1952, Vittles would need every C-54 in the air force. Royall listed daily requirements for the year starting July 1, 1949, as 8,685 short tons, with 11,249 tons required the following year. The present capacity was 6,436. The task force could reach these targets easily if it could replace fifty RAF Dakotas with C-54s, but the larger planes were not available.[79] The British were replacing Dakotas with Handley Page Hastings, but not quickly enough. Several newer and larger U.S. planes were entering production, such as the C-97, C-118, and C-124. But they would not be available in quantity for several years, and none was particularly suited for an operation like Vittles. All three were designed for long-distance missions, not short-haul ones. Runways would have to be lengthened and strengthened to support these larger machines, and integrating them into the traffic flow would recreate the mixed-force problems Tunner had put behind him when he retired the C-47s. Though not insurmountable, these problems were not easily overcome.

Drafting these long-term plans came at an awkward time for the RAF, because Transport Command had renewed its efforts to have more planes and crews released from Plainfare. Aircrew training was not offsetting losses, and the command's crews were losing proficiency in long-distance flying. The War Office also complained that its parachute brigade was no longer operationally ready because planes were unavailable for jump training. The Air Ministry proposed to withdraw two York and two Dakota squadrons, a total of thirty-two planes. Protests from Williams led the ministry to drop the idea, and attention turned to improving maintenance, increasing payloads, borrowing C-54s from the Americans (there were none, of course), combing staffs for fliers, and the like.[80]

Another possibility was to set a limit on Plainfare tours as the Americans had done. In April, Transport Command was able to devise a rotation plan that stationed three-fifths of the force in Germany and the rest in Britain; one-fifth rotated each month, so everyone served three months in Germany and then two months at home. The Air Ministry approved the plan in May and started implementing it on June 1 for York and Dakota squadrons. Hastings squadrons did not come under the scheme until September 1949, and then not fully.[81]

Another project to counter a prolonged blockade was construction of a new power plant in west Berlin. The Soviets had dismantled Kraftwerk West, a 228,000-kilowatt electrical plant, in the summer of 1945 for reparations. City officials had urged the Western powers to rebuild it as long ago as February 1947, but the project was still in its early stages when the blockade began. In January 1949, Western officials announced that 5,000 tons of machinery would be flown in to rebuild the plant, including girders weighing up to 3.5 tons each. Contrary to reports that the airlift delivered it all, shipments had barely begun by early May. Twelve pieces were too large for any available cargo plane. Preparations were under way to sling them underneath a bomber (a U.S. B-29 or a British Lincoln) when diplomatic developments made them and other long-term plans obsolete.[82]

CHAPTER 12

Dealing Sensibly with Established Fact

As Western leaders contemplated Berlin's future in the winter of 1948–1949, they saw few grounds for optimism. Many worried the West had no realistic prospect of ending the crisis on favorable terms. Lewis Douglas told Walter Lippmann, "We are up a blind alley"; the West had lost the "capacity to negotiate." After the technical committee broke up, Douglas's gloom deepened. "I am not clear where we go next," he cabled Acheson. While the airlift could sustain the city physically, Douglas doubted Berliners could endure a permanent blockade. Sooner or later, their morale would fail. In the meantime, the airlift gave Western leaders time to devise a strategy, but Douglas saw none being prepared. Western policy looked no further than maintaining "a precarious status quo . . . through the airlift . . . and [hoping] that some presently unforeseen circumstances in the indefinite future will provide a new basis for a settlement."[1]

Others shared Douglas's doubts. USAFE intelligence estimates echoed his views about the airlift's long-term prospects, while pessimism continued to dominate army calculations. A December 6 memo in Draper's files recommended identifying steps that could be taken to sustain a Western presence in Berlin for one, two, or three years. If the means did not exist or the cost was too high, the Western powers needed to know how much time they had to find "a solution other than by airlift—be that solution a political one, a convoy, or something else."[2] The joint intelligence committee briefed Forrestal in mid-January that the blockade was strangling Berlin's economy and predicted that the West's position "will doubtless deteriorate further."[3] In late March, Murphy questioned whether Berliners' morale could be "indefinitely maintained," and he did not rule out eventual withdrawal. Neither did Royall, who warned that without a definite decision soon, the West's position "will tend to become more and more ridiculous." Jacob Beam thought that if the

Russians lifted the blockade in exchange for a foreign ministers' meeting, the CFM would fail because neither side would make concessions. After that, "it will probably be only a matter of time before war occurs" due to a new flare-up over Berlin.[4]

European leaders reached similar conclusions. Robertson emphasized in mid-December that the airlift was not delivering enough; six weeks later, he was more confident but noted that performance remained well below the rosy forecasts Clay and Marshall had offered in Paris in September. Everything depended on the weather, he told Strang New Year's Day. Into February, he was insisting that the airlift could not sustain Berlin indefinitely.[5]

Sharing Robertson's doubts, Bevin thought a settlement would have to be reached at some point, though he was inclined to let the Russians take the first step. Hector McNeil shared Douglas's view that the airlift was a wasting asset and "worse and worse trouble" lay ahead. In Paris, Jean Chauvel complained about the lack of strategy. In the end, he told Lippmann, the Western powers would be "improvising a policy to make use of the improvisation of the airlift."[6]

The new year proved these gloomy prognostications false. Instead of the interminable deadlock observers expected, 1949 brought an end to the Berlin crisis. Even before the neutrals published their account of failure, talks had begun between American and Soviet representatives that led to a lifting of the blockade.

Yet there was something to those midcourse laments. Policy had not moved beyond its status in July. Western officials were still taking matters one day at a time and hoping something would turn up. When something did, it did not stem from the success of Western strategy. Furthermore, the widespread belief that the breaking of the deadlock was the result of a carefully crafted American probe may be illusory.

THE STORY IS A FAMILIAR ONE. In January, Western newspaperman J. Kingsbury Smith submitted a series of questions to Stalin. Western journalists did this routinely, and usually no answer emerged from behind the Kremlin's grim walls. Stalin chose to answer Smith, however, telling him on January 30 that if the Western powers delayed creation of a west German state until after the foreign ministers met, the Soviets would lift the blockade. On February 15, Jessup asked the Soviet ambassador to the United Nations, Yakov Malik, if Stalin had intentionally omitted an agreement on Berlin's currency as a condition for ending the blockade. On March 15, Malik answered that Stalin's silence had not been "accidental," and six days later, he told Jessup that if a date for the ministers' meeting were agreed on, the blockade could be lifted beforehand. Agreement was announced May 4, the blockade ended at midnight May 11, and the foreign ministers met May 23.

Writers have accepted Western diplomats' interpretation of these events at the time. According to this view, Stalin realized in January that the blockade had failed and was speeding the creation of the Federal Republic of Germany and the North Atlantic Treaty Organization (NATO); he used Smith's questions to cut his losses. The Soviet dictator sent the West a subtle signal that the Americans were discerning enough to see.[7]

Stalin's answers to Smith may have been intended to embarrass the West, not reach an agreement. A Soviet peace offensive had been under way for some weeks. In October, Stalin had called on peace-loving peoples everywhere to treat their warmongering elites the way British voters had treated Churchill in 1945. Lesser lights dismissed both major U.S. parties as "creatures of American monopoly capital" and portrayed Wallace's Progressives as the only true defenders of peace and the interests of the working class. After the November election, Wallace became an unperson and Truman became a tribune of peace. His victory was a repudiation of recent U.S. foreign policy, according to the Soviet press, which predicted Vinson would be the next secretary of state. Suddenly the capitalist elite was not bent on war, only certain members of it were—that is, the "clearly reactionary and aggressive clique of Dewey-Vandenberg-Dulles," which had been rejected at the polls. As one Soviet diplomat put it privately, the election was "a mandate to negotiate with Russia."[8]

The Soviet campaign gathered steam after Christmas. The Russian embassy welcomed the new year by publishing what one scholar described as a statement of "unprecedented and effusive friendliness to the American people"; French Communist leader Michel Cachin called for a Truman-Stalin summit. Italian party boss Palmiro Togliatti declared that collaboration between East and West was possible on the basis of postwar agreements (doubtless meaning Potsdam), and he echoed Cachin's call for new approaches to Stalin. There were mixed signals from Berlin. Colonel Sergei Tulpanov, head of the Soviet Military Administration's "information division," returned from Moscow to give a blistering anti-Western speech to an SED congress. Following hurried telephone consultations with the Kremlin, the edition of the *Berliner Zeitung* carrying the speech was withdrawn from circulation. Ulbricht, who eleven days earlier had proclaimed that someday all Germany would be socialist, said at the same congress that Berlin was not part of the Soviet zone and the SED had no intention of incorporating it into the zone. This was, as Murphy reported, a "complete reversal" of the Soviet position since June and perhaps the "opening shot" in a campaign to settle the crisis.[9]

Cachin's suggestion of a summit was no isolated appeal; indeed, the Soviet effort centered on calls for a Truman-Stalin meeting. Either way the Americans answered, Moscow would benefit. A favorable reply would revive unpleasant memories in European capitals of Smith-Molotov and the Vinson mission; rejection would make Washington appear recalcitrant. Of the two, rejection seemed more likely. Truman had denied suggestions by one of his former speechwriters that he intended to abandon a firm policy toward Moscow—a denial confirmed by his inaugural address.

At a January 13 news conference, the president said he would be glad to meet Stalin—in Washington. A week later, Acheson told reporters that discussions could not occur until the blockade had been lifted and the Berlin question settled. In department meetings, Bohlen dismissed public Soviet maneuvers as propaganda. When the Russians were serious, he commented, they would use private channels.[10]

Stalin's answers to Smith's questions were the capstone of this Soviet effort to portray the Western powers as rejecting peace. Smith, who was chief of the International News Service's European Bureau in Paris, had cabled four questions to Moscow: Would the Soviets consider a joint declaration with the United States pledging that neither government intended to wage war against the other? Would they take steps, such as gradual disarmament, to carry out this "peace pact"? Would the Soviet Union lift the blockade if the Western governments postponed creation of a west German state until the CFM could meet to consider "the German problem as a whole"? And was Stalin willing to meet Truman to discuss the "peace pact"? Smith saw the last question as the most important, as did many others at the time. It was as if the first three set an agenda for the two leaders at the meeting proposed in the fourth.

Stalin gave encouraging answers. His government was willing to consider Kingsbury Smith's peace pact and "of course" stood ready to cooperate in carrying it out. Provided the West removed its counterblockade and postponed action in west Germany, as the journalist described, the Soviet government saw "no obstacle" to ending the blockade. As for a meeting with Truman, Stalin pointed to earlier statements that "there is no objection." When Charles Ross repeated Truman's insistence on a Washington venue, Smith cabled Stalin again on February 1. He put a different spin on Ross's statement. Truman "would be glad" to meet Stalin in the American capital, he telegraphed; would Stalin come? The generalissimo answered within twenty-four hours, thanking the president for his "invitation." Although he had wanted to visit America for many years, unfortunately, his doctors would not let him travel long distances. He would welcome Truman, however, in Poland or Czechoslovakia; in Moscow, Leningrad, or Kaliningrad; or—as Truman and Acheson must have read with a shudder—in Yalta.[11]

The embassy in Moscow concentrated on the summit idea, interpreting Stalin's answer as a propaganda maneuver. As the staff saw it, Stalin had reverted to his terms of August 2. The London program had been the issue from the start; it still was. The only new development was that Smith had allowed Stalin to appear willing to meet the president, putting the onus for continued tension on the West. Soviet handling of the story gave added weight to this analysis. The CIA reported that Soviet radio, especially foreign-language broadcasts, spent more time on the exchange than on any other event since agency monitoring had begun nearly two years before. Two themes dominated: Stalin had given new evidence of the Soviet

Union's desire for peace, and rejection would be final proof of American warmongering. Of the two, the CIA concluded, the Soviets appeared "more concerned with spelling out a propaganda base for subsequent attacks on U.S. policy in the event of negative reaction."[12]

The SED-sponsored German People's Council added another twist on February 1. Denouncing the Western powers' December Ruhr agreement and the Parliamentary Council's work in Bonn, it called on the German people to save their country from division and predatory foreign monopolists. Stalin's declaration had "opened the gate to negotiation on German unity. If the Western powers, following Stalin's proposals, were to *give up* their measures for . . . a German state which threaten both Germany and the peace; if they were to return to the joint consultations with the Soviet Union agreed upon after Potsdam, then there would be no Berlin question any more . . . [and] world peace would be served." By not mentioning Kingsbury Smith, the manifesto implied that Stalin had taken the initiative to lessen tension, contributing to the impression in the West that the Soviets were more interested in public relations than substantive discussion. The call to abandon the London program went beyond the Smith-Stalin exchange, which had involved postponement only. The invocation of Potsdam and joint consultations (a revival of the ACC) suggested the Soviets still stood on the Warsaw declaration of the previous June. Remarks by Hans Jendretzky, the new chairman of the Berlin SED, reinforced that impression. As Jendretzky put it, Stalin's interview was an important step toward three things: restoration of normal life in the city, "*removal* of the destructive B-Mark, . . . [and restoration of] the unity of Germany *on the bases of the Potsdam and Warsaw declarations,*" which hardly signaled a softening of Soviet policy.[13]

Truman shrugged off Stalin's initial answers, joking with his staff that perhaps "we should give a reply to Tass." When he learned of Stalin's second reply on February 2, he reacted more harshly. As Ayers recorded in his diary, Truman wondered what he could say to Stalin. All he could do, the president remarked, was "ask him why he had not lived up to his agreements." The Department of State dismissed Stalin's answers as unworthy of "serious consideration." Delaying the west German government imposed a new condition. Bohlen first thought the Russians wanted to "throw the Western democracies off base, particularly in regard to the Atlantic Pact." While acknowledging to Oliver Franks that Stalin's interview was "most interesting" and might hint at a new Soviet attitude, Bohlen judged that, for the moment, the remarks had to be regarded as propaganda.[14]

Reactions elsewhere were more negative. Stalin's answers helped persuade Brian Robertson that the time had come to make the deutsche mark the sole legal tender in west Berlin. Bevin thought Stalin intended to throw the West off balance regarding the Marshall Plan and west Germany; he and Franks regarded the revival of

Stalin's "insistent wish" as an "additional condition." Stalin's silence about currency was not a portent; the issue was certain to reappear when the Kremlin thought it would be to its advantage. Although Bevin had suggested to General Robertson a few days earlier that the Soviets might raise the blockade "fairly soon"—perhaps in March, when the weather improved—he saw no flexibility in Stalin's answers. Indeed, they seemed so unpromising that Bevin reversed his stance toward the UN technical committee, set a date for introducing the deutsche mark into Berlin, and advocated more speed in creating a west German government. Faced with diplomatic stalemate, Bevin was ready, as noted earlier, to accept the division of Germany as "essential for our plans" for western Europe. Couve de Murville told Sam Reber that Stalin's replies eliminated all doubt regarding Soviet unwillingness to accept a UN solution to the currency dispute. For their part, west German officials told Edward Litchfield of Clay's staff that in light of Stalin's answers, steps toward a separate regime should be accelerated.[15]

Bohlen had second thoughts about the omission of the currency issue, which Dean Rusk had noticed, too. It was worth probing to see if it was significant, he persuaded Acheson. The question was how. Bohlen thought going through the embassies was too direct, would involve too many people, and thus risked leaks; also, the other Western governments would have to be informed. A low-key approach at the United Nations, where "corridor conversations" were commonplace, might be the answer. Acheson liked the idea of a quiet, skeptical response. He worked out the details with Truman on Monday, January 31. He would respond coolly at his weekly press conference on Wednesday but hint that if the Soviets were serious, private channels were open. On Thursday, Truman would avoid questions at his press conference by referring to Acheson's remarks.[16]

Acheson devoted nearly his entire press conference on February 2 to the Smith-Stalin exchange. Speaking from notes, he went over Stalin's answers to Smith—"I stress Mr. Kingsbury Smith and not Ambassador Bedell Smith," he interjected archly—arguing, almost phrase by phrase, that past Soviet performance called into question Stalin's promises. He scorned the notion of a Truman-Stalin meeting. Yet he treated Germany and Berlin differently. For one thing, he took them out of order, discussing them separately at the end. For another, he remarked that this subject had been "the most interesting exchange of the four." If the Soviets were serious about Berlin, he hinted, "all channels are open." To drive the point home, he repeated it moments later and told reporters that if it were up to him, "I would choose some other channel than . . . a press interview." During the question-and-answer session, one reporter noted that Stalin had omitted settlement of the currency question as a condition for agreement on Berlin. Acheson refused to speculate, and no one pressed the subject.[17]

The secretary was pleased with his performance, believing he had answered

Stalin's subtle signals with ones of his own. It did not occur to him that Stalin may have sent no signals or that his own were so subtle as to be undetectable. All he had said was that if the Russians wanted to talk, private diplomatic channels were available, something they already knew. He did not suggest any change in the Western position; in fact, he described the London program as "necessary" for the Western powers to fulfill their responsibilities as occupiers. He reiterated the claim that creation of a west German government would not "in any sense preclude" four-power agreement on Germany; in fact, he contended, "this work facilitates agreement upon Germany as a whole." That would have suggested to any Kremlin observer that the West remained unyielding on west German issues, which was the case. Truman reinforced that impression the next day. As agreed with Acheson, he avoided all questions about the affair by referring reporters to the secretary's remarks.[18]

Several days later, Acheson asked Jessup to come down from New York. He and Bohlen wanted Jessup to ask Malik, as offhandedly as he could, whether Stalin's silence on the currency dispute was significant. Looking back on it, all involved treated the probe as a first step toward peace and implied that the United States was risking its reputation for firmness by seeking talks. Yet what seems most striking is just how ambiguous this maneuver was, how carefully Acheson prepared the ground for disavowal of the probe if Stalin proved to be unyielding. He chose Jessup, he recalled, because a "highly secret, casual approach" to the Russians could be undertaken more easily at the United Nations. "Fewer persons would be involved," and those who were "could act in purely personal and unofficial capacities"; Jessup's personal curiosity would not commit the United States.[19]

Jessup carried out his instructions, striking up a conversation with Malik in the delegates' lounge on February 15. To be sure Malik received the message, Jessup twice repeated that "if there was anything new in what Premier Stalin had said I should be glad to have him let me know."[20] Secrecy in Washington regarding the meeting was extraordinary; no more than five people knew about it. Jessup's nominal superior, Warren Austin, did not learn of it until he read about it two months later in the newspapers, and Clay and the Pentagon were not informed. When Jessup summarized the chat in a memorandum, he stamped it secret and put it in routine classified distribution. Bohlen was aghast, ordering the memo reclassified top secret and all copies at the U.S. mission to the United Nations destroyed.[21]

There matters rested for a month. Bohlen gave up; so did Jessup. The latter endorsed a suggestion from Beam to resume direct talks with the Soviets, using the neutrals' good offices, but only after the introduction of the deutsche mark, five days away. He described his conversation with Malik four weeks earlier, noting there had been no response. He mentioned it, he said, simply to show "we do not seem to have any contact for . . . starting the ball rolling." Then the phone rang.

Malik was on the line, inviting Jessup to the Soviet mission in New York. Perhaps the ball had begun rolling after all.[22]

Stalin's delay is puzzling if, as most accounts agree, his answers to Smith were a bid for talks. The trouble with the usual explanations for the delay—for example, that he was hoping winter weather might defeat the airlift—is that if they were true, Stalin would not have answered Smith in the first place. Instead, Stalin might have taken a month to decide how to answer what he regarded as an *American* probe for terms.[23] Telling Jessup that omission of the currency issue had been deliberate would be admitting defeat. Confessing that the omission had been accidental and that Soviet terms were unchanged would mean continued stalemate, a course that offered Stalin little.

If Stalin had been toying with Kingsbury Smith, Jessup's question posed a dilemma. From the standpoint of Soviet interests, the blockade had become a liability, furthering developments it had been intended to prevent. The Western powers had agreed on a plan for the Ruhr on December 28 that excluded the Soviets. The Parliamentary Council in Bonn presented a draft basic law for the Federal Republic of Germany to the military governors on February 10. The Americans and western Europeans were near agreement on the North Atlantic treaty and would complete a draft March 15.[24] The blockade had not brought Berlin under Soviet control. The Western counterblockade continued its drag on the Soviet zone's economy. This unexpected American query might offer a way out. If official, it suggested that the United States was willing to follow the Kingsbury Smith agenda and postpone the west German government in exchange for an end to the blockade. A delay offered room to maneuver and perhaps disrupt the London program: would the Germans press ahead knowing that four-power talks were under way? Even if the West was not suggesting an implicit trade, it might be maneuvered into one against its will through a "Trollope ploy": pushing it into a position it had not taken by "accepting" a concession it had not made—in this case, Smith's linkage of the blockade and the Bonn government.[25]

Time, it could be argued, was now on the West's side, not Stalin's. The Russians were in the midst of a political competition with the West for the hearts and minds of all Germans. The London program was unpopular in Germany because it meant partition. Furthermore, Germans disliked international controls over the Ruhr and the occupation statute, a list of sovereign powers the Allies planned to retain rather than entrust to the new federal republic. Yet Moscow could not take advantage of the unpopularity of Western policy in Germany because its own policy repelled Germans even more. The prolonged and highly visible spectacle of holding Berliners hostage alienated German opinion, destroying any prospects communism had in western Germany.[26]

The Soviets in Germany paid an economic price for the blockade, not just a political one. When they stopped the flow of goods from the West, they inflicted serious damage on the economy of the eastern zone. Intelligence reports reached Washington during the first week of the blockade that Sokolovsky had held a meeting with industrial leaders from the zone and had been "greatly shocked" to learn how dependent it was on trade with western Germany. British analysts concluded that the zone could not expand production unless interzonal trade resumed.[27] This was bad news not only for the zone but also for the Soviets, who were counting on siphoning off German industrial products and food surpluses as reparations. There was worse news to come. In July, the British and Americans stopped rail and barge traffic across their zones into eastern Germany. They also stopped shipments originating in their zones: reparations plus rail deliveries of coal, steel, machine tools, chemicals, dyes, and other industrial commodities. Western officials attributed the stoppage to "technical difficulties." They extended the embargo to road traffic in September; in January, they introduced measures to prevent west Berlin exports from reaching Soviet-controlled areas. The following month, they stopped freight movements across their zones to and from the entire Soviet bloc, as well as foot traffic to and from the Soviet zone. When Malik opened talks to end the crisis, one of his first questions was whether an end to the blockade would lead to "a full resumption of trade between the Zones," an indication of how effective the counterblockade had been.[28]

Time worked against the Kremlin on a broader stage. The Marshall Plan was infusing new hope and vitality across western Europe and deepening transatlantic political and economic ties. By March 1949, Congress had authorized nearly $5 billion in Marshall aid.[29] The program helped fuel western Germany's economic revival, which had begun with the currency reform in June 1948, and it promoted the western zones' integration into the Western orbit. There were also Europe-wide security trends that ran counter to Soviet interests. Here, too, the blockade backfired, accelerating the creation of an anti-Soviet military coalition. The Americans and western Europeans had begun talking about a North Atlantic security pact long before the blockade began, but the blockade made the threat from the Soviets appear clearer and more immediate. The treaty was nearing completion and would be signed in Washington on April 4. Stalin could see that the blockade was creating exactly what he feared: a Western military alliance centered on a United States that was willing and able to act in the defense of western Europe. At Yalta, Roosevelt had told Stalin that American troops would not stay on the Continent more than two years. Now the United States was committing itself to a central role in European affairs for the indefinite future.[30]

What were the risks involved in rejecting Jessup's probe? Negotiations at the United Nations were at an end, and Jessup's action could be a last maneuver for the record, a prelude to the West's use of force. At the end of January, Stalin could still hope that winter might disrupt the airlift. By mid-February and certainly by mid-March, that hope was clearly in vain. Force would be necessary to stop the airlift. Stalin had avoided that from the start, convinced it was unnecessary. Now the options were escalation, letting the blockade drag on, or telling Jessup a white lie in order to break the impasse. It was a difficult choice, one that could easily take a month to decide.[31]

In the meantime, it was business as usual in Berlin, with the Soviets tightening their grip on east Berlin and expanding control over intersector travel and traffic. Evictions, kidnappings, and arbitrary arrests increased. There may have been some hope that economic collapse was still possible, that the masses might rally and give Stalin a victory before he needed to make concessions. In France, the party's general secretary, Maurice Thorez, pledged that French communists would assist the Red Army if it invaded France, a vow featured prominently in the Cominform Bulletin and echoed immediately by party leaders around the world, including the SED. It is hard to square this public stance, endorsed by Soviet officials, with a decision to reduce tensions and end the blockade.[32]

One possible sign that the decision came in March, not January, was that both Molotov and Sokolovsky, the two men most closely associated with Berlin policy, lost their jobs: Vyshinsky replaced Molotov as foreign minister on March 4, while Sokolovsky turned over his post as Soviet military governor to Marshal Ivan Chuikov on March 29. The last time Stalin had changed foreign ministers was 1939, a precedent that suggested personnel and policy changes in the Kremlin went hand in hand. Observers were unsure how important the changes were. Molotov and Sokolovsky were not the only ones caught in the shuffle, which may have had more to do with internal politics (the "Leningrad Affair") than with Berlin. Molotov retained his post as deputy prime minister, while Sokolovsky returned to Moscow to become first deputy minister of the Soviet armed forces, so neither was cashiered in disgrace. Still, as Molotov himself once declared, "Whenever something goes wrong, there is always someone to blame."[33] Berlin had gone terribly wrong. Stalin was not going to blame himself, and of all his lieutenants, these two had been most involved in Berlin policy.

Whenever Stalin reached his decision, Malik gave his answer March 15: "Moscow says the omission . . . was 'not accidental'"; currency could be discussed at the foreign ministers' meeting. When Jessup asked if the Russians expected the blockade would continue during such a meeting, Malik did not know; Moscow's answer covered only Jessup's initial question. Jessup replied that he would be interested in whatever Malik might learn regarding this point.[34]

The Americans were convinced they were close to a breakthrough, one they had arranged through astute observation and careful follow-through. Rusk casually revealed the talks at Acheson's staff meeting on March 17. Bohlen blandly added that the contact "may be . . . worthwhile" and the British and French should be informed. At a wider meeting at noon, Bohlen explained "the Malik approach to Dr. Jessup" as a shift in Soviet tactics—from insisting on the resolution of currency issues to delaying the creation of a west German government. The group had reservations about informing the other Western governments. Doing so increased the danger of leaks, but leaving London and Paris in the dark would allow the Russians to repeat Smith-Molotov and reveal the talks, undermining European confidence in the United States as the North Atlantic treaty negotiations entered their final round. The group concluded that the British and French should be informed in general terms, work in the Parliamentary Council should continue, and preparations should begin for an early CFM. A member of the American delegation at Lake Success gave the British and French a sketchy summary of developments later that day. Jessup waited four more days, until March 21—the day after the deutsche mark became the sole legal tender in west Berlin—before providing more details. Even then, he tried to portray his action as a casual inquiry, not a carefully orchestrated maneuver. Bevin was not fooled. "Watch this," he scrawled on the report from New York. "Stalin may now raise the blockade."[35]

Jessup saw Malik later that day. The Soviet diplomat had needed less than a week to obtain an answer to Jessup's latest question, an indication of how quickly Stalin could act once he made up his mind. Malik reported that the blockade could be lifted before the foreign ministers met. Having offered a concession, he tried to obtain one. Under the terms of the Smith interview, an end to the blockade was conditional on delaying the establishment of a west German government, and in their next three meetings, Malik tried to extract from Jessup a pledge not only to delay the creation of such a regime but to "call off" all intermediate steps to its creation as well.[36]

Such a stubborn stance surprised American officials and is another sign that the standard assessment of Stalin's policy in early 1949 is incorrect. Malik's firmness was unexpected because the Americans believed they held the upper hand in the discussions, which they were convinced had been initiated by the Soviets. Because Stalin had supposedly approached the West for terms in January, Malik was in no position to demand concessions in March. But if Stalin's answers to Smith had been propaganda, the Soviets would believe the discussions originated at the West's initiative—that Jessup had approached Malik. Both sides thought they held the advantage. By the time the Soviets realized their mistake, the airlift had eliminated the last vestiges of Soviet leverage, and Stalin had to content himself with whatever face-saving concessions the West was willing to grant.

Bevin and Schuman arrived in Washington on March 31. In addition to signing the North Atlantic treaty, they were going to work out the last details of the German occupation statute and consider the next steps in Berlin. For once, the British and French were more suspicious of the Soviets than the Americans were.

Bevin worried that the United States might be rushing into a foreign ministers' meeting before the West had consolidated its position. American actions "might imperil many things," from the west German government to the North Atlantic treaty. Grasping at straws, he fussed that Malik might not have acted under instructions and that the Soviets might reimpose the blockade. He and Schuman were concerned that if word of the talks leaked, progress toward a west German government would end: no German politician could push for a separate Western regime when the four powers were discussing possible unification.[37]

At his next meeting with Malik, April 5, Jessup read a joint statement by the three foreign ministers to the effect that preparations for the Bonn government would continue. The only consolation he offered was to point out that such a government was weeks if not months away. In other words, if the Russians wanted the foreign ministers to confer before the federal republic took shape, they should act quickly. As if to drive Jessup's words home, the Western powers completed the occupation statute and gave it to the Germans on April 10, opening the way for the Parliamentary Council to put the finishing touches on the basic law.[38]

Bevin continued to fret about the Jessup-Malik talks, with the cabinet's Berlin committee providing an echoing chorus. The Americans were ready to start drafting an agreement, but Bevin did not want to put anything on paper before the Soviets did. He worried about the effect on the Germans and urged delay until differences between the Western powers and the Parliamentary Council were resolved. Acheson feared that if the Soviets concluded the Western powers were losing interest, they would reveal the talks. Rumors were circulating already. At press conferences held on April 13 and 20, he had turned aside questions about feelers from the Soviet Union, giving the impression that no talks had occurred and reiterating the demand that the blockade end before the two sides met. Now he worried about being too cool, but Bevin remained stubborn. The American maneuver risked "losing Germany," he complained to Douglas; he wanted to have "Bonn in his pocket before talking to the Russians" and would rather break off talks with Malik than delay the program for west Germany.[39]

Bevin relented on April 26, following agreement in Bonn on the basic law. But as Acheson had feared, *Tass* revealed the talks that day, summarizing developments through April 10, when Jessup and Malik had last met. The Soviet press agency also reported that if a date were set for the foreign ministers' meeting, the blockade and counterblockade could be lifted before the council convened. Bohlen had prepared a statement in case of a Soviet leak, which Acheson hurriedly released. Clay thus learned of the talks from the press and was furious. The fault seems to have been Louis Johnson's. Truman had informed the new secretary of defense of the talks sometime between April 12 and 19 and asked him to notify Royall, Bradley, Clay, and the assistant army secretary, Tracy Voorhees.[40]

Jessup waded through a sea of reporters outside Malik's Park Avenue office on April 27. Inside, he read a statement reiterating that steps toward creating the federal republic would continue; the fact that the foreign ministers were meeting would neither interrupt nor retard those preparations. To sweeten that pill, he repeated pledges that the London program would not preclude four-power agreement and that the Western powers would make a "sincere endeavor" to reach a quadripartite accord.[41]

Ironically, now that the end was in sight and the airlift had triumphed, Soviet harassment peaked. With good flying weather returning, the Soviets began their spring maneuvers in March, taking little care to stay out of the way of British and American planes. There were 51 cases of deliberate buzzing or close flying (within 500 feet) in March, compared with 3 in February. In March alone, there were 96 instances of clear intent to interfere with U.S. planes, roughly one-quarter of 360 such incidents during the airlift. Considering the airlift flew more than half a million sorties (over 277,000 round-trips to Berlin), the number is remarkably low. So, too, are the documented cases of sabotage, which totaled only four.[42]

Close students of the airlift may question the claim that there were only 360 instances of Soviet harassment of American planes. For many years, we have relied on a table listing 733 "corridor incidents." The table summarized a USAFE report, and even a brief perusal of that document makes it clear that pilots were instructed to report anything unusual, not only attempts to interfere with the airlift. Over half the "incidents" involved no hostile intent. A June 1949 report about an unidentified object, for example, referred to a vapor trail twenty to thirty miles away. One crew reported flak in August 1949 about forty miles away. A May 1949 case of deliberate buzzing was by an RAF York. Several reports about searchlights specifically state that the light "did not molest aircraft," "made no attempt to follow aircraft," or "extinguished itself immediately" when the beam touched the plane. There were clearly instances of dangerous interference, including at least five cases of Soviet aircraft passing within fifty feet of an airlift plane, but the total is far less than we thought. Someone converted "incidents" into "interference," and the mistake has been repeated ever since.[43]

Why did the Soviets not do more to interfere? We do not have definitive answers. In the early stages, there must have seemed little point in interfering with something that was certain to fail. It also seems clear that Soviet leaders realized any such efforts ran a serious risk of war. By the spring of 1949, when it dawned on the Kremlin that the airlift might succeed, Berlin was not important enough to Stalin to run such risks. Better to accept a political defeat than risk a military one.

After debating which restrictions would be lifted and the dates on which the blockade would end and the CFM begin, Jessup, Malik, Cadogan, and French UN representative Jean Chauvel reached agreement on May 4. The next day's communiqué reported a Western victory, discussing only the lifting of the blockade (set for May 12) and the day the CFM would convene (May 23). The Soviets had failed to impose any restrictions on steps toward the creation of a west German government.[44]

The clock began ticking down on May 11. At an impromptu press conference, Acheson praised the airlifters' "great morale, great discipline and superb courage," which had made the day possible. That evening, electricity from Soviet power plants began flowing once more into the western sectors. At one minute past midnight, a U.S. Army jeep left Berlin headed west on the autobahn. Five minutes later, a British vehicle passed through the Soviet checkpoint at Helmstedt, bound for Berlin. Shortly thereafter, the first Western passenger train to enter the Soviet zone in over a year chugged across the zonal frontier. The Berlin blockade was over.[45]

THE PARIS MEETING of the Council of Foreign Ministers ratified the division of Germany. Although the foreign ministers came armed with plans to reunite the country, no one expected they would be adopted. Western proposals would extend the London program throughout the country, which the Soviets were bound to reject, while the Soviet program would restore the Kremlin's veto over occupation policy, which the Western powers would never accept. The experiment in four-power cooperation had come to an end. Instead of trying to revive it, the diplomats accepted rivalry as an established fact and sought to regulate it. They achieved modest but important success.

The Policy Planning Staff had been preparing for a CFM since the previous August, on the chance that the Moscow discussions might lead to one. What position should the United States take? Two considerations shaped Kennan's answer—one relating to Berlin, the other global. In his view, the Berlin problem was insoluble in its own terms. Withdrawal would be a humiliating defeat that would demoralize Europeans and encourage the Soviets. Yet the airlift could not sustain the city forever. It might meet basic physical needs, but it could not counter the political and psychological toll imposed by endless privation and uncertainty. The West would someday be compelled to demand an end to the blockade and back up that demand with force. A solution could be found only in an all-German context, one that lifted the blockade by having Soviet troops leave eastern Germany. The Russians, of course, would not withdraw unless the Western powers did too. Thus Kennan envisaged an end to the occupation and the creation of a German government "with real power and independence" that would control the entire country, except for small garrison areas on the periphery, where Soviet and Western armies would remain.[46]

Kennan's evolving sense of the global power balance led him to the same conclusions. There were five centers of military and industrial power in the world: the

United States, Great Britain, Japan, central Europe, and the Soviet Union. In 1948, the key problem was the relationship between the last two. The task facing the West, he told a National War College audience in September, was "maneuvering . . . Russian power back into the Russian border. . . . We must get them out [of central Europe]." Acheson expressed the same point when he said, "You never can get any stability in Western Europe on the long-term basis with Russian troops 100 miles from Hamburg."[47] The London program left them there. As desirable as consolidating Western influence in west Germany might be, Kennan saw that it would prolong the Russian political and military presence in eastern Germany and eastern Europe. The division of Germany and Europe would congeal along the "iron curtain," making impossible the integration of eastern Europe into a free European community. As lines hardened, the Soviets would conclude that the slightest concession might trigger a "landslide." Berlin would remain a hostage and a flash point, vulnerable to Soviet harassment. Kennan also expected that partition would poison Germany's political life by fanning nationalist passions at a time when "Germans must come to regard themselves as Europeans, and not just Germans."

Kennan realized that his "Program A," as it came to be known, had disadvantages. It would complicate the Marshall Plan and defense planning. There was a risk that a united Germany might "go communist," although the mood in the country had swung sharply against the Soviets and the SED due to the blockade. Rather than allowing Russian influence to flow to the Rhine, Kennan expected his proposal would roll it back to the Oder. For that reason, he doubted the Russians would accept it, but for political reasons, it was worth offering anyway. Another problem would be the French. Reluctant as they were to sanction a west German regime, a unified Germany might be more than they could swallow. Kennan also suspected that the Germans were incapable of acting like responsible Europeans: by and large, he thought, they were "a sick people from whom no political impulses emerge in any clear and healthy form." If the French or the British opposed the plan, Kennan was ready to drop it, while Soviet rejection would leave no choice but to "proceed vigorously" with the London program.[48]

Kennan's ideas met a barrage of criticism. John Hickerson considered them an ideal program that "inevitably" meant the "complete substitution of western for eastern political influence in Germany," yet he was convinced they were "highly dangerous." The Russians would cheat, and the plan would "frighten the French out of their wits." Others in the department (including Bohlen), not to mention Clay and Murphy in Berlin, denounced the plan. It was better to press ahead with the London program, develop the western zones, and integrate them with western Europe than to "cast Germany loose" and hope for the best. Murphy was emphatic. The United States must "maintain the political frontiers of western democracy as far east in Europe as possible and should use Western Germany to the greatest possible extent as our political and military bridgehead. . . . [A]ny retreat would be disastrous to the policy of containment." If Kennan and Brian Robertson were willing to take a chance on the Germans, Clay was not. In his view, the only thing assuring European stability was the U.S. Army, not the Marshall Plan and certainly not a German conversion to democratic values. Pull American soldiers out of Germany, he told Forrestal, "and you practically turn the show over to Russia and the Communists without a struggle." He joked with Murphy that if the French learned of Kennan's ideas, they would "immediately reclassify you and I as 'les meilleurs amis.'"[49]

Neither Marshall nor Lovett would approve Program A, but they would not reject it, either. The issue hardly seemed to matter in October and November, with no prospect of a foreign ministers' meeting in sight. That was where matters stood when Acheson became secretary. Two months later, a foreign ministers' conference seemed possible in a matter of weeks, and a decision on Program A could no longer be postponed.

Acheson seemed receptive to Kennan's arguments. Out of the government since July 1947, he had not been involved in the London program and was not wedded to it. One of a group of outside consultants, he had seemed sympathetic to Kennan's ideas the previous September. At a meeting held on March 9, the day before Kennan was to leave on a three-week trip to Germany, the policy planner commented that it was probably too late to change the U.S. position on a west German government. Acheson replied that he was "sorry" to hear this; he had been "almost persuaded" by a recent Kennan paper highlighting the London program's drawbacks. The secretary added that "he did not understand . . . how we ever arrived at the decision" to create a west German government. Hadn't it been "the brainchild of General Clay" and not a governmental decision? Murphy, who had returned to Washington a few days earlier to become acting director of the new Office of German and Austrian Affairs, intervened to defend his former chief and describe the London meetings. Acheson seemed satisfied but put off action until Kennan returned.[50]

Murphy did his best to take advantage of the interval and was aided in this regard when Acheson had him take Kennan's place as head of an NSC working party studying German issues.[51] Murphy's own view was summed up in a comment to Maurice Pope just before he left Berlin: "people who speak of modus vivendi make me sick." He now argued against a "segregated" Germany. Instead, Germany should be integrated into western Europe politically, economically, and militarily. The United States should promote democratic institutions throughout "as much of Germany as possible," a euphemism for the western zones. As long as the "constructive" and "successful" London program went forward, the West's bargaining position vis-à-vis the Soviets "is correspondingly strengthened." Noting that it would be easier to tie only western Germany to the West, rather than the entire country, because of the fears of Germany's neighbors, Murphy concluded that unless America's partners raised questions about the London program, "the US must regard itself as formally and publicly committed." If the foreign ministers met, the United States should propose extending the London program to the entire country. Murphy's first policy recommendation, added to a set of papers drafted by Voorhees, was the flat statement that a separate west German government should "be unreservedly supported by all three powers." While Bevin and Schuman were in Washington during the first week of April, they concentrated on the next steps in pushing the west German government forward, so momentum seemed to be in Murphy's favor.[52]

Kennan had a powerful ally in Philip Jessup, whose judgment Acheson valued, and the debate continued. On April 14, Kennan formally proposed that Program A be taken as the basis of the Western negotiating position, provided the British and French agreed. On May 4, Under Secretary of State James Webb sent the latest "tentative" version of Kennan's program to the Pentagon for comment. It proposed a provisional federal government for all of Germany, rather than a separate government in the western zones. The government would be established on the basis of UN-supervised elections and would draft a permanent constitution, while a civilian Allied high commission, acting by majority vote, would enforce disarmament, demilitarization, and reparations controls. The December plan for international control of the Ruhr would continue, without Soviet participation. Allied armies would move to garrison areas on the German periphery: the Americans to Bremen, the British to Hamburg, the French to the Rhineland, and the Soviets to Stettin.[53]

Acheson had not seen this most recent version of Kennan's paper. He was aware of Clay's response, however, which denounced the proposal as "really stupid," "suicidal," "shocking," and "close to the Cominform proposals." "If you really want to turn Germany over to the Soviets," Clay snorted, "this is the way to do it." The general was convinced the Russians would accept the occupation statute and the basic law and "will permit the states in the Soviet zone to enter the Federal Republic." Kennan's plan would throw away this imminent victory.[54]

Interestingly enough, the joint chiefs disagreed. They thought Kennan's goal—"the early creation of a unified Germany oriented toward the West"—was "essentially sound," although they wanted troops regrouped along the Rhine, not near the North Sea ports. They also opposed arbitrary deadlines for regrouping and national elections. Steps should be taken when conditions were right, not when some predetermined interval had elapsed. The chiefs did not go beyond generalities regarding military aspects of a settlement: the United States should avoid terms that suggested a relaxation of its determination to resist communist aggression; redeployment should contribute to national objectives, enhance western European security, and entail minimum risk.[55]

The British knew nothing of this internal American debate, but Acheson could see that their position was hard to reconcile with Kennan's. Franks brought Acheson a message from Bevin on May 2. Echoing what he had told Massigli the previous July when Roberts, Smith, and Chataigneau were preparing to meet Stalin, Bevin predicted the real trouble would start when four-power talks began, because positions remained irreconcilable. Another British paper sent to Washington on May 10 proposed a line similar to Murphy's: continuing preparations for a west German government and offering to extend the west German basic law and occupation statute throughout the country.[56]

Accepting Kennan's program thus meant a row with the British and the French. It would also rouse fierce opposition from Murphy and other officials within the department, not to mention Clay and his many allies, both inside and outside government, who had invested so much of their time and energy in the last year and a half in the London program and a separate west German state. Germans, who had been less than enthusiastic recruits in this campaign, might feel the rug had been pulled out from under them just as they were putting the finishing touches on the basic law. As sensible as Kennan's ideas might be in the abstract, Acheson could see that they would create enormous practical problems. He would comment a few weeks later that the Europeans would be "utterly terrified if you were to withdraw one soldier one foot at this point"; any hint of weakness would cost the West "all the gains . . . made in the last 2 years."[57]

The secretary dictated an outline of the situation on May 10 and sent it to Bevin and Schuman. Borrowing points from a summary of discussions that Jessup had sent him, Acheson took as his premise the notion that "our concern is with the future of Europe." German reunification was not an end in itself but should be pursued only to the extent it promoted a "free and democratic Europe." Although the West preferred to have Soviet troops leave Germany, the price would be "too high" if British and American troops had to leave, too. In contrast, regrouping such as Kennan suggested deserved "the most careful study." Acheson agreed with the British that the most to be expected was a modus vivendi. The West should try to achieve more, but on its terms, not Moscow's.[58]

Acheson's paper meant the end of Program A, and a leak to James Reston of the *New York Times* was merely the coup de grace. Reston revealed the plan on May 12 and caused, as Bohlen recalled, "a good deal of hell in Europe." Jessup, arriving in Paris for tripartite talks in advance of the CFM, told reporters that Reston's story "in no way represented American policy." Louis Johnson completed Kennan's rout on May 14 by sending Acheson a memo summarizing his firm opposition to Program A.[59]

It would be easy to regard this as a lost opportunity to temper East-West divisions or roll back Soviet influence. The world no doubt would have been a better place if Program A had been adopted. Western diplomacy proved hypercautious and defensive. Ironies abounded. Clay, Murphy, and Acheson hailed progress in Bonn yet feared that "free" west Germans would somehow be more susceptible to Soviet blandishments than "stooge" east Germans would be to the attractions of freedom and democracy.[60] American officials were psychologically on the defensive. A sense of crisis and an awareness of Western economic and military weakness—legacies of 1947 and 1948—made it impossible for them to consider negotiations with the Russians until the West had built positions of strength. Postponing talks meant they would not occur for years.

While one can understand British and French concerns, it is hard to see why Kennan's plan roused such opposition in Washington. As Hickerson, one of its severest critics, noted, it meant the expulsion of Soviet influence from Germany. That, of course, was why it was not a lost opportunity; Stalin never would have accepted it. The CFM meeting in Paris would show that he would not relax his grip on his zone or eastern Europe. At the same time, reactions to Program A showed how deeply entrenched cold war thinking had become in the West. If a plan that even its critics conceded meant Russian defeat could not win acceptance in Western capitals, what hope was there for negotiation? With neither side willing to pull back one soldier one inch, the division of Germany and Europe would deepen. Although that might provide stability in the short run, it left future generations on the brink of a precipice.

WITH PROGRAM A SHELVED, the London program became the centerpiece of Western preparations for the foreign ministers' conference. The Parliamentary Council in Bonn passed the basic law on May 8. The military governors approved it four days later and authorized the minister-presidents to submit it to the *Landtage* for ratification.[61] Jessup, Kirkpatrick, and Parodi met in Paris on May 14 to work out a common position and quickly agreed that the Bonn government must be created before Germany could be reunited. The basic law would be extended throughout the country, which would be allowed to join the Marshall Plan. Four-power controls patterned on the tripartite occupation statute would be revived, with decisions by majority vote. The Soviets would be excluded from the international Ruhr authority.[62]

Analysts were uncertain how Vyshinsky would answer. The Soviet press gave few clear indications beyond ritualistic invocations of Yalta and Potsdam, support for the latest appeals of the People's Congress, and denunciation of the speed with which the West was rushing the west German government to completion. Western press speculation advanced two theories: Vyshinsky would use the meeting as a propaganda forum, or he would accept the Western position as part of a peace offensive aimed at undercutting the North Atlantic treaty. Some thought the second approach more likely. The CIA leaned toward this position, predicting the Russians would seek agreement on Germany to regain maneuvering room. Bohlen worried the West would face a "very delicate and even dangerous situation" if the Kremlin offered reunification on reasonable terms. From Moscow, Foy Kohler agreed. Such a move, he thought, would "shake Western foreign policies to [the] very bottom," disorienting public opinion in western Europe and the United States, weakening support not just for the North Atlantic treaty but for military preparedness in general, and making Germany's integration into western Europe nearly impossible. The president remained blissfully unaware of these pitfalls, telling David Lilienthal in excited and optimistic tones that the West would "get a full settlement in Germany."[63]

Our knowledge of Soviet preparations and expectations is only slightly better than that of Western contemporaries. If Wilhelm Pieck's jottings are to be believed, the Russians approached the CFM with some confidence. Molotov told the SED leader that four-power controls might be reestablished, Western plans for the federal republic shelved, and the eastern mark substituted for the western one in Berlin. The only element of realism here was Pieck's expectation that the SED could not win any new Berlin elections.[64]

Unsure whether his greatest worry was a settlement that threatened Western interests or a failed conference and a new blockade, Acheson arrived in Paris on May 21. He plunged at once into two days of preparations with Bevin and Schuman before the conference opened in the grand salon of the Hôtel Talleyrand-Périgord, better known as the "Palais Rose," on the afternoon of May 23. Built by Comte Boni de Castellane in 1896 for his bride, the daughter of robber baron Jay Gould, the palace's Edwardian elegance suggested to Acheson a "musical comedy setting and atmosphere." A ceiling fresco featured satyrs pursuing nymphs through the clouds, with Aphrodite, "an inattentive referee," reclining at the center. The diplomats were greeted by the *Garde Républicain,* complete with drums and bugles, plumed helmets, breastplates, and shiny black boots. All that was missing, Acheson mused, was a rollicking opening chorus by Victor Herbert.[65]

Acheson quickly lost any impulse to burst into song. The CFM, he wrote later, was "the most impossible institution ever invented by man," one that required eight hours to do fifteen minutes' work. There were no simultaneous translations, so each speech had to be translated twice. As the translations droned on, Acheson found himself gazing at the ceiling, wondering if the satyrs would capture their quarry. Bevin observed to King George in a postmortem report that his three colleagues were "all lawyers by profession. They consequently tended to embark with zest on long legalistic arguments" that he alone found tiresome. He did not mention that his response was to nap through many of the sessions. Acheson complained that it could take an hour and a half to get an answer from Vyshinsky. The delegates were supposed to speak in order, going around the table: Acheson, Schuman, Bevin, then

Vyshinsky, and around again. Invariably, someone spoke out of turn, and the discussion spun out of control. Just as some semblance of order had been restored, Bevin "would wake up and say, 'I didn't quite get that,'" and the cycle began once more. Acheson felt driven "to the limits of human endurance" and told the Senate Foreign Relations Committee, "I felt that I would go out of my mind if this went on any longer."[66]

These procedural difficulties compounded the substantive issues facing the ministers. The discussion proceeded in phases. In the first phase, each side put forward maximum proposals: The Soviets wanted to turn the clock back to Potsdam (with improvements to offset the weakness of their position in Germany), while the West offered to extend the Bonn constitution to the Soviet zone. On Berlin, the Russians endeavored to reestablish the Kommandatura with even greater veto power than before, while the Western powers tried to broaden the authority of the pro-Western Magistrat. The Russians tried to avoid any discussion of access, while the West sought physical control of the Helmstedt autobahn. In the second phase, both sides abandoned their one-sided proposals and worked out a modus vivendi, accepting the division of Germany and affording weak recognition of Western transit rights.

Vyshinsky began the discussion on Germany by proposing that the occupying powers return to the Potsdam accords. The Soviets envisaged a reestablishment of the Allied Control Council and Kommandatura, a unified Berlin government, four-power control of the Ruhr, and an all-German council based on existing zonal economic agencies. The council would exercise governmental power on "all questions of economic and state organisation affecting Germany as a whole." The proposal marked a departure from the Warsaw communiqué of the previous June, in which the Soviets had called for a prompt treaty of peace followed by the withdrawal of occupying forces and the creation of a German government. Vyshinsky was proposing an occupation of indeterminate duration, something few Germans would support. His position on ACC procedure suggested why the Russians had changed their minds about ending the occupation: the council must operate on the basis of unanimity. With ACC approval necessary before any action by the all-German council could take effect, and with Soviet consent needed for ACC approval, the Soviet plan would give Moscow a stranglehold over economic and political developments throughout Germany.[67]

Vyshinsky's stance reflected Soviet political weakness. Only through such a program could the Russians be assured of maintaining their position in a united Germany. The Warsaw program had been excellent propaganda in June 1948 to mobilize nationalist sentiment against the London program, but it risked too much in June 1949. The day Soviet armies left Germany, the SED would be swept from power and the country would align itself with the West. If there were counterparts to George Kennan in the Kremlin who urged Stalin to gamble on an all-German settlement, more cautious heads prevailed. Acheson noticed Vyshinsky's sensitivity about the veto. For the Russians, he realized, this was the "heart of the problem of Germany": whether the Soviets, through organizational means, could gain the power they lacked politically and prevent the emergence of a Germany independent of Soviet control. They insisted on unreasonable advantages, as they had since October 1946, because, as Kennan had put it some months earlier, "without unreasonable advantages they cannot hope to maintain any influence at all."[68]

Western officials were relieved by Vyshinsky's ineptness. Jessup told Canadian ambassador Georges Vanier that the Russian had "thrown away propaganda points," particularly when he insisted on a "return to Potsdam," which could only alienate the Germans. Acheson confessed later his fear that some clever Soviet maneuver would disrupt progress in western Germany and his relief at finding Vyshinsky to be "a long-winded and boring" advocate of sterile policies.[69]

The Western delegates were in a strong position. The west German *Landtage* had approved the basic law and returned it to the Parliamentary Council, which promulgated it May 23, the day the conference convened. Acheson and his colleagues heaped scorn on Vyshinsky's proposals. Acheson compared Vyshinsky's plan to asking a stroke victim who was three-quarters recovered to return to total paralysis. On May 28, after several days of fruitless debate, Bevin presented the Western program, which would extend the Bonn constitution throughout Germany. Under its terms, the four powers would supervise nationwide elections; those in the eastern zone would be held after Soviet occupation forces and police had been withdrawn. Soviet-controlled industries would revert to German ownership, reparations would end, and an occupation statute would reserve a few powers to the four Allied high commanders, whose decisions (with certain exceptions) would be by majority vote. The proposal meant the end of Soviet influence in Germany.[70]

The program was, like its Soviet counterpart, rooted in necessity, for the Western powers faced their own dilemma. They were committed to unification, as they had to be to maintain German support. But they believed, in the words of one U.S. position paper, that "no practicable arrangement for a four-zone German government can now be envisaged." Thus, as Acheson told reporters off the record on May 18, his intent was "to go ahead full steam" toward a west German government, "come hell or high water." His main concern was not Germany but western Europe. He would support integration of the Germans, "or as large a part of them as may prove practicable," into a democratic federated Europe, but only if that strengthened western Europe's ability to resist Soviet pressure. "Our basic policy and aim at Paris is to push freedom as far east as possible," he declared. "If a united Germany contributes to that aim, fine; if not, to hell with it."[71]

The Western proposal at Paris made four-power agreement dependent on acceptance of the basic law. It helped protect west German politicians by taking the onus of the country's division off them and placing it on the Soviets, while at the same time soothing Bevin's and Schuman's fears about being caught between pledges to the west Germans and agreements with the Russians. Anything less than this May 28 proposal would raise doubts about the Western governments' commitment to the Bonn regime, the London program, and, Acheson believed, the North Atlantic treaty, not to mention giving the Soviets an opportunity to subvert an all-German government and use their power over German economic agencies to disrupt the Marshall Plan.[72] When Acheson explained American policy to the Foreign Relations Committee in executive session on May 19, Arthur Vandenberg complained that the secretary had outlined proposals the Soviets must reject and asked, "Is there no sugar that you can put on this sour apple," some "safe concession"? There was none.[73]

Vyshinsky, naturally enough, would have nothing to do with the sour apple, noting that it "aimed to impose [Western] rule on Eastern Germany without participation of Eastern Germans and [the] USSR." He denounced it as undemocratic, a violation of Potsdam, and a repudiation of the aspirations of all peace-loving Germans. He rejected it outright on May 30. His own suggestions were to receive a delegation from the People's Congress, which Bevin and Acheson would not consider, and to call for a peace treaty to be signed within three months, with all occupation troops leaving twelve months after that. The Western delegates were unwilling to contemplate a treaty with so many issues unresolved.[74]

With the meeting deadlocked, the Western delegations concluded that the most that could be achieved was some sort of modus vivendi. The question was whether the Soviets would accept. Bohlen thought so. For all their talk about a new ACC, he noted, their purpose was to hold on to what they had. Acheson agreed, cabling Truman that the "almost hysterical Russian insistence" on the veto stemmed not from hope of interfering with developments in western Germany but from defensive concerns. The Soviets were so worried about preserving their control over the eastern zone that they put forward a program they knew would alienate the Germans and make the need for an iron grip all the greater.[75]

Once again, joint institutions devised in 1945 to promote harmony were only deepening insecurity and mistrust. As long as those institutions yoked the two sides together, defensive motives fueled conflict; each side feared that quadripartite agencies would offer the other side opportunities to extend its influence. A modus vivendi that dispensed with such ties would allow both to consolidate their positions and dampen the fear that all of Germany might slide into the other's sphere.

Western diplomats had been working on terms for such an arrangement. In exchange for a revival of interzonal trade, which Western analysts believed the Soviets desperately wanted, the West would seek guaranteed access to Berlin, if not outright control of routes to the city. The three foreign ministers endorsed the plan on June 10.[76]

Acheson outlined the idea to Vyshinsky over dinner on June 11: discussions by foreign ministers, high commissioners, and Berlin commandants, but no formal quadripartite machinery; expanded trade between the two Germanys (each with its own de facto government); Western control of Berlin access routes; and an Austrian treaty. The three Westerners elaborated the proposal in closed session on June 12, telling Vyshinsky it was a package deal: he could not pick and choose portions. When Douglas asked what the Western delegations would do if the Russian response were evasive, Acheson replied that they would wrap up the meeting and go home.[77]

Acheson seemed as worried about agreement as stalemate, telling Bevin on June 14 that it would be a mistake to accept what appeared to be a substantive accord but in fact was "nothing at all." By seeming to reduce tensions, such a result "might . . . defeat the Military Assistance Bill in the US Congress." That point came up again when the U.S. delegation met the next day. Bohlen argued that any agreement that made it harder for the Russians to reimpose the blockade would be "truly significant in the eyes of the man on the street." Bohlen stood his ground when Murphy warned that an accord might lead to reduced appropriations for the airlift, which had continued past May 12 in order to build up stocks in Berlin.[78] Bohlen condemned a "foreign policy that feeds itself on tension—which is overly afraid of 'relaxing' the American people." Dulles agreed. Although the government should not lead the public to expect the Cold War to end tomorrow, "it would be criminal indeed if we were to reject or even avoid a settlement because we were afraid of lowering a little the intensity of American effort in the present cold war." Acheson saw both sides. He warned Truman that "an illusory agreement is worse than none," but he accepted Bohlen's view that an agreement that made a new blockade less likely would be a "significant and valuable step."[79]

By now, Vyshinsky had his instructions, which were to explore the Western proposal. Discussion began on June 14. The ministers concentrated on Austrian issues and, regarding Germany, the details of interzonal trade and access. After four long meetings, they accepted the broad outlines of the modus vivendi on June 20. In doing so, they confirmed the partition of Germany.[80]

DISCUSSION OF BERLIN'S GOVERNMENT revealed a pattern similar to that affecting Germany: after maneuvering to unify the city on its own terms, each side settled for the status quo. The Western powers opened the discussion on June 1. Under their plan, the occupying powers would supervise citywide elections under the regulations used in October 1946. Political parties authorized in one sector could campaign in all of them. The Magistrat installed by these elections would operate under amended terms of the 1946 temporary constitution and have broad powers. It could not amend the constitution without the Kommandatura's consent, and certain areas (disarmament, reparations, security of occupation forces, control of German prisoners of war and those convicted by the Nuremberg tribunals, and supervision of elections) were reserved for the commandants. Otherwise, it was free to act. Its decisions would take effect unless disapproved by the Kommandatura within twenty-one days, and because the Kommandatura acted by majority vote, Magistrat action could not be blocked by one occupying power. Sector commandants could act on their own if the Kommandatura could not agree, but only in restricted fields: safety of Allied citizens, protection of city officials from interference with the performance of their duties, and control of prisoners of war.[81]

The Western powers were willing to gamble that elections would return a Magistrat favorable to them, and they were content to see such a government exercise broad powers. The "reverse veto," the provision that Magistrat decisions would take effect unless unanimously disapproved by the Kommandatura, protected the Magistrat from Soviet interference. The Western commandants had introduced some of these arrangements into west Berlin in mid-May, supplementing them on June 7 with new procedures for their tripartite Kommandatura. Acheson had summed up the underlying reasoning before he left Washington. "The most dangerous thing in the world," he told the Foreign Relations Committee, was to "enter into any agreement which depends for its execution upon Russian cooperation and Russian good will."[82]

To no one's surprise, Vyshinsky found such arrangements unacceptable and offered his own proposal, which would have given the Kommandatura, in Bevin's words, "the most powerful veto that existed anywhere." The Soviets wanted to give the commandants jurisdiction over day-to-day details of city administration in fields such as police, transport, finance, power, communications, external trade, and personnel. The Magistrat would share authority in these areas, but its actions would not take effect until the Kommandatura voted unanimously to accept them. In other areas, such as "local affairs," housing, education, health, labor, and cultural matters, the Magistrat was free to act, but its decisions would be suspended if one commandant objected.[83] Vyshinsky insisted that unanimity was the "essential basis of all agreements on Germany" and the "only possible basis" for four-power rule. The USSR, he declared, "would never subordinate itself to the rule of the majority." Acheson quipped that the upshot of Moscow's proposal was that the "four powers can do what they like in Berlin so long as it is what [the] USSR wants."[84]

As at the national level, political weakness in Berlin forced the Soviets to insist on unreasonable advantages. Without a veto on the Kommandatura, the Soviets could not protect their position in east Berlin. Absent a Kommandatura veto over the Magistrat, the city government would possess, Vyshinsky complained, too much freedom from Allied—that is, Soviet—control.[85] Once again, the Russians were trying to use institutional arrangements to offset their lack of political support. With agreement on combined agencies impossible, the foreign ministers accepted the status quo. Like Germany, Berlin would remain divided.

WESTERN DIPLOMATS APPROACHED the CFM hoping to win unequivocal recognition of their nations' rights of access to Berlin. As they had on Germany and the city's administration, they developed a maximum program. Faced with Soviet rejection, they settled for much less.

Jessup, Kirkpatrick, and Parodi had grappled with the dilemmas and paradoxes of access during their preliminary talks. All Western officials wanted to strengthen Western rights; no one knew how. A demand that Vyshinsky recognize those rights could backfire. Carelessly phrased, it "might place in question the rights previously agreed upon," while Soviet rejection of the most ironclad wording would have the same effect. The diplomats suggested that the CFM pledge to uphold the May 4 New York agreement and return to the rules in existence on March 1, 1948. Moscow might accept this, they thought, in exchange for a revival of interzonal trade.[86]

Acheson was under political pressure to obtain more. Senator Vandenberg had written to him the day the blockade ended to suggest that he demand formal Soviet recognition of Western rights. Acheson doubted this would be easy but promised to make "every effort." When he met the Foreign Relations Committee in executive session on May 19, Vandenberg and Theodore F. Green of Rhode Island blamed the administration for fumbling access guarantees in 1945 and urged Acheson to remedy the "mistake." He should not only seek formal recognition of Western rights but also demand a land corridor to Berlin. The JCS also insisted on a "clear, favorable written agreement" on a "surface corridor." The Policy Planning Staff wanted a written agreement giving the West "exclusive jurisdiction" over the Helmstedt autobahn and the railways leading to Berlin. Reflecting these views, Acheson told the NSC on May 17 that he hoped to get "a clear corridor to the West" and instructed the delegation on May 30 that the West's "initial demand" should be for a "direct physical channel" that the Soviets could disrupt "only by a clear act of force." He worried about the possibility of a new blockade and asked that a Pentagon study of Western options pay careful attention to probes. Unconsciously echoing John Foster Dulles's comments of nearly a year earlier, Acheson suggested that probes might be a useful way of "testing out Soviet intentions."[87]

An early American draft sought sweeping changes in procedures affecting Western transit. The West would be allowed twenty-five military trains each day, and these trains could enter the zone at any one of five checkpoints, not just Helmstedt. Western authorities would ensure that passengers had proper papers, making Soviet inspection unnecessary. German traffic would be "unlimited" and could use the shortest and most practical route; commercial freight would need only Western permits, not Soviet ones, and all Western trains would be powered by Western locomotives. Western commanders in Berlin would control rail traffic in their sectors, not the east German *Reichsbahn,* which currently directed rail operations throughout the city and the Soviet zone.

Highway travel would be easier. While the Western powers would be limited to the Helmstedt and Munich autobahns, these motorways would be under Western control. German traffic would be free to move by the most direct route, with border crossing points on all major highways. Traffic to Berlin would need only Western permits; no special Soviet pass would be required. Barge travel along east German canals would operate under similar rules.[88]

Few observers expected Soviet acceptance, especially in light of Russian conduct after the blockade. Under the May 4 agreement, traffic was to resume on the basis of rules in effect March 1, 1948, and the Russians had a much narrower interpretation of what that allowed than the Westerners did. Chuikov would allow no more than sixteen military trains to Berlin, observing that in 1945, the ACC had approved only this number. He waved aside Clay's point that the council had accepted this figure as an estimate and that, in practice, the daily average in 1948 had reached thirty-one. Other officials turned deaf ears to reminders that the previous March, Helmstedt had been one of six crossing points; now it was the only place where west German trains could enter the Soviet zone. Similarly, they required that barges be re-registered on the basis of a March 17, 1948, order, a clear violation of the May 4 accord. In addition, Russian officials enforced restrictions they had proclaimed before March 1 but the Western powers had disputed; other restrictions were new: the requirement that trains passing through the eastern zone be pulled by Soviet locomotives, the replacement of east German schedulers and dispatchers with Russians, and the requirement that goods exported from Berlin have Soviet transit permits. For a time, the Russians claimed that goods brought into the city from the western zones must have Russian permits, and they banned German trucks from the autobahn, which was, they said, reserved for use of the occupation forces. Technical talks removed some of these restrictions, but not all of them. Summarizing the situation a week after the blockade had ended, Riddleberger wrote that Berlin remained "in a state of semi-blockade."[89]

The violations were not entirely one-sided. The United States had prohibited exports of certain strategic materials to the Soviet bloc and limited others—the so-called 1A and 1B lists—in late March 1948; the New York agreement required the United States to lift those bans, at least in Germany. Voorhees regarded the problem with "genuine alarm" because of the "real danger that a breach may result in the dam against flow of strategic material to satellite areas," setting a precedent that Europeans, unhappy with the ban, would follow. The view from Clay's headquarters was that because "we'll have to violate it [the pledge to return to the status quo of

March 1, 1948] . . . we might as well do it one way as another." Voorhees's solution was to deliver goods (including 1A and 1B items) promised under the 1948 interzonal trade agreement, but to phrase any new accord to exclude 1A and 1B items. Representatives of the four powers met in Berlin for a month, trying to work out the details, only to adjourn on June 13 without an agreement. By then, trade and access were part of the West's proposed modus vivendi in Paris.[90]

Meanwhile, a strike by west Berlin rail workers had complicated matters. Trouble had been brewing ever since the Western powers banned the Soviet mark. The Soviet-controlled railway administration refused to pay the wages of workers living in west Berlin in deutsche marks. It would not accept payment for fares in what it regarded as illegal Western currency, so it claimed it had no deutsche marks with which to pay wages. Because the Soviet mark, on average, had one-third to one-fourth the purchasing power of the Western currency, even those workers able to convert their wages on the black market suffered a dramatic loss in pay. Matters came to a head when efforts at mediation broke down; the workers left their jobs at midnight May 20.[91]

Western officials supported the strike at first, especially after violent clashes at stations in west Berlin between strikers and Soviet railway police left several people dead. Bevin saw the strike as an opportunity for west Berliners to defeat the Russians in a public test of strength. Howley and his staff saw the strike in similar terms and, as General Pope's staff reported, used it as a way of "baiting the Soviet representatives who have consequently become even more unyielding."[92] This was great sport, especially in the euphoric days after the lifting of the blockade, but traffic from the western zones slowed to a halt. Western officials realized, as Acheson put it, "we were . . . blockading ourselves."[93] The Soviets refused the strikers' offer to work inbound Western trains, and the workers replied by demanding that all their wages be paid in deutsche marks and that their union be recognized. At that point, Acheson determined to end this embarrassing situation. He persuaded Bevin and Schuman to join him in issuing an ultimatum to Vyshinsky: if the four ministers did not instruct their commandants to settle the strike within four days, Acheson and his colleagues would walk out of the conference. The Soviet diplomat was irritated. The strike was not his country's fault; it was organized and directed from the American sector. Personally, this tribune of the proletariat continued, he "did not approve of strikes," and he faulted the Americans for not jailing the strike's leaders. Acheson's four-day deadline came and went with an end nowhere in sight.[94]

Meanwhile, officials in Washington had been trying to devise a response to a new blockade. No one, not even Clay, shared Acheson's enthusiasm for probes. The general, who was in Washington awaiting retirement, considered a new airlift "the only acceptable alternative." The joint chiefs agreed, weighing in against Acheson's probe and forcible efforts to break the blockade. The chiefs thought a new blockade would mean the Soviets were ready to start a war. If hostilities were inevitable, the JCS wanted the Russians to commit the first overt act. Hence, there would be no convoy and no probe; that left an airlift, even though the JCS had not changed their views since October. They declared a new airlift would be "neither a sole nor a final action with respect to solution of a new Berlin blockade" and that an open-ended airlift would progressively weaken America's ability to wage war. Yet it remained "the only practicable step short of great risk of hostilities or [a] decision to leave Berlin." Johnson's deputy, Stephen T. Early, forwarded these views to the NSC. He opposed convoys and probes, recommending a new airlift and counterblockade if the Russians reimposed the blockade. If the CFM adjourned without confirming Western access rights, Early thought the Western powers should continue the airlift until Berlin's emergency stocks had been built up and remain ready to resume the airlift and counterblockade. He also suggested warning the Russians that the United States would regard a new blockade as "a matter of grave concern"—a warning the British and French should be asked to join.[95]

Truman and Webb had already seen the chiefs' report. The president had no particular comment, but Webb sensed he was not enthusiastic about it. Truman's head told him a new airlift was "probably the only answer," but his heart longed for something more assertive. In Paris, Murphy and Acheson also favored a more pugnacious response. Murphy revived his contention that an "unfortunate incident" need not escalate. He was certain that if the West showed it was serious, the Russians would back down. "Fear can be useful as an element of policy," he observed. The Russians had used it during the blockade to restrain the West; next time, Murphy wanted the shoe on the other foot. For his part, Acheson found more and more sense in a probe, not to shoot it out with the Soviets but to see whether they would use force to stop Western troops trying to reach the city. He assured Truman that he would do all he could to get Vyshinsky to confirm Western access rights. He considered warning the Soviet foreign minister that the United States would regard any new blockade as "very close to [an] act of war" and would use whatever means necessary to protect its rights and obligations in Berlin. The best way to handle a new blockade, he seemed to be saying, was to deter one.[96]

Meanwhile, the NSC had approved the Pentagon report with minor changes. There was some controversy about concerting action with the Europeans. The military questioned British and French security; informing London and Paris that the United States would respond to a new blockade with nothing more bellicose than a new airlift meant the Russians might find out and be tempted to impose new restrictions. How, then, to obtain a joint warning to Moscow? The British and French would surely want to know what steps Washington intended. The council essentially passed the problem on to Acheson. As Webb cabled his chief, the NSC had left to him the method, timing, and content of any warning to Vyshinsky, and it delayed submitting the report to the president until Acheson approved it. Acheson endorsed the report on June 11. Despite Johnson's attempt to take away Acheson's discretion regarding a warning, Truman reiterated it on June 15.[97]

Against this background, the Western representatives in Paris began their efforts to win Soviet recognition of Western access rights. From the start, what was possible clashed with what was desirable. On May 31, the American delegation set aside the detailed working paper it had prepared. The conference should concentrate on long-term, general accords, and officials in Berlin could work out specific arrangements using the working paper as a guide. The foreign ministers were to instruct their representatives in Berlin to work out a detailed accord to supplement the May 4 agreement. Under this accord, the Soviets would provide all facilities needed by the Western powers to exercise their "established right of access to and from Berlin" and would facilitate the traffic needed to support the Berlin population. The American paper also proposed that the Western powers be responsible for the "control, operation, and maintenance" of the Helmstedt autobahn.[98]

These proposals stirred controversy when the delegation met to discuss them as part of the proposed modus vivendi on June 10. Bohlen was unhappy with the demand for control of the autobahn, describing it as "throwing a rock at the moon." He asked whether this was a serious proposal or one designed with public relations in mind. Acheson admitted it was "more the latter." Bohlen wanted to know what the response would be when Vyshinsky rejected it. Acheson shrugged: the council would not agree. Bohlen shifted ground, arguing that posturing would backfire: the demand was "too exorbitant . . . for the public to approve." British and French objections tipped the balance in Bohlen's favor. The Europeans were willing to try for control of the autobahn but would not insist on it, nor would they insist on wording that would force the Soviets to recognize the West's "established right of access" to Berlin. The Europeans regarded this as too much like "rubbing [it] in," Paul Nitze reported. The French suggested that quadripartite control of the autobahn was something the Soviets might accept; the Americans and British quashed the idea.[99]

The draft modus vivendi that Acheson gave Vyshinsky on June 12 omitted any demand for Soviet recognition of Western access rights. Instead, it proposed that the military governors devise a new agreement that met "the requirements of the Western allies for facilities for movement by rail, road and water." The Western powers would operate and maintain the Helmstedt autobahn and "control" traffic on it, while the Soviets were to "facilitate" German traffic between west Germany and Berlin.[100]

This took officials in Washington by surprise, especially in light of Acheson's continued hard line about probes. Rusk and Murphy's assistant, Colonel Henry A. Byroade, wired the secretary that the reasoning behind the paper and its failure to insist on a clear reaffirmation of Western rights were "not generally understood here"; they had to deal with vigorous questioning from unnamed quarters—the army, no doubt, and perhaps the White House—and they had no answers. The modus vivendi looked like a retreat. It would require "careful public treatment" to avoid the impression that the Western governments had not even tried to win Soviet recognition of their rights.[101]

Acheson put the best face on his change of position. He argued that the Russians would never explicitly acknowledge Western rights. Soviet acceptance of the proposal "will in fact constitute recognition of our right of access and tacit abandonment of Stalin's contention that we had lost our right," and tacit recognition was the best the West could hope for. At the same time, he observed that the Soviets could evade any accord, no matter how detailed and precise, if they chose to, so any written agreement would be an "illusory victory." Yet if that were so, there was no point to the modus vivendi or anything else.[102]

Vyshinsky's reaction to the Western proposal shaped the West's perception of the minimum it could accept. He had Moscow's answer on June 14. His government would not give the West control of the autobahn, which was, he said, "in the Soviet Union"; Moscow would not be party to the creation of a second Danzig corridor. Acheson had expected as much. Vyshinsky offered a weak substitute for the Western plan: to improve and supplement existing agreements, each zonal commander would act to ensure "normal functioning" of transport and communications in his zone.[103]

Acheson found this unsatisfactory, telling Bevin and Schuman that if they were dealing with people of goodwill, it might be all right, but similar Soviet promises had proved worthless. He feared some illusory meeting of the minds that would allow reimposition of the blockade. A new Western minimum was emerging: Acheson decided to seek assurances that the Western powers would not someday face another blockade. When pressed, Vyshinsky seemed agreeable. Since the purpose of the accord was to improve and supplement existing agreements, he said, clearly "communications were to be improved and not restricted."[104]

Bohlen thought this was enough. Any agreement that made it "a little more difficult for the Soviets to reimpose a sudden or gradual blockade," he argued when the delegation met on June 15, "would be a step forward." Murphy disagreed, as did Jessup, who pointed out that the delegation had first thought in terms of two agreements, a general one reached in Paris and a later, detailed one in Berlin. Now, he said, they were accepting a "final though general agreement here." To counter such criticism, the delegation added a sentence to the effect that the four governments would continue to honor the May 4 agreement. With this change, the Western delegations accepted the Soviet draft. Acheson now saw no need to warn Vyshinsky away from a new blockade.[105] On the assumption that any agreement would make reimposition harder, the Western diplomats had decided that a weak agreement was better than none. There was logic in this, but it was a striking position to take;

just one week before, these same men had been wondering whether they should reject the entire modus vivendi if the Soviets failed to cede them control of the Helmstedt autobahn.

Acheson made only limited claims for success when he returned to Washington, both in executive session before the Senate Foreign Relations Committee on June 22 and at a press conference the following afternoon. The CFM did not decide much, he told the senators. It was, he went on, "more like the gauge on a steam-boiler. It shows you what the pressure is and how much you have accomplished." He reminded reporters of Marshall's comment eighteen months earlier that there would be no progress in the CFM until the great question of whether western Europe would recover had been answered. Paris, Acheson suggested, reflected the gains the West had made and showed that the Soviets had been put on the defensive. He described the modus vivendi as "a very modest document," one that provided "very clearly" that the blockade would not be reimposed. That was something, he mused—not much, but something. It also laid a basis for continued four-power discussion of German issues. "Here again," he commented, "that is not much. It is simply a way of dealing sensibly with . . . established fact."[106]

In the end, both sides preferred to deal with established fact rather than hold out for their maximum programs; both preferred compromise based on minimum goals—the preservation and consolidation of existing positions—even though that meant abandoning the pretense of quadripartite control of Germany and accepting the country's partition. Acceptance rested on the realization that the alternatives were worse. Any attempt to alter the status quo involved risks that neither side would accept, and neither side had compelling reasons to try, because partition satisfied their minimum goals. From the Western point of view, the Paris modus vivendi meant the Soviets recognized that Germany could not be united under their auspices; for the Russians, it meant Western acceptance of the Soviet foothold in eastern Germany. Partition, and the diplomats' acceptance of it, removed Germany and Berlin as causes of East-West conflict for a decade.

Accommodation came at a price. Few regarded partition of Germany as stable or permanent. Berlin remained a potential source of trouble. The western sectors, now a highly visible symbol of Western resolve, remained as exposed to Soviet pressure as ever, and Soviet incentive to absorb them was undiminished. Attitudes had hardened on both sides. Acheson's reference to Marshall's prediction suggested how possibilities had narrowed. Marshall, after all, had linked Europe's economic revival to diplomatic progress at the CFM: the former would lead to the latter. That had not happened. Marshall's great question had an answer, yet the diplomats remained locked in a sterile, dangerous confrontation. Neither side would have the will or the courage to look beyond it for four decades.

Conclusions

"History is lived forwards but it is written in retrospect," C. V. Wedgwood reminds us. "We know the end before we consider the beginning and we can never wholly recapture what it was to know the beginning only."[1] There are few better examples than the causes, course, and ending of the Berlin blockade.

After the blockade, the Western powers' failure to secure access to their sectors in Berlin appeared foolish. The Cold War was inevitable. East-West cooperation depended on the existence of a common enemy, and it would disappear when Hitler died. Not grasping this simple fact, the Western powers put themselves at the mercy of a ruthless dictator. Critics have traced the mistake to American illusions about Stalin and his regime. Like Roosevelt at Yalta and Eisenhower at the Elbe, John Winant sacrificed American national interests in a naive pursuit of Soviet goodwill in the European Advisory Commission.

Naiveté in fact ranked low among the reasons why wartime planners paid little attention to postwar access to Berlin. Planning reflected fixation with the job at hand, which was preventing new German aggression. Germany would be the future enemy, not the Soviet Union. That assumption was national policy at the highest levels, not the invention of midlevel planners or woolly-minded ambassadors. Surrounded by unparalleled death and destruction, no one was inclined to genuflect before alleged historical laws about the fracturing of wartime alliances.[2] What we now see as inevitable, they determined to make impossible. If quarrels among the victors would mock wartime hopes and sacrifices, then those quarrels had to be prevented. To the extent American bureaucratic infighting hampered planning, the cause was the Pentagon's suspicion of the British, not sympathy in Foggy Bottom or Lancaster House for the Soviet Union. Confusion over wartime zones in Rankin C and postwar zones under discussion in the EAC did not help.

Hindsight has distorted our view of what planners were doing. We assume they were arranging to supply an entire city, when in fact they expected the western sectors to meet their needs from the surrounding countryside (the Soviet zone) and that only the garrisons would draw supplies from the western zones. This is why army officers called access a "military problem" and denounced diplomats' attempts to deal with it as intrusions into military affairs. Soviet insistence in July 1945 that each occupying power sustain its own sector created a situation the planners never anticipated.

Hindsight also exaggerates national differences. Critics have focused on American mistakes while absolving British policy. Their perspective draws more on stereotypes—innocent Americans and shrewd Britons—than fact, for the British proved no wiser than the Americans. Indeed, if anyone was to blame for creating the access problem, it was the British. The blueprint used by the EAC to erect the Allied Control Authority structure and establish the zones, after all, was the Attlee plan, not some New Deal foray into international social engineering. The key assumptions that led planners to underestimate the importance of access—that the zones would have no political or economic significance and would merely delineate where each country stationed its troops, that token forces would serve in other zones, that troops from all occupying powers would move freely throughout Germany, and that the occupation would be brief—originated in Whitehall, not Washington.

Another unjustified claim is the assertion that access was ignored. There were more efforts to put it on a sounder footing than historians have realized. Those attempts failed for a variety of reasons. Lack of persistence ranks high among them. Never an immediate priority, access appeared to be a detail that someone else could settle at some other time. Hilldring, Winant, Jebb, Strang, and others assumed the Soviets would grant access when the time came. After Clay met Zhukov in Berlin, he and others were sure that more solid arrangements could be achieved at some point in the future. Hope lived on, sustained by apparent Soviet flexibility. Gusev assured Strang and Winant that access could be worked out. In turning aside Bevin's call for freedom of movement, Molotov cited procedure, not principle: the proper forum was the ACC, not the CFM. Similarly, Zhukov promised additional air corridors "in due course." The Western powers sometimes proved to be their own worst enemies: the Attlee plan rendered Mosely's corridor scheme moot, while Harper's air corridor proposal undercut British calls for unrestricted flights.

Nor was the Western legal position as weak as later critics suggested. Generations of scholars believed that the air corridor agreement was unique and that no written accords protected Western surface access to Berlin. They were mistaken. The ACC defined rail access to Berlin in writing in September 1945. This accord was embodied in a numbered ACC paper, just as the air corridor agreement was, and it was just as binding. Further, the ACA worked out accords at lower levels governing interzonal travel and access to Berlin. The trouble was that if the Soviets chose to ignore these agreements, the Western powers had little recourse. Law mattered less than geography and power.

Access, so often denounced as unsatisfactory, worked reasonably well between 1945 and the end of 1947—far longer than planners expected. Only as relations worsened in 1947 and 1948 did it become contentious. Opportunity, in short, became dangerous when coupled with a willingness to exploit it. Stalin's motives are thus critical to understanding the failure of access and the origins of the blockade. For Western cold warriors, those motives were axiomatic. In reality, Stalin's willingness to risk conflict grew as East-West relations fell prey to the dynamics of mutual fear. No one would confront the world's only nuclear power for light or transient reasons; Stalin did so only when he felt he had no other choice.

The events from April through June 1948 are usually depicted as a failure of Western deterrence, in that the United States and its partners were unable to deter the Soviets from blockading Berlin. Deterrence did fail that spring—Soviet deterrence, not Western. Rather than unprovoked aggression—the standard Cold War interpretation—the blockade was an attempt to deter initiatives in the western zones.

Stalin regarded the revival of Germany under capitalist auspices as a mortal threat. German economic revival and a separate west German government would lead to military resurgence and new aggression. This new war would be more horrible than the last because this time, Russia would face not just German armies but American bombers and British sea power as well. To avert this danger, Stalin resorted to a variety of measures, and as each failed, he saw no alternative but escalation. He believed Berlin was the West's most vulnerable spot, and as the West proceeded with its plans, he ratcheted up pressure on the city. His attempts at deterrence failed. They were too subtle: until July, the Kremlin made no demands and established no link between Berlin and the German question. Stalin also underestimated the Western commitment to the London initiative. Frightened by the power of world capitalism and by German revival, he could not grasp the exaggerated sense of Soviet power in Western calculations and how essential the London program appeared to be to counterbalance it.

The Western powers did not fail to deter the blockade because they never tried. Officials understood that the Soviets might interfere with access, but they could not devise a response. No one had thought seriously about the risks associated with a Western presence in Berlin. The city's importance was undefined, the Western powers' commitment unclear. The garrisons remained due to inertia, not out of a calculated effort to awe the Kremlin. Wishful thinking—the notion that the Russians had no desire to shoulder responsibility for supporting the city's residents, and the belief that the Soviets recognized the political costs of cutting off supplies—led officials to conclude that the Kremlin was bluffing. Officials assumed the Russians would not exploit their geographic advantage, limiting themselves to a war of nerves. Proposals foundered on practical objections. Retaliation would be ineffective, "clearing the decks" by evacuating dependents would panic western Europe, and Clay's convoy involved great risk. Washington's attempt to orchestrate a warning foundered on British and French reluctance.

Clay and Murphy would claim that they had tried to rouse their government to the danger. At the same time, however, they went out of their way to minimize the risk to Berlin inherent in the London program. The Marshall Plan, containment, and the West's policy toward the Soviet Union all hinged on this Anglo-American initiative. British and American officials—Clay and Murphy included—could not allow the Russians (or the French) to hold it hostage because of Berlin. Giving little thought to how the London program appeared in Soviet eyes, the British and Americans underestimated Stalin's motivation to stop it. Nor did they pay much attention to Soviet pressure in Berlin. If the French saw the connection, their Anglo-Saxon partners dismissed French fears as exaggerated, gambling that they could go ahead without eliciting an effective Soviet response. They turned out to be right—but only after an eleven-month confrontation that nearly went the other way.

Stalin did not impose the blockade with the aim of expelling the Western powers from Berlin. His purpose was to compel them to abandon the London program. That aim created unforeseen problems for the Soviets—problems that would not have arisen from the simple, direct goal of compelling Western withdrawal. Because Stalin sought concessions regarding Germany, and because his only leverage to secure them was Western fear of catastrophe in Berlin (e.g., war, starvation, collapse of west Berliners' morale, or residents' turning on the Western garrisons and demanding their departure), he did not want the city to fall into his hands outright. If it did, his bargaining leverage would disappear. Such thinking may be behind what William Stivers calls the "incomplete blockade."[3] From such a perspective, the blockade did not have to be efficient to be effective. Shrewd as this analysis seemed, it led Stalin into a dead end when the Western powers and west Berliners refused to yield. Locked in sterile confrontation with the West, unable to absorb west Berlin or stop the London program, the Soviet leader watched helplessly as the Americans drew western Europe into their economic, political, and military orbit.

He also watched dumbfounded as the airlift circumvented his blockade. He was not alone, for the airlift exceeded everyone's expectations. Historians have assumed that the Western powers' aim in beginning the airlift was to defeat the blockade.[4] This was the furthest thing from their minds. Initially, no one with influence over policy saw the airlift as a counter to Soviet coercion. The airlift did not begin in response to the blockade; it actually started three days before the blockade began, and its initial purpose was to supply the Western garrisons. It evolved into a short-term stopgap to buy time; only later was it transformed into an enormous effort to supply the western sectors indefinitely. That evolution took more than six months. The British and Americans began separate airlifts in June; they did not merge until October. The American air force waited until August before calculating how many airplanes it would need, the National Security Council did not decide to send them until October, and they did not arrive until January. A massive operation required not just planes but also a logistical network that did not exist. Berlin's two airfields needed new runways. A new airfield had to be constructed in the city, and half a dozen more had to be opened in the western zones. Maintenance, supply, and training depots had to be established, some as far away as Montana and California. Tunner had to instill his passion for efficiency and standardization at every level. None of this was certain; all of it took time.

At the start, no one was thinking of the airlift in the way we do today. Doubts went much deeper and lasted far longer than historians have realized. At the same time Clay was ordering LeMay's planes into the air, he was warning Washington that an airlift "cannot supply the German civilian population." In London, Bevin pushed his government into starting a separate British airlift to show "strength and determination" and provide "at least some supplies for the civil population"; the idea that this makeshift effort might sustain the western sectors had no place in his calculations. Weeks later, Cornelius Whitney delivered the considered judgment of the U.S. Air Force: the airlift was "doomed."

Although the airlift could not overcome the blockade, sending as many supplies to Berlin as possible would postpone the day stocks ran out. That bought time for diplomacy, even though prospects for a diplomatic breakthrough remained bleak: Stalin would end the blockade only if the West abandoned the London program, something the Western powers believed they could not do. When diplomacy reached a dead end, the Western powers would face "ultimate" choices. A number of scholars have interpreted the West's reliance on the airlift as reflecting a decision to stay in Berlin, even if it meant war. Truman never chose between withdrawal and war because, thanks to the airlift, he never had to. The airlift represented a policy of putting off the choice between war and retreat for as long as possible.

Scholars have misinterpreted Western thinking for several reasons. One is the role of hindsight. Here again, knowing the ending distorts our view of the beginning. The airlift overcame the blockade, so that must have been its purpose. Decision-making models have been another source of error. The basic structure of these models, stimulus-response, seems sensible: faced with a crisis, governments must devise a response. Game-theory matrices appear to reduce the situation to its essence and outline courses of action. Actor A chooses one of several possibilities, actor B does the same, and their choices determine the outcome. On the assumption that fundamental choices were made at the outset, the historian's task is determining who made them, when, and the rationale behind them. This procrustean model does not allow for the possibility that preferences may be unclear at the start, choices may be ambiguous or deferred, or new alternatives may arise, all of which characterized the West's response to the Berlin blockade. We see what we expect to see, and these models predisposed scholars to expect a pattern of behavior that was not there. Western leaders did not sit down, weigh alternatives, choose airlift as the course of action that would resolve the crisis on their terms, and then implement their decision.

Participants' memoirs have led scholars astray. Success has a thousand fathers. After the airlift triumphed, many people took credit for it. Clay claimed he had foreseen the blockade, calculated the city's requirements, and began a small airlift to "prove that the job could be done."[5] Draper suggested in an oral memoir that the lift was his idea. Truman's claim that on June 26 he ordered the aerial operation put on a full-scale, organized basis is pure invention. Such an order would have passed from the White House to the Pentagon and then to Clay and LeMay in Europe, copies proliferating as it went. There is no trace of it. There was no quick decision, no instant dispatch of a vast aerial armada, no early confidence that a solution had been found and risks brought under control.

The president's account of the July 22 National Security Council meeting has also misled scholars. In his recounting of the discussion, Truman claims he committed the United States to a policy of defeating the blockade by airlift, overruling objections from General Vandenberg and rejecting the alternative, Clay's convoy. Truman's account holds an unshakeable grip on scholars' minds, even though a contemporary summary of the meeting, declassified more than twenty-five years ago, makes it clear that he misrepresented what happened.[6] The president put Clay's words into his own mouth ("if we move out of Berlin we have lost everything we are fighting for") and concocted a showdown with Vandenberg that never took place. Far from opposing an airlift, the air force chief of staff favored an expanded one, declaring, "The Air Force would prefer that we go in wholeheartedly. If we do, Berlin can be supplied." The points he raised, portrayed in Truman's memoirs as objections, were steps necessary to the airlift's success. The transcript makes it clear that few around the table shared Vandenberg's faith in airpower. The NSC ignored his call for a maximum effort. Lovett, Forrestal, and others saw the airlift as a prelude to the convoy, not an alternative to it. They had no doubt that when the airlift failed in October, the West would have to abandon Berlin or send in Clay's tanks.

Because the West would face two alternatives in the end—war or withdrawal—the president's advisers insisted that he decide at once. If the West was going to fight, it needed to mobilize; if it was going to withdraw, steps had to be taken to minimize the damage. Advisers urged Truman time and again to choose. Saltzman, Clay, and Bedell Smith pressed for a decision. So did the joint chiefs. Innumerable scholars have depicted the president as a man predisposed to snap decisions. As Truman would write in *Mr. Citizen,* drift is disaster: "The most dangerous course a President can follow in a time of crisis is to defer making decisions until they are forced upon him and thereupon become inevitable decisions."[7] One would have expected him to listen to his advisers and decide, but that is not what he did. Rather than following the forthright precepts of *Mr. Citizen,* Truman behaved like Mr. Micawber. He waited for something to turn up. We might describe this as a deliberate policy of waiting until the time was right, if there was evidence that Truman saw his actions in such terms. There is none. Nor is there evidence that the president was relying on an intuitive sense of when to act. He drifted without admitting to himself or others what he was doing, insisting all the while that he was not passing the buck.[8]

The British behaved similarly, though with more self-awareness. The airlift's prospects (and much else) depended on the Americans, and Bevin was relentless in pressing them to do their utmost. The British realized they could not decide on war or peace by themselves: the decision rested with the White House. Bevin pushed for an airlift in the early days, not in any expectation that it would break the blockade but to buy time. He hoped a show of Western determination (bombers, not Clay's convoy) would intimidate the Kremlin. Yet he had no desire to push matters to a break. Pressed by the British chiefs of staff whether Britain would go to war over Berlin, Bevin and Attlee gave an equivocal answer: maybe.

No one was making "strategic" choices and commitments in June and July 1948. Instead of the stalwart leadership and calculated strategy described in so many accounts, drift characterized Western policy. Truman's forthright declaration of June 28—"we were going to stay period"—has become legendary; however, a more accurate forecast of his actions came a few minutes later when he said that he would deal with the situation as it developed. The powers resolved neither to be forced from Berlin nor to abandon the London program. At the same time, they wanted to avoid war. How was this balance to be struck? What risks were the powers willing to run? What concessions would they make in order to stay? No one answered these questions. Strategy also reconciles ends and means. In a fundamental sense, the West had no strategy—no set of steps over which it had control that offered a reasonable prospect of bringing the crisis to a favorable conclusion. A successful airlift might allow the West to maintain its position, but it exerted no leverage on Stalin to abandon his. Success—defined as a peaceful outcome that preserved Western interests in Berlin without sacrificing the London program—depended on a change in Soviet policy, and that lay beyond the West's control. To the extent the West had a strategy, it was to wait for Stalin to give up, even though the Western powers believed they were dealing with a ruthless dictator who, in their minds, had no reason to give up. This hardly qualifies as a coherent strategy.

The Western powers avoided these dire prospects for two reasons. First, Tunner transformed the airlift. Concentrating on decisions, scholars have ignored the vital complexities of implementation. Applying Frederick Taylor's theories of scientific management, Tunner brought to the task a firm belief in regimentation and attention to detail. He halved turnaround time in Berlin; replaced C-47s with larger, more efficient C-54s; then put as many C-54s in the British zone, closer to Berlin, as he could. He boosted payloads by removing unneeded equipment and streamlining packaging. He expanded his network of radio communications and navigational aids to control the flow of aircraft. He combined the British and American lifts under a single headquarters, opened a new airfield in Berlin, overcame logistical bottlenecks, and dealt with morale problems.

Despite all these efforts, the airlift would have failed if Berliners had given in to Soviet pressure, and that is the second reason for the West's narrow escape: Berliners' refusal to submit, which had several sources. In some ways, Berliners had endured worse conditions during the war, and they were healthier and better fed in 1948 than in the immediate postwar period. Conditions were not static. At first, when the blockade was not tightly enforced and people believed it would not last long, the situation was relatively easy to tolerate; things worsened in autumn as the Soviets tightened restrictions, unemployment rose, winter loomed, and an end to the crisis receded into the distant future. Winter, though difficult physically, was perhaps less wearing psychologically than the autumn had been; the unusually mild winter weather meant that reality did not match expectations. Life was harder for some Berliners. Economic and class differences mattered, as did where people lived and worked. How much of one's earnings was paid in the more valuable B-mark may have mattered most of all. The poor suffered disproportionately: they were more likely to be unemployed, more likely to receive eastern rather than western marks, more likely to live in substandard housing. But even they, who had the least to lose, proved deaf to Soviet appeals. Strong anticommunist sentiments united the population and helped Berliners endure. So did Reuter's inspiring leadership and the symbolic value of the airlift. Reuter's call to "look to this city" was answered by the constant drone of engines overhead. The airlift's effects on morale were even greater than its material ones. It came to represent a commitment to the city that inspired Berliners and fostered a new self-image as partners of the West. It also reinforced "the remarkable shift in German mentalities" away from authoritarianism and militarism that had begun in 1945 and that one scholar has described as the turning point of twentieth-century European history.[9]

In all this confusion, the Western powers were assuming a commitment in Berlin. As in the case of the airlift, we cannot point to a single conscious decision. That is paradoxical, because of all the American commitments in the Cold War, none seemed more tangible and explicit than the one to west Berlin. The Cuban missile crisis was so stressful for John F. Kennedy and his advisers partly because they feared the Soviets would respond in Berlin. Thomas Risse-Kappen writes that "U.S. decision-makers identified with Berlin as they did with no other place in the world," regarding it as virtually an "American city for which American soldiers were supposed to die."[10] Eight months later, the president obliterated national distinctions when he proclaimed himself a citizen of Berlin. One account calls Berlin America's Cold War "city on a hill," a place of almost mythic importance.[11]

Yet the origins of this commitment remain unclear. When the Western powers assumed responsibility for parts of the city in 1945, they were not committing themselves to defend it against their Soviet ally. Three years later, in the spring of 1948, many Western officials doubted whether such a commitment existed or could be honored if it did. Yet it certainly existed a year later when the blockade ended. The sacrifice of lives and treasure to defeat the blockade transformed the city into a highly visible symbol of Western resolve. Drift, not choice—neither conscious decision nor intuitive judgment—defined a commitment that would last as long as the Cold War itself.

Emergence of what Daniel Yergin has called the concept of "national security" is a widely accepted theme in discussions of the early Cold War. In contrast to previous periods of American history, in which military and diplomatic affairs were kept separate, this new concept fused the two. While Yergin is no doubt correct, one can exaggerate the speed and completeness of this shift. One theme of this book is that considerable divergence remained, well into 1948, between how the military saw national security and how most civilian leaders viewed it. The wartime quarrel about access was largely rooted in the belief that there was a distinction between military and diplomatic affairs and that the other group—the State Department in the eyes of the military; the joint chiefs, according to the diplomats—had crossed the line and exceeded its proper sphere. During the blockade, the October showdown at the NSC pitted two contrasting views of national security and how to protect it. The administration pursued a "strategy of containment" that used American economic power to offset Soviet military power. This was a policy American military leaders could not grasp. The military—and civilians such as Symington and Forrestal, who shared its outlook—viewed the world in purely military terms; that is, the only proper means of securing the administration's ends was military power. No other approach satisfied their definition of military professionalism and the military's proper function. Such men did not regard economic power as an effective means of defense, leading to their complaints about the imbalance of ends and means and about political commitments outrunning the military power to uphold them. That imbalance was nowhere greater than in Berlin, which could not be defended in any military sense.

The difference between military and civilian outlooks in 1948 circumscribed military influence over policy. Although some scholars have suggested that the military's influence increased during the early phase of the crisis, it is hard to find an instance of the president accepting the chiefs' advice.[12] Their clear preference was to withdraw. Truman rejected that course, just as he rejected the diametrically opposite proposal from the military man on the spot, Lucius Clay. Scholars may be unduly influenced by Murphy's assertion that the chiefs restrained an otherwise willing Truman from endorsing Clay's convoy. Murphy's claim is uncorroborated hearsay. Further, one should not put too much emphasis on the July "rejection" of the convoy. Truman and the NSC set aside the convoy idea for the moment, not for all time. It would not be the next step, but it might be the last one. In other words, the president did not rate the chiefs' opposition so highly that he abandoned the convoy option once and for all. Military leaders wanted a definitive statement of what the West would do when the airlift failed, as their planners expected it would. Truman made none. He was more comfortable with the ambiguous world of politics than the generals were, and he was less willing to rush to judgment. We are fortunate he was.

The West's conduct during the crisis exemplifies the adage that it is better to be lucky than good. Incoherent and illogical as Western policy was, it worked. It upheld Western interests in Berlin while avoiding war. The world is lucky that Truman, Bevin, and Attlee did not listen to their all-too-logical advisers pressing them to make ultimate choices. We are all fortunate that these leaders did not make the snap judgments scholars have assumed they made—and that Stalin was not the ruthless burglar the cold warriors assumed he was.

We have been less fortunate in another way: the sources of the West's success have been obscured. The lessons most Westerners derived from the crisis were those critiqued many years ago by Gaddis Smith—the only way to deal with the Soviets was to be tough and unyielding, concessions were signs of weakness, and so forth.[13] That was the message in Clay's memoirs and in Howley's and Truman's. The blockade seemed to confirm earlier lessons: as in Iran two years before, Moscow would retreat when faced with superior strength and resolve; firmness was the only way to stop Soviet expansion, defend democracy, and prevent war. Washington and London rejected Clay's convoy only to accept, in the end, the reasoning behind it. The same premises shaped Cold War scholarship for a generation.

That is only half the story. Restraint is the other. The Western powers did not challenge the blockade with a convoy, they avoided ultimatums, and (thanks to the Europeans) they never backed themselves (or the Russians) into a corner. In delaying American plans to make the B-mark the sole legal tender in Berlin, the British and French avoided a self-inflicted wound that might have proved mortal. Had Clay and other hard-liners had their way and introduced the western mark during the winter, unemployment and the cost of living would have soared at precisely the worst time, adding burdens the airlift might not have been able to meet. The Russians also showed restraint. They could have obstructed the airlift—not just by attacking planes but also by using more subtle and less dangerous means, such as interfering with radio communications or jamming navigational aids. They could have sent troops into the western sectors or triggered riots and sent Markgraf's police into west Berlin to "restore order." They did none of these things.

Restraint rested on the desire to avoid war. Both sides understood that wars are easy to start and hard to stop, and both sides wanted to avoid one. The Second World War was a real and immediate memory that no one wanted to repeat. Truman and Attlee had been in the front lines of the First World War. Stalin had seen war destroy the tsarist regime and nearly topple his own. The French had been stunned by sudden, inexplicable defeat in 1940 and degraded by occupation. If past reality was bad, the image of future war was bleak beyond hope. The Soviets could overrun Europe yet had no way to defeat the United States. The Americans might destroy Soviet cities but could not capture and occupy them. Reality would resemble something out of Orwell's *1984*—perpetual war for perpetual peace. War had to be a last resort—the last step, not the next.

Truman and the men around him chose not to dwell on this side of Western policy in later years, and scholars have neglected it. Doing so overlooks the dilemma Western leaders faced and the solution they devised. Determined to "stay in Berlin, period," they were equally resolved to avoid war. Achieving both goals simultaneously was the fundamental problem confronting them. They solved it through steadfastness and resolve, to be sure, but also through caution and prudence. And they benefited from a large measure of good luck in the form of the airlift's unexpected success and Berliners' willingness to endure. On the other side, Stalin had to balance his goal of derailing the London program with his determination to avoid war. What we see during the blockade as both sides struggled with the resulting dilemmas is the emergence of the tacit rules of what a later generation would call crisis management.[14] These were as much a legacy of the Berlin blockade as were the hard-line lessons perceived by some at the time or in the years that followed, and policy makers would have done well to pay more attention to them.

Perhaps the most important lesson from the blockade for policy makers is how unquestioned assumptions—ideas that seem to be elementary common sense—can inhibit analysis and decisions. The Soviets took for granted that Berlin could not withstand a blockade and that the Western powers would come to terms. The Western powers' most fundamental assumptions—about Berliners' ability to resist, the airlift's ability to deliver, and Stalin's willingness to run risks—were wrong. Stalin's errors resulted in humiliating defeat; the West's mistakes, by unduly narrowing perceived alternatives, might have led to war. Oversimplified through hindsight, the image of the blockade that has come down to us obscures these dangerous possibilities—and how they were averted.

Acknowledgments

Many people—former officials, archivists, friends, teachers, family—helped me over the years as I grappled with this manuscript, and I am deeply grateful to them all. None of them, of course, bears any responsibility for errors of fact or interpretation in these pages; they are my own.

A number of former officials were kind enough to grant me access to private papers and oral history interviews. They all have passed away in the years since, but my debt to them remains. They include Senior Circuit Court Judge George Fahy, Judge Philip C. Jessup, and Generals Curtis E. LeMay and Arthur G. Trudeau. The late Dean Rusk responded patiently to a barrage of questions about George Marshall's idea of turning Berlin over to the United Nations.

A host of archivists also helped me, including Edward Barnes, Richard Boylan, Rebecca Collier, William H. Cunliffe, David Giordano, Milton Gustafson, Michael Hussey, Will Mahoney, Kathy Nicastro, Matthew J. Olsen, Amy Schmidt, and Bill Walsh of the National Archives. I'm especially indebted to Paul Brown and the late Edward J. Reese of the National Archives staff, who took special pains to make sure I saw everything I wanted to see. Ted Jackson of the Leininger Library at Georgetown University; David Keough and Richard J. Sommers of the U.S. Army's Military History Institute; and Hannah Zeidlik and Joana Brignolo of the Center of Military History were invariably kind and helpful. I am also grateful to the staffs at the George Arendts Research Library on the campus of Syracuse University; Columbia Oral History Collection; Dwight D. Eisenhower Library; Library of Congress Manuscript Division; Seeley G. Mudd Manuscript Library, Princeton University; Franklin D. Roosevelt Library; the Western Historical Manuscript Collection at the University of Missouri Library; the University of Rochester's Rush Rees Library; and to Benedict K. Zobrist, Dennis E. Bilger, Philip D. Lagerquist, Irwin Mueller, and Warren Ohrvall of the Harry S. Truman Library.

Dacre P. Cole of the Historical Division of the Canadian Department of External Affairs proved to be a gracious, helpful, and ingenious host. At the Public Archives of Canada (now Library and Archives Canada), Carman V. Carroll, Margaret Mattson, and Ian McClymont of the Manuscript Division and Glenn T. Wright and Denis Boulé of the Public Records Division helped me work through their rich collections. In four trips to Britain's Public Record Office (now the National Archives), I encountered unfailing courtesy and helpfulness. Sebastian Cox and his talented staff at the Ministry of Defence's Air Historical Branch made me feel at home.

In the midst of my wanderings as a civilian working for the Department of Defense, interlibrary loan staffs patiently responded to requests for books and articles, including Randall Moorehead at the University of New Mexico; Susan Cornett, Courtney Wilson, and Isabelle Aldridge at Langley Air Force Base's Bateman Library; Alexandra Keith-Henry at the Offutt Air Force Base library; and Martina Walter and Petra Lutz at the Ramstein Air Base library in Germany. The views expressed in these pages are my own and do not necessarily reflect those of the Department of Defense or any other U.S. government agency.

A grant from the Harry S. Truman Library Institute enabled me to make additional trips to Independence, Missouri, and one from the American Philosophical Society allowed me to make my first trip to Kew. Crown copyright material in the United Kingdom's National Archives is reproduced by permission of the Controller of Her Majesty's Stationery Office. I am also grateful to the editors of the *Historian* and *American History Illustrated* for their kind permission to reprint, in revised form, material that first appeared in their pages. It is also a pleasure to acknowledge permission of the Taylor and Francis Group (http://www.tandfonline.com) to reprint, in revised form, material that originally appeared in the *International History Review*.

On a more personal note, Ken and Karen Harrington aided my research in a special way, as did George and Margaret Cully, Perry and Stephanie Jamieson, Roger Miller and Chrissie Vidas, Joe and Jean Trombly, and Bryan, Silke, and Ted van Sweringen. I am deeply grateful for their friendship and hospitality. Perry took time from his own research at Carlisle Barracks to copy portions of Floyd Parks's diaries. Garry Clifford shared extracts of Walter Lippmann's papers, saving me a research trip. Steve Rearden brought to bear his extensive knowledge of the Truman period on an early version of the manuscript. Ted Wilson and Beverly Jarrett helped me see the forest when I was getting lost in the undergrowth. My parents and stepparents have been constant sources of love and support.

Fellow government historians Bob Beggs, Tom Crouch, Mike Dugre, Ed Longacre, Jerry Martin, Barron Oder, and Tom Snyder listened patiently as I droned on endlessly about my favorite topic, challenged my ideas, and critiqued my prose. George Cully and Bob Duffner deserve special mention for their unflagging encouragement over the years. Ed Gere made history during the airlift and has done more than anyone else to put "ordinary" people back at the heart of its historiography; his friendship and encouragement have been truly inspiring.

Many people at the University Press of Kentucky made this a better book.

Director Steve Wrinn was a constant source of encouragement. Executive assistant Allison Webster was always there with good advice and help, whatever the need. Copy editor Linda Lotz pulled the manuscript together, making improvements on every page; I could not have asked for a better editor. Ila McEntire oversaw editing and production with skill and patience. Richard Gilbreath did an excellent job preparing the maps. I am also deeply grateful to the two anonymous reviewers who critiqued the manuscript for the press. Their praise was generous, their criticisms valid and constructive.

My greatest intellectual debt is to Robert Ferrell, who first supervised this study as a dissertation more years ago than either of us cares to remember and who has patiently read innumerable drafts since then. I have tried to live up to his standards of good sense, clear and unpretentious prose, and empathy for those who went before, and his grasp of essentials.

Last of all, those who are first in my heart. I owe so much to Sylvia, Laura, and Elizabeth, whose love, support, and encouragement never flagged, even though I was often absent, in another decade, in another country.

Abbreviations

AACS	Airways and Air Communications Service
ACA	Allied Control Authority
ACC	Allied Control Council
AEC	Atomic Energy Commission
AFHRA	Air Force Historical Research Agency
AFSWP	Armed Forces Special Weapons Project
AGO	Adjutant General's Office
AMC/HO	Air Mobility Command History Office
BAFO	British Air Forces of Occupation
BASC	Berlin Air Safety Center
BEA	British European Airways
BHL	Bentley Historical Library
BICO	Bipartite Control Office
BTB	British Troops Berlin
CAD	Civil Affairs Division
CALTF	Combined Airlift Task Force
CCAC	Combined Civil Affairs Committee
CCS	Combined Chiefs of Staff
CDU	*Christlich-Demokratische Union* (Christian Democratic Union)
CEEC	Committee for European Economic Cooperation
CFM	Council of Foreign Ministers
CIA	Central Intelligence Agency
CINCEUR	Commander in Chief, European Command
CUOH	Columbia University Oral History Program
DDEL	Dwight D. Eisenhower Presidential Library
DEA	Department of External Affairs Historical Office (Canada)
Dir	director
EAC	European Advisory Commission
ERP	European Recovery Program
EUCOM	European Command
FBIS	Foreign Broadcast Information Service

FDP	*Freie Demokratische Partei* (Free Democratic Party)
FDRL	Franklin D. Roosevelt Presidential Library
FO	Foreign Office
FR	*Foreign Relations of the United States*
GCA	ground-controlled approach
HSTL	Harry S. Truman Presidential Library
IFF	identification friend or foe
JCS	Joint Chiefs of Staff
JIC	Joint Intelligence Committee
JSSC	Joint Strategic Survey Committee
KPD	*Kommunistische Partei Deutschlands* (German Communist Party)
LAC	Library and Archives Canada
LDP	*Liberal-Demokratische Partei Deutschlands* (Liberal Democratic Party)
LOCMD	Library of Congress Manuscript Division
MATS	Military Air Transport Service
MFR	Memo for Record
MG	Manuscript Group
MGLS	Military Government Liaison Section
MHI	U.S. Army Military History Institute
MLC	Military Liaison Committee
MML	Seeley G. Mudd Manuscript Library
MP	military police
NATO	North Atlantic Treaty Organization
NSC	National Security Council
OMGUS	Office of Military Government (United States)
OSD	Office of the Secretary of Defense
P&O	Plans and Operations Division, U.S. Army General Staff
POLAD	political adviser
PORO	Public Opinion Research Office
PPS	Policy Planning Staff
PSF	President's Secretary's File
PSP	pierced-steel plank
RAF	Royal Air Force
RG	Record Group
RIAS	Radio in the American Sector
SAC	Strategic Air Command
SED	*Sozialistische Einheitspartei Deutschlands* (Socialist Unity Party)
SGS	Secretary General Staff
SHAEF	Supreme Headquarters Allied Expeditionary Force

SPD	*Sozialdemocratische Partei Deutschlands* (German Social Democratic Party)
TS	top secret
UKNA	National Archives (United Kingdom)
USAFA	U.S. Air Force Academy
USAFE	U.S. Air Forces in Europe
USAFE/HO	U.S. Air Forces in Europe History Office
USAREUR-MH	U.S. Army Europe Military History Office
USNA	National Archives (United States)
WMD	weapons of mass destruction
WO	War Office
WSC	Working Security Committee

Notes

Introduction

1. Schlesinger, "Origins of the Cold War," 23.
2. Stivers, "Incomplete Blockade," 571.

1. Opportunity

1. Quoted in "Why Ike Didn't Capture Berlin," 72.
2. See Starr, "'Opportunity' and 'Willingness.'"
3. Franklin, "Zonal Boundaries." Other important studies include Mosely, "Occupation of Germany"; Warner, "Our Secret Deal"; Sharp, *Wartime Alliance*; Ziemke, *U.S. Army*; Nelson, *Wartime Origins*; and Slusser, "The Opening Phase."
4. *FR, 1943,* 3:36; WP(43)217, May 25, 1943, CAB 66/37, UKNA; WM(43)86(1), June 16, 1943, CAB 65/34, UKNA; MSC minutes, June 22, 1943, U2887/25/70, 35320, FO 371, UKNA.
5. Sharp, *Wartime Alliance,* 33–39; PHP(43)7b, October 11, 1943, CAB 81/41, UKNA.
6. Sharp, *Wartime Alliance,* 52–53; *FR, 1944,* 1:139–54.
7. Gladwyn, *Memoirs,* 133; Dorn, "Debate over American Occupation Policy," 487; *FR, 1944,* 1:304–5; C. S. A. Ritchie to Wrong, April 3, 1944, pt. 1, AR 405/1/8, and Ritchie memos of conversation, October 2, 1944, pt. 4, AR 405/1/8, RG 25, LAC; WP(43)421, September 27, 1943, CAB 66/41, UKNA; APW(44)17th meeting, September 21, 1944, CAB 87/66, UKNA.
8. PHP(43)7, September 6, 1943, CAB 81/41, UKNA; WM(43)135(3), October 5, 1943, C11296/279/18, 34460, FO 371, UKNA; Nelson, *Wartime Origins,* 122; *FR, Conferences at Malta and Yalta,* 131–32; J. G. Ward quoted in Lewis, *Changing Direction,* 129.
9. For token forces, see WP(43)217, May 25, 1943, CAB 66/37; MSC 22/2, June 8, 1943, WO 193/263; PHP(43)43, November 24, 1943, CAB 81/41; Strang to Eden, June 5, 10, and 13, 1944, PREM 3/137/1, all in UKNA. The idea was an explicit attempt to blend the mixed and zonal approaches and avoid spheres of interest. The British military disliked it; the Soviets and the American military quashed it. Jebb note, June 16, 1943, U2720/25/70, 35320, FO 371, UKNA; APW(44)7th meeting, June 8, 1944, CAB 87/66, UKNA; Hilldring to Wickersham, WAR 50392, June 14, 1944, and JCS 723/3, July 3, 1944, both in "File 144: Zones of Occupation (Germany) I" folder, box 13, Philip Mosely Records, RG 43, USNA; *FR, 1944,* 1:249–50.
10. Cairncross, *Price of War,* 87–88; Mosely, "Occupation of Germany," 593; Rooks to Chief of Staff, Plans Group G, April 10, 1945, "SHAEF/G-5/803/5" folder, box 25, G-5 Numeric File, RG 331, USNA. For the Soviet food demand, see *FR, Conference of Berlin,* 1:632–35.

11. Reynolds, *From World War to Cold War,* 235–48; Yergin, *Shattered Peace,* chap. 2; Folly, *Churchill, Whitehall and the Soviet Union.*

12. Cline, *Washington Command Post,* 104–6, 312–14; Hammond, "Directives," 331–32; Nelson, *Wartime Origins,* 12; Peterson, *American Occupation,* 20.

13. Morgan, *Overture to Overlord,* 104–18; *FR, Conferences at Washington and Quebec,* 1014–15; Franklin, "Zonal Boundaries," 5–7; Elsey to Brown, August 31, 1944, "A/16 Warfare—Germany and German Occupied Countries," folder 1, box 167, Map Room files, FDRL. Despite a comment by Roosevelt about racing the Russians to Berlin, Rankin C's deliberate pace (three stages lasting sixty to seventy-five days), its limited geographic scope (troops would not move beyond the North Sea coast or the Rhine valley until stage three), and planners' repeated emphasis on concerted action with the Russians all belie suggestions that it was a political plan aimed at saving as much of Germany as possible from Bolshevism. Cf. SHAEF SGS Decimal Files 381/5 and 381/7 Rankin, box 82, SGS Decimal File, RG 331, USNA; files 505.10 and 505.11 (and their subfiles), AFHRA; Sharp, *Wartime Alliance,* 32; Kolko, *Politics of War,* 29–30, 317; *FR, Conferences at Washington and Quebec,* 942. For the 1918 analogy's importance in British wartime thinking, see Reynolds, *From World War to Cold War,* 56, 84–91, 111–19.

14. *FR, Conferences at Cairo and Teheran,* 253–61; Matloff, *Strategic Planning for Coalition Warfare,* 341–42.

15. Franklin, "Zonal Boundaries," 11–12, 19–21; for details, see *FR, 1944,* 1:166–341.

16. Stoler, *Allies and Adversaries,* chaps. 1, 2, 4–6; Jones, *Britain, the United States, and the Mediterranean War,* chaps. 1–3.

17. Henry L. Stimson diary, October 28 and 29, 1943 (microfilm edition, reel 8), Sterling Memorial Library, Yale University, New Haven, Connecticut.

18. Coles and Weinberg, *Civil Affairs,* 174–75.

19. Ibid., 114–28, 135–38; Ziemke, *U.S. Army,* 24–25, 34–41; Attlee to Churchill, November 10, 1943, PREM 3/91, UKNA; *FR, Conferences at Cairo and Tehran,* 352–54, 415–22; JCS 126th meeting, November 19, 1943, and 127th meeting, November 22, 1943, both in CCS 334 EAC (12-18-43), box 190, 1942–45 Central Decimal File, RG 218, USNA; Cadogan to Bridges Frozen 191, November 28, 1943, and Bridges to Eden Grand 348, November 30, 1943, both in PREM 3/91, UKNA.

20. *FR, 1943,* 1:57.

21. *FR, Conferences at Cairo and Tehran,* 352–54, 415–20; Cadogan to Bridges Frozen 191, November 28, 1943, and Bridges to Eden Grand 348, November 30, 1943, both in PREM 3/91, UKNA; Halifax to Eden 5138, November 13, 1943, Eden to Halifax 7917, November 16, 1943, Halifax to Eden Citizen 21, January 19, 1944, and Citizen 32, January 22, 1944, all in CAB 122/454, UKNA.

22. *FR, Conferences at Cairo and Tehran,* 260.

23. Franklin, "Zonal Boundaries," 17.

24. Barker to Hilldring, December 18, 1943, CAD 334 EAC (12-18-43)(1), sec. 1, box 105, Classified Correspondence, RG 165, USNA.

25. Sexton memo, November 3, 1943, sec. 1, CCS 381 (8-20-43), box 307, 1942–45 Central Decimal File, RG 218, USNA; Leahy to Roosevelt, November 18, 1943, "MR 371—Germany, Zones of Occupation" folder, box 35, Map Room files, FDRL. Cf. Franklin, "Zonal Boundaries," 9, and Lloyd to Notter, October 15, 1943, "Negotiations with British (Germany)" folder, box 19, Notter files, RG 59, USNA.

26. *FR, 1944,* 1:111; Allen quoted in WSC minutes, December 21, 1943, Shears quoted

in WSC minutes, December 27, 1943, both in "Working Security Minutes 1–25" folder, box 148, Notter files, RG 59, USNA; Hilldring to Secretary JCS, January 29, 1944, CCS 334 (12-18-43), box 190, 1942–45 Central Decimal File, RG 218, USNA; Hammond, "Directives," 320, 333. See also Dunn to Hull, December 22, 1943, "Security Working Committee Miscellaneous" folder, and Leahy to Hull, January 13, 1944, "Working Security Documents 1–45" folder, both in box 148, Notter files, RG 59, USNA.

27. Mosely, "Occupation of Germany," 586–88; Ryan, *Last Battle,* 152.

28. *FR, 1944,* 1:173, 179–80; Roosevelt to Stettinius, February 21, 1944, "A/16 Warfare—Germany and German-Occupied Countries" folder 1, box 167, Map Room files, FDRL.

29. Working Security Minutes, February 24, 26, and 29, 1944, "Working Security Minutes 26—" folder, box 148, Notter files, RG 59, USNA; Hilldring to Dunn, February 25, 1944, and Hilldring to Secretariat, February 25, 1944, both in CAD 334 EAC (12-18-43)(1), sec. 1, box 105, Classified Correspondence, RG 165, USNA.

30. *FR, 1944,* 1:195–96, 208–9; Mosely, "Occupation of Germany," 591–92; Kennan, *Memoirs,* 168–70.

31. Kennan, *Memoirs,* 171; Ryan, *Last Battle,* 157.

32. WS-134 (April 13, 1944), WS-134a (April 15, 1944), and WS-134b (April 17, 1944), "Working Security Documents 121–154" folder, box 149, Notter files, RG 59, USNA.

33. MFR attached to Hilldring to Dunn, April 10, 1944, CAD 334 EAC (12-18-43)(1), sec. 1, box 105, and MFR attached to Hilldring to Marshall, April 17, 1944, sec. 5, CAD 014 Germany (7-10-42)(1), box 21, both in Classified Correspondence, RG 165, USNA; Marshall to Roosevelt, April 28, 1944, "MR 371—Germany, Zones of Occupation" folder, box 35, Map Room files, FDRL. For the cable as sent, see *FR, 1944,* 1:211. Mosely later wrote that Winant suggested a similar idea during a visit to Washington in May 1944, but the CAD vetoed it. Army partisans inverted the story. Both claims may be distorted recollections of these mid-April WSC drafting sessions. Mosely, "Occupation of Germany," 592–93; Warner, "Our Secret Deal," 68.

34. Laufer, "Die UdSSR und die Zoneneinteilung Deutschlands," 325–26.

35. *FR, 1944,* 1:139–54; Sharp, *Wartime Alliance,* 112–19; Ward minute, May 5, 1945, U3598/20/70, 50762, FO 371, UKNA.

36. Strang, *Home and Abroad,* 215; Nelson, *Wartime Origins,* 122; *FR, Conferences at Malta and Yalta,* 131–32.

37. Hopkins quoted in Weil, *Pretty Good Club,* 134. David Reynolds offers a good introduction to the sources of Anglo-American optimism in *From World War to Cold War,* 235–48.

38. Nelson, *Wartime Origins,* 23, 123, 152; Strang, *Home and Abroad,* 204; Winant to Hopkins, December 19, 1944, "Winant" folder, box 257, Hopkins papers, FDRL.

39. CCS 381 (8-20-43), secs. 8–11, boxes 308–9, 1942–45 Central Decimal File, RG 218, USNA. Many writers have pointed to the incongruity of this effort and the contrasting indifference about Berlin. The incongruity rests on hindsight. To the army in 1944 and 1945, routes *out* of Europe mattered more than routes *in.* Its focus was on redeploying divisions to the Pacific, not stationing them in the former German capital. Ziemke, *U.S. Army,* 126.

40. Strang to Eden, November 7, 1944, PREM 3/171/1, UKNA; *FR, 1944,* 1:384.

41. Warner, "Our Secret Deal," 68; Hilldring to McCloy, December 9, 1944, sec. 10, CAD 014 Germany (7-10-42)(1), box 23, Classified Correspondence, RG 165, USNA.

42. Murphy described Riddleberger's suggestion in his memoirs, *Diplomat among Warriors,* 231. From 1948 onward, he blamed Winant for the access problem, and others with no

firsthand knowledge accepted his view. Winant was an easy target, having taken his life the year before. *FR, 1948,* 2:919; Bess, "Will We Be Pushed Out of Berlin?" 92; Clay, *Decision,* 15; Warner, "Our Secret Deal."

43. The EAC amended the protocol on November 14 to reflect FDR's acceptance of the southwestern zone. The British approved it December 5, 1944; the Americans, February 2, 1945; and the Soviets, February 6, 1945. It was amended once more on July 26, 1945, to include the French. U.S. Department of State, *Documents on Germany,* 1–6, 44–48.

44. Sharp, *Wartime Alliance,* 109–10.

45. *FR, 1945,* 3:188–89; CCS 786/1, March 9, 1945, sec. 10, CCS 381 (8-20-43), box 309, 1942–45 Central Decimal File, RG 218, USNA; JCS 1242, February 6, 1945, and JCS 1242/1, February 22, 1945, sec. 11, ibid. For Leahy's stance, see JCS 189th meeting, February 7, 1945, sec. 11, ibid., and MFR attached to memorandum for the president, February 27, 1945, sec. 10, ibid.

46. Memo, Planning Committee to Joint U.S. Advisers, March 21, 1945, with attached Draft Agreement, March 21, 1945, file 519.9744-21, AFHRA; minutes of 61st meeting of the Joint U.S. Advisers, EAC, March 23, 1945, folder 3, box 4, Records Retained by EAC Military Adviser, RG 260, USNA.

47. Mosely, "Occupation of Germany," 603.

48. Nelson, *Wartime Origins,* 125–26. Nelson's identification of the American officer as "Colonel Koontz" rests on a 1969 interview with Mosely. Cf. Nelson, *Wartime Origins,* 126, and "Planning for the Occupation of Germany" (Frankfurt-am-Main, 1947), 105, 178, USAREUR-MH.

49. Ambrose, *Eisenhower and Berlin,* 10.

50. Sharp, *Wartime Alliance,* 37, 147–49; van Cutsem to Kennedy, May 6, 1943, WO 193/263, UKNA; Frederick W. Ganzert, "International Aspects of the Occupation" (Frankfurt-am-Main, 1947), 111–12, USAREUR-MH.

51. *FR, 1945,* 3:326–32; Smith, *Clay Papers,* 1:21–22.

52. *FR, 1945,* 3:133–37.

53. Clay to Parks, June 16, 1945, "ETO 136" binder, Floyd L. Parks papers, MHI; Clay to Parks, June 18, 1945, "SHAEF Post-Hostilities" folder, box 2, G-3 Operational Plans, RG 331, USNA; ETOUSA FWD to Deane S-92155, June 21, 1945, "SHAEF Message File, Soviet Forces" folder, box 1, SHAEF G-3 TS Messages, RG 331, USNA. One can see Mosely's paternity by comparing planning group papers prepared before and after his discussion with Kutz. Cf., for example, file 091.711-3 GPS, box 82, and Parks to Barker, June 2, 1945, "SHAEF/18015/2/GCT 322.01-1/GPS Liaison with the Russians" folder, box 84, both in Post Hostilities Planning Section Decimal File, RG 331, USNA.

54. Harrington, "'As Far as His Army Can Reach.'"

55. Ibid.; Howley, *Berlin Command,* 26–32; Parks diary, June 22–23, 1945, MHI.

56. *FR, Conference of Berlin,* 1:131; SHAEF Main to Parks S-93902, June 28, 1945, SHAEF/G-5/803, jacket 4, box 22, G-5 Numeric File, RG 331, USNA; Parks diary, June 27–28, 1945, MHI.

57. This account of the meeting draws on draft meeting minutes, n.d., "SHAEF Forces: Occupation of Germany, 15 Jan 45–29 Jun 45" folder, box 45, G-3 Subject File, RG 331, USNA; *FR, 1945,* 3:353–61; *FR, Conference of Berlin,* 1:135–37; Clay, *Decision,* 24–27; Clay interview, February 11, 1971, CUOH; Ziemke, *U.S. Army,* 300–301; Murphy, *Diplomat among Warriors,* 262.

58. Clay interview, February 11, 1971, CUOH; Clay, *Decision,* 26.

59. Clay, *Decision,* 26. For critics, see Strang, *Home and Abroad,* 217; and Tusa and Tusa, *Berlin Airlift,* 31–33.

60. Quoted in Butcher, *My Three Years,* 855; Eisenhower, *Crusade in Europe,* 458.

61. Quoted in Backer, *Winds of History,* 16.

62. Smith, *Clay,* 275.

63. Ganzert, "International Aspects," 144–46; Thomas Donovan et al., "Transportation" (Frankfurt-am-Main, 1947), 63, 80–81, both in USAREUR-MH; CONL/P(45)27, September 7, 1945, reprinted in U.S. Department of State, *Documents on Germany,* 65–67.

64. ACC Dir 43 (October 29, 1946), in *Official Gazette of the Control Council for Germany,* no. 11 (October 31, 1946): 215–19; Adams to Riddleberger, August 12, 1948, "Agreements with the Soviets . . ." folder, box 1, Miscellaneous Classified Records, Records of U.S. Political Adviser (hereafter cited as POLAD files), RG 84, USNA; Robertson to Foreign Office 513, April 2, 1948, FO 1049/1507, UKNA; Bathurst, "Legal Aspects," 295; U.S. Department of State, *Documents on Germany,* 83–87; Sokolovsky to Clay, January 16, 1946, "Soviet Russia 1945–1946" folder, box 19, Records Retained for the Military Governor, RG 260, USNA. For the British rail detachment, see FO 1058/9, UKNA.

65. See enclosures with Adams to Riddleberger, August 12, 1948, "Agreements with the Soviets . . ." folder, box 1, Miscellaneous Classified Records, POLAD files, RG 84, USNA; Edden (?) minute, May 22, 1946, W5569/2188/13, 54690, FO 371, UKNA; study, U.S. Army Europe, "The U.S. Army in Berlin, 1945–1961" (Heidelberg, 1962), 109–11, USAREUR-MH; Bathurst, "Legal Aspects," 295.

66. Zhukov to Montgomery, September 11, 1945, and Malinin to Galloway, October 18, 1945, both in AIR 55/257, UKNA; DAIR/P(45)10, September 22, 1945, AIR 55/265, UKNA.

67. Minutes, Chief of Staff Executive Meeting, September 15, 1945; draft, Montgomery to Zhukov, n.d., attached to Douglas to Montgomery, September 20, 1945; DCAD memo, October 1, 1945; and DCAD to Douglas, October 3, 1945, all in AIR 55/257, UKNA; AGWAR to USSTAF WX-44957, August 6, 1945, "TS 811.1" folder, box 4, TS Correspondence, POLAD files, RG 84, USNA.

68. DAIR/M(45)13, November 12, 1945, "DAIR/M(45)1-18" folder, box 435, Air Directorate Records, RG 260, USNA; *FR, 1945,* 3:856, 1576–83, 1586–90; U.S. Department of State, *Bulletin* 45, no. 1159 (September 11, 1961): 432–33, and 45, no. 1162 (September 25, 1961): 511–14. See also Murphy to Marshall 2285, September 9, 1948, "Berlin Cables to SecState, Aug–Sep 1948 TS" folder, box 1, TS Cables, POLAD files, RG 84, USNA.

69. Air HQ (Ops), BAFO to Air Ministry, AO 145, December 19, 1945, and BAFO to Air Ministry AF 17, April 18, 1946, both in AIR 55/257, UKNA. For flight rules, see *FR, 1945,* 3:1596–606, and U.S. Department of State, *Documents on Germany,* 99–109. For creation of the Berlin Air Safety Center, see *FR, 1945,* 3:1585–95.

70. See, for example, Shlaim, "Partition of Germany," 134; Tusa and Tusa, *Berlin Airlift,* 48; George and Smoke, *Deterrence,* 115n8; Buffet, *Mourir,* 34, 107, 169; Larson, "Origins of Commitment," 197. Arnold Offner compounds this error by claiming not only that "ground access had never been guaranteed in writing" but also that "no formal accord" existed authorizing a U.S. presence in Berlin. Access and presence are different things. The EAC protocols authorized a Western presence when they created the Western sectors. Offner, *Another Such Victory,* 258, 271.

71. Minutes of special directors' meeting, January 22, 1946, "Staff Meetings, U.S. Military Government in Germany, May 12, 1945–January 22, 1946" folder, box 31, Charles Fahy papers, FDRL; U.S. Department of State, *Documents on Germany,* 113–14.

72. File "4001—Berlin Airfields," box 20, US ACA Element Records, RG 260, USNA; *FR, 1945,* 3:830–31; Hendry and Wood, *Legal Status,* 92–93; Pernot, "Le pont aérien," 59.

73. Note, "Revision of [July 14, 1945] Tripartite Agreement . . . ," n.d., FO 1032/2009, UKNA; *FR, Conference of Berlin,* 2:493, 502; Butler and Pelly, *Documents,* 1027–28; Gilligan to Hunter, February 1, 1946, C1726/173/18, 55631, FO 371, UKNA; Harrison to Green, August 8, 1945, C4541/4184/18, and Bevin to Lawson, September 5, 1945, C5345/4184/18, both in 46960, FO 371, UKNA.

74. BERCOM to Troopers Argus 47, September 10, 1945, C5665/4184/18, and BERCOM to War Office Argus 72, September 22, 1945, C6142/4184/18, both in 46960, FO 371, UKNA; *FR, 1945,* 3:836, 872–73.

75. Pelly and Yasamee, *Documents,* 164–66; Selby (?) minute, October 11, 1945, on CORC/P(45)68, September 19, 1945, C6419/4184/18, and Molotov to Bevin, October 1, 1945, C6700/4184/18, both in 46960, FO 371, UKNA.

76. Williamson to Spens, September 10, 1945, FO 1032/2009; Working Party report, November 27, 1945, FO 1032/2008; Sec/B(45)263, December 13, 1945, FO 1032/1997, all in UKNA.

77. DAIR/P(45)68, December 3, 1945, W10648/98/802, 54556, FO 371, UKNA; *FR, 1946,* 5:755–56, 760–65.

78. CORC/P(46)361, Secretariat note, November 5, 1946, W10958/98/802; CCG to COGA Argus 699, November 9, 1946, W10958/98/802; CONL/P(46)76, November 18, 1946, W11422/98/802; and CONL/M(46)32, November 20, 1946, W11403/98/802, all in 54556, FO 371, UKNA; *FR, 1946,* 5:765–66; Great Britain, Foreign Office, *Germany No. 2 (1961),* 481.

79. Sokolovsky to Clay, December 19, 1945, and August 22, 1946; Clay to Sokolovsky, July 28, 1946, and July 24, 1947, all in "Soviet Russia, 1945–1946" folder, box 19, Records Retained for the Military Governor, RG 260, USNA. For the Bavarian meat trains, see OMGUS, "Summary of Soviet Violations . . . ," June 3, 1948, 740.00119 Control (Germany)/6-348, Central Decimal Files (entry 205H), RG 59, USNA, and Babcock to Howley, May 28, 1948, "Weekly Reports OMGBS 1948" folder, box 7, Director's files, Berlin Sector Records, RG 260, USNA.

80. Ganzert, "International Aspects," 146, 151; Donovan et al., "Transportation," 130–31; Maginnis, *Military Government Journal,* 329–30; Clay to Sokolovsky, April 16, 1946, "Soviet Russia 1945–1946" folder, box 19, Records Retained for the Military Governor, RG 260, USNA. One should not assume that all bandits were Soviet soldiers and that Clay was being diplomatic. Refugees, deserters from half a dozen armies, and U.S. soldiers added to the crime wave in central Europe in 1945 and 1946. See Naimark, *Russians in Germany,* 145, 152, 357, and chap. 2; Ziemke, *U.S. Army,* 421–22, 437–38; Gimbel, *German Community,* 69–70, 83; Bessel, *Germany 1945,* 116, 143–59.

81. *FR, 1946,* 5:704; Smith, *Clay Papers,* 2:766–67; Clay, *Decision,* 115; Millis and Duffield, *Forrestal Diaries,* 182. OMGUS tried to keep its word, although it acknowledged that Clay's ban was being evaded and Germans were traveling illegally. Howley to OMGUS, July 31, 1947; OMGUS to Howley, October 20, 1947; Gailey to Litchfield, September 5, 1947; and Carrier Sheet, July 23, 1947, all in "AG 200.4 Travel (German)" folder, box 381, OMGUS AGO General Correspondence, RG 260, USNA. See also Babcock to Howley, February 5, 1948, "Staff Studies (1 Jan–30 June) 1948" folder, box 8, Director's files, Berlin Sector Records, RG 260, USNA.

82. Internal Affairs and Communication Instruction 106, July 26, 1946, C9212/173/18, 55631, FO 371, UKNA; Robertson to Kurochkin, February 27, 1947, C4122/1262/18, and

Kurochkin to Robertson, March 4, 1947, C4280/1262/18, both in 64485, FO 371, UKNA; Hynd statement, n.d., C13657/173/18, 55633, FO 371, UKNA; answer to parliamentary question, March 12, 1947, C4299/114/18, 64306, FO 371, UKNA; BERCOMB to CONFOLK 285, March 7, 1947, and Brownjohn to Dratvin, March 21, 1947, both in FO 1049/805, UKNA.

2. Willingness

1. Harbutt, *Yalta*; Trachtenberg, *Constructed Peace,* vii–viii, 15–55.

2. Stalin quoted in Miner, *Between Churchill and Stalin,* 190.

3. Stalin quoted in Trachtenberg, *Constructed Peace,* 10. For the idea of "open spheres," see Mark, "American Policy."

4. Stalin quoted in Narinskii, "Soviet Union," 58. Geoffrey Roberts's gloss does not persuade, especially in light of a similar comment from September 1939. Cf. Roberts, *Stalin's Wars,* 36, 236–37.

5. Stalin quoted in Zubok, "Stalin's Plans," 300; Holloway, *Stalin and the Bomb,* 150–61; Taubman, *Stalin's American Policy,* 5–41. See also Naimark, "Stalin and Europe," 48, 53–54.

6. Smith, *Dean Acheson,* 423–24.

7. Chamberlain quoted in Churchill, *Second World War,* 1:315.

8. Naimark, *Russians in Germany,* 168; Overy, *Russia's War,* 288; Reynolds et al., "Legacies," 429; Laqueur, *Europe since Hitler,* 14.

9. *FR, 1945,* 3:824–29; *FR, 1947,* 2:831–46; Rogers, *Politics after Hitler,* chap. 1.

10. Eisenhower to Marshall, October 26, 1945, "Marshall #3" folder, box 73, Eisenhower prepresidential papers, DDEL.

11. Smith, *Clay*; Backer, *Winds of History,* 46–56, Bowie quoted at 56; Ratchford and Ross, *Berlin Reparations Assignment,* 59; Peterson, *American Occupation,* 57–58.

12. Williamson, *Most Diplomatic General*; Hamilton, *Master of the Battlefield,* 73; Playfair et al., *Mediterranean and Middle East,* 5:854.

13. *New York Times,* May 11, 1968; *London Times,* May 11, 1968; Tusa and Tusa, *Berlin Airlift,* 61–62; Glantz, *Colossus Reborn,* 498; Zubok, *Failed Empire,* 65; Pope, *Soldiers and Politicians,* 297; Clay, *Decision,* 107.

14. *New York Times,* September 4, 1970; *London Times,* September 4, 1970.

15. *FR, Conference of Berlin,* 2:1478–98, reprints the protocol.

16. Lynch, "Resolving the Paradox"; Young, *France, the Cold War and the Western Alliance,* 7–71, quote at 69; Hitchcock, *France Restored,* chaps. 1, 2. For French obstruction in Germany, see Gimbel's *American Occupation, Origins of the Marshall Plan,* "American Reparations Stop," and "Implementation of the Potsdam Agreement," as well as McAllister, *No Exit,* 98–107.

17. Naimark, *Russians in Germany,* 465; Spilker, *East German Leadership,* 5, 9, 56, 69–72, 88, 246; Wettig, *Stalin and the Cold War,* 41–42, 89–92.

18. *FR, 1945,* 3:867.

19. Ibid., 1295; *FR, 1946,* 5:546.

20. *FR, 1945,* 3:1295; *FR, 1946,* 5:546; Farquharson, *Western Allies,* 32; Mai, "United States," 53; Woodhouse, *British Policy towards France,* 48.

21. Gimbel, *American Occupation,* 131–40, 296n12; Spilker, *East German Leadership,* 120–24; Narinskii, "Soviet Union," 61; Overesch, "Senior West German Politicians," 119–23; Steege, *Black Market,* 127–30; Cairncross, *Price of War,* 149–50, 152; Grieder, *East German Leadership,* 15.

22. Naimark, *Russians in Germany,* 142–45, 150–54; *FR, 1945,* 3:1080.

23. Sandford, *From Hitler to Ulbricht,* 38, 189, 197–98.

24. Ibid., 223–24; Naimark, *Russians in Germany,* 467.

25. Naimark, *Russians in Germany,* 272–84, 320, 386–88; Annan, *Changing Enemies,* 188–201; Bruce, *Resistance,* 34–39; Spilker, *East German Leadership,* 38–59.

26. Davison, *Berlin Blockade,* 39–44; Howley, *Berlin Command,* 104–6.

27. Davison, *Berlin Blockade,* 42–43; Military Governor, U.S. Zone, "Special Report: KPD-SPD Merger," May 15, 1946, "KPD-SPD Merger in Berlin and Soviet Zone" folder, box 12, Panuch papers, HSTL.

28. Clare, *Before the Wall,* 121–22.

29. If Clay reached common ground with the Soviets, he horrified Robertson, who protested that the Allies were "turning Germany into a wilderness." *FR, 1946,* 5:484–88. For interpretations that stress the early U.S. commitment to German recovery, see Kuklick, *American Policy*; Paterson, *Soviet-American Confrontation,* chap. 11; and Eisenberg, *Drawing the Line.* For the level-of-industry discussions, see Ratchford and Ross, *Berlin Reparations Assignment*; Cairncross, *Price of War*; and Kramer, "British Dismantling Politics," 131–35.

30. CORC/M(46)22, April 26, 1946, and CORC/M(46)23, May 4, 1946, box 8, and CORC/P(46)139 (Revise), April 25, 1946, box 9, ACC Records, RG 43, USNA; *FR, 1946,* 5:547–48. We have assumed that Clay acted on his own, but, as Fraser Harbutt pointed out long ago, Byrnes authorized the halt. Harbutt, *Iron Curtain,* 270. Even so, the two men's purposes differed. Clay's targets were France and the Soviet Union; Byrnes's, only the latter.

31. *FR, Conference of Berlin,* 2:142, 280–81, 385, 390; Gottlieb, *German Peace Settlement,* 127–28. For Byrnes's assurance, see Gimbel, *Origins of the Marshall Plan,* 82–83.

32. *FR, 1946,* 2:866–68, 896–98; Byrnes to Truman and Acheson, Delsec 687, July 12, 1946, "Council of Foreign Ministers Meetings, June–July 1946" folder, box 9, Naval Aide files, HSTL; Deighton, *Impossible Peace,* 93–97.

33. Byrnes to Truman and Acheson, Delsec 699, July 12, 1946, "Council of Foreign Ministers Meetings, June–July 1946" folder, box 9, Naval Aide files, HSTL; Deighton, *Impossible Peace,* 97–107; Gimbel, *Origins of the Marshall Plan,* 104–11; Cairncross, *Price of War,* 160–61.

34. CP(46)186, May 3, 1946, CAB 129/9, UKNA. Deighton argues that Bevin's paper was a turning point, in that it abandoned cooperation with the Soviets in favor of an independent two- or three-power program in the western zones. Yet policy did not turn. The explicit conclusion of Bevin's paper was to *reject* such a "Western strategy." Deighton, *Impossible Peace,* 74–80, 225.

35. Quoted in Bullock, *Bevin,* 3:271.

36. Gimbel, *Origins of the Marshall Plan,* 110; Smith, *Clay Papers,* 1:217; Clay quoted in Smith, *Clay,* 406, and in Kolko and Kolko, *Limits of Power,* 168.

37. R. M. A. Hankey quoted in Rothwell, *Britain and the Cold War,* 332.

38. Special Report, U.S. Military Governor, "Statistics of Elections in Germany," March 15, 1947, folder 62-10, box 62, Pollock papers, BHL. For the *Land* elections, see Steege, *Black Market,* 74–94, and Creuzberger, "Soviet Military Administration," 92–96.

39. *FR, 1946,* 5:734–36; Davison, *Berlin Blockade,* 51–53. The statistic is an SPD claim from November 1947; Steege, *Black Market,* 135n101.

40. *FR, 1946,* 5:753–54; Tusa and Tusa, *Berlin Airlift,* 74–75; Steege, "More than an Airlift," 72–80.

41. Steege, "More than an Airlift," 80–84.

42. Political—10 June 1947 entry, "Programme of Russian Obstruction . . . ," August 16, 1948, C6740/1/18, 70479, FO 371, UKNA.

43. http://www.berlin.de/rbmskzl/rbm/galerie/ernst_reuter.html, accessed May 7, 2005; report, June 25, 1947, "Memos and Reports Col Glaser" folder, box 71, Records of the Civil Administration and Political Affairs Branch, RG 260, USNA.

44. File "8210—Election of Oberbuergermeister," box 34, Records of U.S. ACA Element, RG 260, USNA.

45. Hogan, "Search for a 'Creative Peace,'" 268–69.

46. W. Averell Harriman quoted in Maier, "Alliance and Autonomy," 286. For FDR, see Gaddis, *United States,* 121; for the French, see Hitchcock, *France Restored,* 41–49, 56–57.

47. Molotov, *Problems,* 462, 466; *FR, 1947,* 3:304; Parrish and Narinsky, "New Evidence," 23–24.

48. Parrish and Narinsky, "New Evidence," 37.

49. Clay's financial adviser, Jack Bennett, mistakenly claimed that the Soviets "dramatically walked out" of the meeting. Cf. Bennett, "German Currency Reform," 45, and Robertson to Pearson, January 17, 1948, file AR 430/16, vol. 2118, RG 25, LAC.

50. *FR, 1947,* 2:822–29; Smith, *Clay Papers,* 1:513–18, 501–2 (the latter misdated by Smith as November 20).

51. C16394/53/18, 64250, FO 371, UKNA; *FR, 1947,* 2:815–17; *FR, 1948,* 3:14–16.

52. *FR, 1948,* 3:21–23.

53. Kaplan, *Short March.*

54. Roberts memo, February 26, 1948, FO 800/502/SU/48/2B, UKNA; Harris, "March Crisis 1948, Act I," 4, Records of the CIA, RG 263, USNA.

55. Robertson to Bevin 336, March 3, 1948, C1727/3/18, 70489, FO 371, UKNA; EUCOM Intelligence Summary 30, March 29, 1948, box 767, Periodic Intelligence Summaries, RG 549, USNA; Wall, "France and the North Atlantic Alliance," 50.

56. Kennan, *Memoirs,* 401; Smith, *Clay Papers,* 2:568–69; Smith, "View from USFET," 75–76; Smith, "Clay and the Russians," 34; Smith, *Clay,* 467. For Walsh's role, see Harris, "March Crisis 1948, Act I," 6–7.

57. See, for example, Yergin, *Shattered Peace,* 351; Howard, "Governor-General"; Shlaim, *United States,* 106–8; Eisenberg, *Drawing the Line,* 387–88, and James Eayrs's essay "The Clay Cable: Analysis or Bureaucratic Ploy?" reprinted in a variety of Canadian newspapers under various titles, folder 28, box 8, Smith papers, Leininger Library, Georgetown University, Washington, D.C. Fred Kofsky made Clay's cable the "centerpiece" of the conspiracy he claimed to have uncovered in his *Truman and the War Scare,* 8, 92–114, 303–4.

58. These quotations are from Interview 22, March 9, 1971, 719–22, CUOH, and folder 91, box 6, Smith papers, Georgetown University. I read all thirty-one numbered interviews at Columbia, plus the Clay interviews and Smith-Clay correspondence at Georgetown. Clay's papers at the George C. Marshall Research Library, Lexington, Virginia, contain no material supporting Smith's claims. Kain to author, September 23, 2011.

59. Smith to author, June 11, 2010. Clay may have made the statements Smith attributes to him during three additional interviews (December 26, 1971, June 6, 1973, and June 2, 1974) listed in his bibliography (Smith, *Clay,* 782), but since Smith has not shared transcripts or tapes of these interviews with researchers, there is no way to know.

60. Millis and Duffield, *Forrestal Diaries,* 387.

61. *FR, 1948,* 3:46–48.

62. *New York Times,* December 20, 1947, 3; ibid., January 12, 1948, 1, 6.

63. Willis, *French in Germany,* 51. For the troubled path to tripartite convergence, see Gimbel, *Origins of the Marshall Plan,* 220–54; Hitchcock, *France Restored,* 78–98; Bungert, "New Perspective"; and Creswell and Trachtenberg, "France and the German Question."

64. *FR, 1948,* 2:75–145; Gimbel, *American Occupation,* 198–201; Eisenberg, *Drawing the Line,* 366–72.

65. "Programme of Russian Obstruction . . . ," August 16, 1948, C6740/1/18, 70479, FO 371, UKNA; "Chronology of Berlin Situation," August 1948, box 17, Howley papers, MHI.

66. Gottlieb, *German Peace Settlement,* 250n; Robertson to Bevin 49, January 10, 1948, FO 1049/1352, UKNA.

67. "Programme of Russian Obstruction . . . ," August 16, 1948, C6740/1/18, 70479, FO 371, UKNA; Hamburg to Washington 89, February 6, 1948, 740.00119 Control (Germany)/2-648, RG 59, USNA; Tusa and Tusa, *Berlin Airlift,* 94–95.

68. Jones memo, January 22, 1948, "AGO 360.1 Flying Regulations and Rules, 1948" folder, box 459, OMGUS AGO General Correspondence, RG 260; Berlin dispatch 319, March 8, 1948, 740.00119 Control (Germany)/3-848, RG 59; DOCS/AIR/A(48)2, March 29, 1948, and DOCS/P(48)5, March 11, 1948, both in "Corridors, Rules of Flight, and Berlin Air Safety Center: Annex #1 to 360.42 Germany (10 Nov 48)" folder, box 806, TS Decimal File, RG 341, all in USNA.

69. Narinskii, "Soviet Union," 62–64; Laufer, "Die UdSSR und die Ursprünge," 574–75.

70. Quoted in Narinskii, "Soviet Union," 65, and Laufer and Kynin, *Die UdSSR und die deutsche Frage,* 3:546.

71. *FR, 1948,* 2:66–68.

72. Naimark, *Russians in Germany,* 370–74.

73. *FR, 1948,* 2:338–39, 346–47; USSR Ministry of Foreign Affairs, *Soviet Union and the Berlin Question,* 18.

74. Robertson to Bevin 434, March 20, 1948, C2211/71/18, 70583, FO 371, UKNA; *FR, 1948,* 2:883–84; USSR Ministry of Foreign Affairs, *Soviet Union and the Berlin Question,* 18–20; Clay, *Decision,* 355–57.

75. Harris, "March Crisis 1948, Act II," 12–14, RG 263, USNA; Berlin airgram A-247, March 29, 1948, 862.00B/3-2948, RG 59, USNA; Robertson to Bevin 494, March 31, 1948, C2473/3/18, 70490, FO 371, UKNA.

76. Talbott, *Khrushchev Remembers,* 191.

3. "The Danger Point Is Berlin"

1. George and Smoke, *Deterrence,* chap. 5.

2. Smith, *Clay Papers,* 2:600–601.

3. Robertson to Bevin 494, March 31, 1948, C2473/3/18, 70490, FO 371, UKNA.

4. Clay to Chamberlin BIW 7, March 31, 1948, "Russia (3)" folder, box 15, Clifford papers, HSTL.

5. Hillenkoetter to Truman, December 22, 1947, "Council of Foreign Ministers, November–December 1947" folder, box 13, Naval Aide files, HSTL.

6. *FR, 1947,* 2:905–7.

7. Wedemeyer to Royall, January 2, 1948, "Germany (1949–50)" folder, box 74, General Correspondence, RG 335, USNA.

8. Royall to Forrestal, January 19, 1948, "Germany (1949–50)" folder, box 74, General Correspondence, RG 335, USNA.

9. Blum to Ohly, n.d., and Blum to Ohly, January 13, 1948, both in folder 1, CD 6-2-9, box 27, OSD Numerical File, RG 330, USNA; Ohly to Greasley, January 22, 1948, case 88/12, "P&O 381 TS (Section V-A)(part 1) . . ." folder, box 102, P&O TS Decimal File, RG 319, USNA.

10. *FR, 1947,* 2:904–5, 908, 1139.

11. CP(48)5, January 5, 1948, CAB 129/23, UKNA.

12. Loftus, "American Response," 47; Royall to Forrestal, January 19, 1948, and Ohly to Forrestal, January 21, 1948, both in folder 1, file CD 6-2-9, box 27, OSD Numerical File, RG 330, USNA.

13. Stone to Pearson, January 22, 1948, folder 1, file W-22-5-G, vol. 119, ser. 18, RG 2, LAC; Pope diary, February 24, 1948, vol. 2, Pope papers, LAC; *New York Times,* January 13, 1948, 10; ibid., January 18, 1948, E7.

14. Staff Study 4052 (revised), May 25, 1948, "P&O 370.05 TS" envelope, box 84, P&O TS Decimal File, RG 319, USNA; *New York Times,* December 17, 1947, 10; ibid., December 21, 1947, E5; ibid., January 13, 1948, 10, E7; ibid., January 18, 1948, E7; Loftus, "American Response," 49.

15. Smith, *Clay Papers,* 2:599–602.

16. Harris, "March Crisis 1948, Act II," 12–25, RG 263, USNA.

17. Elsey interview, July 7, 1970, HSTL.

18. Smith, *Clay Papers,* 2:602–4.

19. Millis and Duffield, *Forrestal Diaries,* 407–8.

20. Mayo to Wedemeyer, March 31, 1948, case 88/18, and draft message, Norstad to LeMay, n.d., case 88/17, both in sec. 1, P&O 381 TS, box 102, P&O TS Decimal File, RG 319, USNA; Nichols, *Road to Trinity,* 260.

21. Saltzman oral history interview, June 28, 1974, HSTL; Elsey interview, July 7, 1970, HSTL; Peterson, *American Occupation,* 23; Eisenberg, *Drawing the Line,* 389, 414, 491.

22. Royall to Forrestal, April 1, 1948, sec. 16, CCS 381 (8-20-43), box 176, 1948–50 Central Decimal File, RG 218, USNA; Truman quoted in Pickersgill and Forster, *Mackenzie King Record,* 4:182.

23. Clay's memory misled him in a fascinating way. Commenting in 1971 on Bradley's instructions, he told an interviewer that his superiors were "pushing me to use these *unarmed* guards" (emphasis added). Clay interview, March 9, 1971, CUOH. For the teleconference, see Smith, *Clay Papers,* 2:604–7.

24. Smith, *Clay Papers,* 2:607; Tusa and Tusa, *Berlin Airlift,* 108; Robertson to Bevin 500, April 1, 1948, C2496/3/18, 70490, FO 371, UKNA.

25. *New York Times,* April 5, 1948, 5.

26. Study, "USAFE and the Berlin Airlift, 1949: Supply and Operational Aspects," February 8, 1950, p. 2, reel Z-0040, USAFE/HO; report, "61st Group," n.d., frame 667ff., reel Z-0039, USAFE/HO; "Chronology of Berlin Situation," August 1948, box 17, Howley papers, MHI.

27. EUCOM to CG OMGUS SX-4053, April 3, 1948, "AG 319.1 Transportation Situation Reports, vol. I, 1948" folder, box 427, OMGUS AGO General Correspondence, RG 260, USNA; "A Report on the Airlift," folder 247, Booton Herndon papers, Western Historical Manuscript Division, University of Missouri, Columbia; Elizabeth S. Lay, "The Berlin Air Lift," 2 vols. (Karlsruhe, 1952), 1:4–5, reel Z-0029, USAFE/HO; *History of USAFE, April 1948,* appendix 37, USAFE/HO; Robertson to Bevin 509, April 1, 1948, FO 1049/1507, UKNA; *New York Times,* April 5, 1948.

28. Loftus, "American Response," 98–99; *Newsweek,* April 12, 1948, 32–34; Pope diary, June 4, 1948, vol. 2, Pope papers, LAC.

29. CSGPO (Wedemeyer) to overseas commands, WX-98734, April 1, 1948, "531 Railroads" folder, box 631, OMGUS AGO Classified Correspondence, RG 260, USNA; memo for the president, April 2, 1948, "Memos for the President: Meeting Discussions (1948)" folder, box 186, PSF, Truman papers, HSTL.

30. Smith, *Clay Papers,* 2:613–15. Clay to Keyes CC-3693, April 2, 1948, and Clay to Bradley and Keyes CC-3710, April 3, 1948, both in "Cables Outgoing Copies Jan through March 1948" folder, box 685, OMGUS AGO Outgoing Cables; Clay to Bradley and Keyes CC-3739, April 5, 1948, "AG 319.1 Transportation Situation Reports, vol. I, 1948" folder, box 427, OMGUS AGO General Correspondence, all in RG 260, USNA; *New York Times,* April 4, 1948, 1E; Buffet, *Mourir,* 107. In light of these events, the usual chronology, which holds that the Soviets relaxed their restrictions around April 10, is incorrect.

31. Hays to EUCOM CC-3740, April 5, 1948, "Cables Outgoing April 1948" folder, box 685, OMGUS AGO Outgoing Cables, RG 260, USNA; *New York Times,* April 6, 1948, 1; Great Britain, Foreign Office, *Germany (1948): Report of the Court of Inquiry.*

32. Clay to Chamberlin BIW 10 and BIW 11, April 5, 1948, both in "Berlin Crisis" folder, box 149, PSF, Truman papers, HSTL; Smith, *Clay Papers,* 2:618–19; Timberman to Wedemeyer, September 8, 1948, case 88/68, sec. 2, P&O 381 TS, box 103, P&O TS Decimal File, RG 319, USNA; *FR, 1948,* 2:890–91.

33. Robertson to Bevin 560, April 6, 1948, and Bevin to Robertson 699, April 7, 1948, C2661/71/18, 70585, FO 371, UKNA; *FR, 1948,* 2:890–91; *New York Times,* April 6, 1948, 3.

34. Hays to EUCOM CC-3795, April 9, 1948, "Cables Outgoing Copies April 1948" folder, box 685, OMGUS AGO Outgoing Cables, and Clay to CSGID CC-3903, April 16, 1948, "AG 319.1 Transportation Situation Reports, vol. I, 1948" folder, box 427, OMGUS AGO General Correspondence, both in RG 260, USNA; Dratvin to Hays, April 12 and 30, May 14, and June 2, 1948, and Soviet accident commission report, all in "Soviet Russia 1948" folder, box 19, Records Retained for the Military Governor, RG 260, USNA; *New York Times,* April 11, 1948, 5; ibid., April 15, 1948, 10. Corridor incidents are detailed in LeMay to Clay UAX-7889, April 22, 1948, case 137/14, "P&O 092 (Section IX)" folder, box 118, P&O Secret Correspondence, RG 319; Berlin telegram 1056, May 5, 1948, 740.00119 Control (Germany)/5-548, RG 59; "Summary of Soviet Violations . . . ," June 3, 1948, 740.00119 Control (Germany)/6-348, RG 59; Murphy to Hickerson, June 28, 1948, 740.00119 Control (Germany)/6-2848, RG 59, all in USNA; Robertson to Bevin 960, May 28, 1948, C4130/3/18, 70493, FO 371, UKNA.

35. Great Britain, Foreign Office, *Germany No. 2,* 16 (hereafter cited as *Command Paper 7534*); *FR, 1948,* 2:887–88; Hays to EUCOM CC-3819, April 11, 1948, "Cables Outgoing Copies April 1948" folder, box 685, OMGUS AGO Outgoing Cables, RG 260, USNA; "Third Year of the Occupation: Fourth Quarter," 1:28–29, USAREUR-MH; Robertson to Bevin 699, April 21, 1948, FO 1049/1507, UKNA; Chase to Marshall 963, April 24, 1948, 740.00119 Control (Germany)/4-2448, RG 59, USNA; Reed to Kvashnin, April 22 and 27, 1948, and minutes of Soviet-British meeting, May 4, 1948, all in FO 1012/618, UKNA; Robertson to Bevin 713, April 23, 1948, C3193/3/18, 70491, FO 371, UKNA.

36. Cf. Millis and Duffield, *Forrestal Diaries,* 409, and Davison, *Berlin Blockade,* 64–65, with *FR, 1948,* 2:889; Robertson to Bevin 687, April 19, 1948, C3080/3/18, 70491; and "Programme of Russian Obstruction . . . ," August 16, 1948, C6740/1/18, 70479, FO 371, UKNA.

37. OMGUS to EUCOM CC-3880, April 15, 1948, "AG 092.2 Treaties and Agreements

1948" folder, box 368, OMGUS AGO General Correspondence, RG 260, USNA; Narinskii, "Soviet Union," 64–65.

38. ORE 29-48, April 28, 1948, box 214, and CIA 4-48, April 8, 1948, "NSC 13th Meeting" folder, box 176, PSF, Truman papers, HSTL; Lovett quoted in Reid, *Time of Fear and Hope*, 50.

39. CIA 4-48, April 8, 1948, "NSC 13th Meeting" folder, box 176, PSF, Truman papers, HSTL; Murphy to Marshall, airgram 269, April 8, 1948, 740.00119 Control (Germany)/4-848, RG 59, USNA; Clay to CSGID CC-3903, April 16, 1948, "AG 319.1 Transportation Situation Reports, vol. I, 1948" folder, box 427, OMGUS AGO General Correspondence, RG 260, USNA.

40. Robertson to St. Laurent 462, April 2, 1948, reel C11051, William L. Mackenzie King papers, LAC; Bevin quoted in *New York Times*, April 7, 1948, 8.

41. Howley(?) to Maginnis, March 11, 1948, Maginnis papers, MHI.

42. Hoover to Truman, April 2, 1948, case 137/24, "P&O 092 (Section IX-B) . . ." folder, box 118, P&O Secret Correspondence, RG 319, USNA. Truman's reply avoided the issues Hoover raised regarding Berlin. Truman to Hoover, April 6, 1948, President's Personal File 3793, Truman papers, HSTL.

43. Caffery to Marshall 1791, April 6, 1948, 740.00119 Control (Germany)/4-648, RG 59, USNA; Tate to CSGID and OMGUS, April 7, 1948, "Cables—Incoming Record Copies—April 1948" folder, box 679, OMGUS AGO Incoming Cables, RG 260, USNA; Buffet, *Mourir*, 111–12.

44. Smith, *Clay Papers*, 2:623.

45. Lay, "Berlin Air Lift," 1:6–8, reel Z-0029, USAFE/HO; report, BAFO, "A Report on Operation Plainfare (The Berlin Airlift) [AP 3257]," April 1950, 5, 95–97, AIR 10/5067, UKNA (hereafter cited as BAFO Report).

46. Cf. *FR, 1948*, 2:888, Robertson to Bevin 494, March 31, 1948, C2473/3/18, 70490, FO 371, UKNA; meeting minutes, April 24, 1948, C3580/3/18, 70492, FO 371, UKNA. For Clay's suggestion and Washington's assessment, see Smith, *Clay Papers*, 2:607; Beam memo, April 1, 1948, sec. 1, "P&O 091 Germany TS" folder, box 13, P&O TS Decimal File, RG 319; Wisner to Lovett, April 2, 1948, 740.00119 Control (Germany)/4-248, RG 59; MFR, April 5, 1948, case 88/23, sec. 1, P&O 381 TS, box 102, P&O TS Decimal File, RG 319; Saltzman to Lovett, April 8, 1948, 740.00119 Control (Germany)/4-848, RG 59, all in USNA.

47. Smith, *Clay Papers*, 2:579–82; misdated in Clay, *Decision*, 358.

48. Smith, *Clay Papers*, 2:613–15, 622–25, 639–42; Clay to Bradley CC-3927, April 18, 1948, "091 Germany—1948" folder, box 74, General Correspondence, RG 335, USNA.

49. For military plans, see Muir to Wedemeyer, April 2, 1948, case 137/17, "P&O 092 (Section IX-A) . . ." folder, box 118, P&O Secret Correspondence, and file P&O 370.05 TS (Section I)(cases 2–12), box 84, P&O TS Decimal File, both in RG 319, USNA; and sec. 1, CCS 370.05 (4-2-48), box 161, 1948–50 Central Decimal File, RG 218, USNA. For Lovett's idea, see Lovett to Murphy 678, April 15, 1948, 740.00119 Control (Germany)/4-1348, RG 59, USNA; and "Chronology of Developments . . . ," n.d., "OUS 000.1 Germany/Berlin Crisis" folder, box 14, Under Secretary of the Army Project Decimal File (hereafter cited as Draper-Voorhees file), RG 335, USNA.

50. Robertson to Kirkpatrick, April 6, 1948; Dean minute, April 13, 1948; and Strang minute, April 14, 1948, all in C2765/3/18, 70491, FO 371, UKNA.

51. CIA 4-48, April 8, 1948, "NSC 13th Meeting" folder, box 176, PSF, Truman papers, HSTL; Robertson to Kirkpatrick, April 6, 1948, C2765/3/18, 70491, FO 371, UKNA.

52. Smith, *Clay Papers,* 2:622–23; *FR, 1948,* 2:176, 179, 892. For the situation in the Austrian capital, see *FR, 1948,* 2:1415–21, and Schmidl, "The Airlift that Never Was."

53. For claims by the two men, see Clay, *Decision,* 239, 365, and Murphy, *Diplomat among Warriors,* 311–12. The Hickerson-Murphy exchange is reprinted in *FR, 1948,* 2:892–93. Strang memo of conversation, April 28, 1948, C3524/3/18, 70492, FO 371, UKNA, contains Clay's prediction.

54. Smith, *Clay Papers,* 2:607; Bradley to Clay WAR 98748, April 1, 1948, "Russia (3)" folder, box 15, Clifford papers, HSTL; Clay to Bradley BIW 17, April 12, 1948, case 88/155, and Bradley to Clay WAR 99614, April 14, 1948, "P&O 092 TS thru 381 TS, 1948 Hot File" folder, box 9, General Administrative File, RG 319, USNA; Robertson to Bevin 510, April 2, 1948, C2529/3/18, 70490, FO 371, UKNA. For the senators' reaction, see Bohlen, *Witness,* 276.

55. Berkowitz et al., "Berlin Airlift," 45; teleconference transcript attached to Mayo to Wedemeyer, April 2, 1948, case 88/26, sec. 1, P&O 381 TS, box 102, P&O TS Decimal File, RG 319, USNA.

56. Batt to Clifford, May 8, 1948, "William L. Batt" folder, box 20, Clifford papers, HSTL; Forrestal manuscript diary, March 4, 1948, Forrestal papers, MML; *FR, 1948,* 4:843–44.

57. *FR, 1948,* 2:896–97.

58. Jamieson and Dean minutes, April 15, 1948, C2923/71/18, 70585, and meeting minutes, April 23, 1948, C3580/3/18, 70492, both in FO 371, UKNA.

59. Minutes of Bevin-Bidault meeting, April 17, 1948, C3175/3/18, 70491, FO 371, UKNA.

60. Strang memo, April 28, 1948, C3524/3/18, 70492, FO 371, UKNA. The much shorter U.S. record is in *FR, 1948,* 2:899–900.

61. Minutes of tripartite meeting, April 28, 1948, C3581/3/18, 70493, FO 371, UKNA.

62. Marshall to Douglas 1555, April 30, 1948, 740.00119 Control (Germany)/4-2848, RG 59, USNA. For an intriguing echo of Marshall's comments, see Laufer and Kynin, *Die UdSSR und die deutsche Frage,* 3:622.

63. Bevin to Attlee PM/48/49, May 5, 1948, and Dean to Sargent, May 7, 1948, both in C3612/3/18, 70493, FO 371, UKNA.

64. Bevin to Inverchapel 673, May 10, 1948, C3713/71/18, 70588, FO 371, UKNA; *FR, 1948,* 2:233; minutes of informal meeting, May 11, 1948, C3884/71/18, 70590, FO 371, UKNA.

65. Davies to Butler, March 19, 1948, "USSR 1946–1950" folder, box 23, PPS Records, RG 59, USNA; *FR, 1948,* 4:834–41. For the connection between this initiative and the stalled note on Berlin, see Loftus, "American Response," 189–95.

66. *FR, 1948,* 4:847–57; Divine, *Foreign Policy,* 202; Gaddis, *George F. Kennan,* 311–14.

67. Robertson to St. Laurent 657, May 11, 1948, AR 5/17, vol. 2078, RG 25, LAC; Bullock, *Bevin,* 3:558; *FR, 1948,* 4:860n2, 861n3.

68. Divine, *Foreign Policy,* 202–3; U.S. Department of State, *Bulletin* 18 (May 23, 1948): 683–84; Millis and Duffield, *Forrestal Diaries,* 442–44; Forrestal to Marshall, May 29, 1948, quoted in Rosenberg, "Berlin and Israel," 166.

69. For the Wallace-Stalin exchange, see Carlyle, *Documents, 1947–1948,* 160–64, and Culver and Hyde, *American Dreamer,* 474–75. Truman quoted in Eben A. Ayers diary, May 17, 1948, box 29, Ayers papers, HSTL, and U.S. Department of State, *Bulletin* 18 (May 30, 1948): 705–6. For Stalin's intentions, see Zubok, *Failed Empire,* 76; for a good summary of this affair, see Walker, "'No More Cold War.'"

70. *FR, 1948,* 2:255–56, 258.

71. Harvey to Bevin 687, May 20, 1948, C3974/71/18, 70590, FO 371, UKNA; Caffery to Marshall 2723, May 21, 1948, 740.00119 Control (Germany)/5-2148, RG 59, USNA; *FR, 1948,* 2:281, 267.

72. *FR, 1948,* 2:272, 3:99; Sargent minute, May 21, 1948, C4022/71/18, 70590, FO 371, UKNA.

73. *FR, 1948,* 2:256, 268, 271, 292, 303–4; record of meeting, n.d. [May 21, 1948], and Bevin to Harvey 426 Saving, May 24, 1948, both in C3974/71/18, 70590; and Dean to Bevin, May 27, 1948, C4241/71/18, 70591, all in FO 371, UKNA; Office of European Affairs paper, May 24, 1948, 740.00119 Control (Germany)/5-2448, RG 59, USNA; Smith, *Clay Papers,* 2:656–57; CP(48)134, May 31, 1948, CAB 129/27, UKNA.

74. Office of European Affairs paper, May 24, 1948, 740.00119 Control (Germany)/5-2448, RG 59, USNA; Dean minute, May 24, 1948, C3974/71/18, 70590, FO 371, UKNA; *FR, 1948,* 2:268–70, 272–73, 283–84, 3:635–37; Strang to Bevin, May 22, 1948, C4022/71/18, 70590; Dean to Bevin, May 27, 1948, C4241/71/18, 70591; Strang minute, May 28, 1948, C4185/71/18, 70591, all in FO 371, UKNA.

75. Dean minute, May 24, 1948, C3974/71/18, 70590, FO 371, UKNA; Draper to Forrestal, June 1, 1948, "P&O 091 Germany TS (Section I)" folder, box 13, P&O TS Decimal File, RG 319, USNA.

76. Dean to Bevin, May 27, 1948, C4241/71/18, 70591, FO 371, UKNA. See also *FR, 1948,* 2:268–70, 275–79.

77. *FR, 1948,* 2:268, 269, 275, 278–79, 284; CP(48)134, May 29, 1948, CAB 129/27, UKNA.

78. Dean to Bevin, May 27, 1948, C4241/71/18, 70591, FO 371, UKNA.

79. *FR, 1948,* 2:284, 272.

80. Ibid., 240–41, 260–62, 285–94, 305–17.

81. Robertson to Bevin 1017, June 7, 1948, C4396/71/18, and Robertson to Bevin 1020, June 8, 1948, C4434/71/18, both in 70592, FO 371, UKNA; Robertson to Bevin 1043, June 10, 1948, C4524/71/18, 70593, FO 371, UKNA; Pope to St. Laurent 810, June 11, 1948, folder 6, file W-22-5-G, vol. 2078, RG 25, LAC; ORE 52-48, July 22, 1948, box 215, PSF, Truman papers, HSTL; OMGUS Opinion Surveys Branch Report 131, August 4, 1948, "ICD Opinion Surveys 1948" folder, box 27, Director's files, Berlin Sector Records, RG 260, USNA.

82. Hitchcock, *France Restored,* 94–95; Young, *Britain, France, and the Unity of Europe,* 93–94; *FR, 1948,* 2:322–23, 336n, 3:637; Harvey to Bevin 824, June 17, 1948, C4703/71/18, 70594, UKNA.

83. "Programme of Russian Obstruction . . . ," August 16, 1948, C6740/1/18, 70479, FO 371, UKNA; Ballard to Howley, May 21, 1948, "Staff Studies (1 Jul–31 Dec) 1948" folder, box 6, Director's files, Berlin Sector Records, RG 260, USNA; Murphy to Marshall 1216, May 25, 1948, 740.00119 Control (Germany)/5-2548, Riddleberger to Marshall 1168, May 20, 1948, 740.00119 Control (Germany)/5-1448, RG 59, USNA; EUCOM Intelligence Summary 36, June 22, 1948, box 767, Periodic Intelligence Summaries, RG 549, USNA.

84. Herbert to Bevin 935, May 25, 1948, C4049/3/18, 70493, FO 371, UKNA.

85. "Programme of Russian Obstruction . . . ," August 16, 1948, C6740/1/18, 70479, FO 371, UKNA; *Command Paper 7534,* 17; U.S. Department of State, *Berlin Crisis,* 3; OMG Bavaria to OMGUS/CAD MGB-1712, June 10, 1948, "AG 092.1 Boundaries and Borders I" folder, box 368, OMGUS AGO General Correspondence, RG 260, USNA; Collier, *Bridge,* 35.

86. Reed to DCOS/Pol, June 10, 1948, FO 1049/1508, UKNA; Dratvin to Hays, June

14, 1948, "Soviet Russia 1948" folder, box 19, Records Retained for the Military Governor, RG 260, USNA; Robertson to Bevin 1057, June 12, 1948, FO 1049/1508, UKNA; Narinskii, "Soviet Union," 65.

87. Pope, *Soldiers and Politicians,* 340; Robertson to Bevin 1061, June 12, 1948, C4612/3/18; Robertson to Bevin 1076, June 15, 1948, C4672/3/18; Robertson to Bevin 1080, June 16, 1948, C4704/3/18; Robertson to Bevin 1085, June 17, 1948, C4705/3/18; and Robertson to Bevin 1086, June 17, 1948, C4706/3/18, all in 70494, FO 371, UKNA; Robertson to Bevin 3220 Basic, June 22, 1948, C4898/3/18, 70495, FO 371, UKNA; Riess, *Berlin Story,* 156.

88. *FR, 1948,* 2:900–902, 905–6; Maring to U.S. Secretariat, July 21, 1948, "1013—Control Council (Misc.) after Soviet Walkout" folder, box 4, Records of US ACA Element, RG 260, USNA; Robertson to Bevin 547, April 5, 1948, FO 1049/1352, UKNA.

89. Howley, *Berlin Command,* 179–82; *FR, 1948,* 2:908–9; minutes, AKB 12th meeting, June 16, 1948, "Quadripartite Kommandatura Stenographic Minutes—Commandants—1948" folder, box 7, and Howley to Ganeval, June 2, 1948, "General Howley—General Ganeval 1948–1949" folder, box 12, both in Director's files, Berlin Sector Records, RG 260, USNA; OMGUS U.S. Secretariat, Special Report 3, June 29, 1948, "G801.4 Berlin I" folder, box 4, Records of the Division of Central European Affairs, RG 59, USNA.

90. Smith to Marshall 1092, June 10, 1948, 740.00119 Council/6-1048, RG 59, USNA; Ruhm von Oppen, *Documents on Germany,* 290; USSR Ministry of Foreign Affairs, *Soviet Union and the Berlin Question,* 32–41.

91. Summary of telegrams, June 14, 1948, "State Department Briefs, May–August 1948" folder, box 21, Naval Aide files, HSTL.

92. Robertson to Bevin, June 12, 1948, Annex to COS(48)120(O), June 25, 1948, DEFE 5/11, UKNA.

93. Huebner to Bradley SX-1057, June 11, 1948, 740.00119 Control (Germany)/6-1148, RG 59, USNA; Lemley memo, June 14, 1948, case 88/41, sec. 1, P&O 381 TS, box 102, P&O Secret Correspondence, RG 319, USNA; Wedemeyer to Clay WARX 83775, June 12, 1948, "Cables Incoming Record Copies June 1948" folder, box 680, OMGUS AGO Incoming Cables, RG 260, USNA; Smith, *Clay Papers,* 2:677.

94. ORE 29-48, April 28, 1948, box 214, PSF, Truman papers, HSTL; CIA 5-48, May 12, 1948, "NSC 11th Meeting" folder, and CIA 6-48, June 17, 1948, "NSC 13th Meeting" folder, both in box 176, PSF, Truman papers, HSTL; Hillenkoetter to Truman, June 9, 1948, file 122, box 19, Chairman's File (entry 47), RG 218, USNA; ORE 21-48, June 14, 1948, box 214, PSF, Truman papers, HSTL.

95. Byroade to Wedemeyer, June 16, 1948, tab K, binder 1, sec. IX, P&O 092 TS, box 118, P&O Secret Correspondence, RG 319, USNA; Loftus, "American Response," 161–62, 185n; minutes of 212th PPS meeting, June 21, 1948, "PPS Minutes of Meetings 1948" folder, box 32, PPS Records, RG 59, USNA.

96. Howley, *Berlin Command,* 90; Gottlieb, *German Peace Settlement,* 112; Smith, *Clay Papers,* 1:209; *FR, 1946,* 5:556–58; Backer, *Decision to Divide,* 121.

97. *FR, 1946,* 5:626; Murphy to Byrnes 2781, December 2, 1946, 862.515/12-246, RG 59, USNA; Narinskii, "Soviet Union," 61.

98. Smith, *Clay Papers,* 1:350–51, 382–83, 398; Playfair to Chambers 266, April 19, 1947, CE1419/22/74, 65005, FO 371, UKNA; *FR, 1946,* 5:625–26; *FR, 1947,* 2:876–82; Narinskii, "Soviet Union," 61.

99. *FR, 1944,* 3:824–32; Gottlieb, *German Peace Settlement,* 24–25; Ziemke, *U.S. Army,* 337; Bennett, "German Currency Reform," 44. Vladimir Petrov points out that notes printed

after the initial run also had a dash ahead of the serial number, confusing the situation further. Petrov, *Money and Conquest,* 201.

100. John C. E. Smith, "Currency Control" (Frankfurt, 1947), USAREUR-MH; Ziemke, *U.S. Army,* 336–37; Morris, *Blockade,* 68n.

101. Murphy to Harriman 86, May 25, 1945, "#190 Treasury—Germany" folder, box 7, Telegrams Maintained by Harriman, RG 84, USNA; SHAEF FWD to AGWAR VOG 457, May 24, 1945, FO 944/78, UKNA; Howley, *Berlin Command,* 186; Clay, *Decision,* 156; Smith, *Clay Papers,* 1:303; *FR, 1946,* 5:626.

102. SHAEF FWD to AGWAR VOG 461, May 31, 1945, FO 944/78, UKNA; Playfair to Chambers 266, April 19, 1947, CE1419/22/74, 65005, FO 371, UKNA; memo of conversation, July 21, 1947, 862.515/7-2147, RG 59, USNA; Ziemke, *U.S. Army,* 336; Backer, *Decision to Divide,* 123–31; Hilldring testimony in U.S. Department of State, *Bulletin* 16, no. 417 (June 29, 1947): 1304–6; Gottlieb, *German Peace Settlement,* 116–22; Gottlieb, "Failure of Quadripartite Monetary Reform," 412–14; DT/KPW minute, September 20, 1948, FO 944/838, UKNA.

103. Smith, *Clay Papers,* 1:382–83; Bennett, "German Currency Reform," 46; DeWilde to Saltzman, October 9, 1947, 862.515/10-947, and Saltzman to Lovett, October 11, 1947, 862.515/10-1147, both in RG 59, USNA; Draper to Snyder, October 20, 1947, "SAOUS 123.7 Germany" folder, box 17, Draper-Voorhees file, RG 335, USNA; Petrov, *Money and Conquest,* 241.

104. Laufer, "From Dismantling to Currency Reform," 80–82; Laufer and Kynin, *Die UdSSR und die deutsche Frage,* 3:411; Hilldring to Saltzman, September 22, 1947, 862.515/6-1247, RG 59, USNA; Lovett to Marshall TELMAR 53, December 8, 1947, and Marshall to Lovett MARTEL 53, December 9, 1947, both in "SAOUS 123.7 Germany" folder, box 17, Draper-Voorhees file, RG 335, USNA; Robertson quoted in Hubert G. Schmidt, "U.S. Military Government in Germany: Policy and Functioning in Industry, vol. III" (Karlsruhe, 1950), 286, USAREUR-MH.

105. Turner, "Great Britain and the German Currency Reform," 698–99; *FR, 1947,* 2:813–14, 819, 822–24.

106. Bennett, "German Currency Reform," 45–46; *FR, 1948,* 2:870; Laufer, "From Dismantling to Currency Reform," 82.

107. Clay to CSCAD CC-3095, February 3, 1948, and CC-3422, March 7, 1948, both in "Cables—Outgoing Copies—January–March 1948" folder, box 685, OMGUS AGO Outgoing Cables, RG 260, USNA. A central bank was indispensable for currency reform; when the West went ahead, it created a special *Bank deutscher Länder* to carry it out. Gottlieb, "Failure of Quadripartite Monetary Reform," 398; Clay, *Decision,* 205–6. For the new American position, see Smith, *Clay Papers,* 2:554, and *FR, 1948,* 2:870–72. The February 11 ACC meeting is summarized in *FR, 1948,* 2:874–75, and Robertson to Bevin 608, April 10, 1948, C2804/71/18, 70585, FO 371, UKNA.

108. Laufer, "From Dismantling to Currency Reform," 82.

109. Clay to Draper CC-3422, March 7, 1948, "SAOUS 123.7 Germany" folder, box 17, Draper-Voorhees file, RG 335, USNA; report, British Office of Financial Adviser, Berlin, September 8, 1949, FO 944/838, UKNA.

110. Smith, *Clay Papers,* 2:578; *FR, 1948,* 2:879–82.

111. Report, British Office of Financial Adviser, Berlin, September 8, 1949, FO 944/838, UKNA; Smith, *Clay Papers,* 2:657, 677–78, 682, 685–86; Murphy, *Diplomat among Warriors,* 313; Murphy to Marshall 1389, June 17, 1948, 740.00119 Control (Germany)/6-1748, RG 59, USNA.

112. Smith, *Clay Papers,* 2:559, 643; *FR, 1948,* 2:891–92, 897–99; CSCAD to CINCEUR W-82922, May 29, 1948, "Cables Incoming Record Copies, May 1948" folder, box 680, OMGUS AGO Incoming Cables, RG 260, USNA. This approach, which assumed that currency agreement with the Russians was possible, weakens George and Smoke's contrast between the lack of Western preparations for a full blockade and what they call the Western governments' thorough, "thoughtful contingency plans" regarding currency reform. George and Smoke, *Deterrence,* 129.

113. Smith, *Clay Papers,* 2:643–44.

114. Bevin to Attlee, PM/48/59, June 16, 1948, FO 800/467/GER/48/25, UKNA.

115. Smith, *Clay Papers,* 2:623, 677; Robertson to Bevin 1043, June 10, 1948, C4524/71/18, 70593, and Williams minute, June 14, 1948, CJ2497/89/182, 71015, both in FO 371, UKNA.

116. Clay to Draper CC-4602, June 8, 1948, "Cables Outgoing Copies, June 1948" folder, box 685, Classified Outgoing Cables, RG 260, USNA; Clay to Sokolovsky, June 18, 1948, "Soviet Russia 1948" folder, box 19, Records Retained for the Military Governor, RG 260, USNA; Gablentz, *Documents,* 57, 61.

117. Vysotsky, *West Berlin,* 81–84; *Newsweek,* June 28, 1948, 30; Robertson to Bevin 1135, June 21, 1948, C4848/3/18, 70495, FO 371, UKNA; *FR, 1948,* 2:910–11; staff conference minutes, June 19, 1948, box 5, OMGUS Minutes, RG 260, USNA; Dean quoted in Robertson to Pearson 925, June 23, 1948, "1948 Robertson, N. A. (Apr–Sep)" folder, vol. 441, King papers, LAC. When I reviewed the OMGUS Minutes, they were housed at the Washington National Records Center; they have since been transferred to College Park, Maryland, and I do not know their current location.

118. *FR, 1948,* 2:911–12; Davison, *Berlin Blockade,* 93; Clay to Bradley CC-4843, June 23, 1948, "AG 319.1 Transportation Situation Reports, vol. II, 1948" folder, box 427, OMGUS AGO General Correspondence, RG 260, USNA.

119. Smith, *Clay Papers,* 2:691; *FR, 1948,* 2:911, 916; MFR, June 21, 1948, case 88/48, "P&O 092 thru 381 TS 1948 Hot File" folder, box 9, General Administrative File, RG 319, USNA.

120. *Command Paper 7534,* 18; Davison, *Berlin Blockade,* 92; Gablentz, *Documents,* 58–62.

121. *New York Times,* June 21, 1948, 1; Bennett, "German Currency Reform," 52; Narinskii, "Soviet Union," 65–66; Gottlieb, *German Peace Settlement,* 192; *FR, 1948,* 2:912–13.

122. Narinskii, "Soviet Union," 61, 66; Laufer, "From Dismantling to Currency Reform," 80–84; Laufer and Kynin, *Die UdSSR und die deutsche Frage,* 3:451–52, 474–79, 606–9; *FR, 1948,* 2:913; Ruhm von Oppen, *Documents on Germany,* 295–300. For arguments that the West could have waited, see Gottlieb, *German Peace Settlement,* 193–94, and Offner, *Another Such Victory,* 256.

123. Smith, *Clay Papers,* 2:692–95, 698–99; Gablentz, *Documents,* 62–63.

124. Gottlieb, *German Peace Settlement,* 196; Smith, *Clay Papers,* 2:695; Murphy to Marshall 1443, June 23, 1948, 862.515/6-2348, RG 59, USNA; Plischke, *Berlin,* 6.

125. Davison, *Berlin Blockade,* 94.

126. Robertson to Bevin 1168, June 24, 1948, C4935/3/18, 70495, FO 371, UKNA; Davison, *Berlin Blockade,* 95–97, 138; *New York Times,* June 23, 1948, 1; ibid., June 24, 1948, 19.

127. Robertson to Bevin 1166, June 24, 1948, C4938/3/18, 70495, FO 371, UKNA; Bennett, *Berlin Bastion,* 38–39; U.S. Department of State, *Berlin Crisis,* 4–5; Charles, *Berlin Blockade,* 47; Smith, *Clay Papers,* 2:701. For Soviet troop movements, see Karber and Combs, "United States," 414. For the late trains and barges, see "Chronology of Berlin Situation," August 1948, box 17, Howley papers, MHI; *Command Paper 7534,* 20; Murphy to Marshall

1528, June 29, 1948, 740.00119 Control (Germany)/6-2948, RG 59; and EUCOM Intelligence Summary 37, July 6, 1948, box 767, Periodic Intelligence Summaries, RG 549, USNA.

128. Howley, *Berlin Command,* 198; Gablentz, *Documents,* 63–64; Davison, *Berlin Blockade,* 99–103; Charles, *Berlin Blockade,* 50–51; Robertson to Bevin 1179, June 25, 1948, C4972/3/18, 70496, FO 371, UKNA; Robertson to Bevin 1170, June 24, 1948, C4939/3/18, 70495, FO 371, UKNA.

129. Howley, *Berlin Command,* 203; Davison, *Berlin Blockade,* 99.

130. Herbert quoted in Charles, *Berlin Blockade,* 47; Clay quoted in *New York Times,* June 25, 1948, 1, and in Loftus, "American Response," 168n; Dean quoted in Robertson to St. Laurent 925, June 23, 1948, "1948 Robertson, N. A. (Apr–Sep)" folder, vol. 441, King papers, LAC.

131. Davison, *Berlin Blockade,* 101–2.

132. *New York Times,* June 25, 1948, 1, 18.

4. Prudence and Resolve

1. CM(48)42, June 24, 1948, CAB 128/13, UKNA.

2. Robertson to Bevin 1162, June 24, 1948, C4921/3/18, 70495, and McNeil to Attlee, June 24, 1948, C5093/3/18, 70597, both in FO 371, UKNA.

3. Douglas to Marshall 2788, June 25, 1948, 740.00119 Control (Germany)/6-2548, RG 59, USNA; meeting minutes, June 25, 1948, C5094/3/18, 70497, FO 371, UKNA (emphasis added). For a similar survey of Bevin's views, see Kirkpatrick to Hollis, June 26, 1948, C5015/3/18, 70496, FO 371, UKNA.

4. Bullock, *Bevin,* 3:575–76.

5. CM(48)43, June 25, 1948, CAB 128/13, UKNA.

6. Great Britain, Parliament, *Parliamentary Debates* (Commons), 5th ser., vol. 435, cols. 1719–22.

7. Bevin to Franks 914, June 25, 1948, C5031/3/18, and Bevin to Franks 915, June 26, 1948, C5032/3/18, 70497, FO 371, UKNA; *FR, 1948,* 2:921–26.

8. *Command Paper 7534,* 19; *London Times,* June 24, 26, and 28, 1948; *New York Times,* June 27, 1948, 1.

9. *FR, 1948,* 2:916–17; Kirkpatrick minute, June 28, 1948, C5134/3/18, and Strang minute, June 28, 1948, C5137/3/18, both in 70498, FO 371, UKNA; Bidault quoted in Narinskii, "Soviet Union," 67; Buffet, *Mourir,* 173–74.

10. *New York Times,* June 27, 1948, 1; ibid., June 28, 1948, 1.

11. Vanier to St. Laurent 361, June 28, 1948, pt. 3, file 7-CA-14(s), DEA files; Rosenberg, "Berlin and Israel," 118. The materials I saw in the DEA files in 1981 have since been transferred to the LAC, and I do not know their current location.

12. Caffery to Marshall 3447, June 30, 1948, 740.00119 Control (Germany)/6-3048, RG 59, USNA; Buffet, *Mourir,* 174; Vanier to St. Laurent 364, June 29, 1948, pt. 3, file 7-CA-14(s), DEA files.

13. CM(48)44, June 28, 1948, CAB 128/13; meeting minutes, June 28, 1948, FO 800/467/GER/48/31, UKNA.

14. COS(48)87, June 28, 1948, DEFE 4/14; Kirkpatrick memo, June 28, 1948, C5070/3/18, 70497; GEN 241/1st meeting, June 28, 1948, C5136/3/18, 70498, FO 371, UKNA.

15. Brook to Tedder, June 28, 1948, AIR 20/7148, UKNA.

16. COS(48)87, June 28, 1948, DEFE 4/14, UKNA; GEN 241/1st meeting, June 28, 1948, C5136/3/18, 70498, FO 371, UKNA.

17. COS(48)88, June 28, 1948, DEFE 4/14, UKNA.

18. GEN 241/1st meeting, June 28, 1948, DEFE 11/321, UKNA; Bevin to Franks 917, June 28, 1948, C5072/3/18, 70497, FO 371, UKNA; Bevin to Robertson 1377, June 29, 1948, C5015/3/18, 70496, FO 371, UKNA.

19. Shlaim, *United States*; Loftus, "American Response," 216.

20. Clay interview, March 9, 1971, CUOH.

21. Dennison interview, September 10, 1971, HSTL.

22. Lilienthal, *Journals,* 2:433–34.

23. Neustadt, *Presidential Power,* 239–40.

24. Jessup interview, 233, CUOH.

25. On such differences among policy makers, see Snyder and Diesing, *Conflict among Nations,* 297–310, and Jervis, *Perception and Misperception,* 104–6.

26. Smith, *Clay Papers,* 2:699–704. For Truman's interest in evacuation, see his *Memoirs,* 2:123. Royall's comment that currency was "a minor issue" is recounted in Dupuy to Draper, July 21, 1948, "SAOUS 123.7 Germany" folder, box 17, Draper-Voorhees file, RG 335, USNA.

27. Clay interview, March 9, 1971, CUOH; Smith, *Clay Papers,* 2:702–3, 706.

28. Smith, *Clay Papers,* 2:696–706.

29. *FR, 1948,* 2:919–21.

30. Draper to Royall, messages 2 and 3, June 27, 1948, "Berlin Crisis, Book I" folder, box 14, Draper-Voorhees file, RG 335, USNA.

31. *New York Times,* June 25, 1948, 1; Summary, Cabinet Meeting, June 25, 1948, in "Cabinet Meetings, 1948" folder, box 2, Connelly papers, HSTL.

32. Truman, *Memoirs,* 2:124. For Marshall's absence, see *New York Times,* June 29, 1948, 1; ibid., July 1, 1948, 1; and Pogue, *Marshall,* 4:303.

33. Forrestal manuscript diary, June 25, 1948, Forrestal papers, MML; Millis and Duffield, *Forrestal Diaries,* 451–52; *FR, 1948,* 2:928–29. Officials at lower levels knew more. Clay's recollections were clearer. Parks had circulated his detailed summary of the June 29, 1945, meeting to the JCS, and the army staff had looked into the matter in May, after Byrnes asked for information for a speech. The colonels feared that Byrnes intended to blame the Pentagon and found a way to avoid answering his questions, but they had summarized—as recently as June 18—the EAC agreements, the Truman-Stalin exchange, and the Clay-Zhukov-Weeks meeting for Royall and Forrestal. See Clay to Parks CC-3865, April 14, 1948, "AG 092.2 Treaties and Agreements 1948" folder, box 368, OMGUS AGO General Correspondence, RG 260, USNA; and Parks to Gruenther, April 1, 1948, sec. 16, CCS 381 (8-20-43), box 176, 1948–50 Central Decimal File, RG 218, USNA. For the Byrnes episode, see case 133, "P&O 092TS (Section VIII) . . ." folder, box 35, P&O TS Decimal File, RG 319, USNA.

34. *FR, 1948,* 2:928–29. For the moral ambiguities of withdrawal, see Jack Raymond's dispatches to the *New York Times,* June 25 and 28, 1948. Truman's instructions to his military advisers are recounted in Leahy diary, June 29, 1948, box 6, Leahy papers, LOCMD, and in meeting transcript 309, June 30, 1948, CD 9-3-13, box 52, OSD Numerical File, RG 330, USNA.

35. Loftus, "American Response," 228–29.

36. Smith, *Clay Papers,* 2:696–97; study, June 26, 1948, case 88/49, "1948—Hot File—P&O 092 TS thru 381 TS" folder, box 9, General Administrative File, RG 319, USNA; Bohlen to Hickerson, June 26, 1948, "Memos CEB 1948 (1946–1948)" folder, box 5, Bohlen papers, RG 59, USNA.

37. "State-National Defense Meeting . . . ," June 27, 1948, "Germany (1949–1950)" folder, box 74, General Correspondence, RG 335, USNA; Millis and Duffield, *Forrestal Diaries*, 452–54; Rearden, *Formative Years*, 290–91. Bradley's "recollections" are in Bradley and Blair, *General's Life*, 479–80.

38. *FR, 1948*, 2:926–28.

39. I have found no record of such a talk. Truman returned the papers to Lovett on Tuesday. Truman to Lovett, June 29, 1948, "Berlin Crisis" folder, box 149, PSF, Truman papers, HSTL.

40. Forrestal manuscript diary, June 28, 1948, and Royall to Bradley, June 28, 1948, filed with this entry, Forrestal papers, MML. For a sound analysis of this meeting, see Loftus, "American Response," 243–46, 287–93.

41. Haynes, *Awesome Power*, 140 ("command decision"); Browder and Smith, *Independent*, 294, and Shlaim, *United States*, 222 ("at all costs"); Miscamble, "Harry S Truman," 309 ("unequivocal . . ."). See also Buffet, *Mourir*, 171–72.

42. From Moscow, Smith summarized policy even as Truman was formulating it. The Western powers sooner or later would confront a choice between withdrawal and remaining under humiliating conditions. That moment had not arrived. The powers could not "back down now without exhausting every possibility of maintaining ourselves and riding out the storm in the hope that improved conditions will give us the opportunity of a reasonable choice of alternatives." Smith to Marshall 1203, June 28, 1948, 740.00119 Control (Germany)/6-2848, RG 59, USNA.

43. *FR, 1948*, 2:930–31; Bohlen memo, June 29, 1948, "Memos CEB 1948 (1946–1948)" folder, box 5, Bohlen papers, RG 59, USNA.

44. *FR, 1948*, 2:917–18, 929–30; Smith, *Clay Papers*, 2:696, 706–7.

45. Report, S-2 Liaison Section, 759th MP Service Battalion, June 26, 1948, "AG 250.1 Incidents 1948" folder, box 405, OMGUS AGO General Correspondence, RG 260, USNA; Clay, *Decision*, 373 (which misdates the meeting and claims the MPs "put a gun in the pit of Sokolovsky's stomach," a detail absent from the MP report); Smith, *Clay Papers*, 2:709–10; Brownjohn to Bevin, June 28, 1948, C5098/3/18, 70497, FO 371, UKNA.

46. Smith, *Clay Papers*, 2:714–15.

47. *FR, 1948*, 2:932, 937; Robertson to Bevin 1229, June 30, 1948, C5148/3/18, 70498, FO 371, UKNA; Schuirman to Connolly, July 1, 1948, file 33, box 7, Chairman's File, RG 218, USNA; Douglas to Marshall 2882 and 2884, June 30, 1948, 740.00119 Control (Germany)/6-3048, RG 59, USNA; Wedemeyer to Clay WX-84885, June 29, 1948, case 137/45, "P&O 092 (Section IX-B) . . ." folder, box 118, P&O Secret Correspondence, RG 319, USNA; Robertson to Bevin 9 Basic, July 1, 1948, CAB 21/1885, UKNA; Strang to Robertson 11820 Basic, June 30, 1948, C5148/3/18, 70498, FO 371, UKNA. For continuing speculation on the prospects of the blockade being eased, see Sterling to Laukhuff, n.d. [July 5, 1948?], "710 Berlin Situation, April–July 15" folder, box 215, Classified General Correspondence, POLAD files, RG 84, USNA.

48. Great Britain, Parliament, *Parliamentary Debates* (Commons), 5th ser., vol. 452, cols. 2233–46; *London Times*, July 1, 1948.

49. U.S. Department of State, *Bulletin* 19 (July 11, 1948): 54; *New York Times*, July 1, 1948, 1.

50. Snyder and Diesing, *Conflict among Nations*, 207ff., 254–56; Young, *Politics of Force*, 223.

51. Paeffgen, "Berlin Blockade and Airlift," 175; *FR, 1948*, 2:940.

52. U.S. President, *Public Papers . . . 1948,* 394; Clifford to Truman, November 19, 1947, box 21, Clifford papers, HSTL. Also see Divine, *Foreign Policy,* 172–73, and Divine, "Cold War and the Election."

53. *FR, 1948,* 2:933–46.

54. Ibid., 378–81; Berlin to Hannover BGCC 5149, July 4, 1948, C5323/71/18, 70595, FO 371, UKNA.

55. *FR, 1948,* 2:941; Smith, *Clay Papers,* 2:719–21; *London Times,* July 3, 1948. The Russians did not physically leave the Kommandatura until August 13; U.S. Department of State, *Germany, 1947–1949,* 201. They continued to participate in the Berlin Air Safety Center, Spandau prison, and liaison and protocol services working with Allied military missions. OMGUS, *Military Government Report, July 1948,* 1.

56. *Command Paper 7534,* 19; *New York Times,* July 4, 1948, 1; Smith, *Clay Papers,* 2:719–22; Forrestal manuscript diary, July 2, 1948, Forrestal papers, MML; *FR, 1948,* 2:944–45.

57. Robertson to Bevin 1287, July 3, 1948, C5294/3/18, 70499, FO 371, UKNA; Smith, *Clay Papers,* 2:722–24; *FR, 1948,* 2:948–50; Clay, *Decision,* 367. Paul Steege claims that Clay's account of this meeting in his memoirs is "the primary source" of or "basis" for the notion that the blockade was a last-ditch effort to prevent the creation of the Federal Republic of Germany, and he leaves the impression that Clay distorted the Soviet position ("Clay *purported* to have gained an insight. . . . Sokolovskii *allegedly* explained" [emphasis added]). Steege is mistaken on both counts. The British and American white papers, published long before Clay's *Decision in Germany,* contain ample evidence that the Soviets imposed the blockade to compel the Western powers to abandon the London program. Clay's memoir is consistent with these reports and contemporary Western records. No one, Steege included, has offered any evidence that Western accounts of the meeting are inaccurate. Cf. Steege, "More than an Airlift," 8n2, 201; Steege, "Totale Blockade," 64n9, and Steege, *Black Market,* 212, with the sources cited above; U.S. Department of State, *Berlin Crisis,* 6–36; *Command Paper 7534,* 19–54; and *FR, 1948,* 2:946–1099.

58. Browder and Smith, *Independent,* 296.

59. Cf. USSR Ministry of Foreign Affairs, *Correspondence,* 1:366–67 and 2:247–48. For Western interpretations of Stalin's cable to Truman, see Draper to Forrestal, June 18, 1948, filed with Forrestal manuscript diary, June 18, 1948, Forrestal papers, MML; Gross to Lovett, June 28, 1948, 740.00119 Control (Germany)/4-1448, RG 59, USNA; and Bohlen memos, June 25, 1948, "1945–48 Meetings between Allied and Soviet Officials" folder, box 12, Berlin Task Force Records, RG 59, USNA. Also see Blum to Forrestal, July 1, 1948, filed with Forrestal manuscript diary, July 1, 1948, Forrestal papers, MML; and *FR, 1948,* 2:927, 933, 942.

60. Bohlen memo, July 6, 1948, "CEB Memos 1948" folder, box 5, Bohlen papers, RG 59, USNA; Leahy diary, July 6, 1948, box 6, Leahy papers, LOCMD; Lilienthal, *Journals,* 2:383.

61. Harrison to Bevin 814, July 10, 1948, CAB 21/1885, and Strang to Bevin, July 8, 1948, C5611/3/18, 70502, FO 371, both in UKNA.

62. COS(48)93, July 7, 1948, DEFE 4/14, UKNA.

63. COS(48)96, July 9, 1948, DEFE 4/14, UKNA.

64. Maddocks to Bradley, June 28, 1948, "1948—Hot File—P&O 092 TS thru 381 TS" folder, box 9, General Administrative File, RG 319, USNA; Saltzman to Lovett, July 4, 1948, 740.00119 Control (Germany)/7-448, RG 59, USNA (emphasis added).

65. *FR, 1948,* 2:960–64.

66. Peterson to Bevin 832, July 15, 1948, C5714/3/18, 70502, FO 371, UKNA; Smith to

Marshall 1335, July 15, 1948, 740.00119 Control (Germany)/7-1548, RG 59, USNA; Harvey to Bevin 944, July 15, 1948, CAB 21/1885, UKNA; *FR, 1948,* 2:965–66.

67. *FR, 1948,* 2:966–67; Truman, *Truman,* 12.

5. "Doomed to Failure"

1. Shlaim, *United States,* 202–11, 260–70; Herken, *Winning Weapon,* 260; Pruessen, *Dulles,* 379–80.

2. Lt. Col. Lester H. Gallogly et al., "Report of Department of the Army Observer Group Concerning Study of Operation VITTLES" (n.p., February 16, 1949), 11 (hereafter cited as Gallogly Report), "PD 381 Berlin Operation Vittles" folder, box 368, Central Decimal File, RG 341, USNA; "USAFE and the Berlin Airlift, 1948: Supply and Operational Aspects," (n.p., April 1, 1949), 11, 38–39, reel Z-0039, USAFE/HO; Lay, "Berlin Air Lift," 1:1–2, 7–8, reel Z-0029, USAFE/HO; press release, USAFE Public Relations Office, "Combined Tonnage," n.d., reel Z-0038, USAFE/HO.

3. BAFO Report, 117, 129.

4. Memo, June 25, 1948, C5094/3/18, 70497, FO 371; CM(48)43, June 25, 1948, CAB 128/13; and Brownjohn to Robertson 1352, June 25, 1948, C4803/3/18, 70495, FO 371, all in UKNA.

5. Bevin to Franks 914, June 25, 1948, C5031/3/18, and Bevin to Franks 915, June 26, 1948, C5032/3/18, 70497, FO 371, UKNA; *FR, 1948,* 2:924.

6. Robertson to Bevin 1204, June 27, 1948, FO 1030/60, UKNA.

7. Robertson to Bevin 1194, June 26, 1948, FO 1030/60, UKNA; Draper to Royall, June 24, 1948, "Cables Incoming Record Copies June 1948" folder, box 680, OMGUS AGO Incoming Cables, RG 260, USNA; Smith, *Clay Papers,* 2:699, 701–2.

8. LeMay to Norstad UAX-8552, June 26, 1948, "AG 319.1 Berlin Transportation Situation Reports, vol. II, 1948" folder, box 427, OMGUS AGO General Correspondence, RG 260, USNA; Miller, *To Save a City,* 44.

9. Collier, *Bridge,* 55; memo, "US Position Regarding the Continued Occupation of Berlin (Gen Clay's Comments)," June 26, 1948, case 88/49, "1948—Hot File—P&O 092 TS thru 381 TS" folder, box 9, General Administrative File, RG 319, USNA; Smith, *Clay Papers,* 2:697, 707–8; Robertson to Bevin 1199, June 27, 1948, C5010/3/18, 70496, FO 371, UKNA. For estimates of existing stocks, see Bohlen to Hickerson, June 26, 1948, "Memos, CEB 1948 (1946–1948)" folder, box 5, Bohlen papers, RG 59, USNA; Smith, *Clay Papers,* 2:699; and Robertson to Bevin, June 24, 1948, C4921/3/18, 70495, FO 371, UKNA.

10. Waite to Spackman, June 26, 1948, AIR 20/7804, UKNA. Waite's analysis is no longer in the file; only the letter of transmittal remains. I assumed it formed the basis of the figures under discussion in London on Monday, which envisaged a daily lift of 2,000 tons.

11. Bullock, *Bevin,* 3:576; Smith, *Clay Papers,* 2:707–8; *FR, 1948,* 2:918–19; Smith interview, 221, file K239.0512-906, AFHRA; "USAFE and the Airlift, 1948," 28, reel Z-0039, USAFE/HO; Murphy, "Berlin Airlift," 90.

12. MFRs, June 28 and 29, 1948, "Movement of Aircraft to Europe," both in "P&O 381 TS (Section V-A)(part 2) . . ." folder, box 103, P&O TS Decimal File, RG 319, USNA; AFOPO to AAC et al., WX-84768 and 84772, June 27, 1948, "AG 319.1 Berlin Transportation Situation, vol. II, 1948" folder, box 427, OMGUS AGO General Correspondence, RG 260, USNA; Bradley to Clay WARX 84774, June 27, 1948, "OAS 580.Germany" folder, box 17, Draper-Voorhees file, RG 335, USNA; Vandenberg to LeMay and Clay W-84775, June 27, 1948,

"Cables—General Clay—June 1948" folder, box 12, Clay papers, RG 200, USNA. Frank Roberts's recollections have led some to exaggerate the effect of Bevin's June 28 appeals to Draper and Wedemeyer to expand the airlift. The order went out the day before Bevin met the two Americans. Tusa and Tusa, *Berlin Airlift,* 155–56; Peplow, "Role of Britain," 210–11.

13. Truman, *Memoirs,* 2:123; Shlaim, *United States,* 208–11. Shlaim qualifies these sweeping assessments by acknowledging the stopgap nature of the airlift at this point. The issues involved in those qualifications (pp. 210–11) are so fundamental as to undermine his characterization of what he thinks the president ordered.

14. USAFE Historical Division, "A Five Year Summary of USAFE History, 1945–1950," May 1, 1952, 183–84, file K570.01, AFHRA; Lay, "Berlin Air Lift," 1:7–8, reel Z-0029, USAFE/HO.

15. Smith, *Clay Papers,* 2:707–8; Clay quoted in Davidson, *Death and Life,* 202–3; Clay to Bradley and Wedemeyer CC-4906, June 27, 1948, "AG 319.1 Berlin Transportation Situation Reports, vol. II, 1948" folder, box 427, OMGUS AGO General Correspondence, RG 260, USNA; *Newsweek,* July 5, 1948, 30. Cf. Smith, *Clay Papers,* 2:701.

16. Draper interview, January 11, 1972, 63–65, HSTL. Another version of the story claims (erroneously) that the two were in Berlin when the blockade began and persuaded Clay to undertake the airlift. Bennett, *Berlin Bastion,* 44–46; Offner, *Another Such Victory,* 256.

17. Timberman to Maddocks, June 28, 1948, case 88/59, and Timberman to Schuyler, June 30, 1948, case 88/43, both in sec. 2, P&O 381 TS, box 103, P&O TS Decimal File, RG 319, USNA.

18. COS(48)87, June 28, 1948, DEFE 4/14, UKNA. For possible evacuations, see CM(48)43, June 25, 1948, CAB 128/13; COS(48)102, July 19, 1948, DEFE 4/14; and file C6208/3/18, 70505, FO 371, all in UKNA; Litchfield to Wedemeyer, July 2, 1948, "G801.4 Berlin II" folder, box 4, Records of the Division of Central European Affairs, RG 59, USNA; plan, July 21, 1948, 740.00119 Control (Germany)/7-2148, RG 59, USNA; and EUCOM plan, August 30, 1948, "OPD 370.05 Berlin, Germany" folder, box 806, TS Decimal File, RG 341, USNA.

19. USAFE to USAF UAX-8474, June 18, 1948, "USAFE UAX 6667 [to] UAX 9859" folder, box 450, Incoming Messages, RG 549, USNA; BAFO Report, 129; Pernot, "Le pont aérien," 56–57; Berlin Magistrat, *Airlift Berlin,* 51.

20. BAFO Report, 325–27; Jackson, *Berlin Airlift,* 82; Downie, "Long Ranger," 20; report, USAFE, "Construction for United States Air Force in Europe," August 1, 1948, box B48, LeMay papers, LOCMD; Harris et al., "Special Study," 58; Barker, *Berlin Air Lift,* 43; Morris, *Blockade,* 120.

21. Report, USAFE, "Berlin Airlift," 40, reel Z-0039, USAFE/HO.

22. Donovan, *Bridge,* 65–66.

23. Robertson to Alexander CCG 21510, June 28, 1948, C5043/3/18, 70497, FO 371, UKNA; COS(48)87 and 88, June 28, 1948, DEFE 4/14, UKNA; GEN 241/1st meeting, June 28, 1948, C5136/3/18, 70498, FO 371, UKNA.

24. Coleridge to Gruenther, June 29, 1948, "1948—Hot File—P&O 092 TS thru 381 TS" folder, box 9, General Administrative File, RG 319, USNA; meeting transcript 309, June 30, 1948, CD 9-3-13, box 52, OSD Numerical File, RG 330, USNA.

25. Meeting transcript 309, June 30, 1948, CD 9-3-13, box 52, OSD Numerical File, RG 330, USNA. For Hays's report, see Mayo to Maddocks, June 30, 1948, case 88/43, sec. 2, P&O 381 TS, box 103, P&O TS Decimal File, RG 319, USNA.

26. Royall to Clay WAR 84975, June 30, 1948, sec. 17, CCS 381 (8-20-43), box 177,

1948–50 Central Decimal File, RG 218, USNA; teleconference, June 30, 1948, 740.00119 Control (Germany)/6-3048, RG 59, USNA; Smith, *Clay Papers,* 2:711–12; *FR, 1948,* 2:936–38; Bevin to Franks 948, June 30, 1948, C5262/3/18, 70499, FO 371, UKNA; MOD to Robertson 954, June 30, 1948, DEFE 11/321, UKNA. Claims that Truman threatened the Russians, who then took down the balloons, are mistaken. Cf. Lebow, *Nuclear Crisis Management,* 106.

27. Meeting at Bückeburg, June 27, 1948, FO 1030/60, UKNA; Robertson to Alexander CCG 21510, June 28, 1948, C5043/3/18, 70497, UKNA; Kirkpatrick to Hollis, June 26, 1948, C5015/3/18, 70496, FO 371, UKNA; Brook to Tedder, June 28, 1948, AIR 20/7148, UKNA; BAFO Report, 117; Jackson, *Berlin Airlift,* 46; Barker, *Berlin Air Lift,* 9. Control of airlift operations by BAFO raised hackles back home; the RAF's Transport Command had planned to direct them itself. A similar and better known "turf battle" divided LeMay's command and MATS in the United States. Cf. Barker, *Berlin Air Lift,* 6; Jackson, *Berlin Airlift,* 45; and Tunner, *Over the Hump,* 159–62, 166, 188–97.

28. Lay, "Berlin Air Lift," 1:1–2, 10–11, reel Z-0029, USAFE/HO; Smith report, July 30, 1948, reel C5113, AFHRA; "USAFE and the Airlift, 1948," 28, reel Z-0039, USAFE/HO; BAFO note, June 30, 1948, AIR 38/384, UKNA; BAFO Report, 129, 557–63; Gallogly Report, 12, 50–52.

29. Fisher, "Berlin Airlift," 9. Fisher spells the officer's name "Willerford," but USAFE rosters omit the first *r*.

30. Kissner to Smith, June 29, 1948, "OPD 381 Berlin (15 Jan 48)" folder, box 807, Plans TS Decimal File, RG 341, USNA; Smith interview, 219–21, file K239.0512-906, AFHRA; *History of USAFE, June 1948,* appendix 18, USAFE/HO; USAFE Press Release 1750, June 29, 1948, reel Z-0039, USAFE/HO.

31. Smith report, July 30, 1948, reel C5113, AFHRA; "USAFE and the Airlift, 1948," 28, and "USAFE Summary," 122, both reel Z-0039, USAFE/HO.

32. For "Vittles," cf. Fisher, "Berlin Airlift," 8; Miller, *To Save a City,* 58; and Vandenberg to LeMay and Clay W-84775, June 27, 1948, "Cables—General Clay—June 1948" folder, box 12, Clay papers, RG 200, USNA. The RAF replaced "Knicker" with "Carter-Paterson" on June 28 but changed the name on July 19 after communist propagandists pointed out that it was the name of a British removals (moving van) company. AHQ BAFO to Air Branch, Combined Svs Div, SYX.805, June 28, 1948, AIR 20/7804, UKNA; Barker, *Berlin Air Lift,* 9; BAFO Report, 146.

33. *History of USAFE, July 1948,* appendix 19, USAFE/HO.

34. Sir Kenneth Cross quoted in Sowrey et al., "Berlin Airlift," 50–52.

35. Quoted in Barker, *Berlin Air Lift,* 16.

36. Launius and Cross, *MAC,* 19–20; "USAFE and the Airlift, 1948," 166, reel Z-0039, USAFE/HO.

37. BAFO Report, 14, 117; minutes of Air Ministry meeting, August 13, 1948, AIR 20/6891, UKNA; COS(48)97th meeting, July 12, 1948, CAB 21/1885, UKNA. The deputy chief of air staff, Air Marshal Sir Hugh Walmsley, later described the training halt as "our first mistake." Walmsley lecture, "Berlin Air Lift," October 25, 1949, AIR 20/6894, UKNA.

38. Robertson to Bevin 1208, June 28, 1948, CAB 21/1885, UKNA; AHQ BAFO to Air Ministry AOX.772, July 1, 1948, AIR 20/7808, UKNA; Barker, *Berlin Air Lift,* 34.

39. COMNAVFORGER to CNO CC-5236, July 20, 1948, "AG 319.1 Berlin Transportation Situation Reports, vol. III, 1948" folder, box 428, OMGUS AGO General Correspondence, RG 260, USNA; Groth to Marshall A-486, August 3, 1948, 740.00119 Control

(Germany)/8-348, RG 59, USNA; EXFOR to BERCOMB MGA.64, August 10, 1948, and report, BEA, August 6, 1948, both in AIR 20/7820, UKNA; Gere, *Unheralded,* 62.

40. Murphy to Marshall 1553, June 30, 1948, 740.00119 Control (Germany)/6-3048, RG 59, USNA; BAFO Report, 113.

41. Smith interview, 223–25, file K230.0512-906, AHFRA; BAFO Report, 120, 130.

42. USAFE Press Release 1771, reel Z-0039, USAFE/HO; BAFO Report, 130; Cox, "Britain and the Airlift," 36; Smith interview, 227, file K239.0512-906, AFHRA; "USAFE and the Airlift, 1948," 17–18, reel Z-0039, USAFE/HO.

43. *London Times,* July 2, 1948; "Operation Vittles," *TI&E Bulletin* 3, no. 34 (August 22, 1948), in tab A, Personnel Division, *History of USAFE, January 1949,* USAFE/HO; Pearcy, "Berlin Airlift," 204; BAFO Report, 16, 36, 261–62; "USAFE and the Airlift, 1948," 167, reel Z-0039, USAFE/HO.

44. *Newsweek,* July 12, 1948, 28; Davison, *Berlin Blockade,* 120; Charles, *Berlin Blockade,* 61.

45. Pope to Pearson, July 7, 1948, Pope diary, July 7, 1948, vol. 2, Pope papers, LAC; Murphy to Marshall 1638, July 8, 1948, 740.00119 Control (Germany)/7-848, RG 59, USNA; *New York Times,* July 6, 1948, 3; ibid., July 9, 1948, 1; ibid., July 10, 1948, 1; *Newsweek,* July 19, 1948, 26–27; Bohlen memo, July 6, 1948, "CEB Memos 1948" folder, box 5, Bohlen papers, RG 59, USNA; *London Times,* July 10 and 14, 1948; "Supply Situation 12 July 1948," n.d., "Airlift Planning Vol. I" folder, box 16, Director's files, Berlin Sector Records, RG 260, USNA; Robertson to Alexander 149 Basic, July 8, 1948, C5483/3/18, 70501, FO 371, UKNA; Robertson to Hannover BGCC 5112, July 2, 1948, FO 1030/61, UKNA.

46. Memo, July 8, 1948, "Director of USAF Public Relations, 1948–49" folder, box 4, Ginsburgh papers, HSTL; draft memo, Vandenberg to JCS, n.d. [early July 1948], "OPD 381 Berlin (15 Jan 48)," sec. 2, box 807, TS Decimal File, RG 341, USNA; memo, July 16, 1948, "Memo for President: Meeting Discussions (1948)" folder, box 186, PSF, Truman papers, HSTL; David MacIssac quoted in Betts, *Nuclear Blackmail,* 28.

47. Clay to Bradley CC-4935, June 29, 1948, "Berlin Crisis Book I" folder, box 14, Draper-Voorhees file, RG 335, USNA; Anderson to Maddocks, June 30, 1948, case 88/65, sec. 2, P&O 381 TS, box 103, P&O TS Decimal File, RG 319, USNA; "USAFE and the Airlift, 1948," 17, reel Z-0039, USAFE/HO; Howley, *Berlin Command,* 209–10. Other tests using C-47s were equally discouraging. Gallogly Report, 62–63. See also BAFO Report, 307–8. When the idea came up in late July Tedder opposed using RAF bombers to drop coal "except as a last resort," citing reasons similar to LeMay's; minutes of Air Ministry meeting, July 27, 1948, AIR 20/6891, UKNA.

48. Charles, *Berlin Blockade,* 61; *Newsweek,* July 19, 1948, 25; OMGUS, *Military Government Report, July 1948,* 7.

49. Charles, *Berlin Blockade,* 61; Donovan, *Bridge,* 131; Smith interim report, July 30, 1948, reel C5113, AFHRA; Barker, *Berlin Air Lift,* 34; Gailey to Clay, August 12 and 17, 1948, "AG 319.1 Berlin Transportation Situation Reports, vol. V, 1948" folder, box 428, OMGUS AGO General Correspondence, RG 260, USNA; report, CALTF, "Preliminary Analysis of Lessons Learned," June 1949, 30–31, 37, reel C5113, AFHRA; Tunner, *Over the Hump,* 205; "USAFE and the Airlift, 1948," 187, reel Z-0039, USAFE/HO.

50. Clay to Bradley CC-4935, June 29, 1948, "Berlin Crisis Book I" folder, box 14, Draper-Voorhees file, RG 335, USNA; Hays to BICO CC-4951, June 29, 1948, and Adcock to Hays BICO-917, July 2, 1948, both in "AG 319.1, Berlin Transportation Situation Reports, vol. II" folder, box 427, OMGUS AGO General Correspondence, RG 260, USNA.

51. Memo, July 8, 1948, AIR 20/7804, UKNA; message, BTB to EXFOR, July 14, 1948, AIR 20/7804, UKNA; *History of USAFE, July 1948,* 14, USAFE/HO; Hays to Bradley CC-5204, July 17, 1948, case 137/69, "P&O 092 (Section IX-C) . . ." folder, box 118, P&O TS Decimal File, RG 319, USNA; Murphy to Marshall 1834, July 27, 1948, 740.00119 Control (Germany)/7-2748, RG 59, USNA; Howley to Chief of Staff, July 17, 1948, "Airlift Planning Vol. I" folder, box 16, Director's files, Berlin Sector Records, RG 260, USNA. The simple word *ton* caused no end of confusion. To Americans, it meant 2,000 pounds; to Europeans, it meant 1,000 kilograms, or 2,204.6 pounds. The difference was important. According to Waite, the goal was 4,500 *metric* tons, but Clay's staff had briefed him that Berlin needed 4,500 *short* tons. The general then publicly committed himself to the lower figure, which understated Berlin's needs by 10 percent. Waite to Herbert, August 31, 1948, AIR 20/7804, UKNA.

52. Harris et al., "Special Study," 13–16; *History of USAFE, April 1949,* 52, USAFE/HO.

53. Smith, *Clay Papers,* 2:730; LeMay to Norstad UAX-8776, July 15, 1948, "094 Berlin" folder, box 353, Classified Correspondence, RG 549, USNA.

54. Smith, *Clay Papers,* 2:730, 736; Lemley memo, July 12, 1948, case 88/94, sec. 3, P&O 381 TS, box 103, P&O TS Decimal File, RG 319, USNA.

55. *History of USAFE, December 1948,* appendix XII, USAFE/HO; BAFO Report, 52; "USAFE Summary," 88, reel Z-0039, USAFE/HO; Dept. of Navy press release, October 20, 1948, "Press Releases 16–30 October 1948" folder, box 237, Post-1946 Command File, SecNav Series, Operational Archives, U.S. Navy Historical Center.

56. BAFO Report, 185, 312; "USAFE Summary," 92, reel Z-0039, USAFE/HO; minutes of Air Ministry meeting, August 13, 1948, AIR 20/6891, UKNA.

57. BAFO Report, 49–50, 316–18; minutes of Air Ministry meeting, August 13, 1948, AIR 20/6891, UKNA; "USAFE and the Airlift, 1948," 105–8, reel Z-0039, USAFE/HO; Harris et al., "Special Study," 98; report, CALTF, "Preliminary Analysis of Lessons Learned," June 1949, 40, reel C5113, AFHRA; "USAFE Summary," 74–79, 92, reel Z-0039, USAFE/HO; Bennett, *Berlin Bastion,* 104.

58. "USAFE and the Airlift, 1948," 91–92, reel Z-0039, USAFE/HO; Bennett, *Berlin Bastion,* 117.

59. "USAFE and the Airlift, 1948," 179, reel Z-0039, USAFE/HO; Gallogly Report, 119; BAFO Report, 121.

60. "USAFE and the Airlift, 1948," 91, 105, 110–14, reel Z-0039, USAFE/HO.

61. Ibid., 95; "USAFE and the Airlift, 1949," 8–9, reel Z-0040, USAFE/HO.

62. "USAFE and the Airlift, 1948," 33–35, 62, 93, 123–24, reel Z-0039, USAFE/HO.

63. *History of USAFE, July 1948* (Air Surgeon Report), USAFE/HO; Moseley, "Medical History," 1253–57; Halvorsen interview, May 13, 1988, 1–3, AMC/HO; Lay, "Berlin Air Lift," 1:41, reel Z-0029, USAFE/HO.

64. Davison, *Berlin Blockade,* 129; Fisher, "Berlin Airlift," 6–8; Slayton, *Master of the Air,* 115; BAFO Report, 191–92, 473–85. The pilot's recollection is from Galligan interview, May 31, 1983, 48, K239.0512-1555, AFHRA.

65. "USAFE and the Airlift, 1948," 20–21, reel Z-0039, USAFE/HO; Lay, "Berlin Air Lift," 1:12–13, reel Z-0029, USAFE/HO; Tusa and Tusa, *Berlin Airlift,* 243.

66. Lay, "Berlin Air Lift," 1:13–19, reel Z-0029, USAFE/HO.

67. Ibid., 21.

68. Ibid., 21–24; "USAFE and the Airlift, 1948," 41, reel Z-0039, USAFE/HO; Barker, *Berlin Air Lift,* 34; note, A. H. Dangerfield, September 6, 1948, AIR 20/7805, UKNA.

69. Lay, "Berlin Air Lift," 1:21–24, 30–32, 43–46, reel Z-0029, USAFE/HO; "USAFE and the Airlift, 1949," 190–94, reel Z-0039, USAFE/HO.

70. "USAFE and the Airlift, 1948," 209–13, reel Z-0039, USAFE/HO; Donovan, *Bridge,* 55–56; Lay, "Berlin Air Lift," 1:18, reel Z-0029, USAFE/HO; Gere, *Unheralded,* 173.

71. Memo for the president, July 16, 1948, "Memo for President: Meeting Discussions (1948)" folder, box 186, PSF, Truman papers, HSTL.

72. For the notion of an airlift as a "conspicuous alternative," see George and Smoke, *Deterrence,* 125.

6. "The Next Step"

1. Betts, *Nuclear Blackmail,* 9; Gelb and Betts, *Irony,* 341; Neustadt, *Presidential Power,* 223–24.

2. Divine, "Cold War and the Election," 104–5; Nicolson, *Diaries and Letters,* 3:146.

3. Barker, *Britain between the Superpowers,* 122; Bevin to Franks 914, June 25, 1948, C5031/3/18, and record of meeting, June 25, 1948, C5094/3/18, both in 70497, FO 371, UKNA; *FR, 1948,* 2:924.

4. Millis and Duffield, *Forrestal Diaries,* 453–54; Smith, *Clay Papers,* 2:707–9.

5. Forrestal manuscript diary, June 27, 1948, and Royall to Bradley, June 28, 1948, filed with Forrestal diary, Forrestal papers, MML; SAC to Commander, 301 Bomb Group, June 28, 1948, file 32, box 7, Chairman's File, RG 218, USNA; AFCCS to SAC WX-84771, June 27, 1948, and WX-84776, June 28, 1948, "AG 360.4 General" folder, box 627, OMGUS AGO Classified Correspondence, RG 260, USNA; *New York Times,* July 1, 1948, 1.

6. Draper to Royall message 3, June 27, 1948, "Berlin Crisis Book I" folder, box 14, Draper-Voorhees file, RG 335, USNA; Brook to Tedder, June 28, 1948, AIR 20/7148, UKNA. Cornelius Whitney claimed that he passed word to the Soviet embassy that the B-29s *were* carrying atomic bombs (possibly true), and the Russians agreed to lift the blockade the following morning (definitely untrue). Whitney, *High Peaks,* 79–84.

7. Lilienthal, *Journals,* 2:377.

8. Meeting transcript 309, June 30, 1948, CD 9-3-13, box 52, OSD Numerical File, RG 330, USNA.

9. Norstad to Forrestal, July 1, 1948, folder 1, CD 6-2-9, box 27, OSD Numerical File, RG 330, USNA; 28th Bomb Group S-2 report, reel B106, frame 1751ff., AFHRA; Williamson and Rearden, *Origins,* 88.

10. Record of meeting, June 28, 1948, C5136/3/18, and Bevin to Franks 924, June 28, 1948, C5183/3/18, both in 70498, FO 371, UKNA.

11. Franks to Bevin 3222, July 1, 1948, and Bevin to Franks 7150, July 2, 1948, both in C5205/3/18, 70498, UKNA.

12. Millis and Duffield, *Forrestal Diaries,* 455–56. Marshall's summary of his conversation with Rayburn, which he said occurred "several weeks" before, is in memo for the president, July 16, 1948, "Memo for the President: Meeting Discussions (1948)" folder, box 186, PSF, Truman papers, HSTL, and in Forrestal manuscript diary, July 15, 1948, Forrestal papers, MML. For a summary of the polls, see Russell to Lovett, July 7, 1948, 740.00119 Control (Germany)/7-748, RG 59, USNA.

13. Marshall to Douglas 2665, July 10, 1948, 740.00119 Control (Germany)/7-248; Douglas to Marshall 3166, July 13, 1948, 740.00119 Control (Germany)/7-1348, both in RG 59, USNA; Bevin to Franks 7709, July 13, 1948, FO 800/467/GER/48/41, UKNA; *FR, 1948,*

2:965; Douglas to Marshall 3194, July 15, 1948, 740.00119 Control (Germany)/7-1548, RG 59, USNA; Smith, *Clay Papers,* 2:740.

14. Millis and Duffield, *Forrestal Diaries,* 457.

15. Memo for the president, July 16, 1948, "Memo for the President: Meeting Discussions (1948)" folder, box 186, and NSC Record of Actions, 15th meeting, July 15, 1948, box 167, both in PSF, Truman papers, HSTL; Forrestal manuscript diary, July 15, 1948, Forrestal papers, MML. Noting that Truman rarely attended council meetings before the Korean War, scholars have offered subtle reasons for his absence. Theodore Sorenson contends that he stayed away from meetings early in the Berlin crisis because he thought his attendance would inhibit discussion. Avi Shlaim counters that in this case, the president had probably been briefed and regarded the deployment as a foregone conclusion. The real reason was more prosaic: Truman did not attend this meeting because he was asleep. He had returned to Washington by train at 5:30 A.M. from the Democratic Party convention in Philadelphia. His first appointment that day was an 11:05 meeting with Forrestal and Royall. Cf. Shlaim, *United States,* 236n, and "Presidential Appointments File . . . 1948—July" folder, box 75, PSF, Truman papers, HSTL. Furthermore, Truman did not view the deployment as a foregone conclusion the day before. *FR, 1948,* 2:967.

16. For additional information on the deployment and its background, see Moody, *Building,* 207–16, and Borowski, *Hollow Threat,* 125–28. Vandenberg explained to LeMay that the deployment was a diplomatic maneuver to induce the Soviets to back down, not preparation for war. Further, it gave the air force a chance to return to Britain and establish supply bases there, which it had wanted to do for some time. Vandenberg to LeMay, July 23, 1948, sec. 1, "OPD 381 Berlin (15 Jan 48)" folder, box 807, TS Decimal File, RG 341, USNA.

17. Kerr, "Secret Hotline." Writers continue to assert, incorrectly, that these bombers carried—or could carry—atomic bombs. There was only one unit trained and equipped for nuclear warfare in 1948—the 509th Bomb Group, stationed near the Los Alamos laboratories in New Mexico. It remained in the Southwest for most of the crisis, deploying to England in April 1949 without atomic bombs or components. Smith to Norstad, August 9, 1948, "452.1 Programming General" folder, Records of the Administrative Office, Deputy Chief of Staff for Operations, RG 341, USNA. For B-29 units rotating to Britain during 1948 and 1949, see "The Third Air Division during Fiscal Year 1949 . . . ," frame 1177ff., reel B5400, AFHRA. Incidentally, after assuming command of SAC, LeMay was unimpressed with the 509th, describing it as "no damn good." LeMay diary, December 16, 1948 entry, box B64, LeMay papers, LOCMD.

18. Quoted in Djilas, *Conversations,* 153.

19. Rearden, *Formative Years,* 426–28; Greenwood, "Emergence," 230; Forrestal manuscript diary, July 10, 1947, and March 15, 1948, Forrestal papers, MML; Millis and Duffield, *Forrestal Diaries,* 393–94.

20. Lilienthal, *Journals,* 2:306–7.

21. Leahy diary, May 6 and 12, 1948, Leahy papers, LOCMD; Barlow, *Revolt,* 92; Millis and Duffield, *Forrestal Diaries,* 432.

22. *FR, 1948,* 1:572–73; memo for the president, June 4, 1948, "Memo for the President: Meeting Discussions (1948)" folder, box 186, PSF, Truman papers, HSTL. For the roots of the army's assumption, see Barlow, *Revolt,* 88–92.

23. Lilienthal, *Journals,* 2:362, 373–74, 377 (emphasis in original); Nichols, *Road to Trinity,* 263.

24. Memo for the president, July 2, 1948, "Memo for the President: Meeting Discussions

(1948)" folder, box 186, PSF, Truman papers, HSTL; Lilienthal, *Journals,* 2:384; Millis and Duffield, *Forrestal Diaries,* 458.

25. "Presidential Appointments File . . . 1948—July" folder, box 75, PSF, Truman papers, HSTL.

26. Lilienthal, *Journals,* 2:388–92; Millis and Duffield, *Forrestal Diaries,* 460–61; Forrestal to Truman, July 21, 1948, and Lilienthal to Truman, July 21, 1948, both in "NSC Atomic: Atomic Energy: Stockpile" folder, box 176; and Webb to Truman, July 22, 1948, "NSC Atomic: Atomic Energy: Budget" folder, box 174, all in PSF, Truman papers, HSTL.

27. Lilienthal, *Journals,* 2:392; Truman to Forrestal, August 6, 1948, "NSC Atomic: Atomic Weapons: Stockpile" folder, box 176, PSF, Truman papers, HSTL.

28. Lilienthal, *Journals,* 2:391. Cf. Ferrell, *Dear Bess,* 555. S. David Broscious offers a good introduction to Truman's views on nuclear weapons in "Longing for International Control."

29. Forrestal manuscript diary, July 28, 1948, Forrestal papers, MML.

30. Robertson memo, July 10, 1948, FO 1030/61; Robertson to Strang, July 20, 1948, C6157/3/18, 70504, FO 371; extract, COS(48)97th meeting, July 12, 1948, DEFE 11/321, all in UKNA.

31. Makins minute, July 14, 1948; Dean minute, July 19, 1948; and Strang to Bevin, July 21, 1948, all in C5540/3/18, 70501, FO 371, UKNA.

32. For the Germans' cold reception of the London program, see *FR, 1948,* 2:380–413, quote at 385. Bevin's rejection is in memo of conversation, July 28, 1948, C6159/3/18, 70504, FO 371, UKNA.

33. COS(48)102(4), July 19, 1948, DEFE 4/14, UKNA; Hollis, Margiobanks, Kirkpatrick, and Strang memos, C6208/3/18, 70505, FO 371, UKNA. See also Litchfield to Wedemeyer, July 24, 1948, "G801.4 Berlin II" folder, box 4, Records of the Division of Central European Affairs, RG 59, USNA.

34. Dean minute, July 18, 1948, C6103/3/18, 70504, FO 371, UKNA; Robertson to Pearson 1185, July 22, 1948, "Robertson, N. A." folder, vol. 441, King papers, LAC.

35. Bullock, *Bevin,* 3:580–82; Dean to Beckett, July 15, 1948, and Jebb minute, July 16, 1948, both in C6254/3/18; and Jebb to Strang, July 23, 1948, C6253/3/18, all in 70505, FO 371, UKNA.

36. Bevin to Franks 52, July 19, 1948, C5808/3/18, 70502, FO 371, UKNA.

37. Bullock, *Bevin,* 3:584–86; Robertson to Pearson 1185, July 22, 1948, "Robertson, N. A." folder, vol. 441, King papers, LAC.

38. *Newsweek,* July 26, 1948, 34; ibid., August 2, 1948, 33; Ashley-Clarke to Bevin 952, July 18, 1948, C5769/3/18, 70502, FO 371, UKNA; Bevin to Strang 272, July 20, 1948, C5854/3/18, 70503, FO 371, UKNA; Bullock, *Bevin,* 3:584–85. For Lovett's comments, see *FR, 1948,* 3:150.

39. Snyder and Diesing, *Conflict among Nations,* 359–60.

40. Young, *Politics of Force,* 215.

41. Schelling, *Arms and Influence,* 69–73, 79–80, 89–91.

42. Minutes of Staff Conference, October 2, 1948, box 5, OMGUS Minutes, RG 260, USNA.

43. Smith, *Clay Papers,* 2:733–35; Trudeau interview, February 17, 1971, MHI; Gobarev, "Soviet Military Plans," 15–17; LeMay interview, March 9, 1971, 13–14, K239.0512-736, AFHRA; LeMay and Kantor, *Mission with LeMay,* 411–12; Osmanski memo, July 13, 1948, case 88/71, sec. 2, "P&O 381 TS (Section V-A)(part 2) . . ." folder, box 103, P&O TS Decimal File, RG 319, USNA. Osmanski noted that the autobahn was 125 miles long, with an average of three bridges to the mile. Destruction of any one of them would delay Trudeau (or later convoys); demolition of several would render the highway unusable.

44. Smith, *Clay Papers,* 2:735–38; Clay interview, March 22, 1971, CUOH; Osmanski memo, July 13, 1948, case 88/71, sec. 2, P&O 381 TS, box 103, P&O TS Decimal File, RG 319, USNA.

45. Smith, *Clay Papers,* 2:739–41; Bradley to Clay, July 15, 1948, case 88/90, and Royall to Clay, July 16, 1948, case 88/91, both in "P&O 092 TS thru 381 TS 1948 Hot File" folder, box 9, General Administrative File, RG 319, USNA. Smith and Shlaim have contended Truman was behind the summons, intending to show support for Clay. More recent evidence indicates otherwise. "My mutton-headed Secretary of the Army ordered Clay home from Germany and stirred up a terrific howdy-do for no good reason," Truman complained in a letter to his wife. "Marshall and I had decided it was not necessary for him to come and so told Forrestal—but you know how smart that Defense setup thinks it is." Cf. Smith, *Defense of Berlin,* 110n; Shlaim, *United States,* 258, 275; and Ferrell, *Dear Bess,* 555.

46. Smith, *Clay Papers,* 2:743–46. Smith's contention that Clay's convoy plan "was based on a cautious, sound judgment of Soviet intent" and Shlaim's contention that it rested on "a complete and coherent analysis of the situation" both seem off the mark. Smith, "View from USFET," 77; Shlaim, *United States,* 193.

47. In a 1973 interview at the Army War College, Clay remained convinced that the Russians would not have interfered with the convoy. Two years earlier, he admitted it would have been only a first step. He told Jean Edward Smith, "If we were going to keep that route open for Germans, we had to take over their highway and guard it. . . . This was always one of the reasons why I was never as sure of going in on the ground, as much as I wanted to do so. . . . I still wish we had, but I don't know what we would have done if . . . the Russians had just let us through and then stopped the next group of German trucks that moved in and out." Clay interviews, January 24, 1973, MHI, and March 9, 1971, CUOH. His recognition that the West would have to take physical control of access routes was not a retrospective judgment; he had said as much in July 1948. See memo for the president, July 23, 1948, "Memo for the President: Meeting Discussions (1948)" folder, box 186, PSF, Truman papers, HSTL.

48. Murphy to Marshall 1662, July 11, 1948, "Berlin Cables to Secretary of State, Jan.–July 1948" folder, box 1, TS Cables, POLAD files, RG 84, USNA; Robertson to Strang 1198, June 27, 1948, DEFE 11/321; Robertson to Bevin 677 Basic, July 16, 1948, CAB 21/1886; and Robertson to MOD Basic 125, July 15, 1948, DEFE 11/322, all in UKNA.

49. Laukhuff to Murphy, July 10, 1948, "710 Berlin Situation Apr–July 15" folder, box 215, Classified General Correspondence, POLAD files, RG 84, USNA.

50. Osmanski memo, July 13, 1948, case 88/71; Anderson to Maddocks, July 15, 1948, case 88/57; Maddocks to Bradley, July 13, 1948, case 88/77; Maddocks to Bradley, July 17, 1948, case 88/74; and Maddocks to Bradley, July 18, 1948, case 88/75, all in sec. 2, P&O 381 TS, box 103, P&O TS Decimal File, RG 319, USNA.

51. Draft memo for Royall, July 17, 1948, case 88/73, sec. 2, P&O 381 TS, box 103, P&O TS Decimal File, RG 319, USNA; Bradley to Royall, July 17, 1948, folder 1, CD 6-2-9, box 27, OSD Numerical File, RG 330, USNA (emphasis added); Bradley to JCS, JCS 1907, July 19, 1948, sec. 17, CCS 381 (8-20-43), box 177, 1948–50 Central Decimal File, RG 218, USNA.

52. Wedemeyer to Bradley, July 23, 1948, "EUCOM Trip, June–July 1948" binder, P&O 319.1 TS (Jun–Jul 48), box 49, P&O TS Decimal File; H. G. S. to Wedemeyer, July 21, 1948, case 137/78, "P&O 092 (Section IX-C) . . ." folder, box 118, P&O Secret Correspondence, both in RG 319, USNA.

53. Memo for the president, July 16, 1948, "Memo for the President: Meeting Discussions (1948)" folder, box 186, PSF, Truman papers, HSTL (emphasis added).

54. Bonnet-Bohlen conversation, July 17, 1948, fiche 635, *FR, Memoranda of Conversations*; Loftus, "American Response," 304–6.

55. Douglas to Marshall 3217, July 15, 1948, 740.00119 Control (Germany)/7-1548, RG 59, USNA; *FR, 1948,* 2:967–70. For Smith's views, see Smith to Marshall 1348, July 19, 1948, 740.00119 Control (Germany)/7-1948, RG 59, USNA.

56. Pruessen, *Dulles,* 375–80; Dulles MFRs, July 19 and 22, 1948, "Berlin and Germany 1948" folder, box 35, Dulles papers, MML. Some contemporaries did not see Dulles as the dove portrayed by Pruessen. Dean thought him "quite determined . . . to bring the United Nations in fairly soon, so that if we do reach a war because of Berlin we shall have trodden the U.N. road as far as possible before the shooting begins." A short while later, James Pollock noted that Dulles "has been insisting on the strongest possible action against the Soviets." Dean to Beckett, July 15, 1948, C6254/3/18, 70505, FO 371, UKNA; Pollock to Clay, August 12, 1948, file 21-17, box 21, Pollock papers, BHL.

57. The phrase, referring to Clay's convoy, is from Pogue, *Marshall,* 4:307.

58. Pruessen, *Dulles,* 376.

59. Millis and Duffield, *Forrestal Diaries,* 459; Truman, *Truman,* 15; Davison, *Berlin Blockade,* 157. Cf. Admiral Dennison's anecdote in Hechler, *Working with Truman,* 53.

60. *FR, 1948,* 2:971–73.

61. Truman, *Truman,* 15; Draper memo of conversation with Harriman, July 17, 1948, and Draper MFR, July 19, 1948, both in "'Lock Up' SAOUS 000.1 Germany" folder, box 12, Draper-Voorhees file, RG 335, USNA.

62. U.S. President, *Public Papers . . . 1948,* 413n. Truman had no comment on Berlin or the international situation at his press conference the next day. Ibid., 411–12.

63. *New York Times,* July 21, 1948, 4; Allen to Dean, July 22, 1948, C6158/3/18, 70504, FO 371, UKNA; Franks to Bevin 3591, July 21, 1948, C5899/3/18, 70503, FO 371, UKNA; Wrong to St. Laurent WA-2088, July 20, 1948, pt. 4, file 7-CA-14(s), DEA files; Wrong to St. Laurent WA-2095, July 21, 1948, folder 1, file W-22-5-G, vol. 119, ser. 18, RG 2, LAC. For Soviet press silence, see Peterson to Bevin 755, June 29, 1948, CAB 21/1885, UKNA; Robertson to St. Laurent, July 8, 1948, "Robertson, N. A." folder, vol. 441, King papers, LAC; and Smith to Marshall 1361, July 19, 1948, 740.00119 Control (Germany)/7-1948, RG 59, USNA.

64. Franks to Bevin 3591, July 21, 1948, C5899/3/18, and Franks to Bevin 3595, July 21, 1948, C5903/3/18, both in 70503, FO 371, UKNA; Marshall to Truman, July 30, 1948, "Berlin Crisis" folder, box 149, PSF, Truman papers, HSTL. Allen to Dean, July 22, 1948, C6158/3/18, 70504, FO 371, UKNA, contains the British embassy's report on American opinion.

65. JCS 1907/2, July 19, 1948; Lalor to JSSC, July 20, 1948; and JCS 1907/3, July 21, 1948, all in sec. 17, CCS 381 (8-20-43), box 177, 1948–50 Central Decimal File, RG 218, USNA; Wedemeyer to Bradley, July 21, 1948, folder 1, CD 6-2-9, box 27, OSD Numerical File, RG 330, USNA.

66. For background to this change, see Combs memo, July 19, 1948; Anderson to Norstad, July 19, 1948; and JBC to Vandenberg, July 20, 1948, all in "OPD 381 Berlin (15 Jan 48)" folder, box 807, TS Decimal File, RG 341, USNA.

67. NSC 24, July 26, 1948, "NSC 17th Meeting, August 5, 1948" folder, box 177, PSF, Truman papers, HSTL. For a similar high-level British analysis, see JP(48)86 (Final), July 26, 1948, DEFE 6/6, and Alexander to Cripps et al., August 2, 1948, DEFE 11/322, both in UKNA.

68. Condit, *History of the JCS,* 2:162; memo for the president, July 23, 1948, "Memo for the President: Meeting Discussions (1948)" folder, box 186, PSF, Truman papers, HSTL; Murphy, *Diplomat among Warriors,* 316–18.

69. Dulles memos, July 19 and 22, 1948, "Berlin and Germany 1948" folder, box 35, Dulles papers, MML.

70. "Agenda for National Security Council Meeting—22 July 1948," "Berlin Crisis Book I" folder, box 14, Draper-Voorhees file, RG 335, USNA. On Truman's loose ties with the council, see Sander, "Truman," 387–88. For similar distance by the JCS, see "Ross Press and Radio Conference, 22 July 1948," box 14, Ayers papers, HSTL.

71. Clay quoted in Forrestal manuscript diary, July 22, 1948, Forrestal papers, MML; memo for the president, July 23, 1948, "Memo for the President: Meeting Discussions (1948)" folder, box 186, PSF, Truman papers, HSTL.

72. Vandenberg diary, July 15, 1948, box 1, Vandenberg papers, LOCMD.

73. Combs memo, July 19, 1948, sec. 1, "OPD 381 Berlin (15 Jan 48)" folder, box 807, TS Decimal File, RG 341, USNA. See also Anderson to Norstad, July 19, 1948; JBC to Vandenberg, July 20, 1948; and Anderson to Vandenberg, July 22, 1948, sec. 1, "OPD 381 Berlin (15 Jan 48)" folder, box 807, TS Decimal File, RG 341, USNA.

74. For Vandenberg's comments to Draper, see "Suggested Agenda for National Security Council Meeting," July 21, 1948, "Berlin Crisis Book I" folder, box 14, Draper-Voorhees file, RG 335, USNA.

75. The best source for this meeting is memo for the president, July 23, 1948, "Memo for the President: Meeting Discussions (1948)" folder, box 186, PSF, Truman papers, HSTL. This memo makes it clear that Truman's memoirs embellished his role. Cf. Truman, *Memoirs,* 2:124–26. Clay's account mistakenly claims that he asked for and the council approved the dispatch of 160 C-54s. Clay, *Decision,* 368.

76. Bohlen to Douglas 2888, July 22, 1948, 740.00119 Control (Germany)/7-2248, RG 59, USNA.

77. *FR, 1948,* 2:994–95; Forrestal to JCS, July 30, 1948, and Royall to Johnson, March 31, 1949, both in folder 3, CD 6-2-9, box 27, OSD Numerical File, RG 330, USNA; Condit, *History of the JCS,* 2:145–46; COS(48)116, August 20, 1948, DEFE 4/15, UKNA; Smith, *Clay Papers,* 2:763. See also Plan, TF Truculent, September 8, 1948, case 88/120, sec. 5, P&O 381 TS, box 103, P&O TS Decimal File, RG 319, USNA; and EUCOM Plan, December 29, 1948, "094 Berlin" folder, box 353, Classified Correspondence, RG 549, USNA.

78. Lovett told Dulles later that day there had been "one new important development." With more aircraft and a third airfield, the airlift could "probably" continue through the winter. This report also reached Ernest Lindley of *Newsweek,* who reported that a "bipartisan decision" had recently been reached, based on "what were supposed to be final figures for the Pentagon on the maximum plane capacity available to supply Berlin." Three days later, the State Department learned the air force could provide enough planes to operate through the winter. "This made possible an important shift in diplomatic tactics," Lindley continued. As welcome as that was, Lindley commented that the episode raised questions about the effectiveness of coordination between Marshall's and Forrestal's departments. Pruessen, *Dulles,* 380; Lindley, "How Many Secretaries of State?" *Newsweek,* August 9, 1948, 23.

79. Rosenberg, "Berlin and Israel," 184–329, quote at 329. See also Shlaim, *United States,* 260–80.

80. NSC Record of Actions, 16th meeting, July 22, 1948, Action 84b, box 167, PSF, Truman papers, HSTL; Bohlen, *Witness,* 277; Leahy diary, July 22, 1948, box 6, Leahy papers, LOCMD. Wedemeyer's comments appear in BJSM to MOD Z0 488, July 28, 1948, DEFE 11/322, UKNA. The general was attempting to use the British to restrain his own government, an astonishing act of insubordination and disloyalty by a serving military officer. That

he, the most Anglophobe member of Marshall's inner circle during the war, would turn to the British now makes the episode all the more extraordinary.

7. The Moscow Discussions

1. AFOPO to COMMATS 50338, July 23, 1948, "AG 319.1 Berlin Transportation Situation Reports, vol. III 1948" folder, box 428, OMGUS AGO General Correspondence, RG 260, USNA; Vandenberg to JCS 50339, July 23, 1948, case 137/91, "P&O 092 (Section IX-C) . . ." folder, box 118, P&O Secret Correspondence, RG 319, USNA; Laurence S. Kuter, "'Vittles'—The Air Supply of Berlin," talk before the Business Advisory Council, December 15, 1948, Kuter papers, USAFA, Colorado Springs, Colorado. I am indebted to Donald J. Barrett of the USAFA's library staff for a copy of this speech.

2. Collier, *Bridge,* 71–72; Donovan, *Bridge,* 47–48, 114–15; Tunner, *Over the Hump,* 160, 167–68; Berlin to Foreign Office 452, July 20, 1948, CAB 21/1882, UKNA.

3. Tunner, *Over the Hump,* 159–60; Milton interview, December 5, 1975, CUOH.

4. Tunner, *Over the Hump,* 166–67. See also Estes interview, August 27–30, 1973, 81–82, K239.0512-686, AFHRA.

5. Milton interview, December 5, 1975, CUOH; Milton, "Berlin Airlift," 60–61. Tunner informed Kuter on August 3 of the estimate that 225 C-54s were needed. Tunner to Kuter, August 3, 1948, AMC/HO. For LeMay's mid-July estimate, see Bradley to Royall, July 17, 1948, folder 1, CD 6-2-9, box 27, OSD Numerical File, RG 330, USNA.

6. Tunner to Kuter, August 3 and 6, 1948, AMC/HO.

7. Tunner, *Over the Hump,* 160.

8. Tunner speech, Dayton, Ohio, n.d., folder 234, Herndon papers, University of Missouri Library.

9. Tunner speech, June 3, 1952, folder 235, Herndon papers, University of Missouri Library.

10. Tunner to Kuter, August 6, 1948, AMC/HO; Tunner, *Over the Hump,* 170–71.

11. Study, USAFE History Office, "USAFE and the Airlift, 1948," 73–75, 78, reel Z-0039, USAFE/HO; Collier, *Bridge,* 82; Gallogly Report, 16–17; BAFO Report, 155, 173. Tunner claimed that every 100 tons of backload cost 41 tons of deliveries. Tunner to Clay MT-142, August 8, 1948, "AG 319.1 Berlin Transportation Situation Reports, vol. IV, 1948" folder, box 428, OMGUS AGO Decimal File, RG 260, USNA.

12. For the unwilling passenger stories, cf. Harty, "Airlift Soars," 16–17, and Bennett, *Berlin Bastion,* 221. For the diplomat's C-47, see *Task Force Times,* September 14, 1948, and Davison, "Human Side," 65.

13. Tunner, *Over the Hump,* 152–55; Tunner to Kuter, August 16, 1948, and Kuter to Tunner, September 2, 1948, AMC/HO.

14. Report, CALTF, "Preliminary Analysis of Lessons Learned," June 1949, 19, reel C5113, AFHRA; BAFO Report, 288; Tunner-Herndon interview, n.d., folder 226, Herndon papers, University of Missouri Library.

15. Harris et al., "Special Study," 20–22; Larson, "Berlin Airlift," 237–38; BAFO Report, 293.

16. Wood, "Thirty Years," 231; MacGregor and Hansen, "Berlin Airlift," 44–45.

17. Barker, *Berlin Air Lift,* 25, 28, 32–33; BAFO Report, 113, 160–61.

18. "USAFE and the Airlift, 1948," 162, 174–75, 181, reel Z-0039, USAFE/HO; BAFO Report, 291; Wood, "Thirty Years," 229–30.

19. Pearcy, "Berlin Airlift," 205; "USAFE and the Airlift, 1948," 167–70, reel Z-0039, USAFE/HO; *History of USAFE, August 1948,* sec. D, p. 4, USAFE/HO.

20. *History of USAFE, July 1948,* Signals Tab; *History of USAFE, August 1948,* sec. D, pp. 1–11; report, 1807 AACS Wing, "Berlin Airlift: Air Traffic Control History," n.d., reel Z-0039, all in USAFE/HO; *History of AACS, July–December 1948,* frames 556–67, reel A3119, AFHRA; "USAFE Summary," 40–42, reel Z-0039, USAFE/HO; CALTF, "Preliminary Analysis," 24, 26.

21. CALTF, "Preliminary Analysis," 17–18; Donovan, *Bridge,* 66–67. See also Kuter, "Berlin Airlift," 379.

22. "USAFE and the Airlift, 1948," 68, reel Z-0039, USAFE/HO; "USAFE and the Airlift, 1949," 139–40, reel Z-0040, USAFE/HO; BAFO Report, 38.

23. Barker, *Berlin Air Lift,* 10, 34; "USAFE and the Airlift, 1948," 67, reel Z-0039, USAFE/HO; Collier, *Bridge,* 125; Milton interview, December 5, 1975, CUOH; Donovan, *Bridge,* 131–32; CALTF, "Preliminary Analysis," 23.

24. AHQ BAFO to AATO Wunstorf AO-836, July 8, 1948, and AHQ BAFO to RAF Wunstorf AO-892, July 14, 1948, both in AIR 55/204, UKNA; Tunner to Kuter, August 6 and 21, 1948, AMC/HO; "USAFE and the Airlift, 1948," 50–61, 197, reel Z-0039, USAFE/HO; *History of USAFE, August 1948,* sec. D1, pp. 15–16, USAFE/HO.

25. "USAFE and the Airlift, 1948," 176–78, reel Z-0039, USAFE/HO.

26. CALTF, "Preliminary Analysis," 10; BAFO Report, 13; Milton, "Berlin Airlift," 61.

27. Tunner to Kuter, September 10, 1948, AMC/HO; "USAFE and the Airlift, 1948," 162, reel Z-0039, USAFE/HO; Murphy to Marshall 2014, August 12, 1948, 740.00119 Control (Germany)/8-1248, RG 59, USNA.

28. "USAFE Summary," 89, reel Z-0039, USAFE/HO; *History of USAFE, January 1949,* appendix 28, and *History of USAFE, November 1948,* tab I, both in USAFE/HO; Moseley, "Medical History," 1254; "Fassberg Diary" (copy in author's possession).

29. Report, BAFO [Trip to Lüneburg and Celle, September 9, 1948], n.d.; Spackman to Stratton, September 17, 1948; memo, September 29, 1948, all in AIR 55/204, UKNA; Pearcy, "Berlin Airlift," 202; *History of USAFE, November 1948,* 25–27, and *History of USAFE, January 1949,* 28, both in USAFE/HO; BAFO Report, 17.

30. Hamburg dispatch 172, April 22, 1949, 740.00119 Control (Germany)/4-2249, RG 59, USNA; BAFO Report, 323; "USAFE and the Airlift, 1949," 246, reel Z-0040, USAFE/HO.

31. CALTF after-action report, reprinted in BAFO Report, 279–332, quote at 311.

32. *History of USAFE, August 1948,* sec. B, p. 8, appendix 40, USAFE/HO; "USAFE and the Airlift, 1948," 64, reel Z-0039, USAFE/HO; BAFO Report, 57.

33. "USAFE and the Airlift, 1948," 95–102, reel Z-0039, USAFE/HO; *History of USAFE, September 1948,* 15, and *History of USAFE, November 1948,* 24, both in USAFE/HO.

34. Anderson to Symington, August 4, 1948, sec. 2, "OPD 381 Berlin (15 Jan 48)" folder, box 808, TS Decimal File, RG 341, USNA; Marshall quoted in memo for the president, September 9, 1948, "Memo for President: Meeting Discussions" folder, box 186, PSF, Truman papers, HSTL.

35. Bohlen, *Witness,* 278–79; Clay, *Decision,* 368–69.

36. Lovett-Douglas teleconference, July 22, 1948, 740.00119 Control (Germany)/6-3048, RG 59, USNA; Franks to Bevin 3591, July 21, 1948, C5899/3/18, 70503, FO 371, UKNA; *FR, 1948,* 2:971–76; Marshall to Douglas 2926, July 24, 1948, 740.00119 Control (Germany)/7-2448, RG 59, USNA.

37. GEN 241/4th meeting, July 22, 1948, CAB 130/38, UKNA; Bevin to Franks 8044,

July 21, 1948, C5815/3/18, 70502; Bevin to Franks 1078, July 22, 1948, C5978/3/18, 70503; Jebb to Strang, July 23, 1948, C6253/3/18, 70505; and Bevin to Franks 1105, July 26, 1948, C6207/3/18, 70504, all in FO 371, UKNA; Douglas to Marshall 3311, July 21, 1948, 740.00119 Control (Germany)/7-2148, RG 59, USNA; Bullock, *Bevin,* 3:588–89; Robertson to St. Laurent 1185, July 22, 1948, "Robertson, N.A." folder, vol. 441, King papers, LAC.

38. Bevin to Foreign Office 272, July 20, 1948, C5854/3/18, and Bevin to Foreign Office 273, July 20, 1948, C5871/3/18, both in 70503, FO 371, UKNA; Bevin to Franks 8043 and 8044, July 21, 1948, C5815/3/18, 70502, FO 371, UKNA; *FR, 1948,* 2:975n, 979; Strang memo, July 23, 1948, C6016/3/18, 70504, FO 371, UKNA; Robertson to St. Laurent 1185, July 22, 1948, "Robertson, N.A." folder, vol. 441, King papers, LAC; Jebb to Strang, July 23, 1948, C6253/3/18, 70505, FO 371, UKNA.

39. *FR, 1948,* 2:975, 980–81; Paeffgen, "Berlin Blockade," 246–47, 255–56; Strang memo, July 23, 1948, C6016/3/18, 70504, FO 371, UKNA; GEN 241/3d, 4th, and 5th meetings, July 21–27, 1948, CAB 130/38, UKNA.

40. Bevin to Franks 1105, July 26, 1948, C6207/3/18, 70504, FO 371, UKNA; Bohlen, *Witness,* 279; *FR, 1948,* 2:986–88. For the exploratory talks in Washington, see *FR, 1948,* 3:148ff.

41. CM(48)54, July 26, 1948, CAB 128/13, UKNA.

42. GEN 241/5th meeting, July 27, 1948, CAB 130/38, UKNA; *FR, 1948,* 2:981–93.

43. Bullock, *Bevin,* 3:589; COS(48)168(O), July 30, 1948, DEFE 5/11; GEN 241/5th meeting, July 27, 1948, CAB 130/38; and Alexander to Bevin, July 31, 1948, CAB 21/1886, all in UKNA.

44. Bullock, *Bevin,* 3:589; Kirkpatrick to Ashley-Clarke, July 31, 1948, DEFE 11/322, UKNA.

45. U.S. President, *Public Papers . . . 1948,* 411–14; Truman, *Truman,* 17. Truman continued to avoid comment on international affairs at his press conferences of July 29 and August 5 and 19. U.S. President, *Public Papers . . . 1948,* 422–23, 434–35, 453.

46. Marshall to Douglas 2929, July 25, 1948, 740.00119 Control (Germany)/7-2548, RG 59, USNA; Wedemeyer to Clay WARX 86521, July 27, 1948, "OAS 580.Germany" folder, box 17, Draper-Voorhees file, RG 335, USNA; Moody, *Building,* 211, 214; Johnson interviews, July 12, 1978, and April 14, 1965, K239.0512-1441 and K239.0512-609, AFHRA.

47. Harrison to Bevin 901, July 30, 1948, C6204/3/18, 70504, FO 371, UKNA; Smith, *My Three Years,* 239–40; U.S. Department of State, *Berlin Crisis,* 15.

48. *FR, 1948,* 2:995–96; Smith, *My Three Years,* 239–40; U.S. Department of State, *Berlin Crisis,* 15–16; Harrison to Bevin 906, July 31, 1948, C6206/3/18, 70504, FO 371, UKNA; *Command Paper 7534,* 21, 54–55.

49. Bohlen, *Witness,* 280; Harrison to Bevin 906, July 31, 1948, C6206/3/18, 70504, FO 371, UKNA; Millis and Duffield, *Forrestal Diaries,* 482.

50. *FR, 1948,* 2:997–98; Harrison to Bevin 913, July 31, 1948, C6218/3/18, 70505, FO 371, UKNA.

51. Mosely, *Kremlin in World Politics,* 3.

52. Beam to Bohlen, August 2, 1948, 740.00119 Control (Germany)/8-248, RG 59, USNA; Smith, *My Three Years,* 242; Smith to Marshall 1559, August 8, 1948, 740.00119 Control (Germany)/8-848, RG 59, USNA. Douglas shared some of Smith's sense of isolation, writing to Marshall on July 28 that he sometimes felt "as lonely as a pine tree on a bald granite mountain." Quoted in Browder and Smith, *Independent,* 298.

53. *FR, 1948,* 2:999–1000; Smith, *My Three Years,* 243–44.

54. *FR, 1948,* 2:1000–1005.

55. Ibid., 1005–6; Smith, *My Three Years,* 245.

56. *FR, 1948,* 2:1006–7; Roberts to Bevin, August 3, 1948, C6546/3/18, 70506, FO 371, UKNA.

57. Smith, *Clay Papers,* 2:749–51; *FR, 1948,* 2:1011–13; Narinskii, "Soviet Union," 69; Davison, *Berlin Blockade,* 176–77. Cf. Eisenberg, "Myth," 182.

58. *FR, 1948,* 2:1012.

59. Ibid., 1008–9, 1013–15; Bohlen "Notes for telecon with Douglas," August 2, 1948, "Memos CEB 1948 (1946–1948)" folder, box 5, Bohlen papers, RG 59, USNA; Millis and Duffield, *Forrestal Diaries,* 469; Wedemeyer to Royall, August 4, 1948, case 88/73, sec. 2, P&O 381 TS, box 103, P&O TS Decimal File, RG 319, USNA; minutes, PPS 239th meeting, August 2, 1948, "PPS Minutes of Meetings, 1948" folder, box 32, PPS Records, RG 59, USNA; Roberts quoted in Robertson to Pearson 1220, August 3, 1948, folder 1, file W-22-5-G, vol. 119, ser. 18, RG 2, LAC; Connelly memo, August 6, 1948, "Cabinet Meetings, 1948" folder, box 2, Connelly papers, HSTL.

60. *Newsweek,* August 16, 1948, 26; Bevin to Harrison 1565, August 3, 1948, C6226/3/18, 70505, FO 371, UKNA.

61. *FR, 1948,* 2:1016–21; *Command Paper 7534,* 24–25.

62. Hillenkoetter to Truman, August 6, 1948, "Central Intelligence Memorandums, 1945–1948" folder, box 211, PSF, Truman papers, HSTL.

63. Harrison to Bevin 979, August 7, 1948, and Bevin to Harrison 1625 and 1626, August 8, 1948, all in C6441/3/18, 70506, FO 371, UKNA; Robertson to Bevin 1578, August 9, 1948, C6474/3/18, 70506, FO 371, UKNA.

64. *FR, 1948,* 2:1024–27.

65. Ibid., 1028–32; Smith, *Clay Papers,* 2:764.

66. *FR, 1948,* 2:1030; Gottlieb, *German Peace Settlement,* 205.

67. Bevin to Harrison 1612, August 7, 1948, C6423/3/18, 70506, FO 371, UKNA. Smith had warned about this good cop–bad cop technique several months before. *FR, 1948,* 4:818–19.

68. Roberts's comments are in Reid to Claxton, October 2, 1948, folder 1, file W-22-5-G, vol. 119, ser. 18, RG 2, LAC; Harrison's are in Harrison to Bevin 1254, September 18, 1948, C7702/3/18, 70515, FO 371, UKNA. Robert Cecil's suggestion that Maclean helped preserve peace by assuring the Soviets of Western restraint needs to be balanced against the likelihood that, by revealing Western doubts about the airlift, he encouraged Soviet recalcitrance and thereby increased the risk of war. Cf. Cecil, *Divided Life,* 86–87, and Kerr, "Secret Hotline." Stalin lost this window into Western deliberations when Maclean's assignment in Washington ended on September 1.

69. Robertson to Bevin 1596, August 10, 1948, and Dean minute, August 11, 1948, C6531/3/18, 70506, FO 371, UKNA.

70. Bevin to Franks 1159, August 11, 1948, C6611/3/18, 70507, FO 371, UKNA; Shlaim, *United States,* 319–20.

71. Dupuy memo, August 9, 1948, "Lockup—SAOUS 000.1 Germany" folder, box 12, and Dupuy memo, August 10, 1948, "Berlin Crisis, Book I" folder, box 14, both in Draper-Voorhees file, RG 335, USNA. For the army's orders to Clay, see Smith, *Clay Papers,* 2:763.

72. *FR, 1948,* 2:1035–38, 1042–47.

73. Ibid., 1047–49. Clay sensed this, too; see Clay to Marshall 2081, August 19, 1948, 740.00119 Control (Germany)/8-1948, RG 59, USNA.

74. Friedensburg to Markgraf, July 26, 1948, and Kotikov to Schroeder, July 26, 1948, both in "Public Safety 1948–1949" folder, box 13, Director's files, Berlin Sector Records, RG 260, USNA.

75. *FR, 1948,* 2:1038–40; Davison, *Berlin Blockade,* 169–81; Charles, *Berlin Blockade,* 76; Murphy to Marshall 2162, August 27, 1948, 740.00119 Control (Germany)/8-2748, RG 59, USNA; *Newsweek,* September 6, 1948, 29; Smith, *Clay Papers,* 2:776.

76. Bohlen memo, n.d. [August 16, 1948?], "Berlin Crisis" folder, box 149, PSF, Truman papers, HSTL; *FR, 1948,* 2:1047–49; Smith to Marshall 1668, August 18, 1948, 740.00119 Control (Germany)/8-1848, RG 59, USNA; CIA 8-48, August 19, 1948, "NSC Meeting 18" folder, box 177, PSF, Truman papers, HSTL.

77. Memo for the president, August 20, 1948, "Memo for President: Meeting Discussions (1948)" folder, box 186, PSF, Truman papers, HSTL.

78. Ibid.; *Newsweek,* August 30, 1948, 31; *FR, 1948,* 3:643–44, 2:1060.

79. Memo for the president, August 20, 1948, "Memo for President: Meeting Discussions (1948)" folder, box 186, PSF, Truman papers, HSTL.

80. *FR, 1948,* 2:1053–54; Douglas to Marshall 3720, August 17, 1948, 740.00119 Control (Germany)/8-1748, and Caffery to Marshall 4285, August 18, 1948, 740.00119 Control (Germany)/8-1848, both in RG 59, USNA. Marshall's caution is reported in *FR, 1948,* 3:221; O'Daniel's in O'Daniel manuscript diary, August 22, 1948, O'Daniel papers, MHI.

81. *Command Paper 7534,* 38; *FR, 1948,* 2:1065–68; Smith, *My Three Years,* 248–52. For the second-front episode, see Kimball, *Juggler,* 192.

82. Dupuy to Draper, August 26, 1948, "Berlin Crisis, Book I" folder, box 14, Draper-Voorhees file, RG 335, USNA; *FR, 1948,* 2:1072–73, 1077.

83. *FR, 1948,* 2:1078–79, 1082–83.

84. Ibid., 1077, 1089, 1093–96.

85. Ibid., 1087–95.

86. Ibid., 1090, 1095–98.

87. Bevin's views are summarized in Hickerson-Douglas teleconference, August 31, 1948, 740.00119 Control (Germany)/6-3048, RG 59, USNA. Batt to Clifford, August 9, 1948, "Russia (folder 3)," box 15, Clifford papers, HSTL; Elsey diary, August 30, 1948, and "Suggested Talk on Berlin," n.d., both in "1948 Campaign—Reference Material—Foreign Affairs" folder, box 33, Elsey papers, HSTL; Kennan, *Memoirs,* 420–23; Curry, *Byrnes,* 299–300; Charles, *Berlin Blockade,* 82.

88. Douglas to Marshall 3899, August 28, 1948, 740.00119 Control (Germany)/8-2848, RG 59, USNA.

89. Millis and Duffield, *Forrestal Diaries,* 480; Clay, *Decision,* 369–70; Smith, *Clay Papers,* 2:771–72, 781–84; Clay to Panuch, August 31, 1948, attached to Panuch to Clay, June 29, 1948, "Military Government of Germany: Personal Correspondence" folder, box 13, Panuch papers, HSTL.

8. The September Crisis

1. Shlaim, *United States,* 328; *FR, 1948,* 2:1099–100.

2. Smith, *Clay Papers,* 2:798–826; *FR, 1948,* 2:1110–12, 1136–38; Murphy to Marshall 2238, September 4, 1948, 740.00119 Control (Germany)/9-448, RG 59, USNA. See also the Dratvin-Hays correspondence in "MG—DMG—C/S Corresp. 1948" folder, box 4, Miscellaneous Berlin Files, RG 466, USNA.

3. Smith, *Clay Papers,* 2:808–9, 812–13, 822–23, 836–39.

4. Ibid., 798–801; *FR, 1948,* 2:1108–9; Douglas to Marshall 3939, September 2, 1948, 740.00119 Control (Germany)/9-248, RG 59, USNA.

5. Douglas to Marshall 3939, September 2, 1948, 740.00119 Control (Germany)/9-248, RG 59, USNA; Smith, *Clay Papers,* 2:800, 802, 814–15.

6. *FR, 1948,* 2:1108–9; Marshall to Lovett, September 3, 1948, 711.00/9-348, RG 59, USNA; Wrong to Pearson WA-2380, September 2, 1948, file 2315, vol. 236, King papers, LAC.

7. Davison, *Berlin Blockade,* 185–86, 376; Howley, *Berlin Command,* 216–17; Winner, "Stadthaus Siege," 8–9; Murphy to Marshall 2247, September 7, 1948, 862.00/9-748, RG 59, USNA; Smith, *Clay Papers,* 2:831–34, 848.

8. Brett-Smith, *Berlin '45,* 163; Davison, *Berlin Blockade,* 189; Collier, *Bridge,* 121; *Newsweek,* September 20, 1948, 38; Robertson to Bevin 1850 and 1857, September 10, 1948, FO 1030/61, UKNA; Steege, *Black Market,* 237–40; Murphy to Marshall 2294, September 10, 1948, 862.00/9-1048, RG 59, USNA.

9. Murphy to Marshall 2294, September 10, 1948, 862.00/9-1048, RG 59, USNA; *Newsweek,* September 13, 1948, 32–34; Glaser, "Political Report No. 14," September 11, 1948, "Political Reports 11–17" folder, box 903, Public Safety Branch Records, RG 260, USNA; Glaser Report, September 10, 1948, "Memos and Reports, Col Glaser" folder, box 71, Records of the Civil Administration and Political Affairs Branch, RG 260, USNA; Smith, *Clay Papers,* 2:857.

10. *FR, 1948,* 2:1132–40; Smith, *Clay Papers,* 2:837–43. For another account of this meeting, misdated September 18, see Smith, *Clay Papers,* 2:862–66. For the Western military governors' report, see *Command Paper 7534,* 56–57. For differing rationales for the air corridors, cf. CONL/P(45)63, paragraphs 2 and 4d, reprinted in *FR, 1945,* 3:1577–79. Sokolovsky did not invent the Soviet argument to use it against the airlift; Soviet officials had voiced it as early as 1946. See U.S. Department of State, *Documents on Germany,* 82, 113–14, and *FR, 1946,* 5:760–62, 764.

11. Gross to Bohlen, September 2, 1948, 740.00119 Control (Germany)/9-248, RG 59, USNA.

12. Kennan lecture, National War College, "Contemporary Problems of Foreign Policy," September 17, 1948, folder 12, box 299, Kennan papers, MML; Browder and Smith, *Independent,* 293, 296, 300, 302; Millis and Duffield, *Forrestal Diaries,* 485.

13. Millis and Duffield, *Forrestal Diaries,* 481–83; Truman to Roosevelt, September 17, 1948, "Harry S. Truman, 1945–1948" folder, box 4560, Eleanor Roosevelt papers, FDRL.

14. "Points on Berlin Situation for NSC," September 7, 1948, "Lockup 000.1 Germany (September)" folder, box 12, Draper-Voorhees file, RG 335, USNA.

15. Memo for the president, September 9, 1948, "Memo for President: Meeting Discussions (1948)" folder, box 186, PSF, Truman papers, HSTL; Millis and Duffield, *Forrestal Diaries,* 483–84.

16. *FR, 1948,* 2:1122–24, 1140–42, 1145–47; Marshall to Douglas 1071, September 6, 1948, 740.00119 Control (Germany)/9-648, RG 59, USNA; memo for the president, September 9, 1948, "Memo for President: Meeting Discussions (1948)" folder, box 186, PSF, Truman papers, HSTL.

17. *FR, 1948,* 2:1142–47.

18. CM(48)59, September 10, 1948, CAB 128/13, UKNA; Bohlen memo, September 11, 1948, "Berlin Crisis" folder, box 149, PSF, Truman papers, HSTL; Browder and Smith, *Independent,* 300; Strang, *Home and Abroad,* 298; *FR, 1948,* 2:1147.

19. Forrestal manuscript diary, September 10, 1948, Forrestal papers, MML; *FR, 1948,* 2:1147–48; Pogue, *Marshall,* 4:314.

20. Rearden, *Formative Years,* 296–97; Forrestal manuscript diary, September 10, 13, 16, and 17, 1948, Forrestal papers, MML; Millis and Duffield, *Forrestal Diaries,* 486–87; Nichols, *Road to Trinity,* 266–68; Hillman, *Mr. President,* 141; sec. 8ff., CCS 381 USSR (3-2-46), 1948–50 Geographic File, RG 218, USNA; Lindsay memo, August 11, 1948, folder 10, box 2, TS Decimal File, RG 341, USNA; "Presidential Appointment File . . . Daily Sheets, Sept. 13–30" folder, box 75, PSF, Truman papers, HSTL.

21. Hillman, *Mr. President,* 141; Lilienthal, *Journals,* 2:406.

22. ORE 22-48 (addendum), September 16, 1948, "Central Intelligence Reports, ORE 1948 numbers 21–29" folder, box 214, PSF, Truman papers, HSTL.

23. *FR, 1948,* 1:625–28; memo for the president, n.d. [September 16, 1948], "Memo for President: Meeting Discussions (1948)" folder, box 186, PSF, Truman papers, HSTL; Rearden, *Formative Years,* 436. Gregg Herken's contention that "NSC-30 determined that the United States would use atomic weapons in the event of a war with Russia" ignores the language approved by the council and gives undue weight to Walton Butterworth's comments (the director of Far Eastern affairs in the Department of State was not a key player in weapons policy and admitted he had given the document "only a brief and cursory examination"). Cf. Herken, *Winning Weapon,* 268–72, and *FR, 1948,* 1:628, 630–31.

24. Forrestal manuscript diary, September 16, 1948, Forrestal papers, MML; Rearden, *Formative Years,* 297, 431. The AFSWP members may have been working on the bomb storage huts. The *New York Times* reported in April 1949 that technical facilities for U.S. atomic bombs were ready, and the 509th Bomb Group arrived in the country that month for a temporary tour of duty. The group brought no atomic bombs or components. Truman did not approve deployment of nonnuclear bomb components overseas until July 1950; Eisenhower authorized overseas deployment of nuclear components in 1953. *New York Times,* April 13, 1949, 1; ibid., May 1, 1949, 16; Rearden, *Formative Years,* 432; Condit, *Test of War,* 463–64.

25. *Command Paper 7534,* 43; *FR, 1948,* 2:1157–60, 1162–73; CM(48)61(3), September 22, 1948, CAB 128/13, UKNA; Harrison to Bevin 1225, September 14, 1948, C7583/3/18, 70515, FO 371, UKNA.

26. Jessup to Marshall 4113, September 14, 1948, 501.BC/9-1448, RG 59, USNA; minute, n.d. [September 14, 1948], C8223/3/18 (emphasis in original), and minute, September 18, 1948, C8224/3/18, 70518, FO 371, UKNA; Jebb minute, September 14, 1948, C7608/3/18, 70515, FO 371, UKNA; GEN 241/8th meeting, September 17, 1948, CAB 130/38, UKNA.

27. Cf. *FR, 1948,* 2:976, and Marshall to Douglas 3657, September 15, 1948, 501.BC/9-1548, RG 59, USNA; Kennan lecture, National War College, December 21, 1948, "1948 September–December" folder, box 17, Kennan papers, MML.

28. Jessup, "Berlin Blockade," 167.

29. Dulles to Vandenberg, September 28, 1948, "Vandenberg 1948" folder, box 39, Dulles papers, MML.

30. Henderson press conference, May 11, 1949, AIR 20/6893, UKNA; Pearcy, "Berlin Airlift," 203–4; BAFO Report, 60, 159, 182, 184; *History of 1st ALTF, January 1949,* 44, reel C5110, AFHRA.

31. DO(48)11th meeting, July 15, 1948, and DO(48)12th meeting, July 21, 1948, both in CAB 131/5, UKNA; minutes of Air Ministry meeting, July 27, 1948, AIR 20/6891, UKNA.

32. Minutes of Air Ministry meetings, August 13 and 23, 1948, and memo, ASTO.2, September 22, 1948, all in AIR 20/6891, UKNA; Robertson to Bevin 1230 Basic, September 3,

1948, AIR 20/7804, UKNA; Bevin to Henderson, August 23, 1948, CAB 21/1882, UKNA; BAFO Report, 140.

33. Melbourne to Air Ministry AX.695, August 3, 1948, AIR 20/7148, UKNA; CRO to Canberra 216, August 13, 1948, and Tedder to Jones MSX.505, August 26, 1948, both in AIR 20/6891, UKNA.

34. BAFO Report, 142; Pearcy, *Berlin Airlift,* 87. For correspondence arranging the Dominions' contributions, see file AIR 20/6891, UKNA. The best explanation of Canada's abstention is Sarty, "Limits of Internationalism"; see also Pickersgill and Forster, *Mackenzie King Record,* 4:189–95; Eayrs, *In Defence of Canada,* 4:38–51; Holmes, *Shaping of Peace,* 2:102–4; file W-22-5-G, vol. 119, ser. 18, RG 2, and file AR 22/19, vol. 2088, RG 25, both in LAC. One other country contributed people. To help manage the many Germans working on the airlift at bases in western Germany, the British used some German-speaking Dutch air force sergeants as interpreters. BAFO Report, 1.

35. James to Cary, DCAS/5963, April 4, 1949, AIR 20/6893; RAF Transport Command to 38 and 47 Groups, APX.672, August 13, 1949, AIR 55/219; minutes of Air Ministry meeting, August 23, 1948, AIR 20/6891, all in UKNA.

36. Cox to Walford, July 1, 1948, AIR 20/7071; Waite to Whitfield, July 5, 1948, AIR 20/7821; Waite to Foreign Office and Air Ministry ALX 99, July 28, 1948, AIR 55/215; Strang to Robertson 926 Basic, July 29, 1948, AIR 55/215, all in UKNA.

37. "USAFE and the Airlift, 1948," 192, reel Z-0039, USAFE/HO; "USAFE and the Airlift, 1949," 151, 383, reel Z-0040, USAFE/HO; Chilver to F.1, July 27, 1948, AIR 20/7071, UKNA; BAFO Report, 199, 215, 221; Pearcy, *Berlin Airlift,* 73.

38. BAFO Report, 15, 51, 193–96, 519; Cox, "Britain and the Airlift," 33; minutes of Air Ministry meetings, July 27 and August 13, 1948, AIR 20/6891; Sanders quoted in report, ACAS(Ops), n.d. [October 5, 1948?], AIR 20/6891; and Atkinson to BEA, n.d., attached to Merer to Hardman, October 7, 1948, AIR 20/7071, all in UKNA. For weekly contracts, see Bevin to Robertson 2211, September 27, 1948, AIR 55/215, UKNA.

39. Tusa quoted in Sowrey et al., "Berlin Airlift," 36; Merer to Williams, February 7, 1949, AIR 55/216, UKNA; Tusa and Tusa, *Berlin Airlift,* 316.

40. BAFO Report, 7–9, 139–41.

41. Merer to Sanders, September 29, 1948, AIR 38/384; report, ACAS(Ops), n.d. [October 5, 1948?], AIR 20/6891; Waite to Cross, September 21, 1948, and Cross to Waite, September 24, 1948, AIR 20/7804; Rainsford minute, September 24, 1948, AIR 20/6891; study, DDBOps, September 20, 1948, AIR 20/6891; Robertson to Williams 7962, October 27, 1948, AIR 55/215; Robertson to Clay, November 1, 1948, FO 1030/64, all in UKNA.

42. "USAFE and the Airlift, 1948," 188–90, reel Z-0039, USAFE/HO; Bennett, *Berlin Bastion,* 127; Smith, *Clay Papers,* 2:867, 877.

43. Memo for the president, July 23, 1948, "Memo for President: Meeting Discussions (1948)" folder, box 186, PSF, Truman papers, HSTL; Smith, *Clay Papers,* 2:761; Timberman to Wedemeyer, August 23, 1948, "P&O 092 TS thru 381 TS 1948 Hot File" folder, box 9, General Administrative File, RG 319, USNA.

44. LeMay to Clay, August 30, 1948, "Air Force in Europe—USAFE" folder, box 12, Gailey Records, RG 260, USNA; Smith, *Clay Papers,* 2:847; memo for the president, September 9, 1948, "Memo for President: Meeting Discussions (1948)" folder, box 186, PSF, Truman papers, HSTL. The U.S. C-47s were withdrawn October 1. "USAFE and the Airlift, 1948," 162, reel Z-0039, USAFE/HO.

45. Smith, *Clay Papers,* 2:852, 878; Bradley to Clay WX-89346, September 17, 1948,

"Cables—Incoming Record Copies—September 1948" folder, box 680, OMGUS AGO Incoming Cables, RG 260, USNA. According to the discussion summary, the council did not settle on a specific number of aircraft, although Forrestal thought it agreed to add seventy-five, unless the JCS disagreed. That makes their decision to provide only forty all the more striking. Memo for the president, September 9, 1948, "Memo for President: Meeting Discussions (1948)" folder, box 186, PSF, Truman papers, HSTL; Millis and Duffield, *Forrestal Diaries,* 484.

46. Smith, *Clay Papers,* 2:867, 875, 877–79.

47. *FR, 1948,* 2:1173–80; Smith, *Clay Papers,* 2:878; Bevin to Foreign Office 1320, September 21, 1948, C7784/3/18, 70516, UKNA (emphasis added); Bullock, *Bevin,* 3:606–7.

48. *FR, 1948,* 2:1178–79.

49. Furlonge minute, September 23, 1948, C7982/3/18, 70516, FO 371, UKNA; *FR, 1948,* 2:1180–81.

50. Great Britain, Parliament, *Parliamentary Debates* (Commons), 5th ser., vol. 456, cols. 907, 917.

51. Record of meeting, September 23, 1948, C8025/3/18, 70517, FO 371, UKNA.

52. *FR, 1948,* 2:1181–84; Harrison to Bevin 1278, September 26, 1948, C7907/3/18, 70516, FO 371, UKNA.

53. *FR, 1948,* 2:1184–87; Bevin to Attlee 1351, September 26, 1948, C8001/3/18, 70517, FO 371, UKNA.

54. *FR, 1948,* 2:1187–93.

55. Robertson memo attached to Strang to Bevin, July 21, 1948, C5540/3/18, 70501, and Robertson to Strang, July 20, 1948, C6157/3/18, 70504, both in FO 371, UKNA.

56. Garvy, *Money,* 9–74; Thieme, "Central Bank," 576–77.

57. Schwartz, *Russia's Soviet Economy,* 469; Garvy, *Money,* 43, 47; Zwass, "Money," 12, 18–19; Zwass, *Monetary Cooperation,* 159.

58. *FR, 1948,* 3:662–63; Harvey to Bevin 4587, September 27, 1948, C7952/3/18, 70516, FO 371, UKNA; Bullock, *Bevin,* 3:607–8.

59. ORE 57-48, September 28, 1948, "Central Intelligence Rpts., O.R.E. 1948 No. 48-57" folder, box 215, PSF, Truman papers, HSTL.

60. Eisenhower to Forrestal, September 27, 1948, "Forrestal" folder, box 38, Eisenhower prepresidential papers, DDEL.

9. A Necessary Failure

1. Document S/1020, September 29, 1948, UN Security Council, *Official Records Supplement for October 1948,* 9–11.

2. Donovan, *Conflict and Crisis,* 424; Scheinman, "Berlin Blockade," 26–27.

3. *FR, 1948,* 2:1215–16; CIA 10-48, October 20, 1948, "NSC 25th Meeting, October 21, 1948" folder, box 177, PSF, Truman papers, HSTL.

4. Jessup, "Berlin Blockade," 170. The two reports were the State Department's *Berlin Crisis* and Britain's *Command Paper 7534.*

5. Bothwell, Drummond, and English, *Canada since 1945,* 102–3; Holmes, *Better Part of Valour,* 11.

6. Iran, not the Western powers, had been the complainant in the 1946 confrontation with the Soviet Union. For concern about the United Nations' ability to cope, see Douglas to Marshall 3810, August 23, 1948, 740.00119 Control (Germany)/8-2348, RG 59, USNA, and Robertson to Pearson, September 27, 1948, "Robertson, N. A." folder, box 13, Pearson papers, LAC.

7. Memo, October 5, 1948, file 2-18-0, vol. 1059, RG 25, LAC.

8. Holmes, *Shaping of Peace,* 2:71.

9. Jessup, "Berlin Blockade," 165. Americans told Canadian George Ignatieff that reference to the international body would also "get through their period of elections." Ignatieff to Pearson, October 6, 1948, folder 1, file W-22-5-G, vol. 119, ser. 18, RG 2, LAC.

10. *FR, 1948,* 2:1225–26.

11. For the currency question, see Murphy to Marshall 1970, August 7, 1948, "Berlin Cables to Secretary of State—Aug–Sep 1948" folder, box 1, TS Cables, POLAD files, RG 84, USNA; Smith, *Clay Papers,* 2:881; *FR, 1948,* 2:1213–14. Meeting minutes, October 4, 1948, C8613/3/18, 70519, UKNA; Holmes memo, n.d., 14, file 2-18-0, vol. 1059, RG 25, LAC. My speculation on the American's identity stems from Gladwyn Jebb's minute of a conversation in which Dulles expressed similar views. Jebb minute, September 22, 1948, C8534/3/18, 70519, FO 371, UKNA.

12. Schoenbaum, *Waging Peace and War,* 183, offers a garbled account of the Marshall-Rusk-Pearson episode, claiming that Marshall was inclined to "pull back," thus "abandoning Berlin." The text relies on Rusk to author, July 16, 1990. The deadlock triggered other startling proposals. Lovett received a suggestion that Germany be turned over to a UN commission that would control all occupation troops and hold nationwide elections; unsigned, undated memo [late November 1948?], "000.1 Germany October–November 1948" folder, box 14, Draper-Voorhees file, RG 335, USNA. See *FR, 1948,* 2:1193–94, for Marshall's discussion with Jessup.

13. Robertson to Reid, October 26, 1948, folder 1, file W-22-5-G, vol. 119, ser. 18, RG 2, LAC; minutes of tripartite meeting, October 4, 1948, C8613/3/18, 70519, FO 371, UKNA; minutes of tripartite meeting, October 6, 1948, fiche 747, *FR, Memoranda of Conversations.*

14. Lie, *In the Cause,* 199–201; Sulzberger, *Long Row,* 409; Barros, *Trygve Lie,* 136–42; *FR, 1948,* 2:1214–16.

15. Stalin quoted in Davison, *Berlin Blockade,* 244.

16. USSR Ministry of Foreign Affairs, *Soviet Union and the Berlin Question,* 58–72; *FR, 1948,* 2:1201–10. Interestingly, Western officials had earlier read article 107 in a similar fashion. See, for example, Bevin to Franks 950, July 2, 1948, FO 800/467/GER/48/39, UKNA.

17. UN Security Council, *Official Records,* no. 113 (361st meeting, October 4, 1948) and no. 114 (362d meeting, October 5, 1948).

18. Ibid., no. 114 (362d meeting, October 5, 1948) and no. 115 (363d meeting, October 6, 1948); Scheinman, "Berlin Blockade," 34.

19. Teletype report, October 6, 1948, "McNaughton Reports, October–November 1948" folder, box 14, McNaughton papers, HSTL. After the election, analysts would cite the failure to offer alternatives on foreign policy, exemplified here, as one cause of Dewey's defeat. Some have suggested that Dewey could have turned the Berlin crisis to his advantage by attacking the Democrats' failure to obtain secure access. Historians have given a variety of reasons why he did not. For instance, doing so might give—or appear to give—ammunition to the Russians, and it was unnecessary. While all this is true, there was perhaps another reason. Dewey's friend and military aide Cornelius Wickersham had helped craft the wartime agreements as a member of CAD and the U.S. EAC delegation. The Democrats could counter attacks on Roosevelt and Winant by pointing to Wickersham, who—unrepentant—cited his wartime experiences as proof that negotiations with the Soviets could succeed. See Wickersham to Dewey, July 21 and August 9, 1948, "Wickersham Cornelius W. Jr.—1948" folder, box 203, ser. 5, Dewey papers, Rush Rees Library, University of Rochester, Rochester, N.Y.

20. Bohlen, *Witness,* 281–82.

21. *Chicago Tribune,* October 9, 1948, 1; *New York Times,* October 9, 1948, 1; *Newsweek,* October 18, 1948, 31–32; Divine, *Foreign Policy,* 256. Truman's aides speculated that the State Department had leaked the story to embarrass him, but Trohan claimed that he first learned of it from former senator Burton K. Wheeler, who had been something of a mentor to Truman in the Senate and was now active in communications law in Washington. Therefore, the initial leaks probably came from someone connected with the networks. James Reston's elaboration of the story in the *New York Times* seems to be derived from State Department sources. Trohan, *Political Animals,* 239–40; Ayers diary, October 9, 1948, box 26, Ayers papers, HSTL.

22. Ayers diary, September 22, 1948, box 26, Ayers papers, HSTL.

23. Ayers to Connelly, September 23, 1948; Connelly to Ayers, September 23, 1948; and Ayers to Ross, September 22, 1948, all in "Subject File: Soviet-U.S. Messages 1948" folder, box 11, Ayers papers, HSTL.

24. Ayers to Daniels, September 24, 1948, "Subject File: Soviet-U.S. Messages 1948" folder, box 11, Ayers papers, HSTL; Ayers diary, September 23–26, 1948, box 26, Ayers papers, HSTL; Ayers interview, April 19, 1967, 131–35, HSTL.

25. Lash, *Eleanor Roosevelt,* 105; Batt to Clifford, July 22, 1948, "William L. Batt" folder, box 20, Clifford papers, HSTL; Carter to Lovett, September 17, 1948, 740.00119 Control (Germany)/9-1748, RG 59, USNA.

26. St. Clair and Gugin, *Vinson*; Truman, *Memoirs,* 1:327–28, 2:489–90.

27. Carr, *Truman, Stalin, and Peace,* 116; Truman, *Memoirs,* 2:212–16. My assessment of Truman's motives also rests on draft speech, October 4, 1948, "Russia, folder 3," box 20, Clifford papers, HSTL, and on Truman's speech to the American Legion Convention on October 17, 1948, reprinted in U.S. President, *Public Papers . . . 1948,* 817.

28. McCullough, *Affection and Trust,* 105.

29. U.S. President, *Public Papers . . . 1948,* 329. J. Garry Clifford outlines Truman's distrust of Soviet motives and policy in "Truman and Peter the Great's Will." Truman's famous remark in Eugene, Oregon, quoted here, was not an isolated slip of the tongue; it was no "irregularity" or "anomaly," as Elizabeth Edwards Spalding would have us believe. Truman had made similar comments time and again since Potsdam. See, for example, Ferrell, *Dear Bess,* 522; Blum, *Price of Vision,* 490; Churchill and Gilbert, *Churchill,* 8:351; Sulzberger, *Long Row,* 364; Truman interview, April 8, 1948, book 1, box 1, Arthur Krock papers, MML; and a post-Vinson episode that unnerved the British in file 74179, FO 371, UKNA. For Spalding's contrary view, see her *First Cold Warrior,* 135, 140. For Molotov's supposed differences with and pernicious influence over an otherwise agreeable Stalin, see *FR, Conference of Berlin,* 2:13, 61; Truman to Davies, October 6, 1945, "Davies" folder, box 101, PSF, Truman papers, HSTL; and Felix Blair memo, April 29, 1946, "Truman" folder, box 58, Krock papers, MML. For the origins of similar views in London, see Folly, *Churchill, Whitehall and the Soviet Union,* 80–85, 122, 144–46.

30. Carr, *Truman, Stalin, and Peace,* 112; Batt to Clifford, May 8, 1948, "William L. Batt, Jr." folder; Batt to Clifford, August 9, 1948, "Russia folder 3"; and Batt to Clifford, August 11, 1948, "Batt . . . Miscellaneous Correspondence" folder, all in box 20, Clifford papers, HSTL.

31. Divine, *Foreign Policy,* 200–202; memo for the secretary, July 29, 1948, "Berlin Crisis" folder, box 149, PSF, Truman papers, HSTL; Forrestal manuscript diary, October 21, 1948, Forrestal papers, MML; "Vinson Mission—Pro" and "Vinson Mission—Con" folders, Official File 220, Miscellaneous, Truman papers, HSTL.

32. Truman to Vinson and Truman to Van Sant, October 5, 1948, "Personal—the President—General—Truman" folder, box 353, Vinson papers, Margaret I. King Library, University of Kentucky, Lexington. These letters refer to meetings the two men held the night before (Monday), and I have followed that chronology here. Most accounts, drawing on the president's memoirs, set the meetings on Sunday. But if the president had told Ross of his plans on Sunday or during the workday Monday and asked him to arrange radio time, it is odd that Ross did nothing about it until Tuesday morning—and then requested time that very evening. Truman's appointment files list no visit by Vinson either Sunday or Monday. Truman, *Memoirs,* 2:213–14; "President's Appointment File . . . Daily Sheets—1948—October" folder, box 75, PSF, Truman papers, HSTL.

33. Lovett quoted in Pogue, *Marshall,* 4:407; Carr, *Truman, Stalin, and Peace,* 118; Marshall quoted in Bohlen, *Witness,* 269; Daniels, *Man of Independence,* 28–29; Ayers diary, October 5, 1948, Ayers papers, HSTL.

34. Vandenberg, *Private Papers,* 457–58; Connally, *My Name,* 331.

35. Divine, *Foreign Policy,* 256.

36. Marshall to Carter, October 9, 1948, 740.00119 Control (Germany)/10-948, RG 59, USNA.

37. Bohlen, *Witness,* 269; Pogue, *Marshall,* 4:407–8.

38. U.S. Department of State, *Bulletin* 19 (October 17, 1948): 483–84.

39. Robert Ferrell described this mood as "residual" in *Marshall,* 252. My view of the political effects of the Vinson story derives from Divine's *Foreign Policy,* 259, 275–76, and "Cold War and the Election," 109. Ayers's efforts in September and the Vinson mission would appear to demolish Wilson Miscamble's claim that Truman did not try to use foreign affairs in general and the Berlin crisis in particular for political advantage during the campaign. Miscamble, "Harry S Truman."

40. Bevin's comment about the superpowers "joining up" is handwritten on Roberts memo, November 25, 1948, AN4214/6/45, 68015A, FO 371, UKNA. For European concern over the Vinson mission, see *FR, 1948,* 3:885–86, 888, 4:926; *New York Times,* October 10, 1948, 1; and "Mr. Truman's Stalin," *Economist,* January 22, 1949, 133–35. See also Dulles to Dewey no. 14, October 10, 1948, "Dewey" folder, box 36, and Dulles to Vandenberg, October 24, 1948, "Vandenberg 1948" folder, box 39, both in Dulles papers, MML.

41. Cadogan to Bevin 1444, October 12, 1948, C8409/3/18, 70519, FO 371, UKNA.

42. Shulman, *Stalin's Foreign Policy,* 31. For rumors of new missions, see Vandenberg, *Private Papers,* 459–60, and Bohlen memo, November 16, 1948, 740.00119 Council/11-1648, RG 59, USNA. The *Pravda* and *Tägliche Rundschau* stories are summarized in Smith to Marshall 2297, October 11, 1948, and Murphy to Marshall 2479, October 11, 1948, both in 740.00119 Control (Germany)/10-1148, RG 59, USNA.

43. McNaughton to Pearson 130, October 6, 1948, folder 1, file W-22-5-G, vol. 119, ser. 18, RG 2, LAC.

44. McNaughton to Pearson 144, October 8, 1948, folder 1, file W-22-5-G, vol. 119, ser. 18, RG 2, LAC; Holmes memo, n.d., 12, file 2-18-0, vol. 1059, RG 25, LAC.

45. *FR, 1948,* 2:1210–16; Bohlen memo, October 12, 1948, "CEB Memos 1948" folder, box 5, Bohlen papers, RG 59, USNA; CIA 10-48, October 20, 1948, "NSC 25th Meeting, October 21, 1948" folder, box 177, PSF, Truman papers, HSTL.

46. Holmes memo, n.d., 12, file 2-18-0, vol. 1059, RG 25, LAC.

47. Holmes, *Shaping of Peace,* 2:70; McNaughton to Pearson 157, October 10, 1948, folder 1, file W-22-5-G, vol. 119, ser. 18, RG 2, LAC.

48. Holmes memo, n.d., 13–14, file 2-18-0, vol. 1059, RG 25, LAC; Cabinet Conclusions, October 20, 1948, vol. 14, ser. 16, RG 2, LAC; Cadogan to Bevin 1443, October 12, 1948, C8408/3/18, FO 371, UKNA.

49. *FR, 1948,* 2:1216–18, 1223; Bohlen to Marshall, October 12, 1948, "CEB Memos 1948" folder, box 5, Bohlen papers, RG 59, USNA.

50. *FR, 1948,* 2:1219–20; McNaughton to Pearson 190, October 14, 1948, and McNaughton to Pearson 207, October 15, 1948, both in folder 1, file W-22-5-G, vol. 119, ser. 18, RG 2, LAC.

51. UN Security Council, *Official Records,* no. 117 (366th meeting, October 15, 1948).

52. McNaughton to Pearson 254, October 22, 1948, folder 1, file W-22-5-G, vol. 119, ser. 18, RG 2, LAC; *FR, 1948,* 2:1217–18; Cadogan to Bevin 1454, October 13, 1948, C8425/3/18, 70519; Gilchrist minute, October 18, 1948, C8490/3/18, 70519; and Cadogan to Bevin 1514, October 22, 1948, C8677/3/18, 70520, all in FO 371, UKNA.

53. McNaughton to Pearson 234, October 20, 1948, folder 1, file W-22-5-G, vol. 119, ser. 18, RG 2, LAC; UN Security Council, *Official Records,* nos. 118 and 120 (370th and 372d meetings, October 22 and 25, 1948).

54. Cadogan to Bevin 1508, October 21, 1948, C8645/3/18, 70520, FO 371, UKNA.

55. Sheinman, "Berlin Blockade," 33; UN Security Council, *Official Records,* no. 120 (372d meeting, October 25, 1948).

56. Holmes memo, n.d., 13–14, file 2-18-0, vol. 1059, RG 25, LAC; *FR, 1948,* 2:1248–49; Bohlen to Kennan, October 25, 1948, "Memos 1948 (1946–48)" folder, box 5, Bohlen papers, RG 59, USNA; Lovett to Smith 1284, November 1, 1948, "1948 'Top Secret'" folder, box 2, Moscow Embassy TS Records, RG 84, USNA. Frank Roberts also complained about the continuing "divergence of view" within the U.S. delegation. Roberts memo, November 25, 1948, AN4214/6/45, 68015A, FO 371, UKNA.

57. *FR, 1948,* 2:1236–38, 1247–49; Bohlen memos, October 27, 1948, 862.00/10-2748, RG 59, USNA; Bevin to Cadogan 384, November 4, 1948, C8956/3/18, and minutes of U.S.-U.K. meeting, October 27, 1948, C8958/3/18, both in 70520, FO 371, UKNA; Pearson to McNaughton 225, November 9, 1948, folder 1, file W-22-5-G, vol. 119, ser. 18, RG 2, LAC.

58. *FR, 1948,* 2:1236–37.

59. Ibid., 1228, 1231–33, 1255–56; Jessup, "Berlin Blockade," 171; Millis and Duffield, *Forrestal Diaries,* 490–91; Dulles to Vandenberg, November 19, 1948, "Vandenberg" folder, box 39, Dulles papers, MML (emphasis in original).

60. Lie, *In the Cause,* 202–5; Barros, *Trygve Lie,* 142–45; Davison, *Berlin Blockade,* 244–45.

61. Lie, *In the Cause,* 209–13; Cadogan to Bevin 286, November 3, 1948, C8956/3/18, 70520, FO 371, UKNA; Douglas to Marshall 4767, November 6, 1948, and Marshall to Smith 1301, November 8, 1948, both in "1948 'Top Secret'" folder, box 2, Moscow Embassy TS Records, RG 84, USNA; Barros, *Trygve Lie,* 146–49; *FR, 1948,* 2:1247–48.

62. Cordier and Foote, *Public Papers,* 1:180–82; Cadogan to Bevin 430, November 16, 1948, C9363/8178/18, 70700, FO 371, UKNA.

63. Jessup interview, 299–300, CUOH; Cadogan to Strang 403, November 14, 1948, C9287/8178/18, 70700, FO 371, UKNA; Barros, *Trygve Lie,* 151–52; Jessup, "Berlin Blockade," 164, 171–72; Bohlen, *Witness,* 282; Marshall to Lovett Martel 138, November 16, 1948, 501.BC/11-1648, RG 59, USNA; CM(48)73, November 15, 1948, CAB 128/13, UKNA; Lippmann diary, November 17, 1948, Lippmann papers, Sterling Memorial Library, Yale University, New Haven, Connecticut. I am indebted to Garry Clifford for extracts from

Lippmann's papers and diaries. For a survey of Evatt's stormy relations with the United States and the reference to his ability to alienate, see Edwards, "Evatt," quote at 549.

64. U.S. Department of State, *Germany, 1947–1949,* 229–30. For the British reply, see Great Britain, Parliament, *Parliamentary Debates* (Commons), 5th ser., vol. 458, cols. 354–55.

65. *FR, 1948,* 2:1253n, 1257–59.

66. Ibid., 1263; Carlyle, *Documents, 1947–48,* 612–14; U.S. Department of State, *Documents & State Papers,* vol. 1 (May 1949), 760–61.

67. U.S. Department of State, *Documents & State Papers,* 1:754–55; Robertson to Pearson 522, December 2, 1948, 800-3-3, vol. 835, RG 19, LAC; Cadogan to Bevin 592, November 29, 1948, C9750/3/18, 70524, and Cadogan to Bevin 622, December 1, 1948, C9837/8178/18, 70700, both in FO 371, UKNA.

68. Robertson to Pearson 522, December 2, 1948, 800-3-3, vol. 835, RG 19, LAC.

69. Davison, *Berlin Blockade,* 219–21; Plischke, *Berlin,* 165; Steege, *Black Market,* 241–42; *New York Times,* October 21, 1948, 5; ibid., November 11, 1948, 6; ibid., November 16, 1948, 7; Charles, *Berlin Blockade,* 101.

70. Memo for the president, November 26, 1948, "Memo for President: Meeting Discussions (1948)" folder, box 186, PSF, Truman papers, HSTL; Charles, *Berlin Blockade,* 102; Plischke, *Berlin,* 136–38; Howley, *Berlin Command,* 226.

71. Bohlen to Jessup, November 30, 1948, "CEB Memos 1948" folder, box 5, Bohlen papers, RG 59, USNA; Lovett quoted in memo for the president, December 3, 1948, "Memo for President: Meeting Discussions (1948)" folder, box 186, PSF, Truman papers, HSTL; Hillenkoetter to Truman, December 10, 1948, file 122, box 19, Chairman's File, RG 218, USNA.

72. Canadian Military Mission Berlin, "Berlin Weekly Summary No. 13," December 10, 1948, 800-3-3, vol. 835, RG 19, LAC; Davison, *Berlin Blockade,* 228–29; Charles, *Berlin Blockade,* 105–6; Plischke, *Berlin,* 165–67.

73. Bohlen to Jessup, November 30, 1948, "CEB Memos 1948" folder, box 5, Bohlen papers, RG 59, USNA.

74. Smith, *Clay Papers,* 2:942–46; Clay to Robertson, December 10, 1948, "Britain-US July 1948–May 1949" folder, box 18, Records Retained for the Military Governor, RG 260, USNA.

75. Norman Robertson (no relation to the British military governor) is the subject of an excellent biography; see Granatstein, *Man of Influence.*

76. U.S. Department of State, *Documents & State Papers,* 1:759–60 (emphasis added).

77. Ibid., 763–71.

78. Robertson to Pearson 862, December 20, 1948, 800-3-3, vol. 835, RG 19, LAC.

79. Bevin to Harvey 3878, December 18, 1948, FO 1030/56, UKNA; *FR, 1948,* 2:1279; Lovett to Douglas 4792, December 29, 1948, C10703/3/18, 70528, FO 371, UKNA; Lovett to Smith 1436, December 30, 1948, "1948 'Top Secret'" folder 2, box 2, Moscow Embassy TS Records, RG 84, USNA.

80. State Department to Truman, December 30, 1948, "State Dept. Briefs, September–December 1948" folder, box 21, Naval Aide files, HSTL; Draper quoted in briefing book, January 4, 1949, "Forrestal" folder, box 38, Eisenhower prepresidential papers, DDEL; *FR, 1949,* 3:644–55.

81. *New York Herald Tribune* extract, December 28, 1948, and Bicknell minute, both in AN17/10338/15; Bevin to Franks 100, January 4, 1949, and minute, January 11, 1949, both in AN70/10338/45, all in 74179, FO 371, UKNA.

82. Coates to Robertson 8910, December 27, 1948; Herbert to Robertson 2361, December

29, 1948; Weir to Robertson, December 28, 1948; minutes, FO meetings, December 29 and 30, 1948; and Bevin to Franks 13712, December 31, 1948, all in FO 1030/56, UKNA; Bevin to Attlee, CPM/49/2, January 4, 1949, C190/14/18, 76538, FO 371, UKNA; N. Robertson to Pearson 2354, December 31, 1948, and U.K. Commonwealth Relations Office to U.K. High Commissioner, Ottawa, Q.2, January 11, 1949, both in file 800-3-3, vol. 835, RG 19, LAC.

83. Minutes, FO meetings, December 29 and 30, 1948, and Bevin to Franks 13712, December 31, 1948, both in FO 1030/56, UKNA; Bevin to Attlee, CPM/49/2, January 4, 1949, C190/14/18, 76538, FO 371, UKNA; Douglas to Murphy 714, December 30, 1948, "Cables—Incoming Record Copies—January 1949" folder, box 681, OMGUS AGO Incoming Cables, RG 260, USNA.

84. Douglas to Lovett 79, January 7, 1949, 740.00119 Control (Germany)/1-749, RG 59, USNA; minutes of meeting, January 7, 1949, Bevin to Robertson 35, January 7, 1949, and Bevin to Robertson 36, January 7, 1949, all in C159/14/18, 76538, FO 371, UKNA; Bevin to Robertson 59, January 13, 1949, C325/14/18, 76539, FO 371, UKNA; Draper to Clay W-82831, January 15, 1949, and Clay to Bradley and Draper FMPC-186, January 15, 1949, both in "Cables—Incoming Record Copies—January 1949" folder, box 681, OMGUS AGO Incoming Cables, RG 260, USNA; *FR, 1949,* 3:652–57; U.K. Commonwealth Relations Office to U.K. High Commissioner, Ottawa, Q.2, January 11, 1949, file 800-3-3, vol. 835, RG 19, LAC.

85. *FR, 1949,* 3:656–57.

86. Ibid., 650–51; Robertson to Bevin 39, January 9, 1949, C226/14/18, 76538, and Bevin to Franks 56, January 11, 1949, C325/14/18, 76539, both in FO 371, UKNA.

87. Robertson to Pearson 77, January 11, 1949, 800-3-3, vol. 835, RG 19, LAC.

88. Reid to Wrong EX-78, January 12, 1949, file 800-3-3, vol. 835, RG 19, LAC.

89. Wrong to Pearson WA-97, January 13, 1949, file 800-3-3, vol. 835, RG 19, LAC; Reid to Robertson 165, January 21, 1949, folder 1, AR 22/23/2, box 2088, RG 25, LAC.

90. *FR, 1949,* 3:658; U.S. Department of State, *Documents & State Papers,* 1:772–79; UN Press Release SC/908, March 15, 1949, Documents Reference and Collections Section, Dag Hammerskjold Library, UN Headquarters, New York, N.Y. I am indebted to Ivan Schwartz of the Hammerskjold Library for providing me with a copy of this document.

91. C. S. A. Ritchie to Pearson 9, January 29, 1949, and Ritchie to Pearson, January 14, 1949, both in file 800-3-3, vol. 835, RG 19, LAC.

92. *FR, 1949,* 3:662–63; Robertson to Pearson 261, January 29, 1949, file 800-3-3, vol. 835, RG 19, LAC; Acheson to Holmes 299, January 27, 1949, C797/14/18, 76542, FO 371, UKNA.

93. Bevin to Robertson 87, January 18, 1949; Robertson to Bevin 114 and 115, January 24, 1949; and Robertson to Bevin 124, January 26, 1949, all in CAB 21/1882, UKNA.

94. Minutes of FO meeting, February 3, 1949, C1035/14/18, 76543, UKNA; Robertson to Bevin 124, January 26, 1949, FO 1030/63, UKNA; Robertson to Clay, February 10, 1949, "British-U.S. July 1948–May 1949" folder, box 18, Records Retained for the Military Governor, RG 260, USNA.

95. *FR, 1949,* 3:671; Bevin to Robertson 139, January 24, 1949, C593/14/18; Robertson to Bevin 124, January 26, 1949, C740/14/18, 76541; Bevin to Robertson 860 Basic, January 28, 1949; and Bevin to Gifford 104, January 29, 1949, C797/14/18, 76542, all in FO 371, UKNA; Bevin memo GEN 241/4, February 2, 1949, CAB 130/38, UKNA; GEN 241 9th meeting, February 7, 1949, CAB 21/1892, UKNA; U.K. Commonwealth Relations Office to Pearson H.61, February 11, 1949; Robertson to Pearson 374, February 16, 1949; Robertson to Pearson 15,

February 4, 1949; and Robertson quoted in Wrong to Pearson WA-240, January 31, 1949, all in file 800-3-3, vol. 835, RG 19, LAC.

96. Geneva to Foreign Office 102, February 5, 1949, C1031/14/18, 76543, FO 371, UKNA; Robertson to Pearson 16, February 6, 1949, file 800-3-3, vol. 835, RG 19, LAC; *FR, 1949,* 3:669–70.

97. Robertson to Pearson 347, February 12, 1949, file 800-3-3, vol. 835, RG 19, LAC.

98. FO report attached to Robertson to Pearson 423, February 26, 1949, file 800-3-3, vol. 835, RG 19, LAC; *FR, 1949,* 3:671–88; Barros, *Trygve Lie,* 153.

99. State Dept. to Truman, February 16, 1949, "State Dept. Briefs, January–April 1949" folder, box 21, Naval Aide files, HSTL; *FR, 1949,* 3:679–80, 690–91; UN Press Release SC/908, March 15, 1949, Hammarskjold Library; C. S. A. Ritchie to A. E. Ritchie, March 17, 1949, AR 22/23/3, vol. 2088, RG 25, LAC; U.S. Department of State, *Bulletin* 20 (1949): 377–79. Jessup's characterization of Alvarez is in Jessup to Beam, March 14, 1949, 740.00119 Control (Germany)/3-1449, RG 59, USNA.

100. Gablentz, *Documents,* 75–76; *FR, 1949,* 3:687.

101. Truman, *Memoirs,* 2:130 (emphasis added).

10. "Lieber Pomm als 'Frau Komm!'"

1. Robertson to Strang, January 1, 1949, FO 943/476, UKNA.

2. Arnold-Forster, *Siege of Berlin,* 81; Special Report 720, December 3, 1948, FO 1005/1860, UKNA.

3. Donovan, *Bridge,* 80.

4. Pennacchio, "United States and Berlin," 120; Heineman, *What Difference,* 98–99, 105–6.

5. Klimov, *Terror Machine,* 101; Schivelbusch, *In a Cold Crater,* 1, 15; Dilks, *Cadogan Diaries,* 762. The American was James Riddleberger, recalling his experiences in his oral history memoir at the Truman Library.

6. Clay, *Decision,* 21, 32; Nettl, *Eastern Zone,* 2; Smith, *Defense of Berlin,* 67; Morris, *Blockade,* 37; Steege, *Black Market,* 20; Balfour and Mair, *Four-Power Control,* 7, 26, 76; Ziemke, *U.S. Army,* 298, 303; Moorhouse, *Berlin at War,* 382; Floyd Parks to Marie Parks, June 24, 1945, "Correspondence, 1945–1946" folder, box 5, Parks papers, DDEL.

7. Elkins, *Berlin,* 37; Plischke, *Berlin,* 3n; Large, *Berlin,* 376; Steege, *Black Market,* 30–31. See also Naimark, *Russians in Germany,* 166–70, 173–83; Merritt, "Postwar Berlin," 154; Merritt, "Political Division," 168–70; Yershov, "Confiscation and Plunder"; Alexandrov, "Dismantling."

8. Table 7a, "The Ten Leading Causes of Death in Berlin 1948," n.d., "Vital Statistics 1949" folder, box 177, Public Health Branch Records, RG 260, USNA.

9. Elkins, *Berlin,* 159, 164–68, 189–90; Ladd, *Ghosts,* 96–104.

10. Plischke, *Berlin,* 2; Diefendorf, *In the Wake of War,* 250; PORO, Reports on Berlin Morale 30 and 37, n.d. [mid-October 1948] and February 3, 1949, FO 1005/1862, UKNA; Howley to Clay, June 22, 1948, "Staff Studies (1 Jul–31 Dec) 1948" folder, box 6, Director's files, Berlin Sector Records, RG 260, USNA; Fuller to Chief, Economics Branch, July 16, 1949, and report, n.d. [May 1949], both in "Special Reports 1949/48" folder, box 570, Building and Housing Section Records, RG 260, USNA.

11. See documents in "Monthly Reports 1948" folder, box 571, Building and Housing Section Records, RG 260, USNA, and BTB Monthly Reports, "Building and Housing Section," FO 1051/804, UKNA.

12. OMGUS Staff Conference, July 24, 1948, "Staff Conferences—July 1948" folder, box

5, OMGUS Minutes, RG 260, USNA; Andreas-Friedrich, *Battleground Berlin,* 234; PORO, Reports on Berlin Morale 29, 32–34, 37, 41, September 28 and November 16–December 17, 1948, February 3 and April 6, 1949, FO 1005/1862, UKNA; Winner, "Berlin Dreads," 14–16; Charles, *Berlin Blockade,* 69; Davison, *Berlin Blockade,* 315; Tusa and Tusa, *Berlin Airlift,* 193, 270–73; Gross, *Memories,* 1:134.

13. Winner, "Berlin Dreads," 16; W. T. C. Berry et al., "The Food and Nutritional Situation in Berlin during the Blockade and After," *Bulletin of the Ministry of Health and the Public Health Laboratory Service* 10, no. 1 (July–August 1951): 155–61, 180–86, in MH 79/636, UKNA; Lay, "Berlin Air Lift," 2:50–51, reel Z-0029, USAFE/HO.

14. Winner, "Berlin Dreads," 16–17; Charles, *Berlin Blockade,* 69; Davison, *Berlin Blockade,* 314–16; Report on Berlin Morale 29, September 28, 1948, FO 1005/1862, UKNA; *Newsweek,* July 19, 1948, 22.

15. Howley to Oberbürgermeister, June 24, 1948, "Public Works & Utilities, 1948/49" folder, box 3, Director's files, Berlin Sector Records, RG 260, USNA.

16. Murphy to Marshall 1638, July 8, 1948, 740.00119 Control (Germany)/7-848, RG 59, USNA.

17. Hays to Bradley and Wedemeyer CC-5092, July 9, 1948, sec. 17, CCS 381 (8-20-43), box 177, 1948–50 Central Decimal File, RG 218, USNA; Charles, *Berlin Blockade,* 69–70.

18. Hillenkoetter to Truman, July 12, 1948, "Central Intelligence—Memos 1945–1948" folder, box 211, PSF, Truman papers, HSTL.

19. Donovan, *Bridge,* 71; Berry et al., "Food and Nutritional Situation," MH 79/636, UKNA; Special Report 720, December 3, 1948, FO 1005/1860, UKNA.

20. PORO, Reports on Berlin Morale 25 and 28, July 27, 1948, and n.d. [mid-September 1948], FO 1005/1862, UKNA.

21. Robertson to Bevin 1086 Basic, August 25, 1948, AIR 20/7804, UKNA. For fat versus coal, see Razzell to Military Assistant, August 4, 1948, and Bransby to Klatt, August 18, 1948, both in FO 943/476, UKNA; and Moran to Howley, August 3, 1948, "Airlift Planning Vol. 1" folder, box 16, Director's files, Berlin Sector Records, RG 260, USNA.

22. Robertson to Williams, November 1, 1948, AIR 55/215, UKNA; Davison, *Berlin Blockade,* 315; "USAFE and the Airlift, 1949," 352, reel Z-0040, USAFE/HO; Smith, *Clay Papers,* 2:890, 964; Stivers, "Incomplete Blockade," 580; Charlesby minute, January 11, 1949, AIR 55/100, UKNA.

23. Davison, *Berlin Blockade,* 315; PORO, Reports on Berlin Morale 29 and 30, FO 1005/1862, UKNA.

24. PORO, Report on Berlin Morale 33, December 3, 1948, FO 1005/1862, UKNA.

25. PORO, Report on Berlin Morale 32, November 16, 1948, FO 1005/1862, UKNA; Davison, *Berlin Blockade,* 315; Tusa and Tusa, *Berlin Airlift,* 244.

26. Bennett, *Berlin Bastion,* 94–95; Special Report 723, February 7, 1949, FO 1005/1860, UKNA.

27. Murphy to Marshall 2811, November 24, 1948, "OUS 000.1 Germany/Berlin Crisis, Oct 4 '48 to Nov 25 '48" folder, box 14, Draper-Voorhees file, RG 335, USNA; Stivers, "Incomplete Blockade," 586.

28. PORO, Report on Berlin Morale 30, FO 1005/1862, UKNA.

29. Charlesby minute, January 11, 1949, AIR 55/100, UKNA; Herbert, "Cold War in Berlin," 174; BAFO Report, 354.

30. Klatt report, June 12, 1948, attached to Klatt to Magee, September 14, 1948, MH 79/636, UKNA; Monthly Report, Food and Agriculture Branch, June 30, 1948, FO 943/476, UKNA.

31. MGLS Weekly Report 39 (August 3, 1948), FO 1005/1830, UKNA; Report of the Special Commission, May 1948, "Nutrition 1948" folder, box 184, Nutrition Reports, RG 260, USNA; Davison, *Berlin Blockade,* 165; Stivers, "Incomplete Blockade," 575. For the August 1947 poll, see Special Report 719, October 14, 1948, FO 1005/1860, UKNA.

32. Steege, *Black Market,* 214–15; Klingelhöfer quoted in Stivers, "Incomplete Blockade," 577.

33. Cf. Stivers, "Incomplete Blockade," 573–79; Steege, "More than an Airlift," 204–8; Steege, *Black Market,* 212–18; PORO, Reports on Berlin Morale 25 and 31, July 25, 1948, and n.d. [early November 1948], FO 1005/1862; MGLS Weekly Reports 37 (July 20, 1948) and 38 (July 27, 1948), FO 1005/1830; Special Report 725, March 31, 1949, FO 1005/1860, UKNA; OMGUS Berlin Sector Political Report no. 7, "Intelligence Reports, 1 Jan 48–2 Oct 48" binder, box 10, Howley papers, MHI; Schuetz to Textor, July 30, 1948, "ICD Opinion Surveys 1948" folder, box 27, Director's files, Berlin Sector Records, RG 260, USNA. For the *Tägliche Rundschau* pun, see Large, *Berlin,* 380.

34. Howley, *Berlin Command,* 230; PORO, Reports on Berlin Morale 29, 32–34, 37, 41, FO 1005/1862, UKNA. The rumors were wrong. Mid-September did see a bottoming out of stocks of meat (twenty-three days' supply) and potatoes (one day), but overall food supplies peaked in late October (forty-two days), helped by a sharp rise in the amount of flour and meat available. See charts by the EUCOM Adjutant's Division, various dates, boxes 1741–43, Berlin Airlift Food and Materiel Position Charts, RG 549, USNA.

35. FO to Berlin (draft), July 14, 1948, DEFE 11/321; Robertson to Strang 479 Basic, July 21, 1948, DEFE 11/322; Klatt memo, July 15, 1948, FO 943/476; Klatt report, August 5, 1948, attached to Klatt to Magee, September 14, 1948, MH 79/636, all in UKNA.

36. Steege, *Black Market,* 112; Robertson to Bevin 1225 Basic, September 3, 1948, and Klatt to Kinnear, September 9, 1948, FO 943/475, UKNA; Steck to Babcock, October 8, 1948, "Staff Studies (1 Jul–31 Dec) 1948" folder, box 6, Director's files, Berlin Sector Records, RG 260, USNA; Steck to Civil Administration and Political Affairs Branch, April 30, 1948, box 79, Kommandatura Records, RG 260, USNA. Martin to Magee, March 25, 1949; Magee to Cheyne, n.d. [March 1949]; Berry et al., "Food and Nutritional Situation"; "Provisional Report on the Nutritional Position in the Western Sectors . . . ," September 28, 1948; Martin minute, October 5, 1948; and Razzell minute, December 1948, all in MH 79/636, UKNA. Klatt to Kinnear, October 5, 1948, FO 943/475, and Razzell to Military Assistant, November 5 and 9, 1948, FO 1012/380, all in UKNA.

37. Robertson to Strang 1823 Basic, October 11, 1948, FO 943/475, UKNA; Razzell memo, December 4, 1948, and Magee to Cheyne, n.d. [March 1949], MH 79/636, UKNA; Herbert to Public Health, December 9, 1948, and Cheyne to Herbert, December 14 and 18, 1948, FO 1012/375, UKNA; Strang to Robertson 141 Basic, January 10, 1949, FO 943/475, UKNA; Klatt minute, December 31, 1948, MH 79/636, UKNA; Razzell to Military Assistant, January 11, 1949, FO 1012/374, UKNA; Robertson to Strang 230 Basic, January 18, 1949; Brownjohn to Seal, January 19, 1949; and Robertson to Strang, January 18, 1949, all in FO 943/475, UKNA; PUHL/R(49)11, March 28, 1949, FO 1112/266, UKNA; Cheyne to Magee, April 14, 1949, MH 79/636, UKNA.

38. "Table 6: Deaths from All Causes . . . ," n.d., "Vital Statistics 1949" folder, and chart, "Public Health Statistics in the US Sector . . . ," n.d., "Vital Statistics" folder, both in box 177, Public Health Branch Records, RG 260, USNA. See also Monthly OMG Berlin Sector Reports, February 1948–January 1949, box 71, Records of Civil Administration and Political Affairs Branch, RG 260, USNA; and Monthly Narrative Reports, June 1948–May 1949, boxes 175–76, Public Health Branch Records, RG 260, USNA.

39. Barker, *Berlin Air Lift,* 59; report, "Average Weight in Kilograms in US Sector of Berlin by Age Groups," n.d., "Public Health, 1949/48 [*sic*]" folder, box 3, Director's files, Berlin Sector Records, RG 260, USNA; W. T. C. Berry and D. J. Cowin, "Nutritional Position in the Western Sector [*sic*] of Berlin, February 1949—Progress Report," n.d. [February 1949], and Magee to Cheyne, n.d. [March 1949], both in MH 79/636, UKNA; Davison, *Berlin Blockade,* 318–19.

40. Report, "General Health Conditions in Berlin . . . ," n.d., and chart, "Public Health Statistics in the US Sector," n.d., both in "Vital Statistics" folder, box 177, Public Health Branch Records, RG 260, USNA.

41. Barker, *Berlin Air Lift,* 54; "Airbridge to Health," *OMGUS Information Bulletin,* no. 159 (April 19, 1949): 25; "USAFE and the Airlift, 1949," 206, reel Z-0040, USAFE/HO; memo, DDASTO, December 1, 1948, AIR 20/6891, UKNA; BERCOMB to CONCOMB Lubbecke CBGCC-6669, September 15, 1948, "AG 200.4 General 1948" folder, box 382, OMGUS AGO General Correspondence, RG 260, USNA; Froistad to Howley, October 5, 1948, "Staff Studies (1 Jul–31 Dec) 1948" folder, box 6, Director's files, Berlin Sector Records, RG 260, USNA.

42. Herbert to Howley, September 30, 1948, Froistad to Howley, October 5, 1948, Babcock to Howley, October 8, 1948, and Kilduff to Babcock, December 8, 1948, all in "Staff Studies (1 Jul–31 Dec) 1948" folder, box 6; Paine to Babcock, October 5, 1948, and Schwarz to Howley, August 2, 1948, both in "Public Health 1949/48" folder, box 3, all in Director's files, Berlin Sector Records, RG 260, USNA. See also report, "Average Weight in Kilograms . . . ," n.d., "Public Health 1949/48" folder, box 3, Director's files, Berlin Sector Records, RG 260, USNA; and Special Report 721, October 1, 1948, FO 1005/1860, UKNA. For a wartime parallel, see Moorhouse, *Berlin at War,* chap. 9.

43. Schwarz to Civil Administration Division, OMGUS, July 8, 1948, "Monthly Narrative Report June 1948" folder, box 175, Public Health Branch Records, RG 260, USNA; excerpt from Deputy Commandants meeting, August 13, 1948, and Babcock to Howley, August 16, 1948, both in "Staff Studies (1 Jul–31 Dec) 1948" folder, box 6, Director's files, Berlin Sector Records, RG 260, USNA.

44. PUHL/R(49)2, February 3, 1949, and PUHL/R(49)4, February 15, 1949, both in FO 1112/266, UKNA; BK/O(49)32, February 24, 1949, "Public Health Committee XVI, 1 Jan 1949–31 [*sic*] Feb 49" folder, box 8, Public Health Committee Records, U.S. Mission Berlin files, RG 84, USNA.

45. Special Report 720, December 3, 1948, FO 1005/1860, UKNA; Manpower Branch to Intelligence Branch, August 16, 1949, "Manpower 1949" folder, box 1, Director's files, Berlin Sector Records, RG 260, USNA; table 7a, "The Ten Leading Causes of Death in Berlin 1948," n.d., "Vital Statistics" folder, box 177, Public Health Branch Records, RG 260, USNA.

46. Naimark, *Russians in Germany,* 126. Also see Diehl, *Thanks of the Fatherland,* 66–71, and Biess, *Homecomings,* chaps. 2 and 4.

47. Heineman, *What Difference,* 115–22; Hilde Thurwald quoted in Moeller, *Protecting Motherhood,* 11.

48. Redding, *Growing Up,* 33, 85–86; Vaizey, *Surviving Hitler's War.*

49. Special Report 720, December 3, 1948, FO 1005/1860, UKNA; Manpower Branch to Intelligence Branch, August 16, 1949, "Manpower 1949" folder, box 1, Director's files, Berlin Sector Records, RG 260, USNA.

50. Winner, "Berlin Dreads," 16; Bennett, *Berlin Bastion,* 78–79; Foggon to Herbert, November 20, 1948, FO 1012/206, UKNA; PORO, Reports on Berlin Morale 30–43, n.d. [mid-October 1948]–May 3, 1949, FO 1005/1862, UKNA.

51. PORO, Reports on Berlin Morale 30 and 37, FO 1005/1862, UKNA.

52. Davison, *Berlin Blockade,* 317; Special Report 720, December 3, 1948, FO 1005/1860, UKNA. For the Siemens payroll, see Berlin Weekly Summary 25, February 25, 1949, file 800-3-1, vol. 835, RG 19, LAC.

53. Ford, "New Mark, Old Mistakes," 11–12; PORO, Reports on Berlin Morale 32 and 37, FO 1005/1862, UKNA; Special Report 720, December 3, 1948, FO 1005/1860, UKNA.

54. Conrad, *Nostromo,* 64.

55. According to one report, 5,800 eastern refugees arrived in one Berlin district, Kreuzberg, in March and April 1949. Froistad to Howley, June 1, 1949, "Public Welfare 1949" folder, box 3, Director's files, Berlin Sector Records, RG 260, USNA.

56. Merritt, *Democracy Imposed,* 335. For worse ordeals in other cities, see (among others) Salisbury, *900 Days*; Ousby, *Occupation,* 117–27; and Mazower, *Inside Hitler's Greece,* chap. 3. For ostracism, see Stivers, "Incomplete Blockade," 577–78.

57. Moeller, *Protecting Motherhood,* 22.

58. Gross, *Memories,* 1:177; Berry et al., "Food and Nutritional Situation," MH 79/636, UKNA.

59. Davison, *Berlin Blockade,* 320; Beck, *Under the Bombs,* 10–13, 23, 186; Richie, *Faust's Metropolis,* 635; Moorhouse, *Berlin at War,* chap. 4. The phrase "enthusiasm for a system of lies" is from Conquest, *Great Terror,* 278.

60. Davison, *Berlin Blockade,* 134; Stivers, "Incomplete Blockade," 579.

61. PORO, Reports on Berlin Morale 32 and 36, November 16, 1948, and January 18, 1949, FO 1005/1862, UKNA.

62. Andreas-Friedrich, *Battleground Berlin,* 84; Naimark, *Russians in Germany,* 79–80.

63. Djilas, *Conversations,* 95.

64. Information Control Division Report 124, June 1, 1948, "ICD Opinion Surveys 1948" folder, box 27, Director's files, Berlin Sector Records, RG 260, USNA; Information Control Division Report 147, November 17, 1948, "Public Opinion—(U.S. Zone)—Germany (. . . Report No. 147)" folder, box 1120, Occupied Area Reports, RG 407, USNA.

65. Halvorsen interview, May 13, 1988, AMC/HO; Donovan, *Bridge,* 148–49. Halvorsen's kindness was not unprecedented. RAF crews used handkerchiefs as parachutes to drop candy over Holland in the last weeks of the Second World War. Onderwater, *Operation Manna/Chowhound,* 69. For the ten-ton donation, see Smith, *Clay Papers,* 2:908. "Little Vittles" received so much publicity that decades later, some residents of the old Soviet sector believed the airlift had delivered only chocolate and other luxuries, not coal and food. Redding, *Growing Up,* 83–84, 142–43.

66. Quoted in Arnold-Forster, *Siege of Berlin,* 99–100.

67. Pennacchio, "United States and Berlin," 9, 25, 232, 234; Heineman, *What Difference,* 106.

68. Howley to OMGUS Economics Division, February 11, 1947, "Staff Studies 1949 (1 Jan–30 Jun) 1949" folder, box 6, Director's files, Berlin Sector Records, RG 260, USNA.

69. Borm to McClusky, May 10, 1949, "Manpower 1949—Trade Unions 1949" folder; minutes, 18th meeting of Informal German Industrial Committee, February 15, 1949, "Economics 1949 (German Industrial Committee) 1949" folder, both in box 2; McEwan study, "The Economic Situation in West Berlin," August 29, 1949, "Economics 1948–1949" folder, box 14, all in Director's files, Berlin Sector Records, RG 260, USNA. Intelligence Branch, OMG, Berlin Sector, "Special Report: Berlin Industrial Unemployment Survey," n.d. [April 13, 1949], II-8, folder 67-5, box 67, Pollock papers, BHL.

70. Manpower Branch to Intelligence Branch, August 16, 1949, "Manpower 1949" folder, box 1, Director's files, Berlin Sector Records, RG 260, USNA.

71. McEwan to Gretton, June 9, 1948, FO 1012/193, UKNA.

72. Ford, "New Mark, Old Mistakes," 11–12.

73. Murphy to Marshall 1757, July 20, 1948, 740.00119 Control (Germany)/7-2048, RG 59, USNA; Summary of Telegrams, July 21, 1948, "State Dept Briefs, May–August 1948" folder, box 21, Naval Aide files, HSTL; Bohlen memo, July 29, 1948, "Memos—CEB 1948 (1946–48)" folder, box 5, Bohlen papers, RG 59, USNA.

74. Wirtschaftsverband Maschinenbau to British Military Government, October 9, 1948, FO 1012/333, UKNA.

75. For the economic committee, see FO 1012/342; for the rubble project, see FO 1012/509, both in UKNA.

76. PORO, Report on Berlin Morale 32, FO 1005/1862, UKNA.

77. Bennett, *Berlin Bastion,* 170.

78. Davison, *Berlin Blockade,* 176; MGLS Weekly Report 40, August 10, 1948, C6767/2/18, 70487, FO 371, UKNA.

79. Davison, *Berlin Blockade,* 176–77.

80. Ibid., 126.

81. Tusa and Tusa, *Berlin Airlift,* 190, 300; Howley to Murphy, October 20, 1948, "Blockade and Counterblockade, 1948–1949" folder, box 11, Director's files, Berlin Sector Records, RG 260, USNA; OMG, Berlin Sector, "Special Report: Berlin Industrial Unemployment Survey," n.d. [April 13, 1949], folder 67-5, box 67, Pollock papers, BHL; Stivers, "Incomplete Blockade," 587.

82. Berry to Murphy, November 24, 1948, "711 Bizone—Berlin Economic Series" folder, box 1, Miscellaneous Classified Records, POLAD files, RG 84, USNA.

83. PORO, Report on Berlin Morale 36, FO 1005/1862, UKNA.

84. Howley to Murphy, October 20, 1948, "Blockade and Counterblockade, 1948–1949" folder, box 11, Director's files, Berlin Sector Records, RG 260, USNA; OMGUS Berlin Sector Weekly Intelligence Reports 9–10, "Intelligence Reports, 1 Jan 48–2 Oct 48" binder, box 10, Howley papers, MHI; "Special Report: Berlin, Winter 1948–49," November 10–17, 1948, and Berry to Murphy, November 24, 1948, both in "711 Bizone—Berlin Economic Series" folder, box 1, Miscellaneous Classified Records, POLAD files, RG 84, USNA; Tusa and Tusa, *Berlin Airlift,* 190; Bennett, *Berlin Bastion,* 150; Davison, *Berlin Blockade,* 316.

85. Howley memo, March 14, 1949, "Civil Administration 1949" folder, and table, "Employed and Unemployed Statistics," March 15, 1949, "Manpower 1949" folder, both in box 1, Director's files, Berlin Sector Records, RG 260, USNA.

86. Berry to Murphy, November 15, 1948, "711 Bizone—Berlin Economic Series" folder, box 1, Miscellaneous Classified Records, POLAD files, RG 84, USNA; Froistad to Howley, June 1, 1949, "Public Welfare 1949" folder, box 3, Director's files, Berlin Sector Records, RG 260, USNA.

87. Research and Analysis Branch, Manpower Division, "Statistical Bulletin No. 1," February 19, 1949, "Manpower 1949" folder, box 1, Director's files, Berlin Sector Records, RG 260, USNA.

88. Curran to Moran, January 29, 1949, "Economics (Commerce and Industry) 1949" folder, box 2, Director's files, Berlin Sector Records, RG 260, USNA.

89. McEwan to BEWAG, July 10, 1948, FO 1012/347, UKNA. Darling to Babcock and Moran, January 7, 1949, "Staff Studies 1949 (Jan–Jun)" folder, box 6; Darling to Moran,

January 20, 1949, and "Resume of Major Decisions," January 12, 1949, both in "Economics (Commerce and Industry) 1949" folder, box 2; Moran to Howley, January 23, 1949, and Gailey to Howley, January 27, 1949, both in "Coal 1948–1949" folder, box 14, all in Director's files, Berlin Sector Records, RG 260, USNA. The U.S.-U.K. sector unemployment comparisons are from pp. II-7 and IV-1–IV-4, Intelligence Branch, OMG, Berlin Sector, "Special Report: Berlin Industrial Unemployment Survey," n.d. [April 13, 1949], folder 67-5, box 67, Pollock papers, BHL.

90. Davison, *Berlin Blockade,* 321.

91. Stivers, "Incomplete Blockade," 570, 580; JGKM to Draper, November 29, 1948, "OUS 000.1 Germany/Berlin Crisis Nov 26, '48 to date" folder, box 14, Draper-Voorhees file, RG 335, USNA; Murphy to Marshall 1614, November 17, 1948, "710 Berlin Situation Apr–July 15" folder, box 215, Classified General Correspondence, POLAD files, RG 84, USNA. Historians discussed this topic, but until Stivers, they underestimated its scope. See, for example, Morris, *Blockade,* 140–41; Davison, *Berlin Blockade,* 196–97, 314; and Gottlieb, *German Peace Settlement,* 198. For gift parcels, see "Logbook Notes," July 8, 1948, "Logbook Notes" folder, box 7, and Babcock to Howley, July 13, 1948, "General Howley—General Ganeval 1948–1949" folder, box 12, both in Director's files, Berlin Sector Records, RG 260, USNA.

92. OMGUS Weekly Intelligence Report 128, October 23, 1948, "OUS 000.1 Germany/Berlin Crisis Nov 26, '48 to date" folder, box 14, Draper-Voorhees file, RG 335, USNA.

93. McEwan to Herbert, August 7, 1948, FO 1012/180, UKNA; Berry to Murphy, November 15, 1948, "711 Bizone—Berlin Economic Series" folder, box 1, Miscellaneous Classified Records, POLAD files, RG 84, USNA.

94. Darling to Babcock and Moran, January 7, 1949, "Staff Studies 1949 (Jan–Jun)" folder, box 6, Director's files, Berlin Sector Records, RG 260, USNA; Gaymer to Brand, October 9, 1948, and Douce to Gaymer, October 4 and 7, 1948, all in FO 1012/333, UKNA; OMGUS Weekly Intelligence Report 128, October 23, 1948, "OUS 000.1 Germany/Berlin Crisis Nov 26, '48 to date" folder, box 14, and Teleconference 1756, December 28, 1948, "SAOUS 000.1 Germany December 1948–February 1949" folder, box 13, both in Draper-Voorhees file, RG 335, USNA; Bolling to Bradley, November 24, 1948, file CD 2-2-4, box 4, OSD Numerical File, RG 330, USNA.

95. Ulbricht and Chwalek quoted in Steege, *Black Market,* 190–91, 209. See also the Allgemeiner Deutscher Nachrichtendienst (a "private" press service sponsored by the Soviet Military Administration) report that Soviet sector police enjoyed "complete success" in stopping goods entering Berlin, cited in Murphy to Marshall A-541, July 9, 1948, "710 Berlin Situation Apr–July 15" folder, box 215, Classified General Correspondence, POLAD files, RG 84, USNA. We know that OMGUS's report of how porous the blockade was took officials in Washington by surprise. Perhaps the most intriguing mystery remaining about the blockade is what Stalin was being told and how effective he thought the restrictions were.

96. Steege, "More than an Airlift," 208–9; Robertson to Bevin 1495, July 29, 1948, C6180/3/18, 70504, FO 371, UKNA.

97. Tunner, *Over the Hump,* 184–85.

98. Stivers, "Incomplete Blockade," 570–71.

99. *FR, 1948,* 2:1261–62; PORO, Reports on Berlin Morale 32–34, FO 1005/1862, UKNA; "US Army in Berlin," 138–39, USAREUR-MH; Huebner to Bradley and Chamberlin SX-91494, October 24, 1948, "Cables—Incoming Record Copies—October 1948" folder, box 681, OMGUS AGO Incoming Cables, RG 260, USNA; Murphy to Marshall 1614, November

17, 1948, "710 Berlin Situation Apr–July 15" folder, box 215, Classified General Correspondence, POLAD files, RG 84, USNA; Royall conference with Howley, December 26, 1948, "General Clay 1947–1949" folder, box 11, Director's files, Berlin Sector Records, RG 260, USNA; Teleconference 1756, December 28, 1948, "SAOUS 000.1 Germany December 1948–February 1949" folder, box 13, Draper-Voorhees file, RG 335, USNA; "Monthly Report, February 1949," n.d., "Civil Administration 1949" folder, box 1, Director's files, Berlin Sector Records, RG 260, USNA; Berlin airgram A-47, January 10, 1949, "OUS 000.1 Germany/Berlin Crisis, November 26, 1948 to date" folder, box 14, Draper-Voorhees file, RG 335, USNA; Berlin Weekly Summaries 13 (December 2, 1948), 17 (December 31, 1948), and 25 (February 25, 1949), all in file 800-3-1, vol. 835, RG 19, LAC; Stivers, "Incomplete Blockade," 581.

100. For PORO reports, see FO 1005/1862 and FO 1012/541 and 590, UKNA. The MGLS reports are in FO 1005/1830 and FO 371, 70613A and B, UKNA. For the OMGUS polls, see boxes 1117–20, Occupied Area Reports, RG 407, and box 27, Director's files, Berlin Sector Records, RG 260, both in USNA. The OMGUS-Berlin reports are in "Intelligence Reports, 1 Jan 48–2 Oct 48" binder, box 10, Howley papers, MHI, and box 903, Political Reports, Public Safety Branch Records, RG 260, USNA. The Canadian reports are in file 800-3-1, vol. 835, RG 19, LAC.

101. MGLS Weekly Report 34 (June 29, 1948), FO 1005/1830, UKNA.

102. Report attached to Schuetz to Textor, July 23, 1948, "AG 014.12 Items of Interest to Military Governor" folder, box 351, OMGUS AGO General Correspondence, RG 260, USNA.

103. Schuetz to Textor, July 30, 1948, "ICD Opinion Surveys 1948" folder, box 27, Director's files, Berlin Sector Records, RG 260, USNA.

104. Crespi to Textor, July 16, 1948, "ICD Opinion Surveys 1948" folder, box 27, Director's files, Berlin Sector Records, RG 260, USNA; MGLS Weekly Report 34 (June 29, 1948), FO 1005/1830, UKNA.

105. OMGUS Director of Intelligence, "Special Intelligence Report: Some German Legal Opinion of the Berlin Crisis," July 24, 1948, box 1117, Occupied Area Reports, RG 407, USNA.

106. Hays to DDMG, September 13, 1948, FO 1012/280, UKNA.

107. MGLS Weekly Reports 39 (August 3, 1948) and 40 (August 10, 1948), FO 1005/1830, UKNA.

108. MGLS Weekly Reports 36 (July 13, 1948) and 37 (July 20, 1948), FO 1005/1830, UKNA.

109. Robertson to Bevin 69, August 14, 1948, C6724/12/18, 70487, FO 371, UKNA.

110. PORO, Reports on Berlin Morale 28 and 30, FO 1005/1862, UKNA; OMGUS Berlin Political Report 13, "Intelligence Reports, 1 Jan 1948–2 Oct 1948" binder, box 10, Howley papers, MHI; Neumann quoted in "Berlin Weekly Summary No. 1," September 7, 1948, file 800-3-1, vol. 835, RG 19, LAC.

111. PORO, Report on Berlin Morale 32, FO 1005/1862, UKNA.

112. OMGUS Berlin Sector Political Reports 8 and 9, "Intelligence Reports, 1 Jan 1948–2 Oct 1948" binder, box 10, Howley papers, MHI.

113. "Special Report: Berlin, Winter 1948–49," November 10–17, 1948, and Berry to Murphy, November 24, 1948, both in "711 Bizone—Berlin Economic Series" folder, box 1, Miscellaneous Classified Records, POLAD files, RG 84, USNA.

114. *FR, 1948,* 2:1242.

115. Clay quoted in Reston to Krock, September 28, 1948, in Schlesinger, *Dynamics of World Power,* 2:398.

116. Stearns to G-2, July 12 and 26, 1948, "War Dept. Daily Cable 1948" folder, box 14, Director's files, Berlin Sector Records, RG 260, USNA.

117. Opinion Surveys Branch, Information Services Division, Report 141, October 4, 1948, "ICD Opinion Surveys 1948" folder, box 27, Director's files, Berlin Sector Records, RG 260, USNA; PORO, Report on Berlin Morale 33, December 3, 1948, FO 1005/1862, UKNA.

118. Murphy to Marshall A-866, November 15, 1948, "800 Political Affairs—Germany—September—" folder, box 220, Classified General Correspondence, POLAD files, RG 84, USNA.

119. Memo of Herbert-Kirkpatrick conversation, January 24, 1949, C577/14/18, 76541, FO 371, UKNA.

120. PORO, Report on Berlin Morale 40, March 18, 1949, FO 1005/1862, UKNA.

121. PORO, Reports on Berlin Morale 25 and 28, FO 1005/1862, UKNA.

122. Berlin Weekly Summary 25, February 25, 1949, file 800-3-1, vol. 835, RG 19, LAC.

123. Stivers, "Incomplete Blockade," 590–92, 602; PORO, Reports on Berlin Morale 30, 31, 40–42, FO 1005/1862, UKNA.

124. Special Report 719, October 14, 1948, FO 1005/1862, UKNA. For "cellar communities," see Tröger, "Between Rape and Prostitution," 101.

11. An Unexpected Success

1. Waite to Spackman, August 24, 1948, AIR 20/7804, UKNA; Herbert quoted in Stratton to Spackman, September 16, 1948, AIR 55/204, UKNA; Smith, *Clay Papers,* 2:878.

2. Waite to Herbert, September 9, 1948, AIR 20/7804, UKNA; memo, "Airlift," n.d. [September 16–17, 1948?], AIR 20/7805, UKNA; BAFO Report, 301; Hays to Cannon, October 20, 1948, "Airlift Correspondence" folder, box 5, Records Regarding Investigations . . . , RG 260, USNA; Robertson to Williams, November 1, 1948, AIR 55/215, UKNA.

3. Waite to Herbert, September 9, 1948, AIR 20/7804, UKNA.

4. Timberman to Wedemeyer, August 23, 1948, case 88/23, "1948—Hot File—P&O 092 TS thru 381 TS" folder, box 9, General Administrative File, RG 319, USNA; P&O Paper, September 29, 1948, sec. 18, CCS 381 (8-20-43), box 177, 1948–50 Central Decimal File, RG 218, USNA; Smith, *Clay Papers,* 2:852, 867, 875, 878–79, 890–91.

5. Kuter to Tunner, August 23, 1948, AMC/HO; Kuter to Vandenberg, September 22, 1948, sec. 2, OPD 381 Berlin (15 Jan 48), box 808, TS Decimal File, RG 341, USNA.

6. Smith, *Clay Papers,* 2:878, 890–91; Loftus, "American Response," 396–97.

7. Minutes of Air Ministry meeting, July 27, 1948, AIR 20/6891, UKNA.

8. Wedemeyer to Draper, October 5, 1948, "OAS 580.Germany" folder, box 17, Draper-Voorhees file, RG 335, USNA.

9. Ibid.; Ohly to JCS, October 4, 1948, sec. 2, OPD 381 (15 Jan 48), box 808, TS Decimal File, RG 341, USNA.

10. P&O Study, September 29, 1948, attached to Wedemeyer to Draper, October 5, 1948, "OAS 580.Germany" folder, box 17, Draper-Voorhees file, RG 335, USNA; Condit, *History of the JCS,* 2:150–53; JCS 1907/11, October 13, 1948, sec. 18, CCS 381 (8-20-43), box 177, 1948–50 Central Decimal File, RG 218, USNA; revised draft memo for secretary of defense, enclosure to JCS 1907/11, n.d., case 88/128, "P&O 381 TS (Section V-A)(part 5) . . ." folder, and enclosure A to JCS 1907/17, October 20, 1948, case 88/107, P&O 381 TS, pt. 4, both in box 103, P&O TS Decimal File, RG 319, USNA.

11. Bohlen to Lovett, July 23, 1948, 740.00119 Control (Germany)/7-2348, RG 59, USNA; Loftus, "American Response," 325–26.

12. Memo for the president, October 1, 1948, "Memo for President: Meeting Discussions (1948)" folder, box 186, PSF, Truman papers, HSTL; *FR, 1948,* 2:1198–99; Loftus, "American Response," 400–405.

13. Mayo to Wedemeyer, October 20, 1948, case 88/133, sec. 6, P&O 381 TS, box 103, P&O TS Decimal File, RG 319, USNA.

14. Condit, *History of the JCS,* 2:153–54; CVRS to Wedemeyer, October 5, 1948, case 88/107, sec. 4, P&O 381 TS, box 103, P&O TS Decimal File, RG 319, USNA; memo for the president, October 8, 1948, "Memo for President: Meeting Discussions (1948)" folder, box 186, PSF, Truman papers, HSTL; Anderson to Vandenberg, October 13, 1948, and Wedemeyer to Bradley, October 12, 1948, both in sec. 2, OPD 381 (15 Jan 48), box 808, TS Decimal File, RG 341, USNA.

15. Clay to Wedemeyer CC-6324, October 14, 1948, "OAS 580.Germany" folder, box 17, Draper-Voorhees file, RG 335, USNA.

16. Condit, *History of the JCS,* 2:154–55; memo for the president, October 15, 1948, "Memo for President: Meeting Discussions (1948)" folder, box 186, PSF, Truman papers, HSTL (emphasis added).

17. Condit, *History of the JCS,* 2:155.

18. For these tenets, see Gaddis, *Strategies,* chap. 3.

19. Condit, *History of the JCS,* 2:155–56; Leahy to Forrestal, October 20, 1948, sec. 19, CCS 381 (8-20-43), box 177, 1948–50 Central Decimal File, RG 218, USNA. Interestingly, one of Lovett's subordinates thought the chiefs' point about the ambiguity in U.S. policy was well taken. The NSC needed to decide, policy planner George Butler wrote, "whether the United States has made an irrevocable decision to maintain its forces in Berlin and to continue operation of the airlift even if that course of action makes war a probability." Butler to Lovett, October 14, 1948, "Chronological July–December 1948" folder, box 33, PPS Records, RG 59, USNA. Lovett's lecture changed few minds. Wedemeyer insisted, "We . . . must get out of Berlin, and regroup our military forces elsewhere." He also persuaded Bradley and Royall to broach the subject of evacuating dependents in Berlin with Lovett and Clay. Muir to chief of plans and policy, October 16, 1948, case 88/135, sec. 6, P&O 381 TS, box 103, and secs. 1 and 2, P&O 370.05 TS, box 84, all in P&O TS Decimal File, RG 319, USNA.

20. Souers to Truman, October 15, 1948, Truman to Pace, October 16, 1948, and Pace to Truman, October 21, 1948, all in "NSC Meeting 24" folder, box 177, PSF, Truman papers, HSTL; Wedemeyer to Clay WARX-91094, October 19, 1948, sec. 19, CCS 381 (8-20-43), box 177, 1948–50 Central Decimal File, RG 218, USNA.

21. Shlaim, *United States,* 364–65.

22. Memo for the president, October 22, 1948, "Memo for President: Meeting Discussions (1948)" folder, box 186, PSF, Truman papers, HSTL.

23. Leahy diary, October 21, 1948, box 6, Leahy papers, LOCMD; Truman to Souers, October 22, 1948, "NSC Meeting 24" folder, box 177, PSF, Truman papers, HSTL.

24. Shlaim, *United States,* 365–66; Schrader, *Blockade Breakers,* 185. In later years, Clay was certain that Truman had overruled his advisers and ordered increases, although he was unsure when. In 1971, Clay told Jean Edward Smith it happened in October; two years later, in an interview at the Army War College, he dated it in July. Cf. Clay interview, March 9, 1971, CUOH, and Clay interview, January 24, 1973, MHI.

25. Tunner to Kuter, August 6, 1948, AMC/HO; Sanders to Robb, July 31 and September 16, 1948, and Anderson to Medhurst, August 30, 1948, all in FO 1030/63, UKNA; LeMay to Vandenberg UAX-9258, August 23, 1948, "AG 319.1 Berlin Transportation Situation Reports,

vol. V" folder, box 428, OMGUS AGO General Correspondence, RG 260, USNA; Medhurst to Anderson, September 28, 1948, and report, "Control of Berlin Airlift," n.d. [September 27, 1948?], both in sec. 2, OPD 381 Berlin (15 Jan 48), box 808, TS Decimal File, RG 341, USNA.

26. Robertson to Sanders 54527 and 54528, September 30, 1948, and Sanders to Robertson AX.469, October 5, 1948, all in FO 1030/63, UKNA; LeMay to Clay, September 29, 1948, "Cables—Incoming Record Copies—September 1948" folder, box 680, OMGUS AGO Incoming Cables, RG 260, USNA; *History of USAFE, November 1948,* 21, USAFE/HO.

27. BAFO Report, 11–12.

28. Memo, Air Staff, BAFO, January 13, 1949, AIR 55/218, UKNA; BAFO Report, 11, 142; "USAFE and the Airlift, 1949," 13, reel Z-0040, USAFE/HO; Tunner, *Over the Hump,* 210.

29. BAFO Report, 19.

30. Strang to Robertson 3212, November 3, 1948, and Robertson to Strang 920 Basic, November 6, 1948, both in AIR 20/6891, UKNA. For Tedder's views, see Sowrey et al., "Berlin Airlift," 71–72.

31. *History of USAFE, November 1948,* 29–33, USAFE/HO; BAFO Report, 326; Berlin Magistrat, *Airlift Berlin,* 21, 51; Gallogly Report, 97, 105–9; *New York Times,* November 6, 1948, 6; Milton interview, December 5, 1975, CUOH; Jackson, *Berlin Airlift,* 61–62. See also Reeves, *Daring Young Men,* 69n.

32. BAFO Report, 326; Donovan, *Bridge,* 137; Bennett, *Berlin Bastion,* 139–40; Harris et al., "Special Study," 64; Pernot, "Le pont aérien," 59–60.

33. Riess, *Berlin Story,* 217–21; Downie, "Long Ranger," 20; Donovan, *Bridge,* 138.

34. Milton interview, December 5, 1975, CUOH.

35. OMGUS Intelligence Division, "Weekly Intelligence Report 119," August 21, 1948, box 3385, Historian's Background Files, RG 549, USNA. For analyses of Soviet restraint, see Adomeit, *Soviet Risk-Taking,* 166–70, and Young, *Politics of Force,* 184, 314. For diplomats' reports, see Narinskii, "Soviet Union," 71–72. Some have criticized Soviet intelligence for telling the Kremlin what it wanted to hear, citing an August 1948 report that the airlift was not providing enough food as one example of distorted reporting. Yet the report was accurate. The criticism rests on hindsight (the airlift's eventual success), not conditions at the time. Murphy, Kondrashev, and Bailey, *Battleground Berlin,* 62–63, 77–78.

36. "Summary of Corridor Incidents," appendix VII-B, "USAFE and the Berlin Airlift, 1949," reel Z-0040, USAFE/HO. British reports (including Robertson's comment about Dallgow [also called Staaken] in a September 9, 1948, cable to Bevin) are in AIR 20/7819, UKNA. There was another period of tension in January, after the Soviets threatened to force down Western planes flying below 3,000 feet. BASC to BAFO Operations CSDX.780, January 15, 1949, Tedder to Williams MSX.845, February 2, 1949, and extract of COS(49)17th meeting, February 3, 1949, all in AIR 20/7819, UKNA; Bevin to Franks 1409 and Franks to Bevin 704, February 4, 1949, C1011/14/18, 76543, FO 371, UKNA; Maddocks to Clay WARX-83789, February 5, 1949, "SAOUS 580.Germany/Airlift" folder, box 17, Draper-Voorhees file, RG 335, USNA.

37. LeMay to Clay, October 14, 1948, "Soviet 1949 [*sic*]" folder, box 63, Vandenberg papers, LOCMD; Clay quoted in memo for the president, October 22, 1948, "Memo for the President: Meeting Discussions (1948)" folder, box 186, PSF, Truman papers, HSTL; BAFO Report, 39; Murphy to Marshall 2298, September 10, 1948, 740.00119 Control (Germany)/9-1048, RG 59, USNA; Davison, *Berlin Blockade,* 198–99.

38. Harris et al., "Special Study," 43; *History of USAFE, October 1948,* 28, USAFE/HO.

39. "USAFE and the Airlift, 1948," 32, 66–67, 204–5, reel Z-0039, USAFE/HO; Harris et al., "Special Study," 11, 47.

40. "USAFE and the Airlift, 1948," 138–41, reel Z-0039, USAFE/HO.

41. Kuter to Tunner, September 2, 1948, AMC/HO; "USAFE Summary," 79, 81, 99, 116, and "USAFE and the Airlift, 1948," 126–27, 130n97, both in reel Z-0039, USAFE/HO.

42. "USAFE Summary," 123, reel Z-0039, USAFE/HO; Donovan, *Bridge,* 118; Bennett, *Berlin Bastion,* 220; Charles, *Berlin Blockade,* 115; Kuter, "Vittles," Kuter papers, USAFA; USAFE press release, November 4, 1948, reel Z-0039, USAFE/HO.

43. *History of USAFE, November 1948,* 19–21, USAFE/HO.

44. Milton, "Berlin Airlift," 63; Tunner, *Over the Hump,* 159, 189; Launius and Cross, *MAC,* 21–22, 26–31; Slayton, *Master of the Air,* 192–201. Tunner acknowledged his initial dependence on USAFE, writing to Kuter, "The organization is not what you wanted, nor what I would have preferred, but higher authority determined it should be under USAFE. As a matter of fact, due to the complete dependence of this thing on the theater for all support, I must now agree with that decision at least for the time being." Tunner to Kuter, August 3, 1948, AMC/HO; Tunner interview, October 5–6, 1976, 81–82, 101–2, K239.0512-911, AFHRA.

45. "USAFE and the Airlift, 1948," 64, 244, and "USAFE Summary," 161, both in reel Z-0039, USAFE/HO; BAFO Report, 141, 143, 187; Milton quoted in Launius and Cross, *MAC,* 32.

46. Launius and Cross, *MAC,* 20; "USAFE and the Airlift, 1948," 180, reel Z-0039, USAFE/HO.

47. BAFO to 85 Wing OX.625, October 15, 1948, and BAFO to 85 Wing O.665, October 14, 1948, both in AIR 55/204, UKNA; BAFO Report, 266; Pearcy, "Berlin Airlift," 201.

48. Barker, *Berlin Air Lift,* 20, 34; Waite to Herbert, December 14, 1948, AIR 20/7808, UKNA.

49. *History of USAFE, November 1948,* 17, USAFE/HO; "USAFE and the Airlift, 1948," 235, reel Z-0039, USAFE/HO; Launius and Cross, *MAC,* 46; USAFE Press Release 2211-A, November 30, 1948, reel Z-0039, USAFE/HO; Kuter, "Vittles," Kuter papers, USAFA.

50. Andreas-Friedrich, *Battleground Berlin,* 253; Draft Report 147, December 10, 1948, AIR 55/100, UKNA.

51. Harris et al., "Special Study," 66–67; "USAFE and the Airlift, 1948," 179, 206–7, reel Z-0039, USAFE/HO; "USAFE and the Airlift, 1949," 306–9, reel Z-0040, USAFE/HO.

52. Study, 1946 Communications Squadron, "The 1946th and the Berlin Airlift," n.d. [1949?], 56–62; "USAFE and the Airlift, 1948," 199–200; "USAFE Summary," 45–46; and report, 1807 AACS Wing, "Berlin Airlift: Air Traffic Control History," n.d., all in reel Z-0039, USAFE/HO; "USAFE and the Airlift, 1949," 112–13, 134, reel Z-0040, USAFE/HO; Bennett quoted in Launius and Cross, *MAC,* 43; MacGregor and Hansen, "Berlin Airlift," 45.

53. "USAFE Summary," 45, reel Z-0039, USAFE/HO; "USAFE and the Airlift, 1949," 116, 129, reel Z-0040, USAFE/HO; MacGregor and Hansen, "Berlin Airlift," 45; BAFO Report, 27, 157.

54. "USAFE and the Airlift, 1949," 27–28, 189–90, reel Z-0040, USAFE/HO; BAFO Report, 183–84, 295.

55. Williams to AOA, December 29, 1948, AIR 55/204, UKNA; "USAFE and the Airlift, 1948," 184, reel Z-0039, USAFE/HO; BAFO Report, 142, 323–24; "USAFE and the Airlift, 1949," 111–12, 117, reel Z-0040, USAFE/HO.

56. "USAFE and the Airlift, 1949," 18, 23–25, 47–49, 51–53, 59, reel Z-0040, USAFE/HO; *History of USAFE, February 1949,* 29, USAFE/HO.

57. Moseley, "Medical History," 1260–62.

58. Report, 7700 TI&E Group, January 24, 1949, appendix 28 in *History of USAFE, January 1949,* USAFE/HO; LeMay and Kantor, *Mission with LeMay,* 418.

59. Dowling quoted in Sowrey et al., "Berlin Airlift," 66; BAFO Report, 62, 155, 179–81.

60. "USAFE and the Airlift, 1949," 262–72, 314–15, reel Z-0040, USAFE/HO; BAFO Report, 61.

61. *History of USAFE, January 1949,* 30–31; ibid., *February 1949,* 19–20, 27; ibid., *March 1949,* 16, 26, all in USAFE/HO; "USAFE and the Airlift, 1949," 238–42, reel Z-0040, USAFE/HO.

62. USAFE to EUCOM UA-9714, September 29, 1948, "USAFE UAX 6667 [to] UAX 9859" folder, box 450, Incoming Messages, RG 549, USNA; Huschke, *Candy Bombers,* 194–95; "USAFE and the Airlift, 1949," 90, 243, reel Z-0040, USAFE/HO; "USAFE Summary," 134, reel Z-0039, USAFE/HO; report, CALTF, "Preliminary Analysis of Lessons Learned," June 1949, 12, 23, reel C5113, AFHRA; BAFO Report, 60.

63. Kuter, "Vittles," Kuter papers, USAFA.

64. Moran to Howley, February 18, 1949, "Staff Studies 1949 (January–June) 1949" folder, box 6, Director's files, Berlin Sector Records, RG 260, USNA; "USAFE and the Airlift, 1949," 352, reel Z-0040, USAFE/HO; BAFO Report, 365; OMGUS Berlin Sector, *Four Year Report,* 31–32.

65. Charlesby minute, January 11, 1949, AIR 55/100, UKNA; BAFO Report, 354.

66. *History of USAFE, February 1949,* appendix XI, USAFE/HO; BAFO Report, 365–70.

67. Tusa and Tusa, *Berlin Airlift,* 335; *History of USAFE, March 1949,* 14, 24, 29, USAFE/HO; "USAFE and the Airlift, 1949," 66–67, reel Z-0040, USAFE/HO; *History of CALTF, March 1949,* 5, 15–17; ibid., *April 1949,* 8–9. For the C-54s, see Launius and Cross, *MAC,* 20; Royall to Johnson, April 25, 1949, folder 3, CD 6-2-9, box 27, OSD Numerical File, RG 330, USNA; and Larson, "Berlin Airlift," 236.

68. BAFO Report, 193, 232, 519; Whitfield to Williams, March 4, 1949, AIR 55/216, UKNA.

69. "USAFE Summary," 30, reel Z-0039, USAFE/HO; Barker, *Berlin Air Lift,* 53; BAFO Report, 199, 227–28.

70. BAFO Report, 237, 519, 529.

71. Ibid., 8–9, 142–44, 187; Air Ministry to BAFO et al., COX.6496, December 10, 1948, AIR 20/6891, and Air Ministry to Transport Command and BAFO AX.2431, April 1, 1949, AIR 20/6893, both in UKNA.

72. BAFO Report, 156; "USAFE and the Airlift, 1949," 95, 117, reel Z-0040, USAFE/HO.

73. "USAFE and the Airlift, 1949," 202–6, 348–50, reel Z-0040, USAFE/HO; BAFO Report, 67; "USAFE Summary," 28, reel Z-0039, USAFE/HO.

74. "USAFE and the Airlift, 1949," 198–99, 209, reel Z-0040, USAFE/HO; Lay, "Berlin Air Lift," 2:50–51, reel Z-0029, USAFE/HO.

75. "USAFE and the Airlift, 1949," 120–21, reel Z-0040, USAFE/HO; Lay, "Berlin Air Lift," 2:52–53, reel Z-0029, USAFE/HO.

76. Tunner, *Over the Hump,* 219–22; "USAFE and the Airlift, 1949," 188, 210, reel Z-0040, USAFE/HO.

77. BAFO and USAFE, "Long Range Plan for Berlin Airlift," February 14, 1949, and memo, S.6 to ACAS(Ops), March 10, 1949, both in AIR 20/6892, UKNA; BAFO Report, 6.

78. Byroade memo, n.d. [March 1949], "OAS 000.1 Germany/Politics" folder, box 15, Draper-Voorhees file, RG 335, USNA.

79. Royall to Johnson, April 25, 1949, folder 3, CD 6-2-9, box 27, OSD Numerical File, RG 330, USNA.

80. Meeting minutes, December 13, 1948, and Walmsley to ACAS(Trg) et al., January 5, 1949, both in AIR 20/6891, UKNA; War Office to Air Ministry, January 25, 1949, and Walmsley to Sanders, January 26, 1949, both in AIR 20/6892, UKNA. For British hopes of obtaining C-54s, see Air Ministry to BAFO MSX.850, February 4, 1949, and minutes, Foreign Office–Air Ministry meeting, February 25, 1949, both in AIR 20/6892, UKNA; and extract of minutes, GEN/241 Committee, February 7, 1949, AIR 20/7184, UKNA.

81. Memo, January 17, 1949, AIR 20/6891, UKNA; BAFO to Air Ministry A.557, January 27, 1949; TO.1(a) memo, February 1949; Rainsford to Walmsley, February 25, 1949; and Sanders to AMP, March 3, 1949, all in AIR 20/6892, UKNA; DDASTO memo, March 31, 1949; Mackworth to Henderson, April 6, 1949; and Transport Command to BAFO OX.1033, May 14, 1949, all in AIR 55/218, UKNA; Walmsley to Mackworth, May 5, 1949, AIR 20/6892, UKNA; BAFO Report, 25.

82. Collier, *Bridge,* 8; Davison, *Berlin Blockade,* 261; Charles, *Berlin Blockade,* 117–18; "USAFE and the Airlift, 1949," 123–24, reel Z-0040, USAFE/HO.

12. Dealing Sensibly with Established Fact

1. Douglas quoted in Lippmann diary, December 2, 11, and 16, 1948, Lippmann papers, Yale University; *FR, 1949,* 3:681–85.

2. USAFE Estimates of the Situation, October 15 and December 1, 1948, "Air Force Intelligence Reports" folder, box 787, Formerly Classified Intelligence Reports, RG 260, USNA; memo, December 6, 1948, "SAOUS 000.1 Germany December 1948–February 1949" folder, box 13, Draper-Voorhees file, RG 335, USNA. See also study, n.d. [December 1948–January 1949], "Alternate Courses . . ." folder, box 1, Records of the Assistant Secretary of State for Occupied Areas, RG 59, USNA.

3. JIC Briefing, January 15, 1949, CD 9-3-38, box 54, OSD Numerical File, RG 330, USNA.

4. *FR, 1949,* 3:82–83, 128–29, 708–9; Beam memo, December 8, 1948, 740.00119 Control (Germany)/12-848, RG 59, USNA.

5. Robertson to Bevin 2677 Basic, December 13, 1948; Robertson to Strang, January 1, 1949; and Robertson to Bevin 124, January 26, 1949, all in FO 1030/63, UKNA; Robertson quoted in meeting minutes, February 3, 1949, C1035/14/18, 76543, FO 371, UKNA.

6. Bullock, *Bevin,* 3:634–35; McNeil and Chauvel quoted in Lippmann diary, December 15, 1948, and November 19, 1948, respectively, Lippmann papers, Yale University.

7. For example, see Smith, *Defense of Berlin,* 128–29; Shlaim, *United States,* 380–81; Pogue, *Marshall,* 4:412; and Eisenberg, *Drawing the Line,* 474–75.

8. Shulman, *Stalin's Foreign Policy,* 31, 52–54; Murphy to Marshall 2684, November 5, 1948, and Douglas to Marshall 584, November 6, 1948, "Miscellaneous Correspondence 1948 Campaign" folder, box 21, Clifford papers, HSTL; *FR, 1948,* 4:932–33; memo, n.d. [November 1948], "Secretary of Defense—Louis Johnson" folder, box 135, PSF, Truman papers, HSTL.

9. Smith, *Acheson,* 83; Shulman, *Stalin's Foreign Policy,* 54–56; *New York Times,* January 17, 1949, 1, 7; Smith, *Clay Papers,* 2:992–93; Davison, *Berlin Blockade,* 255; Murphy to Acheson 149, January 29, 1949, 862.00/1-2949, RG 59, USNA.

10. U.S. President, *Public Papers . . . 1949,* 98; Davison, *Berlin Blockade,* 255; *FR, 1949,* 5:558–59.

11. The original Smith-Stalin exchange is reprinted in *FR, 1949,* 5:562–63; the second is in ibid., 565. See also Ross's press conference, January 31, 1949, "Stalin 1949 (Kingsbury Smith story)" folder, box 7, Ross papers, HSTL, and Ayers diary, February 2, 1949, box 26, Ayers papers, HSTL. The parallels with Stalin's May 1948 peace offensive are striking. See Zubok, *Failed Empire,* 76.

12. *FR, 1949,* 5:561, 563–64, 667–68; FBIS, "Foreign Radio Reactions to Stalin's Replies to Kingsbury Smith," February 3, 1949, "Russia: Moscow" folder, box 164, PSF, Truman papers, HSTL.

13. Carlyle, *Documents, 1949–1950,* 378–80 (emphasis added); Jendretzky quoted in Steege, "More than an Airlift," 262 (emphasis added).

14. Truman quoted in Ayers diary, January 30 and February 2, 1949, Ayers papers, HSTL; Wrong to Pearson WA-241, January 31, 1949, folder 4, file 7-CA-14(s), DEA files; Bohlen to Acheson (marked "not used"), January 31, 1949, "Stalin-INS Exchange" folder, box 8, and Bohlen memo, February 1, 1949, "Memos CEB 1949" folder, box 5, both in Bohlen papers, RG 59, USNA.

15. Robertson quoted in meeting minutes, February 3, 1949, C1035/14/18, 76543, FO 371, UKNA; Bohlen memo, February 1, 1949, "Memos CEB 1949" folder, box 5, Bohlen papers, RG 59, USNA; Bevin to Robertson 139, January 29, 1949, C593/14/18, 76541, FO 371, UKNA; GEN 241/4, February 2, 1949, CAB 130/38, UKNA; *FR, 1949,* 3:668; Litchfield's comments in OMGUS staff conference, February 5, 1949, "Staff Conferences, February 1949" folder, box 6, OMGUS Minutes, RG 260, USNA.

16. Jessup, "Park Avenue Diplomacy," 378; Jessup interview, 305, CUOH; Bohlen, *Witness,* 283; Princeton seminar, July 8–9, 1953, 272–73, box 79, and notes for meetings, pt. 2, box 78, Acheson papers, HSTL. For the Truman-Acheson plan, see Acheson memo, January 31, 1949, "Stalin-INS Exchange" folder, box 8, Bohlen papers, RG 59, USNA; Acheson, *Present,* 267; Truman, *Memoirs,* 2:130.

17. Acheson, *Present,* 267–69; transcript, "Press and Radio News Conference . . . February 2, 1949," in "Press Conferences, Acheson, January–June 1949" folder, box 68, Acheson papers, HSTL.

18. Cf. transcript, "Press and Radio News Conference . . . February 2, 1949," in "Press Conferences, Acheson, January–June 1949" folder, box 68, Acheson papers, HSTL, and U.S. President, *Public Papers . . . 1949,* 127–28.

19. Acheson, *Present,* 269; Princeton seminar, July 8–9, 1953, 281–83, box 79, Acheson papers, HSTL.

20. *FR, 1949,* 3:694–95; Jessup interview, 306, CUOH.

21. Jessup, "Park Avenue Diplomacy," 379–80; Bohlen, *Witness,* 284; Acheson, "Philip C. Jessup," 7; Mazuzan, *Warren Austin,* 135.

22. Bohlen, *Witness,* 284; Beam memo, March 8, 1949, and Jessup to Beam, March 14, 1949, both in 740.00119 Control (Germany)/3-1449, RG 59, USNA.

23. Interestingly, Narinskii writes that the negotiations opened in mid-February "on American initiative." Narinskii, "Soviet Union," 72.

24. *FR, 1948,* 2:581–95; *FR, 1949,* 3:197, 222.

25. For this ploy, see Jervis, *Logic of Images,* 142–69.

26. Davison, *Berlin Blockade,* 281–96.

27. Hillenkoetter to Truman, June 30, 1948, "Central Intelligence—Memos—1945–1948" folder, box 211, PSF, Truman papers, HSTL; SRB/TS/49, July 8, 1948, FO 1012/193, UKNA.

28. Davison, *Berlin Blockade,* 155, 264; Charles, *Berlin Blockade,* 46, 124; Bennett, *Berlin*

Bastion, 202; Smith, *Defense of Berlin,* 127–28. For Malik's question about trade, see *FR, 1949,* 3:706. For a dissenting view on the value of the counterblockade, one that concluded it had little effect, see OIR 4965, May 26, 1949, box 262, Intelligence Reports, RG 59, USNA.

29. Davison, *Berlin Blockade,* 251.

30. Roosevelt quoted in *FR, Conferences at Malta and Yalta,* 617, 628.

31. Alexander Dallin notes that Stalin disliked facing facts that exposed his mistakes, while Hannes Adomeit asks rhetorically, "In the face of Stalin's characteristic refusal to condone failure, who dared explain that the Berlin venture had come to a dead end?" Both points suggest a tardy decision, not one in January, when "General Winter" might still ride to the rescue. Dallin, "Allied Leadership," 12; Adomeit, *Soviet Risk-Taking,* 152.

32. Davison, *Berlin Blockade,* 256–59; Shulman, *Stalin's Foreign Policy,* 58–61; *FR, 1949,* 4:635–37; Leonhard, *Child of the Revolution,* 513. For Ulbricht's echo of Thorez, see Naimark, *Russians in Germany,* 55–56.

33. Molotov quoted in Berezhkov, *At Stalin's Side,* 214. For Western speculation on these and other personnel changes, see *FR, 1949,* 5:585, 601; CIA Intelligence Memo 139, March 18, 1949, "Central Intelligence Memos 1949" folder, box 211, PSF, Truman papers, HSTL; Kennan to Bohlen, March 15, 1949, "Memos CEB 1949" folder, box 5, Bohlen papers, RG 59, USNA.

34. *FR, 1949,* 3:696–97.

35. Acheson, *Present,* 270; summary of daily meeting, March 17, 1949, 740.00119 Control (Germany)/3-1749, RG 59, USNA; *FR, 1949,* 3:698–701; Bevin quoted in Tusa and Tusa, *Berlin Airlift,* 334.

36. *FR, 1949,* 3:700–702, 713–14, 717–19. Other, less substantial obstacles hindered progress. For example, at one point, Jessup said that the United States had an "open mind" about the date and agenda of a CFM. Malik's Russian interpreter stumbled on the phrase, and Jessup asked Malik, who knew some English, if he understood it. The Russian replied that even though "there was no equivalent expression in Russian," he grasped the point. Ibid., 715.

37. *FR, 1949,* 3:179–81, 237, 709–11; Acheson memo, March 31, 1949, "Jessup-Malik Conversations . . ." folder, box 304, RG 43, USNA.

38. *FR, 1949,* 3:179–81, 237, 716.

39. Ibid., 725–30; GEN 241/10th meeting, April 4, 1949, CAB 130/38, UKNA. For Acheson's comments to the press, see press conference transcripts, April 13 and 20, 1949, "Press Conferences—Acheson—January–June 1949" folder, box 68, Acheson papers, HSTL.

40. *FR, 1949,* 3:731; Carlyle, *Documents, 1949–50,* 153–54; Bohlen to Allen, April 19, 1949, "Correspondence A–K" folder, box 1, Bohlen papers, RG 59, USNA; U.S. Senate, Committee on Foreign Relations, *Documents, 1944–1959,* 57–59; Jessup to Acheson, April 12, 1949, and Battle to Secretariat, April 19, 1949, both in "Jessup-Malik Conversations . . ." folder, box 304, RG 43, USNA; Battle to Acheson, April 19, 1949, "Memoranda of Conversation, April 1949" folder, box 64, Acheson papers, HSTL; memo, Truman to Johnson, n.d., "Russia, 1945–1948" folder, box 163, PSF, Truman papers, HSTL; Clay, *Decision,* 390.

41. Jessup, "Park Avenue Diplomacy," 392; *FR, 1949,* 3:732–37.

42. *History of CALTF, April 1949,* 19, reel C5111, AFHRA; appendix VII-B, "USAFE and the Berlin Airlift, 1949," frames 592ff., reel Z-0040, USAFE/HO. For instances of sabotage, see CALTF, "Preliminary Analysis," 22.

43. Appendix VII-B, "USAFE and the Berlin Airlift, 1949," reel Z-0040, USAFE/HO. The most recent instances of the error are Reeves, *Daring Young Men,* 270, and Slayton, *Master of the Air,* 139.

44. U.S. Senate, Committee on Foreign Relations, *Documents, 1944–1961,* 90–91.

45. U.S. Department of State, *Bulletin* 20, no. 516 (May 22, 1949): 662; Riddleberger to Acheson 700, May 12, 1949, 740.00119 Control (Germany)/5-1249, RG 59, USNA; Tusa and Tusa, *Berlin Airlift,* 355; Smith, *Acheson,* 90–91.

46. *FR, 1948,* 2:1287–97.

47. Ibid., 1288; Kennan lecture, National War College, "Contemporary Problems of Foreign Policy," September 17, 1948, folder 12, box 299, Kennan papers, MML; Gaddis, *Strategies,* 30; Acheson quoted in U.S. Senate, Committee on Foreign Relations, *Reviews,* 8.

48. For Kennan's papers, see *FR, 1948,* 2:1240–47, 1287–97, 1320–38; Kennan to Marshall, October 18, 1948, "Memos CEB 1948 (1946–1948)" folder, box 5, Bohlen papers, RG 59, USNA; sec. 1, P&O 091 Germany TS, box 13, P&O TS Decimal File, RG 319, USNA; Kennan to Marshall, September 19, 1948, "Germany 1947–1948" folder, box 15, PPS Records, RG 59, USNA; Kennan to Murphy, December 24, 1948, 740.00119 Control (Germany)/12-748, RG 59, USNA; Kennan, *Memoirs,* 418–29; Mayers, *Kennan,* 145–49; Miscamble, *Kennan,* 145–52; McAllister, *No Exit,* 156–62; and Gaddis, *George F. Kennan*, 328–34. For Kennan's comments about Germans' political impulses, see *FR, 1949,* 3:97.

49. *FR, 1948,* 2:1287n; Hickerson to Carter, November 23, 1948, 740.00119 Control (Germany)/11-2348, RG 59, USNA; Murphy to Carter, January 14, 1949, "Germany 1949" folder, box 15, PPS Records, RG 59, USNA; Clay, *Decision,* 438; Clay quoted in Millis and Duffield, *Forrestal Diaries,* 507; Clay to Murphy, December 3, 1948, "800—Political Affairs—Germany. September—" folder, box 220, Classified General Correspondence, POLAD files, RG 84, USNA.

50. Kennan to Marshall, September 19, 1948, "Germany 1947–1948" folder, box 15, PPS Records, RG 59, USNA; *FR, 1949,* 3:102–5; Gaddis, *George F. Kennan*, 341–43.

51. For this NSC committee, see *FR, 1949,* 3:87–89; Acheson memos, January 24 and 26, 1949, "Memos of Conversations, January–February 1949" folder, box 64, Acheson papers, HSTL; memo for the president, January 27, 1949, "Memo for President—Meeting Discussions (1949)" folder, box 186, PSF, Truman papers, HSTL; and Smith, *Clay Papers,* 2:994–95, 1002–3, 1032–35, 1049–50.

52. Murphy quoted in Pope diary, April 21, 1949, vol. 2, Pope papers, LAC; *FR, 1949,* 3:118–37, 142–55.

53. *FR, 1949,* 3:858–62; Webb to Johnson, May 4, 1949, sec. 1, CCS 092 Germany (5-4-49), box 25, 1948–50 Geographic File, RG 218, USNA; Smith, *Clay Papers,* 2:1139–47.

54. Smith, *Clay Papers,* 2:1148–55; Acheson to Riddleberger 517, May 6, 1949, 740.00119 Council/5-649, RG 59, USNA.

55. Denfeld to Johnson, May 11, 1949, sec. 1, CCS 092 Germany (5-4-49), box 25, 1948–50 Geographic File, RG 218, USNA.

56. For British views, see *FR, 1949,* 3:748–50, 863–64, 867–72, and Patrick Dean's assessment in Robertson to Pearson 967, May 7, 1949, file 7-DE-2(s), DEA files.

57. U.S. Senate, Committee on Foreign Relations, *Reviews,* 5.

58. Cf. Jessup memo, May 7, 1949, "Jessup-Malik Conversations" folder, box 304, U.S. Delegation Records, RG 43, USNA; and *FR, 1949,* 3:872–74.

59. Bohlen, *Witness,* 285; Caffery to Acheson 1976, May 13, 1949, 740.00119 Council/5-1349, RG 59, USNA; *FR, 1949,* 3:875–76.

60. I have borrowed some of Charles Yost's complaints about British and French policy on the eve of the CFM because they describe Acheson's rejection of Program A so aptly. *FR, 1949,* 3:890–92. See also Gaddis, *George F. Kennan*, 348–51, 533–34.

61. *FR, 1949,* 3:252–62, 266.

62. "Tripartite . . . Report to the Foreign Ministers," May 20, 1949, "CFM Paris 1949: Tripartite Conversations—Report to the Foreign Ministers" folder, box 304, U.S. Delegation Records, RG 43, USNA; *FR, 1949,* 3:877–87.

63. FBIS, "Soviet and Satellite Radio Comment . . . ," nos. 1 and 3, May 16 and 20, 1949, both in "Central Intelligence Reports—Foreign Radio Comments—May–August 1949" folder, box 212, PSF, Truman papers, HSTL; FBIS, "Soviet and Satellite Radio Comment . . . ," May 13, 1949, "Russia" folder 3, box 15, Clifford papers, HSTL; Salisbury, *Moscow Journal,* 27–28; ORE 48-49, May 18, 1949, "Central Intelligence Reports, ORE 46-49" folder, box 216, and CIA 5-49, May 17, 1949, "NSC Meeting 40" folder, box 178, PSF, Truman papers, HSTL; Bohlen memo, May 18, 1949, "Memos 1949" folder, box 5, Bohlen papers, RG 59, USNA; *FR, 1949,* 3:909–13. Kohler's comments are in *FR, 1949,* 3:866–67; Truman's are in Lilienthal, *Journals,* 2:526–27.

64. Loth, *Stalin's Unwanted Child,* 115; Spilker, *East German Leadership,* 184.

65. Acheson, *Sketches,* 7–8; Acheson, *Present,* 295.

66. Acheson, *Sketches,* 7–8, 88–89; Acheson, *Present,* 292–93, 298; Smith, *Acheson,* 99; Bevin quoted in Bullock, *Bevin,* 3:695; U.S. Senate, Committee on Foreign Relations, *Reviews,* 29–30.

67. *FR, 1949,* 3:917–18, 979, 1040–41; Acheson to Webb, May 29, 1949, Delsec 1788, May 24, 1949, Delsec 1793, May 26, 1949, and Delsec 1804, May 27, 1949, all in "Paris Conference . . . May 1949" folder, box 141, PSF, Truman papers, HSTL; Princeton seminar, July 16, 1953, box 79, Acheson papers, HSTL.

68. Princeton seminar, July 16, 1953, box 79, Acheson papers, HSTL; Delsec 1804, May 27, 1949, "Paris Conference . . . May 1949" folder, box 141, PSF, Truman papers, HSTL; memo for the president, June 2, 1949, "Memos for President: Meeting Discussions (1949)" folder, box 186, PSF, Truman papers, HSTL; *FR, 1948,* 2:1245.

69. Jessup quoted in Vanier to Pearson 391, June 7, 1949, vol. 1, file 7-DE-2s, DEA files; U.S. Senate, Committee on Foreign Relations, *Reviews,* 38; Acheson, *Present,* 294.

70. Acheson, *Present,* 297; "Statement on CFM Progress," n.d. [May 31, 1949?], and Delsec 1813, May 28, 1949, both in "Paris Conference . . . May 1949" folder, box 141, PSF, Truman papers, HSTL; *FR, 1949,* 3:1041–43. For background of this proposal, see Tripartite Report, May 20, 1949, box 304, U.S. Delegation Records, RG 43, USNA; and *FR, 1949,* 3:881–84, 892–909.

71. *FR, 1949,* 3:144, 153, 872–74; "Secretary's Off-the-Record Press Conference, May 18, 1949," "Press Conferences, Acheson, January–June 1949" folder, box 68, Acheson papers, HSTL.

72. *FR, 1949,* 3:895; "CFM," "Notes for Meetings" folder, box 78, Acheson papers, HSTL.

73. U.S. Senate, Committee on Foreign Relations, *Reviews,* 16–17.

74. Delsec 1813, May 28, 1949; Delsec 1817, May 30, 1949; and Delsec 1818, May 30, 1949, all in "Paris Conference . . . May 1949" folder, box 141, PSF, Truman papers, HSTL; *FR, 1949,* 3:939, 972–73.

75. USDEL Working Paper/23, June 6, 1949, in "USDEL Working Papers Series, Master Set 1-48" folder, box 309, U.S. Delegation Records, RG 43, USNA; Bohlen to Acheson, June 9, 1949, "Correspondence, A–K" folder, box 1, Bohlen papers, RG 59, USNA; *FR, 1949,* 3:977–79.

76. For background of this proposal, see *FR, 1949,* 3:929, 934–37, 960, 975–76, 1051n2; and Division of Historical Research, Department of State, "Negotiation of the Modus

Vivendi for Germany of June 20, 1949, Research Project No. 160," May 1950, "CFM Paris 1949 Research Project No. 160" folder, U.S. Delegation Records, box 310, RG 43, USNA. For the Western belief in interzonal trade as a negotiating card, see Jessup's comments in Vanier to Pearson 391, June 7, 1949, vol. 1, file 7-DE-2s, DEA files; Harriman's comments in Sulzberger, *Long Row,* 445; and *FR, 1949,* 3:929.

77. *FR, 1949,* 3:980–82, 985–87, 992–93, 1051–53; Actel 65, June 12, 1949, "Paris Conference . . . May 1949" folder, box 141, PSF, Truman papers, HSTL; Acheson, *Present,* 297–300; USDEL/MIN/20, June 13, 1949, "USDEL Staff Meetings 1-23" folder, box 309, U.S. Delegation Records, RG 43, USNA.

78. The airlift continued until September 30, 1949. By May 12 and the lifting of the blockade, 195,998 flights had delivered 1,589,567 tons; deliveries through September totaled 2,325,652 tons in 277,682 flights. Fatalities through September included eighteen Commonwealth military, twenty-one British contractors, thirteen Germans, and thirty-two Americans. Gere, *Unheralded,* 187–224. Regrettably, the airlift memorial dedicated at the National Museum of the U.S. Air Force in 2011 lists only thirty-one Americans, omitting U.S. Army Corporal George S. Burns, killed in a construction accident at Tegel on October 29, 1948.

79. *FR, 1949,* 3:995, 1000, 1007; USDEL/MIN/21, June 15, 1949, "USDEL Staff Meetings 1-23" folder, box 309, U.S. Delegation Records, RG 43, USNA; "Status of CFM—June 16, 1949," n.d., "Paris Conference . . . May 1949" folder, box 141, PSF, Truman papers, HSTL.

80. Actel 67, June 13, 1949, "Paris Conference . . . May 1949" folder, box 141, PSF, Truman papers, HSTL; *FR, 1949,* 3:985–1035; Acheson, *Present,* 300.

81. *FR, 1949,* 3:921–22, 942–50, 1043–48; Princeton seminar, July 15–16, 1953, box 79, Acheson papers, HSTL.

82. Acheson quoted in U.S. Senate, Committee on Foreign Relations, *Reviews,* 22; U.S. Senate, Committee on Foreign Relations, *Documents, 1944–1959,* 60–63; Princeton seminar, July 15–16, 1953, box 79, Acheson papers, HSTL.

83. *FR, 1949,* 3:952–56, 1048–51. The Soviet proposal was not as logical as this summary suggests, because it listed certain functions twice. On the one hand, fuel and finance were shared between the Magistrat and the Kommandatura, thus requiring prior unanimous consent by the occupying powers before the city government could act; on the other hand, public utilities were reserved to the Magistrat, so theoretically, it could act on its own. It is hard to disagree with Acheson's description of the plan as a "lot of shenanigans." Princeton seminar, July 16, 1953, box 79, Acheson papers, HSTL.

84. Delsec 1833, June 1, 1949, "Paris Conference . . . May 1949" folder, box 141, PSF, Truman papers, HSTL; *FR, 1949,* 3:942, 954.

85. Delsec 1843, June 3, 1949, and "Status of the CFM—June 7," both in "Paris Conference . . . May 1949" folder, box 141, PSF, Truman papers, HSTL.

86. "CFM Agenda," May 20, 1949, "Preliminary Conversations" folder, box 305, U.S. Delegation Records, RG 43, USNA.

87. Vandenberg to Acheson, May 12, 1949, and Acheson to Vandenberg, May 18, 1949, 740.00119 Council/5-1249, RG 59, USNA; U.S. Senate, Committee on Foreign Relations, *Reviews,* 18–20; memo, May 12, 1949, "Germany 1949" folder, box 15, PPS Records, RG 59, USNA; memo for the president, May 18, 1949, "Memo for President: Meeting Discussions (1949)" folder, box 186, PSF, Truman papers, HSTL; USDEL/MIN/7, May 30, 1949, "USDEL Staff Meetings 1-23" folder, box 309, RG 43, USNA. For JCS views, see Denfeld to Johnson, May 11, 1949, sec. 1, CCS 092 Germany (5-4-49), box 25, 1948–50 Geographic File, RG 218, USNA. For Acheson's interest in probes, see *FR, 1949,* 3:818.

88. U.S. Department of State, "Research Project 160," box 310, RG 43, USNA; *FR, 1949,* 3:789–92, 796–803; USDEL Working Paper/4, "Minimum Access to Berlin," May 26, 1949, "USDEL Working Papers Series, Master Set 1-48" folder, box 309, U.S. Delegation Records, RG 43, USNA.

89. Riddleberger to Acheson 702, May 12, 1949, 740.00119 Control (Germany)/5-1249, and Riddleberger to Acheson 784, May 22, 1949, 740.00119 Control (Germany)/5-2249, RG 59, USNA; Smith, *Clay Papers,* 2:1158–59, 1167; *FR, 1949,* 3:772–73, 779–87; Charles, *Berlin Blockade,* 139. Also see Hays to Voorhees CC-8676, May 22, 1949, "OAS 580.Germany" folder, box 17, Draper-Voorhees file, RG 335, USNA.

90. *FR, 1949,* 3:751–54, 756, 763–65, 769–72, 776–78, 815–18.

91. Ibid., 840–42. For the strike, see "Railroad Strikes 1949" folder, box 13, Director's files, Berlin Sector Records, RG 260, USNA.

92. Charles, *Berlin Blockade,* 140–41; Bevin quoted in Vanier to Heeney 373, May 28, 1949, file 7-DE-2(s), DEA files; Tusa and Tusa, *Berlin Airlift,* 363; Berlin Weekly Review no. 38, June 3, 1949, file 800-3-1, vol. 835, RG 19, LAC.

93. Princeton seminar, July 15–16, 1953, box 79, Acheson papers, HSTL.

94. Charles, *Berlin Blockade,* 141; *FR, 1949,* 3:844, 1007–8; Acheson, *Present,* 298–99. The strike dragged on until June 26, when the Western commandants imposed a settlement by ordering the Magistrat to stop the strikers' unemployment benefits, which, because they were paid in deutsche marks, meant the strikers were better off than if they had been working. The strikers went back to work June 28. Tusa and Tusa, *Berlin Airlift,* 361–65; Charles, *Berlin Blockade,* 140–44; Steege, *Black Market,* 245–47, 276–84; Berlin Weekly Reviews nos. 39 and 42, June 10 and July 2, 1949, both in file 800-3-1, vol. 835, RG 19, LAC; OMGUS Berlin Sector, *Four Year Report,* 119–20.

95. Smith, *Clay Papers,* 2:1168–69; *FR, 1949,* 3:818–24; JCS 1907/27, May 27, 1949, sec. 5, OPD 381 TS Berlin (15 Jan 48), box 809, TS Decimal File, RG 341, USNA.

96. *FR, 1949,* 3:819–20, 825–27; Acheson to Webb Actel 31, June 2, 1949, 740.00119 Control (Germany)/6-249, RG 59, USNA.

97. Rearden, *Formative Years,* 304–6; *FR, 1949,* 3:828–33.

98. USDEL/MIN/8, May 31, 1949, "USDEL Staff Meetings 1-23" folder, and USDEL Working Paper/25 and 25 Rev 1, "Access to Berlin," June 6 and 7, 1949, "USDEL Working Papers Series Master Set 1-48" folder, both in U.S. Delegation Records, box 309, RG 43, USNA.

99. USDEL/MIN/18, June 10, 1949, and USDEL/MIN/19, June 11, 1949, "USDEL Staff Meetings 1-23" folder, box 309; and U.S. Department of State, "Research Project 160," box 310, both in U.S. Delegation Records, RG 43, USNA.

100. *FR, 1949,* 3:1052–53.

101. Telac 81, June 13, 1949, 740.00119 Council/6-249, RG 59, USNA.

102. *FR, 1949,* 3:995.

103. Ibid., 998, 1053n.

104. Ibid., 999–1000, 1005; "Status of the CFM—June 16, 1949," "Paris Conference . . . May 1949" folder, box 141, PSF, Truman papers, HSTL.

105. USDEL/MIN/21, June 15, 1949, "USDEL Staff Meetings 1-23" folder, box 309, U.S. Delegation Records, RG 43, USNA; *FR, 1949,* 3:996, 1027–28; U.S. Senate, Committee on Foreign Relations, *Reviews,* 32–33. For changes made in the Soviet proposal, cf. *FR, 1949,* 3:1052–53 and 1055–57. For the negotiations in general, see also U.S. Department of State, "Research Project 160," box 310, U.S. Delegation Records, RG 43, USNA.

106. U.S. Senate, Committee on Foreign Relations, *Reviews,* 41; U.S. Department of State Press Release 484, June 23, 1949, "Press Conferences, Acheson, June–December 1949" folder, box 68, Acheson papers, HSTL.

Conclusions

1. As quoted in Acheson, *Present,* xvii.

2. Scholars fond of using this supposedly inexorable law to explain the origins of the Cold War never apply it to postwar Anglo-American relations.

3. Stivers, "Incomplete Blockade."

4. Carolyn Eisenberg's phrasing is typical: "In an effort to break the Russian 'blockade,' the Americans and British launched their historic airlift." Eisenberg, "Commentary: H-Diplo Roundtable on Arnold Offner's *Another Such Victory,*" December 19, 2002, http://h-net.msu.edu/~diplo/roundtables/#offner, accessed March 14, 2006. For similar examples, see Ambrose, "Military Impact," 128; Leffler, *Specter of Communism,* 83; Leffler, *Preponderance,* 217; Offner, *Another Such Victory,* 256; Tusa, *Last Division,* 25; Shlaim, *United States,* 206–10; Trachtenberg, *Constructed Peace,* 83; and Spalding, *First Cold Warrior,* 137–38.

5. Clay, *Decision,* 365.

6. Cf. Eisenberg, *Drawing the Line,* 427n67; Olson, *Symington,* 143–44, 151; and memo for the president, July 23, 1948, "Memo for the President: Meeting Discussions (1948)" folder, box 186, PSF, Truman papers, HSTL. The Truman Library declassified the memo in 1982.

7. Truman, *Mr. Citizen,* 261.

8. Cf. Larson, "Truman," 127–28, and Larson, "Origins of Commitment."

9. Bessel, *Germany 1945.* See also Rogers, *Politics after Hitler,* 139–43.

10. Risse-Kappen, *Cooperation,* 160–61.

11. Daum, "America's Berlin," 49.

12. Cf. Shlaim, *United States,* 266.

13. Smith, "Berlin Blockade through the Filter of History."

14. Buchan, *Crisis Management*; Bell, *Conventions of Crisis*; Williams, *Crisis Management*; Snyder and Diesing, *Conflict among Nations,* 207ff.; George, *Avoiding War.*

Bibliography

Manuscripts

Air Mobility Command History Office, Scott Air Force Base, Illinois
  Kuter-Tunner correspondence
Bentley Historical Library, Ann Arbor, Michigan
  James K. Pollock papers
Department of External Affairs, Historical Division, Ottawa, Canada
Dwight D. Eisenhower Library, Abilene, Kansas
  Dwight D. Eisenhower diaries and prepresidential papers
  Floyd L. Parks papers
Margaret I. King Library, University of Kentucky, Lexington, Kentucky
  Frederick M. Vinson papers
Leininger Library, Georgetown University, Washington, D.C.
  Jean Edward Smith papers
Library and Archives Canada, Ottawa
  William Lyon Mackenzie King papers
  Lester Pearson papers
  Maurice A. Pope papers
  RG 2 Records of the Privy Council Office
  RG 19 Records of the Department of Finance
  RG 25 Records of the Department of External Affairs
Library of Congress Manuscript Division, Washington, D.C.
  William D. Leahy papers
  Curtis E. LeMay papers
  Hoyt S. Vandenberg papers
Seeley G. Mudd Manuscript Library, Princeton University, Princeton, New Jersey
  John Foster Dulles papers
  James V. Forrestal diaries and papers
  George F. Kennan papers
  Arthur Krock papers
National Archives, College Park, Maryland
  RG 43, Records of International Conferences, Commissions and Expositions
    Records of the U.S. delegation to the 1949 Paris CFM (Entries 631–40, 654–55, 658)
    Records Relating to the European Advisory Commission (Records of Philip E. Mosely), 1943–45 (Entry 1048)
    Records of the Allied Control Council, 1945–49 (Entry 1056)
  RG 59, General Records of the Department of State

Central Decimal Files, 1940–44, 1945–49 (Entries 205E and 205H)
Records of the Office of European Affairs
General Records of the Division of Central European Affairs, 1944–53 (Entry 381A)
Intelligence Reports, 1941–61 (Entry 449)
Records of Harley A. Notter: Misc. Subject files, 1939–50 (Entry 496)
Records of the Office of the Assistant Secretary of State for Occupied Areas, 1946–49 (Entries 505D/E)
Charles E. Bohlen papers, 1942–71 (Entry 1560)
Records of the Policy Planning Staff, 1947–53 (Entry 1568)
Records of the Berlin Task Force, 1944–88 (Entry 5553)
RG 84, Records of Foreign Service Posts
Records of the U.S. Mission, Berlin
Records of the Public Health Committee, 1945–1952 (Entry 2527P)
Records of the Office of the Political Adviser to OMGUS
Top Secret Correspondence, 1945–1949 (Entry 2530)
Classified General Correspondence, 1945–49 (Entry 2531B)
Miscellaneous Classified Records, 1945–1948 (Entry 2532)
Top Secret Cables to the Secretary of State, 1945–1949 (Entry 2534)
Records of the U.S. Embassy, Moscow
Top Secret General Records, 1941–48 (Entry 3314)
Telegrams Maintained by Ambassador W. Averell Harriman, 1944–45 (Entry 3316)
RG 165, Records of the War Department General and Special Staffs
Records of the Civil Affairs Division, 1943–49
Security Classified General Correspondence, 1943–49 (Entry 463)
RG 200, National Archives Gift Collection/Donated Materials
Papers of General Lucius D. Clay, 1945–49 (Entry 3550)
RG 218, Records of the U.S. Joint Chiefs of Staff
Central Decimal File, 1942–45 (Entry 1)
Central Decimal File, 1948–1950 (Entry 5)
Geographic File, 1948–1950 (Entry 7)
Chairman's File, Admiral Leahy, 1942–48 (Entry 47)
RG 260, Records of U.S. Occupation Headquarters, World War II
Records of the Office of Military Government, United States
Secretary General Staff, Message Control Center, Incoming Messages, 1948–51 (Entry 10)
Records Received and Used by the U.S. Group Control Council: Policy Records Retained by the Military Adviser to the U.S. Delegate, EAC, 1943–45 (Wickersham-Meyer files; "Subject File") (Entry 11)
Executive Office, Chief of Staff, Records Regarding Investigations, Political, Emergency and Other Activities, and Occupation Policies and Requirements, 1947–49 (Entry 20)
Executive Office, Chief of Staff, Correspondence and Other Records of Brigadier General Charles K. Gailey, 1944–48 (Entry 21)
Executive Office, Chief of Staff, Records Retained for the Military Governor, 1945–49 (Entry 22)
Executive Office, Office of the Adjutant General, General Correspondence and Other Records, 1945–49 (Entry 25)

Executive Office, Office of the Adjutant General, Formerly Security-Classified General Correspondence and Other Records, 1945–49 (Entry 26)
Executive Office, Office of the Adjutant General, Formerly Security-Classified Incoming Cables and Other Records, 1946–49 (Entry 40)
Executive Office, Office of the Adjutant General, Security-Classified Outgoing Cables and Other Records, 1946–48 (Entry 41)
OMGUS Minutes
Retained Copies of Records Provided by Other Organizations Retained by AGO: Formerly Security-Classified Intelligence Reports and Other Records, 1945–49 (Entry 61)
Records of the Berlin Sector, 1945–49
General Records of the Director's Office, 1945–1949 (Entry 1152)
General Records of the Civil Administration and Political Affairs Branch, 1945–49 (Entry 1165)
Records Created by the Allied Kommandatura, 1945–1949 (Entry 1169)
Records of the Public Health Branch, 1945–49
Monthly Narrative Reports, 1947–49 (Entry 1192)
Statistical Reports Concerning Causes of Death, 1945–49 (Entry 1193)
Reports Relating to Nutrition, 1946–49 (Entry 1197)
Records of the Economic Branch
Records of the Building and Housing Section, 1946–48 (Entry 1273)
Records of the Public Safety Branch
Political Reports, 1947–48 (Entry 1331)
Records of U.S. Elements of Inter-Allied Organizations
General Records of U.S. Element, Allied Control Authority, 1945–49 (Entry 1790)
General Records of the Air Directorate, 1945–46 (Entry 1825)
RG 263, Records of the Central Intelligence Agency
William Harris, "March Crisis 1948, Act I," *Studies in Intelligence* (Fall 1966)
William Harris, "March Crisis 1948, Act II," *Studies in Intelligence* (Spring 1967)
RG 319, Records of the Army Staff
Records of the Plans and Operations Division
Special Correspondence Maintained by the Top Secret Control Office: General Administrative Files, 1948–52 ("Hot Files") (Entry 101)
P&O Secret General Correspondence 1946–50 (Entry 153)
P&O TS General Correspondence, 1946–50 (Entry 154)
RG 330, Records of the Office of the Secretary of Defense
OSD Numerical File, 1947–50 (Entry 199)
RG 331, Records of Allied Operational and Occupation Headquarters
Records of Supreme Headquarters Allied Expeditionary Force
SGS Decimal File, 1943–45 (Entry 1)
G-3 Subject File, 1942–45 (Entry 23)
G-3 Operational Plans, 1943–45 (Entry 23A)
G-3 TS Incoming and Outgoing Messages, 1944–46 (Entry 24A)
G-3 Post Hostilities Planning Section Decimal File, 1943–45 (Entry 27)
G-5 Numeric File, 1943–45 (Entry 47)
RG 335, Records of the Office of the Secretary of the Army
General Correspondence, Security Classified, Office of the Secretary of the Army, 1947–50 (Entry 3B)

Under Secretary of the Army (Draper/Voorhees) Project Decimal File, 1947–50 (Entry 24)
RG 341, Records of Headquarters, United States Air Force
Plans (Top Secret) Project Decimal File, 1942–54 (Entry 335)
Plans Central Decimal File, 1942–54 (Entry 336)
Administrative Office, Deputy Chief of Staff for Operations, 1947–54 (Entry 345)
RG 407, Records of the Office of the Adjutant General
Records of the Administrative Services Division, Operations Branch
Foreign (Occupied) Area Reports, 1945–54, Special, Germany (U.S. Zone) (Entry 368B)
RG 466, Records of the Office of the U.S. High Commissioner for Germany
Miscellaneous Files Relating Primarily to Berlin (Entry 16B)
RG 549, Records of U.S. Army Europe, 1933–1964
Records of European Command, 1942–1952
Secretary General Staff, Classified General Correspondence, 1946–51 (Entry 6)
Secretary General Staff, Message Control Center, Incoming Messages, 1948–51 (Entry 10)
Intelligence Division, Periodic Intelligence Summaries, 1947–49 (Entry 49)
Adjutant General Division, Berlin Airlift Food and Materiel Position Charts, 1948–49 (Entry 195)
Historian's Background Files, 1945–52 (Entry 327)
National Archives, Kew, U.K.
AIR 10 Air Publications and Reports, 1913–79
AIR 20 Papers Accumulated by the Air Historical Branch, 1874–1983
AIR 38 Transport Command, 1940–1978
AIR 55 British Air Forces of Occupation, 1941–57
CAB 21 Cabinet Office Registered Files, 1916–65
CAB 65 War Cabinet Minutes, 1939–45
CAB 66 War Cabinet memoranda, 1939–45
CAB 81 Post-Hostilities Planning Sub-Committee, 1939–47
CAB 87 War Cabinet Committees ("Attlee Committee" papers and minutes), 1941–46
CAB 122 British Joint Staff Mission, 1940–58
CAB 128 Cabinet Minutes, 1945–78
CAB 129 Cabinet Memoranda, 1945–78
CAB 130 GEN/241 ("Berlin") Committee, 1948–49
CAB 131 Defence Committee, minutes and papers, 1946–1963
DEFE 4 Chiefs of Staff Committee minutes, 1947–79
DEFE 5 Chiefs of Staff Committee memoranda, 1947–77
DEFE 6 Joint Planning Staff Memoranda, 1947–68
DEFE 11 Chiefs of Staff Committee Registered Files, 1946–93
FO 371 Foreign Office General Correspondence (Political), 1906–66
FO 800 Foreign Office Ministers' and Officials' Papers
FO 943 Economic and Industrial Planning Staff and Control Office for Germany and Austria and Successor: Economic Records, 1943–55
FO 944 Foreign Office, German Section and Predecessors, Finance Department Records, 1943–56
FO 1005 Control Commission for Germany (British Element), Records Library Files, 1943–59

FO 1012 Control Commission for Germany (British Element), British Sector, Berlin, 1944–52
FO 1030 Control Commission for Germany (British Element), Military Governor's Private Office, 1944–51
FO 1032 Control Commission for Germany (British Element), Military Sections and HQ Secretariat, Registered Files, 1942–52
FO 1049 Control Commission for Germany (British Element), Political Division, 1943–51
FO 1051 Control Commission for Germany (British Element), Manpower Division, 1944–53
FO 1058 Control Commission for Germany (British Element), Transport Division, 1944–50
FO 1112 Kommandatura, 1945–90
MH 79 Ministry of Health: Confidential Registered Files, 1913–67
PREM 3 Prime Minister's Private Office: Operational Correspondence and Papers, 1937–46
WO 193 War Office Director of Military Operations and Plans, Files re Planning, Intelligence, and Statistics, 1934–58

Rush Rees Library, University of Rochester, Rochester, New York
Thomas E. Dewey papers

Franklin D. Roosevelt Library, Hyde Park, New York
Charles Fahy papers
Harry L. Hopkins papers (Sherwood Collection)
Map Room Files
Anna Eleanor Roosevelt papers

Sterling Memorial Library, Yale University, New Haven, Connecticut
Walter Lippmann papers
Henry L. Stimson diaries (microfilm edition)

Harry S. Truman Library, Independence, Missouri
Dean G. Acheson papers
Eben A. Ayers papers
Clark M. Clifford files and papers
Matthew G. Connelly papers
George M. Elsey files and papers
A. Robert Ginsburgh papers
Frank McNaughton papers
Naval Aide files
J. Anthony Panuch papers
Charles G. Ross papers
Harry S. Truman papers

U.S. Air Force Academy Library, Colorado Springs, Colorado
Laurence S. Kuter papers

U.S. Air Force Historical Research Agency, Maxwell Air Force Base, Alabama

U.S. Air Forces in Europe History Office, Ramstein Air Base, Germany

U.S. Army in Europe Military History Office, Heidelberg, Germany

U.S. Army Military History Institute, Carlisle Barracks, Carlisle, Pennsylvania
Frank L. Howley papers
John J. Maginnis papers

John W. O'Daniel papers
Floyd L. Parks diaries and papers
Arthur G. Trudeau papers
U.S. Navy Historical Center (Operational Archives), Washington, D.C.
SecNav Series, Post-1946 Command File, Press Releases
Western Historical Manuscript Division, University of Missouri, Columbia, Missouri
Booton Herndon papers

Oral History Interviews

Air Force Historical Research Agency, Maxwell Air Force Base, Alabama
Howell Estes, K239.0512-686
Walter T. Galligan, K239.0512-1555
Leon Johnson, K239.0512-609 and K239.0512-1441
Curtis E. LeMay, K239.0512-736
Joseph Smith, K239.0512-906
William H. Tunner, K239.0512-911
Air Mobility Command History Office, Scott Air Force Base, Illinois
Gail Halvorsen
Columbia University Oral History Project, Columbia University, New York, New York
Lucius D. Clay
Philip C. Jessup
Theodore R. Milton
Harry S. Truman Library, Independence, Missouri
Eben A. Ayers
Robert L. Dennison
William H. Draper Jr.
George M. Elsey
James Riddleberger
Charles E. Saltzman
U.S. Army Military History Institute, Carlisle Barracks, Carlisle, Pennsylvania
Lucius D. Clay
Arthur G. Trudeau

Published Documents and Books

Acheson, Dean G. *Present at the Creation: My Years in the State Department.* New York: Norton, 1969.

———. *Sketches from Life of Men I Have Known.* New York: Harper, 1961.

Adomeit, Hannes. *Soviet Risk-Taking and Crisis Behavior.* Winchester, Mass.: Allen and Unwin, 1982.

Ambrose, Stephen E. *Eisenhower and Berlin: The Decision to Halt at the Elbe.* New York: Norton, 1967.

Andreas-Friedrich, Ruth. *Battleground Berlin: Diaries, 1945–1948.* Translated by Anna Boerresen. New York: Paragon House, 1990.

Annan, Noel. *Changing Enemies: The Defeat and Regeneration of Germany.* New York: HarperCollins, 1996.

Arnold-Forster, Mark. *The Siege of Berlin.* London: Collins, 1979.
Backer, John H. *The Decision to Divide Germany: American Foreign Policy in Transition.* Durham, N.C.: Duke University Press, 1978.
———. *Winds of History: The German Years of Lucius Dubignon Clay.* New York: Van Nostrand Reinhold, 1983.
Balfour, Michael, and John Mair. *Four-Power Control in Germany and Austria, 1945–1946.* London: Oxford University Press, 1956.
Barker, Dudley. *Berlin Air Lift: An Account of the British Contribution.* London: His Majesty's Stationery Office, 1949.
Barker, Elisabeth. *Britain between the Superpowers, 1945–1950.* London: Macmillan, 1983.
Barlow, Jeffrey G. *Revolt of the Admirals: The Fight for Naval Aviation, 1945–1950.* Washington, D.C.: Naval Historical Center, 1994.
Barros, James. *Trygve Lie and the Cold War: The UN Secretary-General Pursues Peace, 1946–1953.* De Kalb: Northern Illinois University Press, 1989.
Beck, Earl R. *Under the Bombs: The German Home Front, 1942–1945.* Lexington: University Press of Kentucky, 1986.
Bell, Coral. *The Conventions of Crisis: A Study in Diplomatic Management.* London: Oxford University Press, 1971.
Bennett, Lowell. *Berlin Bastion.* Frankfurt: Fred Rudl, 1951.
Berezhkov, Valentin M. *At Stalin's Side: His Interpreter's Memoirs from the October Revolution to the Fall of the Dictator's Empire.* Translated by Sergei V. Mikheyev. New York: Birch Lane Press, 1994.
Berlin Magistrat. *Airlift Berlin.* Berlin: Arani, 1949.
Bessel, Richard. *Germany 1945.* New York: HarperCollins, 2009.
Betts, Richard K. *Nuclear Blackmail and Nuclear Balance.* Washington, D.C.: Brookings, 1987.
Biess, Frank. *Homecomings: Returning POWs and the Legacies of Defeat in Postwar Germany.* Princeton, N.J.: Princeton University Press, 2006.
Blum, John Morton, ed. *The Price of Vision: The Diaries of Henry A. Wallace, 1942–1946.* Boston: Houghton Mifflin, 1973.
Bohlen, Charles E. *Witness to History, 1929–1969.* New York: Norton, 1973.
Borowski, Harry R. *A Hollow Threat: Strategic Air Power and Containment before Korea.* Westport, Conn.: Greenwood Press, 1982.
Bothwell, Robert, Ian Drummond, and John English. *Canada since 1945: Power, Politics, and Provincialism.* Toronto: University of Toronto Press, 1981.
Bradley, Omar N., and Clay Blair. *A General's Life.* New York: Simon and Schuster, 1983.
Brett-Smith, Richard. *Berlin '45.* London: Macmillan, 1966.
Browder, Robert Paul, and Thomas G. Smith. *Independent: A Biography of Lewis W. Douglas.* New York: Knopf, 1986.
Bruce, Gary. *Resistance with the People: Repression and Resistance in Eastern Germany 1945–1955.* Lanham, Md.: Rowman and Littlefield, 2003.
Buchan, Alastair. *Crisis Management: The New Diplomacy.* Boulogne-sur-Seine: Atlantic Institute, 1966.
Buffet, Cyril. *Mourir pour Berlin: La France et l'Allemagne, 1945–1949.* Paris: Armand Colin, 1991.
Bullock, Alan. *The Life and Times of Ernest Bevin.* 3 vols. London: Heinemann, 1960–1983.
Butcher, Harry C. *My Three Years with Eisenhower.* New York: Simon and Schuster, 1946.
Butler, Rohan, and M. E. Pelly, eds. *Documents on British Policy Overseas.* Ser. 1, vol. 1, *The*

Conference at Potsdam, July–August 1945. London: Her Majesty's Stationery Office, 1984.
Cairncross, Alec. *The Price of War: British Policy on German Reparations, 1941–1949.* Oxford: Basil Blackwell, 1985.
Carlyle, Margaret, ed. *Documents on International Affairs, 1947–1948.* London: Oxford University Press, 1952.
———. *Documents on International Affairs, 1949–1950.* London: Oxford University Press, 1953.
Carr, Albert Z. *Truman, Stalin, and Peace.* Garden City, N.Y.: Doubleday, 1950.
Cecil, Robert. *A Divided Life: A Personal Portrait of the Spy Donald Maclean.* New York: Morrow, 1989.
Charles, Max. *Berlin Blockade.* London: Allan Wingate, 1959.
Churchill, Randolph S., and Martin Gilbert. *Winston S. Churchill.* 8 vols. London: Heinemann, 1966–1988.
Churchill, Winston S. *The Second World War.* 6 vols. Boston: Houghton Mifflin, 1948–1953.
Clare, George. *Before the Wall: Berlin Days, 1946–1948.* New York: Dutton, 1990.
Clay, Lucius D. *Decision in Germany.* Garden City, N.Y.: Doubleday, 1950.
Clements, Kendrick A., ed. *James F. Byrnes and the Origins of the Cold War.* Durham, N.C.: Carolina Academic Press, 1982.
Cline, Ray S. *Washington Command Post.* Washington, D.C.: Government Printing Office, 1951.
Coles, Harry L., and Albert K. Weinberg. *Civil Affairs: Soldiers Become Governors.* Washington, D.C.: Government Printing Office, 1964.
Collier, Richard. *Bridge across the Sky: The Berlin Blockade and Airlift, 1948–1949.* New York: McGraw-Hill, 1978.
Condit, Doris. *History of the Office of the Secretary of Defense.* Vol. 2, *The Test of War, 1950–1953.* Washington, D.C.: Historical Office, Office of the Secretary of Defense, 1988.
Condit, Kenneth. *History of the Joint Chiefs of Staff.* Vol. 2, *1947–1949.* Wilmington, Del.: Glazier, 1979.
Connally, Tom. *My Name Is Tom Connally.* New York: Crowell, 1954.
Conquest, Robert. *The Great Terror: Stalin's Purge of the Thirties.* New York: Macmillan, 1968.
Conrad, Joseph. *Nostromo.* New York: Bantam, 1989.
Cordier, Andrew, and Wilder Foote, eds. *Public Papers of the Secretaries-General of the United Nations.* Vol. 1, *Trygve Lie, 1946–1953.* New York: Columbia University Press, 1969.
Culver, John C., and John Hyde. *American Dreamer: The Life and Times of Henry A. Wallace.* New York: Norton, 2000.
Curry, George. *James F. Byrnes.* New York: Cooper Square, 1965.
Daniels, Jonathan. *Man of Independence.* New York: Lippincott, 1950.
Davidson, Eugene. *The Death and Life of Germany: An Account of the American Occupation.* New York: Knopf, 1959.
Davison, W. Phillips. *The Berlin Blockade: A Study in Cold War Politics.* Princeton, N.J.: Princeton University Press, 1958.
Deighton, Anne. *The Impossible Peace: Britain, the Division of Germany and the Origins of the Cold War.* Oxford: Oxford University Press, 1990.
Diefendorf, Jeffry. *In the Wake of War: The Reconstruction of German Cities after World War II.* New York: Oxford University Press, 1993.
Diehl, James M. *The Thanks of the Fatherland: German Veterans after the Second World War.* Chapel Hill: University of North Carolina Press, 1993.

Dilks, David, ed. *The Diaries of Sir Alexander Cadogan, 1938–1945.* New York: Putnam, 1972.

Divine, Robert A. *Foreign Policy and U.S. Presidential Elections, 1940–1948.* New York: New Viewpoints, 1974.

Djilas, Milovan. *Conversations with Stalin.* Translated by Michael B. Petrovich. New York: Harcourt, Brace and World , 1962.

Donovan, Frank. *Bridge in the Sky.* New York: David McKay, 1968.

Donovan, Robert J. *Conflict and Crisis: The Presidency of Harry S Truman, 1945–1948.* New York: Norton, 1977.

Eayrs, James. *In Defence of Canada.* 5 vols. Toronto: University of Toronto Press, 1964–1984.

Eisenberg, Carolyn Woods. *Drawing the Line: The American Decision to Divide Germany, 1944–1949.* Cambridge: Cambridge University Press, 1996.

Eisenhower, Dwight D. *Crusade in Europe.* Garden City, N.Y.: Doubleday, 1948.

Elkins, T. H., with B. Hofmeister. *Berlin: The Spatial Structure of a Divided City.* London: Methuen, 1988.

Farquharson, John E. *The Western Allies and the Politics of Food: Agrarian Management in Postwar Germany.* Leamington Spa, U.K.: Berg, 1985.

Ferrell, Robert H. *George C. Marshall.* New York: Cooper Square, 1966.

———, ed. *Dear Bess: The Letters from Harry to Bess Truman, 1910–1959.* New York: Norton, 1983.

Folly, Martin H. *Churchill, Whitehall and the Soviet Union, 1940–1945.* Houndmills, U.K.: Palgrave, 2000.

Gablentz, O. M. von der, ed. *Documents on the Status of Berlin, 1944–1959.* Munich: R. Oldenbourg, 1959.

Gaddis, John Lewis. *George F. Kennan: An American Life.* New York: Penguin, 2011.

———. *Strategies of Containment: A Critical Appraisal of Postwar American National Security Policy.* New York: Oxford University Press, 1982.

———. *The United States and the Origins of the Cold War, 1941–1947.* New York: Columbia University Press, 1972.

Garvy, George. *Money, Banking, and Credit in Eastern Europe.* New York: Federal Reserve Bank of New York, 1966.

Gelb, Leslie K., and Richard K. Betts. *The Irony of Vietnam: The System Worked.* Washington, D.C.: Brookings, 1979.

George, Alexander L., ed. *Avoiding War: Problems of Crisis Management.* Boulder, Colo.: Westview Press, 1991.

George, Alexander L., and Richard Smoke. *Deterrence in American Foreign Policy.* New York: Columbia University Press, 1974.

Gere, Edwin. *The Unheralded: Men and Women of the Berlin Blockade and Airlift.* Victoria, B.C.: Trafford, 2002.

Gimbel, John. *The American Occupation of Germany: Politics and the Military, 1945–1949.* Stanford, Calif.: Stanford University Press, 1968.

———. *A German Community under American Occupation: Marburg, 1945–1952.* Stanford, Calif.: Stanford University Press, 1961.

———. *The Origins of the Marshall Plan.* Stanford, Calif.: Stanford University Press, 1976.

Gladwyn, Lord. *Memoirs.* London: Weidenfeld and Nicolson, 1972.

Glantz, David M. *Colossus Reborn: The Red Army at War, 1941–1943.* Lawrence: University Press of Kansas, 2005.

Gottlieb, Manuel. *The German Peace Settlement and the Berlin Crisis.* New York: Paine-Whitman, 1960.

Granatstein, J. L. *A Man of Influence: Norman A. Robertson and Canadian Statecraft, 1929–1968*. Ottawa: Deneau, 1981.

Great Britain, Foreign Office. *Germany (1948): Report of the Court of Inquiry into the Circumstances of the Collision between a Viking Airliner and a Soviet Service Aircraft on 5th April 1948, Berlin, 14th–16th April 1948. Command Paper 7384*. London: His Majesty's Stationery Office, 1948.

———. *Germany No. 2: An Account of Events Leading up to a Reference of the Berlin Question to the United Nations. Command Paper 7534*. London: His Majesty's Stationery Office, 1948.

———. *Germany No. 2 (1961): Selected Documents on Germany and the Question of Berlin, 1944–1961. Command Paper 1552*. London: Her Majesty's Stationery Office, 1961.

Great Britain, Parliament. *Parliamentary Debates*. House of Commons, 5th ser., 1948–1949.

Grieder, Peter. *The East German Leadership, 1946–1973: Conflict and Crisis*. Manchester, U.K.: Manchester University Press, 1999.

Gross, Inge E. Stanneck. *Memories of World War II and Its Aftermath, 1940–1954*. Eastsound, Wash.: Island in the Sky Publishing, 2005.

Hamilton, Nigel. *Master of the Battlefield: Monty's War Years, 1942–1944*. New York: McGraw-Hill, 1983.

Harbutt, Fraser J. *The Iron Curtain: Churchill, America, and the Origins of the Cold War*. New York: Oxford University Press, 1986.

———. *Yalta 1945: Europe and America at the Crossroads*. Cambridge: Cambridge University Press, 2010.

Haynes, Richard F. *The Awesome Power: Harry S. Truman as Commander in Chief*. Baton Rouge: Louisiana State University Press, 1973.

Hechler, Ken. *Working with Truman: A Personal Memoir of the White House Years*. New York: Putnam, 1982.

Heineman, Elizabeth. *What Difference Does a Husband Make? Women and Marital Status in Nazi and Postwar Germany*. Berkeley and Los Angeles: University of California Press, 1999.

Hendry, I. D., and M. C. Wood. *The Legal Status of Berlin*. Cambridge: Grotius Publications, 1987.

Herken, Gregg. *The Winning Weapon: The Atomic Bomb in the Cold War, 1945–1950*. New York: Knopf, 1980.

Hillman, William, ed. *Mr. President*. New York: Farrar, Straus and Young, 1952.

Hitchcock, William I. *France Restored: Cold War Diplomacy and the Quest for Leadership in Europe, 1944–1954*. Chapel Hill: University of North Carolina Press, 1998.

Holloway, David. *Stalin and the Bomb: The Soviet Union and Atomic Energy, 1939–1956*. New Haven, Conn.: Yale University Press, 1994.

Holmes, John W. *The Better Part of Valour: Essays on Canadian Diplomacy*. Toronto: McClelland and Stewart, 1970.

———. *The Shaping of Peace*. 2 vols. Toronto: University of Toronto Press, 1979–1982.

Howley, Frank L. *Berlin Command*. New York: Putnam, 1950.

Huschke, Wolfgang J. *The Candy Bombers: The Berlin Airlift, 1948/49, a History of the People and Planes*. Berlin: Metropol, 1999.

Jackson, Robert. *The Berlin Airlift*. Wellingborough, U.K.: Patrick Stephens, 1988.

Jervis, Robert. *The Logic of Images in International Relations*. Princeton, N.J.: Princeton University Press, 1970.

———. *Perception and Misperception in International Politics*. Princeton, N.J.: Princeton University Press, 1976.

Jones, Matthew. *Britain, the United States, and the Mediterranean War, 1942–1944.* New York: St. Martin's Press, 1996.

Kaplan, Karel. *The Short March: The Communist Takeover in Czechoslovakia, 1945–1948.* New York: St. Martin's Press, 1987.

Kennan, George F. *Memoirs, 1925–1950.* Boston: Houghton Mifflin, 1967.

Kimball, Warren F. *The Juggler: Franklin Roosevelt as Wartime Statesman.* Princeton, N.J.: Princeton University Press, 1991.

Klimov, Gregory. *The Terror Machine: The Inside Story of the Soviet Administration in Germany.* Translated by H. C. Stevens. New York: Praeger, 1953.

Kofsky, Fred. *Harry S. Truman and the War Scare of 1948: A Successful Campaign to Deceive the Nation.* New York: St. Martin's Press, 1995.

Kolko, Gabriel. *The Politics of War: The World and United States Foreign Policy, 1943–1945.* New York: Random House, 1968.

Kolko, Gabriel, and Joyce Kolko. *The Limits of Power: The World and United States Foreign Policy, 1945–1954.* New York: Harper and Row, 1972.

Kuklick, Bruce. *American Policy and the Division of Germany: The Clash with Russia over Reparations.* Ithaca, N.Y.: Cornell University Press, 1972.

Ladd, Brian. *The Ghosts of Berlin: Confronting German History in the Urban Landscape.* Chicago: University of Chicago Press, 1997.

Laqueur, Walter. *Europe since Hitler.* Baltimore: Penguin, 1972.

Large, David Clay. *Berlin.* New York: Basic Books, 2000.

Lash, Joseph. *Eleanor Roosevelt: The Years Alone.* New York: Norton, 1972.

Laufer, Jochen P., and Georgij Kynin, eds. *Die UdSSR und die deutsche Frage, 1941–1948: Dokumente aus dem Archiv für Außenpolitik der Russischen Föderation.* 3 vols. Berlin: Dunker and Humblot, 2004.

Launius, Roger D., and Coy F. Cross II. *MAC and the Legacy of the Berlin Airlift.* Scott Air Force Base, Ill.: Military Airlift Command, 1989.

Lebow, Richard Ned. *Nuclear Crisis Management: A Dangerous Illusion.* Ithaca, N.Y.: Cornell University Press, 1987.

Leffler, Melvyn P. *A Preponderance of Power: National Security, the Truman Administration, and the Cold War.* Stanford, Calif.: Stanford University Press, 1992.

———. *The Specter of Communism: The United States and the Origins of the Cold War, 1917–1953.* New York: Hill and Wang, 1994.

LeMay, Curtis E., with Mackinlay Kantor. *Mission with LeMay.* Garden City, N.Y.: Doubleday, 1965.

Leonhard, Wolfgang. *Child of the Revolution.* Translated by C. M. Woodhouse. Chicago: Henry Regnery, 1958.

Lewis, Julian. *Changing Direction: British Military Planning for Post-War Strategic Defence, 1942–1947.* London: Sherwood Press, 1988.

Lie, Trygve. *In the Cause of Peace: Seven Years with the United Nations.* New York: Macmillan, 1954.

Lilienthal, David E. *Journals.* 6 vols. New York: Harper and Row, 1964–1976.

Loth, Wilfried. *Stalin's Unwanted Child: The Soviet Union, the German Question and the Founding of the GDR.* Translated by Robert F. Hogg. New York: St. Martin's Press, 1998.

Maginnis, John J. *Military Government Journal: Normandy to Berlin.* Amherst: University of Massachusetts Press, 1971.

Matloff, Maurice. *Strategic Planning for Coalition Warfare, 1943–1944.* Washington, D.C.: Government Printing Office, 1959.
Mayers, David. *George Kennan and the Dilemmas of U.S. Foreign Policy.* New York: Oxford University Press, 1988.
Mazower, Mark. *Inside Hitler's Greece.* New Haven, Conn.: Yale University Press, 1993.
Mazuzan, George. *Warren R. Austin at the United Nations.* Kent, Ohio: Kent State University Press, 1977.
McAllister, James. *No Exit: America and the German Problem, 1943–1954.* Ithaca, N.Y.: Cornell University Press, 2001.
McCullough, David, ed. *Affection and Trust: The Personal Correspondence of Harry S. Truman and Dean Acheson, 1953–1971.* New York: Knopf, 2010.
Merritt, Richard L. *Democracy Imposed: U.S. Occupation Policy and the German Public, 1945–1949.* New Haven, Conn.: Yale University Press, 1995.
Miller, Roger G. *To Save a City: The Berlin Airlift, 1948–1949.* College Station: Texas A&M University Press, 2000.
Millis, Walter, and E. S. Duffield, eds. *The Forrestal Diaries.* New York: Viking, 1951.
Miner, Steven Merritt. *Between Churchill and Stalin: The Soviet Union, Great Britain, and the Origins of the Grand Alliance.* Chapel Hill: University of North Carolina Press, 1988.
Miscamble, Wilson D. *George F. Kennan and the Making of American Foreign Policy.* Princeton, N.J.: Princeton University Press, 1992.
Moeller, Robert G. *Protecting Motherhood: Women and the Family in the Politics of Postwar West Germany.* Berkeley and Los Angeles: University of California Press, 1993.
Molotov, V. M. *Problems of Foreign Policy.* Moscow: Foreign Languages Publishing House, 1949.
Moody, Walton S. *Building a Strategic Air Force.* Washington, D.C.: Air Force History and Museums Program, 1996.
Moorhouse, Roger. *Berlin at War.* New York: Basic Books, 2010.
Morgan, Sir Frederick. *Overture to Overlord.* Garden City, N.Y.: Doubleday, 1950.
Morris, Eric. *Blockade: Berlin and the Cold War.* New York: Stein and Day, 1973.
Mosely, Philip E. *The Kremlin in World Politics.* New York: Vintage, 1960.
Murphy, David E., Sergei A. Kondrashev, and George Bailey. *Battleground Berlin: CIA vs. KGB in the Cold War.* New Haven, Conn.: Yale University Press, 1997.
Murphy, Robert D. *Diplomat among Warriors.* Garden City, N.Y.: Doubleday, 1964.
Naimark, Norman M. *The Russians in Germany: A History of the Soviet Zone of Occupation, 1945–1949.* Cambridge, Mass.: Harvard University Press, 1995.
Nelson, Daniel J. *Wartime Origins of the Berlin Dilemma.* University: University of Alabama Press, 1978.
Nettl, J. P. *The Eastern Zone and Soviet Policy in Germany, 1945–1950.* New York: Oxford University Press, 1951.
Neustadt, Richard E. *Presidential Power: The Politics of Leadership, with Reflections on Johnson and Nixon.* New York: Wiley, 1976.
Nichols, K. D. *The Road to Trinity.* New York: Morrow, 1987.
Nicolson, Nigel, ed. *The Diaries and Letters of Harold Nicolson.* 3 vols. New York: Atheneum, 1966–1968.
Offner, Arnold A. *Another Such Victory: President Truman and the Cold War, 1945–1953.* Stanford, Calif.: Stanford University Press, 2002.
Olson, James C. *Stuart Symington: A Life.* Columbia: University of Missouri Press, 2003.

Onderwater, Hans. *Operation Manna/Chowhound.* Weesp, Netherlands: Romen Luchtvaart, 1985.

Ousby, Ian. *Occupation.* London: Pimlico, 1999.

Overy, Richard. *Russia's War.* New York: Penguin, 1998.

Paterson, Thomas G. *Soviet-American Confrontation: Post-War Reconstruction and the Origins of the Cold War.* Baltimore: Johns Hopkins University Press, 1973.

Pearcy, Arthur. *Berlin Airlift.* Shrewsbury, U.K.: Airlift Publishing, 1997.

Pelly, M. E., and H. J. Yasamee, eds. *Documents on British Policy Overseas.* Ser. 1, vol. 5, *Germany and Western Europe, 11 August–31 December 1945.* London: Her Majesty's Stationery Office, 1990.

Peterson, Edward N. *The American Occupation of Germany: Retreat to Victory.* Detroit: Wayne State University Press, 1977.

Petrov, Vladimir. *Money and Conquest: Allied Occupation Currencies in World War II.* Baltimore: Johns Hopkins University Press, 1967.

Pickersgill, J. W., and D. F. Forster, eds. *The Mackenzie King Record.* 4 vols. Toronto: University of Toronto Press, 1960–1970.

Playfair, I. S. O., et al. *The Mediterranean and the Middle East.* 6 vols. London: Her Majesty's Stationery Office, 1954–1988.

Plischke, Elmer. *Berlin: Development of Its Government and Administration.* Westport, Conn.: Praeger, 1970.

Pogue, Forrest C. *George C. Marshall.* 4 vols. New York: Viking, 1963–1987.

Pope, Maurice A. *Soldiers and Politicians: The Memoirs of Lt. Gen. Maurice A. Pope, C.B., M.C.* Toronto: University of Toronto Press, 1962.

Pruessen, Ronald W. *John Foster Dulles: The Road to Power.* New York: Free Press, 1982.

Ratchford, B. U., and William D. Ross. *Berlin Reparations Assignment: Round One of the German Peace Settlement.* Chapel Hill: University of North Carolina Press, 1947.

Rearden, Steven L. *History of the Office of the Secretary of Defense.* Vol. 1, *The Formative Years, 1947–1950.* Washington, D.C.: Historical Office, Office of the Secretary of Defense, 1984.

Redding, Kimberly A. *Growing Up in Hitler's Shadow.* Westport, Conn.: Praeger, 2004.

Reeves, Richard. *Daring Young Men: The Heroism and Triumph of the Berlin Airlift, June 1948–May 1949.* New York: Simon and Schuster, 2010.

Reid, Escott. *Time of Fear and Hope: The Making of the North Atlantic Treaty, 1947–1949.* Toronto: McClelland and Stewart, 1977.

Reynolds, David. *From World War to Cold War: Churchill, Roosevelt, and the International History of the 1940s.* Oxford: Oxford University Press, 2006.

Richie, Alexandra. *Faust's Metropolis: A History of Berlin.* New York: Carroll and Graf, 1998.

Riess, Curt. *The Berlin Story.* New York: Dial Press, 1952.

Risse-Kappen, Thomas. *Cooperation among Democracies: The European Influence on U.S. Foreign Policy.* Princeton, N.J.: Princeton University Press, 1995.

Roberts, Geoffrey. *Stalin's Wars: From World War to Cold War, 1939–1953.* New Haven, Conn.: Yale University Press, 2007.

Rogers, Daniel E. *Politics after Hitler: The Western Allies and the German Party System.* New York: New York University Press, 1995.

Rothwell, Victor. *Britain and the Cold War, 1941–1947.* London: Jonathan Cape, 1981.

Ruhm von Oppen, Beate, ed. *Documents on Germany under Occupation.* London: Oxford University Press, 1955.

Ryan, Cornelius. *The Last Battle.* New York: Simon and Schuster, 1966.

Salisbury, Harrison. *Moscow Journal.* Chicago: University of Chicago Press, 1961.
———. *The 900 Days: The Siege of Leningrad.* New York: Harper and Row, 1969.
Sandford, Gregory W. *From Hitler to Ulbricht: The Communist Reconstruction of East Germany, 1945–1946.* Princeton, N.J.: Princeton University Press, 1983.
Schelling, Thomas. *Arms and Influence.* New Haven, Conn.: Yale University Press, 1966.
Schivelbusch, Wolfgang. *In a Cold Crater: Cultural and Intellectual Life in Berlin, 1945–1948.* Translated by Kelly Barry. Berkeley and Los Angeles: University of California Press, 1998.
Schlesinger, Arthur M., Jr., ed. *The Dynamics of World Power: A Documentary History of United States Foreign Policy, 1945–1973.* 5 vols. New York: Chelsea House, 1973.
Schoenbaum, Thomas J. *Waging Peace and War: Dean Rusk in the Truman, Kennedy, and Johnson Years.* New York: Simon and Schuster, 1988.
Schrader, Helena P. *The Blockade Breakers: The Berlin Airlift.* Chalford, U.K.: History Press, 2008.
Schwartz, Harry. *Russia's Soviet Economy.* 2d ed. New York: Prentice-Hall, 1954.
Sharp, Tony. *The Wartime Alliance and the Zonal Division of Germany.* Oxford: Clarendon Press, 1975.
Shlaim, Avi. *The United States and the Berlin Blockade, 1948–1949: A Study in Crisis Decision-Making.* Berkeley and Los Angeles: University of California Press, 1983.
Shulman, Marshall D. *Stalin's Foreign Policy Reappraised.* New York: Atheneum, 1965.
Slayton, Robert A. *Master of the Air: William Tunner and the Success of Military Airlift.* Tuscaloosa: University of Alabama Press, 2010.
Smith, Gaddis. *Dean G. Acheson.* New York: Cooper Square, 1972.
Smith, Jean Edward. *The Defense of Berlin.* Baltimore: Johns Hopkins Press, 1963.
———. *Lucius D. Clay: An American Life.* New York: Holt, 1990.
———, ed. *The Papers of General Lucius D. Clay: Germany, 1945–1949.* 2 vols. Bloomington: Indiana University Press, 1974.
Smith, Walter Bedell. *My Three Years in Moscow.* Philadelphia: Lippincott, 1950.
Snyder, Glen, and Paul Diesing. *Conflict among Nations: Bargaining, Decision Making, and System Structure in International Crises.* Princeton, N.J.: Princeton University Press, 1977.
Spalding, Elizabeth Edwards. *The First Cold Warrior: Harry Truman, Containment, and the Remaking of Liberal Internationalism.* Lexington: University Press of Kentucky, 2006.
Spilker, Dirk. *The East German Leadership and the Division of Germany: Patriotism and Propaganda, 1945–1953.* Oxford: Oxford University Press, 2006.
St. Clair, James E., and Linda C. Gugin. *Chief Justice Fred M. Vinson of Kentucky: A Political Biography.* Lexington: University Press of Kentucky, 2002.
Steege, Paul. *Black Market, Cold War: Everyday Life in Berlin, 1946–1949.* Cambridge: Cambridge University Press, 2007.
Stoler, Mark A. *Allies and Adversaries: The Joint Chiefs of Staff, the Grand Alliance, and U.S. Strategy in World War II.* Chapel Hill: University of North Carolina Press, 2000.
Strang, Lord. *Home and Abroad.* London: André Deutsch, 1956.
Sulzberger, C. L. *A Long Row of Candles.* New York: Macmillan, 1969.
Talbott, Strobe, ed. and trans. *Khrushchev Remembers: The Last Testament.* Boston: Little, Brown, 1974.
Taubman, William. *Stalin's American Policy: From Entente to Detente to Cold War.* New York: Norton, 1982.
Trachtenberg, Marc. *A Constructed Peace: The Making of the European Settlement, 1945–1963.* Princeton, N.J.: Princeton University Press, 1999.

Trohan, Walter. *Political Animals: Memoirs of a Sentimental Cynic.* Garden City, N.Y.: Doubleday, 1975.

Truman, Harry S. *Memoirs.* 2 vols. Garden City, N.Y.: Doubleday, 1955–1956.

———. *Mr. Citizen.* New York: Geis, 1960.

Truman, Margaret. *Harry S. Truman.* New York: Morrow, 1974.

Tunner, William H. *Over the Hump.* New York: Duell, Sloan, and Pearce, 1964.

Tusa, Ann. *The Last Division: A History of Berlin, 1945–1989.* Reading, Mass.: Addison-Wesley, 1997.

Tusa, Ann, and John Tusa. *The Berlin Airlift.* Rockville Centre, N.Y.: Sarpedon, 1998.

United Nations Security Council. *Official Records, 3rd Year.* Paris, 1948.

U.S. Department of State. *The Berlin Crisis: A Report on the Moscow Discussions.* Washington, D.C.: Government Printing Office, 1948.

———. *Bulletin.* 1947–1949, 1961.

———. *Documents & State Papers.* Washington, D.C.: Government Printing Office, 1949.

———. *Documents on Germany, 1944–1985.* Washington, D.C.: Government Printing Office, 1985.

———. *Foreign Relations of the United States.* Washington, D.C.: Government Printing Office, 1862– .

———. *Foreign Relations of the United States: The Conference of Berlin (The Potsdam Conference), 1945.* 2 vols. Washington, D.C.: Government Printing Office, 1960.

———. *Foreign Relations of the United States: The Conferences at Washington and Quebec, 1943.* Washington, D.C.: Government Printing Office, 1970.

———. *Foreign Relations of the United States: Memoranda of Conversation of the Secretary of State, 1947–1952.* Washington, D.C.: Government Printing Office, 1988.

———. *Foreign Relations of the United States, Diplomatic Papers: The Conferences at Cairo and Tehran, 1943.* Washington, D.C.: Government Printing Office, 1961.

———. *Foreign Relations of the United States, Diplomatic Papers: The Conferences at Malta and Yalta, 1945.* Washington, D.C.: Government Printing Office, 1955.

———. *Germany, 1947–1949: The Story in Documents.* Washington, D.C.: Government Printing Office, 1950.

U.S. Office of Military Government. *Information Bulletins.* Berlin, 1948–1949.

———. *Military Government Reports.* Berlin, 1948–1949.

U.S. Office of Military Government, Berlin Sector. *A Four Year Report: Office of Military Government, U.S. Sector, Berlin, July 1, 1945–September 1, 1949.* Berlin: OMGUS, 1949.

U.S. President. *Public Papers of the Presidents of the United States. Harry S. Truman . . . 1948.* Washington, D.C.: Government Printing Office, 1964.

———. *Public Papers of the Presidents of the United States. Harry S. Truman . . . 1949.* Washington, D.C.: Government Printing Office, 1964.

U.S. Senate. Committee on Foreign Relations. *Documents on Germany, 1944–1959.* Washington, D.C.: Government Printing Office, 1959.

———. *Documents on Germany, 1944–1961.* Washington, D.C.: Government Printing Office, 1961.

———. *Reviews of the World Situation, 1949–1950.* Washington, D.C.: Government Printing Office, 1974.

USSR Ministry of Foreign Affairs. *Correspondence between the Chairman of the Council of Ministers of the U.S.S.R. and the Presidents of the U.S.A. and the Prime Ministers of Great Britain during the Great Patriotic War of 1941–1945.* 2 vols. Moscow: Foreign Languages Publishing House, 1957.

———. *The Soviet Union and the Berlin Question.* Moscow: Ministry of Foreign Affairs, 1948.

Vaizey, Hester. *Surviving Hitler's War: Family Life in Germany, 1939–1948.* New York: Palgrave Macmillan, 2010.

Vandenberg, Arthur H., Jr., ed. *The Private Papers of Senator Vandenberg.* Boston: Houghton Mifflin, 1952.

Vysotsky, V. *West Berlin.* Translated by David Fidlon. Moscow: Progress Publishers, 1974.

Weil, Martin. *A Pretty Good Club.* New York: Norton, 1978.

Wettig, Gerhard. *Stalin and the Cold War in Europe: The Emergence and Development of East-West Conflict, 1939–1953.* Lanham, Md.: Rowman and Littlefield, 2008.

Whitney, C. V. *High Peaks.* Lexington: University Press of Kentucky, 1977.

Williams, Phil. *Crisis Management: Confrontation and Diplomacy in the Nuclear Age.* London: Martin Robertson, 1976.

Williamson, David. *A Most Diplomatic General: The Life of General Lord Robertson of Oakridge.* London: Brassey's, 1996.

Williamson, Samuel R., Jr., and Steven L. Rearden. *The Origins of U.S. Nuclear Strategy, 1945–1953.* New York: St. Martin's Press, 1993.

Willis, F. Roy. *The French in Germany, 1945–1949.* Stanford, Calif.: Stanford University Press, 1962.

Woodhouse, Roger. *British Policy towards France, 1945–51.* New York: St. Martin's Press, 1995.

Yergin, Daniel. *Shattered Peace: The Origins of the Cold War and the National Security State.* Boston: Houghton Mifflin, 1977.

Young, John W. *Britain, France, and the Unity of Europe, 1945–1951.* Leicester, U.K.: Leicester University Press, 1984.

———. *France, the Cold War, and the Western Alliance, 1944–1949: French Foreign Policy and Postwar Europe.* New York: St. Martin's Press, 1990.

Young, Oran. *The Politics of Force: Bargaining during International Crises.* Princeton, N.J.: Princeton University Press, 1968.

Ziemke, Earl. *The U.S. Army in the Occupation of Germany, 1944–1946.* Washington, D.C.: Government Printing Office, 1975.

Zubok, Vladislav M. *A Failed Empire: The Soviet Union in the Cold War from Stalin to Gorbachev.* Chapel Hill: University of North Carolina Press, 2007.

Zwass, Adam. *Monetary Cooperation between East and West.* White Plains, N.Y.: International Arts and Sciences Press, 1975.

Articles, Essays, and Dissertations

Acheson, Dean G. "Philip C. Jessup, Diplomatist." In *Transnational Law in a Changing Society,* edited by Wolfgang Friedmann et al., 3–13. New York: Columbia University Press, 1972.

Alexandrov, Vladimir. "The Dismantling of German Industry." In *Soviet Economic Policy in Postwar Germany,* edited by Robert Slusser, 14–17. New York: Research Program on the USSR, 1953.

Ambrose, Stephen E. "The Military Impact on Foreign Policy." In *The Military and American Society,* edited by Stephen E. Ambrose and James Alden Barber Jr., 121–36. New York: Free Press, 1973.

Bathurst, M. E. "Legal Aspects of the Berlin Problem." *British Yearbook of International Law* 38 (1962): 255–306.

Bennett, Jack. "The German Currency Reform." *Annals* 267 (January 1950): 43–54.

Berkowitz, Morton, et al. "The Berlin Airlift, 1948." In *The Politics of American Foreign Policy: The Social Context of Decisions,* 39–53. Englewood Cliffs, N.J.: Prentice-Hall, 1977.

Bess, Demaree. "Will We Be Pushed Out of Berlin?" *Saturday Evening Post,* July 31, 1948.

Broscious, S. David. "Longing for International Control, Banking on American Superiority: Harry S. Truman's Approach to Nuclear Weapons." In *Cold War Statesmen Confront the Bomb: Nuclear Diplomacy since 1945,* edited by John Lewis Gaddis et al., 15–38. Oxford: Oxford University Press, 1999.

Bungert, Heike. "A New Perspective on French-American Relations during the Occupation of Germany, 1945–1948: Behind-the-Scenes Diplomatic Bargaining and the Zonal Merger." *Diplomatic History* 18, no. 3 (Summer 1994): 333–52.

Clifford, J. Garry. "President Truman and Peter the Great's Will." *Diplomatic History* 4, no. 4 (Fall 1980): 371–85.

Cox, Sebastian. "Britain and the Berlin Airlift." *RAF Air Power Review* 7, no. 1 (Spring 2004): 25–43.

Creswell, Michael, and Marc Trachtenberg. "France and the German Question, 1945–1955." *Journal of Cold War Studies* 5, no. 3 (Summer 2003): 5–28.

Creuzberger, Stefan. "The Soviet Military Administration and East German Elections, Autumn 1946." *Australian Journal of Politics and History* 45, no. 1 (March 1999): 89–98.

Dallin, Alexander. "Allied Leadership in the Second World War: Stalin." *Survey* 21, no. 1 (Winter–Spring 1975): 11–19.

Daum, Andreas W. "America's Berlin 1945–2000." In *Berlin: The New Capital in the East,* edited by Frank Trommler, 49–73. Washington, D.C.: American Institute for Contemporary German Studies, 2000.

Davison, W. Phillips. "The Human Side of the Berlin Airlift." *Air University Review* 10, no. 3 (Fall 1958): 64–73.

Divine, Robert A. "The Cold War and the Election of 1948." *Journal of American History* 59, no. 1 (June 1972): 90–110.

Dorn, W. L. "The Debate over American Occupation Policy in Germany, 1944–1945." *Political Science Quarterly* 72, no. 4 (December 1957): 481–501.

Downie, Don. "Long Ranger." *Wings* 20, no. 2 (April 1990): 10–23, 46–55.

Edwards, Peter. "Evatt and the Americans." *Historical Studies* 18, no. 73 (October 1979): 546–60.

Eisenberg, Carolyn. "The Myth of the Berlin Blockade and the Early Cold War." In *Cold War Triumphalism: The Misuse of History after the Fall of Communism,* edited by Ellen Schrecker, 174–200. New York: New Press, 2004.

Fisher, Paul W. "The Berlin Airlift." *Bee-Hive* 23, no. 4 (Fall 1948).

Ford, Frederick. "New Mark, Old Mistakes in Berlin." *New Republic,* July 19, 1948, 11–12.

Franklin, William. "Zonal Boundaries and Access to Berlin." *World Politics* 16, no. 1 (October 1963): 1–31.

Gimbel, John. "The American Reparations Stop in Germany: An Essay in the Political Uses of History." *Historian* 37, no. 2 (February 1975): 276–96.

———. "On the Implementation of the Potsdam Agreement: An Essay on U.S. Postwar German Policy." *Political Science Quarterly* 87, no. 2 (June 1972): 242–69.

Gobarev, Victor. "Soviet Military Plans and Actions during the First Berlin Crisis, 1948–49." *Journal of Slavic Military Studies* 10, no. 3 (September 1997): 1–24.

Gottlieb, Manuel. "The Failure of Quadripartite Monetary Reform, 1945–1947." *Finanzarchiv* 17, no. 3 (1957): 398–417.

Greenwood, John T. "The Emergence of the Postwar Strategic Air Force, 1945–1953." In *Air Power and Warfare: The Proceedings of the 8th Military History Symposium, United States Air Force Academy,* edited by Alfred F. Hurley and Robert C. Ehrhart, 215–44. Washington, D.C.: Office of Air Force History, 1979.

Hammond, Paul Y. "Directives for the Occupation of Germany." In *American Civil-Military Decisions,* edited by Harold Stein, 311–60. Tuscaloosa: University of Alabama Press, 1963.

Harrington, Daniel F. "'As Far as His Army Can Reach': Military Movements and East-West Discord in Germany, 1945." *Diplomacy and Statecraft* 20, no. 4 (December 2009): 580–94.

Harris, Arthur W. D., et al. "A Special Study of Operation 'Vittles.'" *Aviation Operations* 11, no. 5 (April 1949): 1–120.

Harty, Gerald. "The Airlift Soars On." *Bee-Hive* 24, no. 3 (Summer 1949): 11–17.

Herbert, E. O. "The Cold War in Berlin." *Journal of the Royal United Services Institute* 94, no. 574 (May 1949): 165–77.

Hogan, Michael J. "The Search for a 'Creative Peace': The United States, European Unity, and the Origins of the Marshall Plan." *Diplomatic History* 6, no. 3 (Summer 1982): 267–85.

Howard, Michael. "Governor-General of Germany." *Times Literary Supplement,* August 29, 1979, 969–70.

Jessup, Philip C. "The Berlin Blockade and the Use of the United Nations." *Foreign Affairs* 50, no. 1 (October 1971): 163–73.

———. "Park Avenue Diplomacy: Ending the Berlin Blockade." *Political Science Quarterly* 87, no. 3 (September 1972): 377–400.

Kahn, E. H., Jr. "A Reporter in Germany: *Die Luftbrücke.*" *New Yorker,* May 14, 1949, 37–61.

Karber, Phillip A., and Jerald Combs. "The United States, NATO, and the Soviet Threat to Western Europe: Military Estimates and Policy Options, 1945–1963." *Diplomatic History* 22, no. 3 (Summer 1998): 399–429.

Kerr, Sheila. "The Secret Hotline to Moscow." In *Britain and the First Cold War,* edited by Anne Deighton, 71–87. Houndmills, U.K.: Macmillan, 1990.

Kramer, Alan. "British Dismantling Politics." In *Reconstruction in Post-War Germany: British Occupation Policy and the Western Zones, 1945–55,* edited by Ian Turner, 125–53. Oxford: Berg, 1989.

Kuter, Laurence S. "The Berlin Airlift." In *The Impact of Air Power: National Security and World Politics,* edited by Eugene M. Emme, 377–83. Princeton, N.J.: Van Nostrand, 1959.

Larson, Deborah Welch. "The Origins of Commitment: Truman and West Berlin." *Journal of Cold War Studies* 13, no. 1 (Winter 2011): 180–212.

———. "Truman and the Berlin Blockade." In *Good Judgment in Foreign Policy,* edited by Deborah Welch Larson and Stanley A. Reshon, 127–52. Lanham, Md.: Rowman and Littlefield, 2003.

Larson, Harold. "The Berlin Airlift." In *A History of the United States Air Force, 1907–1957,* edited by Alfred Goldberg, 235–41. Princeton, N.J.: Van Nostrand, 1957.

Laufer, Jochen. "Die UdSSR und die Ursprünge der Berlin Blockade." *Deutschland Archiv* (4/1998): 564–77.

———. "From Dismantling to Currency Reform: External Origins of the Dictatorship, 1944–1948." In *Dictatorship as Experience: Towards a Socio-Cultural History of the GDR,* edited by Konrad H. Jarausch, 73–89. Translated by Eve Duffy. New York: Berghahn, 1999.

———. "Die UdSSR und die Zoneneinteilung Deutschlands (1943/44)." *Zeitschrift für Geschichtswissenschaft* 43, no. 4 (1995): 309–31.

Loftus, Robert A. "The American Response to the Berlin Blockade: Bureaucratic Politics, Partisan Politics, and Foreign Policy Improvisation." Diss., Columbia University, 1979.

Lynch, Frances M. B. "Resolving the Paradox of the Monnet Plan: National and International Planning in French Reconstruction." *Economic History Review*, 2d ser., 37, no. 2 (May 1984): 229–43.

MacGregor, P. L., and K. N. Hansen. "The Berlin Airlift." *South African Air Force Journal* 1, no. 3 (July 1949): 41–46.

Mai, Gunther. "The United States in the Allied Control Council—From Dualism to Temporary Division." In *The United States and Germany in the Era of the Cold War, 1945–1990: A Handbook*, 2 vols., edited by Detlef Junker et al., 1:50–56. Washington, D.C., and Cambridge: German Historical Institute and Cambridge University Press, 2004.

Maier, Charles S. "Alliance and Autonomy: European Identity and U.S. Foreign Policy Objectives in the Truman Years." In *The Truman Presidency*, edited by Michael J. Lacey, 273–98. Cambridge: Cambridge University Press, 1989.

Mark, Eduard. "American Policy toward Eastern Europe and the Origins of the Cold War." *Journal of American History* 68, no. 2 (September 1981): 313–36.

Merritt, Richard L. "Political Division and Municipal Services in Postwar Berlin." In *Public Policy*, edited by John D. Montgomery and Albert O. Hirschmann, 17:165–98. Cambridge, Mass.: Harvard University Press, 1968.

———. "Postwar Berlin: Divided City." In *Berlin between Two Worlds*, edited by Ronald A. Francisco and Richard L. Merritt, 153–75. Boulder, Colo.: Westview Press, 1986.

Milton, T. R. "The Berlin Airlift." *Air Force* 60, no. 6 (June 1978): 57–65.

Miscamble, Wilson D. "Harry S Truman, the Berlin Blockade, and the 1948 Election." *Presidential Studies Quarterly* 10, no. 3 (Summer 1980): 306–16.

Moseley, Harry G. "Medical History of the Berlin Airlift." *United States Armed Forces Medical Journal* 1, no. 11 (November 1950): 1249–63.

Mosely, Philip E. "The Occupation of Germany: New Light on How the Zones Were Drawn." *Foreign Affairs* 28, no. 4 (July 1950): 580–604.

Murphy, Charles J. V. "Berlin Airlift." *Fortune* 38, no. 5 (November 1948): 89ff.

Naimark, Norman M. "Stalin and Europe in the Postwar Period, 1945–1953: Issues and Problems." *Journal of Modern European History* 2, no. 1 (March 2004): 28–57.

Narinskii, Michail M. "The Soviet Union and the Berlin Crisis, 1948–9." In *The Soviet Union and Europe in the Cold War, 1943–53*, edited by Francesca Gori and Silvio Pons, 57–75. New York: St. Martin's Press, 1996.

Overesch, Manfred. "Senior West German Politicians and Their Perceptions of the German Situation in Europe 1945–1999." In *Power in Europe? Great Britain, France, Italy and Germany in a Postwar World, 1945–1950*, edited by Josef Becker and Franz Knipping, 117–34. Berlin: Walter de Gruyter, 1986.

Paeffgen, Hans-Ludwig. "The Berlin Blockade and Airlift: A Study of American Diplomacy." Diss., University of Michigan, 1979.

Parrish, Scott D., and Mikhail M. Narinsky. "New Evidence on the Soviet Rejection of the Marshall Plan, 1947: Two Reports." Cold War International History Project Working Paper No. 9 (March 1994).

Pearcy, Arthur, Jr. "The Berlin Airlift." *Journal of the American Aviation Historical Society* 34, no. 3 (Fall 1989): 196–211.

Pennacchio, Charles F. "The United States and Berlin, 1945–1949." Diss., University of Colorado, Boulder, 1996.

Peplow, Emma. "The Role of Britain in the Berlin Airlift." *History* 95, no. 318 (April 2010): 207–24.

Pernot, François. "Le pont aérien de Berlin et l'armée de l'Air." *Revue historique des Armées* 215 (June 1999): 51–62.

Reynolds, David, et al. "Legacies: Allies, Enemies, and Posterity." In *Allies at War: The Soviet, American, and British Experience, 1939–1945,* edited by David Reynolds, Warren F. Kimball, and A. O. Chubarian, 417–40. New York: St. Martin's Press, 1994.

Rosenberg, Jerry Philipp. "Berlin and Israel 1948: Foreign Policy Decision Making during the Truman Administration." Diss., University of Illinois, 1977.

Sander, Alfred D. "Truman and the National Security Council, 1945–1947." *Journal of American History* 59, no. 2 (September 1972): 369–88.

Sarty, Leigh E. "The Limits of Internationalism: Canada and the Soviet Blockade of Berlin, 1948–1949." In *Nearly Neighbors: Canada and the Soviet Union from Cold War to Détente and Beyond,* edited by J. L. Black and Norman Hillmer, 56–74. Kingston, Ont.: Ronald P. Frye, 1989.

Scheinman, Lawrence. "The Berlin Blockade." In *International Law and Political Crisis: An Analytical Casebook,* edited by Lawrence Scheinman and David Wilkinson, 1–40. Boston: Little, Brown, 1968.

Schlesinger, Arthur M., Jr. "Origins of the Cold War." *Foreign Affairs* 46, no. 1 (October 1967): 22–52.

Schmidl, Erwin A. "The Airlift that Never Was: Allied Plans to Supply Vienna by Air, 1948–1950." *Army History* 43 (Fall 1997–Winter 1998): 12–23.

Shlaim, Avi. "The Partition of Germany and the Origins of the Cold War." *Review of International Studies* 11, no. 2 (1985): 123–37.

Slusser, Robert M. "The Opening Phase of the Struggle for Germany." *Slavic Review* 38, no. 3 (September 1979): 473–80.

Smith, Gaddis. "The Berlin Blockade through the Filter of History: Visions and Revisions of the Cold War." *New York Times Magazine,* April 29, 1973, 13ff.

Smith, Jean Edward. "General Clay and the Russians: A Continuation of the Wartime Alliance in Germany, 1945–1948." *Virginia Quarterly* 64, no. 1 (Winter 1988): 20–36.

———. "The View from USFET: General Clay's and Washington's Interpretation of Soviet Intentions in Germany, 1945–1948." In *U.S. Occupation in Europe after World War II,* edited by Hans Schmitt, 64–85. Lawrence: Regents Press of Kansas, 1978.

Sowrey, Frederick B., et al. "The Berlin Airlift, 1948–1949." *Proceedings of the Royal Air Force Historical Society* 6 (September 1989).

Starr, Harvey. "'Opportunity' and 'Willingness' as Ordering Concepts in the Study of War." *International Interactions* 4 (1978): 363–87.

Steege, Paul R. "More than an Airlift: Constructing the Berlin Blockade as a Cold War Battle, 1946–1949." Diss., University of Chicago, 1999.

———. "Totale Blockade, totale Luftbrücke? Die mythische Erfahrung der ersten Berlinkrise, June 1948 bis May 1949." In *Sterben für Berlin?* edited by Burghard Ciesla et al., 59–77. Berlin: Metropol, 2000.

Stivers, William. "The Incomplete Blockade: Soviet Zone Supply of West Berlin, 1948–49." *Diplomatic History* 21, no. 4 (Fall 1997): 569–602.

Thieme, H. Jörg. "The Central Bank and Money in the GDR." In *Fifty Years of the Deutsche Mark,* edited by Deutsche Bundesbank, 575–617. Oxford: Oxford University Press, 1999.

Tröger, Annemarie. "Between Rape and Prostitution." In *Women in Culture and Politics,* edited by Judith Friedlander et al., 97–117. Bloomington: Indiana University Press, 1986.

Turner, Ian. "Great Britain and the Post-War German Currency Reform." *Historical Journal* 30, no. 3 (September 1987): 685–708.

Walker, J. Samuel. "'No More Cold War': American Foreign Policy and the 1948 Soviet Peace Offensive." *Diplomatic History* 5, no. 1 (Winter 1981): 75–91.

Wall, Irwin M. "France and the North Atlantic Alliance." In *NATO: The Founding of the Atlantic Alliance and the Integration of Europe,* edited by John Gillingham and Francis R. Heller, 45–56. New York: St. Martin's Press, 1992.

Warner, Albert L. "Our Secret Deal over Germany." *Saturday Evening Post,* August 2, 1952, 30ff.

"Why Ike Didn't Capture Berlin: An Untold Story." *U.S. News and World Report,* April 26, 1971, 70–73.

Winner, Percy. "Berlin Dreads the Winter." *New Republic,* October 11, 1948, 14–16.

———. "The Stadthaus Siege." *New Republic,* September 20, 1948, 8–9.

Wood, P. R. "Thirty Years On: The Berlin Airlift—A Reassessment." *Royal Air Force Quarterly* 18, no. 3 (Autumn 1978): 226–38.

Yershov, Vassily. "Confiscation and Plunder by the Army of Occupation." In *Soviet Economic Policy in Postwar Germany,* edited by Robert Slusser, 1–14. New York: Research Program on the USSR, 1953.

Zubok, Vladislav. "Stalin's Plans and Russian Archives." *Diplomatic History* 21, no. 2 (Spring 1997): 295–305.

Zwass, Adam. "Money, Banking, and Credit in the Soviet Union and Eastern Europe." *Eastern European Economics* 17, nos. 1 and 2 (Fall–Winter 1978–1979): 3–233.

Internet Sources

Eisenberg, Carolyn. "Commentary: H-Diplo Roundtable on Arnold Offner's *Another Such Victory*," December 19, 2002. http://h-net.msu.edu/~diplo/roundtables/#offner. Accessed March 14, 2006.

Landesarchiv Berlin. "Ernst Reuter." http://www.berlin.de/rbmskzl/rbm/galerie/ernst_reuter.html. Accessed May 7, 2005.

Index